THE NEW YORK TIMES COOK BOOK

HARPER & ROW, PUBLISHERS, NEW YORK, HAGERSTOWN, SAN FRANCISCO, LONDON

The New York Times
COOK BOOK

BY CRAIG CLAIBORNE

All the photographs in this book were taken by The New York Times Studio except the following: Moussaka, page 129, by Midori.

 For information address Harper & Row, Publishers, Inc., 10 East 53rd Street, New York, N.Y. 10022. Published simultaneously in Canada by Fitzhenry & Whiteside Limited, Toronto.

LIBRARY OF CONGRESS CATALOG CARD NUMBER: 61-10840

Designed by Jacqueline Wilsdon

To Ruth P. Casa-Emellos,
for eighteen years *The New York Times* home economist

CONTENTS

PREFACE

M. F. K. Fisher, that redoubtable writer on food, once noted that the basis of French cuisine is butter, that of Italy olive oil, of Germany lard, and of Russia sour cream. Water or drippings are attributed to English kitchens, and to those of America, the flavor of innumerable tin cans.

Fortunately, there is reason to believe that the circumstance in America is changing for the better. There probably never has been such an absorbing interest in fine cuisine in the home as there is in this decade. While it is true that scarcely a day passes in which some manufacturer or another does not introduce a new "instant" product, it is also true that world travel on a scale unsurpassed in history is making the American palate more sophisticated. Thanks to modern appliances, the amount of time spent in the kitchen for the average homemaker has decreased considerably over the past few years. On the other hand, more and more men, women and children seem to discover the pleasures of the table.

Cooking is at once one of the simplest and most gratifying of the arts, but to cook well one must love and respect food. It is hoped that the major audience for this volume will be those who are willing to pamper the palates of themselves and their friends. To enjoy the pleasures of the palate does not categorize a man either as gourmand or glutton. As Dr. Samuel Johnson once observed, "He who does not mind his belly will hardly mind anything else."

There are many people to whom full credit is due for the quality of *The New York Times Cook Book*. First of all Jane Nickerson, my esteemed predecessor, the first food news editor of *The New York Times*. A woman of exquisite taste and inquiring mind, Miss Nickerson (or more accurately now, Mrs. Alex Steinberg) is the mother of four children and lives in Lakeland, Florida.

Mrs. Ruth P. Casa-Emellos, to whom this book is dedicated, was the tireless and inspired *Times* home economist for eighteen years. Her contributions to this volume are without measure. She retired in the fall of 1961 to Winston-Salem, the place of her birth in North Carolina.

June Owen, Nan Ickeringill and Anne-Marie Schiro of the food news staff were vital in research and inspiration, and the debt to them is strong.

In the styling of the photographs that appear throughout this book, the influence of John Camposa is very much in evidence. His recommendations for backgrounds and for accessories are gratefully acknowledged.

Ultimately, of course, the responsibility for the illustrations as they appear belongs to the *Times* studio photographers, and it has been a genuine pleasure to work closely with Bill Aller, Gene Maggio and Alfred Wegener. They were responsible for most of the photographs included here.

During the course of a single year *The New York Times* publishes more than a thousand recipes. They come from endless sources. Many are translated and adapted from European books on food, others are borrowed from already published regional recipes of America. Some are "heirlooms" from family recipe books and others have been created in *The Times* test kitchen.

This book is a collection of nearly fifteen hundred selected recipes that appeared in the pages of *The New York Times* between 1950 and 1960.

Craig Claiborne

THE NEW YORK TIMES COOK BOOK

CHAPTER ONE

. . . .

APPETIZERS

Appetizers or hors d'oeuvres are the frivolities of a meal, and, like champagne, they are capable of setting a mood. There are several that are almost guaranteed to give a feeling of elegance and richness. These are fresh caviar, genuine foie gras, cold lobster, smoked salmon and thin slices of fine ham such as that of Paris, Parma, Westphalia or Bayonne.

On a lesser but nonetheless appetizing plane are meat and game pâtés, oysters on the half shell, fish or shellfish in aspic and the lowly but elegant stuffed egg.

SERVING CAVIAR

All caviar, whether fresh or pasteurized, should be served thoroughly chilled. To keep it cold, the serving bowl is usually imbedded in ice.

With fresh caviar, many gourmets declare, no embellishments are necessary. They heap it on fresh toast—either buttered or dry—and relish it as is. Others demand a dash of lemon juice. Caviar is also superb, and obviously more economical, when served with blini, melted butter and sour cream.

Chopped hard-cooked egg yolk, chopped hard-cooked egg white and raw onion rings or chopped raw onion often are offered with both fresh and pasteurized caviar. They are particularly recommended with the pasteurized product.

For a delicious spread for buttered bread fingers, mix pasteurized pressed caviar with cream cheese and enough sour cream to make it of spreading consistency.

Fresh caviar is highly perishable and must be kept refrigerated. Never put fresh caviar in a home freezer; freezing ruins it.

Two beverages are eminently suited for service with caviar. They are chilled vodka and chilled dry champagne.

SERVING FOIE GRAS

The foie gras should be chilled. Cut it into quarter-inch or half-inch slices and serve with buttered toast. If the foie gras is coated with aspic, serve a little chopped aspic on the side.

SERVING SMOKED SALMON

The best smoked salmon comes from Nova Scotia, Scotland, Norway and Denmark. Most of that available in the United States is from Nova Scotia. The salmon is generally purchased in wafer-thin slices and it should be served chilled on chilled plates. Classically, it is served accompanied by lemon wedges, capers, buttered toast and a pepper mill. It is also served on occasion with a cruet of olive oil, chopped egg and chopped onion.

SERVING HAM

Fine ham, whether it is a domestic ham such as those from Smithfield or an imported one from France, Italy or Germany, should be served in thin slices. Ham is complemented with small, sour gherkins and buttered toast.

SERVING OYSTERS ON THE HALF SHELL

The flavor of oysters is so delicate they are best savored with a touch of lemon juice and a sprinkling of coarsely ground black pepper. They should be served on a bed of ice and accompanied by buttered toast or buttered black bread fingers. They may, of course, be served with a tomato and horseradish sauce, but this overpowers the flavor of the oysters. The classic drink with oysters is a well-chilled chablis or, when it is appropriate to the occasion, stout.

GALANTINE OF TURKEY *12 to 15 servings*

1 twelve- to fifteen-pound turkey
1 pound lean veal, ground
1 pound lean pork, ground
1 pound salt pork, cubed
¼ cup cognac or sherry wine
1 cup heavy cream
3 tablespoons salt
Black pepper to taste
1 teaspoon nutmeg
1 tablespoon chopped tarragon
½ pound unsalted fatback, cut into strips
½ pound cooked tongue, cut into strips
2 truffles, sliced (optional)
¾ cup pistachio nuts
2 carrots
1 stalk celery
1 sprig parsley

1. Bone the turkey or have it boned by the butcher. Using a sharp knife and fingers, remove all the meat from the skin to leave a shell. Reserve meat and the shell. Make a rich broth with bones.

2. Cut the meat from the drumsticks and the breast into one-third-inch cubes. Grind together the remaining meat from the turkey, the veal and lean pork. Combine this meat mixture with the salt pork, cognac or sherry, cream and seasonings.

(*cont'd*)

1. *To make a galantine,* a turkey or other fowl is boned. Most butchers will do this chore.

2. The skin becomes a shell. It is laid flat, stuffed with meats, sprinkled with pistachios.

3. The stuffed skin is rolled in buttered cheesecloth, tied at both ends and in the middle.

4. The galantine is placed in a suitable kettle, covered with broth and simmered until done.

3. Lay the turkey-skin shell, outside down, on a flat surface and spread with the seasoned mixture. Top with alternate rows of fatback, tongue, truffles and diced turkey. Sprinkle with pistachios.

4. Draw the edges of the skin together to form a sausagelike roll and carefully sew the edges of the skin.

5. Generously butter a large piece of clean linen or several layers of cheesecloth and place the galantine on it. Roll it tightly and tie at both ends and in the middle. The roll should be smooth and even.

6. Place the roll in a large kettle and add the vegetables and enough broth to cover.

(*cont'd*)

7. Cover, bring to a boil and simmer gently about one and one-half hours. Let the galantine cool in the liquid. Remove it from the broth.

8. Unroll the galantine and reroll it in a clean cloth. Weight it down with a heavy plate for two hours or more, then remove the cloth. Remove the thread with which the galantine was sewed. The galantine may be decorated with a sauce chaud froid (page 444) and a clear aspic (see quick aspic, page 431); or it may be glazed merely with an aspic made from the broth in which the turkey was cooked. Chill and cut into thin slices to be served as a first course with buttered toast.

HOW TO DECORATE A GALANTINE:

In decorating any food with aspic there is only one trick: The food on which the gelatin is to be applied must be very cold and the aspic must be cool but still liquid. If the galantine is cold enough the aspic will set almost immediately.

Place the galantine on a wire rack and place the rack in a roasting pan with sides. Chill the galantine briefly in a refrigerator or freezer (do not let it freeze). Remove it and spoon a little of the chaud-froid over the whole of it. Chill again, then repeat until the galantine is covered with a solid glaze.

Using truffle-cutters or a sharp paring knife, make cutouts of truffles, black olives, hard-cooked egg whites or the green part of scallions to form any pattern desired.

Prepare a clear aspic according to recipe. Dip the cutouts in clear aspic and place them on the chaud-froid-covered galantine. Chill.

Cover the galantine with aspic using the same technique as for the chaud-froid.

Keep the galantine chilled until ready to serve.

Some while back Paula Peck and her husband toured the restaurants and bistros of Paris looking for the "perfect" pâté. She took copious notes and, on their return, spent many days duplicating the best pâtés of the lot. The following three (truffled pâté, fine liver pâté and country pâté) were among their favorites:

TRUFFLED PATE *3 quarts*

- 1½ pounds fresh pork fat
- 1 pound lean boneless veal
- 1 pound boneless pork shoulder
- ½ pound ham
- ½ pound tongue
- 4 chicken breast halves, boned, skinned and trimmed
- 1 pound chicken livers
- 4 eggs
- ⅓ cup cognac
- ½ cup chopped black truffles
- ½ cup pistachio nuts
- 4 teaspoons salt
- 1 teaspoon white pepper
- 2 teaspoons monosodium glutamate
- 1 teaspoon allspice
- ½ teaspoon cinnamon
- ¼ teaspoon ground cloves
- ⅓ cup flour

(*cont'd*)

1. Slice two-thirds pound of the pork fat thinly. Grind one-eighth pound each of the veal, pork shoulder, pork fat, ham and tongue. Grind together three times.

2. Wrap each chicken breast half in a thin strip of sliced pork fat.

3. Line two one-and-one-half-quart molds or one three-quart mold with the remaining thin slices of pork fat, letting long ends hang over outside of the pan.

4. In an electric blender, purée half the chicken livers with the eggs and cognac. Gradually add all the ground meats to the blender. Use a little more cognac, an additional egg or a little cream to provide extra liquid if necessary so that the mixture is made as fine as possible.

5. With a sharp knife, cut the remaining pork fat and meats, except the chicken breasts, into cubes less than one-third inch in size. Combine the finely ground meats with the diced meats. Add the truffles, nuts, seasonings and flour. Mix very well.

6. Fill the molds slightly less than halfway with the pâté mixture. Place wrapped chicken breasts over it. Cover with remaining pâté mixture, filling pans to top.

7. Fold hanging strips of pork fat over the top. Cover each mold tightly with a double thickness of aluminum foil. Place in a pan of water and bake in a hot oven (400° F.) three hours. Remove the aluminum foil and continue baking until the top of the pâté is brown, about twenty minutes longer. Weight the pâté (see directions below).

HOW TO WEIGHT A PATE:

Firm pâtés should be weighted so they will slice well. Here are instructions for weighting a pâté.

Do not remove molds from underpan after taking from oven. There will be an overflowing of fat after weights are placed on top.

Place a pan that is slightly smaller than the pâté mold right on top of the baked pâté. Fill pan with heavy objects. Do not remove weights until pâté is completely cool. Refrigerate until needed. Pâté will keep several weeks if surrounding fat is not removed.

FINE LIVER PATE *2 quarts*

- 1 teaspoon rendered chicken or pork fat
- 2 pounds chicken or pork livers
- 3 eggs
- ⅓ cup cognac
- 1½ cups heavy cream
- ⅔ cup diced fresh unrendered chicken fat or fresh pork fat
- 1 onion, coarsely chopped
- ½ cup flour
- 5 teaspoons salt
- 1 teaspoon ground ginger
- 1 teaspoon monosodium glutamate
- 2 teaspoons white pepper
- 1 teaspoon allspice

(*cont'd*)

1. Lightly grease a three-quart mold with rendered fat.

2. In an electric blender, make a fine purée of the livers, eggs, cognac and cream. From time to time add a little diced fat, onion and flour. (It will not be possible to do the entire mixture at one time. Three or four separate blendings will be needed.)

3. To the purée add all the seasonings and mix well. Pour into the mold and cover the top with a double thickness of aluminum foil.

4. Place in a pan of water and bake in a moderate oven (325° F.) two to two and one-half hours. Cool the pâté, then store it in the refrigerator. It is not necessary to weight it. If desired, the top may be decorated with slices of truffle and a clear aspic poured over.

COUNTRY PATE *3 quarts*

- 1½ pounds fresh pork fat
- 1 pound boneless veal
- 1 pound boneless pork shoulder
- 1 pound ham
- ½ pound chicken or pork livers
- 8 cloves garlic
- ¼ cup heavy cream
- 3 eggs
- ½ cup cognac
- 4 teaspoons salt
- 2 teaspoons white pepper
- ½ teaspoon allspice
- ½ teaspoon cinnamon
- ½ cup flour

1. Slice one-half pound of the pork fat thinly. Finely grind half of the remaining pork fat with all the veal and pork shoulder.

2. Line a three-quart mold or two one-and-one-half-quart molds with the thin slices of pork fat, letting long ends hang outside of the pan.

3. Grind the ham and remaining pork fat, using the coarse blade of the meat grinder. If a coarse blade is not available, dice the meat finely with a sharp knife.

4. In an electric blender, purée the chicken livers with the garlic, cream, eggs and cognac. Gradually add to the blender about one-third of the finely ground veal-pork mixture.

5. In a mixing bowl combine all the ground and puréed meats and add the remaining seasonings and flour. Mix all the ingredients thoroughly.

6. Fill the prepared mold with the pâté mixture. Fold the overhanging strips of pork fat over the top. Cover tightly with a double thickness of aluminum foil. Place the mold in a pan of water and bake in a hot oven (400° F.) three hours. Remove the aluminum foil and continue baking until the top of the pâté is brown, about twenty minutes longer. Weight the pâté according to the directions given on page 7.

Note: If desired, the veal and pork shoulder called for in this recipe may be replaced by any available game, such as venison, hare or pheasant. The amount of garlic used may be varied according to taste.

RABBIT OR HARE PATE

About 3 quarts

1 five-pound hare or rabbit
1 cup cognac
3 pounds boneless pork
4 shallots
3 leeks, white part only
1 cup sliced celery
2 teaspoons salt
1 teaspoon freshly ground black pepper
3 eggs plus 2 egg yolks
½ pound foie gras or liver sausage
¼ teaspoon thyme
¼ teaspoon powdered bay leaf
¾ pound salt pork, sliced
Salted water to cover
2 egg whites
3 envelopes unflavored gelatin

1. Reserve the hare liver. Bone the hare and slice the meat, reserving the bones. Add the cognac to the meat and let stand overnight in the refrigerator. Drain, reserving the cognac.
2. Preheat the oven to moderate (325° F.).
3. Grind the hare liver, pork and vegetables, using the finest knife of a food grinder. Add the salt, pepper, eggs and yolks and mix. Reserve the egg shells. Line the bottom of a three-quart casserole with three-quarters of the mixture. Arrange the hare slices and foie gras on top and sprinkle with the seasonings. Cover with the remaining pork mixture and top with the salt pork.
4. Cover the casserole and bake in a pan of hot water three hours.
5. Meanwhile, cook the bones of the hare in salted water to cover two hours. Drain, reserving the broth.
6. Press any excess liquid from the cooked pâté, and add the juice to the broth. Add the cognac marinade. Boil until reduced to four cups. Strain and chill. Chill the pâté.
7. Remove the fat from the broth. Beat the egg whites with the reserved crushed egg shells. Add to the broth and boil five minutes. Let stand twenty minutes and strain through wet cotton flannel.
8. Soften the gelatin in three-fourths cup of cold water, add to the hot broth and stir until dissolved. Add more cognac to taste.
9. Remove the pâté from the casserole. Wash the dish and oil it. Cover the bottom with a layer of thin gelatin and chill until set. Return the pâté to the dish, pour thin gelatin around the sides and chill.

PATE MAISON A LA SARDI

6 servings

¼ cup rendered chicken fat
¼ cup lard or vegetable shortening
2 bay leaves
¼ teaspoon freshly ground black pepper
¼ teaspoon thyme
1 large onion, chopped
1½ pounds chicken livers
2 teaspoons salt
½ teaspoon monosodium glutamate
6 slices hot buttered toast

(*cont'd*)

1. In a large skillet melt the chicken fat and lard over medium heat. Add bay leaves, pepper, thyme and onion, and cook, stirring, five minutes.

2. Add the chicken livers and cook, stirring, until lightly browned. Add the salt and monosodium glutamate, and cook five minutes longer, stirring from time to time. Cool the mixture, discarding the bay leaves.

3. Grind the mixture twice, using the finest knife of a food grinder. Pack in a greased pan and chill. Remove from the pan, wrap in waxed paper and refrigerate until serving time. Serve in one-quarter-inch slices on toast.

PATE BEAU SEJOUR

2 loaves, or about 30 servings

2 pounds salt pork
2 pounds pork liver
2 pounds boneless veal
Boiling water to cover
1½ cups sherry
1 tablespoon cognac
½ teaspoon poultry seasoning
2 teaspoons salt
¼ teaspoon powdered bay leaf
1 cup heavy cream
4 egg yolks, lightly beaten
1 envelope gelatin
1⅓ cups (1 10-ounce can) condensed beef consommé

1. Remove the rind from the salt pork and the tough membranes from the liver and veal. Cut all the meat in one-and-one-half-inch cubes.

2. Place the salt pork in a pan, cover with boiling water and bring to a boil. Boil three minutes, drain and add the pork to the liver and veal.

3. Mix one cup of the sherry with the cognac, poultry seasoning, salt and bay leaf and pour over the meats. Let stand one day, covered, in the refrigerator. Turn the meats occasionally.

4. Preheat oven to slow (300° F.).

5. Drain the meats, reserving the marinade. Grind the meats twice, using first the coarsest and then the finest knife of a food grinder.

6. To the ground meats, add the marinade, cream and egg yolks. Blend.

7. Turn the mixture into two bread pans 9 x 5 x 3 inches. Place in a pan of hot water and bake one and one-quarter hours.

8. Remove the pans from the water and let stand at room temperature two hours. Loosen the loaves with a sharp knife, cover with a platter and invert to unmold. Wash the pans thoroughly, then set the loaves back in the pans.

9. Soften the gelatin in one-half cup of the consommé. Bring the remaining consommé to a boil, add the gelatin mixture and stir until dissolved. Add the remaining half cup of sherry. Pour over the pâté in the pans and chill overnight.

10. To unmold, loosen with a sharp knife or dip the pans for a second in boiling water. Invert on platters.

QUICK CHICKEN-LIVER PATE *About 1½ cups*

½ pound chicken livers
Chicken broth to cover
2 hard-cooked eggs
½ cup chopped onion
2 tablespoons chicken fat or butter
Salt and freshly ground black pepper

1. Simmer the livers in broth until done, eight to ten minutes. Drain. Grind them with the eggs, using the medium blade of a food chopper. Or purée in an electric blender, using a little of the liquid in which the livers were cooked.

2. Brown the onion lightly in the fat and blend all the ingredients to make a paste. Season with salt and pepper to taste. If desired, season further with a pinch of curry powder or a dash of cognac. Serve on buttered toast fingers or in a lettuce cup.

CHICKEN LIVER TERRINE *About 3 cups*

1 quart boiling salted water
1 stalk celery
2 sprigs parsley
6 whole peppercorns
1 pound chicken livers
1½ teaspoons salt
Pinch of cayenne pepper, or ½ teaspoon Tabasco sauce
1 cup soft butter or rendered chicken fat
½ teaspoon nutmeg
2 teaspoons dry mustard
¼ teaspoon powdered cloves
5 tablespoons minced onion
½ clove garlic, finely chopped
2 tablespoons cognac
1 finely chopped truffle (optional)

1. To the boiling water add the celery, parsley and peppercorns. Reduce the heat and simmer five minutes. Add the chicken livers and cook, covered, ten minutes.

2. Drain and grind the livers, using the finest knife of a food grinder. Or grind, a few at a time, in an electric blender.

3. Add the salt, cayenne, butter, nutmeg, mustard, cloves, onion, garlic and cognac. Blend thoroughly. If desired, add chopped truffle and mix. Pack the pâté in a three-cup terrine and chill thoroughly.

4. Garnish the pâté, if desired, with sliced green olives. Serve with buttered toast.

To Render Chicken Fat: Place the fresh fat in the top of a double boiler and heat over boiling water until the fat has been extracted from the tissues. Strain.

COLD VEAL CAUCASIAN STYLE *6 servings*

Cooked round or rump of veal, chilled
½ cup soft butter
2 tablespoons chopped chives
6 anchovy fillets, chopped
Salt and freshly ground black pepper
6 cups bouillon
¼ cup tomato purée
4 envelopes unflavored gelatin
1 cup water

(*cont'd*)

1. Slice enough veal for twenty-four finger-sized pieces.

2. Cream the butter with the chives and anchovies. Season with salt and pepper, spread the mixture between two pieces of veal to form sandwiches and chill.

3. Heat two cups of the bouillon with the tomato purée. Soften the gelatin in the water, add to the hot broth and stir until dissolved. Add the remaining broth. Fill a one-quart mold with the mixture and pour the balance into a bread pan. Chill.

4. To serve, turn out the gelatin mold and stand the sandwiches around it. Chop the pan of gelatin and surround the mold.

SCHWEINSULZE (jellied pork loaf)

About 12 servings

- 6 pigs' feet, split lengthwise
- 1 pound pork shoulder
- 2 quarts water
- ½ cup vinegar
- ½ cup diced celery root or celery
- 1 small carrot, diced
- 1 cup chopped onion
- 1 bay leaf
- 10 peppercorns
- 5 whole allspice
- 1 clove
- ¼ teaspoon thyme
- 2 teaspoons salt
- ⅓ cup or more diced dill pickles or sour gherkins
- 1 hard-cooked egg, sliced
- Sliced cucumber (optional)
- Lettuce leaves

1. Place the pigs' feet in a large kettle and add the pork shoulder, water, vinegar, vegetables, spices tied in a cheesecloth bag, and salt. Cover and bring to a boil. Reduce the heat and simmer until the meat is very tender, about three hours.

2. Strain the broth, discard the spice bag and remove the meat from the bones, discarding the bones. Cut the meat into small pieces, add the pickle, cover and refrigerate.

3. Reduce the broth to one quart by boiling it uncovered. Correct the seasonings. Cool and refrigerate overnight.

4. Skim the fat from the top. Examine the broth and, if it has not jellied enough to hold its shape, either reduce the broth more and refrigerate again, or add one tablespoon gelatin softened in one-quarter cup cold water, bring to the boiling broth and stir until dissolved. Cool.

5. Reheat the broth to liquefy; cover the bottom of a loaf pan or mold with a thin layer of the warm broth and chill until set. Garnish with sliced egg and cucumber and add enough warm broth to just cover. Refrigerate until set.

6. Add the reserved meat and pickle mixture to the remaining broth and turn into the pan or mold. Chill until firm. Unmold, garnish with lettuce and serve with mayonnaise.

RULLEPØLSE (spiced breast of veal) *30 to 40 slices*

The Danes have a word for spiced breast of veal and it is rullepølse. It is delicious for a cold buffet.

- 1 breast of veal
- 1 pound fatback, sliced
- 1 tablespoon freshly ground black pepper
- 2 tablespoons salt
- 1 tablespoon saltpeter
- 1 tablespoon ground allspice
- 1 cup chopped onions
- 5 tablespoons finely chopped dill or parsley
- Brine (see below)

1. Have the butcher bone the breast of veal and flatten it. Trim it to make a large square.
2. Arrange the fatback on the veal and sprinkle with pepper, salt, saltpeter, allspice, onions and dill or parsley.
3. Roll the veal jelly-roll fashion in a clean white cloth.
4. Tie the rolled veal tightly with string and place it in a brine bath prepared according to directions below. Weight it down—a heavy plate will do—and let it rest in a cool place for five or six days.
5. Drain the veal. Place it in a large kettle and cover with water. Add salt to taste and bring to a boil.
6. Simmer, covered, one and one-half hours. Remove from the cooking liquid and weight down once more. Refrigerate at least twenty-four hours. Remove the cloth. Serve in wafer-thin slices.

Brine Bath: To prepare a brine bath, place enough cold water in a crock to cover the rolled veal. Dissolve enough salt in the water so that a medium-sized potato will float in the brine. Stir in a quarter of a teaspoon of saltpeter.

MARINATED PORK STRIPS *32 slices*

An hors d'oeuvre frequently served in the home of Myra Waldo, world traveler and food expert, is this pork dish of Korean origin.

- 2 pork tenderloins
- ½ cup soy sauce
- 3 tablespoons sugar
- 2 tablespoons minced onion
- 2 cloves garlic, minced
- 2 teaspoons ground ginger
- ¾ cup sesame seeds
- 2 tablespoons oil

1. Trim the fat from the tenderloins. If thick, split lengthwise.
2. Combine the remaining ingredients except the oil in a bowl. Marinate the pork in the mixture three hours in the refrigerator, turning and basting frequently. Drain and reserve the marinade.
3. Preheat oven to moderate (375° F.).

(*cont'd*)

4. Transfer the pork to an oiled roasting pan and roast until tender, about forty-five minutes. Simmer the marinade ten minutes.

5. Cut the pork into thin slices and serve on cocktail picks with the marinade as an hors d'oeuvre.

SWEDISH MEAT BALLS, PAGE 108.

CARNITAS (little meat balls)

This is one of the most easily prepared dishes ever created. It is the creation of Elena Zelayeta, perhaps the foremost author of Mexican cookbooks.

Cut fresh pork shoulder into small, even cubes and sprinkle with salt and freshly ground black pepper.

Cook on baking sheet in a preheated slow oven (200° F.) until the cubes are crisp, one and one-half to two hours.

ORIENTAL BEEF BALLS, PAGE 108.

PORK BALLS WITH GINGER

12 to 16 pork balls

- 1 pound ground pork
- 1 cup coarsely chopped water chestnuts
- ¼ cup finely chopped crystallized ginger
- 1 egg, lightly beaten
- 1 teaspoon salt
- Cornstarch
- Peanut oil for deep frying

1. Mix lightly all the ingredients except the cornstarch and peanut oil.
2. Shape the mixture into small bite-sized balls and dust lightly with cornstarch.
3. Heat the peanut oil to 375° F. Deep-fry the pork balls until they are cooked through. Serve hot on toothpicks.

FRICADELLER (DANISH PORK BALLS), PAGE 144.

KEFTEDES (Greek meat balls)

About 32 meat balls

- 1½ pounds ground round steak
- 2 eggs, lightly beaten
- ½ cup fine, soft bread crumbs
- 2 medium onions, finely chopped
- 2 tablespoons chopped parsley
- 1 tablespoon chopped fresh mint
- ¼ teaspoon cinnamon
- ¼ teaspoon ground allspice
- Salt and freshly ground black pepper to taste
- Shortening for pan frying

Combine all the ingredients except shortening and mix thoroughly. Refrigerate for several hours. Shape into small, bite-size balls and fry in hot shortening until browned. Serve hot.

SPARERIBS AND GINGERED PLUM SAUCE *10 to 15 appetizers*

2 pounds lean spareribs
⅓ cup soy sauce
5 tablespoons brown sugar
1 tablespoon cornstarch
2 tablespoons vinegar
5 tablespoons candied ginger, chopped fine
1 clove garlic, chopped fine
1 cup pitted, mashed green plums

1. Simmer the spareribs in salted water to cover until tender, about one hour, and pull out all the bones. Cut the meat into strips about one inch long.

2. Mix the remaining ingredients except the plums and two tablespoons of the ginger. Thoroughly coat the meat with the mixture.

3. Arrange on a roasting pan and set the pan on the middle shelf of the broiler. Turn on the broiler to high, leave the door open and watch carefully. When the tops are brown, turn the meat, brush with sauce and brown. Remove from the broiler and drain the meat on absorbent paper. Refrigerate for twenty-four hours.

4. Meanwhile, mix the plums and remaining ginger and let stand twenty-four hours.

5. When ready to serve the meat, spear each piece on a pick. Place the gingered plum sauce in a small bowl and surround with the meat.

CHINESE BARBECUED SPARERIBS *20 to 30 appetizers*

4 pounds spareribs
1 cup soy sauce
½ cup water
3 tablespoons red wine
1 tablespoon sugar
1 teaspoon salt
1 clove garlic, mashed

1. Score the meat between the ribs, but do not cut all the way through.

2. Place the meat in a large bowl. Combine the remaining ingredients and pour over the ribs. Let stand one hour, turning once. Remove the meat from the marinade. Reserve the liquid.

3. Place the ribs on a grill over medium coals and cook about one and one-half hours. Turn the meat frequently and brush with the marinade. Cut with scissors into individual ribs, if desired.

Spareribs may be baked and basted in a roasting pan in a moderate (350° F.) oven for one and one-half hours.

BACON AND LIVER APPETIZERS *16 appetizers*

¾ cup chicken livers
2 hard-cooked eggs
Chopped chives or finely grated onion to taste
Salt and freshly ground black pepper to taste
2 tablespoons butter, at room temperature
½ teaspoon lemon juice
1 teaspoon cognac (optional)
8 slices bacon, cut in half

(cont'd)

1. Cook the chicken livers in a small amount of boiling, salted water until barely done, five to eight minutes.

2. Rub the livers and hard-cooked eggs through a fine sieve or use a food mill. Blend well and mix with the remaining ingredients except the bacon. Chill.

3. Spread the mixture on the strips of bacon. Roll and fasten with toothpicks. Grill under a preheated broiler until the bacon is crisp. Serve hot.

RUMAKI *6 servings*

This appetizer has become almost as popular as pizza pie in metropolitan America but it is still worth repeating.

- 6 chicken livers (about ½ pound)
- 18 canned water chestnuts
- 9 bacon slices cut in half
- 9 scallions, sliced thin lengthwise
- ½ cup soy sauce
- ¼ teaspoon ground ginger
- ½ teaspoon curry powder

1. Slice the chicken livers into three pieces each and fold each piece over a water chestnut.

2. Wrap a strip of bacon and scallion sliced lengthwise around the liver-chestnut core, pinning each kabob with a toothpick.

3. Marinate the kabobs one hour in the soy sauce spiced with ginger and curry powder. Drain and broil in a preheated broiler, turning frequently, until the bacon is thoroughly cooked, about five minutes. Serve on long picks.

LOBSTER RUMAKI

Remove the shell from raw rock lobster or lobster tails and cut the meat into medallions one-half inch thick. Marinate in equal parts soy sauce and sherry.

Drain and combine each slice with a slice of water chestnut. Wrap in bacon and secure with a toothpick. Bake in a preheated hot oven (400° F.) until the bacon is crisp.

LOBSTER EN BELLEVUE PARISIENNE *6 servings*

- 2 large live lobsters
- Boiling salted water to cover
- Mayonnaise
- 4 cups quick fish aspic (page 431)
- Truffles or black olives for decorating
- Salad greens

1. Plunge the lobsters head first into a large pot of boiling salted water and boil twelve to fifteen minutes.

2. Chill. Turn the lobsters on their backs and trim around the inner edge of the shell, removing the spongelike contents from each body; take care that the back and tail remain in one piece. Pick the meat from the lobster bodies

(*cont'd*)

Lobster en Bellevue Parisienne. Surmounted with aspic-coated medallions, this regal creature is posed on a bed of lettuce and surrounded by stuffed hard-cooked eggs and artichokes.

and from the claws of one of them. Combine the meat with enough mayonnaise to bind it and reserve. Remove the tail meat whole from both lobsters and reserve the lobster with the uncracked claws.

3. Slice the tail meat about one-half-inch thick, as you would bread, to make medallions. Chill well. Chill the shell of the reserved lobster.

4. Place the medallions on a wire rack and spoon chilled but still-liquid aspic over them.

5. Slice the truffles or black olives thin. Cut slices into small fancy shapes. Dip cut-outs into still-liquid aspic and decorate the medallions with a definite pattern. Chill.

6. Spoon another layer of aspic over the medallions and chill again.

7. Cover a platter with salad greens and arrange the reserved lobster shell on it. Dip the base of each decorated medallion into still-liquid aspic and arrange, overlapping, along the back of the shell. Decorate fan-shaped lobster tail with medallions. Decorate the platter with the lobster mayonnaise and, if de-

(cont'd)

sired, with stuffed hard-cooked eggs, artichoke hearts and chopped aspic. If desired, run a decorative skewer garnished with vegetables through the lobster's eyes. Serve with salade Russe (page 419) and additional mayonnaise.

MUSSELS IN BACON *6 servings*

36 mussels
1 cup water
18 slices bacon

1. Scrub the mussels well with a stiff brush or a plastic mesh scrubbing ball. Rinse well and put them into a heavy kettle. Add the water and steam ten minutes. Discard any mussels that do not open. Use a knife to remove the mussels from the shells.
2. Preheat oven to hot (400° F.).
3. Cut the bacon slices in half crosswise and cook in a skillet until half done. Drain on absorbent paper and cool slightly. Wrap a half slice of bacon around each mussel and secure each with a toothpick.
4. Bake in oven five minutes or until the bacon is crisp. Drain on absorbent paper and serve.

ANGUILLES QUO VADIS *8 to 10 servings*

Eels are available on the Eastern seaboard during most of the winter months and may be purchased in many Italian fish markets. One of the finest preparations using them is in a green herb sauce. This delectable eel dish is served at the Quo Vadis in New York.

½ cup olive oil
1½ pounds eels, cleaned, skinned and cut into 1½-inch pieces
1 quart boiling chicken broth
1 cup dry white wine
Juice of one lemon
Salt and freshly ground black pepper to taste
¼ cup chopped parsley
¼ cup chopped mint
¼ cup chopped chives
¼ cup puréed spinach

1. Heat the oil in a skillet, add the eels and cook about five minutes. Add the broth and cook five minutes longer. Drain.
2. Combine the eels, wine, lemon juice, salt, pepper, herbs and spinach. Bring to a boil. Cool and chill.

OYSTERS WITH SAUSAGE

The following idea may strike the mind as odd; it will strike the palate as delicious.

Serve chilled oysters on the half shell with hot, spiced breakfast sausages.

CRABMEAT REMICK *6 servings*

- 2 cups fresh or canned crabmeat in large flakes, picked over well
- 6 slices bacon, fried until crisp
- 1 teaspoon dry mustard
- ½ teaspoon paprika
- ½ teaspoon celery salt
- Few drops of Tabasco sauce
- ½ cup chili sauce
- 1 teaspoon tarragon vinegar
- 1¾ cups mayonnaise

1. Preheat oven to moderate (350° F.).

2. Pile the crab flakes into six buttered individual shells or ramekins. Heat in the oven and top with crisp bacon.

3. Blend together the mustard, paprika, celery salt and Tabasco. Add the chili sauce and vinegar, mix well and add the mayonnaise. Spread the warmed crabmeat with this sauce and brown under a preheated broiler.

The following recipes for oysters and clams call for placing the shells on rock salt. The rock salt, such as that used for freezing ice cream, provides a steady base for the shells and keeps the cooked food warm.

OYSTERS CASINO *6 servings*

- 3 dozen freshly opened oysters
- 3 slices bacon
- ½ cup minced green onion
- ¼ cup minced green pepper
- ¼ cup minced celery
- 1 teaspoon lemon juice
- 1 teaspoon Worcestershire sauce
- 2 drops Tabasco sauce

1. Preheat oven to hot (400° F.).

2. Place two drained oysters on the deep half of one shell. Arrange filled oyster shells on a layer of rock salt in one large baking pan or six individual shallow casseroles.

3. In a skillet cook the bacon until crisp, remove from the pan, drain and crumble.

4. To the bacon fat add the onion, green pepper and celery and cook until almost tender. Season with lemon juice, Worcestershire and Tabasco.

5. Spoon the mixture on the oysters in the shells and top with the crumbled bacon. Bake ten minutes.

OYSTERS ROCKEFELLER I *4 servings*

- 24 oysters on the half shell
- 1 cup butter
- ⅓ cup finely chopped parsley
- ¼ cup finely chopped celery
- ¼ cup finely chopped shallots or scallions
- ½ small clove garlic, finely minced
- 2 cups chopped watercress
- ⅓ cup chopped fennel
- ⅓ cup fine, soft bread crumbs
- ¼ cup anisette or Pernod
- Salt and freshly ground black pepper to taste

(*cont'd*)

1. Preheat oven to hot (450° F.).

2. Fill four tin pie plates with rock salt and arrange six oysters on each.

3. In a skillet heat the butter, add the parsley, celery, shallots and garlic and cook three minutes. Add the watercress and fennel and cook until the watercress wilts, about one minute.

4. Pour the mixture into the container of an electric blender and add the remaining ingredients. Blend until the sauce is thoroughly puréed, about one minute. If a blender is not available, put the ingredients through a food mill or pound in a mortar.

5. Place one tablespoon of the sauce on each oyster and spread to the rim of the shell. Bake the oysters just until the sauce bubbles, about four minutes.

OYSTERS ROCKEFELLER II *6 servings*

½ pound spinach, washed well and drained
6 or 8 scallions
½ head lettuce
1½ stalks celery
½ bunch of parsley
1 clove garlic
1 cup butter
½ cup fine bread crumbs
1 tablespoon Worcestershire sauce
1 teaspoon anchovy paste
½ teaspoon salt
Few dashes of Tabasco sauce
1 ounce (2 tablespoons) absinthe or Pernod
36 oysters

1. Chop finely or grind together the spinach, scallions, lettuce, celery, parsley and garlic.

2. Heat the butter and mix in the greens, bread crumbs, Worcestershire sauce, anchovy paste, salt, Tabasco and Pernod. Refrigerate until ready for use. Spoon the mixture onto thirty-six oysters on the half shell, set the oyster halves on a bed of rock salt and bake in a hot oven (450° F.) until piping hot. Serve immediately.

SESAME BAKED CLAMS *4 to 6 servings*

24 cherrystone clams
4 canned water chestnuts, diced
¼ cup canned bean sprouts, chopped
4 scallions, finely chopped
2 teaspoons soy sauce
½ teaspoon fresh ginger, chopped, or ¼ teaspoon ground ginger
2 tablespoons butter
2 tablespoons flour
1 cup milk
¼ cup grated Parmesan cheese
½ cup sesame seeds

1. Preheat oven to hot (450° F.).

2. Dice the clams, reserving the shells. Mix the clams, water chestnuts, bean sprouts and scallions and season with soy sauce and ginger. Spoon the mixture into the clam shells.

(*cont'd*)

3. In a saucepan, melt the butter, add the flour and stir with a wire whisk until blended. Meanwhile, bring the milk to a boil and add all at once to the butter-flour mixture, stirring vigorously with a whisk until the sauce is thickened and smooth. Add the cheese and stir until melted.

4. Spoon the sauce over the mixture in the shells and sprinkle with sesame seeds.

5. Arrange the shells on a layer of rock salt in baking pans and bake four to five minutes. Serve piping hot.

CLAMS AUX BLINIS *4 servings*

This is a recipe of Jean Vergnes, the distinguished chef of the Colony Restaurant in New York.

36 small clams
1 tablespoon finely chopped shallots
½ cup dry white wine
2 tablespoons fish velouté (page 445)
1 teaspoon finely chopped parsley
½ teaspoon finely chopped tarragon
½ teaspoon finely chopped chives
3 egg yolks, beaten
½ cup heavy cream
2 ounces (¼ cup) Pernod
1 tablespoon hollandaise sauce (page 449)
12 blini (page 487)

1. Have the clams opened and reserve the clams and the clam juice. Discard the shells. Chop the clams and pour the clam juice into a saucepan.

2. Add the shallots and wine and bring to the boil. Cook until wine is reduced by half. Add the fish velouté, parsley, tarragon and chives. Remove the saucepan from the heat.

3. Combine the beaten egg yolks and cream and add to the saucepan. Blend well and return to the lowest possible heat. Stir in half the Pernod and the hollandaise sauce. Stir well and heat thoroughly but do not boil or the sauce may curdle.

4. Add the clams and heat thoroughly. Do not overcook or the clams will toughen. Add the remaining Pernod, blend well and serve immediately on top of warm blini.

SEA SCALLOPS SEVICHE *4 servings*

Attitudes toward food are frequently droll. Many are those who enjoy raw oysters or clams on the half shell but shudder at the thought of eating fish or other shellfish in an uncooked state. Fresh scallops are delicious when marinated in lime juice and seasonings.

1 cup sea scallops (about ½ pound)
Juice of four limes
2 tablespoons chopped onion
1 tablespoon chopped parsley
2 tablespoons chopped green pepper
3 tablespoons olive oil
Salt and freshly ground black pepper to taste

1. Cut the raw scallops into quarters and cover with the lime juice. Marinate one hour or more in the refrigerator. Drain.

(cont'd)

2. Combine the onion, parsley and green pepper with the scallops. Add the olive oil, mix well and season with salt and pepper. Serve as a first course.

SHERRIED SHRIMP *4 servings*

24 medium shrimp, shelled and deveined
¼ cup soy sauce
¼ cup sherry
¼ cup salad oil
1 teaspoon powdered ginger, or 1 tablespoon fresh ginger root, ground
1 clove garlic, finely chopped

1. Marinate the raw shrimp in the remaining ingredients one hour or less.
2. Place the shrimp with a little of the marinade in a skillet and cook three or four minutes, until the shrimp are done. If possible, use an electric skillet.

SHRIMP WITH HERB SAUCE *6 servings*

36 shrimp, cooked, shelled and deveined
Shredded lettuce
½ cup mayonnaise
1 tablespoon chopped parsley
1 tablespoon chopped chives
1 tablespoon chopped cucumber
1 tablespoon finely chopped fennel (optional)
½ teaspoon lemon juice

1. Arrange six shrimp for each person on six beds of lettuce. Cover with waxed paper or Saran wrap and chill.
2. Combine the remaining ingredients and let stand in the refrigerator one hour.
3. Spoon the mayonnaise sauce over the shrimp before serving.

ROQUEFORT-STUFFED SHRIMP *6 servings*

2 quarts salted water
24 jumbo shrimp
3 ounces cream cheese
1 ounce Roquefort or Danish blue cheese
½ teaspoon prepared mustard
1 teaspoon finely chopped scallion
1 cup finely chopped parsley

1. Bring two quarts salted water to a boil in a saucepan. Add the shrimp and, when the water returns to a boil, cook three to five minutes.
2. Drain the shrimp, shell and devein. Split the shrimp down the spine about halfway through. Chill.
3. Meanwhile, blend the cream cheese, Roquefort cheese, mustard and scallion. Using a knife or small spatula, stuff the cheese mixture into the split backs of the shrimp. Roll the cheese side of the shrimp in parsley and serve chilled.

ARTICHOKE BOTTOMS WITH SHRIMP *6 servings*

6 cooked artichoke bottoms
3 tablespoons olive oil
1½ tablespoons wine vinegar
Salt and freshly ground black pepper to taste
1 cup cooked shrimp, cut into small pieces
½ green pepper, finely diced
⅓ cup mayonnaise
2 teaspoons lemon juice
Paprika to taste
6 cooked whole shrimp

1. Prepare artichoke bottoms as for stuffed artichokes (page 347).

2. Marinate the artichoke bottoms in a mixture of the olive oil, wine vinegar, salt and pepper about one hour.

3. Mix the cut-up shrimp, green pepper and mayonnaise seasoned with lemon juice and paprika. Drain the artichoke bottoms and place on individual serving plates. Pile the shrimp mixture atop the artichoke bottoms, cover with a thin layer of mayonnaise and garnish each with a whole shrimp.

ISLANDER SHRIMP LUAU *6 servings*

30 raw jumbo shrimp (about 2 pounds), shelled and deveined
¼ cup lemon juice
½ teaspoon salt
1½ teaspoons curry powder
¼ teaspoon ginger
2 cups flour
1⅓ cups milk
2 teaspoon baking powder
Shaved, toasted coconut
Fat for deep frying

1. Split the shrimp lengthwise with a sharp knife, but do not cut entirely through. Combine the lemon juice, salt, curry powder and ginger and marinate the shrimp in the mixture one hour or longer.

2. Mix the flour, milk and baking powder thoroughly. Add the marinade to the batter.

3. Dredge the shrimp with additional flour, dip in the batter and roll in shaved, toasted coconut. Fry in deep fat at 375° until golden brown, four to six minutes. Serve with curry sauce (page 448).

SHRIMP WITH DILL AND LEMON SAUCE *6 servings*

½ cup sweet butter
2 pounds raw shrimp, shelled and deveined
Salt and freshly ground black pepper to taste
1 tablespoon chopped fresh dill or 2 teaspoons dried dill
Juice of 1 lemon
6 drops Tabasco sauce
1 teaspoon Worcestershire sauce

In a skillet heat the butter, add the shrimp and cook, shaking the skillet occasionally, until the shrimp are red in color and cooked through, about three minutes. Sprinkle with the remaining ingredients and serve on toothpicks.

CHILLED SHRIMP WITH DILL SAUCE *6 servings*

1 quart water
1 tablespoon salt
1 stalk celery
1 carrot
Juice of ½ lemon
¼ teaspoon cayenne pepper
1 small clove garlic
24 medium raw shrimp, shelled and deveined

1. In a deep saucepan combine all the ingredients except the shrimp and boil ten minutes.
2. Drop the shrimp into the boiling liquid and return to a boil. Cook three minutes and drain. Discard the vegetables and chill the shrimp. Serve with dill sauce (see below).

DILL SAUCE:

¾ cup olive oil
3 tablespoons lemon juice
Salt to taste
½ teaspoon dry mustard
1 tablespoon fresh chopped dill, or 2 teaspoons dried dill weed
½ clove garlic (optional)

Combine all the ingredients and mix well. Let stand overnight in the refrigerator. Discard the garlic and serve the sauce chilled.

HERRING SALAD *About 6 cups*

1 salt herring, filleted (or 2 five-ounce jars Bismarck herring)
1½ cups diced boiled potatoes
1½ cups diced cooked beets
½ cup diced peeled apples
¼ cup chopped onion
⅓ cup diced gherkin pickles
¼ cup vinegar
2 tablespoons water
2 tablespoons sugar
White pepper to taste
½ cup whipped cream
1 or 2 hard-cooked eggs, sliced
Chopped parsley
Sour cream

1. Soak the herring overnight in cold water. Drain and dice. Mix carefully with the potatoes, drained beets, apples, onion and gherkin.
2. Blend the vinegar, water, sugar and pepper and add to the herring mixture. Add the whipped cream.
3. Pack the mixture into a mold rinsed out in cold water and chill in the refrigerator.
4. Unmold and garnish with hard-cooked eggs and parsley. Serve with sour cream.

GEFULLTE FISH, PAGES 267, 268.

DANISH FISH BALLS, PAGE 270.

STUFFED EGGS *12 stuffed egg halves*

6 hard-cooked eggs
Small cubes of ham, olive or pimento
3 tablespoons butter, at room temperature
1 teaspoon Worcestershire sauce
Salt and freshly ground black pepper to taste
2 tablespoons mayonnaise

1. Divide the eggs in half lengthwise and remove the yolks. Arrange the egg halves on a cake rack and add a cube of ham, olive or pimento to each cavity.

2. Force the egg yolks through a food mill or fine sieve. Add the remaining ingredients and beat well with a wire whisk or, preferably, at high speed in an electric mixer. Beat until the mixture is perfectly smooth. If desired, anchovy paste, minced ham, lemon juice, dry mustard or mixed herbs may be used as flavoring ingredients.

3. Fit a pastry bag with a large star tube and spoon the egg-yolk mixture into it.

4. Hold the pastry bag close to and almost parallel with the cavity. Force the mixture through the tube, moving in a zig-zag fashion to form a "Turk's head."

Note: The eggs may also be cut in half widthwise and stuffed. If they are to be stuffed in this fashion, use a sharp paring knife to trim off a bit of the round bottom portion of each half and discard. This will permit the egg halves to stand upright. To fill the halves, arrange them on a cake rack and hold the pastry tube directly over the cavity. Fill the halves to produce a spiral effect. At the height of the spiral, raise the tube quickly to form a small peak.

CURRIED STUFFED EGGS, PAGE 312.

HOW TO GARNISH STUFFED EGGS

Top each egg with a round of anchovy stuffed with capers; or flat anchovy fillets cut in half and placed on the filling crosswise; or slices of pimento-stuffed green olives; or thin slices of pickles; or capers, pimento or ham; or truffles or black olives, sliced and cut into various shapes with a truffle-cutter.

EGGS A LA RUSSE *6 servings*

6 hard-cooked eggs, halved lengthwise
1 cup mayonnaise
3 tablespoons chili sauce
1 teaspoon chopped green olives
1 teaspoon chopped chives
1 teaspoon chopped parsley
1 teaspoon chopped onion
Dash of Tabasco sauce
Lemon juice to taste

Arrange two egg halves, cut side down, on each of six small plates. Combine the remaining ingredients and spoon over the eggs. Garnish with watercress.

Tarragon eggs in aspic. Trimmed poached eggs are molded in aspic. The platter is garnished with watercress and aspic.

EGGS CRESSONNIERE

- 1 cup thin, highly seasoned mayonnaise
- ¼ cup finely chopped watercress
- Hard-cooked eggs, chilled and halved lengthwise
- Watercress sprigs

To the mayonnaise add the chopped watercress. Serve over the eggs and garnish with the sprigs of watercress.

TARRAGON EGGS IN ASPIC *6 servings*

This is certainly one of the prettiest of first courses. Poached eggs in clear aspic are garnished with tarragon leaves.

Prepare quick aspic (page 431). Spoon a thin layer of chilled but still-liquid aspic into six egg molds or custard cups. Chill. Dip tarragon leaves in aspic and decorate the bottom of each mold with two leaves in a V shape. (Leaves trimmed from scallion stems may be used if fresh tarragon is not available.) Chill.

Trim six poached eggs with a round cookie cutter or paring knife. Place one

(*cont'd*)

egg and an oval of thin sliced ham in each mold. Fill the mold with chilled but still-liquid aspic. Chill.

To unmold, dip the outside of the mold quickly into a bowl of warm water and turn out on a serving dish. Garnish with watercress and aspic cut-outs.

QUICHE LORRAINE *6 to 10 servings*

It seems odd that this very special pie, traditional in France, was so long in gaining popularity in America. A rich custard with cheese and bacon, it may be served either as an appetizer or as a main luncheon dish. Swiss cheese, which the Swiss know as Ementhaler, may be used in making this dish, but Gruyère has more flavor. Gruyère is available wherever fine cheeses are sold.

Pastry for one-crust nine-inch pie
4 strips bacon
1 onion, thinly sliced
1 cup Gruyère or Swiss cheese, cubed
¼ cup Parmesan cheese, grated
4 eggs, lightly beaten
2 cups heavy cream or 1 cup each milk and cream
¼ teaspoon nutmeg
½ teaspoon salt
¼ teaspoon white pepper

1. Preheat oven to hot (450° F.).
2. Line a nine-inch pie plate with pastry and bake five minutes.
3. Cook the bacon until crisp and remove it from the skillet. Pour off all but one tablespoon of the fat remaining in the skillet. Cook the onion in the remaining fat until the onion is transparent.
4. Crumble the bacon and sprinkle the bacon, onion and cheeses over the inside of the partly baked pastry.
5. Combine the eggs, cream, nutmeg, salt and pepper and strain over the onion-cheese mixture.
6. Bake the pie fifteen minutes, reduce the oven temperature to moderate (350° F.) and bake until a knife inserted one inch from the pastry edge comes out clean, about ten minutes longer. Serve immediately as an hors d'oeuvre or main course.

CRABMEAT QUICHE *6 to 10 servings*

1½ cups crabmeat, fresh or canned
1 tablespoon chopped celery
1 tablespoon chopped onion
2 tablespoons finely chopped parsley
2 tablespoons sherry
Pastry for one-crust nine-inch pie
4 eggs, lightly beaten
2 cups cream, or 1 cup each milk and cream
¼ teaspoon nutmeg
½ teaspoon salt
¼ teaspoon white pepper

1. Pick over the crabmeat to remove bits of shell and cartilage. Combine the crabmeat, celery, onion, parsley and sherry and refrigerate one hour.

(*cont'd*)

2. Preheat oven to hot (450° F.).

3. Line a nine-inch pie plate with pastry and bake five minutes.

4. Sprinkle the inside of the partly baked pastry shell with the crabmeat mixture.

5. Combine the eggs, cream, nutmeg, salt and pepper and strain over the mixture in the pie shell.

6. Bake fifteen minutes, reduce the oven temperature to moderate (350° F.) and bake until a knife inserted one inch from the pastry edge comes out clean, about ten minutes longer. Serve immediately as an hors d'oeuvre or main course.

BAY SCALLOPS QUICHE *6 to 10 servings*

¾ pound bay scallops
2 tablespoons finely chopped parsley
¼ cup sherry
Pastry for a one-crust nine-inch pie
2 tablespoons butter
1 tablespoon finely chopped onion
1 tablespoon finely chopped celery
4 eggs, lightly beaten
¾ cup milk
1 cup cream
¼ teaspoon nutmeg
½ teaspoon salt
¼ teaspoon freshly ground black pepper

1. Combine the scallops, parsley and sherry and let stand in the refrigerator one hour.

2. Preheat oven to hot (450° F.).

3. Line a nine-inch pie plate with pastry and bake five minutes.

4. In a skillet heat the butter, add the onion and celery and cook until the onion is transparent.

5. Combine the eggs, milk, cream, nutmeg, salt and pepper and blend well. Combine the mixture with the scallops, onion and celery and pour into the pastry shell.

6. Return to the oven and bake fifteen minutes. Reduce the oven temperature to moderate (350° F.) and cook until a knife inserted one inch from the pastry edge comes out clean, about ten minutes longer.

EGG AND SPINACH PIE *6 to 8 servings*

Pastry for one-crust eight-inch pie
1 pound spinach, cooked
4 eggs
1 cup sour cream
¾ cup soft bread crumbs
1 tablespoon butter, melted
2 tablespoons grated cheese (optional)

1. Preheat oven to hot (450° F.).

2. Roll the pastry to one-eighth-inch thickness and fit loosely into an eight-inch pie pan. Prick the bottom and sides well with a fork and bake on the lower shelf of the oven until set but not brown, or about five minutes. Remove from oven and lower the temperature to moderate (350° F.).

3. Chop the spinach coarsely and drain well. Spread over the pastry. Break the eggs over the spinach and cover with sour cream. *(cont'd)*

4. Toss the crumbs in the butter and cheese and sprinkle over the top. Return to the oven and bake until the eggs are set, or about fifteen minutes longer.

Fresh Bread Crumbs: Trim crusts from slices of fresh white bread and tear bread into cubes. Blend a few at a time in an electric blender. (If no blender is available, day-old bread may be rubbed through a sieve.)

LEEK AND SAUSAGE PIE *6 servings*

9 leeks
2 cups chicken stock
6 tablespoons butter
6 tablespoons flour
½ teaspoon salt
⅛ teaspoon freshly ground black pepper
½ cup heavy cream
Freshly grated horseradish to taste
1 nine-inch pie shell, baked (page 520)
½ pound pork sausages, fully cooked and drained
1 eight-inch round of pastry, baked

1. Trim the roots and green leaves from the leeks. Split lengthwise, wash carefully and cut into julienne strips.
2. Cook the leeks in the chicken stock until just tender but not mushy, about fifteen minutes. Drain and reserve the liquid.
3. Melt the butter, blend in the flour, salt and pepper. Add two cups of the reserved liquid slowly, while stirring. Bring to a boil, cover, and then cook over hot water, stirring occasionally, for thirty minutes.
4. Preheat the oven to moderate (375° F.).
5. Add the heavy cream and leeks to the sauce and reheat. Season with horseradish to taste and place in the baked pie shell.
6. Arrange the sausages like spokes of a wheel over the sauce mixture and place the pastry round on top.
7. Reheat the pie in the oven for ten minutes. Serve immediately.

ROQUEFORT-CHEESE STRUDEL *16 servings*

Packaged strudel leaves are available at many sources in New York, some of which are listed (under Hungarian specialties) in Chapter 16. This recipe for roquefort-cheese strudel is the creation of Mrs. Silas Spitzer, a charming New York hostess.

2 packages strudel leaves
¾ cup mashed potatoes
½ cup evaporated milk
¾ cup pot cheese
6 ounces Roquefort cheese, crumbled
2 egg yolks
Salt and freshly ground black pepper to taste
½ teaspoon curry powder
2 egg whites
½ cup butter, melted
Dry bread crumbs

(cont'd)

1. Remove the packages of strudel leaves from the refrigerator at least three hours before using.

2. In an electric mixer blend the potatoes, milk, cheeses, yolks, salt, pepper and curry powder. Blend in the slightly beaten egg whites and correct the seasonings.

3. Preheat oven to moderate (375° F.).

4. Spread a large damp towel on a table. Open a sheet of strudel leaves and place on the cloth (keep the remaining dough covered to prevent drying). Brush the leaves with butter and sprinkle with crumbs. Repeat this procedure with three more sheets of leaves, placing each on top of the last.

5. Spread the nearest short edge of the leaves with half the cheese mixture, making a strip about three inches wide.

6. Roll up the strudel, using the towel as an aid and folding in the sides of the leaves. Roll onto a greased baking sheet and brush the top with butter. Repeat the process with the remaining ingredients for a second strudel.

7. Bake until golden brown, or about twenty-five to thirty minutes. Slide onto a bread board, cut into two-inch pieces and serve hot as a first course.

SPINACH-FETA STRUDEL *16 servings*

This is a Greek appetizer often served in the home of Mr. and Mrs. Leon Lianides of New York. Mr. Lianides is proprietor of the Coach House, one of the city's best "American" restaurants.

- 2 packages strudel leaves
- 2 pounds fresh spinach
- 3 tablespoons olive oil
- 1½ cups finely chopped onions
- ½ cup salt butter
- 5 eggs, beaten
- ½ cup chopped scallions, green part and all
- ½ pound Feta cheese, chopped
- ½ cup fresh dill, chopped, or 1 tablespoon dried dill
- ½ cup finely chopped parsley
- Salt and freshly ground black pepper to taste
- 1 cup sweet butter, melted

1. Remove packages of strudel leaves from the refrigerator at least three hours before using.

2. Wash the spinach in several changes of water. Dry it and cut into two-inch lengths. Cook it in oil until wilted. Drain. Brown the onions in the salt butter.

3. Mix the onions, eggs, scallions, cheese, dill and parsley. Add the spinach and season with salt and pepper.

4. Preheat oven to moderate (350° F.).

5. Butter a square 8x8x2-inch pan. Cut two strudel leaves into six squares each by cutting into thirds lengthwise and in half across (keep the remaining strudel leaves covered to prevent drying).

6. Place one of the squares in the prepared pan and brush with butter. Re-

(*cont'd*)

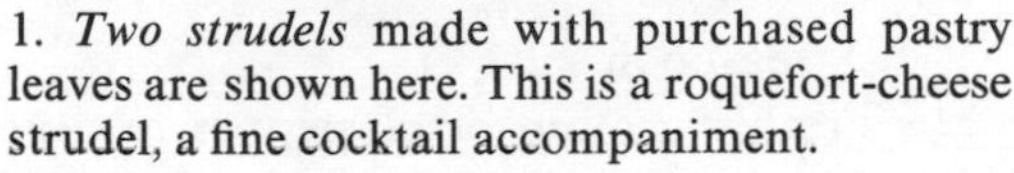

1. *Two strudels* made with purchased pastry leaves are shown here. This is a roquefort-cheese strudel, a fine cocktail accompaniment.

2. An unusual strudel of Greek origin is filled with spinach and Feta cheese. The dish may be served hot or cold.

peat with the remaining eleven strudel squares, placing each on top of the last. Spread with half the spinach-cheese filling and cover with twelve more squares, brushing each with butter. Repeat the process with the remaining ingredients for a second pan.

7. With a sharp knife, cut through the top to mark it into two-inch squares. Bake one hour, or until brown and very puffy. Cut into squares and serve hot as a first course.

PIROZHKI *About 36 servings*

Pirozhki, Russian meat turnovers, are excellent as an appetizer or as an accompaniment to borscht.

PASTRY:

1 package yeast
¼ cup lukewarm water
1 cup milk
3½ cups sifted flour, approximately
2 eggs
1 tablespoon sugar
1 teaspoon salt
2 tablespoons butter, melted

1. Soften the yeast in the water. Bring the milk to a boil and cool to lukewarm. Add the softened yeast. Add about half the flour and beat until smooth. Cover and let stand until light, thirty minutes or longer.

2. Blend one egg yolk with one tablespoon water, cover and set aside.

3. Mix the remaining egg white and whole egg, sugar, salt and melted butter. Add to the yeast mixture and blend. Add enough of the remaining flour to

(*cont'd*)

make a fairly soft dough. Knead until dough is smooth and elastic, about eight to ten minutes. Turn into a greased bowl, grease the top, cover with a towel and let rise in a warm place (80° to 85° F.) until doubled in bulk, about one and one-half hours.

4. Squeeze off small egg-sized pieces of dough and shape into balls. Roll each to less than one-quarter-inch thickness on a floured board. Place a rounded teaspoon of meat filling (see below) in the center, fold the sides of the dough over the filling and roll into a long shape with tapering ends and a plump center. Place on a greased baking sheet, cover and let stand until the dough is light, about twenty minutes.

5. Brush the tops with the reserved egg-yolk mixture and bake in a preheated hot oven (425° F.) fifteen minutes. Lower the oven temperature to 400° and bake until brown, about twenty minutes longer.

MEAT FILLING:

6 tablespoons butter
½ pound lean beef, ground
¾ cup water or meat broth
2 medium onions, chopped
2 tablespoons flour
1 teaspoon salt
Freshly ground black pepper to taste
2 tablespoons chopped parsley or ¼ teaspoon powdered dill

1. In a skillet heat half the butter, add the meat and cook until brown. Remove the meat from the pan and grind again, using the finest knife of a food grinder.

2. Add the liquid to the skillet and heat while scraping loose the browned particles.

3. In a separate skillet heat the remaining butter, add the onions and cook until brown. Stir in the flour. Add the liquid from the first skillet and cook, stirring, until thickened.

4. Mix all the ingredients and season to taste.

MUSHROOM TURNOVERS

About 2 dozen turnovers

3 three-ounce packages cream cheese, at room temperature
½ cup butter, at room temperature
1½ cups flour
Mushroom filling (page 33)

1. Mix the cream cheese and the butter thoroughly. Add the flour and work with the fingers or pastry blender until smooth. Chill well, for at least thirty minutes.

2. Preheat oven to hot (450° F.).

3. Roll the dough to one-eighth-inch thickness on a lightly floured surface and cut into rounds with a three-inch biscuit cutter. Place a teaspoon of mushroom filling on each and fold the dough over the filling. Press the edges together with a fork. Prick top crusts to allow for the escape of steam.

(*cont'd*)

4. Place on an ungreased baking sheet and bake until lightly browned, about fifteen minutes.

MUSHROOM FILLING:

3 tablespoons butter
1 large onion, finely chopped
½ pound mushrooms, finely chopped
¼ teaspoon thyme
½ teaspoon salt
Freshly ground black pepper to taste
2 tablespoons flour
¼ cup sweet or sour cream

1. In a skillet, heat the butter, add the onion and brown lightly. Add the mushrooms and cook, stirring often, about three minutes.

2. Add the thyme, salt and pepper and sprinkle with flour. Stir in the cream and cook gently until thickened.

COCKTAIL PIZZA *Approximately 36 servings*

1 package yeast
⅞ cup lukewarm water
1½ tablespoons salad oil
¾ teaspoon salt
2⅔ cups sifted flour
2 pounds (6 or 7 medium) tomatoes
¼ pound Italian sausage
2 tablespoons olive oil
1 teaspoon crushed dried orégano
½ to 1 teaspoon crushed dried basil
Freshly ground black pepper to taste
¾ pound mozzarella cheese, sliced
4 ounces flat anchovies packed in oil, drained

1. Soften the yeast in the lukewarm water.

2. Add the oil, one-quarter teaspoon of the salt and the flour and mix well. The dough should be soft but not sticky. Add a little more flour if necessary.

3. Turn the dough onto a floured surface and knead until very smooth and elastic.

4. Place in a greased bowl, grease the surface of the dough, cover with a towel and let rise in a warm place (80° to 85° F.) until double in bulk, about one and one-half hours.

5. While the dough is rising prepare tomatoes. Core and peel tomatoes and cut them into wedges. Add the remaining salt and simmer, covered, until very soft, ten minutes or longer. Drain and set the solid part aside.

6. Cook the sausage in a little water five minutes. Drain and continue cooking until lightly browned. Slice the sausage and set it aside.

7. Preheat oven to very hot (500° F.).

8. Grease a 15x10x1-inch jelly-roll pan.

9. Turn the dough out of the bowl onto a floured surface and shape into a ball. Roll the dough into a long strip that is about the size of the pan.

10. Place the dough in the pan and press and stretch with the fingers until the dough touches sides of the pan at all points.

11. Spread the tomatoes over the dough and sprinkle with the oil, orégano, basil and pepper.

(*cont'd*)

12. Arrange the sausage over one-third of the dough and cheese over the other two-thirds. Arrange the anchovies over half of the cheese-covered dough, leaving the other half with cheese only.

13. Bake the pizza on the lower shelf of the oven until it is browned, about fifteen to twenty minutes. Cut into squares or bars and serve hot.

EMPANADAS *About 10 servings*

Empanadas are a Chilean version of meat turnovers. The pastry also contains black olives, raisins and hard-cooked eggs.

FILLING:

- 1 tablespoon salad oil
- 1 tablespoon butter
- 1 Spanish onion, chopped
- ⅓ beef mixture from pastel de choclo recipe (page 112)
- 1 teaspoon paprika
- 8 pitted black olives, quartered
- 3 tablespoons raisins
- 1 tablespoon Kitchen Bouquet
- ¼ teaspoon orégano
- Tabasco to taste
- 2 hard-cooked eggs

1. Heat the oil and butter. Add the onion and brown lightly.

2. Mix all the ingredients except the eggs. Add a little water, if necessary, to moisten the mixture.

PASTRY:

- 5 cups unsifted flour
- ½ cup butter, at room temperature
- 2 egg yolks
- 1 tablespoon vinegar
- 1 teaspoon salt
- 1 cup water, approximately

1. Heap the flour on a board. Make a depression in the center and add the butter, yolks and vinegar. Mix well, using the fingers.

2. Dissolve the salt in the water. Begin sprinkling it over the flour mixture and rub the dough between the hands until it is smooth and fairly stiff. Gather the dough into a ball; continue sprinkling with salt water and kneading until the dough is no longer sticky.

3. Using about one-quarter cup dough at a time, roll into circles one-eighth inch thick and about nine inches in diameter.

4. Place about one-half cup filling on each pastry round. Add two wedges hard-cooked egg. Dip the fingers in the pan juices from the filling and run them around the pastry near the filling. Fold the dough to make a turnover, press around the filling to seal and cut the edges about one inch from the filling, using a pastry wheel to make a half-circle. Mold the curved edge of the pastry to make a triangle. Press tightly at the corners and prick the top with a fork. Brush with an egg yolk diluted with a little water.

5. Place on an ungreased baking sheet and bake in a preheated hot oven (400° F.) until brown, about fifteen minutes. Serve hot.

SPICED SPANISH OLIVES *4 to 6 servings*

1 cup green Spanish olives
¼ cup vinegar
¼ cup olive oil
2 tablespoons chopped chives
1 clove garlic, finely chopped
1 teaspoon paprika
½ teaspoon peppercorns

1. Crush the olives with a hammer or mallet until the pits show.
2. Combine the olives with the remaining ingredients and let stand at room temperature four hours. Chill in the refrigerator.

BLACK OLIVES, GRECIAN STYLE *12 to 18 servings*

2 pounds small, pointed black Greek olives
Vinegar to cover
2 lemons, thinly sliced
Celery stalks, coarsely chopped
Olive oil

1. Crack the olives with a hammer until the pits show and cover them with the vinegar. Let stand two days.
2. Drain and pack into sterilized jars, arranging the olives alternately with layers of lemon slices and celery. Cover with olive oil and keep in a cool place until ready to serve.

MIXED ITALIAN OLIVES *8 to 10 servings*

½ pound green olives
½ pound black olives
3 stalks celery, chopped
1 green pepper, chopped
1 red pepper, chopped
1 clove garlic, crushed
¼ cup olive oil
¼ cup vinegar
Freshly ground black pepper to taste
Orégano to taste

Crack the olives with a hammer until the pits show and combine with the remaining ingredients. Let stand at room temperature two days. Store in refrigerator in sealed, sterilized jars.

OLIVES WITH DILL *8 to 10 servings*

2 pounds large green olives
3 cloves garlic, crushed
2 red chili peppers
2 sprigs fresh dill, or 1 teaspoon dried dill weed
1 bay leaf
¼ cup olive oil
¼ cup vinegar

1. Drain the olives and crack them with a hammer or mallet until the pits show.
2. Combine the olives with the remaining ingredients and let stand a day or so in a cool place. Place in sterilized jars, seal and store in the refrigerator.

BLACK OLIVES WITH GARLIC

2 cloves garlic, cut
Olive oil
1 or 2 jars large ripe olives
Cracked ice

1. Rub a glass or earthenware salad bowl with the garlic and add olive oil to a depth of one-eighth to one-quarter inch. Add the ripe olives, drained, and some cracked ice. Stir thoroughly, cover and let stand at room temperature two hours. Drain and serve.

The olives absorb the oil and garlic and are very delicious.

MUSHROOMS A LA GRECQUE *About 6 servings*

The isles of Greece where burning Sappho loved and sung have contributed a splendid hors d'oeuvre.

1½ pounds whole small mushrooms
2 cups water
1 cup olive oil
Juice of 1 lemon
1 tablespoon white vinegar
1 stalk celery
1 clove garlic, peeled
½ teaspoon rosemary
½ teaspoon sage
1 branch fennel
½ teaspoon thyme
½ bay leaf
¾ teaspoon freshly ground coriander
8 peppercorns
¾ teaspoon salt

1. Combine all ingredients and bring to a boil. Simmer, stirring occasionally, five minutes.
2. Pour into a bowl and marinate overnight in the refrigerator.
3. Serve the mushrooms on toothpicks or, as a first course, on a bed of lettuce leaves.

ARTICHOKES A LA GRECQUE, PAGE 419.

MUSHROOMS UNDER GLASS *4 servings*

Glass domes or bells or cloches are available in many stores where fine imported cookware is sold. This is an inexpensive as well as elegant dish.

1 pound small or medium mushrooms
¼ cup soft butter
2 teaspoons lemon juice
1 tablespoon chopped parsley
½ teaspoon salt
Paprika (preferably imported rose paprika) to taste
4 rounds toast
½ cup cream
2 tablespoons sherry

1. Preheat oven to moderate (375° F.).
2. Trim the stems from the mushrooms and reserve for another use.
3. Cream the butter and add the lemon juice, parsley, salt and paprika. Spread the toast with half the butter mixture and place in four individual bak-

(*cont'd*)

ing dishes. Spread the remaining butter on the mushroom caps and heap them on the toast. Pour the cream over the top.

4. Cover with glass domes and bake twenty-five minutes. Add more cream if the mushrooms become dry. Just before serving, add the sherry.

MARINATED RAW MUSHROOMS *About 3 cups*

½ pound very fresh mushrooms
¼ teaspoon salt
Freshly ground black pepper to taste
½ teaspoon dried tarragon or orégano, crushed
3 tablespoons wine vinegar or lemon juice
½ cup olive oil

1. Cut the ends from the stems of the mushrooms and reserve for another use. Wash the mushrooms thoroughly, dry and slice.

2. Mix the remaining ingredients together, add to the mushrooms and toss until all the pieces are coated. Let stand at room temperature several hours. Serve with picks as a cocktail accompaniment.

MUSHROOMS STUFFED WITH LIVER *12 hors d'oeuvres*

1 pound large mushrooms
5 tablespoons butter
½ pound chicken livers
1 tablespoon minced onion
1 three-ounce package cream cheese, softened
¼ teaspoon powdered tarragon
Salt
Freshly ground black pepper to taste

1. Remove and chop the mushroom stems. In a skillet heat three tablespoons of the butter, add the mushroom caps and sauté five minutes, turning frequently. Remove to a platter.

2. Add the remaining butter to the pan and cook the chicken livers, mushroom stems and onion until the livers are lightly browned. Chop the livers very fine and cool the mixture.

3. Cream the cheese, add the liver mixture and season with the tarragon, salt and pepper. Pile the mixture into the mushroom caps and chill thoroughly.

MUSHROOMS STUFFED WITH SNAILS *6 servings*

½ cup soft butter
1 teaspoon minced shallots
1 large clove garlic, crushed
1 tablespoon minced parsley
1 tablespoon finely minced celery
¼ teaspoon salt
Freshly ground black pepper to taste
12 very large mushrooms
12 canned snails, drained

(*cont'd*)

1. Cream six tablespoons of the butter with the shallots, garlic, parsley, celery, salt and pepper.

2. Remove the mushroom stems and reserve for another use. In a skillet, heat the remaining butter, add the mushrooms caps and turn to coat on all sides. Arrange in the depressions of a snail pan, in scallop shells or in a shallow baking-serving dish.

3. Place a scant teaspoon of the herbed butter in each mushroom cap, add a snail and cover it with a little more butter.

4. Before serving, bake in a preheated moderate oven (375° F.) about fifteen minutes.

Note: Any leftover herbed butter may be used for baked or boiled fish.

BROILED STUFFED MUSHROOMS *12 hors d'oeuvres*

12 large mushrooms
3 tablespoons butter, approximately
1 small onion, chopped
1 cup fine soft bread crumbs
½ cup chopped cooked chicken, ham or shrimp, or ¼ cup chopped unsalted nuts or cooked bacon
2 tablespoons cream or sherry, approximately
Salt and freshly ground black pepper to taste
Sweet marjoram, rosemary or orégano to taste

1. Preheat broiler. Remove and chop the mushroom stems.

2. In a skillet heat one tablespoon of the butter, add the onion and chopped mushroom stems and cook about two minutes. Add the crumbs, the meat, shrimp or nuts, enough cream or sherry to moisten the mixture and the seasonings.

3. Place the mushroom caps on a baking sheet and brush with the remaining butter, melted. Broil, cup side down, in a preheated broiler about two minutes. Invert and fill with the stuffing. Brush with melted butter and broil about three minutes longer.

PLAKY (an Armenian hors d'oeuvre) *10 servings*

1 cup large, dried white beans
2½ cups water
1 teaspoon salt
3 tablespoons olive oil
1 carrot, sliced
2 celery stalks, sliced
2 tablespoons chopped parsley
1 tablespoon chopped fresh dill, or a pinch of dried dill
2 cloves garlic, minced
Freshly ground black pepper to taste
Lemon wedges

1. In a large kettle, combine the beans, water and salt, and let stand overnight. Or boil two minutes and let soak one hour before cooking.

2. Bring to a boil, reduce the heat and simmer, covered, about one and one-quarter hours.

3. Meanwhile, in a skillet heat the oil, add the carrot and celery and cook

(*cont'd*)

until golden brown. Add the parsley, dill and garlic and cook until the garlic is pale yellow. Add the mixture to the beans.

4. Simmer the mixture until the beans are tender, about fifteen minutes longer. Add the pepper and additional salt if desired. Serve at room temperature with lemon wedges.

MARINATED TUNA FISH AND VEGETABLES ITALIENNE

6 servings

There are many ingredients to this recipe but the finished product is worth the effort.

- 1 teaspoon mixed pickling spice
- 1 tablespoon tomato paste
- 3 cups water
- 1 cup olive oil
- ½ cup lemon juice
- 4 cloves garlic, minced
- ¼ teaspoon whole thyme leaves
- 1 teaspoon salt
- ¼ teaspoon freshly ground black pepper
- 1 bay leaf
- ¼ teaspoon whole basil leaves
- 1 large carrot, thinly sliced
- 1 stalk celery, thinly sliced
- 12 small white onions
- 4 mushrooms, quartered
- 2 green peppers, thinly sliced
- 2 pimentos, sliced
- 1 dill pickle, thinly sliced
- 8 green olives, whole or chopped
- 8 black olives, whole or chopped
- 1 eight-ounce can tuna fish

1. Tie the pickling spice in a cheesecloth bag. Combine in a heavy saucepan with the tomato paste, water, oil, lemon juice, garlic, thyme, salt, pepper, bay leaf and basil. Bring the mixture to a boil.

2. Add the carrot, celery and onions, reduce the heat and simmer one-half hour.

3. Add the mushrooms and green pepper and cook until pepper is tender, about ten minutes. Add the pimento, pickle, olives and tuna fish and cook five minutes longer. Discard spice bag. Cool and chill. Drain. Serve as an appetizer on a leaf of lettuce.

GUACAMOLE, PAGE 420.

CUCUMBER APPETIZER *6 servings*

- Salt
- 3 medium cucumbers, peeled and sliced
- 5 scallions, chopped fine
- Pinch of freshly ground black pepper
- ¼ teaspoon cumin powder
- ¼ teaspoon chili powder
- ¼ teaspoon powdered cloves
- 1 cup yoghurt

1. Lightly salt the cucumbers and let stand twenty minutes. Press out excess moisture from the cucumbers by spreading them on a plate and topping with another plate on which a heavy object, such as an iron, may be rested.

(cont'd)

2. Add the scallions, pepper, cumin, chili powder and cloves to the yoghurt. Blend well. Chill both the sauce and the cucumbers well. Serve the cucumbers in individual dishes, topped with the yoghurt sauce.

ANCHOVIES WITH ONION RINGS *About 2 cups*

6 anchovy fillets
1 clove garlic, minced
2 tablespoons parsley
1 teaspoon drained capers
2 tablespoons bread crumbs
1 cup olive oil
¼ cup red wine vinegar
Salt and freshly ground black pepper
1 onion sliced into rings

1. In a mortar, grind the anchovies with one tablespoon oil from the can until smooth. Add the garlic, parsley, capers and crumbs and continue grinding until the paste is well blended. Or use a blender and purée.

2. Add the oil, vinegar and salt and pepper to taste. Blend well and pour the mixture over the onions. Chill. Serve with chilled fish or meats as an hors d'oeuvre.

CELERY WITH RED-CAVIAR STUFFING *6 servings*

Black caviar is the product of the sturgeon. Red caviar comes from salmon and has its virtues, too.

2 bunches celery
½ pound cream cheese
1 tablespoon grated onion
⅓ cup chopped parsley
⅓ cup red caviar
Salt and freshly ground black pepper to taste

1. Use only choice, inner stalks of celery. Wash thoroughly.

2. Mix the softened cream cheese with the onion, parsley, caviar, salt and pepper. Stuff the celery stalks with the mixture and refrigerate until serving time.

CELERY ROOT (CELERI) REMOULADE *6 servings*

3 medium celery knobs
1 cup mayonnaise
1 tablespoon Dijon or Dusseldorf mustard, or to taste
Lemon juice

1. Pare the celery knobs well and, using a sharp knife, cut them into slices about one-sixteenth of an inch thick. Cut the slices into strips as thin or thinner than a toothpick.

2. Combine the mayonnaise and mustard and season to taste with lemon juice. Thoroughly combine celery and mayonnaise and let stand in the refrigerator until serving time.

EGYPTIAN BEANS *4 hors d'oeuvre servings*

½ cup dried pea or navy beans
1½ cups water
½ teaspoon salt
Small clove garlic, crushed
¼ cup olive oil
2 tablespoons lemon juice
1 scallion, sliced fine

1. Soak the beans overnight in the water with the salt; or boil two minutes and soak one hour or longer. Bring to a boil, cover and reduce the heat. Simmer gently until the beans are tender, one and one-half to two hours.
2. Drain the beans thoroughly and add the remaining ingredients. Mix gently but thoroughly. Chill.
3. At serving time correct the seasonings and serve the beans on romaine lettuce garnished with scallions.

BEET AND SCALLION APPETIZER *About 4 servings*

3 medium beets, cooked
¼ cup chopped scallions
½ teaspoon prepared mustard
½ cup sour cream
Freshly ground black pepper or Tabasco sauce to taste
½ teaspoon lemon juice

1. Cut the beets in thin matchlike strips, or chop coarsely. Add the scallions.
2. Mix the remaining ingredients, add to the beets and blend. Chill. Serve on chilled plates with toast.

PICKLED WATERMELON RIND IN BLANKETS

Wrap pieces of pickled watermelon rind in short lengths of bacon. Secure with toothpicks.

At serving time, broil three inches from high heat until the bacon is brown. Serve hot, allowing three per serving.

IRMA'S ONION SANDWICHES *6 servings*

This is one of the finest and most popular appetizers served in New York. Its success depends on the quality of the brioche or bread used and the thinness of the onion-slice filling, which must be nearly transparent.

7 brioche or any fine-textured bread
18 small, wafer-thin slices raw onion
¾ cup mayonnaise
Salt to taste
½ cup minced parsley

1. Slice the brioche across in pieces about one-quarter inch thick; there should be about five slices from each brioche. Cut the slices into rounds with a small biscuit cutter, about one inch in diameter. *(cont'd)*

2. Choose small onions and slice them so that each circle will be a little smaller than the brioche rounds.

3. Spread each piece of brioche with mayonnaise. On half the pieces arrange one onion slice and season with salt. Cover the onion with the remaining pieces of brioche to make sandwiches.

4. Spread the remaining mayonnaise on a wooden board and sprinkle the chopped parsley on another board. Hold each sandwich lightly between thumb and finger so it will turn like a wheel. Roll the edge in mayonnaise, then in parsley. Set the sandwiches, as they are completed, on waxed paper and chill thoroughly.

TUNA AND CHEESE CANAPES *About 12 canapés*

1 cup grated cheddar cheese
½ cup canned tuna fish
2 tablespoons dry vermouth
Freshly ground black pepper to taste
Toast squares

Combine the first four ingredients and blend well. Spread on squares of lightly browned toast and bake in a preheated moderate oven (350° F.) five minutes.

SARDINE CANAPES *About 12 small canapés*

1 can boneless sardines, drained
2 tablespoons lemon juice
1 tablespoon cream
½ teaspoon dry mustard
1 tablespoon mayonnaise
Freshly ground black pepper to taste
Few drops of Tabasco sauce
Toast rounds
Hard-cooked egg slices or sliced green olives

Mash the sardines with a fork and mix with the seasonings. Spread on toast rounds and garnish with hard-cooked egg slices or sliced green olives.

DEVILED SARDINE CANAPES *6 servings*

2 tablespoons prepared mustard
Juice of 1 lemon
1 can sardines
3 tablespoons fine, soft bread crumbs
4 slices buttered toast, cut into strips the size of sardines
Lemon wedges, watercress and parsley

1. Combine the mustard, lemon juice and oil from the can of sardines.

2. Roll individual sardines in the mustard preparation, then in the bread crumbs. Broil two to three minutes on either side in a preheated broiler. Place the sardines on toast strips and spear with toothpicks. Serve hot on a tray garnished with lemon wedges, watercress and parsley.

HOT SARDINE CANAPES

Mash the contents of two small cans of sardines and moisten with a little of the oil from the can. Add a few drops of lemon juice, Tabasco sauce and freshly ground black pepper.

Spread on buttered toast fingers and bake in a preheated moderate oven (350° F.) until the sardine mixture is heated through.

Serve with lemon wedges.

SHRIMP CANAPES A LA SUEDE *6 servings*

18 medium shrimp, cooked, shelled and deveined
12 toast rounds
Butter
Mayonnaise
12 sprigs fresh dill
Lemon wedges
Freshly ground pepper

1. Slice each shrimp in half lengthwise.
2. Butter the toast rounds and arrange three shrimp halves in a spiral on each round.
3. Garnish the canapés, if desired, with mayonnaise "stars" pressed from a pastry tube. Top with dill sprigs. Serve with lemon wedges and freshly ground black pepper.

CURRIED CHEESE CANAPES *8 to 10 canapés*

1 three-ounce package cream cheese
8 pitted ripe olives, chopped
¼ teaspoon curry powder
1 teaspoon chopped chives
Toast rounds

Blend the first four ingredients well and spread on toast rounds. If desired, the mixture may be seasoned with a little lemon juice.

CLAM AND CHEESE CANAPES *About 16 canapés*

1 cup grated cheddar cheese
1 eight-ounce can minced clams, drained
Pinch of cayenne pepper
2 tablespoons chopped parsley
1 tablespoon chopped chives (optional)
Toast rounds

Combine the cheese, clams and seasonings. Spread on toast rounds and broil briefly in a preheated broiler.

ANCHOVY AND PIMENTO CANAPES

Cover squares of buttered toast with pimento slices cut to size. Cover with a latticework of flat anchovy fillets.

EGG AND SMALL-CRESS SANDWICHES

Chop hard-cooked eggs and mix to a paste with melted butter. Season to taste with mustard, salt, freshly ground white pepper, grated onion and vinegar. Spread on one side of a slice of bread, arrange small cress over the egg mixture and top with a slice of bread. Trim the crusts and cut the sandwiches into strips or triangles.

Watercress sprigs may be substituted for mustard cress or small cress, which is often difficult to obtain.

SCHLEMMERSCHNITTE A LA LUCHOW *6 servings*

To make this dish, Lüchow's uses fillet of beef and fresh caviar. But economy-minded cooks can substitute high-quality round steak and pasteurized caviar.

Thickly pile three-quarters pound finely ground raw round steak on six pieces of toast. Garnish with four ounces black caviar.

CUCUMBER CANAPES

Neatly trim the crusts from fresh bread slices and cut each slice into four equal squares. Spread each square with a little softened butter or mayonnaise.

Peel cucumbers and cut into wafer-thin slices. Place a layer of cucumber slices on the bread squares.

Serve with salt, lemon wedges and freshly ground black pepper.

CANAPE SANGRONIZ *12 canapés*

6 tablespoons Roquefort cheese
1 tablespoon butter
1 teaspoon sour cream
3 slices white bread
6 tablespoons caviar
Lemon juice

1. Blend together the Roquefort cheese, butter and sour cream.
2. Toast the bread and spread with the cheese mixture. Top each slice with two tablespoons of the caviar. Add a few drops of lemon juice. Cut each slice into four equal strips.

PARMESAN CHEESE CANAPES *2 dozen canapés*

2 slices bacon
½ cup grated Parmesan cheese
¼ cup evaporated milk
½ teaspoon Worcestershire sauce
24 small toast rounds, squares or triangles
Pimento-stuffed olives, sliced

(cont'd)

1. Preheat oven to hot (400° F.).
2. In a skillet, cook the bacon until crisp. Remove from the pan and crumble.
3. Blend the cheese, milk, Worcestershire sauce and crumbled bacon. Spread the mixture on the toast pieces and top with olive slices.
4. Bake five minutes and serve hot.

BAKED CHEESE CANAPES *12 canapés*

1 three-ounce package cream cheese
1 teaspoon minced onion
1 egg, beaten
¼ teaspoon Tabasco sauce
12 rounds toasted bread

1. Preheat oven to moderate (375° F.).
2. Combine the cheese, onion, egg and Tabasco and beat with a whisk until light.
3. Spread the mixture on the toast and bake until lightly browned.

ANCHOVY AND CURRY CANAPES *8 to 12 canapés*

Finely chop the contents of one can flat anchovy fillets with one-fourth cup softened sweet butter, one teaspoon crumbled blue cheese and one teaspoon curry powder. Add a drop or two of Worcestershire sauce, if desired, and spread on toast fingers.

CRAB AND ARTICHOKE CANAPES *8 to 10 servings*

½ cup Russian dressing
¼ teaspoon dry mustard
1 six-ounce can crabmeat, picked over well
1 ten-ounce can artichoke bottoms, drained
2 tablespoons chopped parsley
Lemon wedges

1. Combine the Russian dressing and mustard and fold in the crabmeat, mixing lightly but thoroughly.
2. Pile the mixture on the artichoke bottoms. Just before serving, brown the canapés in a preheated broiler and sprinkle with chopped parsley. Garnish with lemon wedges and serve immediately.

CANAPES A LA SIMON *About 2 dozen canapés*

Cut small rounds of thinly sliced bread with a biscuit cutter and toast in broiler.

In a skillet, cook six or seven slices bacon until soft, chop and mix with one cup Major Grey's chutney.

(cont'd)

Spread the mixture on the toast rounds and broil in a preheated broiler about five inches from the source of heat until a slight crust is formed on top and the canapés are heated through.

CRABMEAT CANAPES *About 16 canapés*

- 1 can crabmeat, picked over well
- ¼ cup mayonnaise
- 1 tablespoon chopped parsley
- 1 tablespoon chopped chives
- 1 teaspoon lemon juice
- 1 teaspoon Worcestershire sauce
- Tabasco sauce to taste
- Freshly ground black pepper to taste
- Toast rounds

Combine the crabmeat with the mayonnaise, herbs and seasonings. Spread on rounds of toast and serve immediately.

AVOCADO CANAPES

Remove the crusts from very thin slices of white and dark bread. Spread with butter and seasoned mayonnaise. Place wafer-thin slices of cold roast turkey or chicken on white bread and then add a layer of thinly sliced avocado. Top with a slice of dark bread.

Wrap in a damp towel and refrigerate a few hours. Cut into small wedges.

Set upright in tiny pyramids on a tray ringed with parsley. Picks may be used to hold the wedges together.

CUCUMBER SANDWICHES

Slice a cucumber very thin and let soak in vinegar for a few minutes. Drain, season to taste with salt and freshly ground black pepper and place between thin slices of well-buttered bread. Trim crusts, cut into strips or triangles.

ROLLED PICNIC SANDWICHES

Using a sharp knife, remove the crusts from a loaf of unsliced white bread. Cut the bread into very thin slices and spread with a little soft butter or softened cream cheese. Cover each slice with chopped watercress leaves or thin slices of scallions and roll like a jelly roll.

Garnish each end, if desired, with a sprig of watercress. Wrap the sandwiches close together in aluminum foil or Saran wrap and keep chilled in a dry place until ready to serve.

Roquefort or Danish blue cheese mixed with a little soft butter, or the cheese known as petit Suisse, also makes a flavorful spread for these sandwiches.

SWISS FONDUE *8 servings*

1 clove garlic
1½ cups Neuchâtel or Fendant wine
1 pound natural Gruyère cheese, grated (do not use processed Gruyère)
2 teaspoons cornstarch
3 tablespoons kirsch
Freshly ground black pepper

1. Rub the bottom and sides of an earthenware casserole or chafing dish with the garlic. Add the wine and heat to the boiling point, but do not boil.

2. Add the cheese, stirring constantly with a wooden spoon. When the cheese is creamy and barely simmering, add the cornstarch blended with the kirsch. Stir until the mixture bubbles. Add pepper to taste.

3. Place the casserole over an alcohol burner with a slow flame. Keep the fondue hot but not simmering. If it becomes too thick, add a little more wine.

4. To serve, accompany with cubes of crusty bread for dipping into the casserole of melted cheese.

SHRIMP FONDUE, PAGE 291.

FONDUE BRUXELLOISE *10 servings*

¼ cup butter
6 tablespoons flour
1½ cups milk
2 cups grated Gruyère cheese
1 cup grated Parmesan cheese
½ teaspoon salt
Dash of freshly ground black pepper
3 egg yolks, lightly beaten
Flour, egg and fine dry bread crumbs

1. Melt the butter in a saucepan. Stir in the flour, using a wire whisk, until blended. Meanwhile, bring the milk to a boil and add all at once to the butter-flour mixture, stirring vigorously with the whisk. Add the cheeses, salt and pepper and cook, stirring, until the cheese has melted. Remove from the heat, correct the seasonings and let cool. Stir in the egg yolks.

2. Pour the mixture into a nine-inch-square pan. Chill overnight.

3. Cut into two-inch fancy shapes. Coat with flour, egg beaten with a little water and finally with the bread crumbs. Let dry at room temperature or in the refrigerator.

4. Fry a few at a time in deep fat heated to 390° F. until browned. Drain on absorbent paper. Serve at once. If desired, accompany with fried parsley.

BEIGNETS AU FROMAGE *About 3 dozen beignets*

¾ cup flour
¼ teaspoon salt
1 tablespoon salad oil
1 egg, beaten
½ cup beer, at room temperature
1 egg white, stiffly beaten
1 pound natural Gruyère cheese cut into small cubes
Fat for deep frying

(cont'd)

1. Sift one-half cup of the flour with the salt and stir in oil and egg. Add the beer gradually, stirring until the mixture is smooth. Let stand one hour. Fold in the egg white.

2. Lightly dredge the cubes of cheese in the remaining flour and coat with the batter. Brown in deep fat heated to 375° F. Drain on absorbent paper and serve piping hot.

CRUMBED CAMEMBERT

Carefully remove the rind from ripe camembert and roll wheel or individual wedges in fine, soft bread crumbs or finely chopped, toasted almonds.

HUNGARIAN CHEESE *8 to 10 servings*

This is a version of the classic European appetizer known as Liptauer Käse.

- 1 cup cottage cheese
- 1 cup butter
- 1 tablespoon caraway seeds, crushed or whole
- 1 tablespoon capers, minced
- 1 tablespoon chives, minced
- 1 tablespoon dry mustard
- 1 anchovy, chopped
- 1 tablespoon paprika

1. Put the cheese through a ricer or fine sieve.

2. Cream the butter with the caraway seeds, capers, chives, mustard and anchovy and gradually stir in the cottage cheese.

3. Form the mixture into a mound, sprinkle with paprika and garnish with salad greens. Serve as an appetizer or salad.

STUFFED FRENCH BREAD *24 to 36 slices*

- 3 three-ounce packages cream cheese
- 1 can anchovy fillets, rubbed to a paste
- 1 tablespoon capers or chopped sour pickle
- 2 tablespoons chili sauce
- 1 teaspoon grated onion
- 1 teaspoon Worcestershire sauce
- 3 dashes Tabasco sauce
- Salt to taste
- ½ cup butter, at room temperature
- ½ cup minced watercress
- 1 tablespoon fine, soft bread crumbs
- 1 long loaf French bread

1. Cream the cheese until smooth. Add the anchovy paste, capers, chili sauce, onion, Worcestershire, Tabasco and salt. Thin to a stiff spreading consistency with liquid from the caper or anchovy container.

2. Cream the butter, add the watercress and crumbs and mix.

3. Split the bread lengthwise and remove the center. Spread the entire cavity of the upper half with watercress butter. Fill the cavity of the lower half with

(*cont'd*)

the cheese mixture, piling it up so that when the top half of the loaf is pressed over the lower, the entire cavity will be filled. Wrap in foil and chill well. Using a sharp knife, cut into thin slices before serving.

CHEESE STRAWS *4 dozen straws*

- ½ cup butter, at room temperature
- 2 cups shredded sharp cheddar cheese, lightly packed
- ½ cup milk
- ½ teaspoon salt
- ¼ teaspoon Tabasco sauce
- Dash of paprika
- Dash of cayenne pepper
- 1½ cups sifted flour
- 3 cups fine, soft bread crumbs
- Grated Parmesan cheese

1. Cream the butter in the small bowl of an electric mixer. Beat in the cheddar cheese, milk, salt, Tabasco, paprika and cayenne. Gradually mix in the flour and bread crumbs.
2. Turn the mixture out on a smooth surface and knead by hand until the mixture is blended. Divide into halves and wrap each half in waxed paper. Chill in the refrigerator several hours or overnight.
3. Preheat oven to moderate (350° F.).
4. Between two layers of waxed paper, roll out half the dough at a time to one-eighth-inch thickness. Using a pastry wheel, cut into strips six inches long and one-half inch wide. Sprinkle with Parmesan cheese.
5. Place on greased baking sheets and bake until lightly browned, ten to fifteen minutes.

CARAWAY BREAD STICKS *About 3 dozen*

- 1 cup lukewarm water
- 1 package yeast
- 1 tablespoon sugar
- 1½ teaspoons salt
- ½ teaspoon nutmeg
- 2 tablespoons caraway seeds
- 1 tablespoon leaf sage, crumbled
- ¼ cup soft shortening
- 1 egg
- 3 to 3¼ cups sifted all-purpose flour

1. Measure the water into a mixing bowl. Add the yeast, stirring to dissolve. Stir in the remaining ingredients; beat and knead vigorously. Cover with a towel and refrigerate at least two hours, or overnight.
2. About two hours before baking, divide the chilled dough into two parts. Return half to the refrigerator for use in several days.
3. Divide the remaining dough into eighteen small pieces. Roll into eight-inch pencil-like strips and place one inch apart on a greased baking sheet. Brush with melted shortening and cover with a towel. Let rise until doubled in bulk, about two hours.
4. Bake in a preheated hot oven (400° F.) until crisp and golden brown, twelve to fifteen minutes.

GARLIC BREAD *6 to 8 servings*

2 loaves French bread
½ cup butter, melted
1 clove garlic, finely chopped
1 tablespoon Parmesan cheese (optional)

1. Cut the bread diagonally in one-inch slices without cutting through the bottom crust.
2. To the butter add the garlic and cheese and brush the cut surfaces of the bread with the garlic butter.
3. Wrap the bread in aluminum foil and bake in a preheated moderate oven (350° F.) until heated through, about fifteen minutes.

HOT HERB BREAD *3 to 4 servings*

1 loaf French bread
½ cup sweet butter
1 large clove garlic, crushed
¼ cup minced parsley
½ teaspoon or less dried basil, orégano or other herb
Salt and freshly ground black pepper to taste

1. Preheat oven to moderate (375° F.).
2. Slice almost through the bread at one-and-one-half-inch intervals, leaving it attached at the bottom crust.
3. Cream the butter with the remaining ingredients and spread the cut surfaces with the herbed butter. Place on baking sheet and heat about ten minutes. Serve hot.

Note: Before heating, the bread may be wrapped in foil, with the top left exposed, to eliminate need for washing a greasy pan.

CORNMEAL CRACKERS *2 dozen crackers*

1¾ cups sifted flour
½ cup cornmeal
2 teaspoons baking powder
1 teaspoon salt
1 tablespoon sugar
1 egg, lightly beaten
¾ cup sour cream
1 five-ounce jar cheese spread, at room temperature
2 tablespoons caraway seeds
2 tablespoons butter, melted
2 tablespoons poppy seeds

1. Preheat oven to hot (400° F.).
2. Sift together the flour, cornmeal, baking powder, salt and sugar. Gradually add the egg and sour cream, stirring until well mixed.
3. Turn the dough out onto a lightly floured surface and knead gently a few seconds. Roll to one-eighth-inch thickness.
4. Spread half the dough with the cheese spread and sprinkle with the caraway seeds. Cut into shapes with a small floured biscuit cutter, or cut into squares with a knife.

(cont'd)

5. Spread the other half of the dough with the melted butter, sprinkle with poppy seeds and cut into squares.

6. Place on an ungreased cookie sheet and bake eight to ten minutes.

ROQUEFORT AND COGNAC *About 3 cups*

1 pound Roquefort cheese
½ cup butter
Pinch of cayenne pepper
⅓ cup cognac, approximately

1. Blend the cheese with the butter until creamy, using an electric blender or a fork.

2. Season the mixture with cayenne and beat in cognac to taste. Add a little more cognac before using to make the mixture spread easily. Serve with toast or toasted crackers.

Note: The mixture will keep several weeks in small jars in the refrigerator.

CARAWAY AND CHEESE SPREAD *About ½ cup*

1 three-ounce package cream cheese
1 tablespoon capers
2 tablespoons caraway seeds
2 tablespoons sour cream
½ clove garlic, crushed, or one teaspoon finely minced onion

Combine all the ingredients and beat well with a fork or in an electric mixer until well blended. Serve on miniature rounds of rye bread.

CHEDDAR CHEESE AND SHERRY SPREAD *About 2 cups*

¼ pound cheddar cheese, grated
¾ cup sour cream
3 tablespoons sherry

Combine the cheese, sour cream and sherry. Beat vigorously with a wooden spoon or in the bowl of an electric beater until light and fluffy. Add more seasonings, such as Tabasco sauce, if desired. Chill and serve with buttered toast or crackers.

HORSERADISH–CREAM CHEESE DIP *1 cup*

2 three-ounce packages cream cheese
¼ cup sour cream, approximately
2 to 4 tablespoons freshly grated horseradish
Salt and freshly ground black pepper to taste
Paprika
Tabasco sauce
2 tablespoons chopped parsley

1. Mash the cheese and gradually blend in the sour cream. Add the horseradish and seasonings to taste and beat until the mixture is light and fluffy.

2. Chill and sprinkle with parsley. Serve with raw vegetables cut into bite-sized pieces.

GREEK TARAMA SALAD *8 generous servings*

Most people are familiar with black and red caviar. The Greeks have a word for another kind of caviar and it is tarama. *It makes an excellent salad accompaniment or appetizer.*

3 tablespoons bottled tarama (carp roe)
2 tablespoons lemon juice
3 slices white bread
¾ cup olive oil or equal portions olive oil and salad oil

1. Place the tarama and the lemon juice in the bowl of an electric mixer and blend on low speed until thoroughly mixed.

2. Meanwhile, trim crusts from the bread and soak the slices in cold water. Squeeze the bread thoroughly.

3. Break the bread into the mixture and blend at medium high speed until thoroughly blended. Add the oil gradually. The mixture should thicken to the consistency of thick mayonnaise. Serve in the center of a salad tray ringed with slices of green pepper, tomatoes, cucumbers, lettuce and olives. Or serve as an appetizer with buttered toast.

Note: Tarama is available in many Greek grocery stores. See Chapter 16.

BRAZIL-NUT CLAM SPREAD *About 1 cup*

1 three-ounce package cream cheese
1/16 teaspoon curry powder
1 can (10 ounces) minced clams
¼ cup finely chopped Brazil nuts

1. Blend the cream cheese with the curry powder.

2. Drain the clams well and add to the cream cheese. Mix thoroughly and stir in the Brazil nuts. Turn into a serving dish and serve with crackers.

SMOKED SALMON DIP *About ¾ cup*

4 ounces smoked salmon, shredded
⅓ cup heavy cream
½ teaspoon capers (optional)
⅛ teaspoon freshly ground black pepper

Put all the ingredients into the container of an electric blender and blend until smooth. Or grind the salmon and capers, whip the cream and combine all the ingredients. Grind additional pepper over the top of the dip.

GORGONZOLA DIP *About ¾ cup*

4 ounces Gorgonzola or other blue cheese
1 three-ounce package cream cheese
⅓ cup cognac or cream

Mash the Gorgonzola, add the cream cheese and mix until smooth. Add the cognac or cream to give a soft consistency.

Use for sliced apples, pears or crackers.

SOUR CREAM AND RED CAVIAR *About 1¼ cups*

¾ cup sour cream
4 ounces red caviar (salmon roe)

Combine the sour cream with the caviar and chill. Serve as a first course on lettuce leaves, or as a cocktail dip.

DEVILED CHICKEN SPREAD *1 cup*

¼ cup finely chopped scallions
1 cup ground cooked chicken
2 or 3 drops Tabasco sauce
Salt to taste
2 tablespoons mayonnaise

Combine all the ingredients until well blended. Chill, if desired, before serving. Use as sandwich spread.

HERBED CREAM CHEESE *About 1 cup*

1 garlic clove, minced
1 to 2 teaspoons minced onion
¼ teaspoon salt
Pinch of dry mustard
1 three-ounce package cream cheese
¼ cup mayonnaise
1 tablespoon lemon juice
2 tablespoons chopped olives
¼ teaspoon thyme
Dash of Tabasco
Chopped parsley or chives

1. Blend together the garlic, onion, salt and mustard. Add the cream cheese and cream until smooth.

2. Add the mayonnaise, lemon juice, olives, thyme and Tabasco and blend. Sprinkle with parsley or chives. Serve with seafood or raw vegetables such as celery stalks, fennel or cauliflower buds.

SAMBAL DIP *1¾ cups*

1 one-quarter-inch slice medium onion
1 clove garlic
2 stalks celery
½ large cucumber, peeled
½ green pepper, seeded
½ teaspoon salt
½ teaspoon turmeric
½ teaspoon powdered ginger
⅛ teaspoon chili powder
⅛ teaspoon cumin seed, crushed
1 tablespoon tomato paste
1 cup sour cream

1. Grind the onion, garlic, celery, cucumber and green pepper in a food chopper, using the finest knife. Turn into a sieve and press out the juice. (The juice may be added to tomato juice, soup, sauces, stews.)

2. Sprinkle salt, turmeric, ginger, chili powder and cumin seed over the vegetables and mix thoroughly. Blend in the tomato paste.

3. Add the sour cream and stir until mixed. Chill until ready to serve. Use as a dip for cheese cubes or crackers.

CHAPTER TWO

SOUPS

BEEF STOCK OR BOUILLON *3 quarts before concentration*

A good stock is the basis for literally thousands of the world's finest dishes. Although the preparation of beef stock is time-consuming it is not a complicated procedure. It can be made in large quantities and, given sufficient storage space, frozen for future use.

3 pounds shin of beef
2 marrow bones
3 pounds chuck beef, cut into thirds
Water
1½ tablespoons salt
6 peppercorns
1 large onion, peeled or unpeeled, studded with 4 cloves
1 large or 2 small leeks
1 bay leaf
½ teaspoon thyme
2 carrots, washed and trimmed
2 sprigs parsley
2 stalks celery
1 white turnip, quartered (optional)

1. Remove the meat from the shinbone and reserve. Place the shinbone and marrow bones in boiling water, cook five minutes and drain well.

2. Place the bones and all the meat including the trimmings in a large kettle. Add three quarts of water. Bring to a rolling boil and reduce the heat. Skim the surface to remove the foam and fat. Continue skimming until the foam ceases to rise.

3. Add the salt, peppercorns and onion. Trim the leek and split down the center toward the root without cutting through. Wash well under cold running water. Place the bay leaf in the center of the leek and sprinkle with thyme. Tie the cut portion with string and add to the simmering liquid. Add the carrots, parsley, celery and turnip.

4. Cover loosely and simmer gently four or five hours.

5. Strain the liquid through a double thickness of cheesecloth. (The meat may be used for hash.) Taste the stock and, if a greater concentration is desired, simmer uncovered until it reaches the desired flavor.

6. Cool quickly by placing the kettle in cold water. Chill until the fat solidifies. Skim off the fat.

POT AU FEU, PAGE 94.

CLARIFIED BOUILLON

There are several methods of clarifying bouillon. The easiest is with egg whites and eggshells.

4 cups cold bouillon
2 egg whites
2 crushed eggshells

1. Bring the bouillon to a boil.

2. Beat the egg whites to a froth and add them along with eggshells to the stock. Bring to a rolling boil, stirring constantly, and remove from the heat.

3. Wring a flannel cloth with cold water and use it to line a colander. Pour the stock through. Reheat the bouillon before serving.

COURT BOUILLON, PAGE 229.

CONSOMME A LA MADRILENE *About 2 quarts*

Tomatoes are frequently related to the cuisine of Madrid. Thus the name consommé à la Madrilène, or consommé in the style of Madrid.

2½ pounds lean beef, cut in 3 portions
1½ pounds marrow bone
3½ quarts cold water
2 onions, stuck with 3 cloves
3 carrots, cut up
2 stalks celery with leaves
3 leeks, sliced lengthwise and washed
1½ tablespoons salt
6 peppercorns
2 sprigs parsley
Pinch of thyme
1 clove garlic
1 bay leaf
3 egg whites, beaten
3 crushed eggshells
2 cups tomato purée
2 tablespoons finely chopped onion
½ teaspoon dried basil

1. In a large kettle combine the beef, bone and water and bring to a boil. Simmer five minutes and skim. Cover and simmer one hour.

2. Add the onions stuck with cloves, the carrots, celery, leeks, salt, peppercorns, parsley, thyme, garlic and bay leaf. Cover and cook slowly four to five hours. Strain through a double thickness of cheesecloth and skim off the fat. Use absorbent paper towels, if necessary, to remove the remaining particles of fat. Discard bone and vegetables and reserve the meat for another purpose.

3. To clarify the consommé, return it to the heat and add the beaten egg whites and eggshells. Bring to a rolling boil and strain once more through three thicknesses of cheesecloth.

4. Pour six cups of the consommé into a saucepan and reserve the remainder for another use. Add the tomato purée, onion and dried basil. Simmer twenty minutes, remove from the heat and strain through cheesecloth. Serve hot.

HOW TO GARNISH CONSOMME

Bouillon or beef stock becomes a consommé when it is reduced to give a more concentrated flavor. Consommé, in turn, becomes double consommé when it is reduced still further. There are hundreds of garnishes for consommé in French cuisine.

CONSOMME ARGENTEUIL: Just before serving consommé, add one-half cup cooked asparagus tips for each quart and one-half of consommé.

CONSOMME AUX CHEVEUX D'ANGE: Just before serving consommé, add one-half cup cooked vermicelli (thin spaghetti) for each quart and one-half consommé.

CONSOMME LUCETTE: Bring two quarts consommé to a boil and add one-third cup alphabet noodles. Cook until the noodles are tender, or about six minutes. Just before serving, stir in two tablespoons of raw chopped tomato. Serve in soup plates containing a freshly poached egg.

CONSOMME ROYALE: Just before serving consommé, add a few small cubes of royal custard (see below). The custard may be cut in fancy shapes with a French vegetable cutter if desired.

ROYAL CUSTARD

1 whole egg
2 egg yolks
½ cup heavy cream or consommé
Salt and freshly ground black pepper

1. Preheat oven to slow (300° F.).
2. Beat the egg and yolks until light. Stir in the cream. Season with salt and pepper and pour the mixture into a shallow buttered pan. Place the pan in a skillet containing hot water.
3. Bake until firm, fifteen to twenty minutes. Cool and chill. When cold, cut into fancy shapes and serve as a garnish for consommé.

LIVER DUMPLINGS IN SOUP

8 servings, or 3 to 4 dozen dumplings

There is something very middle-European and old-fashioned about liver dumplings in soup. It is also delicious.

¼ pound liver (beef, calf, lamb, pork or chicken)
½ small onion
1 egg yolk
¼ teaspoon salt
Pinch of freshly ground black pepper
Pinch of thyme
Pinch of nutmeg
1½ tablespoons minced parsley
1½ slices bread without crusts
Milk or water
½ cup sifted flour, approximately
2 quarts soup stock

1. Trim the liver and grind with the onion, using the finest knife of food grinder. Add the egg yolk, salt, pepper, thyme, nutmeg and parsley.

(cont'd)

2. Soak the bread in milk or water to moisten and squeeze out excess liquid. Add to the liver. Add enough flour to make a soft dough.

3. Bring the soup stock to a boil. Dip a teaspoon in the soup, then fill it with liver batter and drop the batter into the soup. Re-dip spoon in broth before shaping each dumpling. Cover the pot and simmer ten to fifteen minutes, depending on the size of the dumplings.

DUCK GIBLET SOUP *5 servings*

While a duck roasts on a spit, its giblets can be put to excellent use.

Giblets, wings and necks of two ducks
5 cups water
1 teaspoon salt
1 medium onion
1 slice celery root
1 cup raw long-grain rice
1 tablespoon butter
1 tablespoon flour
Freshly grated nutmeg

1. In a kettle place the giblets, wings and necks and water. Add the salt, onion and celery root and simmer, covered, until the giblets are thoroughly done, about one hour.

2. Strain the soup into another kettle and add the rice. Cook about twenty minutes, or until the rice is tender but still firm.

3. Remove the meat from the necks and wings and reserve along with the giblets, halved or left whole. Combine with the rice and bring to a boil. Blend the butter and flour and add to the soup. Cook four minutes longer. Add a generous dash of nutmeg.

MINESTRONE *6 generous servings*

If Italy can be said to have a national soup, minestrone is it. It is one of the most fortifying of dishes and has few peers for winter meals.

½ pound dry white beans soaked in water overnight
3 quarts salted water
1 teaspoon olive oil
⅛ pound salt pork, cut into small dice
1 clove garlic, chopped fine
1 small onion, chopped
1 leek, diced and washed
1 teaspoon chopped parsley
1 teaspoon chopped basil
1 tablespoon tomato paste
3 tomatoes, peeled, seeded and chopped
3 stalks celery, chopped
2 carrots, sliced
2 potatoes, diced
1 small turnip, peeled and diced
¼ small cabbage, shredded
2 zucchini, diced
1½ quarts water
Salt to taste
½ teaspoon freshly ground black pepper
1 cup elbow macaroni or ditali
6 tablespoons grated Parmesan cheese

(*cont'd*)

Robust soups. From the left: bouillabaisse from France; minestrone from Italy; chicken corn soup, traditionally American.

1. Drain the beans and boil them in the salted water about one hour, or until tender. (Or use quick soaking method on page 64.) Drain.

2. Place the olive oil in a large kettle and add the salt pork, garlic, onion, leek, parsley and basil. Brown lightly. Add the tomato paste thinned with a little water and cook five minutes. Add the tomatoes, celery, carrots, potatoes, turnip, cabbage, zucchini, water, salt and pepper and cook slowly forty-five minutes to one hour. Add the beans.

3. Add the elbow macaroni and cook ten minutes, or until tender. Correct the seasonings and pour into heated bowls. Serve immediately, sprinkled with grated Parmesan cheese.

Note: The number and kinds of vegetables used in making minestrone are optional. They may be included according to season.

UKRAINIAN BORSCHT *12 servings*

The only ingredient that is constant in borscht is beets. It can be made with almost any stock except, perhaps, fish stock. Here is a hearty borscht from the Ukraine.

- 2 pounds soup beef with cracked soup bone
- 2½ quarts cold water
- 1 pound lean fresh pork
- ½ pound smoked pork
- 1 bay leaf
- 10 peppercorns
- 1 clove garlic
- Few sprigs of parsley
- 1 carrot, sliced
- 1 stalk celery, sliced
- 1 leek, sliced
- 8 medium beets
- 1 cup shredded cabbage
- 2 large onions, quartered
- 3 large potatoes, cut into eighths
- ¼ cup tomato purée
- 2 tablespoons vinegar
- 2 teaspoons sugar
- ½ cup cooked or canned navy beans
- 5 frankfurters, sliced thick
- Salt

1. In a heavy six-quart pot, simmer the beef and bone in the water about one hour. Add the fresh and smoked pork, bay leaf, peppercorns, garlic, parsley, carrot, celery and leek. Cover tightly and bring to a boil. Reduce the heat and simmer slowly one and one-half hours.

2. Meanwhile, boil seven of the beets, unpeeled, until tender. Slip off the skins and cut each into eight pieces. Grate the eighth beet raw and mix with three tablespoons cold water. Reserve.

3. Remove the bone and meats from the pot and discard the bone. Strain the soup, discarding the vegetables and flavoring materials. Return the meats and liquid to the pot. Add the cooked beets, cabbage, onions, potatoes, tomato purée, vinegar and sugar. Simmer, covered, forty minutes. Add the beans and frankfurters and simmer, covered, ten minutes.

4. Skim the excess fat from the soup. Add the liquid from the grated raw beet and season with salt to taste.

5. Remove the meats, slice and return to the soup. Return to a boil and serve.

BOUILLABAISSE, PAGE 265.

RUSSIAN BORSCHT *About 2½ quarts*

- 1 pound lean beef, cubed
- 1½ quarts water
- 1 tablespoon salt
- 1½ cups shredded raw beets
- ¾ cup shredded carrots
- ¾ cup shredded white turnips or rutabagas
- 1 medium onion, chopped
- 2 tablespoons tomato purée
- 2 tablespoons vinegar
- 1 teaspoon sugar
- 2 tablespoons butter
- ½ small head cabbage, shredded
- Freshly ground black pepper
- 2 bay leaves
- Sour cream

(*cont'd*)

1. Simmer the beef, covered, in salted water until tender, or about one and one-half hours.

2. Meanwhile, in a large saucepan simmer the beets, carrots, turnips, onion, tomato purée, vinegar, sugar and butter, covered, fifteen minutes. Stir frequently. Add the cabbage and cook ten minutes longer.

3. Add the vegetable mixture, pepper and bay leaves to the meat and broth. Adjust seasonings and cook until the vegetables are tender. Add more vinegar, if desired.

4. Before serving, add sour cream to taste.

CRABMEAT GUMBO, PAGE 277.

LENTIL SOUP *6 to 8 servings*

Lentils are among the most delectable of legumes. They are surprisingly neglected in this country. They make an excellent base for soup.

2 cups dried lentils
2½ quarts water
¼ cup diced salt pork
¾ cup chopped carrots
¾ cup chopped onions
¾ cup chopped celery
1 clove garlic, minced
1 ham bone
1 bay leaf
2 whole cloves
Dash of cayenne pepper
1½ teaspoons salt
¼ teaspoon freshly ground black pepper
Chopped parsley

1. Combine the lentils and water in a large kettle.

2. Sauté the pork five minutes. Add the vegetables and garlic and cook ten minutes. Add to the lentils. Add the ham bone, the bay leaf and cloves tied in a cheesecloth, cayenne pepper, salt and pepper, and bring to a boil. Reduce the heat and simmer gently about two hours.

3. Discard the cheesecloth. Force the mixture through a food mill, adding the lean meat from the ham bone. Reheat the soup and correct the seasonings. Garnish with parsley.

CANADIAN PEA SOUP *4 servings*

Funny how certain dishes are so closely identified with certain regions Speak of yellow pea soup—soupe aux pois—and the map of Canada immediately comes to mind.

1 pound whole dried yellow peas
3 quarts cold water
½ pound salt pork
½ cup diced carrots and turnips
1 chopped white onion
Salt to taste
Freshly ground black pepper

1. Pick over and wash the peas. Soak twelve hours in water with one-half teaspoon baking soda; or use quick method (page 64). *(cont'd)*

2. Rinse the peas well and place in a pot with the cold water and salt pork. Bring to a boil, skim and add the vegetables. Let simmer four hours; add salt and pepper to taste. A little finely chopped herbs or parsley may be added. Serve unstrained.

Quick Soaking Method: The U.S. Department of Agriculture suggests a quick and effective way to soak whole peas or beans. Start by boiling them with the water for two minutes. Remove from the heat, cover and soak one hour before cooking as directed.

DUTCH SPLIT PEA SOUP *6 to 10 servings*

As Canadians are known for yellow pea soup, so are the Dutch identified with split pea soup.

- 1 pound dried green split peas
- 2½ quarts cold water
- ¼ cup diced salt pork
- ½ cup chopped leeks
- ½ cup chopped celery
- ½ cup celeriac (celery root), optional
- ½ cup chopped onions
- ½ bay leaf
- 2 teaspoons salt
- 1 pig's knuckle
- 1 smoked Dutch ring sausage, sliced, or 1 cup sliced Polish sausage
- Chopped parsley

1. Rinse the peas under cold water and pick over to remove all foreign particles. Place the peas in a large kettle, add the water, cover and let stand overnight. Or boil two minutes and let soak one hour.
2. In a skillet, cook the salt pork five minutes. Add the vegetables and cook ten minutes, until tender but not browned.
3. Add the salt pork mixture, bay leaf, salt and pig's knuckle to the peas. Cover and bring slowly to a boil. Reduce the heat, skim foam from the top and simmer gently two hours, or until the meat on the pig's knuckle separates from the bone.
4. Remove the pig's knuckle, shred the meat and reserve. Discard the bone and the bay leaf.
5. Strain the soup and press the vegetables through a sieve, or purée in an electric blender. Return the meat and sieved vegetables to the soup kettle and adjust the seasonings. Add the sliced sausages and simmer five minutes longer.
6. Serve the soup piping hot and garnish each portion with chopped parsley.

RICE, LAMB AND LENTIL SOUP *5 to 6 servings*

- 1 pound cubed lamb
- 5 cups water, approximately
- 1 teaspoon salt
- ¼ teaspoon freshly ground black pepper
- 1 cup lentils
- 1 large onion, sliced
- 1 tablespoon butter
- 1 cup raw rice

(*cont'd*)

1. Brown the lamb in its own or additional fat. Add three cups of the water, the salt and pepper, bring to a boil, reduce the heat and simmer, covered, two and one-half hours.

2. Wash the lentils, add to the lamb and cook fifteen minutes.

3. While the lentils are cooking, brown the onion in the butter and then add to the lentils. Add the remaining water, bring to a boil and add the rice. Cover and continue cooking until the rice, lentils and lamb are tender, stirring occasionally. The soup should be thick.

SAVORY TOMATO SOUP *3 to 4 quarts*

- 3 pounds beef knuckle, cracked
- 2 pounds brisket, cut into two-inch cubes
- 2 quarts cold water
- 1 large onion, quartered
- ½ cup coarsely chopped parsley
- 3 cups coarsely sliced celery
- 2 medium carrots, sliced
- 2 tablespoons salt
- ½ teaspoon whole peppercorns
- 2 small whole dried hot red peppers
- 2 blades whole mace
- 1 bay leaf
- 2½ quarts canned tomatoes, chopped
- 1 teaspoon ground marjoram
- 1 teaspoon ground thyme
- ½ teaspoon ground savory
- 1 whole clove garlic

1. Place the beef knuckle, brisket, water, onion, parsley, celery, carrots, salt, peppercorns, red peppers, mace and bay leaf into an eight-quart soup kettle. Cover and bring to a boil. Reduce the heat and simmer slowly about five hours.

2. Add the tomatoes, herbs and garlic and adjust seasonings. Bring to a boil and boil five minutes. Discard bone and reserve the meat for another purpose. Strain the liquid through a coarse sieve and then through four thicknesses of cheesecloth arranged in a deep colander. Skim off the fat.

3. Bring the strained soup to a boil and serve hot.

Note: If desired, garnish with thin slices of avocado, sprigs of watercress or croutons. Or cook thin noodles or rice in the strained soup.

Any soup not served immediately may be transferred to freezer containers and frozen.

CREAMED CHICKEN SOUP *6 servings*

- 2 pounds chicken backs and wings
- 6 cups water
- 1 stalk celery
- 1 small bay leaf
- 1 small onion, sliced
- 1 teaspoon salt
- 6 peppercorns
- 1 cup light cream
- 1 cup milk
- 3 tablespoons butter
- 3 tablespoons flour

1. Cook the chicken, covered, until tender in the water with the celery, bay leaf, onion, salt and peppercorns, about two hours. Strain, reserving the meat. Remove the skin and bones and discard. (*cont'd*)

2. Add the cream and milk to the broth and heat to a boil. Cream the butter and flour together, add to the soup and cook, stirring, until the mixture boils. Add the chicken meat and reheat.

3. Garnish as desired with chopped parsley, watercress, shredded ham, sliced celery, toasted slivered almonds or cubed avocado.

ESCAROLE CHICKEN SOUP *About 2½ quarts*

- 1 four- to five-pound fowl, cut into pieces
- 2½ quarts water
- 4 stalks celery, sliced
- 2 carrots, sliced
- 2 onions, sliced
- 1 cup canned tomatoes
- 1 tablespoon salt
- 1 bay leaf
- ½ teaspoon peppercorns
- 2 cups small pasta bows or shells
- 4 cups coarsely shredded escarole

1. Simmer the fowl, covered, in water with the celery, carrots, onions, tomatoes, salt, bay leaf and peppercorns until tender, about four hours.

2. Remove the chicken pieces and save for another use. Strain the broth and skim off the excess fat. Heat to boiling and adjust the seasonings.

3. Add the pasta forms and boil until they are half tender, eight to ten minutes. Add the escarole and continue boiling until both the pasta and the escarole are tender, about ten minutes.

CHICKEN CORN SOUP *About 3 quarts*

This chicken corn soup is a gift from the Pennsylvania Dutch.

- 1 three-and-one-half-pound chicken, cut into pieces
- 3 quarts water
- 1 tablespoon salt
- ¼ teaspoon saffron
- 4 ounces noodles
- 2 cups fresh corn, cut from the cob
- Freshly ground black pepper
- Chopped parsley
- 2 hard-cooked eggs, chopped

1. Cover the chicken with water, add the salt and saffron and bring to a boil. Lower the heat and simmer, covered, until tender, about two hours.

2. Remove the chicken from stock and take the meat from the skin and bones. Chop the meat and return to the stock.

3. Bring the broth to a boil, add the noodles and corn and cook until the noodles are tender. Add pepper and salt to taste, a little chopped parsley and the eggs.

AVGOLEMONO SOUP (Greek egg-and-lemon soup) *6 to 8 servings*

- 2 quarts strong, strained chicken broth
- ½ cup raw rice
- 4 eggs
- Juice of 2 lemons

(cont'd)

1. Bring the broth to a boil and add the rice. Cook until the rice is tender, about twenty minutes.

2. Remove the broth from the heat. Just before serving, beat the eggs with a rotary beater until they are light and frothy. Slowly beat in the lemon juice and dilute the mixture with two cups of the hot soup, beating constantly until well mixed.

3. Add the diluted egg-lemon mixture to the rest of the soup, beating constantly. Bring almost to the boiling point, but do not boil or the soup will curdle. Serve immediately.

SUIMONO *4 servings*

There is something exquisitely simple about food as it is presented by the Japanese. Suimono is a plain soup made with bonito, a member of the mackerel family. Bonito is frequently packed in tins and labeled tuna. The ingredients for this soup are available in most metropolitan cities wherever Japanese products are sold.

- 1 cup shaved dried bonito (hanakatsuo)
- 1 piece dried kelp (kobu), about 6 x 6 inches
- 1 quart water
- Salt
- ½ teaspoon monosodium glutamate
- ½ teaspoon Japanese soy sauce (shoyu)

1. Combine the bonito, kelp and water. Simmer together gently twenty minutes. Strain and season to taste with salt, monosodium glutamate and soy sauce.

2. To serve the soup, arrange in each soup bowl one or two small slices canned fish cake (kamaboko), a slice of fresh or canned mushroom, a leaf of boiled spinach and a twist of lemon peel. Pour the hot soup over the top.

BEET SOUP *6 servings*

- 1 cup sliced cooked beets
- ½ small onion, sliced
- 1 teaspoon salt
- ¼ teaspoon freshly ground black pepper
- 2 tablespoons lemon juice
- 1 medium boiled potato or ⅔ cup mashed potato
- 1 cup chicken stock
- 1 cup sour cream
- 1 cup cracked ice

1. Put the beets, onion, salt, pepper, lemon juice and potato into the container of an electric blender, cover and turn the motor on high.

2. Remove the cover and, with the motor running, pour in the chicken stock and the sour cream.

3. Add the cracked ice and blend for one minute.

4. Chill and serve garnished with chopped fresh dill.

CREAM OF BROCCOLI SOUP *6 servings*

1 medium onion, sliced
1 medium carrot, sliced
1 small stalk celery with leaves, sliced
1 clove garlic
½ cup water
2 cups cooked broccoli, coarsely chopped
1 teaspoon salt
Generous pinch of cayenne pepper
½ cup cooked macaroni
1 cup chicken stock
½ cup cream
Sour cream

1. Simmer, covered, the onion, carrot, celery, garlic and water for ten minutes.

2. Transfer to container of electric blender; add broccoli, salt, cayenne and macaroni. Cover and turn motor on high. Remove cover and, with motor running, add the stock and the cream.

3. Chill and serve topped with sour cream.

CREAM OF CARROT SOUP *6 servings*

4 carrots, sliced (1 cup)
1 medium onion, sliced
1 stalk celery with leaves, sliced
1½ cups chicken stock
1 teaspoon salt
Generous pinch of cayenne pepper
½ cup cooked rice
¾ cup cream

1. Place the carrots, onion, celery and one-half cup of the chicken stock in a saucepan. Bring to a boil, cover, reduce the heat and simmer fifteen minutes.

2. Transfer to the container of an electric blender and add the salt, cayenne and rice. Cover and turn the motor on high. Remove the cover and, with the motor running, pour in remaining stock and cream.

3. Chill and serve garnished with diced pimento.

POTAGE CRESSONIERE *6 to 8 servings*

What is in a name? Whether it is called potage cressonière or cream of watercress the result is capital.

¼ cup butter
1 clove garlic, minced
2 cups chopped onions
1 quart thinly sliced raw potatoes
1 tablespoon salt
¼ teaspoon freshly ground black pepper
¾ cup water
1 bunch watercress
1½ cups milk
1½ cups water
2 egg yolks
½ cup light cream

1. Heat the butter in a large saucepan. Add the garlic and onions and sauté until tender, about five minutes.

(*cont'd*)

2. Add the potatoes, seasonings and three-quarters cup water. Cover and bring to a boil. Reduce the heat and simmer fifteen minutes or until the potatoes are almost tender.

3. Cut the watercress stems into one-eighth-inch lengths. Coarsely chop the leaves.

4. To the potato mixture add all the watercress stems, half the leaves, the milk and water. Cook fifteen minutes. Purée in blender or put the mixture through a food mill. Return to the saucepan and reheat.

5. Blend together the egg yolks and cream. Gradually stir into the soup and cook, stirring constantly, until slightly thickened. Garnish with the remaining watercress leaves and serve immediately.

POT HERB SOUP *6 servings*

1 leek, washed and sliced
1 cup fresh shelled green peas
3 cups canned chicken consommé or broth
1 shallot or onion, sliced
Few sprigs of fresh chives
Few sprigs of fresh chervil
6 sprigs fresh parsley
1 tablespoon butter
1 tablespoon flour
½ cup milk
Salt and freshly ground black pepper
2 egg yolks
¼ cup heavy cream

1. Cook the leek and peas in two and one-half cups consommé until tender.

2. Meanwhile, chop the shallot, chives, chervil and parsley very fine.

3. Melt the butter in a saucepan, add the flour and stir with a wire whisk until well blended. Meanwhile bring the milk and remaining consommé to a boil and add all at once to the butter-flour mixture, stirring vigorously with the whisk. Season to taste with salt and pepper.

4. Blend the sauce with the leek and peas and the liquid in which they were cooked. Add the chopped shallot and herbs and mix well.

5. Beat the egg yolks with the heavy cream and add to the soup. Thicken by bringing to the boiling point, but do not let boil. Remove from the heat and serve hot. Add more salt and pepper if desired.

PEA AND LETTUCE SOUP *About 5 cups*

½ cup parsley sprigs
½ small head Boston lettuce, cut into pieces
2 cups chicken broth
1 No. 2 can peas
½ cup cream (optional)
Salt and freshly ground black pepper
Croutons

1. Place the parsley, lettuce, one-half cup of the chicken broth and the peas, undrained, in the container of an electric blender. Run on high speed fifteen seconds, or until the vegetables are puréed.

(cont'd)

2. Turn into a saucepan, add the remaining broth and simmer five minutes. Add the cream and season to taste with salt and pepper. Serve garnished with croutons.

ROMAINE LETTUCE SOUP *8 to 10 servings*

Romaine lettuce is one of the noblest of them all. It is not only an excellent salad ingredient; it can be the basis for a highly creditable soup.

2 tablespoons butter
1 small onion, minced
1 quart chicken broth
2 quarts chopped romaine lettuce
Salt and freshly ground black pepper
4 egg yolks
1 cup heavy cream

1. Melt the butter in a large saucepan, add the onion and cook until tender. Add the chicken broth and bring to a boil. Add the romaine, salt and pepper and cook over low heat ten minutes, or until the romaine is wilted.

2. Beat together the egg yolks and heavy cream. Stir into the soup mixture and cook over low heat, stirring, until the soup begins to thicken but before the boiling point is reached. Correct the seasonings.

MUSHROOM BISQUE *About 2 quarts*

Although cultivated mushrooms lack the character of their wild country cousins they are not to be scorned. They can be the basis for several highly acceptable soups.

1 pound fresh mushrooms
1 quart chicken broth
1 medium onion, chopped
7 tablespoons butter
6 tablespoons flour
3 cups milk
1 cup heavy cream
1 teaspoon or more salt
White pepper
Tabasco sauce
2 tablespoons sherry (optional)

1. Wash the mushrooms and cut off the stems. Slice six caps and reserve. Discard any dried ends from the stems. Grind or chop the remaining caps and stems very fine. Simmer, covered, in the broth with the onion thirty minutes.

2. Sauté the reserved sliced caps in one tablespoon of the butter and reserve for garnish.

3. Melt the remaining butter in a saucepan, add the flour and stir with a wire whisk until blended. Meanwhile bring the milk to a boil and add all at once to the butter-flour mixture, stirring vigorously with the whisk until the sauce is thickened and smooth. Add the cream.

4. Combine the mushroom-broth mixture with the sauce and season to taste with salt, pepper and Tabasco sauce. Reheat and add the sherry before serving. Garnish with sautéed sliced mushrooms.

CREAM OF MUSHROOM SOUP *6 servings*

6 tablespoons butter
1 medium onion, finely chopped
½ pound fresh mushrooms, finely chopped
3 tablespoons flour
½ teaspoon meat concentrate
3 cups stock or bouillon
1 bay leaf
⅛ teaspoon freshly ground black pepper
¾ cup light cream

1. Melt the butter in a heavy pan. Add the finely chopped onion and stir over moderate heat until onion is transparent. Add the mushrooms and cook, stirring, another four minutes.

2. Remove the mixture from the heat and blend in the flour and meat concentrate. Add the stock slowly, stirring constantly. Add the bay leaf and pepper.

3. Bring the mixture to a boil, reduce heat and simmer five minutes. Remove the bay leaf and stir in the cream. If desired, garnish with croutons just before serving.

ONION SOUP CYRANO *4 servings*

More important than onions in a good onion soup is the beef stock with which it is made. If the stock is rich and full-bodied the onions become secondary.

2 cups sliced onions
½ cup butter
1½ quarts beef stock
Salt
Freshly ground black pepper
4 slices French bread, toasted
½ cup grated Parmesan cheese

1. Preheat oven to hot (400° F.).

2. Sauté onions in four tablespoons of the butter until golden, stirring often.

3. Add the stock and boil ten minutes. Season to taste with salt and pepper.

4. Place the toast in one large or four small casseroles, add the soup and sprinkle with cheese. Dot the top with bits of the remaining butter.

5. Bake until the top is golden brown.

CREAM OF CURRIED PEA SOUP *6 servings*

1 cup shelled fresh peas
1 medium onion, sliced
1 small carrot, sliced
1 stalk celery with leaves, sliced
1 medium potato, sliced
1 clove garlic
1 teaspoon salt
1 teaspoon curry powder
2 cups chicken stock
1 cup cream

1. Place the vegetables, seasonings and one cup stock in a saucepan and bring to a boil. Cover, reduce the heat and simmer for fifteen minutes.

(*cont'd*)

2. Transfer to the container of an electric blender. Cover and turn the motor on high. Remove the cover and, with the motor running, pour in the remaining stock and the cream.

3. Chill and serve topped with whipped cream.

CREAM OF PIMENTO SOUP *4 servings*

- 1 small onion, chopped
- 2 pimentos, chopped
- 3 tablespoons butter
- 3 tablespoons flour
- 1½ cups chicken broth
- 1½ cups milk (may be partly cream)
- ¾ cup grated cheese
- Salt and freshly ground black pepper to taste

1. Sauté the onion and pimentos in the butter until the onion is tender but not brown.

2. Blend in the flour, gradually add the broth and milk and cook, stirring, until thickened.

3. Add the cheese and stir until melted. Season with salt and pepper.

PUMPKIN SOUP *8 servings*

This pumpkin soup is a specialty of La Fonda del Sol, New York's carnival-bright Latin American restaurant.

- 2½ pounds pumpkin, peeled and cut into cubes
- 5 cups chicken stock
- 1 cup chopped onion
- ¾ cup white part of scallions
- 2 cups light cream
- Salt and pepper to taste
- 8 thin slices of red-ripe tomatoes
- 1 cup unsweetened heavy cream, whipped
- ¾ cup finely chopped green part of scallions

1. In a large kettle combine the pumpkin, chicken stock, onion and white part of scallions. Bring to a boil and simmer until the pumpkin is tender. Put the mixture through a fine sieve or purée in an electric blender. Cool.

2. Stir the light cream into the soup and season to taste with salt and pepper.

3. Pour the soup into eight chilled cups and float a thin slice of tomato on each serving. Spoon the whipped cream onto each slice or push it through a pastry tube. Garnish each serving with sprinklings of chopped scallions.

CREAM OF TOMATO SOUP *6 servings*

- 1½ pounds (5 or 6 medium) ripe tomatoes
- 1 tablespoon chopped onion
- ¼ teaspoon celery seed
- ½ bay leaf
- 2 cloves
- ¼ cup butter
- ¼ cup flour
- 3 cups milk (may be part light cream)
- 1½ teaspoons salt
- Freshly ground black pepper to taste

(cont'd)

1. Core, peel and chop tomatoes. Add onion, celery seed, bay leaf and cloves and simmer uncovered for fifteen minutes or until tomatoes are very soft; stir occasionally.

2. In a saucepan, melt the butter, add the flour and stir with a wire whisk until blended. Meanwhile bring the milk to a boil and add all at once to the butter-flour mixture, stirring vigorously with the whisk until the sauce is thickened and smooth. Season with salt and pepper.

3. Press tomatoes through a sieve. There should be about two cups.

4. Just before serving, reheat separately sauce and tomato purée. Add purée to sauce while stirring. If mixture curdles, whip until smooth.

TOMATO DILL SOUP *6 servings*

- 3 large tomatoes
- 1 medium onion, sliced
- 1 small clove garlic
- 1 teaspoon salt
- ¼ teaspoon freshly ground black pepper
- 2 sprigs fresh dill
- 1 tablespoon tomato paste
- ¼ cup cold water
- ½ cup cooked macaroni
- 1 cup chicken stock
- ¾ cup cream

1. Peel and slice the tomatoes into a saucepan. Add the onion, garlic, seasonings, dill, tomato paste and water, cover and simmer twelve to fifteen minutes.

2. Transfer to container of electric blender. Add macaroni, cover and turn motor on high. Uncover and, with motor running, add the stock and the cream.

3. Chill and serve garnished with chopped fresh dill and chopped tomato.

NEW ENGLAND CLAM CHOWDER, SOUTH-OF-BOSTON STYLE

8 to 10 servings

- 4 dozen medium hard-shelled clams
- 6 cups cold water
- 1 two-inch cube salt pork, diced
- 1 large onion, chopped very fine
- 4 medium potatoes, diced
- Salt and freshly ground black pepper to taste
- 2 cups milk
- 1 cup light cream

1. Wash clams thoroughly. Place them in a deep saucepan with the cold water, bring to a boil and let boil gently ten minutes, or until the shells open. The water should almost cover the clams.

2. Strain the broth through cheesecloth and reserve. Remove the clams from their shells, clean and chop.

3. Fry the salt pork in the deep saucepan. Add the onion and cook slowly until it begins to turn golden brown. Add the clams and reserved broth. Skim well, if necessary.

4. Add the potatoes and season with salt and pepper. Cook until the potatoes are tender.

5. Remove the mixture from the heat and slowly add the milk and cream, which have been heated. Serve immediately.

TURNIP SOUP *6 servings*

Turnip soup? By all means, for it is startlingly good.

2 cups peeled and diced white turnips
1 quart beef broth
1 cup heavy cream
Salt and freshly ground black pepper
2 egg yolks, beaten
1 tablespoon butter

1. Cook the turnips in the beef broth until tender. Drain, reserving the liquid.
2. Rub the turnips through a sieve or food mill, or purée in an electric blender.
3. Add the reserved broth to the puréed turnips and bring to a boil. Remove from the heat, add the cream, and season to taste with salt and pepper. Reheat but do not boil. Remove from the heat and stir in the egg yolks and butter. Serve piping hot.

ITALIAN CLAM SOUP *4 servings*

40 little-neck clams
¼ cup olive oil
1 clove garlic
3 anchovy fillets, chopped
1 tablespoon chopped parsley
½ cup dry red wine
1 tablespoon tomato paste
1½ cups warm water
½ teaspoon salt
½ teaspoon freshly ground black pepper
¼ teaspoon orégano
8 thin slices Italian bread, fried in olive oil

1. Wash the clams and scrub well with a vegetable brush.
2. Place the oil in a large saucepan, add the garlic and brown. Discard the garlic. Add the anchovies, parsley and wine to the oil and cook five minutes.
3. Add the tomato paste, water, salt and pepper and cook three to four minutes.
4. Add the clams, cover the pan and cook until all the shells are open, or a maximum of five minutes. Add the orégano and cook two minutes longer.
5. Place two slices fried bread in each soup dish; pour the soup over them.

MARYLAND CRAB SOUP *4 to 6 servings*

Whisky is rarely thought of as a flavoring for foods.
It gives a surprising nuance of flavor to a crab soup.

2 tablespoons finely chopped onion
3 tablespoons butter
2 cups (two 6-ounce cans) crabmeat, picked over to remove bits of shell and cartilage
½ teaspoon salt
Freshly ground black pepper
3 cups milk
½ cup heavy cream
2 tablespoons Scotch whisky
Chopped parsley

(cont'd)

1. Cook the onion in the butter until the onion is transparent. Stir in the crabmeat, salt and pepper and cook over low heat ten minutes, stirring occasionally.

2. Add the milk and cook over boiling water fifteen minutes. Add the cream and, when the mixture is piping hot, stir in the whisky. Serve immediately sprinkled with chopped parsley.

FISH CHOWDER *4 servings*

- 4 fish heads, or bones from 4 fish (any kind saved when fish were cooked for a meal)
- 2 cups water
- 1 small onion, chopped
- 1 clove garlic, minced
- 2 tablespoons chopped green pepper
- 2 tablespoons butter or olive oil
- 2 cups chopped, peeled ripe tomatoes
- 2 medium potatoes, finely diced
- ½ cup minced celery
- 1 bay leaf
- 1 teaspoon salt
- ⅛ teaspoon freshly ground black pepper
- 1 tablespoon minced parsley

1. Wash the heads or bones and simmer in water ten minutes. Drain, reserving the broth. Pick the meat from the bones and reserve; discard the bones.

2. Sauté the onion, garlic and pepper in butter until the onion is transparent. Add the reserved stock, tomatoes, potatoes, celery, bay leaf, salt and pepper to taste. Cook until the potatoes are tender.

3. Add the reserved fish meat and the parsley and reheat.

LOBSTER SOUP *6 servings*

- 2 cups water
- ½ teaspoon salt
- ¼ teaspoon peppercorns
- 1 small onion, sliced
- ½ carrot, sliced
- 3 sprigs parsley
- 1 small bay leaf
- ¼ teaspoon thyme
- 2 small live lobsters
- 4 cups chicken broth
- 4 slices white bread, without crusts
- 2 tablespoons Madeira or white wine
- 1½ tablespoons butter

1. Bring the water and salt to a boil in a large saucepan. Tie the peppercorns, onion, carrot, parsley, bay leaf and thyme in cheesecloth, add to the boiling water and simmer five minutes.

2. Return to a boil, add the lobster, reduce heat and simmer, covered, fifteen minutes.

3. Remove the herb bag and strain the stock. Set the lobsters aside to cool, then remove the meat from the shells.

4. Add the chicken broth and bread to the stock and stir until the bread has blended with the stock.

(cont'd)

5. Reserve some of the claw meat for garnishing. Chop the remaining lobster meat coarsely and add to the soup. Add the wine and reheat. Add the butter and garnish with reserved meat.

LOBSTER BISQUE *About 5 servings*

- 1 one-and-one-half-pound live lobster
- 5 tablespoons butter
- ¼ cup diced carrot
- 1 small onion, chopped
- ½ bay leaf
- Pinch of thyme
- 2 sprigs of parsley
- 3 tablespoons cognac
- ⅓ cup dry white wine
- ½ cup fish stock or chicken broth
- 1 tablespoon sherry or Madeira
- ¼ cup flour
- 3 cups boiling milk
- 3 tablespoons heavy cream, approximately
- Red food coloring

1. Have the lobster split and cleaned at the market. Crack the claws and cut the body and tail into four or five pieces.

2. Melt two tablespoons of the butter and sauté the carrot and onion in it until the onion is transparent. Add the bay leaf, thyme, parsley and lobster. Sauté until the lobster turns red, or about five minutes, shaking the pan occasionally.

3. Add two tablespoons of cognac and ignite. Add the wine and stock and simmer twenty minutes.

4. Remove the lobster, cool and remove the meat from the shell. Dice the meat fine, add the sherry and set aside. Reserve the shell and broth.

5. Melt the remaining butter in a saucepan, add the flour and blend with a wire whisk. Meanwhile, bring the milk to a boil and add all at once to the butter-flour mixture, stirring vigorously with the whisk.

6. Grind or crush the lobster shell and add to the sauce. Add the reserved broth with the vegetables and simmer, covered, about one hour. Strain through a fine sieve.

7. Bring the sauce to a boil, and add enough cream to give the desired consistency. If desired, add a few drops of coloring to make the soup a delicate pink color.

8. Add the reserved lobster meat, correct the seasonings and add the remaining cognac.

OYSTER STEW *4 servings*

Nothing is easier to make and few things are more warming and delicious than a rich oyster stew. Care should be taken not to overcook the oysters.

- ¼ cup butter
- 1 pint shelled oysters with liquor
- 1½ cups milk
- ½ cup light cream
- ½ teaspoon salt
- ⅛ teaspoon freshly ground black pepper or paprika
- 2 tablespoons chopped parsley (optional)

(*cont'd*)

In the top of a double boiler over boiling water, place the butter, oysters with their liquor, milk, cream, salt and pepper or paprika. When the oysters float, the butter has melted and the milk and cream are hot, add two tablespoons chopped parsley, if desired. Serve hot.

Note: A richer stew may be made by increasing the cream to one cup and decreasing the milk by one-half cup.

OYSTER CHOWDER *4 to 6 servings*

2 medium potatoes, diced
1 carrot, finely chopped
2 stalks celery, chopped
1 quart milk
1 tablespoon chopped onion
Salt and freshly ground black pepper
2 tablespoons flour
6 tablespoons butter
1 pint shucked oysters
2 tablespoons chopped parsley

1. In a large saucepan, boil the potatoes, carrot and celery in a small amount of boiling salted water until tender. Drain. Add the milk, onion, salt and pepper and bring to a boil.

2. Cream the flour with two tablespoons of the butter and gradually add to the boiling mixture. Cook, stirring, until thickened.

3. Cook the oysters with their liquid in the remaining butter until the edges curl. Add to the soup and serve immediately sprinkled with parsley.

BILLI BI *4 servings*

This may well be the most elegant and delicious soup ever created. It may be served hot or cold. This is the recipe of Pierre Franey, one of this nation's greatest chefs.

2 pounds mussels
2 shallots, coarsely chopped
2 small onions, quartered
2 sprigs of parsley
Salt and freshly ground black pepper
Pinch of cayenne pepper
1 cup dry white wine
2 tablespoons butter
½ bay leaf
½ teaspoon thyme
2 cups heavy cream
1 egg yolk, lightly beaten

1. Scrub the mussels well to remove all exterior sand and dirt. Place them in a large kettle with the shallots, onions, parsley, salt, black pepper, cayenne, wine, butter, bay leaf and thyme. Cover and bring to a boil. Simmer five to ten minutes, or until the mussels have opened. Discard any mussels that do not open.

2. Strain the liquid through a double thickness of cheesecloth. Reserve the mussels for another use or remove them from the shells and use them as a garnish.

3. Bring the liquid in the saucepan to a boil and add the cream. Return to the boil and remove from the heat. Add the beaten egg yolk and return to the heat long enough for the soup to thicken slightly. Do not boil. Serve hot or cold. This dish may be enriched, if desired, by stirring two tablespoons of hollandaise sauce into the soup before it is served.

POTAGE A LA CARAVELLE *About 2 quarts*

This is the recipe of Roger Fessaguet, the outstanding chef of New York's La Caravelle Restaurant.

4 pounds mussels
1 pound fish bones
¼ cup olive oil
3 leeks, trimmed and washed well
3 stalks celery
1 onion, peeled and quartered
½ clove garlic
3 sprigs parsley
4 tomatoes, peeled, seeded and crushed
½ teaspoon each thyme, anise seed and saffron
1 bay leaf
2 cups dry white wine
2 cups water
2 cups fish stock (page 229)
Salt and cayenne pepper to taste
⅓ cup arrowroot

1. Scrub the mussels well and rinse the fish bones under cold running water.
2. Heat the olive oil in a large kettle and add the leeks, celery, onion, garlic and parsley. Cook until the leeks are wilted. Add the tomatoes and seasonings. Add the wine and stir. Add the mussels, fish bones, water and fish stock and cook one hour. When nearly done, season to taste with salt and cayenne pepper.
3. Strain the liquid through a sieve lined with a double thickness of cheesecloth and reserve the meat from the mussels. Chop the mussels.
4. Thicken the soup with arrowroot thoroughly blended with a little cold water. Add the mussels and serve piping hot. Garnish, if desired, with toast croutons rubbed with garlic.

CREME ST. JACQUES *8 servings*

In the world of cuisine the name St. Jacques is synonymous with scallops. The following is a cream of scallop soup.

1½ quarts water
1 pound (3 or 4 medium) potatoes, peeled and quartered
2 medium onions, coarsely chopped
½ bay leaf
¼ teaspoon thyme
Salt and freshly ground black pepper to taste
1 cup sea scallops, coarsely chopped
¼ teaspoon garlic salt
2 egg yolks
½ cup heavy cream

1. Bring the water to a boil and add the potatoes, onions, bay leaf, thyme, salt and pepper. Simmer fifty minutes. Add the scallops and cook five minutes longer. Add the garlic salt.
2. Remove the bay leaf and put the soup through an electric blender until smooth, or purée in food mill. Return the soup to the heat and bring to a boil. Turn the heat off and stir in the egg yolks blended with the cream. Serve hot but do not allow the soup to boil.

SHRIMP SOUP *4 servings*

- 1 small onion, chopped
- 1 small carrot, sliced
- ¼ teaspoon thyme
- 1 bay leaf
- 1 tablespoon chopped parsley
- 2 tablespoons chopped celery leaves
- 3 tablespoons butter
- 1¼ pounds shrimp
- 4½ cups chicken broth
- ½ cup dry white wine
- ¼ cup raw rice, or 4 slices white bread without crusts

1. Sauté the onion, carrot, thyme, bay leaf, parsley and celery leaves in two tablespoons of the butter until lightly browned.

2. Shell and devein the shrimp. Cook, covered, in one cup of the broth and the wine five minutes. Strain. Reserve eight shrimp for garnishing; grind the remainder.

3. Combine the remaining broth with the sautéed vegetables and bring to a boil. Add rice or bread. Cook until rice is tender or bread has blended well with the broth. Strain, rubbing everything possible through the sieve; or remove bay leaf and purée in a blender.

4. Add the ground shrimp to the strained soup. Reheat and season to taste with salt and pepper. Add the remaining butter and the shrimp garnish.

QUICK SEAFOOD BISQUE *8 servings*

- 1½ quarts water
- 4 medium potatoes, peeled and quartered
- 2 medium onions, coarsely chopped
- ½ bay leaf
- ½ teaspoon thyme
- ¼ teaspoon finely minced garlic
- 1 teaspoon salt
- ⅛ teaspoon freshly ground black pepper
- 1 cup chopped sea scallops, shrimp, lobster or crabmeat
- 2 egg yolks
- ½ cup heavy cream
- Paprika

1. Bring two cups of the water to a boil. Add the potatoes, onions, bay leaf, thyme, garlic, salt and pepper and simmer until the vegetables are barely tender, about fifteen minutes, adding the selected seafood during the last five minutes of cooking.

2. Remove the bay leaf and put the mixture through a fine sieve, or purée in an electric blender.

3. Return the puréed mixture to the saucepan and add the remaining water. Bring to a boil and correct the seasonings.

4. Turn off the heat and stir in the egg yolks blended with the cream. Serve hot or chill. Garnish each serving with paprika.

AVOCADO SOUP *4 to 6 servings*

¼ cup butter
¼ cup flour
1 quart milk
Salt to taste
¼ teaspoon powdered ginger
Grated rind of 1 orange
2 avocados
¼ cup cream, whipped
1 to 2 teaspoons minced preserved ginger (optional)

1. Melt the butter in the top of a double boiler, add the flour and blend with a wire whisk. Meanwhile, bring the milk to a boil and add all at once to the butter-flour mixture, stirring vigorously with the whisk. Add the salt, ginger and orange rind and cook, stirring, until the mixture has thickened.

2. Mash or sieve one avocado and add to the sauce. Stir in thoroughly. Chill.

3. Serve the chilled soup in chilled soup bowls or cups. Garnish with the remaining avocado, cubed, the whipped cream and a sprinkling of preserved ginger.

Note: This soup may also be heated before serving.

AVOCADO SOUP GERALD *4 servings*

It was a happy day for ripe avocados when the electric blender came into being. This is a wonderful cold soup made in seconds.

1 to 2 ripe avocados
Few drops onion juice
1 cup chicken consommé
½ cup sour cream
½ cup light sweet cream
Salt and freshly ground black pepper

1. Wash and peel enough avocado to make one cup.

2. Combine all the ingredients in an electric blender, or mash the avocado and beat with the other ingredients until smooth and well blended.

3. Store the mixture in a covered jar in the refrigerator until chilled.

4. Correct the seasonings and top each serving with a sprinkling of paprika.

COLD AVOCADO SOUP *4 servings*

2 cans consommé madrilène
1 large avocado, puréed or mixed in a blender
1 cup sour cream
Salt
Chili powder or cayenne pepper
Scraped onion
Fresh dill, minced, or crushed dill seeds

1. Combine the consommé with the avocado and sour cream. Season with salt, chili powder and a very little scraped onion.

2. Chill thoroughly until the soup jells.

3. Serve, garnishing each portion with the fresh minced dill or crushed dill seeds.

GAZPACHO *8 servings*

Is there anyone left who does not know that gazpacho is a liquid salad from Spain? It is one of the most refreshing of soups, its basic ingredients being tomatoes, garlic, onion, green pepper and cucumber. It must be served ice cold.

1 clove garlic
1 medium onion, sliced
1 cucumber, sliced
3 tomatoes, peeled
1 green pepper, seeded
4 raw eggs
⅛ teaspoon salt
⅛ teaspoon cayenne pepper
¼ cup vinegar
¼ cup olive oil
¾ cup tomato juice

GARNISH:

1 cup bread cubes
2 tablespoons olive oil
1 clove garlic, minced
1 cucumber, diced
1 onion, chopped
1 green pepper, chopped

1. Purée the first six ingredients in a blender, or put the vegetables through a food mill and mix well with the beaten eggs. Season with the salt, cayenne, vinegar, olive oil and tomato juice and chill.
2. For the garnish, brown the bread cubes in the oil with the garlic. Add the croutons, cucumber, onion and green pepper just before serving.

RED CAVIAR MADRILENE *6 servings*

This is an interesting dish. It has unusual eye appeal because it combines the red of salmon roe and madrilène with the white of sour cream and the green of chives. It is served cold, of course.

1 quart (or 2½ thirteen-ounce cans) consommé à la madrilène
2 ounces red caviar
6 tablespoons sour cream
3 teaspoons minced chives

1. Pour the madrilène into six bouillon cups. Stir into each cup a heaping teaspoon of caviar. Refrigerate until the madrilène jellies.
2. Just before serving, top each cup with a tablespoon of sour cream. Sprinkle with minced chives.

COLD CREAM OF SORREL SOUP *6 servings*

½ pound sorrel, finely chopped
1 teaspoon butter
5 cups chicken broth
4 egg yolks
2 cups light cream

1. Sauté the sorrel in the butter until wilted. Set aside.
2. Heat the broth to a boil. Lightly beat together the egg yolks and cream,

(*cont'd*)

remove the broth from the heat and add the egg mixture, stirring with a wire whisk. Cook until slightly thickened, stirring constantly, either over very low heat or over hot water. Do not allow mixture to boil.

3. Remove the mixture from the heat, add the sorrel and set in cracked ice to cool, stirring often. Correct the seasonings. Refrigerate.

There are thousands of versions of cold tomato soup. Few of them are more delicious than the two which follow.

COLD TOMATO SOUP I *4 servings*

1 quart canned tomatoes
2 stalks celery, sliced
1 onion, sliced
1 bay leaf
2 tablespoons minute tapioca
¼ teaspoon ginger
⅛ teaspoon allspice
Salt to taste

1. Boil the tomatoes with the celery, onion and bay leaf one-half hour. Strain. Return to a boil.

2. Add the tapioca and cook until clear. Add the seasonings and chill. To serve, garnish each plate with sour cream, slices of hard-cooked egg, radish and cucumber.

COLD TOMATO SOUP II *5 to 6 servings*

3 cups tomato juice
2 tablespoons tomato paste
4 scallions, minced
Salt to taste
Pinch of powdered thyme
½ teaspoon curry powder
Freshly ground black pepper
Grated rind of ½ lemon
2 tablespoons lemon juice
Sugar
1 cup sour cream
Chopped parsley

1. Mix all the ingredients except the sour cream and parsley, adding sugar to taste. Chill.

2. Before serving blend in the sour cream and sprinkle each portion with parsley.

SENEGALESE SOUP *10 servings*

Curried soup, anyone? Here is one to be served cold.

¼ cup butter
2 medium onions, coarsely chopped
3 stalks celery, chopped
2 tablespoons flour
1 tablespoon curry powder
2 apples, peeled and chopped
1 cup diced cooked chicken
2 quarts chicken broth
1 bay leaf
1 cup light cream, chilled

(*cont'd*)

1. Melt the butter in a skillet, add the onions and celery and cook until the vegetables are limp. Add the flour and curry powder and cook, stirring, several minutes.

2. Transfer the mixture to an electric blender. Add the apples, chicken and about one cup chicken broth. Blend until smooth.

3. In a saucepan combine the puréed mixture with the remaining broth, add the bay leaf and bring to a boil. Remove the bay leaf and chill. Before serving, stir in the chilled cream.

VICHYSSOISE A LA RITZ *8 or more servings*

Someone should start a campaign to instruct Americans that vichyssoise is not pronounced veeshy-swah! Since this creation of the late Louis Diat has become a national favorite, it seems only just that the final consonant be sounded. It is veeshee-swahze.

- 4 leeks, white part, sliced
- 1 medium onion, sliced
- ¼ cup sweet butter
- 5 medium potatoes, thinly sliced
- 1 quart chicken broth
- 1 tablespoon or less salt
- 3 cups milk
- 2 cups heavy cream
- Chopped chives

1. In a deep kettle, brown the leeks and onion very lightly in the butter. Add the potatoes, broth and salt and boil thirty-five minutes, or until very tender. Crush and rub through a fine sieve or purée in an electric blender.

2. Return the sieved mixture to the kettle, add the milk and one cup of the cream and bring to a boil. Cool and rub again through a fine sieve. Chill.

3. Add the remaining cream. Chill thoroughly and serve garnished with chives.

COLD CUCUMBER SOUP *4 servings*

- 2 tablespoons butter
- ¼ cup chopped onion, or one leek sliced and cubed
- 2 cups diced, unpeeled cucumber
- 1 cup watercress leaves
- ½ cup finely diced raw potato
- 2 cups chicken broth
- 2 sprigs parsley
- ½ teaspoon salt
- ¼ teaspoon freshly ground black pepper
- ¼ teaspoon dry mustard
- 1 cup heavy cream
- Chopped chives, cucumber and radishes

1. In a saucepan melt the butter and cook the onion in it until it is transparent. Add the remaining ingredients except the cream and vegetables for garnish and bring to a boil. Simmer fifteen minutes, or until the potatoes are tender.

2. Purée in an electric blender or put the mixture through a food mill and, if desired, through a sieve or cheesecloth. Correct the seasonings and chill. Before serving, stir in the cream. Garnish with chopped chives, cucumber and radishes.

COLD CHICKEN AND PEA SOUP *6 servings*

1 leek
½ head lettuce
2 tablespoons butter
1 quart hot chicken broth
1½ cups cooked peas
1 small bay leaf
1 whole clove
Salt, freshly ground black pepper and nutmeg to taste
¼ cup heavy cream, whipped
1 tablespoon or more chopped chives

1. Cut the leek in quarters lengthwise and wash thoroughly. Wash the lettuce well. Grind both in a food chopper, using the finest knife.

2. Heat the butter, add the leeks and lettuce and sauté until soft but not browned. Add the broth, peas and seasonings and cook until the peas are very tender. Strain the broth and rub the vegetables through a sieve or food mill, or purée in a blender. Chill thoroughly.

3. At serving time, fold in the whipped cream and serve garnished with chopped chives.

Cold fruit soups are not for every palate but those who admire them are voluble in their praise. The ideal time to drink or dine on such soups is at high noon on the hottest day of the year.

CHILLED CHERRY SOUP *6 servings*

½ cup seedless raisins
6 thin slices orange
6 thin slices lemon
¼ cup lemon juice
1 stick cinnamon
2 cups water
2 cups sliced fresh peaches
1½ cups pitted sweet or sour cherries
½ cup sugar, approximately
Dash of salt
1½ tablespoons cornstarch
Whipped cream

1. Simmer together for twenty minutes the raisins, orange and lemon slices, lemon juice, cinnamon stick and water. Remove the cinnamon stick.

2. Add the peaches, cherries, sugar and salt to the mixture and bring to a boil.

3. Blend the cornstarch with a little water and add to the fruit. Cook, stirring, until clear, or about one minute. Adjust the sweetening, adding more if sour cherries are used. Serve chilled, garnished with whipped cream.

COLD BERRY SOUP *4 or 5 servings*

2 cups fresh strawberries or raspberries
½ cup sugar, approximately
½ cup sour cream
2 cups ice water
½ cup red wine

1. Rub the berries through a fine sieve. Add sugar to taste and the sour cream. Mix.

2. Add the water and wine and correct sweetening. Chill.

CHAPTER THREE

MEATS

BEEF

ROAST BEEF (HIGH-TEMPERATURE METHOD)

Preheat the oven to hot (450° F.).

Wipe the roast with a damp cloth and rub it with salt and freshly ground black pepper. Insert a meat thermometer, if one is available, in the thickest part of the roast. Place the meat on a rack in a roasting pan. Cook the meat twenty-five minutes and reduce the heat to slow (300° F.). It is not necessary to baste the roast. Cook the meat until the thermometer registers 140° for rare beef. For medium-rare beef, cook to 150°; for medium, to 160°; and for well done, to 170°. If a meat thermometer is not used, cook it according to the following table. (Times given are for standing rib roast. For rolled roast consult the chart on page 685.)

ROASTING TIMETABLE FOR BEEF COOKED
ACCORDING TO THE HIGH-TEMPERATURE METHOD

Rare . . . . 16 to 18 minutes per pound
Medium rare . . . . . 18 to 20 minutes per pound
Medium . . . . 20 to 22 minutes per pound
Well done . . . . 26 to 30 minutes per pound

ROAST BEEF (LOW-TEMPERATURE METHOD)

Preheat the oven to slow (300° F.).

Wipe the roast with a damp cloth and rub it with salt and freshly ground black pepper. Insert a meat thermometer, if one is available, in the thickest part of the roast. Place the meat on a rack in a roasting pan. It is not necessary to baste the roast. Cook the meat until the thermometer registers 140° for rare beef. For medium-rare beef, cook to 150°; for medium, to 160°; and for well done, to 170°.

If a meat thermometer is not used, cook it according to the following table. (Times given are for standing rib roast. For rolled roast consult the chart on page 685.)

ROASTING TIMETABLE FOR BEEF COOKED ACCORDING TO THE LOW-TEMPERATURE METHOD

Rare	18 to 20 minutes per pound
Medium rare	20 to 22 minutes per pound
Medium	22 to 25 minutes per pound
Well done	27 to 30 minutes per pound

YORKSHIRE PUDDING *4 servings*

2 eggs
1 cup milk
1 cup sifted flour
½ teaspoon salt
Beef drippings

1. Preheat oven to hot (450° F.).
2. Beat the eggs with the milk. Sift together the flour and salt and stir this into the egg mixture. Beat the batter until well blended.
3. Discard most of the fat from the pan in which the beef was roasted. Heat an 11 x 7-inch baking pan or ring mold and pour into it one-quarter cup of the beef drippings. Pour in the pudding mixture and bake ten minutes. Reduce the oven temperature to moderate (350° F.) and bake fifteen to twenty minutes longer, or until puffy and delicately browned. Cut into squares and serve immediately with roast beef.

BROILED STEAK

The best method for broiling a steak in the home is in a skillet. Heat the skillet until it is piping hot and sprinkle it with salt. If the skillet is hot enough it should not be necessary to add fat. If desired, however, the skillet may be rubbed with a piece of suet. Sear the meat quickly on one side, then reduce the heat. Turn the steak and sear on the other side. Cook to desired degree of doneness. The cooking time will depend on the thickness of the steak and the temperature of the skillet. Serve the steak with melted butter seasoned to taste with lemon juice, salt and pepper, Worcestershire sauce, Tabasco and freshly chopped parsley.

MINUTE STEAKS IN PARSLEY BUTTER *4 servings*

½ cup butter, softened
¼ cup finely chopped parsley
Beef suet
8 minute or cubed steaks

1. With a fork, blend the butter and parsley thoroughly.
2. Brush a heavy skillet lightly with beef suet and heat the skillet. Brown

(*cont'd*)

the steaks on one side about two minutes over high heat, turn and brown on the other side about one minute. Top immediately with small balls of the butter-parsley mixture.

BEEF SUKIYAKI *4 servings*

1 small piece beef suet
3 medium onions, thinly sliced
3 stalks celery, thinly sliced
3 cups spinach leaves
1 bunch scallions, cut into two-inch lengths
4 large Japanese canned mushrooms, sliced
½ cup canned bamboo shoots, sliced
1 pound tender beef, sliced thin
¾ cup dashi or canned beef bouillon
½ cup Japanese soy sauce (shoyu)
1 tablespoon sugar
1 cake soy bean curd (tofu), cut into cubes 1x1x½ inch
⅓ cup shirataki

1. With the suet grease a heavy cast-iron pan, nine or ten inches in diameter, and heat. Add the onions, celery, spinach, scallions, mushrooms and bamboo shoots.

2. Arrange the meat over the vegetables, add the bouillon, soy sauce, sugar, bean curd and shirataki. Let simmer uncovered over low to medium heat until the meat is tender and the vegetables are cooked but still crisp. Stir gently two or three times during the cooking. Serve with boiled rice.

Note: The dashi listed in the ingredients is made with shaved dried bonito. The shirataki resembles vermicelli or thin spaghetti and is sometimes called cellophane noodles. These ingredients, and bean curd, are available in many Oriental grocery stores.

STEAK TARTARE LAUSANNE *4 servings*

Champagne is not for all palates and neither is raw beef. For those who fancy it, however, this is a very special version of steak tartare.

2 pounds raw, ground top-quality beef fillet, sirloin or round steak
4 raw egg yolks
8 fillets of anchovy
Capers
½ cup finely chopped onion
4 teaspoons chopped parsley
Salt and freshly ground black pepper
Rose paprika
Cayenne pepper
Tomato catsup
Worcestershire sauce
1 lemon, quartered
Prepared mustard
Cognac or port to taste
Buttered toast

1. Divide the raw beef into four portions and shape into patties. Place the patties on chilled plates. Make a small indentation in the center of each and place one egg yolk in each.

2. Garnish each serving with two anchovies and sprinkle with capers, onion and parsley.

(cont'd)

3. Serve immediately accompanied by the remaining seasonings and toast and butter. Each guest stirs the seasonings into his steak tartare according to his taste. Or one or more of the seasonings may be stirred into the ground steak before it is served to guests.

PEPPER STEAK *4 servings*

1 pound round or flank steak
Salt and freshly ground black pepper to taste
2 tablespoons oil
1 medium onion, chopped
1 clove garlic, minced
2 green peppers, diced
1 cup bouillon
1 cup drained canned tomatoes
1½ tablespoons cornstarch
2 teaspoons soy sauce
¼ cup water

1. Cut the steak into slices one-eighth inch thick (or have this done by the butcher). Sprinkle with salt and pepper.

2. In a large skillet heat the oil, add the steak, onion and garlic and cook until the meat is browned on all sides.

3. Add the green peppers and bouillon, cover and simmer ten minutes. Add the tomatoes and simmer five minutes.

4. Mix the cornstarch, soy sauce and water and stir into the meat mixture. Cook, stirring, until the mixture has thickened. Serve with hot boiled rice.

Note: Old Chinese recipes for this dish call for boiling the pepper halves four minutes before chopping. This gives a milder flavor but takes more time.

BEEF STROGANOFF *About 6 servings*

1½ pounds beef fillet, sirloin or porterhouse steak
Salt and freshly ground black pepper to taste
3 tablespoons butter
1 tablespoon flour
1 cup beef broth or canned consommé
1 teaspoon prepared mustard
1 onion, sliced
3 tablespoons sour cream, at room temperature

1. Remove all the fat and gristle from the meat. Cut into narrow strips about two inches long and one-half inch thick. Season the strips with salt and pepper and refrigerate two hours.

2. In a saucepan melt one and one-half tablespoons of butter, add the flour and stir with a wire whisk until blended. Meanwhile, bring the consommé to a boil and add all at once to the butter-flour mixture, stirring vigorously with the whisk until the sauce is thickened and smooth. Stir in the mustard.

3. In a separate pan heat the remaining butter, add the meat and sliced onion and brown quickly on both sides. Remove the meat to a hot platter, discarding the onion.

4. Add the sour cream to the mustard sauce and heat over a brisk flame for three minutes. Pour sauce over meat and serve.

STEAK AU POIVRE *6 servings*

Coarsely ground black pepper in generous quantity is the secret of the success of this enormously appealing dish. The method listed below is for pan frying. Or try it over charcoal, and serve the steaks with plenty of melted butter to which have been added lemon juice, parsley and chives. Serve with a baked potato.

6 club steaks
2 tablespoons coarsely ground black pepper
Salt
6 teaspoons butter
Tabasco sauce to taste
Worcestershire sauce to taste
Lemon juice to taste
2 tablespoons cognac (optional)
Chopped parsley
Chopped chives

1. Sprinkle the sides of each steak with pepper and, with the heel of the hand, press the pepper into the meat. Let stand thirty minutes.
2. Sprinkle a light layer of salt over the bottom of a heavy skillet. Turn the heat to high and, when the salt begins to brown, add the steaks. Cook until well browned on one side. To produce a very rare steak, cook thirty seconds at high heat. Turn the steaks, lower the heat to moderate and cook one more minute. Adjust the heat and time to cook the steaks to a greater degree of doneness.
3. Place a teaspoon of butter on each steak and add Tabasco, Worcestershire and lemon juice to taste.
4. Turn the heat to low, blaze with cognac and transfer steaks to a platter. Swirl the sauce in the skillet and pour over the meat. Sprinkle the steaks with parsley and chives.

STEAK DIANE *1 serving*

1 ten-ounce sirloin steak
1½ tablespoons butter
1 tablespoon cognac, heated
2 tablespoons sherry
1 tablespoon sweet butter
1 teaspoon chopped chives

1. Trim the meat well and pound very thin with a mallet.
2. Heat one and one-half tablespoons butter in a chafing-dish platter. Add the steak and cook quickly, turning it once.
3. Add the cognac and flame. Add the sherry and the sweet butter creamed with chives.
4. Place the steak on a warm platter and pour the pan juices over it.

LONDON BROIL *4 to 6 servings*

1 two-pound flank steak
1 clove garlic
Salad oil
Salt and freshly ground black pepper to taste
Melted butter

(*cont'd*)

1. Rub the steak on both sides with the cut garlic. Brush with salad oil and place on a preheated greased broiler rack, one and one-half to two inches from the source of heat. Broil five minutes. Season with salt and pepper.

2. Turn the steak and broil five minutes on the second side. Cut in very thin slices diagonally across the grain and serve covered with melted butter.

SIRLOIN STEAK ST. HUBERT, PAGE 182.

FLANK STEAK WITH HERB STUFFING *6 servings*

- 1 two-pound flank steak
- 2 tablespoons butter
- ½ large onion, chopped
- 1 clove garlic, minced (optional)
- ½ cup chopped mushrooms
- ¼ cup pistachio nuts, coarsely chopped (optional)
- ¼ cup chopped parsley
- 1½ cups soft bread cubes
- ¾ teaspoon poultry seasoning, or a mixture of orégano and basil
- ½ teaspoon salt
- Freshly ground black pepper to taste
- 1 egg, slightly beaten
- ½ cup water, dry table wine or bouillon

1. Preheat oven to moderate (350° F.). Pound the steak or score it lightly on both sides.

2. In a skillet heat the butter, add the onion and garlic and cook until lightly browned. Add the mushrooms and cook three minutes. Add the nuts, parsley, bread cubes, poultry seasoning, salt, pepper and egg and mix.

3. Spread the mixture on the steak. Roll lengthwise, as for jelly roll, and tie with string at two-inch intervals.

4. Brown the meat on both sides in a little fat in a skillet or heavy Dutch oven. Add the liquid, cover and bake two hours. To serve, cut into one-inch slices and serve with the pan drippings.

SWISS STEAK *4 servings*

- ¼ cup flour, approximately
- ¾ teaspoon salt
- ⅛ teaspoon freshly ground black pepper
- 1½ pounds beefsteak (rump, round or chuck), cut 1½ inches thick
- 3 tablespoons fat
- 1 medium onion, chopped
- 1¼ cups stewed tomatoes
- ⅓ cup sliced carrots (optional)
- ⅓ cup sliced celery (optional)

1. Mix the flour, salt and pepper. Dredge the steak with the seasoned flour. Pound into both sides of the steak as much more of the flour mixture as it will hold, using the edge of a heavy plate.

2. In a Dutch oven heat the fat, add the steak and brown very well on both sides.

3. Add the vegetables, cover and simmer gently until tender, one and one-half to two hours. Or bake in a covered casserole in a preheated slow oven

(*cont'd*)

(300° F.) two to two and one-half hours. Remove the meat to a warm platter and keep hot.

4. Strain the drippings from the pan and skim the fat from the surface. Serve hot as a gravy with the meat.

TERIYAKI *6 servings*

Teriyaki is Hawaiian for steak marinated in soy sauce, garlic and ginger and broiled, preferably over charcoal.

2 pounds sirloin steak, about ¼ inch thick
1 tablespoon finely chopped fresh ginger, or 2 teaspoons powdered ginger
2 cloves garlic, chopped fine
1 medium onion, chopped fine
2 tablespoons sugar
1 cup soy sauce
½ cup sherry

1. Cut the steak into thin slices or strips.
2. Combine the ginger, garlic, onion, sugar, soy sauce and sherry and pour the mixture over the meat. Let stand one to two hours.
3. Thread the meat on skewers and broil quickly on both sides over charcoal or in a preheated broiler. Serve hot.

EMINCE OF BEEF BOURGEOIS *4 to 6 servings*

Slivers of beef quickly cooked and served with a chicken-liver sauce.

¼ cup butter
½ pound chicken livers
1 bay leaf
¼ teaspoon thyme
1 truffle, finely chopped
2 pounds beef tenderloin tips
Salt and freshly ground black pepper to taste
¼ cup cognac, heated

1. In a skillet heat half the butter, add the chicken livers, bay leaf and thyme and sauté quickly, shaking the pan occasionally, until the livers are barely cooked.
2. Remove the bay leaf. Place the chicken livers and chopped truffle in the container of an electric blender.
3. Cut the beef into very thin strips across the grain. Sprinkle with the salt and pepper and sear quickly in the remaining butter to seal in the juices, one minute or less.
4. Pour the warm cognac over the meat and ignite it. Remove the meat to a warm serving platter. Add the beef juices to the container of the blender and blend until smooth, about thirty seconds. If necessary, add canned beef broth to aid the blending.
5. Reheat the sauce and pour over the beef. Serve immediately.

BOILED BEEF *6 servings*

There is many a man with a sophisticated palate who, when asked to name the dish for his desert island, would nominate boiled beef. It has a classic simplicity, and almost every nation has a version of it.

3 pounds lean first-cut brisket of beef
Boiling water
2 leeks, trimmed and washed well
½ teaspoon thyme
1 bay leaf
1 carrot, scraped and left whole
1 medium onion, peeled
1 small stalk celery with leaves
12 peppercorns, slightly bruised
Salt to taste

1. Place the brisket of beef in a Dutch oven or heavy skillet in which it will fit compactly. Pour over it boiling water barely to cover.

2. Return to a boil and reduce the heat. Spoon off all the grease and scum.

3. Add the remaining ingredients and cover lightly. Simmer three to four hours, until the meat is tender. Serve sliced with horseradish sauce (page 450).

Note: Use remaining broth for soups, or freeze for future use.

POT AU FEU *6 servings*

The French version of boiled beef is pot au feu.

4 pounds beef with bone (brisket, rump, shin, plate, chuck or round)
3 quarts cold water
1 tablespoon salt
1 bouquet garni (bay leaf, ¼ teaspoon thyme, ½ teaspoon peppercorns, 3 cloves, 4 sprigs parsley and a few celery leaves tied in a cheesecloth bag)
2 cups mixed chopped vegetables (onions, carrots, celery, white turnips, parsnips)
6 leeks, white part only
3 carrots, quartered
6 cabbage wedges
6 potatoes, whole or quartered

1. Place the meat in a large soup kettle. Add the water, salt and bouquet garni. Bring to a boil, skimming frequently. Reduce the heat and simmer, covered, until the meat is almost tender, four hours or longer.

2. Add the vegetables and simmer until tender, about forty-five minutes longer. Discard the bouquet garni and correct the seasonings.

3. To serve, remove the meat to a warm serving platter and surround with the large pieces of vegetable.

Note: If a fatty cut of meat is used, the dish is best made a day in advance, refrigerated and the fat removed before reheating the pot au feu and serving. The broth with the chopped vegetables may be served as a first course. Any excess may be refrigerated for later use wherever soup stock is required.

BOLLITO MISTO *12 servings*

A bollito misto is Italian for "mixed boil." It is everything in a pot from chicken to beef to vegetables.

1 three-pound stewing chicken
1 pound boned beef rump or boneless veal
2 pounds zampone or coteghino sausage (optional)
3 bunches medium carrots, scraped
2 pounds (12 medium) onions, quartered
8 small yellow turnips, peeled and quartered
21 leeks
Water to cover
Salt and freshly ground black pepper
1 bay leaf
Pinch of dried thyme
Pinch of dried marjoram
1 one-pound veal tongue
4 pounds (12 medium) potatoes, peeled

1. Place the chicken, beef and sausage in a large pot with one sliced carrot, one quartered onion, one quartered yellow turnip, one chopped leek and cover with cold water. Bring to a boil, skim and season with one tablespoon salt, pepper, bay leaf, thyme and marjoram. Reduce the heat, cover and simmer one hour. Add the veal tongue and continue simmering one hour longer.

2. Thirty minutes before the meats have finished cooking, add the remaining carrots, onions, and turnips and the potatoes to a separate pot of boiling salted water. After cooking ten minutes, add the leeks and cook all the vegetables twenty minutes longer. Drain the vegetables and keep warm.

3. Remove the cooked chicken and meats from the pot. Disjoint the chicken, slice the tongue and sausage and cut the beef into bite-sized pieces. Correct the seasonings and moisten the meats with a little more of the strained broth in which they were cooked. Keep hot.

4. When ready to serve, arrange the meats in a large, deep platter with the vegetables and some of the hot broth poured over all. Serve with salsa verde (page 440) or horseradish sauce (page 450) on the side.

VIENNESE BOILED BEEF *8 servings*

3 carrots, sliced
2 onions, halved
6 stalks celery, sliced
1 tablespoon salt
4 sprigs parsley
1 bay leaf
6 whole peppercorns
4 whole allspice
2 pounds chicken parts (feet, necks, backs, wings)
Water to cover
1 large unpeeled onion
4 pounds beef brisket

1. Place the vegetables, seasonings and chicken parts in a large covered saucepan, cover with water and simmer two hours.

(cont'd)

2. Meanwhile, bake the unpeeled onion in a preheated moderate oven (350° F.) thirty minutes.

3. Place the beef in a Dutch oven or heavy kettle and strain the vegetable-chicken stock over it. Add more water if necessary to cover the meat. Add the baked onion, cover and simmer about three hours.

NEW ENGLAND BOILED DINNER *12 servings*

- 5 pounds corned brisket of beef
- Water to cover
- ½ bay leaf
- 6 whole peppercorns
- 4 large rutabagas (yellow turnips) peeled and sliced
- 6 carrots, scraped and left whole
- 6 parsnips, peeled and left whole (optional)
- 12 small onions, peeled
- 6 medium potatoes, peeled
- 1 head cabbage, cut in wedges

1. Place the meat in a deep kettle, cover with water and add the bay leaf and peppercorns. Bring the water to a boil and skim off the fat. Cover the pot, reduce the heat and simmer three hours.

2. Add the vegetables and simmer until the meat and vegetables are tender, about forty-five minutes longer.

3. Place the meat in the center of a platter and surround with the vegetables. Accompany with horseradish and mustard pickle. (The broth may be reserved for soups.)

BEEF EN CASSEROLE *4 to 6 servings*

- 4 large white mushrooms
- 3 tablespoons butter
- 1½ pounds top sirloin or round beef, cut into 1-inch cubes
- ¼ cup cognac
- 12 small white onions, peeled and left whole
- 6 small carrots, scraped
- 6 small white turnips, peeled
- 1 celery heart, quartered
- ½ teaspoon tomato paste
- 1 teaspoon meat glaze
- 3 teaspoons potato flour, or 3 tablespoons flour
- 1½ cups stock
- ¼ cup red wine
- Salt and freshly ground black pepper to taste
- 1 bay leaf

1. Quarter the mushrooms through the stem without disconnecting stem and cap. Do not peel the mushrooms.

2. In a heavy saucepan heat one tablespoon of the butter, add the meat and brown on all sides. Heat the cognac, ignite it and add to the meat. Remove the meat from the pan.

3. Heat the remaining butter in the pan, add the onions, carrots, turnips and celery and sauté until brown. Add the mushrooms and cook one or two minutes longer.

(cont'd)

4. Remove the pan from the heat and blend in the tomato paste, meat glaze and flour. Add the stock and wine, return to low heat and stir until the mixture boils. Season with salt and pepper.

5. Return the meat with the juices to the pan and add the bay leaf. Cover and simmer until the meat is tender, one to one and one-half hours. Discard the bay leaf.

CARBONNADES A LA FLAMANDE *4 to 6 servings*

Carbonnades à la Flamande is probably Belgium's most famous dish. It is also the one beef stew which, classically, is made with beer. Serve with plenty of cold beer.

Flour for dredging
Salt and freshly ground black pepper to taste
2 pounds boneless chuck, cut into 1-inch cubes
¼ cup salad oil
6 medium onions, sliced
1 clove garlic, finely chopped
1 twelve-ounce bottle or can of beer
1 tablespoon chopped parsley
1 bay leaf
¼ teaspoon thyme

1. Combine flour, salt and pepper. Dredge the meat in the seasoned flour.

2. Heat oil in a skillet. Add onion slices and garlic and cook until tender but not brown. Remove the onions from the skillet.

3. Add the meat and brown on all sides, adding a little more oil if necessary. Return the onions to the skillet.

4. Add the remaining ingredients.

5. Cover and cook over low heat until meat is tender, about one and one-quarter hours. Serve hot with boiled potatoes.

RAGOUT OF BEEF *6 servings*

1½ tablespoons butter
1 medium onion, chopped
1 clove garlic
2 pounds beef shank or bottom round cut into 1-inch cubes
1 teaspoon paprika
Salt to taste
Freshly ground black pepper
2 large tomatoes, chopped
1 cup celery, diced
½ ounce dried black mushrooms
Water
2 tablespoons flour

1. In a large skillet heat the butter, add the onion and garlic and sauté until the onion is transparent. Discard the garlic. Add the meat, paprika, salt and pepper. Cook over medium heat, stirring, until the meat is browned. Add chopped tomatoes. Cover and simmer very gently one hour. Add the celery.

2. Meanwhile, wash mushrooms and soak in one cup water for fifteen minutes. Boil for three minutes in their soaking liquid. Fifteen minutes after the celery

(cont'd)

is added, add the mushrooms and their liquid and continue to simmer gently until tender. The total time is one and one-half to two hours.

3. When the meat is tender, blend the flour with one-quarter cup water and add, stirring, to the ragout. Cook, stirring, until thickened. Serve with steamed rice, buttered noodles or polenta (page 339).

BOEUF BOURGUIGNON I

6 servings

- 2 tablespoons salad or peanut oil
- 2 large slices fatback
- 1½ cups diced carrots
- 2 pounds chuck or rump of beef, cut into ¼-inch slices
- Salt to taste
- Freshly ground black pepper to taste
- 2 medium onions, coarsely chopped
- 1 clove garlic, finely minced
- 2 shallots, finely chopped
- ½ pound mushrooms, chopped
- ½ bottle Burgundy wine
- ⅓ cup cognac

1. Pour the salad or peanut oil into the bottom of a two-quart flameproof casserole and add one slice of the fatback.

2. Add the diced carrots and cover them with a single layer of one-third of the sliced beef. Sprinkle with salt and pepper.

3. Sprinkle the meat with half the onions, garlic, shallots and mushrooms.

4. Cover with a layer of half the remaining beef and sprinkle with more salt and pepper.

5. Add the remaining onions, garlic, shallots and mushrooms and cover with a final layer of the remaining beef. Top with the second slice of fatback.

6. Pour the Burgundy and the cognac over all.

7. Season with additional salt and pepper.

8. Place the casserole over high heat and, when it begins to simmer, cover and lower the heat. Cook three and one-half hours.

Note: While the casserole is cooking, the liquid should barely bubble.

BOEUF BOURGUIGNON II

12 servings

- 5 pounds chuck beef, cut into large cubes
- Flour
- 9 tablespoons butter
- 6 tablespoons olive oil
- Salt and pepper
- ¼ cup cognac, warmed
- ½ pound bacon, diced
- 3 cloves garlic, coarsely chopped
- 2 carrots, coarsely chopped
- 2 leeks, coarsely chopped
- 3 cups coarsely chopped onions
- Chopped parsley
- 1 bay leaf
- 1 teaspoon thyme
- 1 bottle Burgundy wine
- Water
- 36 whole small onions
- Sugar
- 36 mushroom caps
- Juice of half a lemon

(cont'd)

1. Roll the beef cubes in flour and brown them on all sides in a skillet over high heat in four tablespoons each of the butter and olive oil.

2. Sprinkle the meat with salt and pepper, pour the cognac over it and ignite. When the flame dies, transfer meat to a three-quart casserole.

3. Preheat oven to moderate (350° F.).

4. To the skillet add the bacon, garlic, carrots, leeks, chopped onions and two tablespoons chopped parsley. Cook, stirring, until the bacon is crisp and the vegetables are lightly browned. Transfer to the casserole with the meat and add the bay leaf, thyme, Burgundy and enough water to barely cover the meat. Cover and bake one and one-half hours.

5. Prepare a beurre manié by blending one tablespoon each butter and flour and stir into the casserole bit by bit. Return the casserole to the oven and continue cooking two to three hours longer.

6. Brown the small onions in two tablespoons butter with a dash of sugar. Add a little water, cover and cook until the onions are almost tender.

7. Sauté the mushrooms in two tablespoons each of the butter and oil until lightly browned on one side. Sprinkle with lemon juice and turn to brown the other side.

8. To serve, add the onions to the casserole and garnish with the mushrooms and parsley.

LARDED BRAISED BEEF

6 servings

3 to 4 pounds top round of beef
Marinade (page 100)
½ pound salt pork
2 tablespoons fat
3 tablespoons cognac, warmed
1 teaspoon tomato paste
3 tablespoons flour
½ cup stock
Salt and freshly ground black pepper to taste

1. Place the meat in a large bowl, add the marinade and let stand in the refrigerator twenty-four hours, turning occasionally. Remove the meat and dry thoroughly with paper towels. Strain the marinade and reserve.

2. Cut the salt pork into long thin strips and use to lard the beef (page 100).

3. In a Dutch oven heat one tablespoon of the fat, add the meat and brown on all sides.

4. Ignite the cognac and pour over the meat. Remove the meat from the pan.

5. To the pan add one tablespoon of the fat, the tomato paste and flour. Stir in the stock, marinade, salt and pepper, and bring to a boil.

6. Add the meat. Cover, reduce the heat and simmer two to two and one-half hours.

7. Cut enough beef for one meal in thin slices (saving the remainder for another meal) and place on a hot serving platter. Strain the gravy and spoon a little over the meat. Serve the remainder separately. Garnish with Sicilian stuffed tomatoes (page 406).

(cont'd)

MARINADE:

1 teaspoon salt
½ teaspoon freshly ground black pepper
1 large onion, thinly sliced
2 large carrots, sliced
2 cloves
1 bay leaf
1 clove garlic, chopped
10 peppercorns
4 sprigs parsley
¼ teaspoon dried thyme
1½ cups dry red wine
½ cup olive oil
¼ cup wine vinegar

Combine all ingredients. Cubed beef (for stews, casseroles) and pot roasts may be soaked in this mixture in an earthenware, glass or other non-metal vessel for a day or two. Let the meat marinate under refrigeration.

To Lard Meat: To lard meat with a larding needle, thread the needle by placing a long thin strip of salt pork in the open end. Insert the pointed end of the needle into the roast at right angles to the grain. Push, then pull the needle through the roast. Trim off the salt pork flush with the meat.

BEEF STEW WITH WINE AND HERBS *4 to 5 servings*

2 pounds stewing beef, cut into 2-inch cubes
1 cup red wine
1 large bay leaf
1 clove garlic, sliced
1 teaspoon salt
½ teaspoon freshly ground black pepper
2 tablespoons bacon drippings or other fat
1½ cups beef stock
1 stalk celery with leaves, diced
1 onion, sliced
Few sprigs of parsley
¼ teaspoon thyme
8 cloves
1 piece ginger root
Cornstarch

1. Place the meat in a large bowl and add the wine, bay leaf, garlic, salt and pepper. Marinate in the refrigerator several hours, turning frequently.
2. Remove the meat and dry thoroughly with paper towels. Reserve the marinade. In a Dutch oven heat the drippings, add the meat and brown on all sides.
3. Simmer together for ten minutes the reserved marinade, stock and the celery, onion, herbs and spices tied in a cheesecloth. Combine with the meat, cover and simmer until tender, two and one-half to three hours. Add water if necessary. If desired, when meat is just tender, vegetables such as peas, carrots and onions may be added. Cook until vegetables are tender.
4. Discard the herb bag and remove the meat to a hot platter.
5. Thicken the gravy with cornstarch mixed with a little cold water, using one-half tablespoon cornstarch for each cup of broth. Boil, stirring, two minutes. Serve the sauce over the meat with the vegetables, if used, arranged attractively around it.

COLLOPS *6 servings*

3 pounds top round beef
2 cups beef stock
Salt and freshly ground black pepper to taste
Pinch dried thyme
Pinch of marjoram
Pinch of winter savory
1 onion, chopped
½ cup dried bread cubes
6 anchovies, coarsely chopped
1 tablespoon butter
Bread triangles
1 thinly sliced lemon
1 tablespoon capers

1. Have the butcher cut the meat into thin slices and pound them flat.
2. Place the meat in a heavy saucepan and add the stock, salt, pepper, herbs and onion. Cover and simmer until the meat is tender, one to one and one-half hours.
3. Transfer the meat to a warm platter and keep hot. Strain the juices in the pan and add the bread cubes and anchovies. Simmer until slightly thickened. Stir in the butter.
4. Pour the sauce over the meat and surround with bread triangles. Garnish the top with sliced lemon dotted with capers.

JAMAICAN POT ROAST *6 generous servings*

Flour for dredging
Salt and freshly ground black pepper to taste
3-pound boneless chuck or rump roast of beef
3 tablespoons lard
½ cup chopped onion
1 clove garlic, finely chopped
⅓ teaspoon thyme
2 cups canned tomatoes, undrained
½ teaspoon powdered ginger

1. Mix flour, salt and pepper. Dredge the meat with the seasoned flour. In a Dutch oven heat the lard, add the meat and brown well on all sides. Pour off the fat.
2. Add the onion, garlic and thyme. Stir until onion begins to brown and then add the tomatoes and ginger. Cover tightly and simmer until tender, about two and one-half hours. Remove to heated platter. Thicken the gravy, if desired, with a little flour mixed with water.

RUMP ROAST WITH CARAWAY SEEDS *6 to 8 servings*

1½ cups chopped onion
1 teaspoon salt
2 tablespoons caraway seeds
4 pounds rolled rump roast
5 strips bacon
2 to 3 pounds beef bones, sawed into pieces
⅓ cup vinegar
Water
1 tablespoon flour

(*cont'd*)

1. Preheat oven to moderate (325° F.).

2. Combine one-half cup of the onions with the salt and one tablespoon of the caraway seeds. Using a spoon and spatula, work the mixture into the folds of the roast.

3. In a large roasting pan cook the bacon until crisp. Add the remaining onions and cook, stirring, until the onions are transparent. Place the beef bones around the edge of the pan and add the meat. Sprinkle with the remaining caraway seeds and the vinegar and add enough water to cover the bottom of the pan to a depth of one-half inch. Bake until tender, about two hours, basting frequently. Remove the meat to a warm platter and keep hot.

4. Mix the flour with a little water and stir into the boiling liquid. Cook until the gravy thickens. Strain and serve with the roast.

Note: Bones give additional body and flavor to gravy.

POTTED BEEF ITALIAN STYLE *4 generous servings*

¼ cup olive oil
3-pound chuck or rump roast of beef
1 carrot, chopped
1 stalk celery, chopped
1 onion, chopped
2 cloves garlic, chopped
2 bay leaves
Salt and freshly ground black pepper to taste
1 ounce dried mushrooms
Water
1 cup red wine
1 small can tomato paste
2 cups warm beef broth or consommé

1. In a heavy saucepan, heat the oil and brown the beef quickly on all sides. Add the carrot, celery and onion and sauté until the onion is golden brown. Add the garlic, bay leaves, salt and pepper. Continue cooking over low heat.

2. Soak the mushrooms in warm water several minutes. Drain off the water, chop the mushrooms and add to the meat and vegetables. Cook, uncovered, over low heat four minutes. Add the wine and the tomato paste diluted with the warm beef broth, cover and bring to a boil. Continue cooking, covered, until the meat is tender, about two and one-half hours. Stir occasionally, basting the meat from time to time. If the gravy becomes too thick, add more warm beef broth.

3. When the meat is done, remove from the pan and serve separately. Serve the gravy, unstrained, over any kind of pasta, polenta or gnocchi.

RIB ROAST BRAISED IN WINE *About 12 servings*

1 five-pound boned and rolled rib roast
Flour for dredging
¼ cup butter
½ cup chopped onion
½ cup chopped leeks
½ cup chopped carrots
1 clove garlic, crushed
2 cups dry red wine, approximately
Salt to taste
8 crushed peppercorns
1 bay leaf
¼ teaspoon marjoram
½ teaspoon thyme
2 tablespoons cognac, warmed

(*cont'd*)

1. Preheat oven to moderate (325° F.).

2. Dredge the roast with flour. In a Dutch oven, heat the butter, add the meat and brown on all sides.

3. Add the onions, leeks, carrots and garlic and sauté until browned.

4. Add the wine and seasonings. Ignite the cognac and add. Cover and bake until the meat is tender, about four hours. If necessary, add more wine.

5. Transfer the meat to a warm platter and keep hot. Strain the sauce, correct the seasoning and pour over the beef.

Note: Five pounds boneless chuck or rump roast may be substituted for rib roast.

SAUERBRATEN I *8 to 10 servings*

- 4 pounds boneless chuck or rump roast
- Salt and freshly ground black pepper to taste
- 2 cups wine vinegar
- 2 cups water
- 1 clove garlic
- ¾ cup sliced onion
- 1 bay leaf
- 10 peppercorns
- ¼ cup sugar
- 3 whole cloves
- Flour
- 2 tablespoons bacon drippings
- 1½ cups sour cream

1. Season the meat with the salt and pepper and place in a large bowl.

2. Bring the vinegar and water to a boil and add the garlic, onion, bay leaf, peppercorns, sugar and cloves. Pour the marinade over the beef, cover and refrigerate twelve hours or overnight.

3. Remove the meat and dry thoroughly with paper towels. Reserve the marinade. Dredge the meat with flour.

4. In a heavy kettle heat the bacon drippings, add the meat and brown on all sides. Add two cups of the marinade, cover tightly and simmer gently until the meat is tender, two and-one-half to three hours. Remove the meat to a warm platter and keep hot. Thicken the gravy with a little flour mixed with water. Stir in the sour cream and serve over the sliced meat.

SAUERBRATEN II *8 to 10 servings*

- 1 four- to six-pound eye round pot roast
- ¼ pound salt pork
- Salt and freshly ground black pepper to taste
- 2 onions, sliced
- ½ parsnip, sliced
- 2 leeks, sliced
- 2 carrots, sliced
- 2 bay leaves
- 6 whole cloves
- 12 peppercorns
- 12 juniper berries
- 1 quart red wine vinegar
- 2 tablespoons lard or drippings
- Rye bread heel

(*cont'd*)

1. Lard the roast with salt pork (as page 100) and season with the salt and pepper.

2. Place the meat in a large bowl and add the vegetables, bay leaves, cloves, peppercorns and juniper berries. Bring the vinegar to a boil and pour over the top. Let the meat marinate, covered, a week or more in the refrigerator, turning it twice daily.

3. Remove the meat and dry thoroughly with paper towels. Reserve the marinade. In a Dutch oven heat the fat, add the meat and brown on all sides. Add the marinade with the vegetables, making sure the liquid does not come more than halfway up the meat.

4. Cover and simmer until the meat is tender, three to four hours. Toward the end of the cooking period, add a heel of rye bread.

5. Remove the roast to a warm platter and keep hot while preparing the gravy.

SAUERBRATEN GRAVY:

¼ cup butter
1 tablespoon sugar
¼ cup flour, approximately
1 cup sauerbraten marinade (left after cooking meat)
1 cup red wine

1. In a large saucepan heat the butter, add the sugar and enough flour to produce a thick roux. Stir constantly and let the flour darken as much as possible without burning.

2. Slowly add the marinade, stirring. Add the wine and simmer, stirring, until the sauce has the thickness of heavy cream.

3. Strain the mixture through a very fine sieve and keep warm.

Note: The sauce should be pungent, with just a suspicion of sweetness. In some parts of Germany sour cream is used instead of wine.

To Serve Sauerbraten: Slice the roast evenly and place the slices, slightly overlapping, on a hot platter. Coat with some of the sauce and serve the rest separately. Serve with potato pancakes (page 396).

BEEF WITH OLIVES *6 to 8 servings*

3 pounds chuck beef, cut into 1½-inch cubes
Flour
Salt and freshly ground black pepper
3 tablespoons olive oil
12 small white onions, peeled and left whole
1 clove garlic, finely chopped
½ teaspoon thyme
1½ cups beef stock or bouillon
1 cup pitted green olives
¼ cup chopped parsley
2 tablespoons butter
2 tablespoons flour

1. Preheat oven to slow (300° F.).

2. Dredge the meat with flour seasoned with salt and pepper. In a Dutch

(*cont'd*)

oven heat the oil, add the meat and brown on all sides. Add the onions and garlic and brown lightly. Sprinkle with the thyme and add the stock.

3. Cover and bake one and one-half hours. Add the olives and parsley, cover and cook until the meat is tender, thirty to forty-five minutes longer.

4. Blend the butter with the flour and add it, bit by bit, to the simmering liquid in the casserole, stirring constantly until thickened. Correct the seasonings.

PRAGUE THREE-MEAT GOULASH *8 servings*

- 1½ pounds onions, coarsely chopped (about 4 cups)
- ¼ cup shortening
- 1½ pounds chuck beef, cubed
- 2 teaspoons salt
- 1 small can tomato paste
- ½ pound veal shoulder, cubed
- ½ pound fresh pork shoulder, cubed
- 1 cup dry white wine
- 1 cup sour cream

1. In a heavy three-quart saucepan or Dutch oven, sauté the onions in the fat until the onions are golden. Add the beef and cook over medium heat until it loses its bright redness.

2. Add the salt and tomato paste, reduce the heat, cover and simmer slowly thirty minutes. Add the veal and pork and continue to simmer slowly, covered, one hour. Add the wine.

3. Simmer, covered, thirty minutes longer, or until the meats are tender. Stir in the sour cream and heat for a few minutes; do not boil.

BUDAPEST BEEF GOULASH I *5 servings*

- ¼ cup shortening
- 1½ pounds onions, coarsely chopped (about 4 cups)
- 1½ pounds chuck beef, cubed
- 1½ teaspoons salt
- 1 tablespoon sweet paprika
- 1 small can tomato paste

1. In a heavy two-quart saucepan, heat the fat, add the onions and sauté until golden brown. Add the beef and cook over medium heat, stirring, until the beef loses its bright redness. Add the remaining ingredients.

2. Simmer very slowly, covered, until the beef is tender, one and one-half to two hours. If necessary, to prevent sticking, one-quarter cup water may be added.

BUDAPEST BEEF GOULASH II *5 servings*

- 2 tablespoons fat
- 2 large onions, chopped
- 1 small tomato, chopped
- 1 small green pepper, seeded and chopped
- 1 tablespoon sweet paprika
- 1½ pounds chuck beef, cubed
- 1 teaspoon tomato paste
- 2 teaspoons salt
- 1 cup boiling water
- 2 large raw potatoes, diced

(*cont'd*)

1. In a heavy two-and-one-half-quart saucepan, heat the fat, add the onions and cook until golden brown. Add the tomato, green pepper, paprika, beef, tomato paste and salt. Cook, stirring, over medium heat until the beef loses its bright redness.

2. Reduce the heat, add the water, cover and simmer one and one-half hours. Remove the meat, strain the gravy and return to the pan with the meat. Add the potatoes and simmer until tender, about one hour.

BEEF WITH SOUR CREAM *6 servings*

- ⅓ cup flour
- 1 teaspoon salt
- 1 teaspoon freshly ground black pepper
- 2 pounds boneless chuck, cut into 1-inch cubes
- ¼ cup salad oil or bacon drippings
- 1 cup water or tomato juice
- 3 tablespoons grated onion
- ½ teaspoon thyme
- ½ bay leaf
- 1 package frozen peas
- 1 cup sour cream
- 1 tablespoon horseradish

1. Mix the flour, salt and pepper. Dredge the meat with the seasoned flour. In a Dutch oven heat the oil, add the meat and brown quickly on all sides. Add the water, onion, thyme and bay leaf. Cover tightly and simmer gently about two and one-fourth hours or until meat is tender.

2. Add the peas and simmer about ten minutes, or until done. Stir in the sour cream and horseradish and heat but do not let boil.

HAMBURGERS AU POIVRE *4 servings*

Here is a ground-beef version of steak au poivre.

- 2 pounds chopped beef
- 4 teaspoons coarsely ground black pepper
- Salt
- 4 teaspoons butter
- Tabasco sauce to taste
- Worcestershire sauce to taste
- Lemon juice to taste
- 2 tablespoons cognac, warmed (optional)
- Chopped parsley
- Chopped chives

1. Shape the beef lightly into four cakes and sprinkle each side with pepper. With the heel of the hand, press the pepper into the meat and let stand thirty minutes.

2. Sprinkle a light layer of salt over the bottom of a heavy skillet, place over high heat and, when the salt begins to brown, add the hamburgers. Cook until well browned on one side. Turn and, to produce a rare hamburger, cook thirty seconds over high heat, then lower the heat to medium and cook one more minute. (Adjust heat and time to cook the hamburger to a greater degree of doneness.)

3. Place a teaspoon of butter on each cake in the pan and add Tabasco, Worcestershire and lemon juice to taste. Ignite the cognac and add.

(cont'd)

4. Transfer the patties to a warm platter and keep hot. Lower heat. Swirl the sauce in the skillet, pour it over the meat and sprinkle the patties with parsley and chives.

HAMBURGERS WITH DILL *6 servings*

Ground beef can be glorified and glorious. It should be a good grade of beef.

- 3 pounds ground round steak
- 1½ tablespoons freshly chopped dill or 1½ teaspoons dried dill
- Salt
- 6 teaspoons butter
- Freshly ground black pepper to taste
- Worcestershire sauce to taste
- Juice of one-half lemon
- Tabasco sauce to taste
- Buttered toast

1. Combine the meat lightly with the dill and divide into six equal portions. Shape into flat patties.

2. Heat a heavy skillet over moderate heat eight to ten minutes and sprinkle with a thin, even layer of salt. Sear the meat on both sides, reduce the heat and continue cooking to the desired degree of doneness.

3. Top each patty with a teaspoon butter, sprinkle with pepper and add a few drops of Worcestershire sauce. Sprinkle with lemon juice and a little Tabasco sauce.

4. Serve on toast with the pan gravy.

HAMBURGER POTATO ROLL *5 to 6 servings*

One of the most frequently requested recipes ever printed in The Times *is this novelty: a hamburger roll filled with mashed potatoes.*

- 1 tablespoon drippings
- 1 medium onion, chopped
- 1 small clove garlic, crushed
- 1 pound ground chuck beef
- 1 egg, lightly beaten
- 2 slices bread, crusts removed
- Water
- 1 teaspoon salt
- ¼ teaspoon orégano, rosemary or basil
- Freshly ground black pepper to taste
- 2 tablespoons dry bread crumbs
- 2 cups seasoned mashed potato
- 1 tablespoon minced parsley or green pepper (optional)
- 3 strips bacon (optional)

1. Preheat oven to moderate (350° F.).

2. Heat the drippings, add the onion and garlic and sauté until the onion is transparent. Remove to a mixing bowl and add the ground beef. Add the egg.

3. Soften the bread in water, press out the excess water and add bread to the meat. Add the salt, orégano and pepper. Mix thoroughly.

4. Sprinkle a piece of waxed paper with crumbs. Press the meat out on the crumbs to make a rectangle about one-half inch thick.

5. Beat the mashed potatoes with the parsley and spread on top of the meat. (If leftover potato is used, reheat it in a double boiler before spreading.)

(cont'd)

6. Using the waxed paper as an aid, roll the meat and potatoes, jelly-roll fashion, and place in a loaf pan or on a shallow baking pan. Grease the pan if the meat is very lean. Place the bacon on top or brush with additional drippings; baste at least once during baking.

7. Bake about one hour and serve with a brown sauce made from the pan drippings, or with mushroom, tomato or other sauce.

STUFFED CABBAGE, PAGE 368.

SWEDISH MEAT BALLS *6 servings*

2 tablespoons butter
3 tablespoons minced onion
1 cup fresh bread crumbs
1 cup milk, or equal parts milk and cream
¾ pound ground round steak
¼ pound ground veal
¼ pound ground pork
1 egg
Salt and freshly ground black pepper
¼ cup flour
¾ cup cream or evaporated milk

1. In a large skillet melt the butter and sauté the onion until it is golden brown.

2. Soak the bread crumbs in the milk, add the meats, egg, onion, salt and pepper and mix thoroughly. Shape the mixture into balls about one and one-half inches in diameter and roll in the flour. Reserve one tablespoon of the flour.

3. Melt enough additional butter in the skillet to cover the bottom and brown the meat balls over medium heat. Shake the pan occasionally so the meat balls will retain their round shape. Remove to a serving dish and keep warm.

4. Combine the reserved flour with the cream and, using a wire whisk, stir gradually into the pan juices. Simmer three to four minutes, stirring occasionally. Pour the gravy over the meat balls and serve hot.

ORIENTAL BEEF BALLS *6 servings*

1 pound ground chuck
1 teaspoon salt
⅛ teaspoon freshly ground black pepper
3 tablespoons oil
¼ cup chopped onion
1 clove garlic, minced
1 bunch watercress
1 cup diagonally cut celery slices
1 cup diagonally cut carrot slices
1 can (1 pound) bean sprouts, drained
1 cup beef bouillon
1 teaspoon powdered ginger
2 tablespoons cornstarch
1 tablespoon soy sauce
¼ cup water

1. Season the meat with salt and pepper and shape into one-inch balls. In a skillet heat the oil, add the meat balls, a few at a time, and brown on all sides. Remove from the pan. Add the onion and garlic and cook until tender but not browned.

2. Cut the watercress stems into one-eighth-inch lengths and add. Coarsely chop the watercress leaves and reserve.

(cont'd)

3. Add the celery, carrots, bean sprouts and bouillon to the skillet, cover and cook until the vegetables are tender, about ten minutes.

4. Blend together the ginger, cornstarch, soy sauce and water. Stir into the vegetable mixture and cook until thickened. Add the meat balls and cook until heated through.

5. Before serving, stir in the watercress leaves. Serve with hot cooked rice.

KEFTEDES (GREEK MEAT BALLS), PAGE 14.

GROUND BEEF AND EGGPLANT CASSEROLE *6 to 8 servings*

- 12 slices eggplant, ½ inch thick
- Boiling salted water
- 2 pounds ground beef
- 3 tablespoons olive oil or bacon fat
- ¼ cup chopped onion
- ¼ cup chopped green pepper
- 2 tablespoons flour
- 2 teaspoons salt
- ¼ teaspoon freshly ground black pepper
- ½ teaspoon orégano
- 2 cups canned tomato sauce
- 1½ cups grated Cheddar cheese

1. Preheat oven to slow (300° F.).

2. Cook the peeled eggplant slices in boiling salted water until tender, about five minutes.

3. Brown the meat in two tablespoons of the oil, stirring occasionally. Cook the onion and green pepper in the remaining oil until the vegetables are wilted. Combine the meat and vegetables in the skillet and stir in the flour, salt, pepper and orégano. Add the tomato sauce and cook until thickened.

4. Arrange half the eggplant slices in a shallow, two-quart buttered baking dish. Spoon over them half the meat mixture and half the cheese. Repeat the layers and bake, uncovered, for thirty minutes.

WESTERN BEEF AND RICE CASSEROLE *6 to 8 servings*

- 1 cup pitted ripe olives
- 1 pound ground lean beef
- 2 tablespoons oil
- ½ cup chopped onion
- 1 cup sliced celery
- ¼ cup chopped green pepper
- 1 cup raw rice
- 2½ cups canned tomatoes
- 1 cup water
- 2 teaspoons salt
- 2 or 3 teaspoons chili powder
- ¼ teaspoon freshly ground black pepper
- ½ teaspoon Worcestershire sauce

1. Preheat oven to moderate (325° F.).

2. Cut the olives into large pieces.

3. Brown the beef in the oil. Remove the meat from the pan and add the onion, celery, green pepper and rice. Cook, stirring, until browned.

4. Add the tomatoes, water, seasonings, meat and olives and bring to a boil. Pour into a two-quart casserole and cover. Bake forty-five minutes to one hour.

CHILI CON CARNE *4 servings*

3 tablespoons butter or olive oil
1 large onion, minced
2 cloves garlic, minced
1 pound chopped beef
3 cups water
1⅓ cups canned tomatoes
1 green pepper, minced
½ teaspoon celery seed
¼ teaspoon cayenne
1 teaspoon cumin seed, crushed
1 small bay leaf
2 tablespoons chili powder
⅛ teaspoon basil
1½ teaspoons salt

1. Heat the butter in a skillet, add the onion and garlic and sauté until golden brown. Add the meat and brown.

2. Transfer the meat mixture to a large saucepan and add the remaining ingredients. Bring to a boil, reduce the heat and simmer, uncovered, until the sauce is as thick as desired, or about three hours. If desired, add one can of kidney beans just before serving.

HERBED MEAT LOAF *6 servings*

1 pound ground beef
½ pound ground veal
½ pound ground lean pork
2 eggs
½ cup fine bread crumbs
¾ cup chopped parsley
¼ cup finely chopped chives
2 tablespoons fresh basil, finely chopped, or 1 tablespoon dried basil (optional)
¼ cup green pepper, coarsely chopped (optional)
1½ teaspoons salt
½ teaspoon freshly ground black pepper
Bacon slices to cover top

1. Preheat oven to moderate (350° F.).

2. In a mixing bowl combine all the ingredients except the bacon slices. Using the hands, blend well; do not overwork the meat or it will produce a meat loaf that is too tightly packed.

3. Line a nine-inch pie plate with aluminum foil and shape the meat mixture into an oval loaf. Place the loaf on the foil and cover with bacon slices.

4. Bake one and one-half hours. Serve with mushroom sauce (page 452) or fresh tomato sauce (page 454).

HALLACAS *12 to 16 hallacas*

Hallacas are the Venezuelan version of tamales. They are normally wrapped in banana leaves, but aluminum foil is a reasonable substitute.

THE PASTE:

1 quart beef consommé
2 tablespoons paprika
½ cup butter
3 cups white cornmeal

(*cont'd*)

1. Combine the consommé and paprika and bring to a boil.

2. Add the butter and, when it has melted, gradually stir in the cornmeal. Cook, stirring, until the mixture is smooth and thick, ten to fifteen minutes. Remove from the heat and set aside.

THE FILLING:

3 tablespoons olive oil
2 cloves garlic, finely chopped
1 onion, chopped
1 pound ground round steak
1 three-pound chicken, simmered until tender, or 3 cups cooked chicken
6 scallions, sliced
2 tablespoons capers
2 teaspoons sugar
1 teaspoon salt
1 chili pepper, chopped (or ¼ teaspoon crushed dried chili pepper)
¼ cup vinegar
4 ripe tomatoes, peeled and chopped
⅓ cup soft bread crumbs
¼ cup minced parsley
½ cup Spanish sherry

1. Heat the oil in a large skillet. Add the garlic, onion and round steak and brown.

2. Add the chicken, which has been removed from the bones and cut up coarsely, the scallions, capers, sugar, salt, chili pepper and vinegar.

3. Simmer ten minutes. Stir in the remaining ingredients and cook five minutes longer. Remove from the heat.

THE GARNISHES:

2 hard-cooked eggs, sliced and each slice cut in half
Pitted ripe olives, sliced
Stuffed green olives, sliced
Seedless raisins

1. Tear off a strip of heavy-duty aluminum foil about eight inches wide. Place it on a flat surface. Pinch off a small amount of the hallaca paste and flatten it down on the foil to make a strip five inches long, two and one-half inches wide, and one-quarter inch thick. Top the dough with about two tablespoons of the filling and flatten it out. Add a little of each garnish.

2. Pinch off enough of the paste to top the hallaca, flatten it and pinch the top and bottom edges of the paste together to seal in the filling.

3. Pull up the ends of the foil and fold the lengthwise edges over themselves several times. Twist the ends firmly and pull the twisted ends under the hallaca. The idea is to make a watertight seal.

4. Drop the foil-wrapped hallacas into boiling water to cover and cook one hour. Unwrap and serve. Garnish as desired.

EMPANADAS (CHILEAN MEAT TURNOVERS), PAGE 34.

PIROZHKI (RUSSIAN MEAT TURNOVERS), PAGE 31.

PASTEL DE CHOCLO *10 to 12 generous servings*

This is a hearty and unusual Chilean casserole that is somewhat tedious to prepare but well worth the effort. It contains an amplitude of chicken, beef and corn.

Salad oil
Butter
3½-pound chicken, cut into pieces
1 onion, sliced
Salt
Orégano
3 pounds lean round steak, cut into ¼-inch cubes
Paprika
1½ teaspoons Tabasco sauce
16 ears corn, grated
Sugar
6 cups chopped onion
12 black olives, pitted
4 hard-cooked eggs, quartered
2 raw egg yolks

1. Heat two tablespoons oil and three tablespoons butter in a large skillet and brown the chicken on all sides. Add the sliced onion, one teaspoon salt and one tablespoon orégano, and sauté until onion is golden brown. Remove from skillet and set aside.

2. In the same skillet, heat two tablespoons oil and four tablespoons butter and brown the beef. Season with two teaspoons salt, one tablespoon paprika, one-half teaspoon orégano and the Tabasco. Cover. Cook, stirring often, until the meat is tender. Set aside.

3. Combine the grated raw corn with one tablespoon sugar, one teaspoon salt and four tablespoons butter in a heavy pot. Cook, stirring constantly, until the mixture boils and thickens. Set aside.

4. Sauté six cups chopped onion in two tablespoons oil and four tablespoons butter until golden brown. Combine with the beef mixture and turn into two three-quart casseroles.

5. Arrange olives and quartered eggs over the beef, place the chicken pieces on top and cover with the corn. Paint the corn with egg yolks diluted with a teaspoon of water and sprinkle very lightly with sugar.

6. Bake in a preheated hot oven (400° F.) until the top is golden brown, about twenty-five minutes.

BRAISED SHORT RIBS OF BEEF *3 servings*

3 tablespoons flour
2 teaspoons salt
Freshly ground black pepper to taste
¼ teaspoon powdered rosemary
3 pounds short ribs of beef, cut into serving pieces
3 tablespoons bacon drippings
½ cup chopped onion
½ cup chopped celery
1½ cups boiling beef broth or consommé

1. Preheat oven to slow (300° F.).

2. Combine the flour, salt, pepper and rosemary. Dredge the ribs with the seasoned flour.

(cont'd)

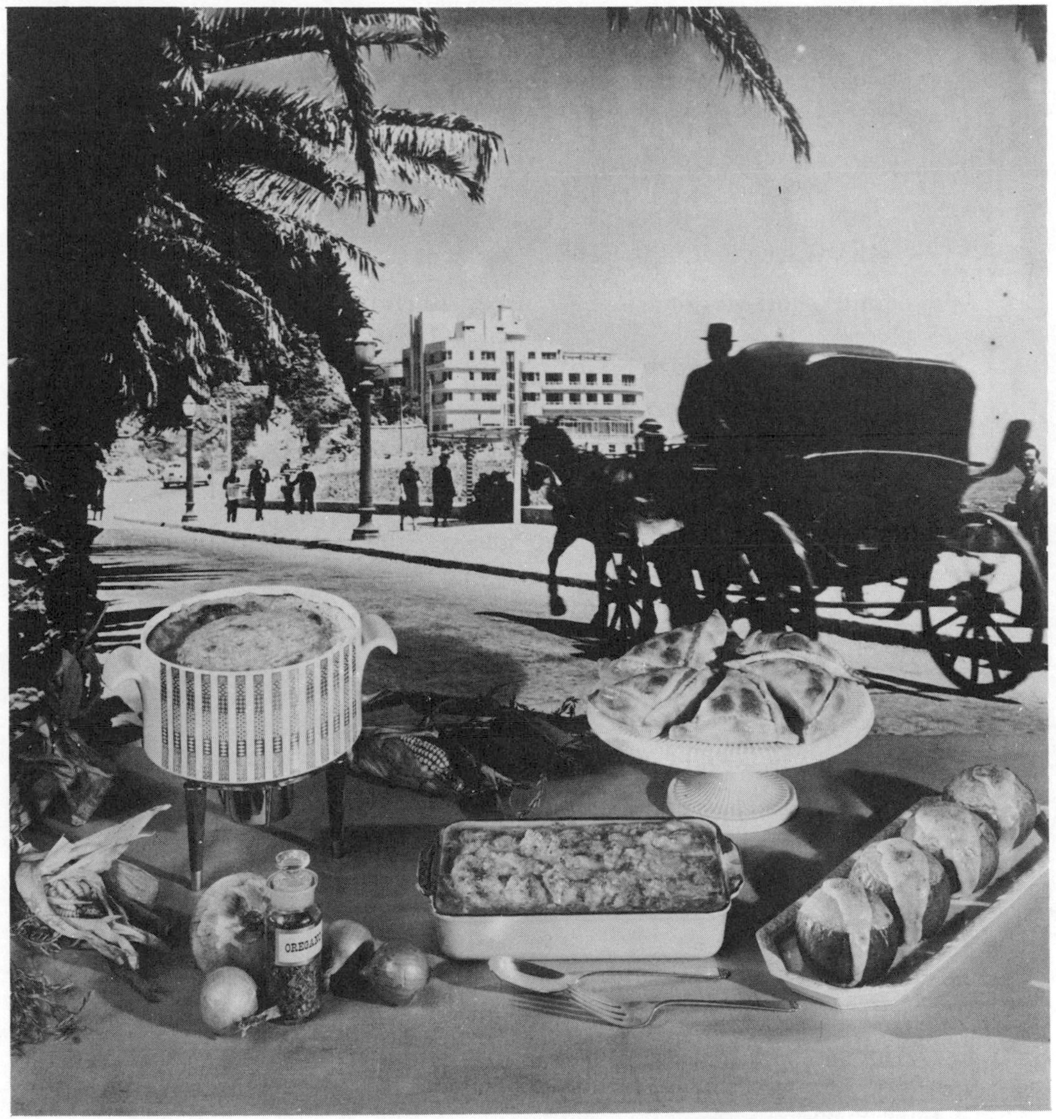

The cuisine of Chile includes appetizing fare such as (left to right) pastel de choclo (a corn and beef casserole), chupe (a mélange of seafood), empanadas (pastry turnovers) and manjar blanco (a custard) served in apples. In the background is Viña del Mar, Chile.

3. In a skillet, heat the bacon drippings, add the onion and celery and sauté five minutes. Transfer the vegetables to a heavy kettle with a lid.

4. Brown the ribs well on all sides in the same fat and transfer them to the kettle. Add the boiling broth and cover tightly.

(*cont'd*)

5. Bake two and one-half hours. If desired, skim off excess fat and thicken the juices by stirring in a little of the seasoned flour mixed with cold water. Simmer five minutes and serve with the meat.

Note: The ribs may also be simmered slowly on top of the stove over low heat.

DEVILED SHORT RIBS *3 servings*

- 3 pounds short ribs, cut into serving pieces
- 2 tablespoons prepared mustard
- 2 teaspoons salt
- ½ teaspoon chili powder
- ½ teaspoon sugar
- 2 tablespoons lemon juice
- ¼ cup oil
- 1 clove garlic, crushed
- Freshly ground black pepper to taste
- 1 small onion, chopped
- Flour
- ⅔ cup stock or water

1. Place the short ribs in a deep bowl. Mix the remaining ingredients, except the flour, and pour over the ribs. Cover and refrigerate several hours, turning the meat once or twice. Drain, reserving the marinade.

2. Preheat oven to hot (425° F.). Arrange the ribs on a rack in a roasting pan and bake until browned, about thirty minutes. Reduce the oven temperature to moderate (350° F.). Add the reserved marinade to the ribs, cover and bake until tender, about one and one-half hours. Uncover and bake until the fat on the ribs is crisp. Pour off the fat from pan. Add stock or water to pan. Boil for two minutes.

3. Thicken the broth with flour mixed with a little water and serve with the ribs.

LENTIL AND SHORT-RIB STEW *3 generous servings*

- 3 pounds short ribs, cut into 3-inch pieces
- 3 cups water
- 1 teaspoon salt
- 1 bay leaf
- 1 clove garlic, minced
- 1 onion, chopped
- 1 small stalk celery, chopped
- 1 cup dried lentils, washed and picked over
- ¼ teaspoon thyme or orégano
- 1 cup elbow macaroni, cooked (optional)

1. Place short ribs in a heavy saucepan and add water, salt, bay leaf, garlic, onion and celery. Simmer, covered, until the meat is tender, about two hours.

2. Add the lentils and thyme and continue cooking, stirring often, until the lentils are tender, about thirty minutes longer. Correct the seasonings and add macaroni. Reheat.

3. If the bones have separated from the short ribs, remove them before serving.

OXTAIL STEW *3 servings*

2 pounds oxtail, disjointed
Flour for dredging
3 tablespoons fat
1 large onion, chopped
2 cups canned beef bouillon
1 tablespoon vinegar
Salt and freshly ground black pepper to taste
3 carrots, sliced
1 cup diced celery
1 green pepper, chopped
2 teaspoons butter

1. Dredge the oxtail in flour. In a large skillet, heat the fat. Brown the oxtail pieces on all sides. Add the onion, then the bouillon, vinegar, salt and pepper. Cover tightly and simmer until the meat is almost tender, about two and one-half hours.
2. Add the carrots, celery and green pepper. Cover and simmer until the meat and vegetables are tender, about thirty minutes longer. Remove the meat and vegetables to a warm platter and keep hot.
3. Cream the butter with two teaspoons flour and stir into the liquid remaining in the skillet. Bring to a boil, stirring, and boil one minute. Pour over the vegetables and meat.
4. Serve with rice, mashed potatoes or baked barley.

BRAISED OXTAIL *4 servings*

3 pounds oxtail, disjointed
Flour for dredging
Salt and freshly ground black pepper
3 tablespoons shortening
1 cup diced carrots
1 clove garlic, minced
12 small whole white onions, peeled
2 cups dry red wine
1 bay leaf
Pinch of thyme
Beef stock or consommé
1 cup mushrooms (optional)
Chopped parsley

1. Preheat oven to moderate (350° F.).
2. Have the oxtail disjointed and roll in flour seasoned with salt and pepper. Brown the meat in the shortening in a hot skillet and transfer it to a casserole.
3. Add the carrots, garlic and onions to the pan and brown well. Transfer to the casserole and add the wine and seasonings. Add enough beef stock to barely cover and sprinkle with salt and pepper.
4. Cover and bake two and one-half to three hours, or until the meat is tender. If desired, sauté the mushrooms in a little butter and add to the casserole for the last half hour of cooking. Serve sprinkled with chopped parsley.

STEAK AND KIDNEY PIE *6 servings*

1¾ teaspoons salt
4¼ cups sifted all-purpose flour, approximately
3 medium eggs, lightly beaten
½ cup milk
1 cup butter
2 pounds round steak, cut ½ inch thick
½ pound beef kidney
½ teaspoon freshly ground black pepper

(*cont'd*)

1. Mix one-quarter teaspoon of the salt with four cups sifted flour. Mix the eggs with the milk and reserve about four tablespoons for a glaze. Add the milk mixture to the flour and stir together to form a stiff dough. Knead until smooth.

2. Roll into a thin sheet and dot with bits of half a stick of butter. Sift a light dusting of flour over the butter. Fold the corners of the dough to the center, fold in half, pound to flatten and roll into a sheet. Repeat process until all the butter has been folded in. Chill between each rolling if the butter softens. When all the butter has been used, chill the dough.

3. Preheat the oven to hot (425° F.).

4. While the pastry is chilling, cut the steak into three-inch squares and pound lightly. Place a piece of kidney on each slice of beef and roll jelly-roll fashion. Mix one tablespoon flour, one and one-half teaspoons salt and the pepper and sprinkle over the rolls. Stand the rolls on end in a shallow six- to eight-cup casserole.

5. Roll the chilled pastry to about one-quarter-inch thickness and cut out a shape that is one inch larger than the top of the casserole. Cut a one-inch hole in the center of the pastry. Cut six small "leaves" from scraps of pastry and use the balance of the pastry scraps to line the rim of the casserole. Place top on pie loosely, moisten the rim and seal the edge. Brush bottoms of leaves with the diluted egg reserved earlier and arrange the leaves as a trim on top of pie. Brush whole of top with the egg.

6. Bake at 425° twelve minutes, lower the heat to moderate (325° F.); bake two hours longer.

BEEF PIE WITH HERBS *4 to 6 servings*

¼ cup flour
1 teaspoon salt
½ teaspoon freshly ground black pepper
1 pound boneless chuck cut into one-inch cubes
¼ cup salad oil or shortening
½ cup chopped onion
½ cup chopped celery
2 cups water
½ bay leaf
¼ cup chopped fresh basil or 1 teaspoon dried basil
2 tablespoons finely chopped parsley
2 cups peeled, cubed cooked potatoes
1½ cups sliced cooked carrots
Pastry for a single-crust pie

1. Mix flour, salt and pepper and dredge the meat with the seasoned flour. In a large skillet, heat the fat and brown the meat on all sides.

2. Add the onion and celery and sauté five minutes. Stir in the remaining seasoned flour and gradually add the water. Cook, stirring, until thickened.

3. Add bay leaf, cover the skillet and simmer over low heat until meat is tender, about one and one-half hours. Discard the bay leaf.

4. Preheat oven to hot (425° F.). Add parsley, potatoes and carrots to the meat and allow the mixture to cool until lukewarm.

(cont'd)

5. Turn the mixture into a one-and-one-half-quart casserole and top with pastry. Flute the edge and cut gashes in the top for the escape of steam. Bake twenty-five minutes.

ENGLISH BEEF AND KIDNEY PIE *6 or more servings*

2 pounds chuck beef
1 pound beef kidney, carefully trimmed
Beef suet (a piece the size of a large egg)
1 large onion, coarsely chopped
1 cup rich beef stock
1 teaspoon salt
Freshly ground black pepper
Cayenne pepper
1½ teaspoons Worcestershire sauce
Flour
Pastry for a single-crust pie

1. Cut the beef and kidney into one-and-one-half-inch cubes.
2. Try out the suet in a heavy kettle or Dutch oven, and remove the suet cracklings. Add the onion and sauté until transparent.
3. Add the beef and kidney and cook, stirring almost constantly, until thoroughly browned.
4. Add the beef stock, salt, pepper and cayenne to taste and the Worcestershire sauce. Stir well, cover and simmer until the meat is tender, or about one hour and forty-five minutes.
5. If necessary, add enough water to almost cover the meat. Thicken the broth with flour which has been blended with cold water, allowing one and one-half teaspoons flour for each cup of broth. Transfer the mixture to a casserole and cool until lukewarm.
6. Preheat oven to hot (450° F.).
7. Roll the pastry to one-eighth-inch thickness and place over the meat, sealing it to the sides of the casserole. Cut gashes for the escape of steam. If desired, the pastry can be cut in strips and arranged lattice-fashion over the meat.
8. Bake about ten minutes, lower heat to moderate (350° F.) and bake until the crust is delicately browned, or about fifteen minutes longer.

CORNED BEEF HASH *4 servings*

1 pound cooked corned beef (approximately 2 cups)
3 to 4 medium cooked potatoes
1 small onion
½ large green pepper
1 small stalk celery
1 or 2 sprigs parsley

1. Preheat oven to hot (425° F.).
2. Grind all the ingredients in a food grinder, using the finest knife. Mix well.
3. Turn into a shallow greased nine-inch pan. Bake until the crust is brown, twenty to twenty-five minutes. Fold as you would an omelet. Serve with poached eggs, catsup or thickened tomato sauce.

RED FLANNEL HASH *6 servings*

1½ cups chopped cooked corned beef
1½ cups chopped boiled potatoes
1½ cups chopped boiled beets
1 minced onion
½ cup milk
1 teaspoon Worcestershire sauce
Salt and freshly ground black pepper to taste
2 tablespoons butter

1. Mix together the beef, potatoes, beets, onion, milk, Worcestershire, salt and pepper.

2. Heat the butter in a skillet and add the meat mixture. Cook over low heat, stirring occasionally, until thoroughly hot. Let cook until browned and crusted underneath.

3. Fold over the hash as you would an omelet and turn out on a hot platter.

ROAST BEEF HASH *4 to 5 servings*

1½ pounds cold roast beef (about 3 cups)
1 pound cooked potatoes, diced (about 2 cups)
1 large onion, grated
¼ green pepper, chopped
1 cup meat stock or gravy
⅓ cup tomato paste
Salt and freshly ground black pepper to taste

1. Chop or grind the roast beef, add the remaining ingredients and mix well.

2. Turn the mixture into a greased preheated frying pan and cook, stirring occasionally, until the hash is thoroughly hot. Let cook until browned and crusted underneath.

3. Fold the hash over as you would an omelet and turn out on a hot platter.

CHIPPED BEEF WITH ARTICHOKE HEARTS *4 servings*

2 packages frozen artichoke hearts
1½ cups ripe olives, pitted
6 tablespoons butter
6 tablespoons flour
1½ cups milk
½ to 1 teaspoon salt, depending on the saltiness of the chipped beef
2 cups sour cream
½ cup dry white wine
1 cup shredded chipped beef

1. Cook the artichoke hearts according to package directions and drain.

2. Cut the olives into small pieces.

3. Melt the butter in a saucepan, add the flour and stir with a wire whisk until blended. Meanwhile bring the milk to a boil and add all at once to the butter-flour mixture, stirring vigorously with the whisk. When the mixture is thickened and smooth, add the salt, sour cream, wine, beef, olives and artichoke hearts.

4. Heat the mixture until it is piping hot, but do not boil. Serve hot with cooked rice.

LAMB

ROAST LEG OF LAMB *6 servings*

1 five-pound leg of lamb, trimmed
1 clove garlic, sliced
1 teaspoon rosemary
Lemon juice
Salt and freshly ground black pepper

1. Preheat oven to slow (300° F.).
2. Cut small slits in the lamb and insert the garlic. Rub the meat with rosemary and lemon juice and sprinkle with salt and pepper.
3. Place the meat on a rack in a roasting pan and roast, uncovered, eighteen minutes per pound for well done (175° F. on a meat thermometer), twelve for rare (140° F.).
4. Transfer the lamb to a warm serving tray and let stand for twenty minutes before carving. Serve with pan gravy, a white-bean casserole and tossed green salad.

ROAST LAMB WITH HERBS

Combine one clove crushed garlic, one teaspoon salt, one teaspoon pepper, one-half teaspoon powdered ginger, a bay leaf, and one-half teaspoon each thyme, sage and marjoram with one tablespoon soy sauce and one tablespoon salad oil. Make slits in the lamb and rub the sauce thoroughly over and into the meat. Proceed as for roast leg of lamb, above.

CROWN ROAST OF LAMB *8 servings*

1 crown roast of lamb, at room temperature
Salt and freshly ground black pepper
Center stuffing

1. Have the butcher prepare a crown roast with rib sections of two loins of lamb by tying the sections together in a crown shape.
2. Preheat oven to moderate (325° F.).
3. Cover the tips of the roast's bones with aluminum foil to prevent them from charring as the roast cooks. Place the meat on a rack in an open roasting pan.
4. Salt and pepper the roast and cook it about one hour or one hour and fifteen minutes. It should be rare when served.
5. Remove the aluminum foil and replace with paper frills. Fill the center with the desired stuffing and serve immediately.

Recommended stuffings include buttered or creamed whole onions, mushrooms cooked lightly in butter, and puréed peas.

SWEDISH LAMB *6 to 8 servings*

- 1 tablespoon salt
- 1 tablespoon freshly ground black pepper
- 1 five-pound leg of lamb
- 3 onions, sliced
- 3 carrots, sliced
- 1 cup hot beef broth
- 1½ cups hot strong coffee
- ½ cup heavy cream
- 1 tablespoon sugar

1. Preheat oven to hot (425° F.).
2. Rub the salt and pepper into the lamb and place the meat on a rack in a roasting pan surrounded with the onions and carrots. Roast thirty minutes, then skim off the fat.
3. Reduce the oven temperature to moderate (350° F.) and add the broth, coffee, cream and sugar. Continue roasting, basting frequently, forty minutes to one hour, depending on desired degree of doneness.
4. Transfer the lamb to a warm platter and force the gravy through a sieve, or purée in an electric blender.

LEG OF LAMB A LA MOLLY ELLSWORTH *6 to 8 servings*

- 1 five-pound leg of lamb
- 2 tablespoons butter
- ¼ pound mushrooms, chopped
- 1 clove garlic, chopped
- ¼ pound ham, chopped
- 1 teaspoon chopped parsley
- 1 tablespoon chopped onion
- Grated rind of one lemon
- Pinch of nutmeg
- Salt and freshly ground black pepper to taste
- ¼ cup soft fresh bread crumbs
- 4 egg yolks, beaten
- ¼ cup olive oil
- 2 bay leaves
- Pinch of thyme
- Pinch of marjoram
- 2 cloves garlic, chopped
- 3 cups chicken or meat stock, or canned broth

1. Have the butcher bone the lamb, leaving a small portion of the bone protruding two inches from the narrow end of the meat. (This is for appearance only.) Trim and save any lean scraps.
2. Preheat oven to moderate (325° F.).
3. Melt the butter in a skillet, add the mushrooms, garlic, ham, parsley, onion, lemon rind, nutmeg, salt and pepper and cook until the mushrooms wilt.
4. Chop the scraps of lamb. Combine with the bread crumbs and egg yolks and add to the mushroom mixture. Stuff the mixture into the lamb cavity. Sew up the cavity and brown the meat in hot oil. Transfer to a casserole.
5. Add the remaining ingredients and cover tightly. Cook three hours, turning the lamb occasionally.
6. When the meat is tender, remove to a hot platter and keep warm. Strain the gravy and boil until reduced to one-half the original quantity.
7. Brown the lamb under a broiler, basting occasionally with the gravy, until it acquires a brown glaze.

ARNI PSITO (roast leg of lamb, Greek style) *6 servings*

Lamb is most loved by the Greek people. Arni tou galatos psito, or roast baby lamb, is traditional at Easter and is a dish of great delicacy. Lamb is never fried but roasted or lightly browned and cooked or baked in sauces.

1 five-pound leg of lamb
Salt and freshly ground black pepper
1 tablespoon orégano
1 clove garlic, halved
¼ cup butter
Juice of 1 large lemon
2 small onions, chopped
3 or 4 sprigs parsley
2 or 3 dried mushrooms, washed and chopped
1 cup water

1. Preheat oven to very hot (500° F.).
2. Place lamb, skin side up, on a rack in an open roasting pan. Rub the meat with salt, pepper, orégano and garlic.
3. Melt the butter, add the lemon juice and pour over the meat. Add onions, parsley, mushrooms and one-half cup water to the pan. Place in oven and roast twenty minutes.
4. Add the remaining water, lower oven temperature to 350° F. and roast to desired degree of doneness (see roast leg of lamb, page 119). Baste occasionally. Serve with pilaff Greek style (page 321).

CUSHION SHOULDER OF LAMB WITH CHICKEN LIVER STUFFING *6 to 8 servings*

1 three- to four-pound cushion lamb shoulder
Salt and freshly ground black pepper to taste
½ pound chicken livers
2 tablespoons butter
1 tablespoon grated onion
2 cups soft bread cubes or crumbs
¾ cup finely chopped celery
2 tablespoons chopped chives
2 tablespoons sherry
⅓ cup cream or stock
1 egg, slightly beaten

1. Have the butcher remove the bones from a square-cut lamb shoulder to form a cushion roast. Close three sides of the roast with metal skewers. Season the pocket lightly with salt and pepper.

3. Chop the chicken livers coarsely and brown them lightly in the butter.

4. Add the remaining ingredients, mix well and season with three-quarters teaspoon salt and pepper to taste. Fill the pocket with the mixture, without packing. Fasten the edges together with skewers.

5. Place the roast, fat side up, in an open roasting pan and roast about two and one-half hours (170° for medium and 180° for well done on a meat thermometer). Serve with the pan drippings, from which the excess fat has been removed.

STUFFED SHOULDER OF LAMB *6 servings*

3 tablespoons butter
1 cup diced mushrooms
1 clove garlic, minced
½ pound ham, chopped fine
1 tablespoon finely chopped parsley
¼ cup finely chopped onion
Grated rind of 1 lemon
Salt and freshly ground black pepper to taste
¼ cup soft fresh bread crumbs
2 eggs, lightly beaten
1 boned shoulder of lamb prepared for stuffing

1. Preheat oven to slow (300° F.).

2. In a large skillet melt the butter, add the mushrooms and sauté until browned. Add the remaining ingredients (except the lamb) and mix. Stuff the shoulder with the mixture and tie securely with string.

3. Place the shoulder on a rack in a roasting pan and roast approximately forty minutes per pound.

LEG OF LAMB, MIDDLE EASTERN STYLE *6 servings*

5-pound leg of lamb, trimmed
Salt and freshly ground black pepper to taste
1 bunch scallions, chopped
8 stalks fresh mint, chopped
1 cup stock or bouillon

1. Preheat oven to hot (450° F.). Rub the meat with salt and pepper.

2. Place the roast on a rack in an open pan and bake until browned, about fifteen minutes. Reduce the temperature to moderate (325° F.) and continue roasting until the meat is rare (140° on a meat thermometer).

3. Cover the lamb with the scallions and mint. Add the stock to the pan and return the meat to the oven. Roast until done (175° on a meat thermometer), basting frequently with the broth in the pan.

4. Serve the meat with the cooked scallions around and on top of it. Make a gravy, if desired, from the drippings in the pan.

LEG OF LAMB WITH TURNIPS *8 servings*

1 six- to eight-pound leg of lamb, trimmed
Salt
2 tablespoons olive oil
3 onions, sliced
3 carrots, sliced
2 stalks celery, sliced
3 sprigs parsley
1 bay leaf
½ teaspoon thyme
1 tablespoon flour
1 to 2 cups water or stock
1 cup canned tomatoes, undrained
12 white turnips, quartered and parboiled
12 small white onions, peeled and parboiled

(*cont'd*)

1. Preheat oven to hot (400° F.). Season the meat with salt.

2. In a heavy kettle or Dutch oven place the oil, onions, carrots, celery, parsley, bay leaf and thyme. Sprinkle with flour and place the lamb on top.

3. Roast uncovered, turning frequently, until the lamb is browned on all sides. Add the water and tomatoes, cover closely and reduce the oven temperature to moderate (325° F.). Braise the lamb three to three and one-half hours, basting the meat occasionally. Fifteen minutes before the lamb is done, add the parboiled turnips and onions and cook until done.

4. Remove the lamb to a hot platter and keep warm. Strain the gravy and skim the fat from the surface. Thicken the gravy with a little flour mixed with water.

5. Slice the lamb and serve with the vegetables and gravy.

BROILED LAMB CHOPS *6 servings*

6 double lamb chops
5 tablespoons olive oil
1 clove garlic, sliced
Salt and freshly ground black pepper
Butter
Herbs

1. Marinate the lamb chops in the olive oil with the garlic for at least an hour.

2. Broil on a rack about two inches from the source of heat in a very hot preheated broiler. Brown both sides, cooking a total of ten minutes for rare, fifteen for medium, twenty for well done. Transfer to a warm platter, season with salt and pepper and place a pat of butter on each chop. Sprinkle with dill or parsley and lemon juice if desired. Serve with French-fried potatoes and watercress.

VARIATIONS:

Herb-Stuffed Lamb Chops: Before cooking, slit the chops in the thickest part. Cream a little butter with parsley, tarragon or rosemary and stuff the chops with the mixture. Seal the opening with picks. Broil and serve as indicated above.

Marinated Lamb Chops: Marinate chops for several hours in a mixture of three-fourths cup red wine, one-fourth cup olive oil, two crushed cloves garlic, one teaspoon salt, six peppercorns and a teaspoon of orégano. Broil as above.

Herbed Lamb Chops: Rub chops with a cut clove of garlic on each side, then rub with olive oil. Combine one tablespoon dried basil and one tablespoon dried marjoram and sprinkle the chops with the mixture. Refrigerate, covered, about two hours before cooking. Broil as above.

MUSLIM KEBABS *4 servings*

1 pound very lean lamb, ground
1 small onion, minced
1½ teaspoons yoghurt
1 teaspoon curry powder
¼ teaspoon salt
1 teaspoon lemon juice

(*cont'd*)

1. Mix all the ingredients very thoroughly. Divide into eight portions and pat each around a skewer in a long cigar shape.

2. Cook over hot coals until brown all over. Or cook on a kitchen range in a skillet in shallow, very hot fat.

SATAY KAMBING MADURA *6 servings*

Satay kambing madura is an Indonesian dish which is, in effect, skewered lamb in a peanut and red-pepper sauce. It is a very special version of shish kebab.

½ cup Indonesian soy sauce (or ½ cup regular soy sauce mixed with 1 teaspoon dark molasses)
1 teaspoon ground hot red pepper
¾ cup hot water
⅓ cup peanut butter
½ cup roasted peanuts, ground
1 clove garlic, minced
Juice of 1 lemon
3 pounds well-trimmed leg of lamb, boned and cut into 1-inch cubes

1. Combine all ingredients except lamb in a saucepan. Bring to a boil and stir until smooth. Cool to room temperature.

2. Pour half the sauce over the lamb cubes. Mix well and let stand one hour. Reserve remaining marinade for later use.

3. Preheat broiler. Arrange the lamb on small skewers, broil quickly on all sides and serve with hot sauce (see below).

HOT SAUCE:

Reserved marinade
½ can tomato sauce
¼ cup water or stock
Juice of 1 lemon
1 teaspoon Tabasco sauce

Combine all ingredients and bring to a boil. Use as a dip for skewered lamb.

SHASHLIK *6 servings*

Skewered meat dishes are called shish kebab in Armenian and shashlik in Russian.

1 small leg of lamb
1 cup red wine
¼ cup olive oil
2 cloves garlic, crushed
1 tablespoon salt
Freshly ground black pepper to taste
1 teaspoon orégano
Mushroom caps
Tomato wedges
Green pepper squares
Onion squares
Sliced bacon squares
Eggplant cubes

1. Trim the leg of lamb and remove the bone, gristle and remnants of fat. Cut the meat into two-inch cubes and marinate overnight in a mixture of the wine, oil, garlic, salt, pepper and orégano. *(cont'd)*

2. Preheat broiler. String the meat on skewers, alternating with mushrooms, tomato, green pepper, onion, bacon and eggplant.

3. Brush with the marinade and broil beneath high heat five minutes on each side.

LAMB CURRY *4 servings*

¼ cup butter
4 onions, chopped
1 clove garlic, minced
1 pound boneless lamb shoulder, cut into 2-inch cubes
1 cup yoghurt
1 teaspoon ground ginger
2 teaspoons ground coriander
¼ teaspoon ground cinnamon
½ teaspoon ground cardamom
¼ teaspoon ground cloves

1. In a heavy kettle melt the butter. Add the onions and garlic and sauté until the onion is tender and transparent. Remove onions and garlic.

2. Add the meat to the kettle and brown on all sides. Return the onions to the pot and add the yoghurt and remaining ingredients. Simmer until tender, about thirty minutes. If desired, thin the sauce with water before serving.

RICHARD KENT'S BENGAL CURRY OF LAMB *4 to 5 servings*

2½ pounds lean lamb shoulder
¼ cup butter
⅔ cup finely chopped onion
3 tablespoons chopped preserved or crystallized ginger
½ teaspoon granulated sugar
⅛ teaspoon freshly ground black pepper
2 teaspoons salt
2 to 3 tablespoons curry powder
¼ teaspoon crushed dried mint
2 cups milk
½ cup fresh coconut milk (see page 139)
½ cup freshly grated coconut
½ cup freshly squeezed lime juice
½ cup heavy cream

1. Cut the lamb into one-inch cubes, removing the bones and fat.

2. Melt half the butter in a large, heavy pan. Add the onion and cook until tender, about five minutes. Remove with a slotted spoon to a paper towel.

3. Add the remaining butter to the pan and brown the lamb cubes in it. Return the onion to the pan and add the ginger, sugar, pepper, salt, curry powder, mint and milk. Mix well. Cover and simmer over low heat one hour.

4. Add the coconut milk and freshly grated coconut. Cover and cook five minutes. Gradually stir in the lime juice and cream, adding them separately and in the order given. Cook without boiling ten to fifteen minutes, or until the lamb is tender.

5. Serve on hot, fluffy rice.

LAMB STEW *4 to 6 servings*

- 2 pounds shoulder of lamb, cut into 1½-inch cubes
- 5 tablespoons butter
- 3 tablespoons flour
- 6 cups water
- Salt and freshly ground black pepper to taste
- 2 tomatoes, peeled and diced
- 18 small whole white onions, peeled
- 6 small whole carrots, scraped, or 3 large carrots, scraped and cut into quarters
- 1 medium turnip, peeled and cut into 1-inch cubes
- 18 small potatoes, peeled, or 6 medium potatoes, cut up
- 1 pound freshly shelled peas
- 2 teaspoons chopped parsley

1. Brown the meat on all sides in three tablespoons of the butter in a hot skillet. Transfer to a Dutch oven or heavy kettle.

2. Sprinkle the lamb with flour and add the water, salt, pepper and tomatoes. Bring slowly to a boil, cover, reduce the heat and simmer one and one-half hours.

3. Heat the remaining butter in the skillet, add the onions, carrots and turnip and sauté until the onions are lightly browned.

4. Add the browned vegetables and the potatoes to the stew. Cook, uncovered, until the potatoes are tender, thirty to forty minutes. Twenty minutes before the potatoes are done, add the peas. Serve sprinkled with chopped parsley.

GORMEH SABZEE (lamb and parsley stew) *6 to 8 servings*

This is a Persian stew made with meat and parsley, mostly parsley. It calls for four large bunches.

- 6 tablespoons butter
- 4 large bunches parsley (3 quarts chopped)
- 16 scallions, chopped
- 3 pounds lean lamb, cut into 1-inch cubes
- Salt and freshly ground black pepper to taste
- Water to cover
- 3 lemons
- 5 cups canned kidney beans undrained

1. In a heavy four-quart pot or Dutch oven, heat four tablespoons of the butter, add chopped parsley and scallions and cook until the parsley is dark green.

2. In a large skillet heat the remaining butter, add the meat and brown lightly. Season with salt and pepper. Combine with the vegetable mixture in the pot and add water to cover, the juice of two of the lemons and quarters of the third. Cover and simmer until the meat is almost tender, one to one and one-half hours.

3. Add the kidney beans and correct the seasonings. Continue cooking until the lamb is tender. Serve with pilaff Greek style (page 321).

Note: Beef may be substituted for the lamb.

LAMB STEW WITH OKRA *4 to 6 servings*

¼ cup olive oil
2 pounds lamb shoulder, cut into 2-inch cubes
½ cup finely chopped onion
1 pound trimmed fresh okra, or 1 package frozen okra, defrosted
4 large tomatoes, peeled and chopped, or 3 cups canned tomatoes, drained and chopped
1 tablespoon chopped parsley
1 lemon, sliced and seeded
1 cup water
½ teaspoon thyme
Salt and freshly ground black pepper to taste

1. Heat the oil in a heavy kettle, add the meat and brown on all sides. Add the onion and cook until lightly browned.

2. Add the remaining ingredients, cover and simmer gently until tender, about one and one-quarter hours. Serve with fluffy rice.

LAMB STEW WITH CARAWAY *3 to 4 servings*

1 tablespoon fat
1 to 1½ pounds boneless lamb cut into 1-inch cubes
Salt and freshly ground black pepper to taste
1 clove garlic, finely chopped
2 tablespoons flour
¼ cup dry white wine
Water
1 teaspoon caraway seeds
4 medium potatoes, peeled and cut in large cubes
8 small whole onions, peeled
4 to 6 carrots, scraped and sliced thick
Chopped parsley

1. Melt the fat in a skillet and brown the lamb well on all sides, using moderate heat. Sprinkle with salt, pepper, garlic and flour, stirring well to coat the lamb. Add the wine and enough water to almost cover the meat. Add more water later if the liquid cooks too low. Sprinkle with caraway seeds. Cover and cook one hour.

2. Add potatoes, onions and carrots, cover tightly and cook slowly until the lamb is tender, about thirty minutes. Serve sprinkled with chopped parsley.

RAGOUT OF LAMB *5 servings*

2 pounds lean lamb, cut from the leg, in 1½-inch cubes
¼ cup flour
½ teaspoon salt
Generous dash of freshly ground black pepper
¼ cup olive oil
1½ cups consommé, approximately
⅓ cup Spanish sherry
1 clove garlic, crushed
2 tablespoons lemon juice
2 tablespoons chopped parsley

(*cont'd*)

1. Preheat oven to moderate (350° F.).

2. Dredge the lamb with the flour seasoned with the salt and pepper. Heat the oil and sauté the lamb in it until browned on all sides. Stir in the remaining ingredients, except the lemon juice and parsley, and heat.

3. Transfer the mixture to a two-quart casserole, cover and bake until the lamb is tender, or one to one and one-half hours. Stir in the lemon juice and garnish with the parsley.

BRAISED LAMB SHANKS *6 servings*

6 lamb shanks
Flour for dredging
Salt and freshly ground black pepper to taste
½ teaspoon orégano
⅓ cup salad oil
¾ cup chopped onion
¾ cup chopped celery
¾ cup chopped carrots
1 clove garlic, finely chopped
Pinch of thyme
¾ cup dry red wine
¾ cup beef bouillon

1. Preheat oven to moderate (350° F.).

2. Wipe the lamb shanks well with a damp cloth. Combine flour, salt, pepper and orégano and dredge the lamb shanks with the seasoned flour. Brown in the oil and transfer to a large earthenware casserole or Dutch oven. Add the vegetables, garlic and thyme to the skillet and cook, stirring, five minutes.

3. Pour the vegetables over the lamb and add the liquids. Cover and bake one and one-half hours, or until the meat is tender. Thicken the gravy with a little flour mixed with cold water.

MOUSSAKA A LA TURQUE *8 servings*

*Moussaka, pronounced moos-ah-*kah, *with an accent on the last syllable, is a meat and eggplant dish found in many Middle Eastern countries. Here is a Turkish version.*

4 medium eggplants
¾ cup salad oil
1 tablespoon lemon juice
6 tablespoons hot water
½ cup flour
1 tablespoon butter
1 clove garlic, minced
3 tablespoons minced onion
½ cup chopped mushrooms
2 tablespoons minced parsley
1½ cups (2 medium) diced fresh tomatoes
1 cup ground or diced cooked lamb
4 teaspoons salt
½ teaspoon freshly ground black pepper
2 eggs, slightly beaten

1. Cut three of the eggplants into halves lengthwise. Run a sharp pointed stainless steel knife around the inside of the skins, separating them from the pulp. Score the pulp deeply, cutting almost through but being careful not to pierce the skin.

(cont'd)

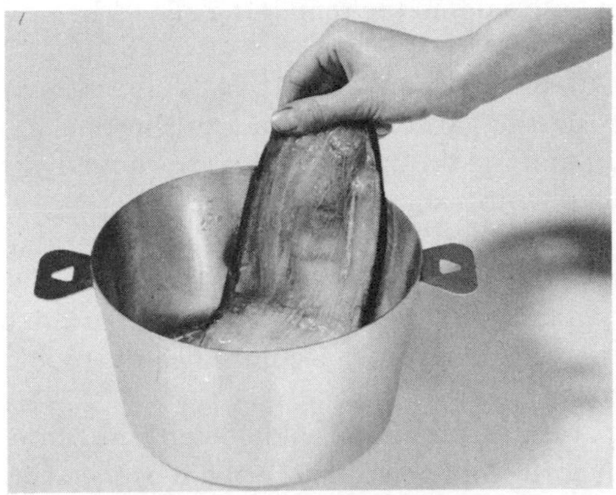

1. *To prepare a moussaka à la Turque,* an unusual eggplant and ground lamb casserole of Near Eastern origin, a charlotte mold is lined with eggplant skins. The purple exteriors of the skins are placed next to the sides of the mold and extended well over the rim.

2. The meat and vegetable mixture, which also contains mushrooms and spices, is spooned into the center of the mold and the overhanging eggplant skins are folded toward the center. The mold is placed in a pan of hot water and baked for one and a half hours.

3. When done, the casserole is left to stand ten minutes and then unmolded onto a hot serving plate.

4. The moussaka should be served immediately upon unmolding, accompanied by a rich tomato sauce. The skin in which the moussaka has been baked is edible.

2. In a large skillet heat two tablespoons of the oil, add two eggplant halves, cut side down, and cook one minute. Combine one teaspoon of the lemon juice with two tablespoons of the hot water and add. Cover and cook over medium heat ten minutes. Remove from the pan and scoop out the pulp, leaving the skins intact. Place the pulp in a bowl and reserve. Repeat the process, using the remaining eggplant halves.

3. Peel the fourth eggplant and cut into slices one-half inch thick. Coat the

(cont'd)

slices lightly with flour and brown on both sides in the remaining oil, adding two tablespoons at a time.

4. Preheat oven to moderate (375° F.).

5. In a skillet heat the butter, add the garlic, onion and mushrooms and sauté until the onion is transparent. Combine the mixture with the cooked eggplant pulp. Stir in the parsley, tomatoes, lamb, salt, pepper and eggs.

6. Line an oiled two-quart charlotte mold or casserole with the eggplant skins, having the purple exterior next to the sides of the mold and extending over the edge. Place a one-inch layer of eggplant-and-lamb mixture in the bottom of the mold. Over this place a layer of fried eggplant slices. Repeat until the mold is filled, ending with a layer of the mixture.

7. Bring the skins, which extend over the side of the mold, toward the center. If the skins are not long enough to cover the top, place a piece of foil over the uncovered portion.

8. Place the mold in a pan of hot water and bake one and one-half hours. Remove from the oven and let stand ten minutes. Unmold onto a serving plate and serve hot with tomato sauce (page 454).

MOUSSAKA A LA GRECQUE *8 to 10 servings*

This moussaka is of Greek origin. It is a splendid item for buffets since it should be prepared in advance. It may be served lukewarm or at room temperature.

3 medium-sized eggplants
1 cup butter
3 large onions, finely chopped
2 pounds ground lamb or beef
3 tablespoons tomato paste
½ cup red wine
½ cup chopped parsley
¼ teaspoon cinnamon
Salt to taste
Freshly ground black pepper to taste
6 tablespoons flour
1 quart milk
4 eggs, beaten until frothy
Nutmeg
2 cups ricotta cheese or cottage cheese
1 cup fine bread crumbs
1 cup freshly grated Parmesan cheese

1. Peel the eggplants and cut them into slices about one-half inch thick. Brown the slices quickly in four tablespoons of the butter. Set aside.

2. Heat four tablespoons of butter in the same skillet and cook the onions until they are brown. Add the ground meat and cook ten minutes. Combine the tomato paste with the wine, parsley, cinnamon, salt and pepper. Stir this mixture into the meat and simmer over low heat, stirring frequently, until all the liquid has been absorbed. Remove the mixture from the fire.

3. Preheat the oven to moderate (375° F.).

4. Make a white sauce by melting eight tablespoons of butter and blending in the flour, stirring with a wire whisk. Meanwhile, bring the milk to a boil and add it gradually to the butter-flour mixture, stirring constantly. When the mixture is thickened and smooth, remove it from the heat. Cool slightly and stir in the beaten eggs, nutmeg and ricotta cheese.

(*cont'd*)

5. Grease an 11 x 16-inch pan and sprinkle the bottom lightly with bread crumbs. Arrange alternate layers of eggplant and meat sauce in the pan, sprinkling each layer with Parmesan cheese and bread crumbs. Pour the ricotta cheese sauce over the top and bake one hour, or until top is golden. Remove from the oven and cool twenty to thirty minutes before serving. Cut into squares and serve.

Note: The flavor of this dish improves on standing one day. Reheat before serving.

EGGPLANT-LAMB CASSEROLE *6 servings*

2 medium eggplants, pared and diced
Water
1 pound mushrooms
3 tablespoons butter
½ cup chopped onion
1 clove garlic, crushed
1 tablespoon bacon fat
2 tablespoons flour
½ cup chopped green pepper
2 cups diced cooked lamb
1 teaspoon orégano
½ cup soft bread crumbs

1. Cook the eggplant in boiling salted water fifteen minutes. Drain well and mash.
2. Peel and stem the mushrooms. Simmer the stems and peelings in two and one-half cups water fifteen minutes.
3. Preheat oven to hot (400° F.).
4. Chop the mushroom caps coarsely and sauté in two tablespoons of the butter.
5. Sauté the onions and garlic in the bacon fat until the onions are golden. Add the flour and blend. Add stock drained from the mushroom stems and stir until smooth and thick.
6. Add the eggplant, sautéed mushrooms, green pepper, lamb and orégano. Pile the mixture in a buttered two-quart casserole.
7. Cover the mixture with the crumbs and dot with the remaining butter. Bake, uncovered, thirty minutes.

LAMB HASH *4 servings*

1 tablespoon butter
1 large onion, minced
3 sprigs parsley, chopped
1 clove garlic, minced
2 slices bacon, minced
3 cups chopped cooked lamb
1 cup meat gravy or stock
½ cup canned tomato sauce
Salt and freshly ground black pepper to taste
1 cup heavy cream, approximately
2 tablespoons grated Parmesan cheese

1. Preheat oven to moderate (325° F.).
2. Melt the butter in a heavy skillet, add the onion and sauté until golden. Add the parsley, garlic and bacon and cook briefly.

(*cont'd*)

3. Mix in the remaining ingredients except the cream and cheese and bake, covered, one hour, stirring from time to time.

4. Place the hash in four greased individual deep casseroles, cover with cream and sprinkle with cheese. Brown under a hot broiler.

. . . .

PORK

. . . .

ROAST PORK *6 servings*

Salt and freshly ground pepper to taste
1 four-pound pork loin
1 cup stock

1. Preheat oven to moderate (350° F.).
2. Rub the meat with salt and pepper and place, fat side up, on a rack in an uncovered roasting pan. Roast about two and one-half hours, or thirty-five to forty-five minutes per pound (185° F. on a meat thermometer).
3. When meat is done, remove roast to a hot platter and pour off the fat in the roasting pan. Add stock to the pan and bring to a boil. Thicken, if desired, with a little flour mixed with water. Serve with the meat.

ROAST PORK WITH THYME

Combine three tablespoons olive oil, two tablespoons lemon juice, one teaspoon thyme and one clove garlic, finely chopped, with salt and freshly ground pepper to taste. Rub the mixture into the pork loin and roast as above.

LOIN OF PORK WITH PRUNES *6 to 8 servings*

The Swedes enjoy braised pork stuffed with prunes. It is not only delicious to dine on but it has a most interesting design.

1 four- to five-pound loin of pork
20 prunes, pitted
Hot water
2 teaspoons salt
½ teaspoon white pepper
¼ teaspoon powdered ginger

1. Have the meat boned and a pocket cut to the center along the length of the roast.
2. Cover the prunes with hot water and soak thirty minutes. Drain, reserving the liquid.
3. Insert the prunes in the pocket. Season the meat with the salt, pepper and ginger and tie it into a good shape with a string.

(*cont'd*)

4. In a Dutch oven brown the meat on all sides. Cover and cook over low heat until tender, about one and one-half hours, basting occasionally with the prune juice. Serve the meat sliced with the strained pan juices in a gravy boat.

BRAISED PORK LOIN FOR A FEIJOADA, PAGE 363.

HERBED PORK CHOPS *4 servings*

1 teaspoon rosemary
½ teaspoon sage
½ clove garlic, chopped
Salt and freshly ground black pepper
4 large pork chops, about 1 inch thick
1 cup water
½ cup dry white wine

1. Mix the rosemary, sage, garlic, salt and pepper. Rub the chops with the mixture.

2. Place the chops in a large greased skillet, add the water and cover. Simmer until all the water has evaporated, about forty-five minutes. Remove the cover and brown the chops in their own fat.

3. Add the wine and cook about one minute, turning the chops occasionally. The wine should be almost evaporated before service.

PORK CHOPS WITH PAPRIKA *6 servings*

6 loin pork chops, ¾ inch thick
1 clove garlic, finely chopped
1 teaspoon caraway seeds
2 teaspoons paprika
Salt and freshly ground black pepper to taste
1 cup dry white wine

1. Arrange the chops in a shallow heatproof casserole so that they do not touch. Mix the garlic, caraway seeds, paprika, salt and pepper and sprinkle over the chops. Add the wine. Cover and let the chops marinate in the refrigerator two to three hours.

2. Preheat oven to slow (300° F.).

3. Bake the chops in the marinade, uncovered, until tender, about one hour. Add more wine if necessary. Serve with buttered noodles and the pan sauce.

PORK CHOPS WITH BASIL *8 servings*

Flour for dredging
Garlic salt to taste
8 loin pork chops, trimmed
Olive oil
2 teaspoons chopped fresh basil, or ½ teaspoon dried basil
½ cup Marsala wine, apricot or plum juice

1. Preheat oven to slow (250° F.).

2. Combine flour and garlic salt in a paper bag, add the chops and toss

(*cont'd*)

lightly until they are thoroughly coated with the mixture. Brown chops in a heavy skillet, using just enough olive oil to cover bottom of skillet.

3. Arrange the chops neatly in a shallow ungreased baking dish without letting them overlap. Sprinkle with basil. Cover the dish closely with aluminum foil.

4. Bake until the chops are tender, about one and one-half hours. Skim off the fat. Add the wine or fruit juice to the baking dish, remove the cover and continue to cook, basting occasionally, until the liquid bubbles.

KEY WEST PORK CHOPS *6 servings*

3 tablespoons salad oil
6 lean pork chops
1½ cups raw rice
Salt to taste
6 large onion slices
6 lime or lemon slices
6 tablespoons chili sauce
3 cups tomato juice or water
½ teaspoon Tabasco sauce

1. Preheat oven to moderate (325° F.).

2. In a Dutch oven, heat the oil, add the chops and brown on both sides. Remove the chops and drain off all but four tablespoons of the fat. Stir in the raw, dry rice, coating all the grains with fat. Arrange the chops on top and sprinkle with the salt.

3. Place a slice of onion, a slice of lime and a spoonful of chili sauce on each chop. Add the tomato juice and Tabasco, cover closely and bake until the chops are tender, about one hour.

PORK CHOPS ZINGARA *4 servings*

4 loin pork chops
1 small white onion, chopped
¼ pound mushrooms, cut in thin strips julienne style
1 cup tomato sauce
2 tablespoons julienne-cut cooked ham
2 tablespoons julienne-cut cooked tongue
3 tablespoons dry sherry
Salt and freshly ground black pepper to taste

1. In a lightly greased skillet brown the chops on both sides over brisk heat. Cover, reduce the heat and cook slowly until the chops are almost tender, about twenty minutes.

2. Add the onion and mushrooms and cook slowly, covered, until the chops are tender and the onion is soft, about five minutes.

3. Add the tomato sauce, heat to simmering and add the remaining ingredients.

Note: If desired, finish off by adding bits of butter to the sauce just before serving and swirling it in to give the sauce a gloss.

POLISH PORK CHOPS *4 servings*

4 loin pork chops
3 tablespoons chopped onion
1 cup tomato sauce
½ cup sour cream
1 small dill pickle, chopped
3 tablespoons dry sherry
Salt and freshly ground black pepper to taste

1. In a lightly greased skillet brown the chops on both sides over brisk heat. Cover, reduce the heat and cook slowly until the chops are almost tender, about twenty minutes.

2. Add the onion, cover and continue cooking until the chops are tender and the onion is soft, about five minutes longer.

3. Add the tomato sauce and sour cream and heat to simmering. Do not boil sauce after sour cream has been added or it will curdle. Stir in the pickle, sherry, salt and pepper.

NEAPOLITAN PORK CHOPS *6 servings*

2 tablespoons olive oil
1 clove garlic
6 lean pork chops
Salt and freshly ground black pepper to taste
3 tablespoons tomato paste
3 tablespoons dry white wine
1 green pepper, finely chopped
1 pound fresh mushrooms, sliced

1. In a heavy skillet heat the oil, add the garlic and cook until browned. Discard the garlic. Add the pork chops and brown on both sides.

2. Sprinkle the meat with salt and pepper. Add the remaining ingredients, cover and simmer over low heat until the chops are tender and cooked through, about thirty to thirty-five minutes.

PORK CHOPS CHARCUTIERE *6 servings*

6 lean pork chops
Salt and freshly ground black pepper
2 tablespoons vegetable or peanut oil
¼ cup each finely chopped shallots and onion (or all onion if shallots are not available)
¾ cup dry white wine
1½ cups brown sauce (page 445) or canned beef gravy
2 tablespoons cold butter
1 tablespoon Dijon or Dusseldorf mustard
3 small sour gherkins, cut into julienne strips

1. Trim the pork chops, leaving a quarter-inch layer of fat. Sprinkle with salt and pepper.

2. Heat the oil in a skillet and brown the chops on both sides. Cook twenty minutes, or until cooked through. Transfer to a warm platter. Pour off all but two tablespoons of fat from the pan and add the shallots and onions to the skillet. Cook, stirring, two minutes.

3. Add the wine to the skillet and stir to dissolve brown particles in the bot-

(*cont'd*)

tom of the pan. Cook until the wine is almost totally reduced. Add the brown sauce and cook about twelve minutes.

4. Turn off the heat and stir in the cold butter. Add the mustard and stir. Do not reheat. Add the gherkins. Spoon a little sauce over each chop and serve the remainder in a sauceboat.

BRAISED BUTTERFLY PORK CHOPS *6 servings*

6 loin pork chops, 1 inch thick
3 tablespoons butter or bacon fat
1 large onion, chopped
1 teaspoon flour
2 teaspoons salt
2 teaspoons prepared mustard
Freshly ground black pepper to taste
1 cup beef stock
2 tablespoons chopped pickle

1. Remove the bones from the pork chops with a sharp knife. Holding the knife parallel to the surface of the meat, split the chops in half, but do not cut entirely through. Spread the split chops so that they lie fairly flat.

2. In a skillet heat two tablespoons of the butter, add the chops and brown on both sides. Remove the chops. Heat the remaining butter in the pan, add the onion and sauté three minutes. Add the flour, salt, mustard and pepper and stir until well blended. Gradually add the heated stock and chopped pickle and simmer five minutes.

3. Return the chops to the skillet and spoon the sauce over them. Cover and simmer until the chops are tender, about fifteen minutes.

PORK CHOPS WITH RYE-BREAD STUFFING *6 servings*

6 loin pork chops, 1 inch thick
2 tablespoons butter
1 medium onion, chopped
1 large clove garlic, minced
1½ cups soft rye-bread crumbs
¾ teaspoon salt
½ teaspoon caraway seeds
¼ cup chopped parsley
1 egg, slightly beaten
3 tablespoons water
1 cup stock or water
2 tablespoons flour

1. Have the butcher cut pockets in the pork chops. Preheat oven to moderate (350° F.).

2. In a skillet, heat the butter and sauté the onion and garlic about five minutes. Remove from heat. Combine with the bread crumbs, salt, caraway, parsley, egg and three tablespoons water and mix well. Stuff the chops with the mixture, closing the openings with toothpicks.

3. Place the chops in a baking pan and season to taste with additional salt and pepper. Cover closely and bake thirty minutes. Uncover and continue baking until brown and tender, about thirty minutes longer. Remove chops to a heated platter.

4. Pour off fat from the pan. Add stock to the pan and bring to a boil. Thicken with flour mixed with a little water.

HERB-STUFFED PORK CHOPS WITH WINE SAUCE *6 servings*

6 double pork chops
Salt and freshly ground black pepper to taste
¼ cup butter
¾ cup chopped onion
¼ cup chopped celery
1½ cups bread cubes
1 teaspoon crushed fennel seeds
½ cup chopped parsley
¼ cup heavy cream, approximately
Dry white wine
1 teaspoon cornstarch for each cup of liquid to be thickened

1. Have the butcher cut pockets in the pork chops. Preheat oven to moderate (350° F.).

2. Sprinkle the chops inside and out with salt and pepper.

3. In a heavy skillet heat three tablespoons of the butter, add the onion and celery and cook until the onion is transparent. Add the bread cubes, fennel seeds and parsley and remove from the heat. Add enough heavy cream to moisten the mixture.

4. Stuff the pork chop cavities with the mixture and close the openings with toothpicks. In a Dutch oven melt the remaining butter, add the pork chops and brown on both sides. Add wine to a depth of one-quarter inch, cover and bake one hour.

5. Transfer the chops to a warm platter and keep hot. Bring the remaining sauce to a boil. Mix the cornstarch with a little water and stir into the sauce. Correct the seasonings and serve with the pork chops.

STUFFED PORK CHOPS WITH SOUR-CREAM GRAVY *4 servings*

4 double rib pork chops
2 tablespoons drippings or other fat
1 medium onion, chopped
1 cup chopped mushrooms
1 cup bread cubes or coarse crumbs
1 tablespoon chopped parsley
¼ teaspoon salt
¼ teaspoon sage or poultry seasoning (optional)
Freshly ground black pepper to taste
2 tablespoons sour cream, approximately
¼ cup water

1. Have the butcher cut pockets in the pork chops. Preheat oven to moderate (350° F.).

2. In a skillet heat the drippings, add the onion and sauté until transparent. Add the mushrooms and cook, stirring often, about two minutes. Add the bread crumbs, parsley and seasonings and stir together well. Add enough sour cream to moisten the mixture.

3. Stuff the chops with the mixture and close the openings with toothpicks. Sprinkle lightly with additional salt, sage and pepper.

4. Arrange the chops in a baking pan, add one-quarter cup water and bake, covered, thirty minutes. Remove the cover and bake until brown and tender, about thirty minutes longer. Serve with sour-cream gravy (page 138).

(cont'd)

SOUR-CREAM GRAVY:

Pork drippings
1½ cups water
3 tablespoons flour
½ cup sour cream
Salt
Freshly ground black pepper

1. Pour the drippings from the baking pan into a bowl. Add the water to the pan and scrape loose all the brown particles.

2. Skim the fat from the drippings and place three tablespoons fat in a saucepan. Stir in the flour and brown. Slowly add the water from the pan and the drippings from the bowl and cook, stirring, until thickened.

3. Add the sour cream and heat gently, while beating with a whisk or rotary beater. Do not let boil. Correct the seasonings.

PORK SATAY *5 to 6 servings*

This recipe is adapted from the late Pearl Metzelthin's World Wide Cook Book. *It is a genuine Indonesian masterpiece and it may be cooked over charcoal or under a broiler flame. The marinade is made with ground Brazil nuts.*

8 shelled Brazil nuts
2 tablespoons ground coriander seeds
⅛ teaspoon ground red pepper
¼ teaspoon freshly ground black pepper
1 clove garlic, finely chopped
2 tablespoons finely chopped onion
1 teaspoon salt
1 tablespoon brown sugar
3 tablespoons fresh lemon juice
¼ cup soy sauce
1½ pounds lean pork
Olive oil or melted butter

1. Grind the Brazil nuts very fine, using a food mill, mortar and pestle or electric blender. Mix with the remaining ingredients except the pork and olive oil.

2. Cut the pork into one-and-one-half-inch cubes and add to the marinade. Mix well and let stand two or three hours.

3. String the meat on skewers and broil slowly over a charcoal fire or under a broiler flame, turning to brown on all sides. Cook twenty to twenty-five minutes or until meat is well done. While cooking, baste often with olive oil or butter. Serve hot.

MALAYAN PORK CHOPS *4 servings*

1 pound boneless pork loin
Salt and freshly ground black pepper to taste
1 cup coconut milk (page 139)
2 teaspoons brown sugar

1. Cut the pork into bite-sized cubes. Sprinkle with salt and pepper. Thread on skewers and marinate in coconut milk at least one hour.

2. Drain, sprinkle with sugar and barbecue or broil fifteen to twenty minutes, turning frequently and basting often with coconut milk. Serve with satay sauce (page 139).

To Prepare Coconut Milk: Coconut milk as it exists in tropical countries is taken from green coconuts, generally unavailable here; ripe coconuts contain a tasteless fluid which must be discarded. To prepare coconut milk from a ripe coconut, pare the brown skin from the coconut meat. Chop the meat and blend with one cup fresh scalded milk. Let stand for twenty minutes, then strain. (About one cup of packaged shredded coconut may be substituted for freshly grated coconut.)

SATAY SAUCE:

1 clove garlic
1 small onion, chopped
1 cup shelled peanuts
3 dried hot chili peppers (or ½ teaspoon crushed hot pepper)
2 pieces preserved or candied ginger
1 tablespoon soy sauce
½ teaspoon salt
1 teaspoon turmeric
Juice of ½ lemon
1 cup water, approximately

1. In a mortar crush the garlic, onion, peanuts, peppers and ginger. Stir in the remaining ingredients. Or put all the ingredients in an electric blender and blend thirty seconds.

2. Pour the sauce into the top part of a double boiler, place over direct heat and bring to a boil, stirring. Place over boiling water and cook thirty minutes, stirring occasionally. Thin to desired consistency with more water or with coconut milk (see above).

SATAY KAMBING MADURA, PAGE 124.

CHINESE-STYLE PORK *4 servings*

3 tablespoons oil
½ cup chopped onion
1½ cups roast pork, cut into thin small strips
1½ cups chicken broth
½ cup thinly sliced celery
½ cup sliced raw mushrooms
1 can bean sprouts, drained
2 tablespoons cornstarch
¼ teaspoon sugar
¼ teaspoon salt
Freshly ground black pepper to taste
1½ tablespoons soy sauce
2 tablespoons water
Chinese noodles

1. In a skillet heat the oil, add the onion and cook until transparent. Add the pork, chicken broth, celery, mushrooms and bean sprouts and simmer five minutes.

2. Blend the cornstarch, sugar, salt, pepper, soy sauce and water. Add to the simmering mixture and cook, stirring, until thickened. Correct the seasonings and serve over crisp Chinese noodles.

MARINATED PORK STRIPS, PAGE 13.

SWEET AND PUNGENT PORK CUBES *6 servings*

- 1½ pounds lean pork cut into 1-inch cubes
- 2 cups water
- 1 teaspoon salt
- ¼ cup soy sauce
- 1 clove garlic
- ⅓ cup sugar
- ¼ cup cornstarch
- ¼ cup cider vinegar
- ⅓ cup pineapple juice
- ⅔ cup pineapple chunks
- 2 tablespoons sherry

1. Place the pork, water, salt, soy sauce and garlic in a two-quart saucepan and bring to a boil. Reduce the heat, cover and simmer gently until the meat is tender, about fifty minutes. Discard the garlic. Drain the broth and reserve.

2. In a saucepan, blend the sugar, cornstarch, vinegar and pineapple juice until smooth. Gradually stir in the meat broth and cook over medium heat, stirring, until the sauce is thick and transparent.

3. Combine the sauce with the pork cubes, pineapple chunks and sherry.

PORK WITH WATERCRESS *6 servings*

- 4 large bunches watercress
- Salted water
- ¼ cup peanut oil
- 1 small clove garlic, chopped
- 1 pound pork shoulder cut in thin slices
- 3 tablespoons soy sauce

1. Wash the watercress well and drain. Cut off the bottoms of the stems. Soak in cold salted water to cover thirty minutes. Drain, rinse in fresh water and dry gently.

2. In a skillet heat the oil, add the garlic and pork and brown the meat quickly on all sides.

3. Add the soy sauce and watercress. Cook, stirring, until the mixture reaches a boil. Cover and cook two minutes longer. Serve immediately.

CASSOULET, PAGE 360.

BARBECUED SPARERIBS WITH BEER AND HONEY *8 servings*

- 8 pounds spareribs, cut into serving pieces
- 3 cups beer
- 1 cup honey
- 1½ teaspoons dry mustard
- 2 teaspoons chili powder
- 2 teaspoons sage
- 1 tablespoon salt
- 2 tablespoons lemon juice

1. Place the ribs in a large shallow pan. Mix the remaining ingredients and pour over the ribs. Let stand in the refrigerator twenty-four hours, turning at least once.

2. Remove the ribs from the marinade. Reserve the liquid. Weave the spare-

(cont'd)

ribs on a spit or long skewers or place flat on the rack of a hot charcoal grill or broiler, about four inches from the heat. Cook, turning frequently and brushing with the marinade, until brown, about one hour and fifteen minutes, or bake in a preheated moderate oven (350° F.) about one and one-half hours, or till ribs are brown and glazed, basting frequently.

HERBED BARBECUED SPARERIBS *6 servings*

6 pounds spareribs
Boiling salted water
1 onion, studded with cloves
1 teaspoon rosemary
1 teaspoon thyme
1 teaspoon marjoram
1 teaspoon orégano
1 cup dry red wine
⅓ cup tomato catsup or chili sauce
1 tablespoon soy sauce
¼ teaspoon powdered ginger
2 tablespoons honey
1 teaspoon minced garlic

1. Cut the spareribs into generous serving pieces. Cover with boiling salted water and add the onion and herbs. Bring to a boil, reduce the heat and simmer until just tender, about fifty minutes. Drain and place the meat in a shallow pan.
2. Blend all the remaining ingredients and pour over the meat. Let stand in the refrigerator at least two hours, or until ready to barbecue. Drain spareribs. Reserve marinade.
3. Grill ribs slowly over hot coals, or bake in a preheated moderate oven (350° F.) about thirty minutes, until the ribs are browned and glazed, basting frequently with marinade.

CHINESE BARBECUED SPARERIBS, PAGE 15.
SPARERIBS AND GINGERED PLUM SAUCE, PAGE 15.

CHOUCROUTE A L'ALSACIENNE (sauerkraut with meats)

6 servings

Choucroute à l'Alsacienne—sauerkraut garnished with meat—is one of the most easily prepared of dishes whether it is made for two or two dozen. Here is a recipe from the world-famed gastronome, James A. Beard. Serve it with iced beer or well-chilled champagne.

2 quarts sauerkraut, canned or in bulk
Pork rind or salt pork
2 cloves garlic, chopped
Freshly ground black pepper
Dry white Alsatian wine
1 onion, stuck with 4 cloves
Frankfurters or other meats (see note on variations, page 142)

1. Wash the sauerkraut, drain and squeeze out liquid.
2. Line a heavy kettle with pork rind or thin slices of salt pork. Add the sauerkraut, garlic, pepper and enough wine to cover. Add the onion stuck with cloves.

(cont'd)

3. Cover tightly and cook in a preheated moderate oven (325° F.) or simmer gently on top of the stove three and one-half to four hours. Add more wine as necessary.

VARIATIONS:

Many combinations of meats may be used in the preparation of this dish.

Pigs' Knuckles: Cook on the sauerkraut four hours.

Polish Sausages or Italian Coteghino: Add for the last thirty-five minutes of cooking.

Knockwurst: Add for the last fifteen or twenty minutes of cooking.

Salt Pork: Cut into serving pieces, parboil and cook with the sauerkraut one hour.

Cooked Ham Slices: Heat through in a little white wine.

Frankfurters: Cook on the sauerkraut five minutes.

SPARERIBS AND KRAUT *3 or 4 servings*

3 pounds spareribs
3–4 cups sauerkraut
1 tart apple, peeled, cored and sliced
1 teaspoon caraway seeds

1. Cut the spareribs into individual portions and brown in a heavy pan. Add the juice from the sauerkraut and enough water barely to cover. Simmer, covered, about forty-five minutes.

2. Add the kraut, pushing it down into the liquid in the pan.

3. Add the apple and caraway and cook thirty minutes to one hour longer. Use a shorter time if canned kraut is used and a longer period for bulk kraut. The liquid should evaporate during cooking.

Note: If desired, this dish may be baked in a moderate oven (350° F.).

PIGS' KNUCKLES WITH SAUERKRAUT *6 generous servings*

6 pigs' knuckles
2 quarts sauerkraut, canned or in bulk
1 tablespoon caraway seeds
Dry white wine or water
1 onion studded with cloves
12 medium potatoes, peeled
6 to 12 frankfurters (optional)

1. Scrub the pigs' knuckles thoroughly and drain. Place, with alternate layers of sauerkraut, in a large heavy kettle. Sprinkle throughout with the caraway seeds.

2. Add enough white wine to cover. Insert the onion, cover and simmer gently until the knuckles are tender, three to four hours.

3. One-half hour before the knuckles are done, add the potatoes. Replace the cover and continue cooking until done. If desired, add frankfurters to the kettle five minutes before the knuckles are done.

GRILLED PIGS' FEET *4 servings*

- 4 pigs' feet
- 1½ quarts water
- 1 carrot, sliced
- 1 onion, sliced
- 1 clove garlic
- 1 sprig fresh thyme or a pinch of dried thyme
- 2 sprigs parsley
- 1 bay leaf
- 3 or 4 cloves
- 1 tablespoon salt
- 6 peppercorns
- 2 tablespoons butter, melted
- Fine dry bread crumbs

1. Have the butcher prepare the pigs' feet for cooking. Wash them well.
2. Prepare a stock with 1½ quarts water, the carrot, onion, garlic, thyme, parsley, bay leaf, cloves, salt and peppercorns. Bring to a boil and simmer one-half hour.
3. To keep the skin on the pigs' feet from breaking, tie each foot tightly in cheesecloth before cooking. Add the pigs' feet to the stock and let simmer until very tender, four to five hours. Cool in the liquid and, when cooled, drain. (Reserve and freeze broth for soups.)
4. Brush the pigs' feet with melted butter and roll in bread crumbs. Broil slowly until golden brown on all sides or roast in a hot oven (450° F.) until well browned. Serve with strong mustard.

ROAST SUCKLING PIG *8 to 12 servings*

- 1 ten- to fifteen-pound pig
- 1 tablespoon salt
- 1 teaspoon freshly ground black pepper
- ¾ teaspoon powdered thyme
- Fruit-almond stuffing (page 144)
- 2 teaspoons dry mustard
- 3 tablespoons water

1. Preheat oven to moderate (350° F.).
2. Wash the pig thoroughly under cold running water and dry inside and out with paper towels. Mix the salt, pepper and thyme and rub the mixture over the inside of the pig. Fill the cavity with the stuffing and run skewers through both sides of opening, lacing it with strings to close. Place a raw potato or a tightly packed ball of aluminum foil the size of an apple in the pig's mouth. Cover the ears with small pieces of brown paper.
3. Place a piece of heavy-duty foil about twelve inches longer than the pig on a rack placed diagonally in an open roasting pan. Place the pig on the foil with the back legs forward. Turn the foil up loosely around the pig.
4. Place in the oven and roast three and one-half to four hours, or about eighteen minutes per pound. About fifteen minutes before the pig is done, mix the mustard with three tablespoons water and brush over the skin.
5. Transfer the pig to a hot platter and remove the skewers, lacings and covering on the ears. Replace the foil in the mouth with a small apple. Place cranberries or cherries in the eyes and parsley in or around the ears.

(cont'd)

6. Pour the drippings in the foil into a saucepan and skim off the fat. Reheat and serve as a sauce.

7. For carving purposes, place the platter before the host with the head to his left.

Note: The pig's bones should separate easily at the joints. There is more meat on the shoulders than on the hind legs. Cut along the backbone to remove the chops.

FRUIT ALMOND STUFFING FOR SUCKLING PIG:

1 pound almonds
1½ pounds prunes
10 large apples
¼ cup butter
Salt and freshly ground black pepper to taste

1. Drop the almonds in boiling water and let stand until the skins slip easily. Drain, remove the skins and shred the almonds lengthwise.

2. Cook the prunes in water to cover until just tender. Drain and pit.

3. Peel, core and slice the apples. Cook in the butter over moderately high heat until half tender. Mix the apples, almonds, prunes, salt and pepper.

TOURTIERE (pork pie) *6 servings*

The French-Canadian pork-and-spice pie is known as tourtière.

1 pound ground lean pork (shoulder or leg)
1 teaspoon salt
¼ teaspoon pepper
¼ teaspoon nutmeg
1 clove garlic
⅛ teaspoon mace
1½ teaspoons cornstarch
1 cup water
Pastry for a 2-crust 8-inch pie

1. In a saucepan combine pork, seasonings, cornstarch and water. Cover and simmer thirty minutes. Uncover and cook ten minutes more. Remove garlic.

2. Preheat oven to hot (425° F.).

3. Line an eight-inch pie pan with pastry; pour in the mixture and cover with remaining pastry. Press edges together and prick top to allow escape of steam.

4. Bake the pie ten minutes, reduce heat to 350° F. and bake thirty minutes longer. Serve hot.

FRICADELLER *24 to 36 pork balls*

Fricadeller or Danish pork balls appear on many Scandinavian buffets.

2 pounds lean pork, ground
½ cup flour
1 egg
1 small onion, grated
Salt and freshly ground black pepper to taste
¾ cup club soda, or plain water
2 tablespoons butter

(*cont'd*)

1. In a mixing bowl combine the ground pork with the flour, egg, onion, salt and pepper. Work with a fork until the ingredients are well blended.

2. Stir in the club soda or water, a little at a time, and shape the meat mixture into small balls or patties.

3. Melt butter in a skillet. Brown the patties on all sides in the butter, turning gently with a fork or a spatula. Continue to cook over low heat, uncovered, until the pork is cooked through.

PORK BALLS WITH GINGER, PAGE 14.

CARNITAS (LITTLE MEAT BALLS), PAGE 14.

FRANKFURTER GOULASH A LA WALTER SLEZAK

6 generous servings

Walter Slezak is not only a versatile artist, he is also a good cook. Here is a family favorite.

- ¼ cup vegetable oil or shortening
- 6 large onions, coarsely chopped
- 2 cloves garlic, crushed
- 10 large green peppers, cut into 1½-inch cubes
- 1½ tablespoons caraway seeds
- 2½ cups canned tomatoes, undrained
- 2 tablespoons paprika
- Salt and freshly ground black pepper to taste
- 2 pounds frankfurters, sliced ½ inch thick

1. In a large heavy kettle, heat the oil and add the onions and garlic. Cook over moderate heat, stirring with a wooden spoon, until the onions begin to take on color. Add the green peppers and cook, stirring, five minutes longer. Cover and continue cooking twenty minutes, stirring occasionally.

2. Add the caraway seeds, half the tomatoes and the paprika and cover again. Simmer twenty minutes longer, stirring occasionally. Add the remaining tomatoes, if necessary, to prevent the vegetables from becoming dry.

3. When the goulash has thickened slightly, add the salt and pepper and frankfurter slices. Cover and heat thoroughly. Serve with plain boiled potatoes and a crisp green salad.

SCRAPPLE OR PAWNHAAS

About 12 servings

Scrapple, a Pennsylvania Dutch specialty, is traditionally made with pork trimmings of whatever nature. Here is a recipe for it, perfected by Mrs. Ruth P. Casa-Emellos, that is a genuine culinary tour de force.

- 4 large pigs' knuckles
- ½ pound lean pork
- 3 quarts water
- 1 tablespoon salt
- 1 hot red pepper (optional)
- ½ teaspoon freshly ground black pepper
- ½ to 1 teaspoon sage
- 2¾ cups cornmeal

(cont'd)

1. Simmer the pigs' knuckles and pork in water with the salt and red pepper until the meat almost falls from the bones, about two and one-half hours.

2. Remove the meat from the broth, discard the bones and grind the meat. Strain the broth and skim off the fat, if desired. Measure two quarts of broth into a large heavy kettle. Return the meat to the broth and add ground black pepper and sage. Bring to a rapid boil.

3. Mix the cornmeal with one quart of cool broth, add to the boiling broth and cook, stirring, until thickened. Place on an asbestos pad over lowest heat and cook covered, stirring often, about thirty minutes longer. Adjust the seasonings.

4. Turn into two large bread pans, cool, cover and chill overnight.

5. To serve, cut into one-half-inch slices, coat with flour and brown over moderately high heat in butter or other fat.

SCHWEINSULZE (JELLIED PORK LOAF), PAGE 10.

KNOCKWURST IN BEER *8 servings*

8 knockwurst
1 pint beer
2 tablespoons vinegar
1 to 2 teaspoons sugar

1. Simmer the knockwurst in the beer very slowly fifteen minutes. Remove to a heated shallow baking dish.

2. Reduce the beer to one-third cup, by rapid boiling, and stir in the vinegar and sugar. Pour over the knockwurst and broil briefly, turning to brown on all sides.

BASIC SAUSAGE RECIPE *About 9 pounds*

There are several good commercial pork sausages on the market. None, however, can compare with homemade versions.

9 pounds fresh lean pork
¾ teaspoon red pepper
3 tablespoons salt
1½ tablespoons freshly ground black pepper
1½ tablespoons crushed sage
6 yards sausage casing

1. Cut the meat into cubes and grind, using the fine knife of the meat grinder. Sprinkle the seasonings over the ground meat and mix well.

2. Remove the cutting blade from the grinder and attach the sausage stuffer. Using a yard of casing at a time, work all but a few inches of casing onto the sausage stuffer. Tie a knot at the end of the casing.

3. Refeed the meat through the grinder and into the casing. Twist into links.

Note: This sausage should be kept refrigerated since it is perishable.

LEEK AND SAUSAGE PIE, PAGE 29.

CREOLE PORK SAUSAGE

About 7 pounds

- 7 pounds fresh pork
- 2 large onions, chopped
- 1 clove garlic, crushed
- 2 tablespoons salt
- 2 teaspoons freshly ground black pepper
- 1 teaspoon crushed chili pepper
- ½ teaspoon paprika
- ½ teaspoon cayenne pepper
- 3 sprigs parsley, chopped
- ½ teaspoon allspice
- ¼ teaspoon powdered bay leaf
- 5 yards sausage casing

1. Grind the pork, using the coarse knife of a meat grinder. Add the onions and garlic and regrind. Add the seasonings and mix thoroughly.

2. Remove the cutting blades from the grinder and attach the sausage stuffer. Attach casing as in basic sausage recipe (page 146). Refeed the mixture into the grinder and through the sausage stuffer.

CHORIZO (Spanish hot sausage)

About 2 pounds

- 2 pounds lean pork
- ¼ cup vinegar
- 1 teaspoon orégano
- 3 cloves garlic, crushed
- 2 tablespoons chili powder
- 1 teaspoon freshly ground black pepper
- 2 teaspoons salt
- ¼ teaspoon ground cumin
- 2 small hot red peppers, minced, or ½ teaspoon crushed hot peppers
- 1 yard sausage casing

1. Grind the pork, using the coarse blade of the meat grinder. Add the remaining ingredients and mix thoroughly. Attach casing as in basic sausage recipe (page 146).

2. Force the mixture through the sausage stuffer into casings and twist into links. If desired, hang the links in a cool place to dry. The dried sausage may be kept for several weeks. Cook as you would fresh sausage.

ITALIAN PEPPER SAUSAGE

About 6 pounds

- 4½ pounds fresh lean pork
- 1½ pounds fresh fat pork (fresh pork siding)
- 1 medium onion, chopped
- 1 large clove garlic, minced
- 3 tablespoons salt
- 1½ tablespoons freshly ground black pepper
- 1½ teaspoons paprika
- 2 tablespoons crushed dried red peppers
- 2 teaspoons fennel seeds
- ½ teaspoon crushed bay leaf
- ¼ teaspoon thyme
- Pinch of coriander
- ⅔ cup red wine or water
- 2½ yards sausage casing

(cont'd)

1. Grind the lean and fat pork, onion and garlic. Add the seasonings and mix thoroughly. Add the wine and mix well.

2. Force through a sausage stuffer into casing (see basic sausage recipe, page 146).

. . . .

HAM

. . . .

BAKED GLAZED HAM

1 uncooked tenderized ham
Whole cloves
1 cup brown sugar, packed
2 teaspoons dry mustard

1. Preheat oven to slow (300° F.).

2. Place the ham under cold running water and scrub the rind well with a stiff brush.

3. Dry the ham and place it in a roasting pan with the skin and fat side up. Insert meat thermometer through fat side into the thickest part of the ham.

4. Bake the ham, uncovered, twenty or twenty-five minutes to the pound, or until it registers 160° F. on a meat thermometer. Hams weighing fifteen pounds or more need only be baked about seventeen minutes to the pound.

5. When the ham is done, remove it from the oven and, using ordinary kitchen shears or a sharp knife, cut off the rind. Score the fat diagonally about one-eighth inch deep to make a diamond pattern. Stud the corners of the diamond pattern with cloves. Combine brown sugar with dry mustard and a little of the ham fat from the roasting pan. Spread this mixture over the top of the ham.

6. Increase the oven heat to 400° and return the ham to the oven. Bake until the sugar forms a glaze.

BAKED HAM IN BEER *25 servings*

1 thirteen-pound canned ham
¾ cup raisins
Water
Whole cloves
2 teaspoons dry mustard
½ cup molasses
1 pint beer
2½ tablespoons cornstarch
2 tablespoons wine vinegar

1. Preheat oven to moderate (350° F.).

2. Remove the top of the ham can and heat the ham in the oven until the gelatin softens. Invert the ham on a rack in a pan, punch holes in the bottom of the can and lift it off. Pour off the can liquid.

3. Cover the raisins with warm water. *(cont'd)*

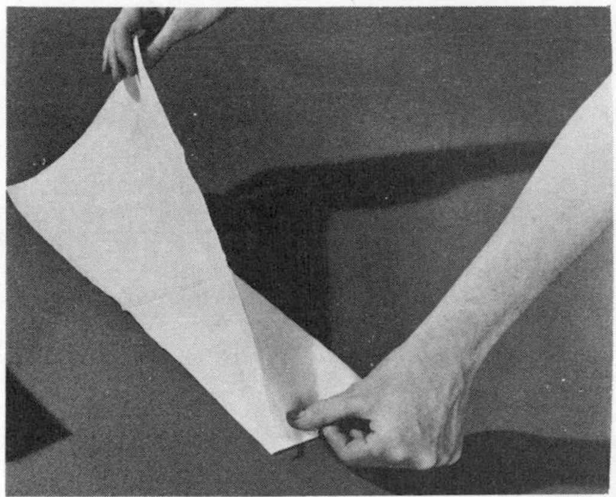

1. To make a frill for the shank bone of a ham, a large dinner napkin of fairly stiff material is folded in half.

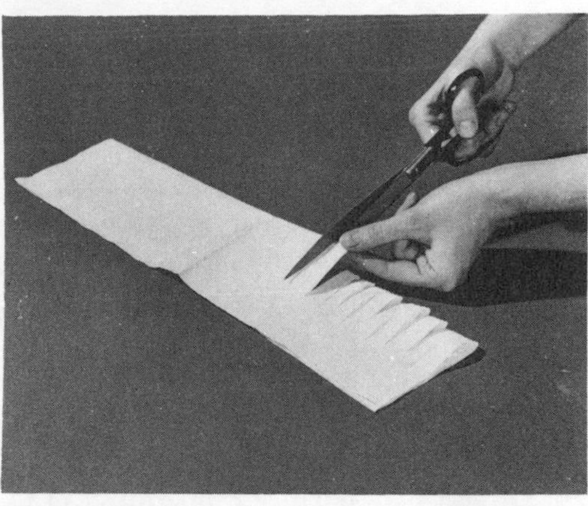

2. With a pair of kitchen scissors, the fold is cut at half-inch intervals to within about one inch of the open edge.

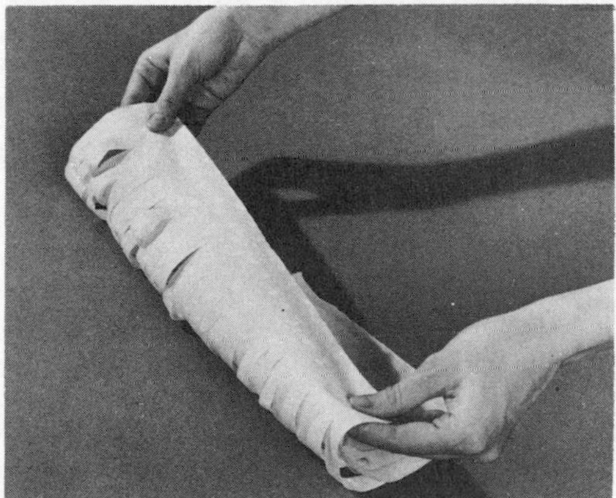

3. The napkin fold is then reversed and the edges are brought together again. This gives the frill a puffed effect.

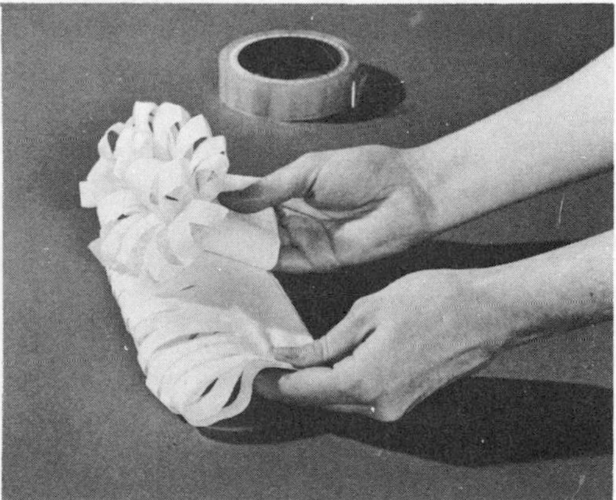

4. Starting at one end, the uncut portion of the napkin is rolled to the size desired and then fitted onto the bone.

5. There are several ways of securing the ends of a paper frill. They may be glued together, secured with a strip of cellophane tape or easily fastened with a stapling machine.

4. Score the ham in diamonds and stud with cloves. Mix the mustard and molasses and spread on the ham. Bake one hour, basting with the beer.

5. Transfer the ham to a platter and boil the drippings until reduced to one and one-half cups. Drain the water from the raisins into a measuring cup and add more water to make one cup. Add to the drippings and bring to a boil.

6. Mix the cornstarch with one-third cup water, add to the boiling broth and boil, stirring, one minute. Add the vinegar and raisins and serve the sauce with the ham.

BAKED COUNTRY HAM

Scrape mold and pepper from the surface of a country-cured Smithfield or Virginia ham. Wash well with baking soda, soap and hot water and rinse thoroughly. Soak the ham overnight in water to cover and then drain.

Place ham in a deep kettle. Add water to cover, bring to a boil and simmer until tender, about twenty minutes per pound. Cool in the water.

Remove the skin and excess fat. Score the remaining fat, stud with cloves and glaze with brown sugar or honey (see instructions for baked glazed ham, page 148). Bake in a preheated hot oven (400° F.), basting with the pan drippings, until well glazed, about thirty minutes.

COUNTRY-FRIED HAM

Cut ham slices about one-quarter inch thick and place in a heavy cold skillet. Cook over moderate heat, turning often, until the ham is brown and the fat is crisp.

If the ham is very salty, first simmer briefly in water to cover, turning frequently. Pour off the water and fry as directed.

Serve with red-eye gravy (see below), grits and hot biscuits.

RED-EYE GRAVY:

Drain off the excess fat in the pan after the ham is removed. To the drippings left in the pan add a little water and a tablespoon of strong coffee, if desired. Bring to a boil and serve hot.

BOILED HAM

Place a whole, scrubbed ham in a kettle or other container large enough to hold it and add water to cover. Bring to a boil and lower the heat until the water barely simmers. Cook fifteen to twenty minutes to the pound. The broth in which the meat has cooked may be used in dried bean soups or casseroles.

SLICED HAM WITH ASPARAGUS SPEARS AND EGG SAUCE

6 servings

6 tablespoons butter
6 tablespoons flour
2 cups milk, or half milk and half cream
Salt and freshly ground black pepper to taste
¼ cup Parmesan cheese
3 hard-cooked eggs, sliced
6 slices baked ham
12 triangles toast
30 asparagus spears, trimmed and cooked

1. Melt the butter in a saucepan, add the flour and stir with a wire whisk until blended. Meanwhile, bring the milk to a boil and add all at once to the butter-flour mixture, stirring vigorously with the whisk. When thickened, reduce the heat and simmer one minute. Season to taste with salt and pepper, turn off the heat and add the cheese, stirring until smooth. Gently stir in the egg slices to complete the sauce.

2. Sauté the ham slices in a little butter until heated through. Place on toast triangles and top each slice with five freshly cooked and drained asparagus spears.

3. Spoon the egg sauce over the asparagus spears and serve immediately.

SAUTEED SWEETBREADS AND MUSHROOMS ON HAM, PAGE 173.

. . . .

VEAL

. . . .

ROAST LEG OF VEAL *6 servings*

1 four-pound boneless leg of veal
Salt and freshly ground black pepper
½ pound salt pork
2 cloves garlic
1 carrot, coarsely chopped
1 onion, quartered
Pinch of thyme
1 bay leaf
½ cup butter, melted
1 cup dry white wine

1. Have the butcher lard the veal with fat and tie it securely.

2. Preheat oven to slow (300° F.).

3. Rub the roast with salt and pepper and cover it with thin strips of salt pork.

4. Place the veal in a roasting pan and insert a meat thermometer in the thickest part of the roast. Surround the meat with the garlic, carrot, onion, thyme and bay leaf. Roast the meat, basting frequently with melted butter and wine, until the meat thermometer registers 170° F., about two hours. Skim fat from surface of sauce.

VEAL RUMP WITH SOUR CREAM *8 or more servings*

1 four-pound boned rump of veal
2 cloves garlic, crushed
1½ tablespoons anchovy paste
¼ teaspoon powdered basil
5 tablespoons butter
2 cups dry white wine
2 tablespoons cornstarch
Water
½ cup sour cream
2 tablespoons capers
Salt and freshly ground black pepper to taste
Watercress

1. Place the roast flat with the boned surface up. Cream together the garlic, anchovy paste, basil and two tablespoons of butter. Spread over the meat, roll and tie securely.

2. Place the veal in a bowl, add the wine and marinate four hours or longer, turning occasionally.

3. Remove and dry the meat with paper towels, reserving the marinade. Heat the remaining butter in a Dutch oven, add the meat and brown on all sides. Place a rack under the meat, add the marinade, cover and let simmer until the meat is tender, about two hours.

4. Slice the veal and arrange the slices on a hot serving platter. Blend the cornstarch with a little water and add, stirring, to the broth. Boil one minute.

5. Stir in the sour cream, capers, salt and pepper and heat but do not let boil. Pour over the veal or serve separately. Garnish the platter with watercress.

SAVORY POT ROAST OF VEAL *10 or more servings*

3½ tablespoons fat
1 five-pound rolled veal rump
Flour for dredging
1 medium onion, chopped
1 clove garlic, crushed
¼ cup chopped celery
1 tablespoon minced parsley
1 teaspoon meat glaze
1 teaspoon tomato paste
¼ teaspoon powdered dry mushrooms or 3 dry mushrooms washed and soaked in hot bouillon for 15 minutes, then chopped
1 cup concentrated bouillon
1 cup water

1. Preheat oven to hot (450° F.). Place two tablespoons of the fat in a baking pan and heat in the oven.

2. Dredge the veal with flour. Brown in the baking pan in the oven, turning veal over once so both sides brown. Remove from the oven, drain off the fat and lower the oven temperature to slow (300° F.).

3. Heat the remaining fat in a skillet, add the onion, garlic, celery and parsley and cook slowly until the onion is transparent. With a slotted spoon, remove the vegetables and add to the veal. Add the glaze, tomato paste, mushrooms, bouillon and water. Cover.

4. Bake about four hours, adding more bouillon if necessary to keep the bot-

(*cont'd*)

tom of the pan covered with liquid. Turn the meat over when the cooking is half finished. When the veal is tender, transfer it to a hot platter and keep warm.

5. Strain the liquid in the pan, skim off the fat, thicken with a little flour mixed with water and serve with the veal.

VEAL ROAST WITH ROSEMARY *6 servings*

1 three-pound veal rump roast, boned, rolled and tied
Salt and freshly ground black pepper to taste
Flour
2 tablespoons fat
½ cup water
½ cup white wine
1 clove garlic, chopped
1 teaspoon rosemary
3 medium onions, halved
3 carrots, halved

1. Sprinkle the roast with salt and pepper and dredge with flour.
2. Melt the fat in a heavy kettle or roasting pan, add the meat and brown on all sides. Place a rack under the meat, add the water, wine, one and one-half teaspoons salt, the garlic and rosemary.
3. Cover the kettle or pan and cook slowly over surface heat or in a moderate oven (350° F.) two hours. Thirty minutes before the meat is done, add the onions and carrots.
4. Remove the roast and vegetables to a hot platter. Slice meat and serve with unthickened sauce remaining in pan.

BREADED VEAL CHOPS *4 servings*

1 cup fine, dry bread crumbs
1 tablespoon chopped parsley
1 teaspoon orégano
½ cup grated Parmesan or American cheese
4 loin veal chops
Salt and freshly ground black pepper
1 egg, well beaten and diluted with 2 tablespoons water
¼ cup butter

1. Combine the bread crumbs, parsley, orégano and cheese.
2. Sprinkle the chops with the salt and pepper, dip them into the beaten egg and roll in the bread-crumb mixture.
3. Melt the butter in a skillet, add the chops and cook over moderate heat until tender, about ten minutes on each side.

VEAL CHOPS SAUTE *4 servings*

4 veal rib chops, about ½ inch thick
Flour for dredging
Salt and freshly ground black pepper
3 tablespoons butter
6 tablespoons dry white wine
1 teaspoon lemon juice
¼ cup firm butter
Minced parsley

(cont'd)

1. Dredge the chops with flour seasoned with salt and pepper. Heat the butter in a heavy skillet, add the meat and brown on both sides.

2. Reduce the heat to low, cover the pan and cook about twenty minutes. Turn the chops two or three times. Transfer to a hot platter and keep warm.

3. To the juices in the pan add the white wine. Reduce by cooking uncovered over fairly high heat two or three minutes. Add the lemon juice.

4. Add the firm butter to the sauce in little curls, swirling the pan to incorporate the butter without its melting rapidly.

5. When the butter has barely melted, pour the sauce over the chops and sprinkle with minced parsley.

VEAL CHOPS WITH OLIVES *6 servings*

5 tablespoons butter
6 loin veal chops
2 tablespoons chopped onion
1 clove garlic, chopped
½ cup finely diced ham
½ cup green olives, pitted and coarsely chopped

1. Heat the butter in a skillet, add the chops and cook until golden brown on both sides.

2. Add the onion, garlic and ham and cook, stirring, until the onion is transparent. Cover and continue cooking over low heat until the chops are tender, about twenty minutes. Transfer the chops to a heated platter and keep warm.

3. Add the olives to the pan and heat. Pour over the chops and serve at once.

VEAL CHOPS WITH PEPPERS ITALIAN STYLE *4 servings*

3 tablespoons olive oil
4 large green peppers, seeded and cut into thin slices
1 medium onion, chopped
1 clove garlic, minced
6 green olives, chopped
1 tablespoon capers
1 or 2 anchovies, chopped (optional)
Salt and freshly ground black pepper to taste
4 large loin veal chops
Flour
2 tablespoons butter

1. In a skillet heat the oil, add the peppers, onion and garlic and sauté until tender, stirring often. Transfer to a bowl, add the olives, capers, anchovies, salt and pepper. Keep warm.

2. Dredge the chops lightly with flour. Heat the butter in the same skillet, add the chops and brown on both sides. Add the pepper mixture, cover and cook over low heat until the chops are tender, about twenty-five minutes. Remove the chops to a platter and arrange the peppers over and around them.

3. Add one or two tablespoons water to the pan and heat, scraping loose all the brown particles. Pour over the chops.

VEAL CHOPS GUILDERLAND *6 servings*

7 tablespoons butter
1 small onion, chopped
½ pound mushrooms, chopped
3 inner stalks celery, chopped
1 tablespoon chopped parsley
Salt to taste
6 rib veal chops about 2 inches thick
Flour
Freshly ground black pepper to taste
3 tablespoons sherry
1 cup stock or water
½ cup sour cream

1. Heat four tablespoons of the butter in a skillet, add the onion and cook two minutes. Add the mushrooms and celery, cover and cook five minutes. Remove the cover and continue cooking until most of the moisture has evaporated. Add the parsley and salt.
2. Preheat oven to moderate (350° F.).
3. Place the chops on a board. With a sharp knife, cutting from the bone toward the center, make a pocket in each chop and stuff with two tablespoons of the mushroom mixture. Fasten securely with toothpicks.
4. Dust the chops lightly with flour and sprinkle with pepper.
5. Heat two tablespoons of the butter in the skillet, add the chops and brown on both sides. Remove to a casserole, add the sherry, cover with waxed paper and a lid and bake until tender, about thirty minutes.
6. While the chops are baking, make the sauce in the pan in which the chops were browned. Melt the remaining butter, add one tablespoon flour and blend. Add the stock and bring to a boil, scraping loose all the brown particles. Cook, stirring, until thickened. Stir in sour cream. Remove from the heat.
7. To serve, place the chops on a platter. Combine the cream sauce with the juices in the casserole, correct the seasonings and spoon over the chops. Garnish with additional chopped parsley.

BARBECUED VEAL CHOPS *6 servings*

6 veal chops with kidney
½ teaspoon crumbled thyme leaves
½ teaspoon ground cumin seeds
½ teaspoon chili powder
¼ teaspoon ground dry red pepper
1½ teaspoons salt
1 small onion, minced
½ cup cider vinegar
¼ cup salad oil
¼ cup catsup
1 clove garlic, sliced

1. Have the butcher cut the veal chops one and one-half inches thick.
2. Combine the remaining ingredients in a mixing bowl. Add the meat to this marinade and let stand two to three hours.
3. Broil the chops slowly over a charcoal fire or under a medium broiler flame until brown on both sides, basting with the sauce left in the bowl as often as the meat looks dry.

BAKED VEAL CHOPS *6 servings*

2 leeks, sliced lengthwise, washed and chopped, or ½ cup thin onion slices
½ cup thin carrot slices
1 stalk celery, chopped
Thyme
6 loin veal chops, 1 inch thick
Salt and freshly ground black pepper to taste
Dry white wine or chicken stock or both
Flour

1. Preheat oven to moderate (375° F.).

2. Arrange the vegetables over the bottom of a shallow casserole and sprinkle with thyme.

3. Sprinkle the chops with salt and pepper and place on the vegetables. Add enough liquid barely to cover the vegetables.

4. Bake uncovered, basting frequently with the liquid in the casserole, until the chops are browned and tender, about one hour and fifteen minutes. Add more liquid if necessary and turn the chops occasionally while cooking. Strain the gravy and thicken with a little flour mixed with water.

ESCALOPES DE VEAU PANEES (breaded veal scallops) *4 servings*

Wonderfully simple to prepare and delicious to eat are escalopes de veau panées, or, more simply put, breaded veal scallops. They should be made with fresh bread crumbs.

4 six-ounce veal cutlets
Salt and freshly ground black pepper
Flour for dredging
1 egg
1 teaspoon water
1 cup fresh bread crumbs (page 29)
¼ cup butter
Lemon wedges

1. Pound the cutlets until thin and sprinkle lightly on both sides with salt and pepper. Dredge them lightly but thoroughly with flour.

2. Beat the egg lightly with the water and dip the floured cutlets in the mixture; coat with the crumbs. Using the side of a kitchen knife, tap the cutlets lightly so crumbs will adhere well to the meat. Transfer them to a wire rack. Refrigerate one or two hours. This will help the breading to adhere to the cutlets when they are being cooked.

3. Heat the butter in a large skillet and, when it is hot but not brown or smoking, sauté the cutlets in it until golden brown on both sides.

4. Arrange the cutlets on a heated serving platter and garnish with lemon wedges. Serve immediately.

VARIATIONS:

Escalopes de Veau à la Viennoise: Cook the cutlets as above. Garnish each cutlet with a lemon slice and top each slice with a rolled fillet of anchovy stuffed with a caper. Sprinkle with chopped parsley. If desired, garnish one end of the platter with sieved egg white and the other end with sieved egg yolk.

(cont'd)

1. *For perfect breaded veal cutlets,* place meat between waxed paper sheets and pound it wafer-thin.

2. Sprinkle meat with salt and pepper and, using fingers or tongs, coat lightly but thoroughly with flour.

3. Dip cutlets, one at a time, in egg lightly beaten with a little water. Egg makes the crumbs adhere.

4. Dredge in bread crumbs. If desired, tap breaded cutlets lightly with the side of a kitchen knife.

5. Transfer cutlets to a rack to dry for fifteen minutes. They may be stored in refrigerator for several hours. Sauté in butter until brown.

6. Golden-brown breaded veal cutlets gain character with piquant garnishes. They are served here with lemon slices and anchovy fillets. Recipe for the dish (escalopes de veau à la Viennoise) is given.

Escalopes de Veau à la Holstein: Cook veal cutlets as page 156. Top each slice with an egg fried in butter. Top the egg, if desired, with crossed flat fillets of anchovy.

Escalopes de Veau à la Milanaise: Cook cutlets as page 156. Arrange them on a bed of cooked spaghetti covered with Milanaise sauce (page 342).

VEAL SCALOPPINE ALLA MARSALA *3 servings*

- 1 pound veal, cut into thin, even slices
- Flour for dredging
- Salt and freshly ground black pepper to taste
- 3 tablespoons butter
- ¼ cup Marsala wine
- 2 tablespoons canned concentrated bouillon

1. Pound the veal lightly until very thin. Dredge with flour seasoned with salt and pepper.
2. Heat the butter in a skillet, add the veal and brown on both sides. Add the Marsala and cook one minute longer over moderately high heat. Transfer the meat to a warm platter.
3. Add the bouillon to the pan drippings. Scrape loose all the brown particles and bring to a boil. Pour over the veal.

VARIATIONS:

Veal Scaloppine with Prosciutto: Cook the veal as above. Transfer to a warm serving platter. Add one-eighth pound slivered prosciutto to the drippings in the skillet. Sauté briskly one or two minutes, adding more butter if needed. Arrange the prosciutto on the veal. Add to the drippings two tablespoons concentrated bouillon, one teaspoon chopped parsley and one teaspoon lemon juice. Bring to a boil and pour over the meat.

Veal Scaloppine with Mushrooms: Sauté one-half pound sliced mushrooms in two tablespoons butter. Arrange mushrooms on a warm platter. Add three tablespoons butter to the pan and in it cook the scaloppine as indicated for scaloppine alla Marsala. Serve the veal and sauce on the same platter with the mushrooms.

VEAL SCALOPPINE WITH CHEESE *6 servings*

- 2 pounds veal, cut into thin, even slices
- ½ cup butter
- 3 tablespoons sherry or Marsala
- 1 tablespoon flour
- ½ cup milk
- ½ cup water
- 1 bouillon cube
- Dash of nutmeg
- Freshly ground black pepper to taste
- ½ pound Swiss or Gruyère cheese, sliced very thin

1. Pound the veal lightly until very thin.
2. Heat six tablespoons of the butter in a skillet, add the veal and cook until brown on both sides. Add the sherry and cook a few seconds longer. Remove from the heat.

(cont'd)

3. To make the sauce, melt the remaining butter in a saucepan, add the flour and stir with a wire whisk until blended. Meanwhile, bring the water and milk to a boil and dissolve the bouillon cube in the mixture. Add all at once to the butter-flour mixture, stirring vigorously with the whisk until the sauce is thickened and smooth. Season with the nutmeg and pepper.

4. Arrange the veal in a single layer in a shallow baking dish. Scrape loose the brown particles from the skillet and pour the drippings over the meat. Top with the sauce and arrange the cheese over all.

5. If desired, refrigerate several hours. Before serving, heat in a preheated hot oven (425° F.) until the cheese melts and turns brown, about twenty minutes.

VEAL SCHNITZEL WITH KIDNEYS *4 servings*

4 six-ounce veal cutlets
Flour for dredging
6 tablespoons butter
2 veal kidneys
8 large mushroom caps
½ cup canned bouillon
½ cup dry white wine
Salt and freshly ground black pepper to taste

1. Pound the cutlets lightly until very thin. Dredge with the flour.

2. Heat four tablespoons of the butter, add the cutlets and brown on both sides. Remove to a warm platter.

3. Trim the kidneys and remove the hard core of fat in centers. Cut each kidney into eight slices.

4. Add the remaining butter to the pan, add the kidneys and mushrooms and cook over high heat for only two or three minutes, until brown. Garnish each cutlet with two slices of kidney and two mushroom caps.

5. Add the bouillon and wine to the pan and boil until reduced one-half. Season with salt and pepper and pour over the meat.

VEAL SCALLOPS A LA PROVENCALE *6 to 8 servings*

1½ to 2 pounds veal, cut into thin, even slices
Flour for dredging
¼ cup olive oil
½ pound fresh mushrooms, sliced
2 cloves garlic, minced
½ cup dry white wine
4 medium tomatoes, peeled and chopped
Salt and freshly ground black pepper to taste
Chopped parsley

1. Pound the veal lightly until very thin. Dredge with flour. Heat the oil in a skillet, add the veal and brown on both sides. Push the veal to the side of the pan, add the mushrooms and cook, stirring often, two or three minutes.

2. Arrange the mushrooms on the veal and spoon around them the garlic, wine, tomatoes, salt and pepper. Simmer about ten minutes. Serve sprinkled with parsley.

VEAL PAPRIKA *6 servings*

2 pounds veal cut into thin, even slices
Salt and freshly ground black pepper to taste
3 tablespoons olive or salad oil
1 tablespoon butter
2 shallots, finely chopped
1 tablespoon paprika
¼ cup dry white Bordeaux wine
¼ cup chicken broth
1 cup sour cream

1. Cut the veal slices into one-quarter-inch strips. Sprinkle with salt and pepper. Heat the oil in a skillet, add the veal and cook quickly over high heat until browned. Transfer to a heated serving dish or casserole.

2. Melt the butter in the same skillet, add the shallots and sauté until tender but not browned. Stir in the paprika. Add the wine and cook until it is reduced almost completely.

3. Add the broth and gradually stir in the sour cream. Combine the sauce with the meat and heat, but do not let boil. Serve with hot, buttered noodles.

VEAL WITH PEPPERS *4 servings*

4 large green peppers
1 tablespoon fat
½ pound raw veal, cut into thin slivers
2 teaspoons sugar
1 teaspoon monosodium glutamate
½ teaspoon salt
1 cup veal or chicken stock, or water
2 teaspoons cornstarch
1 teaspoon soy sauce

1. Remove the seedy portions from the peppers and cut each pepper into eighths. Parboil in water to cover three minutes and drain.

2. In a skillet heat the fat, add the veal and sauté two minutes, stirring often. Add the peppers, sugar, monosodium glutamate, salt and stock. Cover and simmer six minutes.

3. Mix the cornstarch and soy sauce with a little water and add, stirring, to the veal. Cook, stirring, two minutes. Serve with rice.

ITALIAN STUFFED VEAL CUTLET *3 to 4 servings*

1 pound veal cutlet, cut in serving pieces about ½ inch thick
¼ pound Swiss cheese, sliced very thin
¼ pound prosciutto, sliced very thin
⅔ cup fine, fresh bread crumbs
½ cup grated Parmesan cheese
1 tablespoon finely chopped parsley
2 teaspoons finely chopped celery leaves
1 clove garlic, minced
Pinch each of orégano, basil and rosemary
Salt and freshly ground black pepper
Flour
1 egg
3 tablespoons milk
¼ cup butter

(cont'd)

1. With a short, sharp-bladed knife, cut a deep pocket in each piece of veal. (Insert the knife in the longest side and cut through almost the entire area of the meat.)

2. Wrap a slice of Swiss cheese around a slice of prosciutto for each piece of veal. Fit into the veal pocket and press tightly closed.

3. Mix the bread crumbs with the Parmesan cheese, parsley, celery, garlic and herbs to make breading mixture.

4. Season the meat on both sides with salt and pepper and dredge with flour. Beat the egg well with the milk and dip the cutlets into the mixture, then roll in the seasoned crumbs.

5. Melt the butter in a heavy skillet, add the cutlets and cook uncovered over moderate heat twenty minutes, turning to brown evenly.

VEAL BREAST WITH SPINACH STUFFING *6 servings*

3 tablespoons butter
1 medium onion, chopped
½ pound mushrooms, chopped
1 pound spinach, cooked
½ teaspoon rosemary or basil
½ teaspoon salt
Freshly ground black pepper to taste
1 cup cooked rice
1 egg, slightly beaten
1 three-pound boned veal breast cut with a pocket
4 slices salt pork
1 cup water or meat broth
Flour

1. Heat the butter, add the onion and cook until transparent. Add the mushrooms and cook, stirring often, about three minutes.

2. Chop the spinach and drain thoroughly.

3. Preheat the oven to moderate (350° F.).

4. Mix the vegetables with the seasonings, rice and egg. Use the mixture to fill the pocket in the veal breast and close with metal skewers.

5. Place the meat on a low rack in a roasting pan. Arrange the salt pork over the veal and add the water to the pan. Cover with aluminum foil and bake two hours. Uncover and bake thirty minutes longer. Thicken the broth with a little flour mixed with water and serve with the hot meat.

ROLLED BREAST OF VEAL *6 servings*

1 three- to four-pound boned breast of veal
Salt and freshly ground black pepper to taste
1 small clove garlic, crushed
¼ pound sliced prosciutto
1 small mozzarella cheese, cut into small pieces
1 to 2 teaspoons chopped parsley
2 tablespoons olive oil
1 small onion, sliced
1 carrot, sliced
½ cup white wine
½ cup water
2 tablespoons butter
½ pound mushrooms, sliced
2 tablespoons flour

(*cont'd*)

1. Reserve the bones from the veal. Spread the meat flat and season with the salt, pepper and garlic.

2. Preheat oven to moderate (375° F.).

3. Cover the meat with the prosciutto and arrange the mozzarella on top. Sprinkle with parsley.

4. Roll the meat lengthwise and tie with string at one-and-one-half-inch intervals. Place in a shallow baking pan and brush with the olive oil. Add to the pan the onion, carrot, wine, water and veal bones. Roast one and one-half hours, basting occasionally with the pan juices. Remove the veal to a hot platter and keep warm.

5. Heat the butter, add the mushrooms and sauté until lightly browned. Remove from the heat and blend in the flour. Strain the pan juices and add enough water to make two cups. Pour the liquid into the pan with the mushrooms and stir over moderate heat until the sauce comes to a boil. Correct the seasonings and serve with the meat.

STUFFED SHOULDER OF VEAL *12 or more servings*

1 ounce salt pork, cubed
¼ cup butter
1 onion, chopped
½ cup chopped celery with leaves
1 clove garlic, crushed (optional)
¼ cup chopped parsley
½ teaspoon salt
Freshly ground black pepper to taste
½ to 1 teaspoon dried rosemary or summer savory
4 cups soft bread crumbs or cubes
1 veal shoulder, boned (4 to 5 pounds)
1 stalk celery
3 sprigs parsley
1 onion, sliced
1 cup heated veal or chicken broth

1. Preheat oven to hot (425° F.).

2. Cook the salt pork in two tablespoons of the butter until yellow. Add the onion, celery and garlic and cook until the onion is transparent, stirring often.

3. Add the parsley, salt, pepper and rosemary. Mix well with the bread cubes.

4. Spread the meat out on a board, skin side down. If desired, sprinkle with salt and pepper. Cover with the stuffing and roll. Tie into a neat shape.

5. Place the celery stalk, sprigs of parsley and sliced onion in a roasting pan or Dutch oven and place the meat on the vegetables. Rub the veal with the remaining butter.

6. Roast until the top of the meat is brown, about fifteen minutes. Reduce the heat to moderate (350° F.), add the broth, cover and cook until tender, about two hours longer. Baste often with the drippings in the pan. Fifteen minutes before the meat is done, uncover and baste frequently.

7. Place the meat on a hot platter, strain the drippings and pour over the veal.

VEAL SHOULDER WITH CHICKEN-LIVER STUFFING

6 to 8 servings

- ¼ pound ground pork
- ¼ pound chicken livers, chopped
- ¼ cup chopped onion
- ¼ cup fine, soft bread crumbs
- ½ pound mushrooms, chopped and cooked in a little butter
- Pinch of thyme or marjoram
- 1 egg, lightly beaten
- Salt and freshly ground black pepper to taste
- Water or dry white wine, if necessary
- 1 three-pound boneless veal shoulder
- 2 tablespoons butter or bacon fat
- 2 cups chicken stock

1. Combine the pork, chicken livers, onion, bread crumbs, mushrooms, thyme, egg, salt and pepper and mix well. If mixture seems dry, add a little water or dry white wine, tossing it lightly. Stuff the veal as in stuffed shoulder of veal (page 162), and tie securely.

2. Heat the butter in a Dutch oven, add the meat and brown on all sides. Add the chicken stock, cover closely and simmer gently over low heat until the veal is fork tender, two to three hours. Turn the meat occasionally as it cooks.

3. Transfer the meat to a hot platter and keep warm. Cook the sauce, uncovered, over moderate heat until it is reduced to one cup. Strain and serve with the meat.

STUFFED BREAST OF VEAL

5 to 6 servings

- 1 three- to four-pound boned veal breast, cut with a pocket
- Salt and freshly ground black pepper
- 1 medium onion, chopped
- 1 clove garlic, crushed (optional)
- ½ cup butter
- 3 cups soft bread crumbs or cubes
- 2 tablespoons minced parsley
- ½ teaspoon dried summer savory, rosemary or marjoram
- ¼ teaspoon dried basil or thyme
- Flour
- ¼ cup water
- ¼ cup sour cream or 2 tablespoons dry white wine (optional)

1. Sprinkle the inside of the veal pocket with salt and pepper.

2. Sauté the onion and garlic lightly in one-third cup of the butter. Mix the crumbs with the parsley, herbs and salt and pepper to taste. Add the onion with the butter in the pan and mix. Stuff the veal breast with the mixture and skewer to close.

3. Dredge the meat with flour and brown well in the remaining butter in a Dutch oven. Add one-quarter cup water, cover and simmer until tender, about two hours.

4. Thicken the drippings with flour and, if desired, add the sour cream or wine.

BLANQUETTE OF VEAL *6 servings*

- 2 pounds shoulder or breast of veal, cut into 1½-inch cubes
- Water
- 3 carrots, cut into pieces
- 12 small white onions, peeled and left whole
- 3 sprigs parsley
- 1 stalk celery
- 1 leek
- 1 bay leaf
- 1 clove garlic
- ¼ teaspoon peppercorns
- ¼ teaspoon thyme
- 2 teaspoons salt
- 2 tablespoons butter
- 2 tablespoons flour
- 1 cup heavy cream
- 2 egg yolks
- ½ pound small mushrooms, sautéed in a little butter
- Croutons

1. Parboil the meat in a deep kettle in water to cover five minutes. Drain and add to the meat about four cups water and the carrots and onions.
2. Tie the parsley, celery, leek, bay leaf, garlic, peppercorns and thyme in a cheesecloth bag and add to the meat. Add the salt, bring the mixture to a boil, skimming as necessary, and simmer, covered, until the veal is tender, or about one and one-half hours.
3. Remove the meat, carrots and onions to a serving dish and keep warm. Remove the cheesecloth bag and discard.
4. Boil the broth until reduced about two-thirds. Cream the butter with the flour, add to the broth and boil, stirring, one minute.
5. Mix the cream and egg yolks, add to the broth and heat, stirring, until the mixture thickens. Do not let it boil or the cream will curdle. Strain over the meat and vegetables. Garnish with mushrooms and croutons.

VIENNESE VEAL GOULASH *6 servings*

- 2 pounds boneless veal shoulder, cut in 1½-inch cubes
- 2 teaspoons salt
- 2 teaspoons sweet Hungarian-style paprika (rose paprika)
- 4 small onions, coarsely chopped (about 2 cups)
- ¼ cup butter
- ¼ cup canned tomato sauce
- 2 small fresh tomatoes, peeled and cubed
- 2 tablespoons sour cream

1. Sprinkle the veal with the salt and paprika. Let stand while preparing the onions.
2. In a heavy two-quart saucepan, heat the butter, add the onions and cook until golden. Add the veal and cook, stirring, over medium heat until the meat loses its surface color. Reduce the heat and add the tomato sauce and tomatoes, cover and simmer until the veal is tender, about one and one-half hours.
3. Stir in the sour cream and correct the seasonings. Do not let sauce boil after sour cream has been added.

VEAL STEW WITH SOUR CREAM *6 to 8 servings*

Flour for dredging
Salt and freshly ground black pepper
3 pounds boneless veal shoulder, cut into 1½-inch cubes
½ cup shortening or lard
3 medium onions, peeled and quartered
1 cup sliced celery
2 cups water
Pinch of thyme
1 small head of cauliflower, broken into flowerettes
12 small mushrooms, quartered
Butter
1 cup sour cream
¼ cup chopped parsley

1. Combine flour, salt and pepper and dredge the veal with the seasoned flour. Heat the shortening in a heavy saucepan, add the veal and brown on all sides.

2. Pour off the drippings from the pan and add the onions, celery, water and thyme to the meat. Cover tightly and simmer one hour and fifteen minutes. Add the cauliflower and continue simmering thirty minutes, or until tender.

3. Cook the mushrooms in a little butter and add. Stir in the sour cream and parsley and reheat, but do not let boil.

VEAL WITH RIPE OLIVES *6 servings*

2 pounds lean veal, cut into 1½-inch cubes
Flour for dredging
Salt and freshly ground black pepper
¼ cup salad oil
1 clove garlic, chopped
1 small onion, sliced
⅔ teaspoon dried rosemary
½ cup dry white wine
1 tablespoon tomato paste
Chicken stock (approximately 1 cup)
12 pitted ripe olives, sliced
Chopped parsley

1. Preheat oven to slow (300° F.).

2. Dredge the veal with flour seasoned with salt and pepper. Heat the oil in a Dutch oven, add the meat and brown on all sides. Add the garlic and onion and cook three minutes longer, stirring with a wooden spoon.

3. Add the rosemary, wine, tomato paste and enough stock to cover. Cover and bake two hours. Add the ripe olives and cook thirty minutes longer.

4. Before serving, sprinkle with chopped parsley.

VEAL ROLLS WITH ANCHOVIES *4 servings*

1 pound veal, cut into thin, even slices
¼ pound mozzarella cheese
1 can anchovy fillets
½ cup butter
½ cup canned, concentrated bouillon
1 teaspoon chopped parsley

(cont'd)

1. Pound the veal slices lightly until very thin. On each slice place a small piece of cheese and an anchovy fillet. Roll and fasten securely with toothpicks.

2. Heat half the butter in a skillet, add the rolls and brown on all sides. Add one tablespoon of the bouillon, cover the pan, and cook the rolls slowly ten minutes. Remove the meat to a hot platter and keep warm.

3. Add the remaining bouillon to the pan drippings and simmer a few minutes. Swirl in the remaining butter (as for veal chops sauté, p. 153). Add the parsley and pour over the rolls.

ITALIAN VEAL BIRDS *6 servings*

1½ pounds veal, cut into thin, even slices
¾ cup ham, finely chopped
1 clove garlic, finely chopped
2 tablespoons chopped parsley
Salt and freshly ground black pepper to taste
Flour for dredging
3 tablespoons butter
3 tablespoons olive oil
¼ cup dry white wine
2 cups chicken stock
½ cup finely chopped onion
½ cup finely chopped carrot
½ cup finely chopped celery
½ teaspoon rosemary

1. Pound the veal slices lightly until very thin.

2. Combine the ham, garlic, parsley, salt and pepper. Spoon a little of the mixture onto the veal slices, roll and fasten securely with toothpicks.

3. Dredge the meat with flour and brown on all sides in the butter and oil. Add the wine and cook until it is almost completely reduced. Add the chicken stock and simmer gently twenty minutes. Add the vegetables and rosemary and cook twenty minutes longer.

VEAL BIRDS WITH CHICKEN LIVERS *6 servings*

½ cup butter
10 chicken livers
2 thin slices cooked ham
1 teaspoon chopped parsley
½ teaspoon dried sage, or 2 sage leaves
Salt and freshly ground black pepper
1½ pounds veal, cut into thin, even slices
1 teaspoon flour
1 cup sherry
12 slices toasted French bread

1. Heat two tablespoons butter, add the chicken livers and cook over high heat until lightly browned, about four minutes. Chop the livers into fine pieces. Cut the ham into small pieces and add to the livers, along with the parsley, sage, salt and pepper.

2. Pound the veal slices lightly until very thin and spread with the liver-ham mixture. Roll the slices and fasten securely with toothpicks.

3. Melt the remaining butter in a skillet and brown the veal rolls well. Sprinkle with flour, add the sherry and cook until it is almost completely reduced.

(cont'd)

4. Place the meat on the toast. Add a little stock to the pan gravy. Heat, stirring, and pour over the meat.

VITELLO TONNATO *6 servings*

- 2 tablespoons olive oil
- 3½ pounds boneless rolled leg of veal
- 1 large onion, sliced
- 2 carrots, chopped
- 2 celery stalks, chopped
- 2 large cloves of garlic, finely minced
- 1 two-ounce can anchovy fillets
- 1 six- to seven-ounce can tuna
- 1 cup dry white wine
- 3 sprigs parsley
- 2 bay leaves
- Pinch of thyme
- Salt and freshly ground black pepper
- 1 cup mayonnaise
- Lemon juice to taste

1. Heat the olive oil in a large, heavy kettle or Dutch oven with a tight-fitting cover. Add the veal and brown lightly on all sides.
2. In the same pan sauté the onion, carrots, chopped celery, and garlic. Add the anchovy fillets, tuna, dry white wine, parsley, bay leaves, thyme, salt and pepper to taste. Cover and cook gently for two hours.
3. Remove the meat from the kettle and chill. Boil the sauce remaining in the kettle until reduced by half and purée in an electric blender or sieve. Chill, then blend in the mayonnaise. Season to taste with lemon juice.
4. Slice the veal thin and serve with the sauce.

OSSO BUCO *6 servings*

- 3 whole shanks of veal, cut by butcher into 3-inch pieces
- Flour for dredging
- ½ cup olive oil, approximately
- 1 onion, sliced thin
- 1 bay leaf
- 2 small carrots, sliced thin
- 1 stalk celery, diced
- ½ cup dry white wine
- 2½ cups canned tomatoes, undrained
- 1 teaspoon tomato paste
- 1½ tablespoons chopped parsley
- 1 clove garlic, crushed
- 1 tablespoon grated lemon peel
- Salt and freshly ground black pepper to taste

1. Dredge the shanks with flour. Heat the oil in a skillet, add the shanks and brown on all sides. Remove to a warm platter.
2. If necessary, add more oil to the skillet. Add the onion, bay leaf, carrots and celery and cook over medium heat five minutes. Add the wine and simmer until all the wine has evaporated.
3. Add the shanks, tomatoes and tomato paste, cover and simmer until tender, about one and one-half hours. If necessary, add a small amount of wine or water during cooking.

(cont'd)

4. Remove the shanks from the skillet and strain the sauce. Place the sauce and meat back in the pan and stir in the parsley, garlic, lemon peel, salt and pepper. Simmer five minutes longer. Serve with risotto alla Milanaise (page 321).

VEAL LOAF *4 servings*

2 tablespoons butter
1 medium onion, chopped
½ green pepper, seeded and chopped
2 cups chopped cooked veal
2 cups cooked rice
1 egg
¾ cup chicken broth
1 teaspoon salt
¼ teaspoon freshly ground black pepper
¼ teaspoon rosemary or orégano

1. Preheat oven to moderate (350° F.).
2. Heat the butter in a skillet, add the onion and green pepper and cook until tender. Add the remaining ingredients and mix well.
3. Turn the mixture into a greased loaf pan and bake one hour. Serve with tomato or mushroom sauce.

COLD VEAL CAUCASIAN STYLE, PAGE 11.

RULLEPØLSE (SPICED BREAST OF VEAL), PAGE 13.

SPECIALTY CUTS

BRAINS IN BLACK BUTTER *6 servings*

3 veal brains
Salted water
1 cup beef bouillon
1 carrot, sliced
¼ cup sliced celery
1 onion, halved
1 bay leaf
¼ teaspoon thyme
½ cup butter
1 teaspoon cider vinegar
1 tablespoon capers

1. Soak the brains in water to cover with two teaspoons salt for fifteen minutes. Remove the covering membrane and veins.
2. Drop the brains into boiling bouillon and add the carrot, celery, onion, bay leaf and thyme. Reduce heat and simmer, covered, for thirty minutes.
3. Remove the brains, slice and place on a hot serving dish. Brown the butter, add the vinegar and capers and pour over the brains.

VEAL KIDNEYS BORDELAISE *8 servings*

Salt and freshly ground black pepper to taste
6 veal kidneys, trimmed and cut into 1-inch slices
⅓ cup butter
¼ cup chopped shallots
½ cup red Bordeaux wine
2 cups brown sauce (page 445) or canned beef gravy
2 tablespoons chopped beef marrow
1 tablespoon chopped parsley

1. Salt and pepper the kidneys and brown them quickly in the butter in a skillet. Place in a chafing dish or casserole. Drain the fat from the pan.

2. To the skillet add the shallots and wine and boil until the wine is reduced one-third. Add the brown sauce, marrow and parsley and pour over the kidneys. Heat just to simmering.

VEAL KIDNEYS FLAMBE *6 servings*

¼ cup butter
1 tablespoon chopped shallots
6 veal kidneys, trimmed and cut into 1-inch cubes
6 fresh mushrooms, sliced
2 tablespoons cognac
¼ cup heavy cream
Salt and freshly ground black pepper to taste
Chopped parsley

1. Melt the butter in a skillet, add the shallots and sauté until tender but not browned. Add the kidneys and mushrooms and cook over moderate heat until lightly browned.

2. Warm the cognac and sprinkle over the kidney mixture. Ignite it and, when the flame dies, stir in the heavy cream. Cook one minute, or until the sauce thickens slightly. Season with salt and pepper and sprinkle with parsley.

BEEF KIDNEY STEW *2 to 4 servings*

1 beef kidney
Water
3 tablespoons wine vinegar
Salt and freshly ground black pepper
Flour for dredging
¼ cup butter
3 tablespoons olive or peanut oil
1 clove garlic, finely chopped
½ cup chopped onion
½ teaspoon rosemary
½ teaspoon thyme
1 bay leaf
½ cup dry red wine
½ cup beef broth

1. Remove all membranes from the kidney and place it in a small mixing bowl. Add water barely to cover and the vinegar. Let stand two hours.

2. Drain the kidney and wipe it dry. Cut into thin slices and sprinkle with salt and pepper. Dredge lightly in flour and brown quickly on all sides in hot butter and oil.

3. Add the garlic, onion and herbs and cook five minutes. Add the wine and beef broth and simmer fifteen minutes longer. Serve with boiled potatoes.

VEAL KIDNEYS IN WHITE WINE *6 servings*

3 tablespoons olive oil
2 tablespoons butter
4 veal kidneys, trimmed and cut into 1-inch squares
2 tablespoons chopped parsley
1 tablespoon chopped shallots or chives
3 tablespoons flour
1½ cups dry white wine
½ cup water
2 teaspoons butter
2 teaspoons lemon juice
Salt and freshly ground black pepper to taste

1. Heat the oil and butter in a skillet, add the kidneys and brown on all sides. Reduce the heat and add the parsley and shallots. Cook three minutes, stirring occasionally. Remove the kidneys from the pan. (If kidneys are cooked too long, they will toughen.)

2. Stir the flour into the juices in the pan and gradually add the wine and water. Cook, stirring, until smooth. Remove from the heat and add the butter. Season with lemon juice, salt and pepper. Pour the sauce over the kidneys and serve hot.

VEAL SCHNITZEL WITH KIDNEYS, PAGE 159.

SAUTEED CALVES' LIVER *6 servings*

6 slices calves' liver, trimmed
Flour
Salt and freshly ground black pepper to taste
3 tablespoons butter

1. Dredge the liver with flour seasoned with salt and pepper and sauté in the butter over medium heat until golden brown on both sides. Reduce the heat and cook to the desired degree of doneness. (Two minutes on each side will produce rare meat; six will produce well done.)

2. Transfer the liver to a heated platter and serve immediately.

FLAMED CALVES' LIVER

Sauté liver as above. After cooking, sprinkle with one-fourth cup heated cognac and ignite. Transfer the liver to a heated platter and pour the pan juices over it.

LIVER AND BACON ROLLS *4 servings*

4 thin slices liver, trimmed
Boiling water
¼ pound pork sausage
1¼ cups soft bread crumbs
¼ teaspoon salt
⅛ teaspoon freshly ground black pepper
¼ teaspoon celery salt
4 bacon slices

(cont'd)

1. Cover the liver slices with boiling water and leave one minute. Drain.

2. Break the sausage into small pieces and brown in a skillet. Add the remaining ingredients except the bacon.

3. Place a spoonful of the mixture on each liver slice and roll up. Wrap a slice of bacon around each and fasten with a toothpick.

4. Preheat oven to moderate (375° F.).

5. Place the rolls in a baking dish and add hot water to the depth of one-quarter inch. Cover and bake thirty minutes. Remove the cover during the last ten minutes to brown the bacon and evaporate any remaining water.

Note: Steps 1 to 3 may be done in advance and the liver rolls refrigerated until the final cooking.

BRAISED SWEETBREADS *6 servings*

3 pairs sweetbreads
Water
1 teaspoon lemon juice
3 tablespoons butter
1 onion, sliced
1 carrot, sliced
1 bay leaf
Pinch of thyme
3 sprigs parsley
1 tablespoon flour
½ cup dry white wine
1 cup chicken stock
Salt and freshly ground black pepper to taste
2 tablespoons dry sherry

1. Soak the sweetbreads in ice water one hour. Drain and place in boiling water to cover. Add the lemon juice and simmer ten minutes. Drain and cool immediately in ice water. Remove all the connective and covering tissues.

2. Preheat oven to moderate (350° F.).

3. In a flameproof casserole, melt the butter. Add the onion, carrot, bay leaf, thyme and parsley and cook slowly until the onion is golden.

4. Sprinkle the mixture with the flour, add the sweetbreads, wine, stock, salt and pepper and heat to simmering. Cover and transfer to the oven. Bake twenty minutes. Uncover and bake ten minutes longer.

5. Transfer the sweetbreads to a platter. Stir the sherry into the liquid in the casserole and strain over the sweetbreads. Serve with puréed green peas (page 391).

SAVORY SWEETBREADS *4 servings*

2 pairs sweetbreads
Water
1 tablespoon vinegar
Salt and freshly ground black pepper to taste
½ cup butter
1 tablespoon chopped onion
¼ cup flour
1 cup chicken consommé
1 cup light or heavy cream
Chopped parsley or paprika

(*cont'd*)

1. Soak the sweetbreads in ice water to cover forty-five minutes. Drain and cook slowly fifteen to twenty minutes in water to cover with the vinegar and one teaspoon salt. Drain, cool in ice water and remove all the connective and covering tissues.

2. Split each sweetbread and sprinkle lightly with salt and pepper.

3. Preheat broiler. Melt half the butter and brush the sweetbreads generously with part of it. Broil about three inches from high heat until golden brown on both sides, brushing often with more of the melted butter. Cut the sweetbreads into cubes.

4. While the sweetbreads are broiling, make the sauce. Melt the remaining four tablespoons butter, add the onion and cook until the onion is transparent. Blend in the flour. Stir over low heat for five minutes. Add the consommé. Bring slowly to a boil, continuing to stir constantly. Season to taste with salt and pepper and stir in the cream.

5. Pour sauce over broiled sweetbreads. Garnish with parsley or paprika.

SWEETBREADS IN PATTY SHELLS *6 servings*

3 pairs sweetbreads
Water
1½ cups dry white wine
¼ bay leaf
¼ teaspoon thyme
½ teaspoon salt
¼ cup butter
¼ cup flour
1 cup milk
½ pound boiled ham, cubed (about 1 cup)
½ cup stuffed olives, sliced
White pepper to taste
6 patty shells, purchased
Chopped parsley

1. Soak the sweetbreads in ice water to cover for forty-five minutes.

2. In a saucepan, combine one and one-half cups water, the wine, bay leaf, thyme and salt and bring to a boil. Drop the cold sweetbreads into the boiling liquid and simmer gently twenty-five minutes.

3. Remove the sweetbreads from the broth with a slotted spoon and cool in ice water. Remove all the connective and covering tissues and cut the sweetbreads into large cubes. Strain and measure the broth; if necessary add water or stock to make two cups of liquid.

4. Melt the butter in the top part of a double boiler over direct heat. Add the flour and stir with a wire whisk until blended. Meanwhile, bring the milk with the broth to a boil and add all at once to the butter-flour mixture, stirring vigorously with the whisk until the sauce is thickened and smooth. Add the sweetbreads, ham and olives and season with white pepper and more salt, if necessary. Place over boiling water and cook for thirty minutes.

5. Meanwhile, heat the patty shells for ten minutes on a baking sheet in a preheated moderate oven (375° F.). Pour the sweetbread mixture into the patty shells and serve hot. Garnish with chopped parsley.

SAUTEED SWEETBREADS AND MUSHROOMS ON HAM

6 servings

3 pairs sweetbreads
Water
2 tablespoons lemon juice
2 slices onion
1 stalk celery
5 tablespoons butter
¾ pound mushrooms, sliced
6 slices cooked ham, about ⅛ inch thick
2 tablespoons flour
1½ cups chicken stock or consommé
¾ cup heavy cream
1 egg yolk
Salt and paprika to taste

1. Soak the sweetbreads in ice water forty-five minutes. Drain and cook slowly fifteen to twenty minutes in simmering water to cover, flavored with the lemon juice, onion and celery. Drain and cool immediately in ice water. Remove all the connective and covering tissues.

2. Cut the sweetbreads into bite-sized pieces. Melt three tablespoons of the butter in a skillet, add the sweetbreads and mushrooms and cook until brown, about six minutes.

3. While the sweetbreads are sautéing, place the cooked ham slices in a preheated moderate oven (350° F.) and heat thoroughly.

4. Melt the remaining butter in a skillet, stir in the flour and blend until smooth. Gradually add the chicken stock.

5. Beat together the cream and egg yolk and add slowly to the sauce. Cook, stirring, until thickened and smooth. Add more cream or stock if the sauce becomes too thick. Season with salt and paprika.

6. Arrange the ham slices on a platter, cover with the mushrooms and sweetbreads and top with the sauce.

BROILED SWEETBREADS VIRGINIA *6 servings*

3 pairs sweetbreads
Water
1 tablespoon vinegar
Salt and freshly ground black pepper to taste
¾ cup butter, melted
1 cup fine, dry bread crumbs
6 slices cooked ham, ⅛ inch thick
6 mushroom caps
6 slices buttered toast

1. Soak the sweetbreads in ice water forty-five minutes. Meanwhile, bring to a boil enough water to cover the sweetbreads, and add the vinegar and one teaspoon salt. Drop the sweetbreads into the boiling liquid and simmer until white, fifteen to twenty minutes. Drain, cool in ice water and remove all covering and connective tissues. Preheat broiler.

2. Split the sweetbreads and season with salt and pepper. Roll in the melted butter, then in the crumbs. Sprinkle with more butter and broil about five inches from the source of heat until well browned. Broil the ham and mushrooms brushed with butter at the same time, or sauté the mushrooms in butter.

3. Place a slice of ham on each slice of toast, add the sweetbreads and top with a mushroom. Lightly brown remaining butter and pour over the top.

SWEETBREADS A LA KING *4 servings*

2 pairs sweetbreads
Water
6 tablespoons butter
12 fresh mushrooms, sliced
1 green pepper, seeded and chopped
1 canned pimento, chopped
½ cup sherry
1 cup heavy cream
2 tablespoons flour
1 cup milk
1 teaspoon salt
4 patty shells, purchased

1. Soak the sweetbreads in ice water forty-five minutes. Drain and cook slowly in simmering water to cover until white, fifteen to twenty minutes. Drain, cool in ice water and remove all covering and connective tissues. Cut into small cubes.

2. Melt half the butter in a saucepan, add the mushrooms, green pepper and pimento and cook about ten minutes. Add half the sherry and cream.

3. Simmer until the sauce is reduced by about half. Add the diced sweetbreads.

4. In a saucepan melt the remaining butter, add the flour and stir with a wire whisk until blended. Meanwhile, bring the milk to a boil and add all at once to the butter-flour mixture, stirring vigorously with the whisk. Add to the sweetbread mixture and season with salt.

5. Add the remaining cream and sherry just before pouring the mixture into the heated patty shells.

BOILED SMOKED TONGUE *About 8 servings*

1 four-pound smoked beef tongue
Water to cover
1 onion studded with 1 clove
1 clove garlic
1 stalk celery, with leaves
1 carrot, sliced
5 peppercorns
1 bay leaf

1. Cover the tongue with water, add remaining ingredients and cook, covered, until tender, three hours or longer.

2. Remove the root portion and the skin as for boiled fresh beef tongue, page 175. Serve whole or sliced, with horseradish sauce (page 450).

TONGUE IN ASPIC *About 8 servings*

1 four-pound smoked tongue
1 egg white and shell
2 envelopes unflavored gelatin
½ cup dry white wine
1 teaspoon Worcestershire sauce
Few drops of Tabasco sauce
2 teaspoons sugar (optional)
Salt to taste

1. Cook the tongue as above and cool in the broth. Remove the root portion and the skin and chill. Strain the broth, chill and remove the fat.

(cont'd)

2. Beat the egg white with a fork till frothy and crush the eggshell. Add three and one-half cups broth, bring slowly to a boil, reduce the heat and simmer ten minutes. Let cool and then strain through wet cotton flannel or several thicknesses of cheesecloth, making a clarified broth.

3. Soften the gelatin in one-half cup of the cleared, cool broth. Heat the remaining broth, add the gelatin and stir until dissolved. Add the wine, Worcestershire, Tabasco, sugar and salt. Pour a thin layer into a loaf pan and chill until firm. Chill the remaining aspic in another pan until beginning to set.

4. Cut the tongue into thin slices and arrange in alternate layers with the aspic in the loaf pan. Chill until firm. Turn out and serve surrounded with sliced stuffed olives, hard-cooked egg slices, cucumbers, tomatoes, endive, etc.

BOILED FRESH BEEF TONGUE *About 8 servings*

1 fresh beef tongue, about 4 pounds
1 onion studded with 3 cloves
1 leek, or an extra onion
1 stalk celery with leaves
4 sprigs parsley
1 bay leaf
Few whole black peppercorns
1 tablespoon salt

1. Wash the tongue and place it in a large kettle with the remaining ingredients. Add cold water to just cover. Cover tightly, bring to a boil, lower the heat and simmer until tender, about three and one-half hours.

2. Let tongue cool in its broth. When cool, remove it and cut off bones and gristle at the thick end of the tongue. Slit the skin from the thick end to the tip on the underside. Use a paring knife to loosen the skin at the thick end, and pull and peel off the skin from the thick end to the tip.

3. Return the tongue to the broth to reheat, if desired; or serve cold.

SPICED BEEF TONGUE *6 servings*

1 fresh beef tongue, about 3 pounds
1 tablespoon salt
1 small onion, sliced
Few whole black peppercorns
1 bay leaf
Water to cover
3 strips lemon peel
1 teaspoon cinnamon
2 teaspoons brown sugar
1/8 teaspoon freshly ground black pepper
2 cups dry white wine

1. Place the tongue, salt, onion, peppercorns and bay leaf in a saucepan. Cover with cold water and bring to a boil. Reduce heat, cover the pan and simmer until the tongue is fork tender, two and one-half to three hours.

2. Remove the tongue from the water and cool slightly. Trim as for boiled fresh beef tongue, above. Cut the meat into thin slices.

3. Place the tongue slices in a casserole and add the remaining ingredients. Bake, covered, in a preheated moderate oven (375° F.) until the meat absorbs nearly all the liquid, about thirty-five minutes. Serve hot or chilled.

TRIPES A LA MODE DE CAEN *8 to 10 servings*

4 pounds honeycomb tripe
4 calves' feet
Water
2 large carrots, scraped
1 onion, peeled
1 stalk celery
2 large leeks, split and washed well
Bouquet garni (10 peppercorns, 1 clove garlic, 1 teaspoon thyme, 1 bay leaf, 1 clove and 2 sprigs parsley, tied in cheesecloth bag)
Salt and freshly ground black pepper
2 large thin slices beef fat (obtained from the butcher)
Thick paste made with flour and water
½ cup aged Calvados

1. Heat oven to slow (300° F.).

2. Wash the tripe carefully in several changes of cold water. Drain and slice the tripe into pieces two inches square.

3. In two separate kettles, cover the tripe with cold water and the calves' feet with cold water. Bring each to a boil. Immediately add two cups of cold water to each kettle to stop the cooking. Drain.

4. Line a large earthenware casserole or tripe pot with the blanched calves' feet and cover with the tripe. Add the carrots, onion, celery, leeks and bouquet garni. Sprinkle with salt and pepper. Cover with cold water and top with the beef fat. The lid of the casserole or pot should have a small hole to permit escape of steam.

5. Cover the pot with the lid and prepare a thick paste with flour and water. Seal the cover with the paste. Bring to boiling point on top of stove, then place in oven. Bake twelve hours.

6. Break and discard the pastry seal. Uncover and discard the vegetables and bouquet garni. Transfer the tripe to a serving casserole and add the meat from the calves' feet, discarding the bones. Skim the fat from the liquid and season to taste with salt and pepper. Add the Calvados and strain the liquid through a double thickness of cheesecloth over the tripe. Serve piping hot with boiled potatoes on the side.

HEAD CHEESE *About 12 servings*

1 calf's or pig's head
Water
Dry white wine
1 large onion, quartered and studded with 4 cloves
6 celery tops
4 sprigs parsley
1 carrot
1 bay leaf
12 peppercorns
2 teaspoons salt
Cayenne pepper
Nutmeg
Sage

1. Have the butcher clean the head, removing the snout and reserving the tongue and brains.

2. Scrub the head well and place in a deep kettle. Cover with equal parts water and wine. Add the reserved tongue and the onion.

(cont'd)

3. Tie the celery tops, parsley, carrot, bay leaf and peppercorns in a cheesecloth bag and add. Add the salt, bring to a boil and skim the surface carefully. Reduce the heat, cover and simmer very slowly until the meat is so tender that it falls easily from the bones, about four hours. Remove the tongue from the water after it has cooked one and one-half hours. Remove the root portion and skin from the tongue.

4. After four hours' cooking, lift the head onto a large platter. Strain and reserve the liquid in the kettle. Carefully remove all the rind from the head and cut the meat and tongue into pieces the size of large walnuts.

5. Drop the brains into a little of the cooking liquid and simmer, covered, about fifteen minutes. Drain and place in a mixing bowl, together with the meat and tongue. Season lightly with cayenne, nutmeg and sage. Toss thoroughly until well mixed.

6. Pack the mixture into a loaf pan or a mold, pressing it in firmly. Pour over it one-half cup of the cooking liquid, cooled to lukewarm.

7. Cover the pan and put a weight on top to keep meats submerged in broth. Allow to cool so that the mixture will jell. Refrigerate at least forty-eight hours before using. Head cheese should be served well chilled, cut in slices.

GAME

**

HASSENPFEFFER *6 to 8 servings*

- 2 packages frozen roasting rabbit, about 4 pounds
- 1½ cups mild vinegar
- 1½ cups water
- 1 cup red Bordeaux wine
- 2 cups sliced onion
- 2 teaspoons salt
- 1 teaspoon dry mustard
- 1 teaspoon freshly ground black pepper
- 1 tablespoon mixed pickling spices
- 8 whole cloves
- 3 bay leaves
- Flour
- ⅓ cup butter
- 1 tablespoon sugar
- 1 cup sour cream

1. Partly thaw the rabbits and place them in a large bowl. Add the vinegar, water, wine, onion, salt, mustard, pepper, pickling spices, cloves and bay leaves. Refrigerate twenty-four hours or longer, turning the rabbit occasionally.

2. Remove the rabbit, dry the pieces well, dust them lightly with flour and brown in the butter in a heavy saucepan or Dutch oven.

3. Strain the marinade and add to the rabbit. Cover, bring to a boil, lower the heat and simmer until tender, about forty minutes.

4. Arrange the rabbit on a heated platter. Add the sugar to the broth and

(*cont'd*)

correct the seasonings. Blend six tablespoons flour with a little water. Stir into the broth and cook, stirring, one minute. Just before serving, stir in the sour cream. Reheat but do not let boil. Pour over the rabbit and serve with buttered noodles.

RABBIT OR HARE PATE, PAGE 9.

ROAST PHEASANT *2 servings*

1 two- to three-pound pheasant
Salt and freshly ground black pepper to taste
1 bay leaf
1 clove garlic
Few celery leaves
1 slice lemon
4 slices bacon
Melted butter
Madeira sauce (see below)

1. Preheat oven to moderate (350° F.).
2. Sprinkle the pheasant inside and out with salt and pepper. Place the bay leaf, garlic, celery leaves and lemon in the cavity. Tie the legs together with string and turn the wings under.
3. Cover the breast with bacon and a piece of cheesecloth soaked in melted butter. Place the pheasant, breast up, on a rack in a baking pan and roast until tender, about thirty minutes per pound, basting frequently with melted butter.
4. Remove the cheesecloth and string. If desired, serve the pheasant on a bed of rice accompanied by Madeira sauce.

MADEIRA SAUCE:

Remove the pheasant to a warm serving platter and add one cup consommé to the pan. Stir over moderate heat, scraping loose the browned particles. Blend two tablespoons flour with two tablespoons butter and stir into the gravy bit by bit. When the gravy is thickened and smooth, add two to three tablespoons Madeira wine and the cooked pheasant liver, finely chopped.

QUAIL WITH WINE *8 servings*

8 quail
Salt and freshly ground black pepper
1½ cups Madeira wine
½ cup raisins
3 cloves
1 cup cooked white rice
¼ teaspoon powdered ginger
1 teaspoon grated orange peel
1 tablespoon butter, melted
⅔ cup chopped pecans
½ cup butter, melted
Juice of one orange
½ cup cognac, heated

1. Preheat oven to hot (450° F.).
2. Wash and dry the quail. Sprinkle inside and out with salt and pepper.
3. In a saucepan combine the Madeira, raisins and cloves. Bring to a boil, reduce the heat and simmer five minutes. Strain the mixture, discarding the cloves and reserving the wine and raisins. *(cont'd)*

4. In a mixing bowl combine the raisins, rice, ginger, orange peel, tablespoon of melted butter and the nuts. Mix well and use the mixture to stuff the quail.

5. Place the quail on a rack in a shallow open roasting pan and brush with part of the butter. Bake five minutes. Reduce the oven temperature to slow (300° F.) and bake twenty-five minutes longer, basting frequently with a mixture of the remaining butter, the reserved Madeira and orange juice.

6. Place the quail in a chafing dish. Season the liquid in the roasting pan with salt and pepper to taste and pour over the quail. When steam rises from the chafing dish, pour the warmed cognac over the quail, ignite and serve at once.

ROAST WILD GOOSE *6 to 8 servings*

1 six- to eight-pound young wild goose
Juice of 1 lemon
Salt and freshly ground black pepper to taste
¼ cup butter
¼ cup chopped onion
1 cup chopped tart apple
1 cup chopped dried apricots
3 cups fine, soft bread crumbs
4 to 6 slices bacon
Melted bacon fat

1. Preheat oven to moderate (325° F.).

2. Sprinkle the goose inside and out with lemon juice, salt and pepper.

3. In a large saucepan, heat the butter, add the onion and cook until tender. Stir in the apple, apricots, bread crumbs, one-half teaspoon salt and one-eighth teaspoon pepper.

4. Spoon the stuffing lightly into the goose cavity. Close the opening and truss with skewers and string. Cover the breast with bacon slices and cheesecloth soaked in melted bacon fat. Place the goose, breast up, on a rack in an open roasting pan.

5. Roast until tender, two to three hours, basting frequently with bacon fat and the drippings in the pan. If the age of the goose is uncertain, pour one cup water into the pan and cover for the last hour of cooking. Remove the cheesecloth, skewers and string.

MALLARD DUCK WITH BING CHERRIES *4 servings*

2 tablespoon butter
1 four-pound mallard (or domestic duck), quartered
2 tablespoons very dry sherry
¼ teaspoon crushed garlic
¾ cup pitted Bing cherries
2 teaspoons potato flour or cornstarch
1 teaspoon tomato paste
½ bay leaf

1. In a skillet heat the butter, add the duck and brown on all sides. Drain off the fat. Pour the sherry over the duck and remove it to a platter.

2. To the pan add the garlic and cherries, reserving the juice. Boil two or three minutes. Blend the potato flour with the reserved cherry juice and tomato

(*cont'd*)

paste and add, stirring, to the cherries. Cook, stirring, until thickened. The sauce should have the consistency of heavy cream. If too thick, thin with chicken broth.

3. Return the duck to the pan, skin side down. Add the bay leaf, cover with waxed paper and skillet lid and simmer until done, forty to fifty minutes. Arrange the duck on a platter and garnish with the cherries.

ROAST GAME HENS OR SQUABS *3 servings*

- 3 one-and-one-quarter-pound Rock Cornish game hens or squabs
- ½ lemon
- Salt and freshly ground black pepper to taste
- 3 tablespoons butter
- 9 chicken livers, halved
- ½ cup chopped mushrooms
- ¼ cup ham, cut in thin strips
- ¼ cup shelled pistachio nuts
- 12 strips bacon

1. Preheat oven to moderate (350° F.). Rub the game hens or squabs with the lemon half and sprinkle inside and out with salt and pepper.

2. In a skillet heat two tablespoons of the butter, add the chicken liver halves and cook until barely done. Remove from the pan and chop fine.

3. Heat the remaining butter in the same skillet, add the mushrooms and cook briefly. Combine the livers, mushrooms, ham and pistachio nuts and stuff the game hens or squabs lightly with the mixture. Close the opening with skewers and string and tie the legs with string.

4. Place the birds, breast side up, on a rack in an open roasting pan and cover the breasts with the bacon slices. Roast, basting occasionally with the pan drippings, until tender, forty-five minutes to one hour. Serve hot or cold.

PAKISTANI PIGEONS AND PILAU *6 servings*

- ¼ cup butter
- 6 squabs or Rock Cornish game hens
- 5 cups water
- 2 pieces preserved or candied ginger root or 1 teaspoon ground ginger
- 2 cloves garlic
- 2 teaspoons coriander seeds
- 2 teaspoons fennel seeds
- 1 small onion, quartered
- ½ cup chopped onions
- 6 cloves
- ¼ teaspoon ground cardamom
- 2 tablespoons chopped candied or preserved ginger
- ¾ teaspoon cumin seeds
- ¼ teaspoon saffron
- 1½ cups raw long-grain rice
- 2 tablespoons pistachio nuts, chopped
- 1 cup sultana raisins

1. In a heavy kettle heat two tablespoons of the butter, add the squabs and brown on all sides.

2. Remove the kettle from the heat and pour five cups water over the birds. Add the ginger root, garlic, coriander, fennel and the quartered onion. Return the

(cont'd)

kettle to the heat and bring the liquid to a boil. Cover the kettle tightly, reduce the heat and simmer until the birds are tender, about thirty minutes.

3. Remove the birds from the kettle, place on a warm platter and keep hot.

4. Strain the liquid from the kettle into a saucepan and wash the kettle. Return the kettle to the heat, melt the remaining butter, add the chopped onions and cook until golden.

5. Add the cloves, cardamom, chopped ginger, cumin seeds, saffron and rice and stir until all the ingredients are thoroughly mixed. Add three cups of the strained liquid in which the birds were cooked and bring to a boil. Cover the kettle, reduce the heat to the lowest point and cook until the rice is tender, fifteen to twenty minutes. Stir in the chopped pistachio nuts and the sultana raisins.

6. Cut each squab or game hen in half and arrange on top of the rice mixture. Cover and keep hot until ready to serve.

ROAST HAUNCH OF VENISON *10 to 12 servings*

1 six-pound haunch of venison
1 bottle claret or Burgundy
1 large onion, sliced
1 clove garlic, crushed
1 bay leaf
3 juniper berries
6 strips fat bacon

1. If the lower part of the leg is used, remove the shank bone from the venison. Place the meat in a large bowl and marinate overnight in the wine with the onion, garlic, bay leaf and juniper berries.

2. Preheat oven to hot (450° F.).

3. Remove the meat from the marinade and skewer and tie it into a compact shape. Strain and reserve the marinade. Insert a thermometer in the thickest portion of muscle and place the meat on a rack in an open roasting pan. Place the bacon strips on top of the meat.

4. Roast the meat twenty minutes. Reduce the oven temperature to moderate (325° F.) and cook fifteen to eighteen minutes per pound to an internal temperature of 140° for very rare; 150° for medium well done. While the meat is roasting, baste occasionally with the marinade. Serve with boiled puréed chestnuts (page 375).

VENISON GOULASH *6 servings*

2 pounds venison (any cut) cut into 1½-inch cubes
3 tablespoons flour
3 tablespoons bacon fat
1 large onion, sliced or chopped fine
2 cloves garlic, chopped
1 tablespoon Hungarian paprika
½ cup red wine
1 quart boiling water or stock
Salt to taste
1 small can tomato paste
1 cup sour cream (optional)

(*cont'd*)

1. Roll the meat in the flour, pressing the flour into the cubes.

2. Melt the fat in a skillet, add the onion and garlic and cook until browned. Add the meat and brown well. Add all the remaining ingredients except the sour cream. Stir well, cover and simmer gently until the meat is tender, two to three hours, adding more stock, water or wine if necessary.

3. Just before serving, stir in the sour cream. Serve with red cabbage cooked with apples, and buttered noodles, or boiled new potatoes covered with sour cream.

VENISON STEAK ST. HUBERT *4 servings*

4 venison round steaks, 8 to 9 ounces each, cut ½ to ¾ inch thick
2 shallots, chopped
2 carrots, sliced
2 onions, sliced
1 clove garlic, chopped
⅛ teaspoon thyme
2 bay leaves
⅓ teaspoon freshly ground pepper
Small pinch of ground cloves
2 cups dry white wine
1 cup mild vinegar (¾ cup cider vinegar of 5 per cent acidity mixed with ¼ cup water)
½ cup olive oil
Sauce poivrade (page 452).

1. Place the steaks in an enamel, glass or earthenware bowl. Add the remaining ingredients and let stand in the refrigerator twenty-four hours. Turn the meat several times. Remove the steaks and dry.

2. Reserve one cup of the strained marinade. Cook marinade over high heat until reduced by half and use this liquid in lieu of the vinegar called for in the sauce poivrade recipe.

3. Sauté the steaks in shallow, hot fat until brown on both sides. The steaks should be rare. Serve on a hot platter with sauce poivrade.

VARIATION:

Sirloin Steak St. Hubert: Four sirloin steaks about seven ounces each and cut one-half to three-quarters inch thick may be substituted for the venison in the above recipe.

CHAPTER FOUR

POULTRY

CHICKEN

ROAST CHICKEN *4 servings*

1 four-pound roasting chicken, at room temperature
½ lemon
Salt and freshly ground black pepper
1 small onion, peeled
Herbs, such as a half teaspoon of thyme or rosemary, a bay leaf, a sprig of tarragon or parsley
½ cup butter, melted

1. Preheat oven to moderate (350° F.).

2. Rub the inside of the chicken with half a lemon and sprinkle with salt and pepper. Add a small onion to the cavity and the herbs, if desired, or stuff with basic bread crumb stuffing, page 222. Truss the chicken and place it in a roasting pan in the oven.

3. Bake eighteen to twenty minutes per pound, or about one hour and fifteen minutes for a four-pound bird. Baste the chicken as it roasts with the melted butter. Test for doneness by moving the leg of the chicken up and down. If it moves easily, the chicken is done.

TO BONE CHICKEN BREASTS

Boneless chicken breasts are the basis for many of the world's most elegant dishes. Boning them is no great chore and almost any butcher is willing to perform the task. It is easily done in the home, however, and here is how to go about it.

Buy one whole chicken breast split in two for each two people to be served. Place the halved chicken breasts on a flat surface and, using the fingers, pull off the skin of the chicken. It has a tenuous attachment to the flesh and comes off with a minimum of effort.

(cont'd)

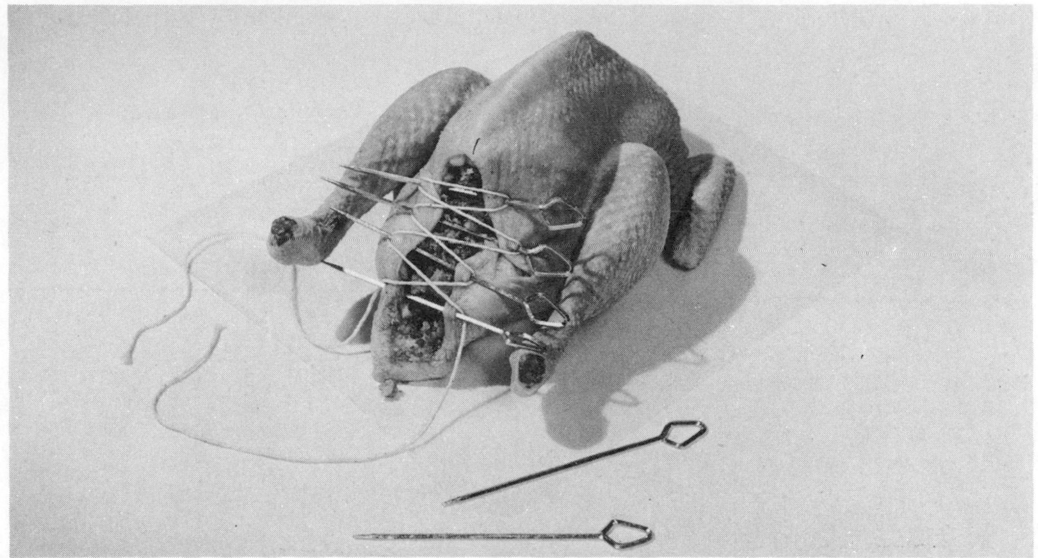

Before a stuffed chicken is roasted, truss it with string and skewers as shown here.

Using a paring knife, make a small incision between the meat and the breastbones at a point away from the main wing portion. Using the fingers and the knife, carefully pull and scrape the meat away from the bones, taking care not to tear the meat. If the breasts are to be boned "French style" the butcher must be instructed to leave the main wing bones attached to the breasts.

CHICKEN A LA KIEV *6 servings*

Chicken à la Kiev is a dish created during the Czarist days in Russia. It is, in effect, rolled boneless breast of chicken stuffed with butter and chives. When a knife slices into it, the butter should spurt forth. This is a dish still found on menus in Moscow.

3 whole breasts of chicken with or without main wing bones attached, boned and halved
½ cup chilled, firm butter
Salt and freshly ground black pepper
2 tablespoons chopped chives
Flour for dredging
2 eggs, lightly beaten
1 cup fresh bread crumbs
Fat for deep frying

1. Place the chicken breasts between pieces of waxed paper and pound until thin with a mallet or the flat side of a butcher knife. Do not split the flesh. Remove the waxed paper.

2. Cut the butter into six finger-shaped pieces. Place a piece in the middle of each breast, sprinkle with salt, pepper and chives and roll up, envelope fashion,

(*cont'd*)

letting the wing bone protrude and making the sides overlap. The flesh will adhere without skewers.

3. Dredge each roll lightly with flour, dip into the beaten eggs and roll in bread crumbs. Refrigerate one hour or more so the crumbs will adhere.

4. Fill a fryer or kettle with enough fat to completely cover the breasts. Heat until hot (360° F.). Add chicken gradually and brown on all sides. Drain on absorbent paper and place a paper frill on the main wing bones before serving.

CHICKEN BREASTS ALL' ALBA *4 servings*

This is one of the most incredible of dishes when made with white Italian truffles and topped with Fontina cheese. These ingredients are available wherever fine Italian delicacies are sold.

2 whole chicken breasts, boned and halved
Flour for dredging
2 tablespoons butter
Salt and freshly ground black pepper
Slices of white or black truffles, or 4 sliced mushrooms sautéed in a little butter
4 slices Fontina or mozzarella cheese

1. Remove and discard skin from chicken breasts. Place the chicken breasts between pieces of waxed paper and pound until thin.

2. Dredge the chicken with flour. In a skillet heat the butter, add the chicken and cook until tender, five to six minutes on each side. Remove to a shallow pan and sprinkle with salt and pepper. Arrange on each breast half a dozen small slices of truffles or mushrooms and cover with a slice of cheese.

3. Place the chicken breasts under a hot broiler just long enough to melt the cheese. Serve at once.

VIENNESE CHICKEN BREASTS *6 servings*

This is a variation of a continental dish known as escalopes de veau Viennoise, or veal scallops Vienna-style. Breaded boneless breast of chicken is garnished with lemon slices and anchovies.

3 whole chicken breasts, boned and halved
Salt and freshly ground black pepper
Flour for dredging
2 eggs, beaten
1 cup fine fresh bread crumbs
½ cup butter
6 lemon slices
6 anchovy fillets, stuffed with capers
Chopped parsley

1. Remove skin from chicken breasts. Place the chicken breasts between slices of waxed paper and pound until thin.

2. Sprinkle both sides with salt and pepper, dredge with flour and dip in the beaten eggs. Coat with the bread crumbs and tap lightly with the flat edge

(cont'd)

of a knife to make the crumbs stick. Refrigerate one hour or more so crumbs will adhere.

3. In a skillet heat the butter, add the chicken and cook until brown on both sides. Garnish with the lemon slices, anchovy fillets and parsley. Serve with plain boiled potatoes.

BREAST OF CHICKEN FLORENTINE *8 servings*

As will be noted many times throughout this book, Florentine means spinach. This is breast of chicken on a bed of spinach. The dish is also called Gismonda.

Flour for dredging
Salt and freshly ground black pepper to taste
4 whole chicken breasts, boned and halved
1 egg
1 tablespoon water
¼ cup grated Parmesan cheese
½ cup dry bread crumbs
¾ cup butter
2 pounds spinach, cooked and drained
1 tablespoon lemon juice
1 pound mushrooms, sliced
Chopped parsley

1. Remove skin from chicken breasts. Mix the flour, salt and pepper and dredge the chicken breasts with the seasoned flour. Dip them in the egg lightly beaten with the water and then coat with a mixture of the cheese and crumbs. Refrigerate one hour or more.

2. In a large skillet heat one-half cup of the butter, add the chicken and brown on both sides. Lower heat, cover and cook until tender, about twenty-five minutes.

3. Meanwhile, chop the spinach coarsely and season with the lemon juice. Pile the spinach on a platter, arrange the chicken breasts on top and keep hot.

4. To the skillet add two tablespoons of the remaining butter and the mushrooms and sauté until the mushrooms are tender. Spoon over the chicken.

5. Brown the remaining butter in the same pan and pour through a fine sieve over the dish. Sprinkle with chopped parsley.

BREAST OF CHICKEN EN PAPILLOTE *6 servings*

En papillote means roughly "baked in a bag." This is breast of chicken baked in aluminum foil.

3 chicken breasts, halved
Chicken broth or lightly salted water
¼ cup butter
2 tablespoons flour
½ cup milk
½ cup dry white Bordeaux wine
1 egg yolk, beaten
Salt and freshly ground black pepper to taste
Pinch of cayenne pepper
Pinch of mace or nutmeg
Pinch of ground cloves
¼ cup finely chopped mushrooms
1 teaspoon chopped chives

(cont'd)

1. Place the chicken breasts in a small kettle and add chicken broth barely to cover. Bring to a boil, reduce the heat, cover and simmer gently until the meat is tender, twenty-five to forty minutes, depending on the size of the breasts. Remove the chicken from the broth and cool. Carefully remove skin and the meat from the bones.

2. Preheat oven to hot (400° F.).

3. Cut six pieces of aluminum foil large enough to make an envelope for each breast half and spread the foil with half the butter.

4. In a saucepan melt the remaining butter, add the flour and stir with a wire whisk until blended. Meanwhile, bring the milk, wine and one-half cup of the chicken broth to a boil and add all at once to the butter-flour mixture, stirring vigorously with the whisk until the sauce is thickened and smooth. Add the egg yolk lightly beaten with a little of the hot sauce, stirring gently until thickened. Do not let boil. Add the seasonings and stir in the mushrooms and chives.

5. Place half a chicken breast in the center of each square of aluminum foil and spoon some sauce over the top. Fold the edges of the foil and seal tightly by crimping the edges. Arrange on baking sheet and bake ten minutes. Serve wrapped in the foil.

CHICKEN BREASTS WITH TARRAGON *6 servings*

White wine, heavy cream and the delicate herb known as tarragon are three of the foundations for classic French cuisine.

- 3 whole chicken breasts, boned and halved
- Salt and freshly ground pepper
- ¼ cup flour
- ¼ cup butter
- 1 tablespoon chopped shallots or onion
- ¼ cup dry white Bordeaux wine
- 1 teaspoon freshly chopped tarragon, or ½ teaspoon dried tarragon
- ¼ cup chicken broth
- ¼ cup heavy cream

1. Skin the chicken breasts. Sprinkle with salt and pepper and dredge with the flour. Reserve the remaining flour.

2. In a large skillet heat three tablespoons of the butter, add the chicken and brown on both sides. Transfer to a heated platter. Add the shallots to the skillet and sauté briefly. Add the wine.

3. Cook the liquid over high heat until it is nearly evaporated, while scraping loose all the brown particles.

4. Add the reserved flour and stir to make a thick paste. Sprinkle with the tarragon and stir in the chicken broth.

5. Return the chicken to the skillet, cover and cook until tender, about twenty-five minutes. Transfer the chicken to a heated platter and keep hot. Add the remaining butter and the cream to the skillet; heat, stirring, and pour the sauce over the chicken.

CANNELLONI ALLA NERONE, PAGE 330.

EGYPTIAN KEBABS *4 servings*

2 whole chicken breasts
1 tablespoon yoghurt
¼ teaspoon salt
¼ teaspoon turmeric
⅛ teaspoon dry mustard
½ teaspoon curry powder
⅛ teaspoon ground cardamom
1 teaspoon lemon juice
1 teaspoon vinegar
8 thin slices onion
4 small tomatoes, halved

1. Skin and bone the chicken breasts and cut each into sixteen squares. Combine with the yoghurt, salt, turmeric, mustard, curry powder, cardamom, lemon juice and vinegar and let stand one-half hour.
2. Thread on skewers two chicken pieces, one slice of onion, two chicken pieces, one-half tomato. Repeat until all the ingredients are used.
3. Broil slowly, turning occasionally, over hot coals or in a kitchen broiler until the chicken is tender, about ten minutes.
4. Transfer to a hot platter, sprinkle with lemon juice and garnish with fresh tomatoes, green pepper rings and fresh mint or parsley.

CHICKEN WITH GINGER *6 servings*

½ cup butter
3 whole chicken breasts, halved
Salt and freshly ground black pepper to taste
1 clove garlic, finely minced
1 cup chicken broth
¼ cup ginger syrup
2 slices preserved ginger, chopped
Juice of ½ lemon
1 tablespoon cornstarch
3 tablespoons cold water
2 tablespoons chopped parsley

1. Heat the butter in a large skillet and brown the chicken in it on all sides. Sprinkle with the salt and pepper.
2. Add the garlic to the skillet and cook until golden. Stir in the chicken broth, cover and cook until the chicken is tender, about thirty minutes.
3. Remove the chicken to a warm serving platter. To the juices in the pan add the ginger syrup, chopped ginger and lemon juice. Simmer one minute.
4. Stir in the cornstarch mixed with the cold water and cook, stirring, until the sauce is thickened. Add the parsley and return the chicken to the skillet. Cook five minutes.
5. Arrange the chicken on a platter and spoon the sauce over it. Serve with cooked rice.

INDIAN CHICKEN *10 or more servings*

⅓ cup butter
8 small chicken breasts, skinned, boned and quartered
1 cup chopped onion
1 clove garlic, chopped
2 teaspoons salt
1 tablespoon powdered ginger
¼ teaspoon chili powder
½ cup drained canned tomatoes
1 cup clear chicken broth or yoghurt
½ cup ground cashew nuts
½ cup flaked coconut
2 tablespoons cornstarch
1 cup heavy cream

1. In a three-and-one-half-quart Dutch oven or deep skillet melt half the butter. Brown the chicken about eight pieces at a time, adding the remaining butter as necessary. Remove the chicken.
2. To the pan add the onion and garlic and cook five minutes. Return the chicken to the pan.
3. Add the salt, ginger, chili, tomatoes and broth. Mix lightly, cover and cook fifteen minutes.
4. Add the nuts and coconut, cover and cook over low heat until the chicken is tender, about ten minutes longer.
5. To the cornstarch slowly add the cream, then stir into the cooking liquid. Stir constantly until the sauce returns to a boil. Simmer over low heat another five minutes. If desired, cool and refrigerate. Near serving time, bring up to room temperature. Reheat over very low heat. Serve with noodles.

CHICKEN CURRY JAIPUR *6 servings*

1 four-pound stewing chicken, cut up
3 cups hot water
2½ teaspoons salt
3 peppercorns
1 onion, studded with four cloves
1 small carrot
2 tablespoons butter
⅔ cup minced onion
3 tablespoons curry powder
1 cup coconut milk (page 139)
⅛ teaspoon freshly ground black pepper
3 tablespoons chopped preserved or crystallized ginger
¼ teaspoon ground cloves
1 teaspoon chopped fresh mint, or ½ teaspoon crushed dried mint
¼ cup lime juice
½ cup heavy cream

1. Place the chicken in a deep kettle or Dutch oven with the water, two teaspoons of the salt, the peppercorns, onion and carrot. Cover and simmer one hour.
2. Remove the chicken from the broth and cool. Reserve broth. Cut the chicken into small pieces, removing the skin and bones.
3. Melt the butter in a large skillet. Add the onion and sauté until tender, but not brown. Stir in the curry powder.
4. Gradually stir in the coconut milk and one cup of the strained chicken

(cont'd)

broth. Add the pepper, remaining salt, ginger, cloves and mint. Cover and cook over low heat thirty minutes.

5. Add the chicken pieces and continue cooking until the chicken is tender, about thirty minutes longer. Just before serving, stir in the lime juice and then the cream.

6. Serve on hot rice with chutney and other condiments.

CHICKEN AND SPAGHETTI CASSEROLE, PAGE 336.

CURRIED CHICKEN *6 servings*

½ cup butter
1 medium onion, chopped
1 clove garlic, chopped
1 stalk celery, diced
½ bay leaf
Sprig of parsley
¼ teaspoon dry mustard
1 tart apple, peeled and diced
¼ pound raw ham, chopped
2 tablespoons flour
½ teaspoon mace
1¼ teaspoons or more curry powder
2½ cups chicken broth
3 cups cubed, boned raw chicken

1. In a large kettle heat the butter, add the onion, garlic, celery, bay leaf, parsley, mustard, apple and ham and cook eight minutes, stirring occasionally. Stir in the flour, mace and curry powder and cook four minutes longer.

2. Add the broth and simmer, covered, one hour. Rub the mixture through a sieve and return to the saucepan. Add the chicken and simmer until tender, about ten minutes longer. Serve hot with boiled rice.

MEXICAN CHICKEN *6 or more servings*

½ cup butter
2 frying chickens, cut into pieces
Water to cover
2 cloves garlic, minced
Salt to taste
4 medium onions, chopped
4 green peppers, seeded and chopped
¼ cup flour
1 quart stewed tomatoes, undrained
2 cups pitted ripe olives
2 cups whole-kernel corn, frozen, canned or cut from the cob
6 slices bacon

1. In a skillet heat the butter, add the chicken and brown on all sides. Remove the chicken to a kettle and cover with water. Add the garlic and salt, bring to a boil, reduce the heat and simmer, covered, until the chicken is tender, about one-half hour. Remove the meat from the bones and discard the bones. Reserve two cups of the broth.

2. To the skillet add the onions and green peppers and cook until the vegetables are wilted. With a wire whisk stir in the flour, add the chicken broth, tomatoes and olives and cook, stirring, until thickened and smooth.

3. Preheat the oven to hot (400° F.).

(cont'd)

4. Place a layer of corn in a buttered baking dish, add a layer of chicken and a layer of the tomato mixture. Repeat the process until all the ingredients are used, ending with a layer of corn.

5. Place slices of bacon on the top and bake until the bacon is crisp, about twenty minutes.

CHICKEN TAMALE PIE *4 to 6 servings*

1 three-pound frying chicken, cut in serving pieces
Water to cover
2 teaspoons salt
12 peppercorns
2 stalks celery with leaves
½ bay leaf
½ cup yellow cornmeal
2 tablespoons butter
¼ cup chopped onion
1 clove garlic, finely chopped
2 ripe tomatoes, peeled and chopped
¼ teaspoon dried orégano
¼ teaspoon dried thyme
¼ teaspoon dried tarragon
Chili powder to taste
1½ cups whole-kernel corn, fresh, frozen or canned
Grated Parmesan or Cheddar cheese

1. In a deep kettle, combine the chicken, water to cover, salt, peppercorns, celery and bay leaf. Bring to a boil, lower the heat and simmer gently, skimming as necessary, until the chicken is tender, about thirty to forty-five minutes. Let the chicken cool in the broth. Remove the meat from the bones and reserve. Strain broth.

2. In a saucepan bring one and one-half cups of the broth to a boil. Combine the cornmeal with one-half cup of the remaining broth, stir into the boiling broth, cover and cook until the mixture thickens, ten to fifteen minutes.

3. Preheat oven to moderate (350° F.). Cool the mush slightly and use to line the bottom and sides of a two-and-one-half-quart casserole.

4. Meanwhile, melt the butter and cook the onion and garlic in it until the onion is transparent. Add the tomatoes and seasonings and simmer fifteen minutes. Add the corn and salt to taste.

5. Spread the chicken over the center of the mush-lined casserole and cover with the tomato-and-corn mixture. Sprinkle with cheese and bake thirty minutes.

HERBED BAKED CHICKEN *4 to 6 servings*

2 plump broiling chickens, quartered
Flour for dredging
Salt and pepper to taste
4 teaspoons chopped fresh or dried tarragon
4 teaspoons chopped parsley
4 teaspoons chopped chives
½ lemon
½ cup butter
¼ cup lemon juice
½ cup dry sherry
Thin slices of toast

1. Preheat oven to slow (250° F.). Remove the necks and backbones from the chicken parts and reserve for another use. *(cont'd)*

2. In a paper bag combine the flour, salt, pepper and two teaspoons each of the tarragon, parsley and chives. Add a few chicken parts at a time and shake to coat well with the seasoned flour. Place the chicken, skin side down, in a shallow buttered baking dish. Sprinkle with the juice from the lemon half and cover with aluminum foil.

3. In a saucepan combine the butter, lemon juice, sherry and the remaining herbs. Heat until the butter melts.

4. Bake the chickens one to one and one-half hours, lifting the foil and basting every twenty minutes with the butter sauce. Toward the end of the cooking time, increase the oven temperature to hot (400° F.), remove the foil, and turn the chicken to let it brown lightly. If necessary add a little more wine or water to the pan so that there will be ample sauce.

5. Sprinkle the chicken with additional freshly chopped herbs and serve on thin slices of toast, accompanied by the pan juices.

CHICKEN BAKED IN CREAM *6 servings*

6 tablespoons butter or bacon fat
2 two-and-one-half-pound frying chickens, cut into serving pieces
3 cups light cream
⅔ cup sherry
Salt and freshly ground black pepper to taste

1. Preheat oven to moderate (350° F.).

2. In a skillet heat the butter, add the chicken and brown on all sides.

3. Arrange the chicken in a casserole and add the remaining ingredients. Cover tightly.

4. Bake until the chicken is tender, about forty minutes. The cream will be reduced to a rich clotted sauce, needing no further thickening. Serve with rice mixed with peas.

CHICKEN BAKED IN SOUR CREAM *4 servings*

1 two-and-one-half-pound frying chicken, cut into serving pieces
Flour for dredging
Salt and freshly ground black pepper to taste
¼ cup butter
½ cup sliced mushrooms
1 cup sour cream
1 cup water
¼ teaspoon thyme

1. Preheat oven to moderate (325° F.).

2. Dredge the chicken pieces with seasoned flour. In a large skillet heat the butter and brown the chicken on all sides. Transfer to a casserole.

3. Add the mushrooms and sour cream diluted with the water. Sprinkle with thyme and cover closely. Bake until the chicken is tender, about one hour. Serve with fluffy rice or boiled potatoes.

ARROZ CON POLLO *6 to 8 servings*

Arroz con pollo is chicken with rice.

- 1 four-pound frying chicken, cut into serving pieces
- 1¼ teaspoons salt
- ½ teaspoon pepper
- ⅛ teaspoon paprika
- ¼ cup olive oil
- 1 clove garlic, minced
- 1 medium onion, chopped
- 2 cups water
- 3½ cups canned whole tomatoes
- 2 chicken bouillon cubes
- ¼ teaspoon powdered saffron
- 1 bay leaf
- ½ teaspoon orégano
- 2 cups raw rice
- 1 package frozen peas or artichoke hearts, defrosted
- 3 pimentos, cut in pieces

1. Preheat oven to moderate (350° F.).

2. Season the chicken with one teaspoon of the salt, the pepper and paprika. In a skillet heat the oil, add the chicken and brown on all sides. Remove to a baking dish.

3. To the skillet add the garlic and onion and sauté until the onion is tender. Add the water and heat while scraping loose the brown particles. Add the tomatoes and their liquid, bouillon cubes, seasonings and remaining salt. Bring to a boil and pour over the chicken. Add the rice and stir. Cover tightly.

4. Bake twenty-five minutes. Uncover and toss the rice. Stir in the peas, arrange the pimentos on top, cover and cook ten minutes longer.

ISLANDER CHICKEN *6 servings*

Here is another dish flavored with cumin. Cumin is a principal ingredient in chili powder and smells like it. It is a spice that is becoming increasingly popular in America.

- ⅓ cup olive oil
- 1 three-pound frying chicken, cut into pieces
- ¾ cup diced raw ham
- 1 cup sliced onions
- 2 cloves garlic, minced
- 3 medium tomatoes, peeled and chopped
- 2½ cups water
- 2½ cups raw rice
- ¾ cup chopped green pepper
- 1 small bay leaf
- 2½ teaspoons salt
- ½ teaspoon cumin seed
- ⅛ teaspoon saffron

1. Heat the olive oil in a Dutch oven, add the chicken, ham, onions and garlic and brown the chicken on all sides.

2. Add the tomatoes, cover and simmer twenty minutes.

3. Add the remaining ingredients and bring to a boil. Lower the heat, cover and simmer slowly until the rice is tender, about twenty minutes. Add more liquid if necessary.

4. Remove the chicken. Heap the rice mixture in the center of a large platter and surround with the chicken. Garnish with strips of pimento, if desired.

CHICKEN WITH ALMONDS *4 servings*

- ¼ cup butter
- 1 frying chicken, 2½ to 3 pounds, cut into serving pieces
- 1 clove garlic, chopped
- 2 tablespoons chopped onion
- 1 tablespoon tomato paste
- 2 tablespoons flour
- 1½ cups chicken stock
- 2 tablespoons sherry
- 2 tablespoons slivered almonds
- Salt and freshly ground black pepper to taste
- 1 teaspoon dried tarragon
- ¾ cup sour cream
- 1 tablespoon grated Parmesan cheese

1. In a skillet heat the butter, add the chicken and brown on all sides. Remove the chicken and keep hot. To the pan add the garlic and onion and cook over low heat three minutes. Add the tomato paste and flour and stir with a wire whisk until the mixture is smooth.

2. Stir in the stock and sherry. When the mixture returns to a boil return the chicken to the pan and add the almonds, salt, pepper and tarragon. Cover and simmer slowly forty-five to fifty minutes.

3. Transfer the chicken to a shallow casserole. Stir the sour cream into the sauce remaining in the pan and heat thoroughly. Do not boil. Pour the sauce over the chicken and sprinkle with the cheese. Brown lightly under a preheated broiler.

CHICKEN IN PARMESAN CREAM SAUCE *4 to 6 servings*

One of the simplest and most flavorful of cheeses is that from the region around Parma. Known as Parmesan, it should be freshly grated when possible—either by hand or in an electric blender.

- 1 three-pound frying chicken, cut into serving pieces
- Salt and freshly ground black pepper to taste
- 5 tablespoons butter
- 2 tablespoons flour
- ¾ cup light cream
- ½ cup freshly grated Parmesan cheese
- 3 egg yolks, beaten
- ½ cup fresh bread crumbs

1. Season the chicken with salt and pepper. In a skillet heat half the butter, add the chicken pieces, skin side down, and cook until browned. Turn the pieces, partly cover the skillet and cook until the chicken is tender, about thirty minutes.

2. Preheat oven to moderate (350° F.).

3. In a saucepan, melt the remaining butter, add the flour and stir with a wire whisk until blended. Bring the cream to a boil and add all at once to the butter-flour mixture, stirring vigorously with the whisk until the sauce is thickened and smooth. Stir in one tablespoon of the cheese. When it has melted, stir in the egg yolks lightly beaten with a little of the hot sauce.

4. Sprinkle the bottom of a flat casserole with one-quarter cup of the cheese, arrange the chicken on the cheese and spoon the sauce over the top. Place the casserole in the oven and bake five minutes or until thoroughly heated. *(cont'd)*

5. Combine the remaining cheese with the bread crumbs, sprinkle over the chicken and broil until golden brown.

COQ AU VIN *6 servings*

Chicken with wine is coq au vin. The classic vin for coq au vin is Chambertin but any good dry red wine will do.

1 five-pound roasting chicken, cut into serving pieces
Flour for dredging
½ cup butter
1 slice raw ham, chopped
10 small white onions, peeled and left whole
1 clove garlic, finely chopped
¼ teaspoon thyme
1 sprig parsley
1 bay leaf
8 whole mushrooms
Salt and freshly ground black pepper to taste
2 ounces (¼ cup) warmed cognac
1 cup dry red wine

1. Preheat oven to slow (300° F.).
2. Dredge the chicken with flour. In a skillet heat the butter, add the chicken and brown on all sides. Transfer the chicken to an earthenware casserole and add the ham, onions, garlic, thyme, parsley, bay leaf, mushrooms, salt and pepper.
3. Pour the cognac over the chicken and ignite. When the flame dies, add the wine.
4. Cover and bake until the chicken is tender, about two and one-half hours.

CHICKEN BORDEAUX *6 to 8 servings*

This is a favorite recipe of Mme. Fernande Garvin of the Bordeaux Wine Information Bureau.

2 three-pound broiler-fryers, quartered
¾ cup flour
1 teaspoon salt
Freshly ground black pepper to taste
½ cup salad oil
1 cup canned tomatoes
1½ cups dry white Bordeaux wine
1 cup sliced mushrooms, cooked in a little butter until wilted
1 clove garlic, finely chopped and cooked briefly in a little butter (optional)

1. Dredge the chicken with one-half cup of the flour, seasoned with the salt and pepper.
2. In a heavy skillet heat the oil, add the chicken and brown on all sides. Cover the pan and cook slowly twenty-five minutes. Pour the oil from the skillet and add the tomatoes with their juice. Bring to a boil.
3. Combine the remaining flour with a little water and stir into the simmering tomatoes. Cook, stirring, until the mixture thickens.
4. Add the wine, mushrooms and garlic, cover and cook until the chicken is tender, about twenty minutes longer. Serve hot.

COUNTRY CAPTAIN *4 servings*

Country Captain sounds as though it originated in the southern United States. It is, according to authoritative sources, a dish from India, and the word "captain" is a corruption of "capon." This is a recipe from Cecily Brownstone, food editor of the Associated Press.

- 1 two-and-one-half-pound frying chicken, cut into serving pieces
- ¼ cup flour
- 1 teaspoon salt
- ¼ teaspoon freshly ground black pepper
- 4 to 5 tablespoons butter
- ⅓ cup finely diced onion
- ⅓ cup finely diced green pepper
- 1 clove garlic, crushed
- 1½ teaspoons curry powder
- ½ teaspoon thyme
- 2 cups canned stewed tomatoes
- 3 tablespoons dried currants, washed and drained
- Blanched toasted almonds
- Chutney

1. Dredge the chicken pieces in the flour seasoned with the salt and pepper.

2. Heat four tablespoons of butter in a large skillet and brown the chicken parts on all sides. If necessary, add more butter. Remove the chicken from the skillet and add the onion, green pepper, garlic, curry powder and thyme. Cook briefly, stirring, until the onion wilts. Add the tomatoes with the liquid from the can. Return the chicken to the skillet, skin side up. Cover the skillet and cook until tender, twenty to thirty minutes. Stir the currants into the sauce.

3. Serve with blanched toasted almonds and chutney.

PORTUGUESE CHICKEN *4 servings*

- 3 tablespoons or more butter
- 1 two-pound frying chicken, cut into pieces
- 1 tablespoon chopped onion
- 1 tablespoon flour
- 1 clove garlic, finely chopped
- ¼ cup dry white wine or water
- ½ cup chicken broth
- ½ cup canned tomatoes, drained
- Salt and freshly ground black pepper to taste
- 2 fresh tomatoes, peeled and chopped
- Chopped parsley

1. In a large skillet heat the butter, add the chicken and brown on all sides. Remove chicken and keep hot.

2. Add the onion to the skillet and cook slowly, stirring occasionally, three to four minutes. Add the flour and garlic and, stirring with a wire whisk, add the wine and broth and cook until the mixture is thickened and smooth.

3. Add the canned tomatoes, salt and pepper. Return the chicken to the skillet, cover and simmer until tender, about thirty minutes.

4. Remove the chicken from the skillet to a warm serving platter and keep hot. Add the fresh tomatoes to the skillet and simmer fifteen minutes. Pour the sauce over the chicken and serve sprinkled with chopped parsley.

LIME-BROILED CHICKEN *6 servings*

3 broiler-fryer chickens, quartered
3 teaspoons monosodium glutamate
Salt and pepper
Lime barbecue sauce (see below)

1. Preheat broiler to moderate.
2. Sprinkle each piece of chicken with monosodium glutamate, salt and pepper. Place skin side up on rack six inches from broiler heat. Brush with sauce.
3. Cook slowly until tender, turning and basting occasionally, one to one and one-quarter hours.

LIME BARBECUE SAUCE:

½ cup corn oil
½ cup lime juice
2 tablespoons chopped onion
2 teaspoons dried tarragon
1 teaspoon salt
½ teaspoon Tabasco

Combine all ingredients. Brush on chicken. For a richer herb flavor, marinate chicken in sauce several hours.

BRUNSWICK STEW *4 to 6 servings*

1 broiling chicken, cut into serving pieces
3 teaspoons salt
Paprika to taste
¼ cup butter
2 medium onions, sliced
1 medium green pepper, diced
3 cups water
2 cups canned tomatoes, undrained
2 tablespoons chopped parsley
½ teaspoon Tabasco sauce
1 tablespoon Worcestershire sauce
2 cups whole-kernel corn
1 package frozen lima beans, defrosted
3 tablespoons flour

1. Sprinkle the chicken with one teaspoon of the salt and paprika.
2. In a deep kettle heat the butter and brown the chicken on all sides. Add the onions and green pepper and cook until the onion is transparent.
3. Add the water, the tomatoes with their liquid, the parsley, remaining salt, the Tabasco and Worcestershire and bring to a boil. Cover, reduce the heat and simmer for thirty minutes.
4. Add the corn and lima beans and cook twenty minutes longer.
5. Blend the flour with a little cold water and gradually stir into the stew. Cook, stirring, ten minutes longer.
6. Serve in flat soup plates.

CHICKEN SAUTE CHASSEUR *4 servings*

1 two-and-one-half- to three-pound frying chicken, cut into pieces
Flour for dredging
Salt and freshly ground black pepper
Dried thyme
¼ cup butter
¼ cup chopped shallots or onions
¼ pound mushrooms, chopped
½ cup white wine
¾ cup canned tomatoes
2 tablespoons chopped parsley
¼ teaspoon tarragon or chervil

(*cont'd*)

1. Dredge the chicken in the flour seasoned with the salt, pepper and thyme. In a large skillet heat the butter, add the chicken and brown on all sides.

2. Add the shallots, mushrooms, wine, tomatoes and herbs. Cover and cook slowly until the chicken is tender, thirty to forty-five minutes.

POULET MARENGO *6 servings*

Poulet Marengo, like chicken chasseur, contains tomatoes and mushrooms. This dish, according to Larousse Gastronomique, *was created by Napoleon's chef after the battle of Marengo. The original creation was garnished with crawfish and fried eggs.*

½ cup flour
1 teaspoon salt
½ teaspoon freshly ground black pepper
1 teaspoon dried tarragon
1 three-pound roasting chicken, cut into pieces
¼ cup olive oil
¼ cup butter
1 cup dry white wine
2 cups canned tomatoes
1 clove garlic, finely chopped
8 mushrooms, sliced
Chopped parsley

1. Preheat oven to moderate (350° F.).

2. Mix the flour, salt, pepper and tarragon and dredge the chicken with the seasoned flour. Reserve the remaining flour.

3. In a large skillet heat the olive oil and butter, add the chicken and brown on all sides.

4. Remove the chicken to a heavy casserole. Add the reserved flour to the fat remaining in the skillet and, using a wire whisk, gradually stir in the wine. When the sauce is thickened and smooth, pour over the chicken and add the tomatoes, garlic and mushrooms. Cover the casserole with a heavy lid and bake until the chicken is tender, about forty-five minutes. Before serving, sprinkle with chopped parsley.

CHICKEN VALLE D'AUGE *4 servings*

6 tablespoons butter
2 broiling chickens, quartered
¼ cup warmed Calvados (or other apple brandy)
2 small white onions, minced
1 tablespoon minced parsley
Pinch of dried thyme
Salt and freshly ground black pepper to taste
6 tablespoons cider
6 tablespoons heavy cream

1. In a large skillet heat the butter, add the chicken and brown on all sides. Continue cooking, uncovered, twenty minutes. Add the Calvados and ignite. When the flame has subsided, add the onions, parsley, thyme, salt, pepper and cider. Cover tightly and cook over low heat until the chicken is tender, about twenty minutes.

(cont'd)

2. Remove the chicken to a warm platter and keep hot. Slowly stir the cream into the pan and heat thoroughly. Do not boil. Correct the seasonings. Pour some of the sauce over the chicken and serve the remainder separately.

CHICKEN DIVAN *6 servings*

This dish is said to have originated many years ago in a New York restaurant, the Divan Parisien. It is poached chicken on broccoli with a Hollandaise sauce. Turkey may be substituted for the chicken.

1 five-pound stewing chicken
Water
2 teaspoons salt
¼ cup butter
3 tablespoons flour
2 cups milk
½ teaspoon nutmeg
1 large bunch broccoli
1 cup grated Parmesan cheese, approximately
½ cup Hollandaise sauce (page 449)
½ cup heavy cream, whipped
3 tablespoons sherry
1 teaspoon Worcestershire sauce

1. Place the chicken on a rack in a large kettle. Add about five cups boiling water and the salt. Bring to a boil, lower the heat, cover and simmer until tender, about three hours. Cool the chicken in the broth.

2. Meanwhile, make white sauce: In a saucepan melt the butter, add the flour and stir with a wire whisk until blended. Bring the milk to a boil and add all at once to the butter-flour mixture, stirring vigorously with the whisk until the sauce is thickened and smooth. Stir in the nutmeg. Keep hot.

3. When the chicken has cooled in the broth, remove the skin and slice the breast and leg meat. Reserve the remainder of the chicken for another purpose.

4. Cook the broccoli in salted water until tender, drain and arrange on a deep heatproof serving platter. Sprinkle lightly with some of the cheese. Arrange the chicken meat on the broccoli.

5. Make the Hollandaise sauce and combine with the white sauce. Add the whipped cream, sherry, and Worcestershire sauce. Pour the sauce over the chicken and broccoli and sprinkle with the remaining cheese.

6. Place about five inches below high heat in a preheated broiler and broil until browned and bubbly.

CHICKEN IN A PINEAPPLE SHELL *4 servings*

1 three-and-one-half-pound stewing chicken cut into pieces
3 cups boiling salted water
1 cup fine noodles
½ cup slivered toasted almonds
Chicken broth
½ cup heavy cream
2 egg yolks, beaten
Pinch of cayenne pepper
Salt and freshly ground black pepper to taste
2 medium-sized fresh ripe pineapples
Cognac (optional)

(*cont'd*)

1. Cook the chicken in salted water until tender. Remove the chicken and reserve the broth. Remove the meat from the bones. Discard the bones and slice the meat.

2. Cook the noodles in the chicken broth. Drain, reserving the broth.

3. Preheat oven to moderate (375° F.).

4. Combine the chicken, noodles and toasted almonds.

5. Heat one-half cup of the broth and the cream together. Add the egg yolks lightly beaten with a little of the hot mixture. Season with cayenne, salt and pepper and cook over low heat, stirring, until smooth and slightly thickened. Combine with the chicken mixture.

6. Halve the pineapples, leaving on the fronds, and remove the meat, leaving a shell three-quarters to one inch thick. Cube the pineapple meat. If desired, add a few tablespoons cognac and let stand until ready to use.

7. Fill the pineapple shells with the chicken mixture and place each shell on a large piece of heavy-duty aluminum foil. Seal the foil at the top and on the sides, being sure to cover the fronds. Place on a baking pan and bake forty minutes.

8. Partially open the foil around the shell, leaving the fronds covered. Cover the top of the filled pineapple with cubes of pineapple meat and broil under a preheated broiler four to five minutes.

CHICKEN LIVER RISOTTO, PAGE 323.

BROILED CHICKEN MAINTENON *8 servings*

The Marquise de Maintenon was a consort of Louis XIV. The monarch's chef named this dish, of broiled chicken on toast, after her.

2 small broiling chickens, split in half
½ lemon
Salt and freshly ground black pepper to taste
½ cup butter
Juice of ½ lemon
2 chicken livers
1 cup sliced mushrooms
½ cup cooked tongue, cut in thin slices (optional)
½ teaspoon thyme
8 large rounds toast, buttered
½ cup dry white wine or sherry
Chopped parsley

1. Rub the chicken with the lemon and sprinkle with salt and pepper.

2. Heat half the butter in a skillet and add the lemon juice. Broil the chicken under a preheated broiler, basting occasionally with the lemon butter, until tender, about fifteen minutes on each side. Cut into quarters, transfer to a warm platter and keep hot until ready to serve.

3. Meanwhile in a skillet heat one tablespoon of the remaining butter, add the chicken livers and cook briefly. Remove and slice. Heat the remaining butter in the pan, add the mushrooms, tongue and thyme and cook slowly ten minutes. Spread the mixture on the toast rounds and top each round with a quarter of chicken.

(cont'd)

4. Pour the drippings from the broiling pan into a saucepan, add the wine and bring to a boil. Correct the seasonings, add the chicken-liver slices and heat thoroughly. Pour over the chicken and sprinkle with parsley.

CHICKEN NEWBURG *4 servings*

How often has the story been told about Mr. Wenburg who was much admired by a chef? A lobster dish was named after Mr. Wenburg but he had a falling-out with the chef and the dish became forevermore Newburg. Here is a similar dish made with chicken.

¼ cup rendered chicken fat or butter
¼ cup sliced mushrooms
2 cups cubed, cooked chicken (pieces should be fairly large)
¼ cup dry sherry
¼ teaspoon salt
Dash of white pepper
1 cup light cream
3 egg yolks
Hot toast or fluffy rice
Paprika

1. In a skillet heat the fat, add the mushrooms and cook until almost tender. Add the chicken, half the sherry, the salt and pepper and cook slowly until the mushrooms are tender.

2. Transfer the mixture to the top of a double boiler, add the cream and heat thoroughly over boiling water.

3. Add the remaining sherry and the egg yolks lightly beaten with a little of the hot sauce. Cook, stirring, until thickened. Correct the seasonings. Serve on hot toast or fluffy rice and sprinkle with paprika.

SHERRIED CHICKEN WITH GREEN NOODLES *4 to 6 servings*

1 three-pound broiler-fryer chicken, cut into serving pieces
3 cups chicken broth
½ pound flat green spinach noodles
6 tablespoons butter
6 tablespoons flour
Salt and freshly ground black pepper to taste
½ teaspoon paprika
¼ cup sherry
¼ pound fresh mushrooms, sliced thin and cooked until tender in a little butter or olive oil
Grated Parmesan cheese

1. Place the chicken in a heavy kettle and cover with the broth. Bring to a boil, reduce the heat and simmer, covered, until the meat can be easily removed from the bones, thirty to forty minutes. Remove the chicken parts. Strain the broth and return to a boil.

2. Meanwhile, cook the noodles according to package directions and drain. Return to the pot in which noodles were cooked, add a little melted butter and stir to prevent the strands from sticking together.

(*cont'd*)

3. In a saucepan melt six tablespoons butter, add the flour and stir with a wire whisk until blended. Add the boiling broth all at once, stirring vigorously with the whisk until the sauce is thickened and smooth. Season with salt, pepper and paprika and stir in the sherry.

4. Remove the meat from the chicken bones, discarding skin and bones. Add the meat and mushrooms to the sauce. Serve the sauce on individual beds of noodles, accompanied by grated Parmesan cheese.

Note: If desired, this dish may be served as a casserole. Cook the noodles until barely tender, drain and arrange in a buttered baking dish. Cover with sauce and sprinkle with cheese. Bake, uncovered, in a preheated oven (400° F.) until the top is brown and bubbling, about twenty minutes.

CHICKEN TETRAZZINI *6 servings*

Luisa Tetrazzini, the coloratura soprano, was distinctly Italian. This dish, named for her, is quite good but distinctly American.

1 five-pound stewing chicken, cut into serving pieces
1 onion studded with 2 cloves
2 stalks celery with leaves
Salt
½ bay leaf
1 carrot
3 cups water
Chicken fat or butter
¼ cup flour
Tabasco sauce
½ pound mushrooms, sliced
1 egg yolk, lightly beaten
1 tablespoon dry sherry
3 tablespoons light cream
1 eight-ounce package spaghetti
2 tablespoons grated Parmesan cheese
1 teaspoon butter
Toasted almonds (optional)

1. In a heavy kettle place the chicken, onion, celery, one tablespoon salt, bay leaf, carrot and three cups water. Bring to a boil, reduce the heat and simmer, covered, until the chicken is tender, three to four hours. Remove the chicken from the broth and let cool. Remove the meat from the bones, discarding skin and bones.

2. Skim the fat from the top of the broth and place four tablespoons of the fat (or an equal amount of butter) in a saucepan. Add the flour and salt to taste, stirring with a wire whisk until blended. Meanwhile, bring two cups of the strained chicken broth to a boil and add all at once to the fat-flour mixture, stirring vigorously with the whisk until the sauce is thickened and smooth. Season with Tabasco sauce.

3. In a skillet heat three tablespoons of the remaining fat or butter, add the mushrooms and cook until brown.

4. To the sauce add the egg yolk lightly beaten with a little of the hot sauce and stir in the sherry, cream, chicken and mushrooms. Cook, stirring, until heated through. Do not let boil.

5. Cook the spaghetti according to package directions. Place alternate layers

(*cont'd*)

of spaghetti and sauce in a buttered casserole, sprinkle with grated Parmesan cheese and dot with the butter. Brown quickly in a preheated broiler and serve with toasted almonds, if desired.

CHICKEN STUFFED WITH MACARONI *4 servings*

1 four-pound stewing chicken
Water to cover
1 stalk celery, with leaves
Sprig of parsley
Salt
¼ cup butter
2 tablespoons flour
½ cup cream
⅛ teaspoon nutmeg
¼ teaspoon freshly ground black pepper
½ pound elbow macaroni
Grated Parmesan cheese

1. Place the whole chicken in a kettle and add water barely to cover. Add the celery stalk, parsley and a little salt. Bring to a boil, cover and simmer until the chicken is tender, two to three hours. Remove the chicken to a warm platter and keep hot. Strain the stock and reserve one cup.

2. In a saucepan melt the butter, add the flour and stir with a wire whisk until blended. Meanwhile, bring the reserved stock and the cream to a boil and add all at once to the butter-flour mixture, stirring vigorously with the whisk until the sauce is thickened and smooth. Season with the nutmeg, one-half teaspoon salt and the pepper.

3. Preheat oven to hot (400° F.).

4. Cook the macaroni in two quarts boiling salted water until tender, about ten minutes. Drain and mix with half the sauce. Stuff the chicken with the mixture, close the opening and truss. Place, breast side up, in a buttered baking dish. Pour the remaining sauce over the top and sprinkle with grated cheese. Bake until the cheese is browned, about ten minutes.

STEWED CHICKEN WITH PARSLEY DUMPLINGS *6 servings*

1 four-pound stewing fowl, cut into pieces
Water to cover
Salt
10 peppercorns, bruised
1 stalk celery, with leaves
1 medium onion, peeled
1 carrot, scraped
½ bay leaf
Parsley dumplings (page 206)
3 tablespoons flour (approximately)

1. Rinse the chicken pieces under cold running water. Place in a heavy kettle or Dutch oven and barely cover with water. Sprinkle with a little salt and the peppercorns.

2. Add the celery, onion, carrot and bay leaf and cover. Bring to a boil, reduce the heat and simmer gently until the chicken meat begins to loosen from the bones, two to three hours.

(cont'd)

3. Drop the dumpling dough from a wet tablespoon onto the boiling stew, letting the dumplings rest on the meat. Cover tightly, reduce the heat and cook, without raising the cover, fifteen minutes.

4. Transfer the dumplings to a hot platter and thicken the stew with flour mixed with water. Serve immediately, using the dumplings as a border around the chicken.

PARSLEY DUMPLINGS:

1½ cups sifted flour
2 teaspoons baking powder
¾ teaspoon salt
2 tablespoons chopped parsley
½ teaspoon crushed rosemary
3 tablespoons shortening
¾ cup milk, approximately

1. Sift together the flour, baking powder and salt. Add the parsley and rosemary and mix.

2. Chop in the shortening until the mixture resembles coarse cornmeal. Add enough milk to make a thick batter that can be mounded up in a spoon and dropped.

FRICASSEE OF CHICKEN WITH HERBS *6 to 8 servings*

3 cups chicken broth
1 onion studded with 4 cloves
1 small carrot, diced
3 peppercorns
1 tablespoon chopped chives
2 tablespoons chopped parsley
1 teaspoon salt
½ bay leaf
2 three-and-one-half-pound frying chickens, cut into pieces
6 tablespoons flour
6 tablespoons butter
12 small white onions, peeled and left whole
½ teaspoon rosemary
½ teaspoon marjoram
¼ teaspoon powdered saffron
3 tablespoons light cream
2 egg yolks
1 teaspoon lemon juice

1. In a heavy kettle combine the broth, onion, carrot, peppercorns, chives, parsley, salt and bay leaf. Bring to a boil.

2. Dredge the chicken pieces in three tablespoons of the flour. In a skillet, heat three tablespoons of the butter, add the chicken and brown on all sides. Add to the simmering broth and cook, covered, over low heat until the chicken is tender, about forty-five minutes.

3. Remove the chicken pieces to a warm platter and keep hot. Strain the stock, return it to the heat and add the onions. Cover and cook forty-five minutes. Remove the onions to the platter and keep hot.

4. In a heavy saucepan melt the remaining butter, add the remaining flour and stir with a wire whisk until blended. Add the simmering chicken broth all at once to the butter-flour mixture, stirring vigorously with the whisk until the sauce is thickened and smooth. Add the herbs and additional salt to taste.

(cont'd)

6. In a small mixing bowl combine the cream and egg yolks. Add a little of the hot sauce to the yolk mixture and stir it into the remaining sauce. Do not let boil. Stir in the lemon juice. Pour the sauce over the chicken and onions.

CHICKEN PAPRIKA *4 servings*

Chicken paprika is of Hungarian origin. It is best when made with genuine Hungarian rose paprika, available in many spice shops.

2 tablespoons butter
½ cup chopped onion
1 clove garlic, minced
1½ tablespoons paprika
1 teaspoon salt
1 tomato, peeled and chopped
1 green pepper, seeded and chopped
¾ cup chicken stock
1 three-pound broiler-fryer chicken, cut into pieces
¼ cup flour
¼ cup light cream
½ cup sour cream

1. In a heavy kettle heat the butter, add the onion and garlic and sauté until lightly browned. Add the paprika, salt, tomato, green pepper and stock. Cover and cook ten minutes.

2. Add the chicken, cover and cook until tender, about forty minutes. Add water or additional chicken stock, if necessary, to make one and one-quarter cups broth.

3. Add the flour blended with the light cream and a little of the hot sauce and cook, stirring, until thickened.

4. Add the sour cream and cook until heated through. Do not let boil. Serve over noodles or rice.

PINK CHICKEN SAUTE *4 servings*

This is similar to the recipe for chicken paprika but it uses fresh rather than sour cream.

2 two-pound frying chickens, quartered
Flour for dredging
⅓ cup clarified butter (page 456)
1 small onion, finely chopped
1 tablespoon paprika
Salt and freshly ground black pepper to taste
1 cup hot chicken broth, made from the giblets and chicken backs
1 cup heavy cream
1½ tablespoons firm butter
½ teaspoon lemon juice
Chopped parsley

1. Dredge the chicken lightly with flour. In a large skillet heat the butter, add the chicken and brown lightly on all sides.

2. Add the onion, paprika, salt and pepper. Cover and cook very slowly until

(cont'd)

the chicken is tender, about twenty minutes. Remove the chicken to a hot platter and keep warm.

3. Add the broth, cream and firm butter to the skillet and cook one minute. Remove from the heat and stir in the lemon juice and parsley. Pour over the chicken.

SPAGHETTI WITH CHICKEN AND MUSHROOMS, PAGE 335.

HERB-FRIED CHICKEN *6 servings*

½ cup flour
1½ teaspoons salt
1 teaspoon freshly ground black pepper
½ teaspoon dried rosemary, crushed
2 two-pound frying chickens, cut into pieces
Fat for deep frying

1. In a paper bag combine the flour, salt, pepper and rosemary. Add a few chicken parts at a time and shake to coat well with the seasoned flour.

2. Place fat to a depth of one inch in a heavy skillet and heat to 375° F. Drop the chicken pieces into the fat and cook until golden brown on one side. Turn and cook the other side until brown. Drain on absorbent toweling.

MIZUTAKI *2 to 4 servings*

Undoubtedly the most popular of all Japanese dishes in America is sukiyaki. Equally delicious in its own way is a simmered chicken dish known as mizutaki. To prepare it, uncooked chicken is cut into bite-sized pieces and simmered in chicken broth. Vegetables are added and everything is served piping hot with chopsticks and a soya and lemon sauce. A word of warning: The dish must be eaten with chopsticks or it loses character.

1 three-pound broiler-fryer chicken
Chicken stock or water to cover
Salt
6 scallions, cut into 1-inch lengths
1 medium onion, peeled and sliced thin
1 bunch watercress, trimmed
¼ cup lemon juice
¼ cup soy sauce
¼ cup Japanese wine (sake)
¼ teaspoon monosodium glutamate

1. Have the butcher divide the chicken in half and cut or chop both halves into one-and-one-half-inch cubes with the bones.

2. Place the pieces in a heavy saucepan and cover with chicken stock or water. Add a little salt and simmer gently, uncovered, forty-five minutes after the boiling point is reached.

3. Bring to the table in the cooking utensil and place over a charcoal or alcohol burner so that the liquid barely boils.

4. When the guests are seated, commence adding the vegetables to the simmering broth, a few at a time. To serve, spoon a few portions of the meat and barely cooked vegetables into small serving bowls. Using chopsticks or forks, guests dip bite-sized pieces of chicken into a sauce made by combining the lemon juice, soy sauce, sake and monosodium glutamate.

CHICKEN HASH *5 servings*

- 2 cups cubed, cooked chicken or turkey
- 1 cup light cream
- 3½ tablespoons butter
- 2½ tablespoons flour
- 1½ cups milk
- 1 teaspoon salt, approximately
- 3 egg yolks
- ¼ teaspoon grated onion
- 2 tablespoons grated Parmesan or Swiss cheese

1. Simmer the chicken in the cream until the cream is reduced to one-half its original quantity.

2. Meanwhile, prepare a white sauce: In a saucepan melt two and one-half tablespoons of the butter, add the flour and stir with a wire whisk until blended. Bring one and one-fourth cups of the milk to a boil and add all at once to the butter-flour mixture, stirring vigorously with the whisk until the sauce is thickened and smooth.

3. Add one-half cup of the white sauce to the chicken mixture, season with salt and set aside. Stir in one of the egg yolks.

4. Mix the remaining white sauce with the remaining egg yolks slightly beaten with a little of the hot sauce. Add the remaining milk and the grated onion and cook, stirring, until thickened and smooth. Add the remaining butter and one tablespoon of the cheese.

5. Place the reserved hash in a heatproof dish and cover with the sauce. Sprinkle with the remaining cheese. Brown under a hot broiler.

JOSIE McCARTHY'S CHICKEN WINGS WITH SPANISH RICE

4 to 6 servings

- 2 pounds chicken wings
- ¼ cup olive oil
- 1 cup chopped onions
- 1 clove garlic, crushed
- 1 cup raw rice
- 2 teaspoons salt
- ¼ teaspoon freshly ground pepper
- 1 cup canned tomatoes with liquid
- 1¼ cups chicken stock
- ¼ teaspoon powdered saffron
- 1 cup cooked green peas
- 2 canned pimentos, diced

1. Wash the chicken wings, drain them and pat dry.

2. Heat the oil over moderate heat until hot but not smoking. Add the onions and garlic and cook until soft and lightly browned, stirring constantly.

3. Remove the onions from the skillet and set aside. Add the chicken wings to the remaining oil in the pan and cook, uncovered, until evenly browned, turning frequently.

4. Place the chicken wings and onions in a saucepan. Add the rice, salt, pepper, tomatoes and chicken stock. Dissolve the saffron in one tablespoon hot water and add to the chicken.

5. Cover and simmer forty-five to fifty minutes, or until the rice and chicken are tender and the liquid has been absorbed.

6. Add the peas and pimentos, stirring gently into the rice. Reheat and serve.

SAMBAL GORENG (spiced chicken livers with vegetables) *6 servings*

Sambal Goreng is an Indonesian dish that is unusual but should appeal to Western palates. It is made with chicken livers, vegetables, spices and a great deal of garlic.

- 1 pound chicken livers, cut in half
- 3 tablespoons peanut oil
- 10 cloves garlic, finely minced
- 1 teaspoon finely minced fresh ginger
- 3 shallots or 1 small onion, minced
- 1 pound string beans, cut into half-inch pieces
- ¼ cup ground Indonesian almonds (optional)
- 2 tablespoons tamarind pulp or juice of 2 lemons
- 1 tablespoon Indonesian soy sauce
- 1 cup chicken stock
- 1 tablespoon salt
- 1 teaspoon hot red pepper
- 2 teaspoons brown sugar or dark molasses
- 2 teaspoons turmeric
- 1½ teaspoons kentjur (optional)
- 2 teaspoons seren leaves (optional)
- ½ teaspoon laus (optional)

1. In a large skillet sauté the chicken livers in peanut oil over high heat until lightly browned, stirring constantly. Remove the livers from the skillet.

2. Reduce the heat and add the garlic, ginger and shallots. Cook until the vegetables are soft, stirring occasionally. Add the string beans and cook three minutes.

3. Add the remaining ingredients, cover the pan and cook over low heat until the string beans are just tender, about ten minutes.

4. Return the livers to the pan and cook five minutes longer.

Note: If Indonesian soy sauce is unavailable, substitute regular soy sauce mixed with half as much dark molasses. For sources for foreign ingredients see Chapter 16.

CHICKEN-OKRA GUMBO *8 to 10 servings*

- 2 tablespoons butter
- 1 three- to three-and-one-half-pound chicken, cut into pieces
- 1½ to 2 pounds ham slices, cut into 1-inch cubes
- 1 onion, chopped
- ½ pod hot red pepper, seeded
- 1 sprig thyme or parsley, chopped
- 6 large tomatoes, peeled and chopped
- 1 quart (1 pound) okra, sliced
- 3 quarts boiling water
- 1 bay leaf
- Salt and cayenne pepper to taste
- 2½ cups boiled rice

1. Heat the butter in a heavy kettle or Dutch oven, add the chicken and ham and cook, covered, about ten minutes.

2. Add the onion, red pepper, thyme and solid part of the tomatoes, reserving the juice. Simmer a few minutes, stirring often.

3. Add the okra and simmer, stirring, until brown.

4. Add the reserved tomato juice, the boiling water and bay leaf. Season with salt and cayenne and simmer, covered, about one hour. Serve with rice.

CHICKENBURGER *4 to 6 patties*

"Chickenburger" is a much more descriptive name for this dish than "chicken cutlet à la Pojarski." That is what it is, however, and it is Russian in origin. Note that vodka is an ingredient.

1 three-pound broiling chicken
1 pound veal shoulder, skinned and trimmed of the fat
3 slices white bread
½ cup milk
Salt and nutmeg to taste
2 jiggers (6 tablespoons) vodka or dry sherry
1 cup light cream

1. Remove the chicken meat from the bones and cut the chicken into strips. Cut the veal into pieces.
2. Grind the veal and chicken in a meat grinder, using the finest blade.
3. Soak the bread in the milk and squeeze it dry. Mix the bread with the meat. Add the remaining ingredients and form into flat patties.
4. Broil the patties in a preheated broiler or sauté in butter until browned on both sides. Serve with cream sauce (page 444).

CHICKEN LIVERS MARSALA *4 servings*

1 pound chicken livers
¼ cup butter
½ teaspoon salt
¼ teaspoon freshly ground black pepper
½ teaspoon sage
2 slices prosciutto, diced
8 bread triangles, sautéed
¼ cup Marsala
1 tablespoon butter

1. Cut the livers in half and simmer in melted butter, together with the seasonings and prosciutto, five minutes.
2. Remove the livers from the pan and place them on the sautéed bread triangles. Add the wine to the pan gravy and cook three minutes. Add the remaining butter, mix well and pour over the livers.

CHICKEN LIVERS WITH PINEAPPLE *4 servings*

1 pound chicken livers
Soy sauce
¼ cup peanut or vegetable oil
1 cup canned pineapple chunks, drained
½ cup blanched almonds
1¼ cups pineapple juice
¼ cup vinegar
¼ teaspoon salt
¼ cup sugar
2 tablespoons cornstarch
1 cup Chinese peas (optional)

1. Cut the livers in half and dip the pieces in soy sauce. Heat the oil and brown the livers in it quickly. Add the pineapple and almonds and remove from the heat.

(*cont'd*)

2. Combine the pineapple juice, vinegar, salt, sugar and cornstarch and stir over low heat until clear, thickened and smooth. Pour over the chicken livers and, if desired, add the Chinese peas cooked in a little boiling salted water until barely tender. Serve with rice.

CHICKEN GIBLETS WITH MUSHROOMS *4 servings*

- 6 tablespoons butter
- 1 pound mushrooms, sliced
- 1 medium onion, sliced thin
- ½ pound raw chicken livers
- ½ pound chicken gizzards and hearts, cooked
- Salt and freshly ground black pepper to taste
- ½ cup dry white wine
- 4 slices toasted white bread

1. Heat the butter, add the mushrooms and onion and cook until brown, stirring occasionally.

2. Add the chicken livers and cook three minutes. Add the gizzards and hearts and cook about three minutes longer. Season with salt and pepper, add the wine and cook two minutes. Serve hot on toast squares.

TURKEY

HIGH-TEMPERATURE ROASTING OF TURKEY

Season a stuffed turkey with salt and place it on its side in a roasting pan fitted with a rack. Place slices of fat salt pork over the breast and spread the bird generously with butter. Cook in a preheated hot oven (425° F.) fifteen minutes, then turn on the other side and cook fifteen minutes longer.

Reduce the oven heat to moderate (375° F.) and continue roasting, turning the bird from side to side and basting often with fat from the pan. If the fat tends to burn, add a few tablespoons of water.

Allow twenty minutes a pound for roasting.

Place the turkey on its back for the last fifteen minutes of cooking. Pierce the thigh for doneness; if the juice that runs out is clear with no tinge of pink, the bird is done.

Note: For stuffing directions and recipes, see pages 221–225.

LOW-TEMPERATURE ROASTING OF TURKEY

Place stuffed turkey, breast side up, on a rack in an open roasting pan. Grease the surface well with shortening and place a fat-moistened cheesecloth—large enough to drape down over the sides of the bird—on top. (*cont'd*)

Roast in a constant moderate oven (325° F.). Do not add water; baste only once or twice with fat or drippings in the pan. Remove the cloth for the last half hour to brown.

Allow three to four hours for a four- to eight-pound turkey, four to four and one-half hours for an eight- to twelve-pound turkey, four and one-half to five hours for a twelve- to sixteen-pound turkey.

To test for doneness, move the leg joint up and down. It should give readily or break. Or, using a cloth or paper, press the fleshy part of the drumstick. It should feel soft.

Note: For stuffing directions and recipes, see pages 221–225.

GIBLET GRAVY *About 3 cups*

Giblets from 1 turkey or chicken
Salted water to cover
Pan drippings from roast turkey or chicken
¼ cup flour
½ cup cream (optional)
1 hard-cooked egg, chopped (optional)
Salt and freshly ground black pepper

1. Clean the giblets well and simmer, covered, in salted water until tender. Drain, reserving the broth. Cool the giblets and chop.

2. After bird has been removed to serving platter, pour four tablespoons fat from the roasting pan into a saucepan. If necessary, add enough butter to make the four tablespoons. Add two cups giblet broth to the drippings in the roasting pan and scrape loose all the brown particles. If necessary, add enough water to make two cups.

3. Add flour to the drippings in the saucepan and cook, stirring, until browned. Gradually add the giblet broth from the roasting pan and cook, stirring, until thickened.

4. Add the cream, chopped giblets and hard-cooked egg, season with salt and pepper and reheat.

TURKEY FLORENTINE *6 servings*

3 tablespoons butter
3 tablespoons flour
1 cup milk
½ cup cream
Salt and freshly ground black pepper to taste
2 pounds spinach, cooked and puréed
¼ teaspoon nutmeg
Sliced cooked turkey, enough for six servings
Parmesan cheese

1. Melt the butter in a saucepan, add the flour and stir with a wire whisk until blended. Meanwhile bring the milk and cream to a boil and add all at once to the butter-flour mixture, stirring vigorously with the whisk until the sauce is thickened and smooth. Season with salt and pepper.

(*cont'd*)

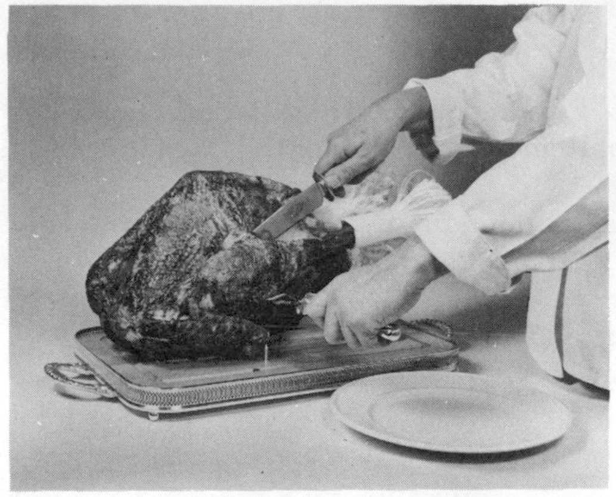

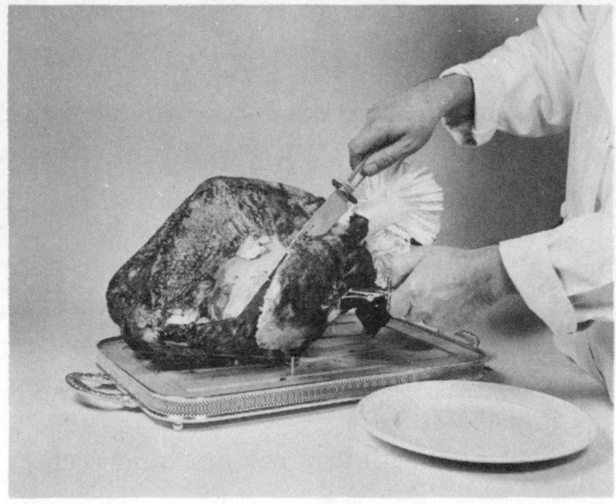

1. *Carving a turkey.* Insert prongs of a carving fork firmly into joint of drumstick and thighbone.

2. With sharp knife, cut strip of skin holding leg to body. Pull leg away with fork.

3. Hold leg upright at tip and cut downward between drumstick and thighbone.

4. Sever joint connecting drumstick and thigh. Carve meat in slices from bones.

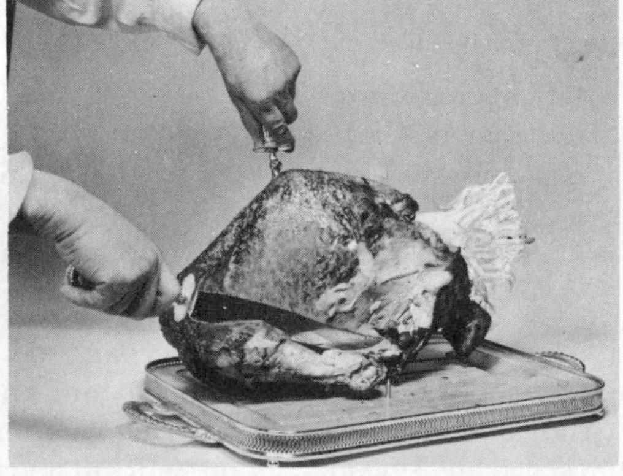

5. Insert fork into small wing bones and cut between small and main wing bones.

6. Hold the knife horizontally and cut above wing joint through to body frame.

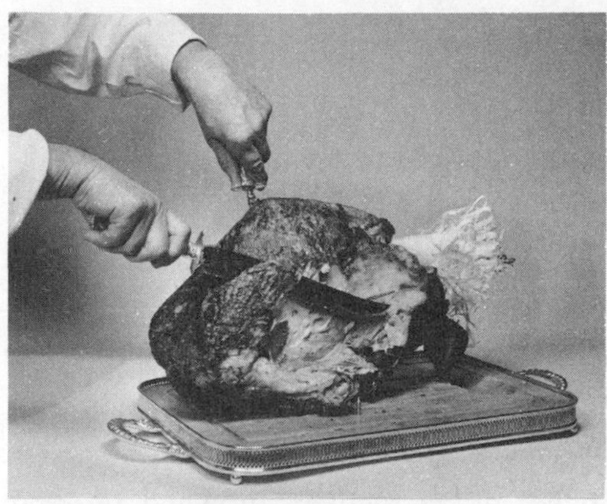
7. Beginning halfway up breast, slice downward until each slice falls free.

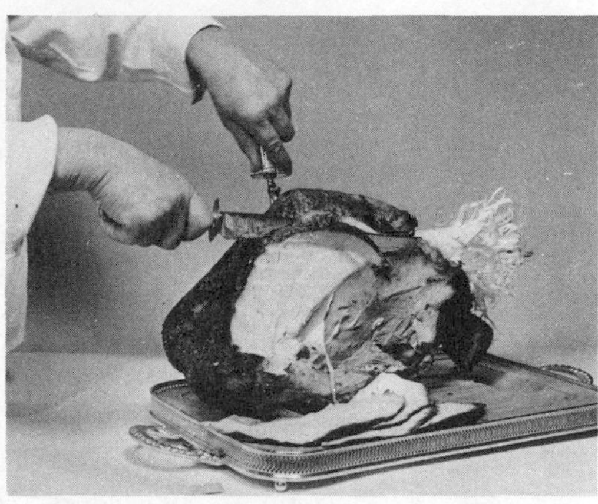
8. Continue slicing, beginning at higher point until crest of bone is reached.

9. When meat is sliced from one side, remove wing bone. Repeat on other side.

2. In a saucepan, combine the spinach, nutmeg and one-half cup of the sauce. Heat thoroughly but do not let boil.

3. Spoon the spinach onto a warm heatproof platter and arrange the sliced turkey on top.

4. Stir a little Parmesan cheese into the remaining sauce and spoon over the turkey slices. Sprinkle with additional Parmesan cheese, dot with additional butter and brown lightly under the broiler.

TURKEY TURNOVERS *6 servings*

3 tablespoons butter
2 teaspoons minced onion
3 tablespoons flour
¼ teaspoon salt
⅛ teaspoon freshly ground black pepper
¼ teaspoon celery salt
⅛ teaspoon ground ginger
1 cup milk
2 cups chopped, cooked turkey
Plain pastry made from 2 cups flour

(cont'd)

1. Preheat oven to hot (450° F.).

2. Melt butter; add onion and flour and stir until smooth. Add the seasonings. Slowly add the milk, stirring constantly, and cook until thickened. Add the turkey; adjust the seasonings. Let mixture cool.

3. Meanwhile, roll out the pastry to one-eighth-inch thickness. Cut dough into three-inch circles or squares, place a rounded tablespoon of the turkey mixture over one half and fold the other half over the filling, pressing the edges together. Or put the turkey mixture in the center of a square or circle, place another square or circle over the top and press the edges together to seal. Slash the top crust to allow for the escape of steam.

4. Place on a cookie sheet and bake until attractively browned, or about twenty to thirty minutes. Serve with mushroom sauce (page 452) or with a creamed vegetable.

TURKEY HASH *4 servings*

3 cups ground cooked turkey
3 cups finely chopped, cooked potatoes
3 tablespoons chopped green pepper
½ cup finely chopped onion
2 teaspoons salt
Freshly ground black pepper to taste
¾ cup turkey broth or canned chicken consommé
4 poached eggs
Tabasco sauce

1. Preheat oven to moderate (350° F.).

2. Mix together the turkey, vegetables, seasonings and broth. Place in one large greased casserole or four individual greased casseroles. Cover.

3. Bake one hour for large casserole, or about forty minutes for individual casseroles. Halfway through the baking, remove cover to permit browning.

4. Arrange poached eggs on top of the hash and serve with Tabasco sauce.

Note: Turkey may also be substituted in the chicken hash recipe, page 209.

DUCK

ROAST DUCK

Preheat oven to moderate (350° F.).

Rub the skin of the duck with half a lemon. Sprinkle the inside of the duck with salt and pepper. Place the duck on a rack in a roasting pan and roast, without basting, about twelve minutes per pound, or longer if desired. Fifteen minutes before the duck is done, sprinkle the outside with salt and pepper.

If desired, before roasting, fill the cavity of the duck with any desired stuffing. Roast a stuffed duck approximately fifteen minutes per pound.

ROTISSERIE CHINESE DUCK *4 servings*

This is a splendid recipe developed for an electric rotisserie. When done the duck should be crisp on the outside and almost jet black.

1 five- to six-pound duckling
Salt to taste
Few sprigs of parsley
½ lemon
¼ cup dark molasses (preferably Chinese bead molasses available in most Oriental grocery stores)
½ cup soy sauce
½ cup sherry
1 small clove garlic, minced

1. Wash the duck and dry well with paper towels inside and out. Sprinkle the duck cavity with salt and insert the parsley and lemon. Truss the bird securely. Fold the wings under and tie close to the body. Tie the legs together, then bring the cord under the tail and over the breast and tie securely. Make certain the thighs are tied close to the body so they will not break away during cooking.

2. In a saucepan combine the molasses, soy sauce, sherry and garlic and cook over low heat five minutes.

3. Insert the spit rod through the center of the duck cavity, balancing it carefully. Be sure one set of skewers is inserted firmly into the legs before tightening the screws.

4. Roast until tender, about two hours, basting every fifteen minutes with sauce. The duck skin will darken considerably while cooking. When done, the drumstick meat is soft when pressed with the fingers and the thigh joint moves easily.

LONG ISLAND DUCKLING IN PORT *4 servings*

1 duckling, 5 to 6 pounds
3 tablespoons fat
1 cup port or dry red wine
½ cup orange juice
2 teaspoons lemon juice
1 tablespoon cognac
1 teaspoon Kitchen Bouquet
1 tablespoon cornstarch
½ teaspoon salt
Dash of freshly ground black pepper
⅛ teaspoon Tabasco sauce
Pinch of allspice
2 tablespoons pâté de foie gras or the duck liver, cooked and puréed

1. With a sharp pointed knife, cut through the duck skin along the center of the breast from neck to vent. Loosen the skin by pulling away from the flesh and at the same time running the knife underneath. Cut the skin where necessary but keep the flesh intact. Quarter the duck.

2. In a skillet heat the fat, add the duck and brown on all sides. Add half the port, cover and cook until the duck is tender, about forty-five minutes. Remove the duck to a warm platter and keep hot.

3. Blend together and stir into the pan the remaining ingredients. Cook, stirring constantly, until the sauce thickens. Return the duck to the sauce and simmer over low heat five minutes. Serve with a garnish of orange slices and watercress.

DUCKLING IN WINE WITH GREEN GRAPES *4 servings*

1 five-pound duckling, cut into pieces
1 teaspoon Kitchen Bouquet
1 teaspoon salt
⅛ teaspoon nutmeg
2 tablespoons fat
¾ cup muscatel wine
2 tablespoons currant jelly
1½ tablespoons cornstarch
1 cup halved, seedless green grapes

1. Remove the outer layer of skin and fat from the duck by pulling it away from the flesh and at the same time running a knife underneath. Place duck in a bowl with the Kitchen Bouquet, salt and nutmeg and stir to coat evenly.

2. In a skillet heat the fat, add the duckling and brown on all sides. Add the wine and jelly, cover and bring to a boil. Reduce the heat and cook slowly until the duck is tender, about forty-five minutes. Remove the duck to a warm platter and keep hot.

3. Blend the cornstarch with two tablespoons water and stir into the sauce. Cook, stirring, until thickened and smooth. Add the grapes and heat thoroughly. Pour over the duck.

CASSOULET, PAGE 360.

DUCK WITH BEANS *6 servings*

1 pound dried pea or marrow beans
Water to cover
2 teaspoons salt
4 sprigs parsley
2 stems celery tops with leaves
1 bay leaf
2 cloves garlic
1 five-pound duck, cut into serving pieces
6 strips bacon
1 onion, chopped
½ teaspoon thyme
Tabasco sauce or cayenne pepper to taste

1. Soak the beans overnight in water to cover. Or boil two minutes and let stand one hour.

2. Add the salt and additional water to cover if necessary. Add the parsley, celery, bay leaf and one sliced clove of garlic all tied in a piece of cheesecloth. Cook, covered, until tender, for two hours or longer. Drain, reserving the broth and beans.

3. Sprinkle the duck lightly with additional salt. Broil in preheated broiler, skin side up, until brown. Turn, brush the second side with the drippings in the pan and broil until brown. (If desired, the duck may be pan fried.)

4. Reduce oven heat to slow (300° F.).

5. Rub the inside of an earthenware casserole with the second clove of garlic and place three strips of bacon on the bottom of the casserole. Add the onion, thyme and Tabasco to the beans and place half the mixture in the casserole. Add the broiled duck and cover with the remaining beans.

6. Pour off the fat from the broiler pan, add one cup bean broth to the pan

(cont'd)

and scrape loose all the browned particles. Pour over the beans. Place the remaining bacon on top.

7. Cover and bake until the duck is tender, or about one and one-half hours. The cover may be removed during the last fifteen minutes to crisp the bacon.

DUCK SPANISH STYLE *4 servings*

- 1 five-pound duck, cut into serving pieces
- Salt and freshly ground black pepper to taste
- 2 tablespoons olive or salad oil
- 1 onion, chopped
- ½ green pepper, chopped
- 1 clove garlic, minced
- 1 cup sliced carrots
- 1 cup chopped celery
- 1½ cups tomato juice
- 1 bay leaf
- ½ pound mushrooms, cooked until wilted in a little butter
- ¼ cup sliced stuffed olives

1. Preheat oven to moderate (350° F.).

2. Sprinkle the duck with salt and pepper. In a skillet heat the oil, add the duck and brown on all sides. Transfer the duck to a casserole or covered baking dish and pour off all but two tablespoons of the fat.

3. To the fat remaining in the skillet add the onion, green pepper and garlic and cook until the onion is transparent. Add the carrots, celery, tomato juice, bay leaf and one teaspoon salt. Pour the mixture over the duck.

4. Cover and bake about one hour. Five minutes before the duck is done, add the mushrooms and olives. Serve with noodles or spaghetti.

DUCK WITH RICE *4 servings*

- 1 five-pound duck, quartered
- 3 cups water
- 2 teaspoons salt
- ¼ teaspoon freshly ground black pepper
- ½ cup raw rice
- 2 carrots, sliced
- 2 leeks, sliced
- 2 turnips, sliced
- 4 small onions, halved
- 1 egg, lightly beaten
- Parsley

1. Broil the duck in a preheated broiler until brown on all sides. Place in a kettle with three cups water, the giblets, salt and pepper and bring to a boil. Cover, reduce the heat and simmer until the duck is tender, about forty minutes. Remove the duck and, if desired, remove the meat from the bones. Skim the fat from the broth.

2. Preheat oven to moderate (350° F.).

3. To two cups of the duck broth add the rice and cook two minutes. Turn the rice and broth into a casserole and add the vegetables and the duck.

4. Cover and bake until the vegetables and rice are tender, about twenty-five minutes. Blend the egg with an additional one-half cup duck broth or water and stir gently into the casserole. Heat but do not boil. Serve sprinkled with chopped parsley.

BRAISED DUCK *4 to 6 servings*

- 1 tablespoon fat
- 1 four- to five-pound duck, cut into serving pieces
- ½ pound mushrooms, sliced
- 3 tablespoons flour
- 3 cups water
- 1½ teaspoons salt
- ¼ teaspoon freshly ground black pepper
- 1 bay leaf
- Dash of rosemary
- 1 onion studded with 3 cloves
- ½ cup port
- ½ cup stuffed olives (optional)

1. In a skillet heat the fat, add the duck and brown on all sides. Transfer the pieces to a deep pan and drain off all but three tablespoons of the fat.
2. Add the mushrooms to the reserved fat and cook five minutes. Add the flour and blend. Stir in the water and bring to a boil.
3. Season the mixture with salt and pepper and pour over the duck. Add the bay leaf, rosemary and onion.
4. Cover and simmer very gently until tender, one to one and one-half hours. Or bake, covered, in a moderate oven (350° F.).
5. Discard the bay leaf and onion. Add the port and olives and serve with wild rice.

DUCK WITH BING CHERRIES, PAGE 179.

GOOSE

HIGH-TEMPERATURE ROASTING OF GOOSE

Stuff the goose (see page 225) and truss as directed on page 222. Rub the outside with a little salt, place in a shallow roasting pan on its side and brush with two tablespoons goose fat. Pour one cup hot water into the pan and roast in a hot oven (425° F.), allowing fifteen to sixteen minutes for each pound ready-to-cook weight. Baste often. If the water evaporates and juice that comes out of the bird gets too brown, add a little hot water to the pan. Skim off the fat from time to time. After the first hour turn the bird on the other side, then turn every half hour, roasting the goose the last fifteen minutes on its back so that the breast will brown. To test for doneness, move the legs up and down—they should move freely.

LOW-TEMPERATURE ROASTING OF GOOSE

After stuffing and trussing the goose, place the bird, breast up, on a rack in a shallow open pan and roast in a moderate oven (325° F.) until the leg joints

(cont'd)

move readily or twist out. Toward the end of cooking time, test by moving the drumstick up and down. During the roasting, spoon or siphon off the fat as it gathers in the pan. Save the fat for use in other cooking.

An eight-pound goose (ready-to-cook weight) will take four hours to roast; a ten-pound goose will take four and one-quarter hours; a twelve-pound goose will take five hours, and a fourteen-pound goose six hours.

ROAST WILD GOOSE, PAGE 179.

DANISH ROAST GOOSE

8-pound goose serves 6 to 8

Greenings or other tart apples
Prunes
Ready-to-cook goose
Salt to taste

1. The amount of stuffing depends on the size of the goose. Allow one cup for each pound of the bird, ready-to-cook weight. Apples and prunes may be used in equal measure.
2. Soak the prunes two hours or longer, drain and remove the pits. Peel, core and slice the apples. Mix the fruits and sweeten to taste.
3. Preheat oven to moderate (325° F.).
4. Sprinkle the goose inside with salt and fill its cavities with the fruits. Truss as directed on page 222, tying the legs loosely to the tail.
5. Place the goose, breast up, on a rack in an open roasting pan and roast until the leg joints move easily and the flesh is soft. Remove the fat from the pan as it is extracted. See above for roasting time.
6. Make a gravy from the drippings in the pan. Danish cooks sometimes finish off the gravy for roast goose by stirring in a little tart currant jelly.

STUFFINGS

POULTRY STUFFINGS

Stuffing for poultry can be moist or dry and can be made as family tradition indicates, with a basis of white bread, cornbread, rice or even sauerkraut. Preparing a stuffing consumes precious time Thanksgiving or Christmas morning and many cooks like to make it the day before. Stuffings are highly perishable and have been suspected in food-poisoning outbreaks. The American Institute of Baking suggests the following safe-for-health procedures:

Moist Stuffings: Prepare the liquid ingredients and refrigerate. Prepare the dry ingredients and store at room temperature. Combine the two just before stuffing and roasting the bird.

(*cont'd*)

Dry Stuffings: Combine the ingredients except raw egg, oysters and other such moist foods and refrigerate. Stuff the bird just before roasting.

TO TRUSS POULTRY

Allow three-quarters to onc cup of stuffing for each pound of ready-to-cook bird. Stuff wishbone cavity lightly and skewer or sew the skin to the back. Shape the wings akimbo, bringing tips onto back of wings. Sprinkle the body cavity with salt and fill lightly with stuffing. Do not pack it, as it expands on cooking. To close the cavity, place skewers across it and lace it closed with cord. Tie the drumsticks securely to the tail. (Many frozen birds do not require trussing nowadays because the legs are held in place through a slit made in the skin.)

BASIC BREAD CRUMB STUFFING

Enough for 5-pound chicken or turkey

1 small onion, chopped
1 stalk celery with leaves, chopped
⅓ to ½ cup butter
1 to 2 teaspoons poultry seasoning or sage
½ teaspoon salt
Freshly ground black pepper
2 tablespoons chopped parsley (optional)
5 cups stale bread cubes or crumbs
Water, milk or giblet broth (optional)

1. Sauté the onion and celery in the butter until tender but not brown.
2. Combine the seasonings and the bread crumbs, toss together with the onion mixture and, if a moist dressing is desired, add enough liquid to barely moisten crumbs.

VARIATIONS:

Bread Crumb–Chestnut Stuffing: Use not more than one-third cup butter and reduce bread crumbs to three and one-half cups. Add one pound boiled, coarsely chopped chestnuts. To prepare the chestnuts, cut a cross in the flat side of each shell. Boil in water to cover twenty minutes or until tender. Shell, peel and chop.

Mushroom Stuffing: Cook one-half pound sliced mushrooms with the onion and proceed as directed.

Giblet Stuffing: Simmer giblets in water until tender. Chop and measure. Substitute for an equal amount of the bread crumbs.

Cornbread Stuffing: Substitute cornbread crumbs for all or part of the bread crumbs. Ham or bacon drippings may be used in place of part of the butter.

Sausage Stuffing: Crumble four to six ounces sausage meat and brown in a skillet. Remove sausage and sauté onion and celery in part bacon fat and part butter. Add all to crumbs and proceed as directed.

NEW ENGLAND DRESSING

Enough for 10-pound turkey

- 2 quarts cubed stale bread, crusts removed
- 1 cup minced onion
- ½ cup butter
- ¾ teaspoon powdered thyme
- ¾ teaspoon sage
- 1 tablespoon salt
- 1½ teaspoons white pepper
- ¼ teaspoon powdered bay leaf
- ½ cup diced celery
- ½ cup coarsely chopped celery leaves
- ½ cup diced peeled tart apple

1. Dry out the bread cubes in a slow oven (300° F.). Do not let brown.
2. Cook the onion in the butter until transparent, stirring often. Add the thyme, sage, salt, pepper and bay leaf and blend.
3. Add the celery, the leaves of the celery and the apple. Cook three to five minutes. Add to the bread and mix well.

OLD-FASHIONED BREAD AND EGG DRESSING

About 8 servings

- ¼ cup chopped onion
- ¼ cup chopped celery
- ¼ cup butter or drippings
- 5 cups stale bread cubes or crumbs
- 1 hard-cooked egg, chopped
- ¾ teaspoon salt
- ⅛ teaspoon pepper
- 1 teaspoon mixed herbs (sage, thyme and marjoram)
- 1 egg, beaten
- ¾ cup giblet stock

1. Sauté the onion and celery in the butter until the onion is transparent. Mix with the bread, hard-cooked egg and seasonings.
2. Blend the beaten egg with the stock and stir into the bread mixture.
3. Turn into a greased pan and place in the oven with the turkey about one hour before the turkey is done. Bake, uncovered, until the dressing is a deep golden brown. Cut into pieces to serve.

PENNSYLVANIA DUTCH FILLING

Enough for 2 4-pound chickens or 6-pound turkey

- 2 cups hot, unseasoned, mashed potatoes
- 1 egg, well beaten
- 1 quart dry bread cubes
- 3 tablespoons butter or other fat
- ¼ cup chopped parsley
- ½ cup chopped onion
- 1 teaspoon salt
- ½ teaspoon poultry seasoning
- Freshly ground black pepper to taste

1. Combine the potatoes and egg.
2. Sauté the bread cubes in butter. Combine the potato mixture with the bread and stir in the remaining ingredients. Mix well.

BALTIMORE STUFFING

Enough for 2 4-pound chickens or 6-pound turkey

2 tablespoons bacon fat
1 tablespoon chopped parsley
2 teaspoons chopped chives
1 quart stale bread cubes or crumbs
1 teaspoon marjoram or thyme
1 teaspoon salt
Freshly ground black pepper to taste
25 oysters, drained

1. Melt the bacon fat, add the parsley and chives and cook until wilted. Add the mixture to the bread and season with marjoram, salt and pepper.

2. Lightly mix in the oysters. If the stuffing seems too dry, moisten with a little of the liquor which has been drained from the oysters.

CHESTNUT STUFFING

Enough for 12-pound turkey

2 quarts (about 4 pounds) chestnuts
4 teaspoons olive oil or salad oil
6 cups beef broth
1 onion, chopped
2 tablespoons butter
½ pound sausage meat
1 teaspoon chopped parsley
1 teaspoon chopped chives
½ teaspoon powdered thyme
¼ teaspoon powdered marjoram
Salt and freshly ground black pepper to taste
¾ cup soft bread crumbs
½ cup cognac (optional)

1. Cut gashes in the flat side of each chestnut. Heat the oil, add the chestnuts and cook over brisk heat three minutes, stirring or shaking the pan constantly. Drain and let cool. Remove the shells and inner skins.

2. Cook the chestnuts in the broth about twenty minutes, or until tender. Drain, reserving the broth for soup. Chop half the nuts coarsely and mash the rest. Set aside.

3. Cook the onion in the butter until golden brown. Add the sausage and seasonings and cook, stirring constantly, four to five minutes. Add to the chestnuts.

4. Soften the bread crumbs in milk or water. Press out the excess liquid and add to the chestnuts. Add the cognac, if desired, and mix well.

BRAZIL NUT–MUSHROOM STUFFING

Enough for 2 4-pound chickens or a 6-pound turkey

½ cup butter
½ pound mushrooms, finely chopped
½ cup diced celery
½ cup chopped Brazil nuts
¼ cup chopped onion
½ teaspoon salt
1 package (8 ounces) prepared stuffing mix
2 tablespoons chopped parsley

1. Melt the butter in a skillet, add the mushrooms, celery, Brazil nuts and onion. Sprinkle with salt and cook about ten minutes, stirring occasionally.

2. Add the stuffing mix and parsley and toss to combine.

HAM AND OLIVE STUFFING

Enough for a 12- to 15-pound turkey

1 quart boiled rice
1 quart toasted bread cubes
4 eggs, lightly beaten
1 cup diced cooked ham
⅔ cup chopped stuffed green olives
1 teaspoon salt
1 teaspoon ground sage
1 teaspoon ground marjoram
½ teaspoon freshly ground black pepper
¼ teaspoon garlic powder
½ cup chopped fresh parsley
1 cup chopped fresh onion
1 cup diced celery

Combine all the ingredients.

STUFFING A GOOSE

When stuffing a goose, Germans sometimes use mashed potatoes, sometimes sauerkraut and sometimes quartered apples, cored and peeled or not, as preferred.

The French like chestnuts and at least two chefs we know use them in combination with pork sausage and cognac. Sausage is an unusual ingredient, for most experts feel goose is so fatty that a tart or at least dry stuffing is better than one containing fat.

TANGERINE STUFFING FOR GOOSE

Enough for 9-pound goose

¼ cup butter
½ cup diced celery with leaves
3 tangerines
1 eight-ounce package prepared bread stuffing
½ pound chestnuts (1 cup cooked and chopped)
½ teaspoon poultry seasoning
3 cups cooked rice
½ cup stock or water

1. Melt the butter in a skillet, add the celery and cook over medium heat about ten minutes.

2. Meanwhile, peel the tangerines, removing the white membranes. Cut the sections into halves and remove the seeds.

3. Combine the tangerines, bread stuffing, chestnuts (to prepare see page 224), poultry seasoning, rice and stock. Add the cooked celery and butter and mix together lightly with a fork.

Other Stuffings for Goose: See Danish roast goose, page 221, and roast wild goose, page 179.

CHAPTER FIVE

FISH AND SHELLFISH

FISH

COURT BOUILLON *About 2 quarts*

A court bouillon is any liquid used for poaching fish or shellfish. It may be merely salted water. The best court bouillon, however, is made with fish trimmings and herbs.

1 stalk celery
3 sprigs parsley
½ bay leaf
1 cup white wine or ½ cup cider vinegar
Bones and head of any white-meat fish
2 quarts water
10 bruised peppercorns
Pinch of thyme
1 small onion
1 teaspoon salt

Tie the celery, parsley and bay leaf together with string. Combine all ingredients in a deep saucepan or kettle and simmer, uncovered, twenty minutes. Strain the liquid through a double thickness of cheesecloth. Cool it before using it for poached fish. Plunge shellfish into boiling court bouillon.

FISH STOCK *About 3 quarts*

3 pounds fish bones
2 tablespoons butter
4 quarts water
1 teaspoon thyme
3 bay leaves
3 cloves garlic, unpeeled
2 onions, coarsely chopped
10 peppercorns
2 large carrots, coarsely chopped
1 cup chopped leeks
2 stalks celery with leaves
2 teaspoons salt

1. Wash the fish bones in several changes of water.
2. Put the butter into a large kettle over medium heat and when it melts add fish bones and water.

(*cont'd*)

3. Cook, stirring, about five minutes. Add remaining ingredients and bring to the boil. Simmer thirty minutes and strain.

Note: This stock may be frozen and defrosted as needed. Or it may be kept a week or longer in the refrigerator.

STUFFED STRIPED BASS WITH SHRIMP WINE SAUCE

6 to 8 servings

1 four- to five-pound striped bass, dressed for baking
Salt and freshly ground black pepper to taste
Shrimp stuffing (see below)
1 carrot, sliced
1 cup sliced celery
1 small onion, minced
1½ cups dry white wine
1 bay leaf
2 tablespoons butter, melted
Shrimp wine sauce (see below)

1. Preheat oven to hot (400° F.).

2. Sprinkle the inside of the fish with salt and pepper and stuff loosely with shrimp stuffing. Close with skewers and lace with string.

3. Line an open roasting pan with foil, as page 231. On it make a bed of the carrot, celery and onion. Add the wine and bay leaf and place the fish on the vegetables. Brush the fish with butter. Bake, uncovered, until the fish flakes easily when tested with a fork, forty-five to fifty minutes. Baste frequently during baking with any remaining butter and with the liquid in the pan.

4. Place the fish on a hot platter and serve with shrimp wine sauce.

SHRIMP STUFFING:

1¼ pounds shrimp
¼ cup butter
1 small onion, minced
½ cup minced celery
½ cup chopped parsley
2 tablespoons dry white wine
1½ cups soft bread crumbs or cubes
Salt and freshly ground black pepper to taste

1. Shell and devein the raw shrimp. Coarsely chop enough to yield one-half cup and reserve for the sauce. Chop the remaining shrimp in small pieces.

2. In a skillet heat the butter, add the onion and celery and cook until the onion is transparent. Add the shrimp pieces and cook until they are pink. Add the parsley and cook until wilted.

3. Remove the pan from the heat, add the wine, mix, and add the bread crumbs. Season to taste with salt and pepper.

SHRIMP WINE SAUCE:

Dry white wine
2 teaspoons flour
½ cup chopped raw shrimp, reserved from the stuffing
2 egg yolks, lightly beaten
1 cup heavy cream
Salt and freshly ground black pepper to taste

(cont'd)

1. Strain the pan drippings from the fish and rub the vegetable residue through a fine sieve.

2. Add enough wine to the strained portion to make one and one-fourth cups. Blend the flour with a little wine and add, stirring, to the mixture. Add the shrimp and bring to a boil.

3. Mix the egg yolks and the cream. Add to the shrimp mixture and cook over the lowest heat, stirring constantly, until the mixture thickens. Do not let boil. Season with salt and pepper.

Preparing Whole Baked Fish: The following procedure will prevent the cooked fish from breaking when it is transferred from the pan to the serving platter: Line a greased baking dish with a double thickness of aluminum foil, allowing foil to overlap at both ends. Grease the foil, place the fish on it and bake as directed. When fish is done, use the foil as handles to transfer the fish to a heated serving platter.

SEA BASS STUFFED WITH CRABMEAT *6 servings*

1 three- to four-pound sea bass
Salt
1 pound crabmeat, picked over well
¼ cup chopped chives or green onion
¼ cup chopped parsley
¼ cup butter, melted
3 tablespoons chopped celery
½ cup fresh bread crumbs
¼ cup heavy cream
Freshly ground black pepper to taste
Olive or salad oil

1. Preheat oven to hot (400° F.).

2. Sprinkle the fish inside and out with salt. Combine the remaining ingredients, except the oil, and mix. Stuff the fish with the mixture and close with skewers and string. Sprinkle the fish with oil and place in a foil-lined baking pan (see above).

3. Bake, uncovered, until the fish flakes easily when tested with a fork, about thirty to forty minutes. Serve with rémoulade sauce I (page 453) to which has been added one-half cup crabmeat.

STRIPED BASS WITH OYSTERS AND HERBS *4 servings*

1 three- to four-pound striped bass
¼ cup butter, melted
2 cups soft white bread crumbs
⅛ teaspoon dried marjoram
2 tablespoons minced parsley
Salt and freshly ground black pepper to taste
Cayenne pepper to taste
2 thin slices salt pork
1 cup oysters

1. Have the fish cleaned but have the head and tail left intact.

2. Preheat oven to hot (400° F.).

3. In a skillet heat the butter and lightly brown the crumbs in it. Add the

(cont'd)

marjoram, parsley, salt, pepper and cayenne and mix. Stuff the fish loosely with the mixture and close with skewers and string.

4. Line a pan with foil, as page 231, grease the foil, place the fish on it and arrange the salt pork on top. Bake, uncovered, until the fish flakes easily when tested with a fork, thirty to forty minutes. Using the foil as handles, transfer the fish to a heated platter. Garnish with oysters that have been simmered in their juices one minute.

STRIPED BASS STUFFED WITH TOMATOES AND MUSHROOMS

6 servings

6 tablespoons butter
¼ cup chopped onion
1 cup chopped mushrooms
1 tomato, peeled, seeded and chopped
1 teaspoon chopped chives
1 tablespoon chopped parsley
¾ cup fresh bread crumbs
Salt
Freshly ground black pepper to taste
1 three-pound striped bass
1 tablespoon lemon juice
½ cup dry white wine or water

1. Preheat oven to hot (400° F.).

2. In a skillet heat half the butter, add the onion and cook until it is transparent. Add the mushrooms and cook until wilted. Add the tomato and simmer five minutes. Add the chives, parsley, bread crumbs, salt and pepper and mix. Stuff the fish loosely with the mixture and close the opening with skewers and string.

3. Place the fish in a baking pan lined with foil, as page 231, and sprinkle with the lemon juice, wine and additional salt and pepper. Dot with the remaining butter and bake, uncovered, basting occasionally, until the fish flakes easily when tested with a fork, about thirty to forty minutes. Sprinkle with additional butter and lemon juice.

BAKED BLUEFISH *4 to 6 servings*

1 four-pound bluefish, cleaned and split
4 strips bacon
Chopped parsley
Lemon wedges

1. Preheat oven to hot (425° F.).

2. Place the fish, skin side down, on an oiled baking sheet and place the bacon strips across it. Bake, uncovered, until the fish flakes easily when tested with a fork, twenty to twenty-five minutes.

3. Sprinkle with parsley and serve with lemon wedges and sour cream dill sauce (page 453).

CARP IN RED WINE *4 to 6 servings*

1 five-pound carp, dressed
1 cup water
1 cup red wine
1 teaspoon salt
1 slice each lemon and orange
1 tablespoon chopped parsley
Pinch of marjoram
Pinch of thyme
2 medium onions, chopped
2 anchovy fillets, chopped
2 teaspoons flour
2 teaspoons butter
1 egg yolk, lightly beaten

1. Combine the carp head, water, wine, salt, fruit, parsley and herbs and simmer, uncovered, twenty minutes; strain.
2. Preheat oven to moderate (350° F.).
3. Place the onions in a foil-lined baking dish (page 231) and place the fish on top. Add the seasoned wine and anchovies and bake, uncovered, until the fish flakes easily, about thirty-five minutes. Baste often with the pan liquid.
4. Transfer the fish to a hot platter. Strain the liquid and reheat. Stir in the flour creamed with the butter and boil one minute. Add a little of the hot mixture to the egg yolk, then return this to the sauce. Heat but do not boil. Adjust the seasonings and pour over the fish.

CURRIED COD *6 servings*

¾ cup flour
¼ cup curry powder
2 pounds cod fillets, cut into 2-inch strips
½ cup butter
Chopped parsley

1. Mix the flour and curry powder and dip the fillets into the mixture.
2. Heat the butter in a skillet over moderate heat and brown the fish in it on both sides. Serve sprinkled with chopped parsley.

BAKED COD WITH OYSTER STUFFING *4 to 8 servings*

5 tablespoons butter
6 whole scallions, chopped
¼ cup minced celery
¼ cup minced green pepper
½ cup fresh bread crumbs
½ cup chopped parsley
½ pint oysters, with their liquor
¼ teaspoon freshly ground black pepper
1 teaspoon salt
½ teaspoon thyme
1 two- to four-pound cod

1. Preheat oven to hot (400° F.).
2. In a skillet heat the butter, add the scallions, celery and green pepper and cook until tender. Add the crumbs, parsley, oysters and oyster liquor and cook five minutes. Add the remaining seasonings.

(cont'd)

3. Stuff the fish loosely with the mixture and close with skewers and string. Place the fish on a foil-lined pan (page 231). Dot with additional butter. Bake, uncovered, until the fish flakes easily when tested with a fork, thirty to forty minutes.

COD PROVENCAL *8 servings*

¼ cup olive oil
1 large onion, sliced thin
2 cloves garlic, chopped
1 green pepper, shredded
1 two-ounce can anchovies with oil, chopped
½ cup black olives, pitted
¼ teaspoon fennel seed
8 thin cod steaks
4 slices tomato
Salt and freshly ground black pepper to taste
½ cup tomato purée
1 cup red wine
Chopped parsley

1. Preheat oven to hot (400° F.).
2. In a skillet, heat half the oil, add the onion, garlic and green pepper and cook until the onion is transparent. Add the anchovies, olives and fennel.
3. Place four cod steaks in a greased baking dish, spread with the anchovy mixture and top each with a slice of the remaining cod, then of tomato. Brush with the remaining oil and season with salt and pepper.
4. Mix the tomato purée with the wine and pour over the fish. Bake about thirty minutes, basting often. Sprinkle with the parsley.

CODFISH LOAF *6 servings*

2½ cups cooked codfish, flaked
¼ cup chopped onion
3 tablespoons chopped celery
3 tablespoons chopped green pepper
⅓ cup chopped walnuts
¼ cup chopped parsley
2 toast slices, crumbled
Salt and freshly ground black pepper
Few drops of Tabasco sauce
1 teaspoon Worcestershire sauce
1 teaspoon dried tarragon
2 eggs, separated
½ cup light cream
½ cup butter, melted

1. Preheat oven to moderate (375° F.).
2. Combine the fish, onion, celery, green pepper, walnuts, parsley, toast crumbs, salt, pepper, Tabasco, Worcestershire sauce and tarragon.
3. Beat the egg yolks until light and lemon colored and add them to the mixture. Add the cream and melted butter. Fold in the egg whites, stiffly beaten, and pour the mixture into a buttered ring mold or bread pan.
4. Set in a pan of hot water and bake until the loaf is set, about forty minutes. Unmold on a hot plate and serve with egg sauce (page 447).

CODFISH CAKES *4 servings*

½ pound salt cod, soaked overnight
Water
1 cup mashed potatoes
1 or 2 eggs
Freshly ground black pepper to taste
Butter or bacon fat
Flour or crumbs, if desired

1. Cut the cod into small pieces, cover with water and bring to a boil. Taste for saltiness; if excessively salty, discard the water and repeat until the water is almost fresh.

2. Mix the fish with the potatoes, eggs and pepper. Form into eight cakes and sauté in plenty of hot butter or bacon fat. Or roll in flour or crumbs and fry in deep fat heated to 370° F.

Note: A little ground ginger does wonders for codfish cakes.

EELS IN TOMATO SAUCE *6 servings*

3 pounds fresh eels, cleaned and skinned
½ cup olive oil
1 onion, finely minced
2 cloves garlic, crushed or minced
1 tablespoon minced parsley
½ cup boiling rich meat or fish stock
2 tablespoons tomato paste, or ¾ cup tomato purée
Salt and freshly ground black pepper to taste

1. Cut the eels into small sections. Wash and dry thoroughly.

2. Heat the oil in a skillet, add the onion, garlic and parsley and cook until the onion is transparent. Add the eels and cook very slowly, turning the sections so they absorb the flavor of the sauce.

3. When the sauce has almost cooked away, slowly add the stock and blend in the tomato paste. Add salt and pepper, bring to a boil and cook five to ten minutes over low heat. Serve very hot.

ANGUILLES QUO VADIS, PAGE 18.

EELS A L'ORLY *4 servings*

3 pounds eels
2 tablespoons lemon juice
2 tablespoons cognac
Salt and freshly ground black pepper to taste
1 cup sifted flour
½ teaspoon baking powder
1 egg, beaten
½ cup milk
Fat for deep frying

1. Skin and clean the eels and cut them into three-inch lengths. Wash and drain. Add the lemon juice, cognac, salt and pepper. Let stand an hour or longer.

2. Sift together the flour, baking powder and one-fourth teaspoon salt. Mix the egg and milk and combine with the dry ingredients. Stir until smooth.

3. Dip the eels in batter and fry in deep hot fat (360° F.) until well browned.

FINNAN HADDIE DELMONICO *5 to 6 servings*

1½ pounds finnan haddie
¼ cup butter
3 tablespoons flour
2 cups cream or milk
Salt and freshly ground black pepper
4 hard-cooked eggs, quartered
Mashed potatoes (about 2 cups)
Grated Parmesan cheese

1. Place the fish in a shallow pan, barely cover with water and simmer, covered, fifteen minutes. Drain and cool the fish; remove the bones and flake into good-sized pieces.

2. Preheat oven to hot (400° F.).

3. Melt the butter in the top of a double boiler, add the flour and stir with a wire whisk until blended. Meanwhile, bring the cream to a boil and add all at once to the butter-flour mixture, stirring vigorously with the whisk until thickened and smooth. Season the sauce with salt and pepper.

4. Add the fish and eggs and mix carefully to avoid mashing the fish. Pour into a casserole and border the mashed potatoes around the dish, using a pastry tube if desired.

5. Sprinkle the Parmesan cheese over the top and bake until the top is golden brown. Serve immediately.

PICKLED FLOUNDER *8 or more servings*

2 pounds flounder fillets
Lemon or lime juice for dipping
Flour
Butter
1 clove garlic, crushed
3 tablespoons lemon or lime juice
⅓ cup orange juice
⅓ cup olive oil
¼ cup minced scallions
Dash of Tabasco
Salt to taste
Ripe olives
Quartered limes or lemons

1. Dip the fillets in the lemon or lime juice, rub with flour and sauté in hot butter until golden brown. Arrange in a dish about two inches deep in a symmetrical fashion.

2. Combine the garlic, lemon juice, orange juice, olive oil, scallions, Tabasco and salt. Pour this sauce over the fish. Cover and refrigerate twenty-four hours or more.

3. To serve as a first course or as one of the dishes at a buffet supper, garnish with ripe olives and quartered limes. If desired, accompany with mayonnaise.

GULF COAST STUFFED FLOUNDER *6 servings*

¼ cup butter
2 tablespoons chopped green pepper
¼ cup finely chopped onion
1 cup fresh or canned crabmeat, picked over well
1 teaspoon chopped parsley
Salt and freshly ground black pepper to taste
1 tablespoon lemon juice
Tabasco sauce to taste
6 one-pound flounders, backbones removed

(*cont'd*)

1. In a saucepan heat the butter, add the green pepper and onion and cook until the onion is transparent. Add the crabmeat, parsley, salt, pepper, lemon juice and Tabasco sauce and mix well.

2. Stuff the flounders loosely with the mixture and close with skewers and string. Arrange the fish on a buttered baking pan and sprinkle with salt and pepper.

3. Broil slowly on both sides in a preheated broiler, basting frequently with lemon juice and additional butter, until golden brown.

HADDOCK STUFFED WITH CLAMS *4 to 6 servings*

- 1 three-pound haddock
- ¼ cup butter
- ½ cup finely chopped onion
- 1½ cups fresh bread crumbs
- ¼ cup finely chopped parsley
- 1 can (7 ounces) minced clams with liquid
- Salt and freshly ground black pepper to taste
- ¼ teaspoon nutmeg
- 2 eggs, beaten
- Bacon or salt pork

1. Have the haddock cleaned and split for stuffing. Preheat oven to hot (400° F.).

2. In a skillet heat the butter, add the onion and cook until it is transparent. Combine the onion with the remaining ingredients, except the bacon. Stuff the fish loosely with the mixture and close with skewers and string. Lace strips of bacon or salt pork on top of the fish.

3. Place the fish in an oiled baking dish and bake, uncovered, twenty-five to thirty-five minutes. Serve sprinkled with additional chopped parsley.

FILLETS OF HADDOCK IN CREAM SAUCE *6 servings*

- ¼ cup butter
- 3 tablespoons flour
- ¼ cup bottled clam juice
- ¼ cup dry white wine
- 1 cup cream
- Salt and freshly ground black pepper
- Nutmeg
- 2 tablespoons sherry
- ½ bulb fresh fennel, thinly sliced, or ½ teaspoon fennel seed, ground
- 6 haddock fillets
- Chopped parsley

1. Preheat oven to moderate (325° F.).

2. In a saucepan heat the butter, stir in the flour with a wire whisk and cook until slightly colored. Add the clam juice and wine and stir until smooth. Gradually add the cream and continue stirring until smooth and moderately thick. Cook five minutes and season to taste with salt, pepper and nutmeg. Add the sherry and fennel.

3. Place the fillets in a greased baking dish and pour the sauce over them. Bake, uncovered, twenty-five to thirty minutes. Remove to heated serving platter and sprinkle liberally with chopped parsley.

OVEN-FRIED HADDOCK FILLETS *6 servings*

1 tablespoon salt
1 cup milk
3 haddock fillets
¾ cup fine, dry bread crumbs
¼ cup grated Parmesan cheese
¼ teaspoon thyme
¼ cup butter, melted
Paprika
Lemon wedges

1. Preheat oven to very hot (525° F.).

2. Add the salt to the milk. Cut the fillets into serving pieces and dip first in the milk and then in the crumbs mixed with the cheese and thyme.

3. Arrange the fish pieces in a well-greased baking dish and pour the butter over them evenly. Bake on the top shelf of the oven about twelve minutes. Garnish with paprika. Serve with lemon wedges.

CURRIED HADDOCK *6 servings*

2 pounds haddock fillets
1 cup water
1 cup dry white wine
½ bay leaf
3 tablespoons butter
¼ cup finely chopped shallot or onion
¼ cup finely chopped green pepper
1 stalk celery, finely chopped
1 tablespoon curry powder
3 tablespoons flour
½ cup dry white wine
Tabasco sauce
Salt and freshly ground black pepper to taste
Chopped parsley

1. Wipe the fillets with a damp cloth and place in a skillet. Cover with the water and wine and add the bay leaf. Cover closely with aluminum foil and simmer over low heat until the fish flakes easily with a fork, about ten minutes. Drain and reserve the stock. Transfer fish to a heated serving dish and keep warm.

2. In a saucepan, heat the butter and add the vegetables. Cook over low heat ten minutes. Stir in the curry powder and flour. Bring the reserved stock and wine to a boil and, using a wire whisk, add the stock all at once to the vegetable mixture, stirring vigorously until the sauce is thickened and smooth.

3. Simmer gently five minutes and season to taste with Tabasco sauce, salt and pepper. Strain or not, as desired, and pour the sauce, piping hot, over the fish. Garnish with chopped parsley.

BAKED HALIBUT IN CREAM *6 servings*

1 three-pound halibut steak
Flour
Salt and freshly ground black pepper
5 tablespoons butter
½ pound mushrooms, sliced
½ cup thinly sliced onion
½ bay leaf
1 whole clove garlic
1 cup dry white wine
1 cup heavy cream
Chopped parsley

(*cont'd*)

1. Preheat oven to moderate (350° F.).

2. Wipe the fish with a damp cloth and dredge with flour seasoned with salt and pepper. Place the fish in a buttered baking dish and dot with butter. Bake twenty minutes, basting often.

3. Sprinkle the fish with the mushrooms and onion and add the bay leaf, garlic and white wine. Cover with buttered waxed paper or aluminum foil (butter side down) and bake twenty minutes longer, basting occasionally.

4. Transfer the fish, mushrooms and onion to a heated platter and discard the bay leaf and garlic. To the liquid remaining in the pan add the heavy cream. Heat the sauce to the boiling point but do not let it boil. Correct the seasonings and pour over the fish. Garnish with chopped parsley.

SESAME HALIBUT STEAKS *6 servings*

3 halibut steaks, 1¼ inches thick
Dash of salt
6 teaspoons butter
3 cups soft bread crumbs
1 teaspoon salt
⅛ teaspoon freshly ground pepper
3 tablespoons toasted sesame seeds
½ teaspoon whole thyme leaves, crumbled
⅓ cup butter, melted

1. Preheat oven to moderate (350° F.).

2. Place the steaks in a buttered baking pan, sprinkle with salt and top each with two teaspoons of butter.

3. Combine the remaining ingredients and sprinkle each steak with one cup of the mixture. Bake, uncovered, until the fish flakes easily when tested with a fork, twenty-five to thirty minutes.

STUFFED HALIBUT STEAKS *6 to 8 servings*

3 tablespoons butter
¼ cup finely chopped onion
½ cup coarsely chopped mushrooms
¼ cup finely chopped parsley
1 teaspoon salt
Freshly ground black pepper to taste
¼ teaspoon thyme
½ cup fresh bread crumbs
2 tablespoons heavy cream
2 halibut steaks, weighing 2 pounds each
Lemon wedges

1. Preheat oven to hot (400° F.).

2. In a skillet heat the butter, add the onion and cook until it is transparent. Add the mushrooms, parsley and seasonings and cook five minutes longer. Stir in the bread crumbs and cream.

3. Oil a baking dish and place one of the fish steaks on the bottom. Cover the center with the stuffing and top with the second steak. Skewer with toothpicks.

4. Brush the top steak with butter and sprinkle with salt and pepper. Bake until the fish flakes easily when tested with a fork, thirty to forty minutes. Baste with a little melted butter while cooking. Serve with lemon wedges.

BAKED KIPPERED HERRING *6 servings*

Baked kippered herring is a wonderful idea for Sunday brunch. Serve the herring with scrambled eggs to which a little whipped cream has been added, broiled tomato halves, and toast. Pickled walnuts provide a flavorful garnish. Serve tea with lemon or cups of piping hot coffee.

6 plain smoked kippered herring (canned or packaged)
Butter
Juice of ½ lemon
Few drops of Tabasco sauce
Worcestershire sauce (optional)
Chopped parsley

1. Preheat oven to hot (400° F.).
2. Line a heavy skillet with aluminum foil and arrange the herring on it. Dot with butter and bake until the butter melts and the fish is heated through.
3. In a small saucepan or butter warmer, combine three tablespoons butter, the lemon juice, Tabasco and Worcestershire. Pour over the hot herring and serve sprinkled with chopped parsley.

HERRING SALAD, PAGE 24.

MACKEREL WITH OLIVES *4 servings*

Salad oil
4 Boston mackerel
Small pitted green olives
Salt and freshly ground black pepper to taste
Black Italian or Greek olives
Lemon slices

1. Preheat oven to moderate (350° F.). Lightly grease the bottom of a shallow glass or earthenware baking dish with salad oil.
2. Stuff each mackerel with five or six green olives. Arrange the fish in the baking dish, sprinkle with a little more oil and with salt and pepper. Scatter the black olives around the fish.
3. Bake, uncovered, until the fish flakes easily when tested with a fork, about twenty-five minutes. Garnish the mackerel with lemon slices and serve from the baking dish.

BROILED MACKEREL *3 to 4 servings*

1 three-pound mackerel
Flour
Butter
Salt and freshly ground black pepper
Paprika
Lemon wedges
Chopped parsley

1. Preheat broiler ten minutes.
2. Split the mackerel, dust with flour, place skin side down in a greased baking pan and dot heavily with butter. Sprinkle with salt, pepper and paprika.

(*cont'd*)

3. Broil the fish two to three inches from the source of the heat in a preheated broiler, basting occasionally. Cook until the fish flakes easily when tested with a fork, six to ten minutes.

4. Serve immediately with lemon wedges and, if desired, sprinkle with chopped parsley.

SAUTEED WALL-EYED PIKE *About 6 servings*

1 small wall-eyed pike, 5 to 6 pounds
½ cup milk
Flour or cornmeal
Salt and freshly ground black pepper to taste
¾ cup butter, approximately
1 tablespoon lemon juice
1 teaspoon chopped parsley

1. Cut fillets from the pike and cut the fillets into serving pieces. The thicker portions should be split if more than one inch thick.

2. Dip the pieces of fish in the milk and then in flour or cornmeal seasoned with salt and pepper.

3. In a skillet heat one-fourth cup of the butter and sauté the fish in it until brown on both sides. Add more butter as necessary and cook until the fish flakes easily when tested with a fork.

4. Cream the remaining butter (about one-third cup) with the lemon juice and dot over the hot, cooked fish. Sprinkle with the chopped parsley. Serve with broiled tomatoes and marinated cucumbers.

PIKE BAKED WITH HERBS *5 to 6 servings*

1 five- to six-pound pike
½ cup butter
1 teaspoon salt
1 tablespoon minced parsley
Pinch of thyme
Pinch of marjoram
Pinch of winter savory
2 anchovy fillets, chopped
1 cut clove garlic
1 cup white wine
2 teaspoons flour
2 teaspoons butter
Lemon juice to taste
White pepper (optional)

1. Preheat oven to moderate (350° F.).

2. Thoroughly clean and scale the pike; do not remove the head or tail. Dot the inside with six tablespoons of the butter and sprinkle the cavity with the salt, parsley, herbs and anchovies. Close the fish with skewers and string.

3. Oil a baking pan, cover the bottom with a double thickness of aluminum foil, as page 231, and rub the foil with a cut garlic clove. Oil the foil and place the pike on top. Dot with the remaining butter.

4. Bake, uncovered, until the fish flakes easily when tested with a fork. Baste every five or, at the most, ten minutes with the wine.

5. Lift the foil with the fish on it and set on a heated platter. Tuck the foil around the fish.

(cont'd)

6. Strain the pan juices into a saucepan and set over low heat. Stir in the flour creamed with the two teaspoons of butter and boil one minute. Add a dash of lemon juice and season with additional salt and white pepper if desired. Serve the sauce with the fish.

POMPANO A LA SIEPI *4 servings*

4 Florida pompanos, cleaned
Salt and freshly ground black pepper
Olive oil
4 tomatoes
8 anchovy fillets
¼ cup sweet butter
2 teaspoons dry mustard
2 teaspoons chopped chives
2 tablespoons lemon juice

1. Season the pompano lightly with salt and pepper and brush with olive oil.
2. Broil the fish about three inches from the source of heat in a preheated broiler five to seven minutes on each side. Brush the second side with oil after turning the fish.
3. Cut a slice from the top of each tomato, season lightly with salt and pepper and brush with olive oil. Place on the broiler rack after turning the fish and broil until hot but not soft. Place two anchovy fillets on each tomato.
4. In a small saucepan, melt the butter and add the mustard and chives. Add the lemon juice just before serving.
5. To serve, place the fish on a hot platter, garnish with the tomatoes and pour the sauce over the fish, or serve separately.

POMPANO BAKED IN WINE *2 servings*

1 one-and-one-half-pound pompano, split
2 tablespoons chopped pimento
2 tablespoons chopped onion
¾ cup sliced mushrooms
2 tablespoons chopped parsley
2 tablespoons buttered crumbs
½ teaspoon salt
Freshly ground black pepper to taste
1 cup chicken stock
¼ cup dry red or white wine

1. Preheat oven to moderate (375° F.).
2. Place the fish, skin side down, on a greased heatproof platter.
3. Mix the pimento, onion, mushrooms, parsley, buttered crumbs, salt and pepper and spread over the fish. Mix the stock and wine and pour around the fish.
4. Bake, uncovered, about twenty-five minutes, basting occasionally with the wine-and-broth mixture.

PORGY SAUTE MEUNIERE *6 servings*

6 porgies, cleaned
Milk
Flour
Salt and freshly ground black pepper
Salad oil
Lemon juice
Chopped parsley
6 slices peeled lemon
6 tablespoons butter

1. Dip the fish in milk, then in flour seasoned with salt and pepper.
2. In a skillet add salad oil to a depth of one-quarter inch and heat until very hot. Add the fish and cook until golden brown, about three minutes on each side.
3. Remove the fish to a warm serving platter and sprinkle with lemon juice and chopped parsley. Place a slice of lemon on top. Heat the butter until it is light brown and pour over the fish.

BROILED PORGIES *6 servings*

6 porgies, cleaned
Salt and freshly ground black pepper to taste
¼ cup butter
Flour
Paprika

1. Season fish with salt and pepper and place on greased foil in a shallow pan. Brush half the butter over the fish and sprinkle lightly with flour.
2. Broil three to five inches from the source of heat in a preheated broiler for three minutes. Turn, brush with the remaining butter and sprinkle lightly with flour and paprika to give a light crust. Continue broiling until the fish flakes easily when tested with a fork, about six minutes in all.

WHOLE SALMON BAKED IN FOIL *About 12 servings*

Here is a dish for a New England Fourth of July feast. Salmon and peas are traditional in that region on Independence Day.

1 seven- to ten-pound salmon, cleaned
¾ cup dry white wine, or equal parts lemon juice and water
¼ teaspoon dried thyme leaves
8 fresh basil leaves, or ½ teaspoon dried basil
3 sprigs fresh tarragon, or ¼ teaspoon dried tarragon
2 sprigs rosemary, or ¼ teaspoon dried rosemary
Celery leaves from a small stalk
3 minced shallots or 1 small onion freshly minced
2 slices lemon with peel
Salt

1 Leave the salmon whole or remove the head. Rinse under cold running water and place on paper towels to dry.
2 Place the wine in a saucepan and add the remaining ingredients, except the salt. Let the mixture simmer, uncovered, one-half hour without boiling.

(cont'd)

3. Preheat oven to moderate (375° F.).

4. Place the fish lengthwise on a long sheet of foil, bring up the edges and pour the wine mixture over the fish. Sprinkle with salt.

5. Completely enclose the fish, crimping the foil to seal the edges tightly. Place the foil-wrapped fish in a large baking pan and transfer to the oven. Bake until the fish flakes easily when tested with a fork, about two hours.

6. Serve hot with Hollandaise sauce (page 449) or with a white wine sauce (see below).

Note: If there is leftover salmon, serve it cold with mayonnaise.

WHITE WINE SAUCE:

½ cup butter
2 shallots, finely minced
6 tablespoons flour
Liquid in which salmon was baked
Equal parts dry white wine and boiling water
½ cup heavy cream
Salt and freshly ground black pepper to taste
2 egg yolks

1. While the salmon is baking, melt the butter in a saucepan and add the shallots. Cook until transparent but not brown. Using a wire whisk, stir in the flour until it is well blended. Cook over low heat three minutes. Let stand until the fish is done.

2. When the fish is removed from the oven, use a large spoon to dip out the juices and add to the butter mixture in the saucepan, stirring constantly over moderate heat. Continue stirring vigorously and add enough wine and boiling water to make five cups of liquid.

3. Cook the liquid, stirring, until thickened and smooth. Add the cream and season with salt and pepper. Strain through a fine sieve. Just before serving, reheat and add the egg yolks lightly beaten with a little of the hot sauce. Cook two minutes over low heat but do not let boil.

Note: A small three- or four-pound center cut of salmon may be baked in exactly the same manner as the whole salmon. For a center cut of that size, use half the wine-herb mixture and prepare half the amount of sauce. Cook fifteen minutes a pound in a moderate oven (375° F.).

GRILLED SALMON STEAKS *8 servings*

8 salmon steaks, ¾ inch thick
¾ cup dry vermouth
¾ cup olive or salad oil
1½ tablespoons lemon juice
¾ teaspoon salt
Dash of freshly ground black pepper
¼ teaspoon thyme
¼ teaspoon marjoram
⅛ teaspoon sage
1 tablespoon minced parsley

1. Place the salmon steaks in a large pan. Mix the remaining ingredients and pour over the top. Allow to stand three to four hours, turning once.

(*cont'd*)

2. Preheat broiler. Remove the steaks from the marinade, reserving the marinade. Place the fish on greased broiler rack and broil until brown. Turn carefully and brown on the other side. Cook until fork tender, or about fifteen minutes, brushing frequently with the reserved marinade.

Note: The salmon steaks may be grilled over charcoal.

BROILED SALMON *6 servings*

2 pounds salmon steaks
1 teaspoon salt
¼ teaspoon freshly ground black pepper
½ cup butter, melted
Finely chopped parsley
Lemon slices

1. Sprinkle both sides of each steak with salt and pepper and let stand about ten minutes to absorb the salt.

2. Place the steaks on a preheated greased broiler pan and brush with about two tablespoons of the butter. Place the pan in the preheated broiler about two inches from high heat and cook three to five minutes. Turn, brush the other side with two tablespoons butter and cook three to five minutes.

3. Serve on a hot platter. Pour the remaining melted butter, to which the parsley has been added, over the fish. Garnish with lemon slices.

BAKED SALMON LOAF *6 servings*

2 cups cooked or canned salmon
⅔ cup evaporated milk
2 cups soft bread crumbs
1 egg, well beaten
1 tablespoon minced parsley
2 tablespoons minced onion
½ teaspoon salt
¼ teaspoon poultry seasoning

1. Preheat oven to moderate (375° F.).

2. Turn the salmon with the liquid into a mixing bowl. Add the milk and bread crumbs and mix with a fork until well blended. Add the egg and remaining ingredients and mix well.

3. Turn the mixture into a well-greased loaf pan and bake until the center is firm, about forty minutes. Serve with a sauce made by heating one cup white sauce with one-quarter cup each mayonnaise, chopped almonds and olives.

SALMON FLORENTINE *4 servings*

Here is another Florentine dish. This time it is salmon on a bed of spinach.

2 cups cooked or canned salmon
Milk
¼ cup butter
¼ cup flour
½ teaspoon dry mustard
¼ teaspoon salt
¼ teaspoon Tabasco sauce
1½ cups grated cheese
2 cups cooked spinach, drained

(*cont'd*)

1. Preheat oven to hot (425° F.).

2. Drain and flake the salmon. Add enough milk to the salmon liquid to make one and one-half cups.

3. In a saucepan melt the butter, add the flour and stir with a wire whisk until blended. Meanwhile, bring the milk mixture to a boil and add all at once to the butter-flour mixture, stirring vigorously with the whisk until the sauce is thickened and smooth. Season with the mustard, salt and Tabasco and mix in one cup of the cheese.

4. Place the spinach in four individual greased casseroles, top with the salmon and sauce and sprinkle with the remaining cheese. Bake, uncovered, fifteen minutes.

POACHED SALMON STEAK *6 servings*

2 tablespoons butter
⅓ cup chopped onion
⅓ cup chopped carrot
⅓ cup chopped celery
1 quart water
½ cup dry white wine, or ¼ cup vinegar
Salt
Peppercorns
1 three-pound salmon steak
Hollandaise sauce or mayonnaise

1. In a large skillet heat the butter, add the vegetables and cook five minutes. Add the water, wine and seasonings and simmer five minutes.

2. Wrap the salmon in cheesecloth and place in the boiling liquid. Lower the heat, cover and simmer gently about twenty-five minutes, or eight minutes per pound.

3. Remove the salmon carefully, unwrap and serve hot with Hollandaise sauce (page 449) or cold with mayonnaise.

SALMON FROMAGE *6 servings*

2 cups cooked or canned salmon
½ cup milk
¼ cup butter
2 tablespoons finely chopped onion
¼ cup flour
Dash of Tabasco sauce
1½ cups cottage or pot cheese
Hot biscuits
Pimento strips
Parsley

1. Drain the salmon and add its liquid to the milk. Gently break the salmon into large pieces.

2. Melt the butter in a heavy saucepan, add the onion and cook until it is transparent. Using a wire whisk, stir in the flour. Add the milk and salmon liquid all at once and cook over moderate heat, stirring constantly, until the mixture begins to thicken. Add the Tabasco.

3. Immediately fold in the cottage cheese and reheat, stirring gently. Add the salmon and reheat, stirring gently. Serve at once on hot biscuits. Garnish with pimento strips and parsley.

SALMON ARCHIDUC *4 to 6 servings*

Salmon archiduc is salmon in a sherry-and-cream sauce.

¼ cup minced onion
¼ cup butter
4½ tablespoons flour
1½ cups milk (if canned salmon is used, the liquid from the can may be substituted for part of the milk)
½ teaspoon salt
¼ teaspoon freshly ground black pepper
Dash of cayenne pepper
½ cup heavy cream
¼ cup sherry
2 tablespoons cognac
2 cups cooked salmon, canned or fresh
1 tablespoon finely chopped parsley
Toast points

1. In a saucepan sauté the onion in butter until it is transparent. Using a wire whisk, stir in the flour. Meanwhile, bring the milk to a boil and add all at once to the butter-onion mixture, stirring vigorously with the whisk until the sauce is thickened and smooth.

2. Stir in the salt, pepper, cayenne, cream, sherry and cognac. Stir in the flaked salmon and parsley and heat until very hot. Serve over toast points.

SARDINES ORIENTALE *4 servings*

2 tablespoons olive oil
2 leeks (white part only), cut in thin strips
1 onion, cut in thin strips
2 cloves garlic, crushed
2 tomatoes, peeled and chopped
1 cup white wine
Pinch of saffron
Salt and freshly ground black pepper to taste
4 three-and-three-quarter-ounce cans sardines

1. In a skillet heat the oil, add the leeks and onion and cook ten minutes. Add the garlic, tomatoes, wine and saffron. Simmer, uncovered, about twenty-five minutes. Season with salt and pepper.

2. Place all but fifteen of the drained sardines in an earthenware dish. Pour the sauce over the top and arrange the reserved sardines over the sauce. Bake in a preheated moderate oven (350° F.) five minutes. Serve hot in the baking dish.

Shad and shad roe are among the noblest gifts of spring. Despite the delicate texture and flavor of shad, however, it is loaded with bones. There are only about a dozen professional shad boners in New York, and if the cost of boned shad seems somewhat elevated, it is justifiable.

SHAD BAKED IN CREAM *6 servings*

1 three-pound boned shad
Butter
Salt and freshly ground black pepper to taste
1 cup heavy cream
Chopped parsley

(cont'd)

1. Preheat oven to hot (400° F.).

2. Butter a baking dish and place the shad on it. Dot with butter and sprinkle with salt and pepper. Bake, uncovered, twenty minutes.

3. Add the cream and bake ten minutes longer, basting occasionally with the cream. Sprinkle with chopped parsley.

STUFFED BAKED BUCK SHAD *6 servings*

1 four-pound buck shad, cleaned and boned
Salt
Butter
1 cup chopped onion
½ cup thinly sliced celery
4 cups bread crumbs
⅛ teaspoon freshly ground black pepper
¼ teaspoon each thyme, rosemary and tarragon, or ½ teaspoon sage
2 tablespoons lemon juice
1 or 2 strips bacon

1. Preheat oven to moderate (350° F.).

2. Sprinkle the shad inside and out with salt.

3. In a skillet, heat one-quarter cup of butter, add the onion and celery and cook until almost tender. Mix with the bread crumbs, herbs and lemon juice. Stuff the fish loosely with the mixture and close with skewers and string. Place on a foil-lined baking dish.

4. Brush the shad with additional melted butter and place a strip or two of bacon over the top. Bake until the fish flakes easily, about thirty-five to forty-five minutes. Baste with butter as necessary. Serve with lemon butter.

BAKED SHAD WITH SPINACH STUFFING *5 to 6 servings*

1 three-and-one-half- to four-pound shad
Salt and freshly ground black pepper
2 pounds spinach, cooked
⅓ cup butter
1 tablespoon minced onion
1½ tablespoons flour
½ cup heavy sweet or sour cream (optional)
1 tablespoon lemon juice
½ cup dry white wine (optional)

1. Have the shad boned at the fish market. Sprinkle inside with salt and pepper.

2. Preheat oven to moderate (350° F.).

3. Drain the spinach and rub through a coarse sieve, or chop fine.

4. In a large skillet heat two tablespoons of the butter, add the onion and cook until lightly browned. Using a wire whisk, stir in the flour. Add the spinach and cook, stirring, until thickened. Add the cream and lemon juice and season with salt and pepper.

5. Stuff the shad with the mixture and tie into shape. Place the shad in a greased baking pan lined with foil, as page 231, and add the wine to the pan, if

(cont'd)

desired. Sprinkle the fish with salt and pepper and dot with bits of the remaining butter.

6. Bake the shad until it flakes easily when tested with a fork, about thirty-five to forty-five minutes. Baste frequently with butter, or the butter and wine in the pan.

PLANKED SHAD *6 servings*

1 three-pound shad, boned and split
Salt and freshly ground black pepper to taste
Melted butter
Duchesse potatoes (page 394)
Assorted cooked vegetables

1. Oil an oak or hickory plank with salad oil and heat it in a hot oven (450° F.). Arrange the shad, skin side down, in the center. Sprinkle with salt and pepper and brush well with melted butter.

2. Bake fifteen minutes, basting with the butter. Reduce the oven temperature to moderate (350° F.) and bake until the fish is lightly browned and flakes easily when tested with a fork, ten or twelve minutes longer.

3. Remove the planked fish from the oven and surround it with a border of duchesse potatoes. Brush the potatoes with butter and broil until lightly browned. Fill the spaces between the fish and potatoes with assorted hot, cooked vegetables such as peas, string beans or grilled tomatoes. Serve immediately.

PLANKED SHAD WITH SHAD ROE DRESSING *6 to 8 servings*

1 four-pound shad, boned
1 pair shad roe
Water
¾ teaspoon salt
1 tablespoon vinegar
1 tablespoon butter
1 small onion, minced
1 tablespoon chopped parsley
1 tablespoon lemon juice or dry white wine
2 tablespoons grated Parmesan cheese
Freshly ground black pepper
Tomatoes, halved
Hot duchesse potatoes (page 394)

1. Have boned shad prepared for stuffing.

2. Preheat oven to hot (400° F.) and heat a well-oiled wooden plank.

3. Simmer shad roe in water to cover with one-half teaspoon of the salt and the vinegar for ten minutes. Drain, skin and chop.

4. In a skillet heat the butter, add the onion and cook until it is transparent.

5. Mix roe, onion and the remaining ingredients, except the vegetables, until well blended.

6. Sprinkle the fish with additional salt, stuff with roe mixture, sew cut surfaces together loosely and place on the plank. Bake until the fish flakes easily when tested with a fork, about one hour.

7. Garnish plank with the tomatoes and duchesse potatoes put through a pastry tube. Brush the vegetables with additional melted butter and broil until the potatoes are lightly browned.

TO POACH SHAD ROE

Handle the roe carefully in pairs with the membrane intact. Cover with boiling water and for each quart of water add one tablespoon vinegar or lemon juice, one-half teaspoon salt and, if desired, one-half teaspoon pickling spice. Lower the heat and simmer until white and firm, from five to twenty minutes depending on size. Drain, cover with cold water, cool and drain again. Remove the membrane or not, as desired.

BROILED SHAD ROE

Dry poached roe. Dredge with flour and baste generously with melted butter. Broil about two inches from the source of heat in a very hot preheated broiler about three minutes on one side and five minutes on the other.

FRIED SHAD ROE WITH BACON

Fry bacon and set aside. Blend one beaten egg with one tablespoon milk or water. Dip poached roe into the egg mixture, then in flour, cornmeal or sifted crumbs. Fry in the bacon fat until brown on both sides, turning the roe carefully. Garnish with the bacon.

SHAD ROE A L'OSEILLE *3 servings*

2 tablespoons sweet butter
2 tablespoons finely chopped shallot or green onion
¼ cup canned sorrel
1 cup dry white wine
3 pairs shad roe
Salt and white pepper to taste
1 cup heavy cream

1. Grease a skillet with the butter. Place the shallot, sorrel and wine in it and arrange the roe on top. Season with salt and pepper.
2. Cover the pan and bring the mixture to a boil. Reduce the heat and simmer slowly about twenty minutes. Remove the roe to a warm plate and keep warm.
3. Add the cream to the sauce remaining in the skillet, bring to a boil, reduce the heat and cook down to the consistency of a thin white sauce, leaving the skillet uncovered. Adjust the seasonings and spoon the sauce over the roe.

SHAD ROE WITH TOAST POINTS *6 servings*

½ cup butter
2 pounds fresh shad roe
3 slices fresh bread
Salt and freshly ground black pepper
Lemon slices
½ cup chopped parsley

(*cont'd*)

1. In a ten-inch skillet melt the butter until warm but not hot. Arrange the fresh roe in it, cover the pan and cook over low heat, turning once, until tender, about twelve minutes. Add more butter if necessary.

2. Toast the bread and cut diagonally in half. Arrange the toast on a warm platter and place the roe on top. Season with salt and pepper, garnish with lemon slices and sprinkle generously with parsley.

SHAD ROE AUX FINES HERBES *2 to 4 servings*

The "fines herbes" of French cuisine are parsley, tarragon, chervil and chives.

¼ cup butter
2 medium shad roe
Salt and pepper
2 teaspoons lemon juice
1 tablespoon chopped parsley
2 teaspoons chopped chives
1 teaspoon freshly chopped tarragon
1 teaspoon freshly chopped chervil

1. In a large, heavy skillet heat the butter and add the shad roe. Sprinkle with salt and pepper. Cook the roe on both sides, turning once carefully, about twelve minutes. When the roe is lightly browned and cooked through, transfer to a hot platter.

2. Add the remaining ingredients to the skillet. Heat, stirring, and pour over the shad roe.

DEEP-FRIED SMELTS IN BATTER *6 servings*

Fat for deep frying
1 cup sifted flour
1 teaspoon baking powder
1 teaspoon salt
1 egg, beaten
1 cup water
12 smelts

1. Heat fat to 370° F.

2. Sift together the flour, baking powder and salt. Add the egg and water and stir until smooth.

3. Coat smelts with batter and lower into fat. Do not crowd the fish. Fry until brown, about four minutes, turning once. Drain thoroughly on paper towels.

PAN-FRIED SMELTS *6 servings*

3 pounds smelts
1 tablespoon salt
¼ teaspoon freshly ground black pepper
¾ cup flour
2 eggs
2 tablespoons water
1½ cups finely ground bread crumbs
¾ cup shortening or oil

1. Wipe the smelts with a damp cloth. Mix salt and pepper with the flour and sprinkle the mixture over the fish. Dip floured fish into the eggs lightly beaten with the water and then roll in the bread crumbs. *(cont'd)*

2. In a shallow skillet heat the shortening, add the smelts and sauté until browned on both sides, above five minutes. The fish should be turned carefully with a spatula.

BAKED RED SNAPPER *6 servings*

- 1 four-pound red snapper
- 1 teaspoon salt
- ¼ teaspoon freshly ground black pepper
- ⅔ cup butter
- 1 small onion, chopped
- 4 cups fine stale bread crumbs
- 1 cup chopped cucumber
- 2 teaspoons capers or chopped sour pickle
- ¾ teaspoon powdered sage
- ½ cup white wine
- Salt pork or bacon slices

1. Preheat oven to hot (400° F.).
2. Sprinkle the fish inside with salt and pepper.
3. In a skillet heat one-third cup of the butter, add the onion and brown lightly. Add the crumbs, cucumber, capers, sage and half the wine and mix. Stuff the fish with the mixture and close with skewers and string.
4. Place the fish in a well-greased shallow pan lined with foil (page 231). Cut gashes at one-serving intervals and place a piece of salt pork or bacon in each. Brush with the remaining butter and pour the remaining wine over the top.
5. Bake, uncovered, until the fish flakes easily when tested with a fork, about fifty minutes. Baste frequently with the drippings in the pan or with additional butter and wine. Serve with the pan drippings seasoned to taste.

BAKED RED SNAPPER WITH GRAPEFRUIT *6 to 8 servings*

- 1 four- to five-pound red snapper
- Salt
- 6 tablespoons butter
- ½ small onion, minced
- 1 cup stale bread crumbs or cubes
- ½ cup fine cracker crumbs
- ½ teaspoon basil or dill
- 2 teaspoons chopped parsley
- Freshly ground black pepper to taste
- 1 grapefruit, sectioned, with its juice

1. Preheat oven to hot (400° F.).
2. Sprinkle the fish inside and out with salt.
3. In a skillet heat four tablespoons of the butter, add the onion and cook until it is transparent. Add the bread and cracker crumbs, the basil, parsley, one-quarter teaspoon salt and the pepper and mix. Stuff the fish with the mixture and close with skewers and string.
4. Place the fish in a greased, foil-lined pan, as page 231, and bake until it flakes easily when tested with a fork, about fifty to sixty minutes. Brush frequently with the remaining butter, melted and mixed with the grapefruit juice. Three minutes before removing the fish from the oven, arrange the grapefruit sections on top and brush with the remaining mixture or additional butter.

SOLE FILLETS IN WHITE WINE SAUCE *6 servings*

6 fillets of sole
1 cup water or court bouillon
Salt and freshly ground black pepper to taste
6 tablespoons butter
2 shallots, chopped, or 1 tablespoon chopped onion
½ cup dry white wine
1 tablespoon flour
½ cup cream

1. Halve the fillets lengthwise and roll each half. Fasten with picks and place in a skillet. Add one cup boiling water, or court bouillon, salt, pepper, half the butter, the shallots and wine. Bring to a boil, reduce the heat and simmer until the fish is white in the center, about twelve minutes. Remove to a hot platter and keep warm.

2. Boil the liquid in the pan until reduced to one-third. Add the flour blended with the cream, then the remaining butter. Heat, stirring, until smooth. Strain and pour over the fish.

FILLETS OF SOLE WITH MORNAY SAUCE *6 servings*

6 small fillets of sole
Water to cover
Salt and freshly ground pepper to taste
Water or white wine
¼ cup butter
¼ cup flour
1 cup milk
1 cup cream
¾ cup grated Gruyère or Swiss cheese (Cheddar may be used)
Grated Parmesan cheesc

1. Sprinkle the fish with salt and pepper and simmer in water barely to cover just until the fish flakes easily when tested with a fork. The liquid in which the fish is cooked may be reserved and used in place of part of the milk to make the sauce. Remove the fish to a heatproof dish and keep warm.

2. In a saucepan melt the butter, add the flour and stir with a wire whisk until blended. Meanwhile bring the milk, with the fish broth, if desired, and cream to a boil and add all at once to the butter-flour mixture, stirring vigorously with the whisk until the sauce is thickened and smooth.

3. Remove the sauce from the heat and let cool one minute. Stir in the Gruyère cheese and correct the seasonings.

4. Pour the sauce over the fish and sprinkle with Parmesan cheese. Place under the broiler to glaze. Serve with toast points, if desired.

SOLE ALBERT *8 servings*

1½ cups dry vermouth
3 tablespoons chopped shallot
2 tablespoons chopped parsley
8 small fillets of sole
Salt and freshly ground pepper
1¼ cups butter, cut into small pieces
8 egg yolks
2 tablespoons heavy cream

(*cont'd*)

1. In a skillet bring the vermouth, shallot and parsley to a boil. Lower the heat and simmer ten minutes. Add the sole and poach gently until the fish flakes easily when tested with a fork. There should be enough of the wine to cover the fish. Add more wine if necessary.

2. Remove the fish to a flat baking dish, season with salt and pepper and keep warm. Boil the liquid until it is reduced to one-half cup.

3. In the top of a double boiler, mix the cooking liquid, butter and egg yolks. Whisk the sauce with a wire whisk over simmering water until it thickens. Add the heavy cream and pour the sauce over the fish fillets. Set under a hot broiler for a few seconds to glaze the top and serve at once.

SOLE DEAUVILLE *6 servings*

- 1 pint mussels, scrubbed well and debearded
- Water
- ½ teaspoon lemon juice
- 12 small mushrooms
- 6 small fillets of sole
- ½ cup butter
- 1 tablespoon flour
- 2 egg yolks
- ½ cup heavy cream
- Salt and freshly ground black pepper

1. Place the mussels in a saucepan with a small amount of water and the lemon juice, cover and steam until the shells open. Drain, reserving the liquid.

2. Cook the mushrooms in two tablespoons water about five minutes. Drain, reserving the liquid.

3. Place the fillets in a saucepan with one and one-half cups of the mixed liquids from the mussels and mushrooms. If there is not enough liquid to make one and one-half cups add enough water or white wine to fill. Simmer gently ten minutes. Remove the fish to a serving dish, arrange the mussels and mushrooms around it and keep warm.

4. In a saucepan heat two tablespoons of the butter, add the flour and cook, stirring with a wire whisk, until golden. Add the cooking liquid from the fish, stirring vigorously, and boil about four minutes.

5. Mix the egg yolks with the cream, combine with the sauce and bring to the boiling point, stirring constantly. Do not let boil. Add the remaining butter, season with salt and pepper and strain through a fine sieve over the fish.

FILLETS OF SOLE VALENCIENNES *6 servings*

- 1 teaspoon salt
- ⅛ teaspoon freshly ground black pepper
- ⅛ teaspoon mace
- ⅛ teaspoon thyme
- 6 fillets of sole (2 pounds)
- ½ cup dry vermouth
- 2 tablespoons lemon juice
- 2 tablespoons butter, melted
- 1 tablespoon minced chives
- 2 tablespoons minced onion
- 24 medium mushroom caps
- Chopped parsley
- Lemon quarters

(*cont'd*)

1. Preheat oven to moderate (325° F.).

2. Combine the salt, pepper, mace and thyme and sprinkle the mixture on both sides of the fillets. Place the fish in a buttered heatproof skillet.

3. Combine the vermouth, lemon juice and butter and pour over the fish. Sprinkle with the chives and onion. Place the mushrooms on and around the fish.

4. Cover the pan and very slowly bring to a boil over low heat. Immediately uncover the pan and place in the oven. Bake, basting often with the wine-butter mixture, fifteen minutes. Garnish with parsley and lemon quarters. Serve the fish from the pan in which it was cooked.

SOLE DUGLERE *4 servings*

In French cuisine the name Duglère indicates the presence of tomatoes.

4 fillets of sole or flounder
2 tablespoons butter
2 tablespoons finely chopped onion
¼ cup fish stock or bottled clam juice
½ cup dry white wine or water
½ cup canned tomatoes, drained and coarsely chopped
2 tablespoons minced parsley
⅛ teaspoon freshly ground black pepper

1. Roll the fillets and secure with toothpicks. In a skillet heat the butter, add the onion and cook until it is transparent.

2. Arrange the fillets in the pan and pour the fish stock and wine over them. Add the tomatoes and parsley and bring to a boil. Reduce the heat and cook gently until the fish flakes easily when tested with a fork, ten to twelve minutes. Turn carefully once while cooking.

3. Remove the fillets to a serving dish and keep warm. Stir the sauce over high heat two or three minutes, until slightly reduced. Add the pepper and pour the sauce over the fillets.

FILLETS OF SOLE VERONIQUE *6 servings*

The name Veronique in French cuisine indicates that white seedless grapes are used in preparing the dish.

1 cup small white seedless grapes
¼ cup butter
2 shallots, finely chopped
6 fillets of sole
Salt and white pepper to taste
¼ cup dry white wine
¼ cup water
1 tablespoon flour
¼ cup milk
¼ cup cream
1 egg yolk
3 tablespoons whipped cream

1. Simmer the grapes in water to cover three minutes. Drain. (If fresh grapes are not available, use canned.)

2. In a shallow skillet heat one tablespoon of the butter and sprinkle with shallots.

(*cont'd*)

3. Sprinkle the fish with salt and pepper and arrange on the shallots. Add the wine and water. Cut a circle of waxed paper the size of the skillet, butter it and place it, buttered side down, on top of the fish.

4. Bring the liquid in the pan to a boil and cook gently ten to twelve minutes. Using two spatulas, carefully remove the fish to a heatproof serving dish and keep warm.

5. Cook the liquid remaining in the skillet until reduced to one-half cup.

6. In a saucepan melt one tablespoon of the butter, add the flour and stir with a wire whisk until blended. Meanwhile, bring the milk and cream to a boil and add all at once to the butter-flour mixture, stirring vigorously with the whisk until the sauce is thickened and smooth. Season with salt and pepper. Add the egg yolk lightly beaten with a little of the hot sauce, the remaining butter and the cooking liquid from the skillet. Cook, stirring, until the butter has melted.

7. Place the grapes around the fish. Fold the whipped cream into the sauce and pour over the fish. Brown quickly under a preheated broiler and serve immediately.

FILLETS OF SOLE MARGUERY *4 to 6 servings*

Court bouillon (page 229)
½ pound shrimp
12 large mussels, scrubbed well and debearded
5 tablespoons butter
4 to 6 fillets of sole
Salt and white pepper
2 tablespoons chopped shallot
½ pound mushrooms, sliced
¼ cup dry white wine
¼ cup water
2 tablespoons flour
½ cup light cream
1 egg yolk, beaten
Parsley or thyme

1. Bring the court bouillon to a boil. Add the shrimp, cover and cook three minutes. Remove the shrimp with tongs, leaving the court bouillon in the pan.

2. Add the mussels, cover and steam gently three to four minutes, or until they open.

3. Shell and devein the shrimp, and cut in half lengthwise. Remove the mussels from their shells and keep the mussels and the shrimp warm.

4. Gently boil the court bouillon left in the pan while preparing the fish.

5. In a large skillet melt three tablespoons of the butter. Brush the fillets with the butter and sprinkle with salt and pepper. Place the shallot in the bottom of the skillet and arrange the fillets and mushrooms over the top. Add the wine and water and cover with a circle of buttered waxed paper the size of the skillet.

6. Bring the wine mixture to a boil and poach the fillets gently until the fish flakes easily when tested with a fork, four to five minutes. Using two wide spatulas, remove the fillets and mushrooms to a heated broilerproof buttered serving platter and keep warm.

(*cont'd*)

7. Strain the liquid left in the pan and strain the boiling court bouillon.

8. Melt the remaining butter in the same skillet, add the flour and stir with a wire whisk until blended. Meanwhile, bring one and one-half cups of the strained liquid with the light cream to a boil and add all at once to the butter-flour mixture, stirring vigorously with the whisk until the sauce is thickened and smooth.

9. Add the egg yolk lightly beaten with a little of the hot sauce and cook, stirring, one minute. Correct the seasonings.

10. Arrange the mussels and shrimp over the fillets and pour the sauce over the top. Heat very quickly under a preheated broiler and garnish with parsley or sprigs of thyme.

SOLE MEUNIERE *6 servings*

6 fillets of sole
Milk
Seasoned flour
Peanut oil
3 tablespoons butter
Lemon juice
Finely chopped parsley

1. Divide the sole down the center line and discard the tiny bone structure from the center line. Add milk barely to cover and let stand about fifteen minutes.

2. Pat the fillets dry and dredge in seasoned flour. Add peanut oil to a large skillet to a depth of one-quarter inch. When it is hot, cook the fillets on both sides until golden brown. Transfer the fillets by means of a spatula to a hot dish and pour off and discard the oil in the skillet.

3. Add the butter to the skillet and, when it starts to brown, pour it over the sole fillets. Sprinkle with lemon juice and chopped parsley and garnish with lemon slices dipped in parsley.

BROILED SWORDFISH STEAKS *4 servings*

1½ pounds swordfish steaks, about 1 inch thick
¾ teaspoon salt
¼ teaspoon freshly ground black pepper
⅛ teaspoon paprika
¼ cup butter, melted
Lemon juice or lemon butter
Watercress

1. Sprinkle the fish with the salt, pepper and paprika; rub the seasonings in lightly.

2. Place the fish on a preheated, greased broiler rack about two inches from the source of heat. Brush the top of the fish with two tablespoons of the melted butter and broil three minutes. Turn, brush the second side with the remaining butter and broil until lightly browned, or four to five minutes. Serve with lemon or lemon butter and a garnish of watercress.

SWORDFISH STEAK WITH ROSEMARY

4 servings

1 swordfish steak, 2 inches thick
Flour
2 teaspoons dried rosemary
Olive oil
6 tablespoons butter
Salt to taste
¼ cup white wine

1. Dredge the steak with the flour. Press the rosemary into the fish and brush with oil.

2. Heat five tablespoons of the butter in a skillet, add the fish and cook, turning once, until the fish flakes easily when tested with a fork, about fifteen minutes. Sprinkle with salt and remove the fish to a hot platter.

3. Add the wine and remaining butter to the pan and heat. Pour over and around the fish.

SWORDFISH STEAKS POACHED IN BEER AND SAUCED

8 servings

1 quart beer
1 carrot, sliced
1 onion, sliced
1 stalk celery, sliced
4 sprigs parsley
8 peppercorns
5 whole cloves
1 bay leaf
8 swordfish steaks
3 tablespoons butter
2 tablespoons flour
1 cup milk
¼ cup grated Parmesan cheese
½ cup chopped natural Gruyère cheese
2 egg yolks
¼ cup heavy cream, whipped
Salt and freshly ground black pepper to taste

1. In a large skillet bring the beer, carrot, onion, celery, parsley, peppercorns, cloves and bay leaf to a boil. Reduce the heat, cover and simmer fifteen minutes.

2. Arrange four of the steaks in the broth one layer deep. Simmer, covered, turning once, until the fish flakes easily when tested with a fork, about ten minutes. Transfer to a shallow greased baking dish and repeat with the remaining steaks.

3. Boil the broth, uncovered, until reduced to one cup. Strain through four thicknesses of cheesecloth.

4. In a saucepan, melt two tablespoons of the butter, add the flour and stir with a wire whisk until blended. Meanwhile, bring the milk to a boil and add all at once to the butter-flour mixture, stirring vigorously with the whisk until the sauce is thickened and smooth. Add the strained broth and cheeses and stir. Add the egg yolks lightly beaten with a little of the hot sauce and cook over low heat, stirring, until the sauce has thickened. Stir in the remaining butter and the cream and season with salt and pepper.

5. Pour the sauce over the fish and broil in a preheated broiler until lightly browned.

(cont'd)

Note: For a made-in-advance dish, pour the sauce on the fish and refrigerate. At serving time bake in a preheated moderate oven (375° F.) until the fish is heated through, or about twenty minutes.

SWORDFISH BAKED IN FOIL *4 servings*

1 cup sliced mushrooms
1 medium onion, sliced
2 tablespoons chopped green pepper or parsley
2 tablespoons lemon juice or wine vinegar
2 tablespoons olive or salad oil
Salt and freshly ground black pepper to taste
½ teaspoon dill seed
1½ pounds swordfish steak, cut into 4 servings
4 small pieces bay leaf
4 thick slices tomato

1. Preheat oven to hot (425° F.).
2. Mix the mushrooms, onion, green pepper, lemon juice, oil, salt, pepper and dill.
3. Line a baking pan with aluminum foil, spread half the seasoning mixture over the bottom and add the swordfish steaks.
4. Sprinkle the fish with salt and pepper, place a piece of bay leaf and a slice of tomato on each steak and cover with remaining seasoning mixture.
5. Cover the pan with foil and bake until the fish flakes easily when tested with a fork, forty-five minutes for fresh steaks or sixty minutes for frozen.
6. To serve, remove cover and set pan of fish on a tray or platter. Serve juices and vegetables in the pan as a sauce for the fish.

BLUE TROUT LUCHOW *2 servings*

¼ cup white vinegar
2 tablespoons wine vinegar
Juice of ½ lemon
1 pint water
½ teaspoon salt
½ bay leaf
1 clove
2 peppercorns
¼ onion, chopped
¼ carrot, chopped
¼ celery heart, chopped
1 pound fish bones and heads
2 fresh brook trout

1. Combine all the ingredients except the trout and bring to a boil. Lower the heat and simmer twenty minutes. Strain the mixture through a cheesecloth.
2. While the liquid is boiling, clean the fish. Do not wash, and handle as little as possible.
3. Bring the strained liquid to a boil, reduce the heat, add the trout and simmer, uncovered, until the trout turns blue and the fish flakes easily when tested with a fork, seven or eight minutes. Remove from the liquid and serve with boiled potatoes.

A quartet of trout in aspic. Fish shown here are decorated with scallion stems and white of egg to simulate lily of the valley.

COLD TROUT IN ASPIC *6 servings*

6 trout
Salted water
4 cups quick fish aspic (page 431)
Green onion stems and hard-cooked egg whites, sliced thin

1. Cook the trout in simmering salted water four to six minutes, or until the fish flakes easily when tested with a fork. Place on a wire rack. Make two diagonal incisions on one side of the fish, a few inches apart. Pry under the cuts to loosen the skin and peel it off, leaving the head and tail intact. Chill the fish.
2. Spoon chilled but still-liquid aspic over the fish.
3. Make a flower design on the fish as follows: Use trimmed green parts of onions as the stems. Cut the egg white slices with a paring knife to simulate petals. Dip the decorations in still-liquid aspic and arrange on the fish. Chill.
4. Cover with layers of aspic as desired, chilling after each layer is applied. To serve, garnish the fish platter with chopped aspic and serve with mayonnaise.

BROOK TROUT MEUNIERE *6 servings*

6 brook trout
Milk
⅓ cup flour
½ teaspoon salt
Pepper
Peanut oil
⅔ cup butter
Lemon slices
Chopped parsley

1. Clean the trout, remove the fins but leave the heads and tails on. Dip in milk and drain well.

2. Mix flour, salt and pepper. Roll fish in mixture.

3. Heat enough peanut oil in a skillet to cover the bottom to a depth of about one-fourth inch. When hot, add trout and brown well on both sides. When cooked, remove to a hot serving platter.

4. Pour off the fat from the skillet and wipe well with paper towels. Add the butter and cook until it is hazelnut brown. Pour the butter over the trout. Garnish with lemon and parsley.

FISH TAHITI STYLE *8 appetizer or 4 main-course servings*

This is a raw fish dish that is surprisingly good. Serve it in summer on a cold buffet.

2 pounds fresh tuna or red snapper
Lime juice
1 teaspoon salt
1 small onion, chopped
1 cup coconut milk (page 139)
1 small tomato, chopped
1 green pepper, chopped
1 cucumber, chopped
1 hard-cooked egg, chopped

1. Cut the raw fish into paper-thin slices. Cover with lime juice, add the salt and let the mixture stand at least two hours in the refrigerator, stirring occasionally.

2. Add the onion, coconut milk and half each of the remaining ingredients. Mix lightly and chill.

3. Transfer the mixture to a serving dish and garnish the top with the remaining ingredients.

GRILLED FRESH TUNA *6 servings*

6 half-pound tuna steaks, each 1 inch thick
½ cup olive oil
Juice of 1 lemon
1 clove garlic, finely chopped
Salt and freshly ground black pepper

1. Marinate the tuna steaks for an hour or more in a mixture of olive oil, lemon juice, garlic, salt and pepper to taste.

(*cont'd*)

2. Grill the tuna over charcoal or in a preheated broiler, basting well with additional oil. Cook eight to ten minutes, turning once. Remove to a hot platter and serve with Hollandaise sauce (page 449) or melted butter and lemon wedges.

TUNA PUDDING *5 to 6 servings*

6 medium potatoes, unpeeled
3 seven-ounce cans tuna
½ cup milk, approximately
¼ cup butter
½ teaspoon dry mustard
Salt and freshly ground black pepper to taste
1 cup mayonnaise, approximately

1. Boil the potatoes in a small amount of salted water.

2. While the potatoes are cooking, turn one can of the tuna, bit by bit, with its oil into the container of an electric blender. Add one tablespoon of the milk at a time and blend until smooth. Repeat the process until all the tuna and milk are used. If a blender is not available, mash the tuna very fine and mix with the milk.

3. Peel the potatoes, mash and whip until fluffy with the butter, mustard, salt, pepper and tuna purée. Add more milk if necessary to give a fairly firm mashed-potato consistency.

4. Turn the mixture into a well-oiled five- or six-cup ring or fish-shaped mold. Chill.

5. To serve, unmold and frost with mayonnaise. Garnish as desired with cucumbers, shrimp, salad greens, hard-cooked eggs, hearts of artichokes, cooked carrots or other vegetables.

MARINATED TUNA FISH AND VEGETABLES ITALIENNE, PAGE 39.

STEAMED WHITEFISH WITH EGG SAUCE *4 servings*

1 two-pound whitefish
1 clove garlic, minced
Salt and freshly ground black pepper to taste
3 tablespoons butter
3 tablespoons flour
1½ cups milk
2 or 3 hard-cooked eggs, diced
½ teaspoon Worcestershire sauce
3 tablespoons dry white wine or 2 tablespoons lemon juice
1 teaspoon prepared mustard (optional)
Chopped parsley or paprika

1. Place the fish in a wire steaming basket or on a large piece of cheesecloth. Sprinkle with garlic, salt and pepper. Cover with cheesecloth, place in a steamer or on a rack in a kettle with about one-half inch water. Cover and steam fifteen minutes. Remove to a hot platter and keep warm.

2. In a saucepan, melt the butter, add the flour and stir with a wire whisk until blended. Meanwhile, bring the milk to a boil and add all at once to the butter-flour mixture, stirring vigorously with the whisk until the sauce is thickened and smooth. Add the remaining ingredients and correct the seasonings. Pour the sauce over the fish and garnish with parsley.

PAN-FRIED WHITING *4 servings*

4 whole whiting, ¾ to 1 pound each
½ teaspoon salt
Freshly ground black pepper to taste
½ cup milk
½ cup white cornmeal
½ cup shortening (may be half butter)
⅛ teaspoon rosemary or thyme (optional)
Lemon wedges

1. Sprinkle inside of the fish with salt and pepper. Dip in the milk, and then roll in the cornmeal.

2. Heat the shortening in a skillet and fry the fish in it until brown on one side. Sprinkle with the rosemary, turn carefully and cook until the fish flakes easily when tested with a fork. Serve with lemon wedges.

BAKED FISH PARMIGIANA *4 servings*

Parmigiana means in the style of Parma and probably that Parmesan cheese is used as an ingredient.

4 servings fish fillets or steaks
Salt and freshly ground black pepper to taste
1 cup canned tomato sauce
½ cup grated Parmesan cheese
2 tablespoons melted butter

1. Preheat oven to hot (425° F.).

2. Place the fish in a shallow buttered baking dish and season with salt and pepper.

3. Spread the tomato sauce over each fillet and sprinkle with the cheese. Drizzle with melted butter.

4. Bake, uncovered, until the fish flakes easily when tested with a fork, fifteen to twenty minutes.

FILLETS PLAZA ATHENEE *6 servings*

2 tablespoons butter
1 teaspoon chopped shallot or onion
6 large mushrooms, thinly sliced
1 tablespoon chopped parsley
6 medium tomatoes, peeled, seeded and chopped
6 fillets of fish
Salt and freshly ground black pepper
¼ cup dry white wine, water or fish stock
1 or 2 egg yolks
½ cup heavy cream
18 cooked shrimp
1 teaspoon chopped chives

1. In a large skillet melt the butter and add the shallot, mushrooms, parsley and tomatoes.

2. Season the fillets with salt and pepper and arrange side by side on the tomatoes. Pour the wine over the top.

(cont'd)

3. Cover with a circle of buttered waxed paper. Bring to a boil, cover the pan, reduce the heat and simmer until the fish flakes easily when tested with a fork, ten to twelve minutes. Remove the fillets to a serving dish.

4. Cook the sauce in the pan until it is reduced about one-half. Add the egg yolk lightly beaten with a little of the hot liquid and the cream. Combine by swirling it in, moving the pan in a circular motion.

5. Reheat the sauce but do not let boil. Pour over the fish and garnish with shrimp and chopped chives.

FISH FILLETS BONNE FEMME *4 servings*

Bonne femme means that the good wife cooked with mushrooms.

2 shallots, chopped, or 1 small onion
¾ cup sliced mushrooms
Salt and freshly ground black pepper to taste
2 pounds fish fillets
1 cup dry white wine
2 tablespoons white sauce (page 443)
¼ cup heavy cream
1 tablespoon butter
1 tablespoon chopped chives
1 tablespoon chopped parsley

1. Preheat oven to moderate (350° F.).

2. Butter a heatproof baking dish. Arrange the shallots and mushrooms on the bottom of the dish and sprinkle with salt and pepper. Place the fish on top, add the wine and cover with buttered waxed paper or foil.

3. Bake until the fish flakes easily when tested with a fork, about fifteen minutes.

4. Drain the juices from the baking dish into a saucepan. Cook over moderately high heat until reduced about one-half. Add the white sauce and cream and cook until the sauce has thickened a little. Add the butter in little curls, rotating the pan all the time; this incorporates the butter without rapidly melting it.

5. Pour the sauce over the fillets and sprinkle with the chives and parsley.

FISH FILLETS WITH GINGER *6 servings*

3 tablespoons olive oil
3 tablespoons butter
6 fish fillets
1 clove garlic, chopped
12 wafer-thin slices green ginger, or 1 teaspoon ground ginger
1½ tablespoons sugar
1 tablespoon cider vinegar
2½ tablespoons soy sauce
1 tablespoon cornstarch
6 tablespoons water
2 scallions, cut in thin diagonal slices

1. In a skillet, heat the olive oil and butter. Add the fish fillets and cook until the fish flakes easily when tested with a fork, about three to four minutes on each side. Transfer the fish to a warm serving platter.

2. To the fat remaining in the skillet, add the garlic and ginger. Add the sugar mixed with vinegar and soy sauce.

(*cont'd*)

3. Combine the cornstarch and water and gradually stir into the liquid in the skillet. Cook, stirring with a wire whisk, until the sauce is smooth and thickened. Pour the sauce over the fish, sprinkle with the scallions and serve immediately.

BOUILLABAISSE *6 servings*

In some circles it is impossible to mention bouillabaisse without someone telling you that you cannot make bouillabaisse unless you are from Marseille or the region from Nice to Menton. They add that the reason it cannot be made elsewhere is that the ugliest fish in the world swims in the waters of that area. It is called the rascasse, they say, and it is essential in a genuine bouillabaisse. Nevertheless, here is an adapted recipe for the dish, about which William Makepeace Thackeray could not make up his mind as to whether it is "a soup or broth, or brew, or hotchpotch."

¼ cup olive oil
1 stalk celery, chopped
1 medium onion, chopped
1 clove garlic, finely chopped
1 leek, diced
½ teaspoon thyme
½ bay leaf
2 cups crushed tomatoes
1 cup bottled clam juice
1 cup dry white wine
¼ cup fennel, chopped, or ½ teaspoon crushed fennel seeds
Pinch of saffron
Salt and pepper to taste
2 tablespoons chopped parsley
1 small lobster, cut into pieces (see page 279)
12 mussels, well scrubbed and debearded
12 raw shrimp, shelled and deveined
12 scallops
1 pound red snapper or cod, cut into serving pieces

1. In a large kettle heat the oil, add the celery, onion, garlic, leek, thyme and bay leaf and cook five minutes.

2. Add the tomatoes, clam juice, wine, fennel, saffron, salt, pepper and parsley and simmer fifteen minutes.

3. Add the seafood and cook fifteen minutes longer.

CATALAN BOUILLABAISSE *4 servings*

The Spanish version.

3½-pound red snapper
Water
¼ cup olive oil
2 tablespoons sweet butter
2 medium onions, minced
2 large ripe tomatoes, peeled, seeded and chopped
2 tablespoons minced parsley
1 bay leaf
1 pinch thyme
2 cups dry white wine
Salt and freshly ground black pepper to taste
18 blanched, toasted almonds
2 cloves garlic

(cont'd)

1. Have the flesh of the red snapper cut into slices two inches thick and reserve. Add the bones and trimmings of the fish to four cups boiling salted water and boil slowly thirty minutes. Strain and reserve two cups of the stock.

2. In a heavy saucepan or Dutch oven heat the oil and butter, add the onions and cook until transparent. Add the tomatoes and simmer until very tender, about five minutes.

3. Add the reserved fish stock, parsley, bay leaf and thyme. Bring the mixture to a boil, add the wine, salt and pepper and simmer fifteen minutes.

4. Meanwhile, preheat the oven to hot (400° F.). Chop the almonds and garlic fine, then grind them together to a paste, using a mortar and pestle or electric blender. Add the paste to the simmering wine sauce and stir until well blended.

5. Place the red snapper slices in the bottom of a well-buttered two-and-one-half- to three-quart earthenware casserole. Pour the sauce over the fish, cover and bake in the oven until the broth begins to simmer. Bake twenty minutes longer and serve from the casserole.

CRABMEAT BOUILLABAISSE, PAGE 278.

CACCIUCCO (Italian seafood stew) *4 servings*

Lobster is sometimes used in cacciucco. The seasonings also may include chopped parsley and grated lemon rind. Squid are always customary. Though Americans hold them in somewhat nervous regard, they are delicious. One old Boston fisherman holds they are "twice as sweet as lobster and only half the trouble to fix."

Those who never have cleaned squid would do well to enlist assistance from a fish dealer. The general procedure is to remove the spiny portion, which looks like a translucent rod. Then the head and legs are pulled from the envelope-like covering. The ink sac at the base of the head may be retained or removed. Europeans think the ink adds to the flavor.

The squid, sometimes known as the cuttlefish, is plentiful and inexpensive. A distant cousin of the octopus, it is shaped roughly like a pen. Its length is about a foot.

½ cup olive oil
1 clove garlic, minced
1 tiny, hot red pepper
½ pound raw shrimp, shelled and deveined
½ pound squid, skinned and cleaned
½ cup dry white wine
2 tablespoons tomato paste
3 cups water
½ teaspoon salt
1 pound cod fillet, cut in pieces
½ pound scallops, cut in pieces
½ pound halibut, cut in pieces
4 slices Italian bread
1 clove garlic, cut

(cont'd)

1. In a deep kettle heat the oil, add the garlic and red pepper and brown the garlic lightly.

2. Cut the shrimp and squid into small pieces and add. Cover the pan and cook over low heat until the squid is tender, about thirty minutes. Add the wine and continue cooking, uncovered, until the wine evaporates. Add the tomato paste, water and salt and cook five minutes longer.

3. Cut the remaining fish into small pieces and add. Cover and simmer until tender, about fifteen minutes. Add more water if necessary; the stew must be thick.

4. While the stew is cooking, toast the bread and rub with a cut clove of garlic. Place a slice in each soup bowl.

5. Remove the hot red pepper from the stew and correct the seasonings. Ladle a generous serving of stew over the bread.

There are nearly as many recipes for gefüllte fish as there are for bouillabaisse. Here are three. The first is that of Mrs. Judah Nadich, the wife of the rabbi of the Park Avenue Synagogue in New York.

GEFULLTE FISH I *15 to 20 fish balls*

5 pounds fish fillets (equal amounts of whitefish and pike plus a small amount of carp)
Heads, bones and trimmings from fish
5 onions, sliced
1 stalk celery, sliced
2 large carrots, sliced
Water to cover
Salt and pepper
3 or 4 eggs, depending on size
2 tablespoons matzo meal
Horseradish

1. Have butcher grind the fish or put it through the finest blade of a food grinder.

2. In a large kettle, combine heads, bones and trimmings of fish with four of the onions, celery and carrots. Cover with water and season with salt and pepper. Bring to a boil.

3. Meanwhile, place the remaining sliced onion and the eggs in an electric blender and blend well. If a blender is not available, chop the onions to a pulp with the eggs. Add the onion-egg mixture to the ground fish and blend well. Add matzo meal and salt and pepper to taste. Add one quarter cup of water and blend well.

4. Shape the fish mixture into balls and drop into simmering fish broth. Lower the heat so that the broth barely simmers and cook, covered, two hours. When cool, remove the balls to a platter. Garnish with the cooked carrots and strain the fish broth. Chill. Serve the gefüllte fish with the jellied fish broth and horseradish.

GEFULLTE FISH II *15 to 20 fish balls*

5 pounds fish (carp, whitefish and pike)
5 medium onions, sliced
3 carrots, sliced
2 raw eggs
2 hard-cooked eggs, finely chopped
Sugar
Salt and freshly ground black pepper to taste
¼ cup ice water, approximately

1. Remove the heads, skin and bones from the fish and reserve. Cut the fish into pieces and put through a food grinder with two of the onions. If desired, place the fish in a wooden bowl and chop finer.

2. Place the skin, bones and heads in a deep pot. Add the remaining onions, the carrots and cold water to cover. Bring to a boil.

3. Meanwhile, add the raw eggs to the chopped fish, then the hard-cooked eggs, sugar, salt and pepper. Sugar should be used sparingly. Add enough ice water to make a light, soft mixture and shape into balls.

4. Drop the fish balls into the boiling broth, reduce the heat and simmer, covered, for about two hours. Remove the fish from the broth and serve either warm or chilled. Strain the liquid in the pot and serve either warm or cool as a sauce.

GEFULLTE FISH III *6 servings*

1½ pounds whitefish
1½ pounds yellow pike
2 teaspoons salt
3 medium onions
2 medium carrots
8 almonds, blanched
1 egg
¼ teaspoon freshly ground black pepper
1 tablespoon cracker meal
Watercress or parsley

1. Clean, fillet and season the fish with half the salt. Reserve the heads, skins and large bones. Refrigerate overnight.

2. Slice two of the onions and the carrots fine and arrange in a four-quart pot. Add one quart of cold water. Add the fish bones, heads and skins, cover and boil ten minutes.

3. Grind the fish fillets and remaining onion with the almonds. Place in a wooden bowl and add one-third cup water, the remaining salt, egg, pepper and cracker meal. Mix thoroughly.

4. Mold fish patties out of the mixture, using one-half cup for each patty. Gently lower them into the boiling stock. Replace the cover, return to a boil, then reduce the heat and let simmer two and one-half hours.

5. After one hour, correct the seasonings. When cooked, let the patties cool in the stock. Remove them to a platter with the carrot slices and garnish with watercress. Strain the liquid in the pot and serve either warm or cool as a sauce.

SWEDISH FISH MOLD *8 servings*

1 to 1¼ pounds haddock
½ cup butter, softened
1 teaspoon salt
⅛ teaspoon freshly ground black pepper
Dash of cayenne pepper
4 eggs, separated
3 tablespoons flour
1 cup milk
1 cup heavy cream
Sifted bread crumbs
Chopped parsley

1. Preheat oven to moderate (350° F.).
2. Grind the raw fish three or four times. Blend in the butter and seasonings and cream until smooth.
3. Beat together the egg yolks, flour and milk. Add by spoonfuls to the fish, beating constantly until the mixture is blended. Should the mixture curdle, add two teaspoons hot butter and beat until the mixture is smooth. If desired, the blending can be done in an electric mixer at low speed.
4. Beat the egg whites until stiff but not dry. Whip the cream until stiff. Fold egg whites, then cream into the fish mixture.
5. Pour the mixture into a greased two-quart mold that has been sprinkled with fine bread crumbs; the mixture should fill the mold only three-quarters full. Cover with greased waxed paper.
6. Place the mold in a pan of warm water and bake one to one and one-half hours.
7. Unmold on a platter and garnish with parsley. Serve with Hollandaise sauce (page 449).

PEIXADA *8 servings*

*A peixada, pronounced pay-*shah*-dah, is a Brazilian specialty. As it is made in Bahia it is worth a trip to South America. There they employ a fish not available in North American waters, but red snapper will do.*

1 four-pound red snapper
6 medium tomatoes, peeled and chopped
2 scallions with green tops, sliced
¼ cup chopped parsley
2 bay leaves
1 teaspoon ground coriander
¼ teaspoon freshly ground black pepper
2 teaspoons salt
2 pounds small raw shrimp, shelled and deveined
Tabasco sauce

1. Clean the red snapper and remove the head. Cut the body into slices about one inch thick. Place the slices and the head, if desired, in a large saucepan and add the tomatoes, scallions, parsley, bay leaves, coriander, pepper and salt. Let stand several hours in the refrigerator.
2. Add water just to cover the fish and bring to a boil. Reduce the heat and simmer, covered, until the fish flakes easily when tested with a fork, about twenty

(cont'd)

minutes. Carefully remove the fish steaks to a hot platter. Discard the bay leaves and the fish head, if used.

3. Add the shrimp to the mixture in which the fish was poached and add Tabasco and additional salt and pepper to taste. Simmer until the shrimp are pink, about three minutes. Serve the sauce over the fish.

JANSON'S TEMPTATION *5 to 6 servings*

Who was Janson, what was he? This anchovy and potato dish of Swedish origin bears his name.

5 medium potatoes, cut into fine strips
2 yellow onions, sliced thin
10 anchovies or 20 anchovy fillets
¼ cup butter
1½ cups cream

1. Preheat oven to moderate (325° F.).

2. In a buttered baking dish, place a layer of half the potatoes. Add a layer of onions, the anchovies, then the remaining potatoes. Dot with butter and the anchovy juice.

3. Bake ten minutes. Add half the cream and cook ten minutes longer. Add the remaining cream and bake forty minutes longer.

DANISH FISH BALLS *6 servings*

1 pound cod
⅓ cup butter
½ cup potato flour
½ teaspoon salt
White pepper
2 cups milk, approximately
2 eggs

1. Grind the raw fish and mix with the butter, flour, salt and pepper. Grind the mixture eight times.

2. Add the milk, a little at a time, beating constantly. Use an electric mixer at low speed, if desired. Beat in the eggs.

3. Form the mixture into small balls with a teaspoon. Drop into boiling water, cook slowly for a few minutes and drain.

TEMPURA *About 6 servings*

Almost every nation has some version of the "mixed fry" in which many foods are dipped in a batter and deep fried. In Japan it is known as tempura; *in Italy* fritto misto. *Both include bits of fish seafood and vegetables.*

18 medium shrimp
2 flounder fillets
1 medium squid (optional)
6 sea scallops
1 carrot
12 long string beans
1 sweet potato
4 cups vegetable oil or, preferably, 3 cups vegetable oil and 1 cup sesame seed oil
Tempura batter (page 271)
Tempura sauce (page 271)

(*cont'd*)

1. Insert the small blade of a pair of scissors under the shell of each raw shrimp. Starting at the head portion, cut down to, but not through, the last tail segment.

2. Peel the shrimp, leaving the tail segment intact. Cut off the lower half of the tails. Split the peeled shrimp down the backs and rinse under cold running water to remove sand and intestinal tract.

3. Using a sharp knife, make shallow cuts across the underside of each shrimp in three equidistant places. This permits "straightening" the shrimp lengthwise.

4. Cut the flounder into small sections measuring about two by three inches. Remove the tentacles from the squid and peel off the outer and inner skins. Cut into square bite-sized pieces. Cut the scallops into quarters.

5. Cut the carrot into one-eighth-inch-thick slices. Cut string beans into three-inch lengths. Peel the sweet potato and cut into one-eighth-inch-thick slices and cut each slice into quarters.

6. Dry all the seafood and vegetables well between clean cloths or absorbent toweling.

7. Using a deep-fry kettle or thermometer or electric skillet, heat the oil to 375° F. This temperature must be maintained for the entire frying process. Hold shrimp by the tail, dip into the batter and gently drop, one at a time, into the hot fat. Deep fry a few shrimp at a time until the batter is golden brown, or about thirty seconds to one minute. Dip the flounder in the batter and cook the same length of time. Continue with remaining seafood and vegetables.

8. Remove the deep-fried foods, as they are cooked, to paper napkins or other absorbent toweling to drain briefly. To eat tempura, the fried food should be dipped in tempura sauce (below).

TEMPURA BATTER:

3 egg yolks
2 cups cold water
2½ cups sifted flour

Combine the egg yolks with the water and mix well. Gradually stir in the flour, stirring from the bottom of the bowl, preferably with thick chopsticks. Do not overstir; this is the secret of a light batter. Flour should remain floating on top of the batter.

TEMPURA SAUCE: *About 2 cups*

1 cup water
2 tablespoons dried bonito flakes
⅓ cup soy sauce
⅓ cup mirin, or ⅓ cup sake mixed with
1 teaspoon sugar
Freshly grated Japanese white radish
Freshly grated ginger (powdered ginger may be used)

1. In a saucepan, bring the water to a boil and add the bonito flakes. Cook three minutes and strain. This stock is known as dashi. *(cont'd)*

2. Combine the dashi with the soy sauce and mirin. Pour a little of the sauce into individual serving bowls and let guests add radish and ginger to taste.

FRITTO MISTO *6 to 8 servings*

- 2 cups sifted flour
- 1½ teaspoons salt
- ¼ teaspoon freshly ground black pepper
- 4 eggs, separated
- 1 can beer (12 ounces)
- ¼ cup butter, melted
- Pieces of vegetables, fish, seafood, cheese
- Fat for deep frying

1. Sift together the flour, salt and pepper.

2. Beat the egg yolks until light. Add the beer and mix into the dry ingredients, stirring only until well blended.

3. Stir in the butter. Let stand at room temperature one and one-half hours. Beat the egg whites until stiff, then fold into the batter.

4. Heat the fat to 375° F. Dip pieces of vegetables, fish, seafood and cheese into the batter and fry until golden brown, about two or three minutes.

VARIATIONS:

Almost any vegetable, fish or seafood is suitable in one form or another for a mixed fry. The following are especially recommended:

Onions: Cut into quarter-inch rings and coat with flour before dipping into the batter.

Eggplant: Slice without peeling into half-moons or rectangular fingers about one-half inch thick. Coat with flour before dipping into the batter.

Cauliflower: Break into flowerettes.

Broccoli: Peel stems and cut vegetables into bite-sized bits.

Tomatoes: Do not peel. Cut into one-half-inch slices. Discard the seeds and coat with flour before dipping into the batter.

Shrimp: Shell and devein raw shrimp, leaving the last segment of the tail intact, if desired. To "butterfly" shrimp, slit deeply down the back with a sharp knife, without cutting right through. Wash and dry with absorbent toweling. Dust with flour.

Crabmeat: Select large pieces of lump crabmeat. Dust with flour.

Oysters: Use whole. Dust with flour before dipping into batter.

Lobster or Rock Lobster Tail: Cut meat into one-half-inch medallions and dust with flour before frying.

Fish Fillets: Cut into strips about one inch wide. Dust with flour.

Cheese: Use Gruyère, Swiss or Fontina cheese cut into one-inch squares one-half inch thick.

SHELLFISH

WASHBOILER CLAMBAKE *8 servings*

Wet seaweed, well washed
1 quart water
4 Idaho potatoes, wrapped in foil
2 chickens cut up, each part wrapped in cheesecloth
2 1½-pound lobsters
4 ears corn, husked and wrapped in foil
24 steamer clams

1. Fill the bottom of a washboiler or large enamel pot with a layer of washed seaweed. Add the water and place over high heat. When water boils, add potatoes and more washed seaweed. Cover.

2. About fifteen minutes later, add the chicken and a layer of seaweed. Cover.

3. Fifteen minutes later, add the lobster and more seaweed. Cover.

4. About eight minutes later add the corn.

5. Ten minutes later add the clams. Cover and steam until clams open. Serve with butter and kettle liquid as a dip.

CLAMS ON TOAST *4 to 6 servings*

1 cup shucked raw clams, minced
2 tablespoons butter
2 tablespoons flour
1 cup milk
1 teaspoon chopped chives
1 cup heavy cream
Cayenne pepper
Dry toast

1. Simmer the clams in their own juice five minutes. Grind, using the finest knife of a food chopper.

2. In a saucepan melt the butter, add the flour and stir with a wire whisk until blended. Meanwhile, bring the milk to a boil and add all at once to the butter-flour mixture, stirring vigorously with the whisk until the sauce is thickened and smooth.

3. Add the chives, cream, cayenne and clams and reheat. Serve on toast.

SCALLOPED CLAMS *4 to 6 servings*

½ cup butter
½ cup toasted bread crumbs
1 cup cracker crumbs
Salt and freshly ground black pepper to taste
Paprika
2 cups shucked clams, minced
2 tablespoons finely minced onion
2 tablespoons finely minced parsley
⅓ cup cream

(*cont'd*)

1. Preheat oven to moderate (375° F.).

2. Melt the butter, add the bread and cracker crumbs, the salt, pepper and paprika and mix. Reserving a third of the mixture for the top of the casserole, mix the remainder with the clams, onion and parsley.

3. Pour the mixture into a well-buttered baking dish and top with the reserved crumbs. Dot with additional butter and pour the cream over the top. Bake, uncovered, twenty to twenty-five minutes.

SESAME BAKED CLAMS, PAGE 20.

SOFT-SHELLED CRABS SAUTE

Kill the crabs by piercing between the eyes with a knife. Lift the pointed ends of the shells and scrape out the spongy portions between the shells and the body. Put the crabs on their backs and cut off the tails.

Wash thoroughly and dry. Sprinkle with salt and pepper and dip in flour. Fry quickly in hot shallow butter until golden brown.

Serve each crab on a slice of toast, sprinkled with chopped parsley.

SOFT-SHELLED CRABS AMANDINE *4 to 6 servings*

8 to 12 soft-shelled crabs, dressed for the pan (see above)
Flour
6 to 8 tablespoons butter
1 teaspoon Worcestershire sauce
Salt and freshly ground black pepper to taste
½ cup blanched, sliced almonds
Lemon wedges

1. Dip the crabs in flour. In a skillet heat the butter, add the crabs and Worcestershire sauce and cook until the crabs are delicately browned and crisp on the edges, about three to four minutes on each side. Remove the crabs to a hot serving dish and sprinkle with salt and pepper.

2. Add the almonds to the butter in the pan in which the crabs were cooked. Sauté until golden, then pour them, with the butter, over the crabs. Serve with lemon wedges.

BROILED SOFT-SHELLED CRABS *6 servings*

12 soft-shelled crabs, dressed for cooking (see above)
Flour for dredging
½ cup butter, at room temperature
½ cup chopped parsley
1 tablespoon finely chopped chives
2 teaspoons paprika
1 teaspoon salt
Melted butter
Lemon juice and lemon wedges

(*cont'd*)

1. Dredge the crabs lightly with flour. Arrange them in a flat broiling dish or on a broiling rack.

2. Cream the butter with the parsley, chives, paprika and salt and dot the crabs with the mixture.

3. Broil the crabs about three inches from the source of heat in a preheated broiler five to eight minutes. Baste often and turn once during cooking. Serve with melted butter and lemon juice. Garnish with lemon wedges. If desired, serve with crisp bacon slices.

DEEP-FAT-FRIED SOFT-SHELLED CRABS

Prepare the crabs as for sauté (page 274) and season with salt and pepper. Dip in flour, then in slightly beaten egg that has been mixed with a little water, and then in sifted cracker or bread crumbs.

Fry the crabs in deep hot fat (370° F.) until golden brown. Drain on absorbent paper.

HARD-SHELLED CRABS

Wash live crabs in several changes of cold water, handling them with tongs. Plunge them head first into boiling salted water to cover and boil fifteen to twenty minutes, or until shells turn red. Drain, plunge into cold water, drain again and cool. To clean crabs, break off claws and legs close to body, crack the claws with a nutcracker and remove the meat. Break off the pointed apron, or tail. Take the crab in both hands and pull the upper and lower shells apart, beginning at tail. Wash away loose matter under running water and remove membranous covering round side. Remove meat between sections, picking out any cartilage. Six crabs yield about one cup of meat.

HERBED CRABMEAT *6 servings*

1½ pounds crabmeat
6 tablespoons butter
Salt
Coarsely ground black pepper
Juice of half a lemon
1 tablespoon each chopped chives and parsley
1 teaspoon freshly chopped tarragon (optional)

1. Pick over the crabmeat to remove all bits of shell and cartilage. Heat the butter until it bubbles and cook the crabmeat in it just until it is heated through.

2. Season the crab with salt, coarsely ground black pepper, lemon juice and the herbs. Serve on toast points and garnish with lemon wedges.

CRABMEAT SAUTEED WITH ALMONDS *4 servings*

7 tablespoons butter
1 pound fresh or canned crabmeat, picked over well
⅔ cup almonds, blanched and split in half
Salt and freshly ground black pepper to taste
½ cup heavy cream
3 tablespoons chopped parsley

1. In a medium-sized skillet heat four tablespoons of the butter, add the crabmeat and toss lightly until delicately browned.

2. Meanwhile, in a separate skillet heat the remaining butter, add the almonds and cook over brisk heat until lightly browned. Add the salt and pepper, then add the crabmeat.

3. Add the cream and parsley and bring the mixture to a boil. Reduce the heat and simmer two minutes. Serve on rice.

CRABMEAT VIRGINIA *1 serving*

6 ounces fresh lump crabmeat, picked over well
3 tablespoons butter
1½ tablespoons fresh lemon juice
Chopped parsley
Lemon wedge

1. Preheat oven to hot (400° F.).

2. Arrange the crabmeat in a lightly greased, individual casserole and dot with butter. Sprinkle with lemon juice.

3. Bake, uncovered, until golden brown, about eight minutes. Garnish with parsley and serve with a lemon wedge.

CRABMEAT REMICK, PAGE 19.

DEVILED CRAB *6 servings*

2 tablespoons butter
2 tablespoons flour
½ cup milk
½ cup cream
¼ teaspoon nutmeg
¼ teaspoon dry mustard
2 egg yolks
¼ cup sherry
Salt and freshly ground black pepper to taste
3 cups crabmeat, fresh or canned, picked over well
Buttered bread crumbs
Lemon wedges

1. Preheat oven to hot (400° F.).

2. In a saucepan, melt the butter, add the flour and stir with a wire whisk until blended. Meanwhile bring the milk and cream to a boil and add all at once to butter-flour mixture, stirring vigorously with the whisk until the sauce is smooth.

3. Remove the sauce from the heat and stir in the nutmeg and mustard.

(cont'd)

Add the egg yolks lightly beaten with a little of the hot sauce and heat, stirring, until thickened. Add the sherry, salt, pepper and crabmeat.

4. Spoon the mixture into individual crab shells, flameproof ramekins or a baking dish. Sprinkle with buttered crumbs and bake until the crab is thoroughly hot and the crumbs have browned, about ten minutes. Serve with lemon wedges.

CRABMEAT GUMBO *4 to 6 servings*

- 1/4 pound salt pork or bacon, cubed
- 1/4 cup butter
- 1/4 cup chopped onion
- 2 cups sliced fresh, frozen (defrosted) or canned okra
- 2 cups canned tomatoes, undrained
- 1 clove garlic, finely minced
- 1/4 lemon, thinly sliced
- 1 bay leaf
- 3 cups boiling water
- 1/2 teaspoon salt
- 1/4 teaspoon paprika
- Few drops of Tabasco sauce
- 1 teaspoon Worcestershire sauce
- 2 tablespoons flour
- 2 cups cooked fresh or canned crabmeat, picked over well

1. In a heavy kettle, cook the salt pork or bacon briefly over low heat until rendered of its fat. Add two tablespoons of the butter and the onion and cook until the onion is transparent.

2. Add the okra, tomatoes, garlic, lemon and bay leaf. Bring to a boil and add the boiling water, salt, paprika, Tabasco sauce and Worcestershire sauce. Lower the heat and simmer, partially covered, one hour.

3. Blend the remaining butter with the flour and stir the mixture, bit by bit, into the simmering vegetables. When thickened and smooth, stir in the crabmeat. Heat to boiling and serve with steamed rice.

CRABMEAT STEW *6 servings*

- 2 cups crabmeat, fresh or canned, picked over well
- 1/2 cup dry sherry
- 2 tablespoons butter
- 1 clove garlic, crushed
- 1 1/2 tablespoons flour
- 1/2 teaspoon rosemary
- 1/4 cup finely chopped onion or chives
- 3 tablespoons green pepper, finely chopped
- 3/4 cup peeled, chopped tomato
- Salt and freshly ground black pepper to taste
- 1 cup cream

1. Marinate the crabmeat in the sherry one hour in the refrigerator. In a skillet heat the butter, add the garlic and sauté. Add the flour, rosemary, onion, green pepper, tomato, salt and pepper and simmer five minutes.

2. Stir in the crabmeat with the sherry and add the cream.

3. Cook five to ten minutes longer, adding more cream if necessary. Correct the seasonings and serve with buttered toast.

CRABMEAT SCRAMBLED WITH EGGS *2 to 3 servings*

1 cup crabmeat, picked over well
4 eggs
½ teaspoon salt
¼ teaspoon freshly ground black pepper
1 tablespoon chopped scallions
3 tablespoons oil or butter

1. Flake the crabmeat. Beat the eggs with the salt, pepper and scallions.
2. In a skillet heat half the oil, add the crabmeat and cook gently until hot. Add the remaining oil and heat.
3. Add the eggs and adjust the heat at high. With a fork draw the solidified egg to the center of the skillet, tilt the skillet and let the uncooked egg run over the pan. Repeat until most of the egg has set. Serve immediately.

CRABMEAT BOUILLABAISSE *6 servings*

¼ cup salad oil
3 onions, chopped
2 green peppers, cut into thin strips
2 potatoes, pared and sliced
2 teaspoons salt
1 clove garlic, minced
1 bay leaf
¼ cup tomato paste
1 quart boiling water
1 pound white fish fillets, cut into 1-inch chunks
½ pound raw shrimp, shelled and deveined
½ pound fresh crabmeat or 1 can (6½ ounces) crabmeat, picked over well
Chopped parsley

1. In a large kettle heat the oil, add the onions and cook until transparent.
2. Add the green peppers and potatoes and cook several minutes. Add the salt, garlic, bay leaf, tomato paste and boiling water. Cover and simmer twenty minutes.
3. Add the fish fillets and cook ten minutes. Add the shrimp and crabmeat and simmer fifteen minutes longer.
4. Serve in deep soup bowls and garnish each serving with chopped parsley.

CATALAN BOUILLABAISSE, PAGE 265.

CRABMEAT CASSEROLE *6 servings*

1 green pepper, seeded
¾ pound mushrooms
4 small sweet gherkins
3 small white onions
2 tablespoons chopped parsley
1½ pounds fresh crabmeat, or 3 seven-ounce cans crabmeat, picked over well
6 tablespoons butter
5 tablespoons flour
1½ cups milk
½ cup light cream
½ teaspoon salt
Freshly ground black pepper
Few grains of cayenne pepper
½ cup dry sherry
½ cup dry bread crumbs

(*cont'd*)

1. Chop fine the pepper, mushrooms, sweet gherkins and onions and mix with the parsley and crabmeat, which has been broken into small pieces.

2. Preheat oven to moderate (350° F.).

3. In a saucepan melt the butter, add the flour and stir with a wire whisk until blended. Meanwhile, bring the milk and cream to a boil and add all at once to the butter-flour mixture, stirring vigorously with the whisk until the sauce is thickened and smooth.

4. Combine the sauce with the crabmeat mixture and season with salt, pepper and cayenne. Remove from the heat and add the sherry. Pour into a buttered casserole, sprinkle with bread crumbs, dot with additional butter and bake thirty minutes.

CRABMEAT QUICHE, PAGE 27.

BOILED LIVE LOBSTER

Plunge the lobster, head first, into a large pot of rapidly boiling salted water. Cover the pot, return to a boil and boil twelve to fifteen minutes for a one-and-one-half- to two-pound lobster. When done, remove from water with tongs and place the lobster on its back. Slit the undershell lengthwise with a sharp knife or scissors. Remove and discard the dark vein, the sac near the head and spongy tissue, but save the green liver and coral, if any. Serve hot, cut side up, with drawn butter (page 447). Garnish with parsley and lemon wedges.

To Cut Up Live Lobster: Wash the lobster and cut its spinal cord by inserting a knife where the tail and body meet. Turn lobster on its back and split lengthwise. Clean as above. Cut each tail crosswise into three pieces. Cut off the claws and crack them.

HOMARD A L'ABSINTHE

2 to 3 servings

2 live lobsters, about 1½ pounds each
2 teaspoons chopped fresh tarragon
2 teaspoons chopped fresh chervil
Chopped parsley
4 egg yolks
½ cup butter
¼ cup heavy cream
1 teaspoon salt
Dash of white pepper
1 cup dry white wine
3 tablespoons absinthe (or Pernod)
2 cups light cream
Dash of Tabasco sauce

1. Kill the lobsters, as above, and cut the lobster tails into pieces about one inch thick. Remove the large front claws and cut each in half. Split the body lengthwise, scrape out the liver, near the head, and reserve. Remove the waste near the head. Remove the small claws for another use.

2. Mix the lobster liver with the herbs, one-half teaspoon parsley, the egg yolks, three tablespoons of the softened butter and the heavy cream. Cream together and set aside.

3. Heat a skillet over high heat. Add the remaining butter and cook the

(cont'd)

cut-up lobster in it over high heat only until the shell turns red, shaking the pan almost constantly. Season with one teaspoon salt and a dash of white pepper.

4. Turn the lobster mixture into a saucepan, add the wine and cook, uncovered, over medium heat about fifteen minutes. (The wine will evaporate.) Heat two tablespoons of the absinthe, add to the lobster and ignite.

5. While the lobster is cooking, heat a two-and-one-half-quart casserole. Heat the light cream over low heat.

6. Turn the cooked lobster into the heated casserole and keep warm.

7. Add the heated cream and the Tabasco to the saucepan in which the lobster was cooked. Remove from the heat and add the liver mixture, stirring vigorously with a wire whisk. Cook over low heat, stirring constantly, until the sauce has just thickened.

8. Stir in the remaining absinthe and pour the sauce over the lobster. Sprinkle with chopped parsley. Serve with oyster forks.

LOBSTER RUMAKI, PAGE 16.

LOBSTER EN BELLEVUE PARISIENNE, PAGE 16.

SPAGHETTI WITH LOBSTER, PAGE 335.

PAELLA *6 to 8 servings*

- 1 one-and-one-half-pound lobster, cooked
- 1 pound shrimp
- 1 dozen or more small clams
- 1 quart mussels
- 1 one-and-one-half-pound chicken
- 1 teaspoon orégano
- 2 peppercorns
- 1 clove garlic, peeled
- 1½ teaspoons salt
- 6 tablespoons olive oil
- 1 teaspoon vinegar
- 2 ounces ham, cut in thin strips
- 1 chorizo (hot Spanish sausage), sliced
- 1 ounce salt pork, finely chopped
- 1 onion, peeled and chopped
- 1 green pepper, seeded and chopped
- ½ teaspoon ground coriander
- 1 teaspoon capers
- 3 tablespoons tomato sauce
- 2¼ cups rice, washed and drained
- 4 cups boiling water
- 1 teaspoon saffron
- 1 can peas, drained
- 1 can pimentos

1. Remove the meat from the lobster. Shell and devein the shrimp. Scrub the clams and mussels.

2. Cut the chicken into medium-sized serving pieces.

3. Combine the orégano, peppercorns, garlic, salt, two tablespoons of the olive oil and the vinegar and mash with the back of a kitchen spoon or in a mortar. Rub the chicken with the mixture.

4. Heat the remaining olive oil in a deep, heavy skillet and brown the chicken lightly over moderate heat. Add the ham, chorizo, the salt pork, onion, green pepper, coriander and capers. Cook ten minutes over low heat. Add the tomato sauce and rice and cook five minutes.

5. Add the boiling water, saffron and shrimp. Mix well and cook rapidly,

(*cont'd*)

covered, until the liquid is absorbed, about twenty minutes. With a large spoon turn the rice from top to bottom.

6. Add the lobster meat and peas, cover and cook five minutes longer.

7. Steam the mussels and clams in a little water until the shells open. Heat the pimentos and drain. Use the mussels, clams and pimentos as a garnish.

LOBSTER THERMIDOR *4 servings*

4 live lobsters, 1½ pounds each
¾ cup butter
1 cup chopped mushrooms
Salt and freshly ground black pepper to taste
½ cup soft bread crumbs
1 tablespoon Worcestershire sauce
1½ teaspoons Maggi seasoning
Tabasco sauce
4 teaspoons chopped parsley
4 teaspoons chopped pimento
¾ cup sherry
¼ cup cognac
2 cups heavy cream
4 egg yolks
½ cup grated Parmesan cheese
Paprika

1. Cook and clean the lobsters as for boiled live lobster (page 279). Twist off the claws, reserving the small claws for garnish. Remove meat from the bodies and cut into small pieces. Crack the large claws, remove meat and cube. Reserve the shells.

2. Preheat oven to moderate (350° F.).

3. Heat one-half cup of the butter, add the mushrooms and cook three minutes. Season with salt and pepper.

4. Add the lobster meat, crumbs, seasonings, sherry, cognac, cream and egg yolks. Mix well.

5. Fill the lobster shells with the mixture, sprinkle with cheese, dot with the remaining butter and sprinkle with paprika.

6. Place in a shallow pan and bake fifteen minutes. Serve immediately.

LOBSTER BISQUE, PAGE 76.

LOBSTER MOANA *About 5 servings*

1 live lobster, 2 to 2½ pounds
2 tablespoons oil
1 small clove garlic, minced
2 tablespoons rum
½ cup chicken or veal broth
1 cup bean sprouts
1 cup sliced water chestnuts
1 cup snow peas
1½ cups coarsely cut Chinese cabbage
Salt and freshly ground black pepper
1 egg, beaten

1. Cook the lobster as for boiled live lobster (page 279). Cool, clean and remove the meat from the shell.

2. In a skillet heat the oil and the sliced lobster meat and garlic and cook briefly. Add the rum, broth and vegetables and simmer, uncovered, five minutes. Season with the salt and pepper. Add the egg beaten lightly with a little of the hot sauce and cook, stirring, until hot. Do not let boil.

LOBSTER A L'AMERICAINE *4 to 6 servings*

Arguments have raged for decades over the origin of this lobster-and-tomato dish. American chefs say it was created by an American and French chefs say no such thing unless it was a Frenchman lured to this country by the Yankee dollar.

- 2 live lobsters, 1½ pounds each
- ¼ cup olive oil
- 3 tablespoons butter
- ¼ cup finely chopped onion, or 3 tablespoons finely chopped shallot
- 1 clove garlic, finely chopped
- 6 firm tomatoes, peeled, seeded and chopped
- 3 tablespoons chopped parsley
- 1 tablespoon chopped fresh tarragon
- Dried thyme
- ½ bay leaf
- ¾ cup dry white wine or water
- 3 tablespoons tomato paste
- Cayenne pepper
- Salt to taste
- ¼ cup warmed cognac

1. Kill the lobsters by plunging a knife into the thorax (see page 279). Cut through the markings on the tail to make round medallions. Cut the body in half, clean it and save the coral and liver for the sauce.

2. If the lobster is to be cooked shortly after it is purchased, these advance preparations may be made by the fish dealer; in this case, the lobster must be kept cold to prevent spoilage.

3. In a large heavy skillet, heat the olive oil and add the lobster pieces. Toss and stir the pieces until the shells turn red and the meat is seared. Transfer the meat and shells to a hot platter.

4. Add the butter to the skillet and cook the onion and garlic until the onion is wilted. Add the tomatoes, herbs and wine and simmer one-half hour. Add the tomato paste, cayenne and salt.

5. Pour the cognac over the lobster pieces and ignite. Transfer the lobster to the sauce, cover and simmer fifteen to twenty minutes. Just before serving, stir in the liver and lobster coral.

Note: If desired, the lobster meat may be removed from the shell before it is transferred to the sauce. The shells, however, give the sauce additional flavor.

MUSSELS MARINIERE *4 to 6 servings*

This is one of the most glorious dishes ever created. Many home cooks avoid it, however, thinking the mussels too sandy and difficult to clean to make it worthwhile. A plastic mesh scrubbing ball simplifies the task of cleaning.

- 6 tablespoons butter
- 1 clove garlic, chopped
- 3 tablespoons chopped shallot or onion
- 2 small leeks, chopped
- 1 small bay leaf
- 36 fresh mussels, scrubbed well and debearded
- Salt and freshly ground black pepper to taste
- ¾ cup dry white wine
- 4 teaspoons flour
- ½ cup cream
- 2 egg yolks
- Chopped parsley

(*cont'd*)

1. In a deep kettle or saucepan, heat three tablespoons of the butter, add the garlic and shallot and cook over low heat one minute. Add the leeks and bay leaf and cook two minutes longer.

2. Add the mussels, sprinkle with salt and pepper and pour the wine over the top. Cover and simmer gently until the mussel shells open, about ten minutes.

3. Remove the mussels, discard the top shell but leave the mussels in the bottom shell. Arrange in soup dishes.

4. Strain the liquid in the saucepan and bring to a boil. Thicken slightly with beurre manié, made by creaming the remaining butter with the flour. Remove saucepan from the heat and add the cream mixed with the egg yolks.

5. Heat the sauce, without letting it boil, and pour over the mussels. Sprinkle with finely chopped parsley and serve immediately.

MUSSELS IN BACON, PAGE 18.

FRENCH-FRIED OYSTERS *4 to 6 servings*

Fat for deep frying
2 eggs
2 tablespoons cream
1 teaspoon salt
Freshly ground black pepper
1 quart shucked oysters
Flour
Cracker crumbs or cornmeal

1. Heat the fat to 380° F.

2. Beat the eggs lightly and add the cream, salt and pepper.

3. Dredge the oysters individually in flour, dip in the egg mixture and roll in crumbs or cornmeal.

4. Fry the oysters until golden brown, about two minutes. Drain on absorbent paper and sprinkle with additional salt and pepper.

OYSTERS EN BROCHETTE *6 servings*

24 shucked oysters
Lemon juice
Salt and freshly ground black pepper to taste
12 strips bacon, cut in half
12 mushroom caps
Melted butter
Minced parsley

1. Sprinkle the oysters with the lemon juice, salt and pepper. Wrap half a strip of bacon around each oyster.

2. Using six long brochettes, arrange on each a mushroom cap, four bacon-wrapped oysters and another mushroom. Brush with butter and broil over charcoal or under a broiler until the bacon is crisp. Serve sprinkled with parsley.

OYSTERS CASINO, PAGE 19.

OYSTERS ROCKEFELLER, PAGE 19.

OYSTERS BALTIMORE *4 servings*

4 thin slices country-cured ham, cut to fit toast slices
4 slices buttered toast
6 tablespoons butter, melted
1 pint shucked oysters, drained
1 teaspoon lemon juice
Salt and freshly ground black pepper to taste

1. In a large skillet cook the ham gently until tender. If it is lean, add a little fat to the pan. Place the ham on the toast and keep hot.

2. Heat the butter and add the oysters and lemon juice. When the oysters are plump, in one or two minutes, ladle them with the butter over the ham and toast. Season with salt and pepper.

PAN ROAST GRAND CENTRAL *1 serving*

This is only a variation of the genuine pan roast served at the oyster bar in Grand Central Station. To make the real McCoy one would have to own one of the round-bottom aluminum cooking utensils used by the chefs there.

8 freshly opened oysters
¼ cup butter, at room temperature
1 tablespoon chili sauce
1 teaspoon Worcestershire sauce
Few drops of lemon juice
Celery salt and paprika to taste
½ cup cream
1 piece dry toast

1. Boil the oysters with their liquor, one tablespoon butter, chili sauce, Worcestershire sauce, lemon juice, celery salt and paprika one minute, stirring constantly.

2. Add the cream, return to a boil and pour over the toast. Top with remaining butter and sprinkle with additional paprika.

OYSTERS A LA KING *6 servings*

1 pint shucked oysters
¼ cup butter
¼ cup diced celery
¼ cup diced green pepper
5 tablespoons flour
2 cups milk
1 egg, beaten
1 tablespoon pimento, chopped
1 teaspoon salt
⅛ teaspoon freshly ground black pepper

1. Simmer the oysters in their liquor until the edges begin to curl, about five minutes. Drain.

2. In a saucepan heat the butter, add the celery and green pepper and cook until tender. With a wire whisk stir in the flour. Meanwhile, bring the milk to a boil and add all at once to the mixture, stirring vigorously with the whisk until thickened.

3. Add the egg, lightly beaten with a little of the hot sauce, stirring constantly. Add the simmered oysters and the seasonings. Heat thoroughly but do not let boil. Serve on buttered toast or rice.

OYSTER CHOWDER, PAGE 77.

OYSTER PIE *5 servings*

3 tablespoons butter
1 cup sliced mushrooms
3 tablespoons flour
1 cup milk
½ teaspoon salt
¼ teaspoon celery salt
Dash of freshly ground black pepper
1 teaspoon lemon juice
1 pint shucked oysters
Pastry for a 2-crust 8-inch pie

1. Preheat oven to hot (425° F.).
2. In a saucepan heat the butter, add the mushrooms and cook until wilted. With a wire whisk stir in the flour. Meanwhile, bring the milk to a boil and add to the mixture, stirring vigorously until thickened.
3. Add the seasonings, lemon juice and oysters with their liquor.
4. Line the bottom and sides of an eight-inch pie pan or small casserole with pastry, rolled to one-eighth-inch thickness. Add the oyster mixture and cover with the remaining pastry. Seal the edges and cut gashes in the top to allow steam to escape.
5. Bake until brown, about thirty minutes.

OYSTERS WITH SAUSAGE, PAGE 18.

OLD-FASHIONED SCALLOPED OYSTERS *4 servings*

⅔ cup soft bread crumbs
1 cup fine cracker crumbs
½ cup butter, melted
1½ pints small shucked oysters, or 18 large oysters
¾ teaspoon salt
Freshly ground black pepper to taste
2 tablespoons chopped parsley (optional)
½ teaspoon Worcestershire sauce
3 tablespoons milk or cream

1. Preheat oven to moderate (350° F.).
2. Mix the bread crumbs, cracker crumbs and butter.
3. Place half the crumb mixture on the bottom of a greased one-quart casserole. Add half the oysters, reserving the liquor, and sprinkle with half the salt, pepper and parsley. Add the remaining oysters and sprinkle with the remaining salt, pepper and parsley.
4. Mix one-third cup oyster liquor with the Worcestershire sauce and milk and pour over the oysters. Top with the remaining crumb mixture.
5. Bake, uncovered, until puffy and brown, about forty-five minutes.

SCALLOPS EN BROCHETTE *4 servings*

1 pound sea or bay scallops
8 strips bacon
3 tablespoons butter, melted
½ teaspoon salt
⅛ teaspoon freshly ground black pepper
Lemon wedges

(cont'd)

1. Wash the scallops and dry thoroughly.

2. On each of four skewers, intertwine a strip of bacon with about three sea scallops or four to six bay scallops. Brush the scallops with the melted butter and sprinkle with salt and pepper.

3. Broil in a preheated broiler three to five inches from the source of heat five to ten minutes, turning once. Serve with lemon wedges.

BROILED SCALLOPS *4 servings*

Scallops in vermouth is an unusual and good idea.

- 1½ pounds scallops
- ½ cup dry vermouth
- ½ cup olive oil
- ½ teaspoon finely chopped garlic
- ½ teaspoon salt
- 2 tablespoons minced parsley

1. Marinate the scallops in the vermouth mixed with the remaining ingredients several hours in the refrigerator.

2. When ready to serve, place the scallops and the marinade in a shallow pan. Place under a preheated broiler, two inches from the source of heat, and broil five to six minutes, turning once.

SEA SCALLOPS SEVICHE, PAGE 21.

BAY SCALLOPS QUICHE, PAGE 28.

CURRIED SEA SCALLOPS *6 servings*

- ½ cup butter
- ½ cup chopped onion
- 1 clove garlic, finely chopped
- 1 stalk celery, diced
- ½ bay leaf
- Sprig of parsley
- ¼ teaspoon powdered mustard
- ½ cup diced tart apple
- 2 tablespoons flour
- ½ teaspoon mace
- 2 tablespoons curry powder
- 1½ cups clam broth (bottled)
- 1 cup dry white wine or water
- 1½ pounds sea scallops, cut in half
- ½ cup heavy cream

1. In a large saucepan heat the butter, add the onion, garlic, celery, bay leaf, parsley, mustard and apple and cook eight minutes, stirring occasionally.

2. With a wire whisk stir in the flour, mace and curry powder and cook four minutes longer. Add the clam broth and wine and simmer, partially covered, forty-five minutes. Strain into another saucepan, rubbing the solids through a sieve.

3. Add the scallops to the sauce and simmer until the scallops are tender when tested with a fork, five to ten minutes. Stir in the cream and heat briefly but do not boil. Serve with chutney, chopped egg and coconut.

SCALLOPS SAUCE VERTE *6 to 8 servings*

This is a cold scallop dish in which they are covered with a green mayonnaise sauce.

½ cup dry vermouth
½ onion, chopped
Sprig of parsley
1 bay leaf
Salt and freshly ground black pepper to taste
1 pound sea scallops, halved
1 cup mayonnaise, approximately
¼ cup finely chopped parsley
½ cup finely chopped spinach
¼ cup chopped chives or green onion
1 tablespoon fresh dill, chopped, or ½ teaspoon dried dill
Lettuce leaves

1. In a saucepan heat the vermouth with the onion, sprig of parsley, bay leaf, salt and pepper. Add the scallops and simmer gently until tender, shaking the pan occasionally, about seven minutes. Drain and cool.
2. Meanwhile, blend the mayonnaise, chopped parsley, spinach, chives and dill. Add more mayonnaise, if desired.
3. Place the scallops in a bowl lined with lettuce leaves, cover with the green sauce and top with a sprinkling of additional finely chopped parsley. Chill.

SCALLOPS SAUTEED IN GARLIC BUTTER *4 servings*

¼ cup butter
1 small clove garlic, split
1 pound scallops, fresh or frozen (defrosted)
Salt and freshly ground black pepper to taste
Tartar sauce
Lemon wedges

In a saucepan heat the butter and garlic slowly. Discard garlic. Add the scallops and cook five minutes. Season with salt and pepper and serve immediately with tartar sauce and lemon wedges.

SCALLOPS SAUTE *4 servings*

This is a delectable scallop creation that is quickly prepared.

1 pound sea or bay scallops
¼ cup butter
½ teaspoon salt
⅛ teaspoon freshly ground black pepper
¼ teaspoon paprika
1 clove garlic, minced
1 tablespoon minced parsley
3 tablespoons lemon juice

1. Wash the scallops and dry thoroughly. If sea scallops are used, cut them into thirds or quarters.
2. In a large skillet heat two tablespoons of the butter and add the salt, pepper, paprika and garlic.
3. Add enough scallops to cover the bottom of the skillet without crowding. Cook quickly over high heat, stirring occasionally, until golden brown, five to

(cont'd)

ten minutes. Transfer the scallops to a heated platter. Repeat the process until all the scallops are cooked.

4. In the same skillet place the parsley, lemon juice and remaining butter. Heat until the butter melts and pour over the scallops.

BOILED SHRIMP *4 servings*

1 quart water
½ stalk celery, sliced
1 carrot, sliced
1 small white onion, sliced
Juice of ½ lemon
1 teaspoon salt
½ teaspoon freshly ground black pepper
1 pound shrimp, shelled and deveined

1. In a large saucepan bring one quart of water to a boil, add the remaining ingredients except the shrimp and boil fifteen minutes.

2. Add the shrimp and simmer, uncovered, until pink, two to five minutes. Drain or leave the shrimp in the broth until serving time, as desired. Refrigerate.

COLD RICE WITH SHRIMP, PAGE 428.

SHRIMP BOILED IN BEER *4 servings*

Beer makes a marvelous cooking liquid for shrimp.

2 pounds shrimp
2 twelve-ounce bottles or cans of beer
1 clove garlic, peeled
2 teaspoons salt
½ teaspoon thyme
2 bay leaves
1 teaspoon celery seed
1 tablespoon chopped parsley
⅛ teaspoon cayenne pepper
Juice of ½ lemon

1. Wash the shrimp, if desired, but do not remove the shells.

2. Combine the remaining ingredients and bring to a boil. Add the shrimp. Return to a boil, reduce the heat and simmer, uncovered, for two to five minutes, depending on the size of the shrimp.

3. Drain and serve hot with plenty of melted butter seasoned with lemon juice and Tabasco sauce; or cold with a mayonnaise and cognac sauce for shrimp. The shrimp may, of course, be shelled and deveined before serving.

SHRIMP MARINATED IN BEER *6 servings*

2 pounds shrimp, shelled and deveined
1 tablespoon chopped chives
1 tablespoon chopped parsley
2 teaspoons dried basil (optional)
1 teaspoon finely chopped garlic
2 teaspoons dry mustard
½ teaspoon freshly ground black pepper
½ teaspoon celery salt
1 teaspoon salt
1 bottle or can of beer

(cont'd)

1. Marinate the shrimp in the remaining ingredients at least eight hours in the refrigerator, stirring frequently. Drain.

2. Place the shrimp in a preheated broiler pan three inches from the source of heat and broil about five minutes, turning once.

SAYUR LODEH (vegetables with shrimp) *About 10 servings*

Sayur lodeh is a vegetable and shrimp dish of Indonesian origin, with a heavy accent of garlic.

- 4 shallots or 1 small onion, chopped
- 6 whole scallions (green onions), sliced
- 1½ tablespoons chopped fresh ginger or ½ teaspoon powdered ginger
- 12 cloves garlic, minced
- ¾ cup peanut oil
- 2 pounds shrimp, shelled and deveined
- 3 cups coarsely shredded cabbage
- 3 cups coarsely chopped Chinese cabbage
- 2 cups peeled, cubed eggplant
- 2 cups sliced zucchini
- 1 green pepper, seeded and chopped
- 1 bay leaf
- 1 teaspoon ground sereh leaves (optional)
- 1 tablespoon salt
- 1 teaspoon hot red pepper
- ¾ cup coconut milk (page 139)
- 2 teaspoons arrowroot or cornstarch
- 2 tablespoons water

1. Cook the shallots, scallions, ginger and garlic in half the peanut oil for five minutes or until the vegetables are soft and wilted. Add the shrimp and continue cooking over high heat until shrimp turn pink. Stir constantly. Remove the shrimp to a platter.

2. Add the remaining oil to the pan. Cook the cabbages, eggplant, zucchini and green pepper for five minutes, stirring constantly. Add the seasonings and coconut milk. Cover the pan and simmer ten minutes, or until the vegetables are barely tender. Return the shrimp to the pan and cook five minutes longer.

3. Mix the arrowroot with the water and stir it into the simmering stew. When thickened, serve immediately.

Note: Sources for foreign ingredients are listed in Chapter 16.

TEMPURA, PAGE 270.

FRIED SHRIMP *3 servings*

- 1 pound raw shrimp, shelled and deveined
- 1 tablespoon cognac, rum or lemon juice
- ½ teaspoon Worcestershire sauce
- Frying batter (page 290)
- Fat for deep frying

1. Marinate the shrimp in the cognac and Worcestershire sauce about fifteen minutes. *(cont'd)*

2. Dip a few shrimp at a time in the batter and fry in deep hot fat (375° F.) until golden brown. Drain on absorbent paper. Serve with mayonnaise seasoned with horseradish or capers.

FRYING BATTER (WITH BEER):

½ cup flour
Pinch of salt
1 tablespoon melted butter
1 egg, beaten
½ cup beer
1 egg white, stiffly beaten

1. Sift the flour and salt into a mixing bowl. Stir in the butter and egg. Add the beer gradually, stirring only until the mixture is smooth.

2. Let the batter stand in a warm place one hour, then fold in the beaten egg white.

SWEET AND PUNGENT SHRIMP *3 to 4 servings*

¼ cup brown sugar, firmly packed
2 tablespoons cornstarch
½ teaspoon salt
¼ cup vinegar
1 tablespoon soy sauce
¼ teaspoon ground ginger
2½ cups canned pineapple chunks
1 green pepper, cut in strips
2 small onions, cut in rings
1 pound shrimp, cleaned and cooked

1. In a saucepan mix the sugar, cornstarch and salt. Add the vinegar, soy sauce, ginger and syrup drained from the pineapple and cook slowly until slightly thickened, stirring constantly.

2. Add the green pepper, onions and pineapple and simmer two minutes.

3. Add the shrimp, bring to a boil, stirring constantly, and serve immediately with hot rice.

SHRIMP TOLLIVER *3 servings*

1 pound small raw shrimp, shelled and deveined
¼ cup olive oil
3 tablespoons lemon juice
2 tablespoons butter
1 clove garlic
½ cup chopped almonds
Few dashes of Tabasco sauce
2 tablespoons dry vermouth
Pinch of saffron
2 tablespoons chopped chives
2 cups cooked rice

1. Marinate the shrimp in a mixture of the olive oil and lemon juice two hours, turning the shrimp once. Drain, reserving the marinade.

2. In a skillet heat the butter, add the shrimp and garlic and cook until the shrimp turns pink. Discard the garlic and transfer the shrimp to a hot platter.

3. To the skillet add the chopped almonds, reserved marinade, Tabasco and vermouth. Heat and pour over the shrimp.

4. Serve with shrimp-boat rice, made by mixing the saffron and chives with the cooked rice. Stir and let steam a few minutes.

SHRIMP FONDUE *4 servings*

1 pound shrimp, shelled and deveined
2 tablespoons butter
½ teaspoon dry mustard
4 slices bread, crusts removed
1½ cups grated cheese
2 eggs, beaten
1 cup milk
½ teaspoon salt
Freshly ground black pepper

1. Preheat oven to moderate (350° F.). Cook shrimp, covered, in one-half cup water five minutes. Drain, reserving the broth.

2. Cream the butter with the mustard and spread on the bread. Cut into cubes. Arrange the bread cubes, cheese and shrimp in layers in a greased one-quart casserole.

3. Mix the eggs, milk, reserved shrimp broth, salt and pepper and pour over the shrimp mixture. Set in a pan of hot water and bake until a knife inserted in the center comes out clean, one hour or longer. Serve immediately.

SHRIMP WITH SAFFRON *3 servings*

1 pound shrimp, shelled and deveined
1 cup dry white wine
1 tablespoon olive oil
1 cup tomato juice
Juice of 1 lemon
2 sprigs parsley
1 branch fennel or celery
1 sprig fresh thyme
½ bay leaf
2 garlic cloves, crushed
6 peppercorns
1 teaspoon powdered saffron
Salt to taste

1. Combine all the ingredients and cook, covered, over high heat eight to ten minutes. Correct the seasonings, which should be sharp.

2. Chill the shrimp. Serve cold with the sauce strained over the top.

SHRIMP WITH DILL-FLAVORED CREAM SAUCE *4 servings*

5 tablespoons butter
1 tablespoon chopped shallot or onion
1 pound raw shrimp, cleaned
¾ cup white wine
3 tablespoons flour
1½ cups milk
1½ teaspoons chopped fresh dill, or ¾ teaspoon dried dill

1. In a saucepan heat two tablespoons of the butter, add the shallot, shrimp and wine and cook five minutes.

2. In a separate saucepan melt the remaining butter, add the flour and stir with a wire whisk until blended. Meanwhile, bring the milk to a boil and add all at once to the butter-flour mixture, stirring vigorously with the whisk until the sauce is thickened and smooth.

3. Add the sauce and the dill to the shrimp mixture and cook slowly five minutes longer. Serve immediately.

GRILLED SHRIMP *4 servings*

- 32 large shrimp, shelled and deveined
- ½ cup cognac or dry white wine
- ½ teaspoon salt
- ¼ teaspoon freshly ground black pepper
- ½ teaspoon basil or marjoram
- 32 thin strips ham or half slices bacon
- ¼ cup sifted dry bread crumbs
- Lemon wedges

1. Place the shrimp in a bowl, add cognac, salt, pepper and basil and marinate in refrigerator one hour or longer.

2. Wrap each shrimp in a strip of ham and string on skewers, allowing four or eight for each skewer.

3. Place in a preheated broiler about four inches from the source of the heat and cook until the fat of the ham is partially browned. Roll in the crumbs, return to the broiler and cook until golden brown. Serve with lemon wedges.

SHRIMP PIERRE *4 servings*

- 2 pounds jumbo shrimp, shelled and deveined
- 3 cloves garlic, finely chopped
- 1 medium onion, finely chopped
- ¼ cup chopped parsley
- 1 teaspoon dried basil
- 1 teaspoon dry mustard
- 1 teaspoon salt
- ½ cup olive oil or peanut oil
- Juice of 1 lemon

1. Place the shrimp in a bowl with the remaining ingredients and let marinate at room temperature several hours.

2. Broil the shrimp over charcoal or in preheated kitchen broiler about four or five minutes, or until the shrimp are just cooked through. Turn once.

ITALIAN-STYLE SHRIMP *4 servings*

- ½ cup olive or salad oil
- ½ teaspoon salt
- ¼ teaspoon freshly ground black pepper
- 2 tablespoons finely chopped parsley
- 2 pounds large shrimp, shelled and deveined
- ¼ cup butter
- Juice of 1 lemon

1. Mix the oil, salt, pepper and parsley. Dip the shrimp in this mixture, then place in a preheated broiler about two inches from the source of heat. Broil two minutes on each side.

2. Place the broiled shrimp in a baking dish, sprinkle with four tablespoons of the oil mixture and bake in a hot oven (450° F.) ten minutes. Remove the shrimp to a hot serving dish and keep warm. Add the butter and lemon juice to the baking dish and return to the oven for two to three minutes. Remove as soon as the butter is hot and pour over the shrimp.

GARLIC BROILED SHRIMP *4 servings*

24 large shrimp, shelled and deveined
1 cup lemon juice
1 cup olive oil
6 cloves garlic, crushed
2 teaspoons chopped parsley
1 teaspoon red pepper (optional)

1. Wash the shrimp in cold water, dry and arrange in a pan.
2. Mix the remaining ingredients and pour over the shrimp. Let stand in the refrigerator overnight.
3. Remove the shrimp from the marinade and place in the broiler three inches from the source of heat. Broil until brown, about five minutes on each side.

SHRIMP CURRY *6 or more servings*

¼ cup butter
4 large onions, chopped
3 cloves garlic, chopped
3 cups water or coconut milk (page 139)
3 large tomatoes, peeled and chopped
2 large apples, peeled and chopped
1 cup chopped celery
1 tablespoon shredded coconut
1 piece fresh ginger root, or ¾ teaspoon powdered ginger
1 tablespoon sugar
1½ tablespoons curry powder, or more
1½ tablespoons flour
1½ teaspoons salt
¼ teaspoon freshly ground black pepper
3½ pounds raw shrimp, shelled and deveined

1. In a large skillet heat the butter, add the onions and garlic and cook until lightly browned. Add the water and bring to a boil.
2. Add the tomatoes, apples, celery, coconut and fresh ginger, if used.
3. Blend the sugar, curry powder, flour, salt and pepper and powdered ginger, if used. Add enough cold water to make a paste and add gradually, stirring, to the boiling mixture. Simmer, partially covered, stirring occasionally, until the vegetables are very tender, about forty minutes.
4. Add the shrimp and cook five minutes longer. Serve on rice.

SHRIMP AU GRATIN *4 servings*

1 cup water
1 small onion, sliced
1 small clove garlic, sliced
Leaves from 2 stalks celery
1 small bay leaf
6 peppercorns
1¼ to 1½ pounds raw shrimp
¼ cup butter
¼ cup flour
1 cup light cream or evaporated milk
2 tablespoons sherry
¾ to 1 cup grated Parmesan cheese
Salt and freshly ground black pepper to taste

1. In a saucepan bring one cup water to a boil, add the onion, garlic, celery leaves, bay leaf and peppercorns. Cover and boil five minutes. Add the shrimp

(cont'd)

and simmer four minutes. Drain, reserving the broth. Discard the bay leaf. Shell and devein the shrimp.

2. In a saucepan melt the butter, add the flour and stir with a wire whisk until blended. Meanwhile, bring the cream and shrimp broth to a boil and add all at once to the butter-flour mixture, stirring vigorously with the whisk until the sauce is thickened and smooth.

3. Add the sherry, half the cheese and the shrimp. Season with salt and pepper.

4. Turn the mixture into a shallow six-cup baking dish and sprinkle with the remaining cheese. Bake in a preheated moderate oven (375° F.) until the top is brown and bubbly.

SHRIMP WITH RICE *4 to 6 servings*

- ½ cup butter
- 1 large onion, finely chopped
- 1 cup sliced mushrooms
- 1 green pepper, finely chopped
- 1¼ cups raw rice
- ¼ teaspoon nutmeg
- 1 teaspoon salt
- ½ teaspoon freshly ground pepper
- 1 cup dry white wine
- 3 cups hot chicken stock or water
- 2 tablespoons chopped parsley
- ¼ teaspoon thyme
- ½ bay leaf
- 2 pounds raw shrimp, shelled and deveined

1. In a large skillet heat the butter, add the onion, mushrooms, green pepper, rice, nutmeg, salt and pepper and cook, stirring, until the rice is golden brown.

2. Add the wine and simmer five minutes. Add the stock, parsley, thyme and bay leaf, cover and cook ten minutes, stirring occasionally.

3. Add the shrimp and simmer five to ten minutes, depending on the size of the shrimp.

4. Remove the bay leaf and serve immediately.

ORIENTAL SHRIMP *6 servings*

- 2 tablespoons salad oil
- 2 pounds raw shrimp, shelled and deveined
- 1 scallion or small onion, chopped
- ½ cup hot chicken broth
- ½ cup thinly sliced water chestnuts
- 1 package frozen peas
- 3 thin slices fresh ginger root, or ½ teaspoon powdered ginger
- 1 teaspoon salt
- 2 tablespoons soy sauce
- 2 tablespoons sherry
- 2 teaspoons cornstarch
- 1 tablespoon water

1. In a skillet heat the oil, add the shrimp and onion and cook, stirring, until the shrimp turn pink and the onion is tender but not brown, about one minute.

(*cont'd*)

2. Add the broth, water chestnuts, peas, ginger and salt. Cover and cook until the peas and shrimp are tender, about three minutes.

3. Remove the cover and stir in the soy sauce, sherry and cornstarch dissolved in the water. Cook until the sauce is clear and slightly thickened.

BAKED PERIWINKLES *4 servings*

6 dozen periwinkles
½ cup soft butter
⅓ cup minced parsley
2 cloves garlic, minced
Salt to taste

1. Soak the periwinkles in warm water long enough to break the membranes that seal them in their shells. Discard any that do not emerge from the shells. Cover the periwinkles with salted water and bring to a boil. The periwinkles will recede into their shells because of the heat. Drain.

2. Using a nut pick or tip of a small paring knife, remove the periwinkles from their shells. Rinse several times in cold water.

3. Cream together the butter, parsley, garlic and salt.

4. Grease the inside of twenty-four large snail shells, insert three periwinkles in each and fill the shells with the garlic butter. Arrange butter side up in a baking dish and let stand two hours.

5. Bake in a preheated hot oven (450° F.) ten minutes.

SEAFOOD IN RAMEKINS *4 servings*

7 tablespoons butter
½ cup raw shrimp, cut into bite-sized pieces
½ cup canned or fresh crabmeat, picked over well and flaked
½ cup bay or sea scallops, cut into bite-sized pieces
1 tablespoon finely chopped onion
2 tablespoons sherry
½ teaspoon salt
¼ teaspoon freshly ground black pepper
3 tablespoons flour
1½ cups milk
½ cup bread crumbs
¼ cup grated Parmesan cheese

1. Preheat oven to hot (400° F.).

2. In a large skillet heat four tablespoons of the butter, add the seafood and onion and cook four minutes, stirring occasionally. Sprinkle with the sherry, salt and pepper.

3. In a saucepan melt the remaining butter, add the flour and stir with a wire whisk until blended. Meanwhile, bring the milk to a boil and add all at once to the butter-flour mixture, stirring vigorously with the whisk until the sauce is thickened and smooth. Combine the sauce with the seafood mixture.

4. Spoon the mixture into individual buttered ramekins or shells and sprinkle with the bread crumbs mixed with the cheese.

5. Bake twelve to fifteen minutes, or brown under a broiler. Garnish with lemon wedges.

CHUPE *10 servings*

Chupe is a Chilean seafood casserole that is thickened with bread soaked in milk. It is a splendid buffet dish. The chupe below is served on occasion in the home of Leonard Bernstein, the conductor of the New York Philharmonic. His wife, the former Felicia Montealegre, was born in Montevideo.

- 3 small loaves French bread, about five cups cubed
- 5 cups milk
- 1 quart water
- 1 tablespoon salt
- 1 bay leaf
- 2 pounds scallops, washed
- 1 pound raw shrimp, shelled and deveined
- 2 tablespoons paprika
- 1 teaspoon Tabasco sauce
- Butter
- ½ teaspoon orégano
- ¼ teaspoon freshly ground black pepper
- 1 onion, sliced
- 2 large lobster tails
- ½ pound crabmeat
- ½ pound mozzarella cheese, diced
- 4 hard-cooked eggs
- Parmesan cheese

1. Cut the bread into cubes and soak in the milk.
2. Bring the water with the salt and bay leaf to a boil. Add the scallops and cook about three minutes. Remove the scallops, add the shrimp and cook until pink. Remove the shrimp.
3. Add about one and one-half cups of the broth to the bread mixture. Add the paprika, Tabasco and four tablespoons of melted butter. Mix well and sieve, or run through a food mill.
4. Add enough water to the remaining broth to make about three quarts. Add the orégano, black pepper and onion and bring to a boil. Add the lobster tails and boil about eight minutes. Cool the lobster, remove from shell and cut the meat into one-inch slices.
5. Discard the broth, wash the pot and place in it all the seafood, bread purée, mozzarella and three tablespoons of butter. Mix.
6. Spread half the mixture in two shallow buttered three-quart casseroles. Add the eggs, cut into wedges, and the remaining seafood mixture. Sprinkle with Parmesan cheese and dot with bits of butter.
7. Bake in a preheated hot oven (400° F.) until golden brown, about twenty minutes. If prepared ahead and chilled, let warm to room temperature before baking.

FROGS' LEGS PROVENCALE *6 servings*

- 18 jumbo frogs' legs, trimmed
- Water
- Milk
- Seasoned flour for dredging
- Peanut oil
- 3 tablespoons butter
- 1 clove garlic, finely chopped
- Lemon juice
- Finely chopped parsley

(cont'd)

1. Soak the frogs' legs in water to cover for two hours. Drain and dry well. Dip the frogs' legs in milk, then dredge in seasoned flour.

2. Add peanut oil to a skillet to the depth of one-quarter inch. When it is hot, cook the frogs' legs on all sides, six to eight minutes.

3. Transfer the frogs' legs to a hot platter and pour off and discard the oil from the skillet. Add the butter to the skillet and cook to a golden brown. Add the garlic, then pour the butter over the frogs' legs. Sprinkle with lemon juice and chopped parsley and serve immediately.

SNAILS IN WINE *6 servings*

3 cups dry white wine
1 teaspoon chopped shallot or onion
6 dozen canned snails and shells
Snail butter (see below)

1. Boil the wine with the shallot until reduced by one-half. Strain.

2. Add a little wine to each shell, insert a snail and cover the opening with snail butter. Bake in a preheated hot oven (450° F.) ten minutes.

SNAIL BUTTER:

½ cup butter, at room temperature
2 cloves garlic, minced
¼ cup minced parsley
Salt and freshly ground black pepper to taste

Cream the butter and garlic, add the parsley, salt and pepper and mix well.

CHAPTER SIX

EGGS, CHEESE, RICE AND PASTA

EGG DISHES

There are people in the world who literally do not know how to boil water. There are also those who cannot scramble an egg. Not properly, that is. Eggs, for the most part, should be cooked slowly, which is the treatment they deserve. The one exception is in making French omelets, when the eggs must be cooked over high heat.

BAKED OR SHIRRED EGGS

Butter

Eggs at room temperature

1. Preheat oven to moderate (350° F.).
2. Melt one teaspoon butter in an individual ramekin or any small heatproof dish. Break one or two eggs into each dish and bake ten to twelve minutes, until the white is milky and still creamy.

Note: There are many variations of this dish. To make shirred eggs Florentine, for example, buttered ramekins are lined with cooked, well-drained buttered spinach over which the eggs are broken.

Other ingredients which may be combined with the eggs to be shirred are tongue slices, cooked sausages, chicken livers or shrimp and other seafood.

Hot chicken gravy or veal gravy flavored with tarragon may be poured over the eggs after they are cooked.

BAKED EGGS GRUYERE *1 serving*

1 teaspoon butter
2 eggs
Grated Gruyère cheese
¼ cup hot heavy cream

(*cont'd*)

1. Preheat oven to moderate (350° F.).
2. In an individual heatproof ramekin melt the butter. Break the eggs into it and cook over low heat one minute.
3. Cover the eggs with grated Gruyère cheese and pour hot cream over the top. Place the ramekin in a pan of hot water and bake until eggs are set and the cheese has melted.

FRIED EGGS

Butter or bacon fat
Eggs at room temperature

1. Melt enough butter or bacon fat in a heavy skillet to cover the bottom. Break the desired number of eggs into a saucer and slip them carefully in the pan.
2. Cook over low heat, basting the eggs with the hot fat until the whites are set. If the eggs are to be cooked on both sides, turn with a pancake turner.

OEUFS AU BUERRE NOIR

The most famous fried-egg dish, other than plain fried eggs, is the French specialty, fried eggs au beurre noir or in black butter. Eggs are fried in butter and transferred to a warm serving dish. A little additional butter is added to the pan and cooked quickly until dark brown. A few drops of vinegar are added for each egg and the mixture is poured over the eggs. Each egg is garnished with one-half teaspoon capers.

HARD- OR SOFT-COOKED EGGS

Water
Eggs at room temperature

1. In a saucepan bring enough water to a rapid boil to cover the eggs to be cooked.
2. Place each egg on a spoon and lower it into the water. Reduce the heat until the water barely simmers and cook the eggs to the desired degree of doneness. For soft-cooked eggs, leave in the water three to four and one-half minutes. For hard-cooked, leave in the water ten minutes, drain immediately and plunge the eggs into cold water; this causes a jacket of steam to form between the egg and shell to facilitate peeling.

EGGS MOLLET

Eggs soft-cooked in the above fashion for exactly six minutes are called eggs mollet. The white is set and firm and the yolks remain liquid. They are shelled and used in much the same way as poached eggs. Plunge the eggs immediately in cold water after removing from the pan to arrest the cooking process.

POACHED EGGS

Water
3 tablespoons white vinegar
1 teaspoon salt
Eggs at room temperature

1. Put water to a depth of one inch in a skillet, add the vinegar and salt and bring to a boil.

2. Reduce the heat immediately. Break the eggs one at a time into a saucer, then slip them gently into the water. Let the eggs steep until the whites are firm.

3. Using a slotted spoon or pancake turner, remove the eggs and drain on absorbent paper. Trim with a knife or cookie cutter. Serve topped with butter, or a sherry or cheese sauce.

Note: Eggs may be poached in advance and reheated briefly in boiling salted water, about thirty seconds, just before serving. This is advantageous if a quantity of eggs are to be poached for special occasions.

EGGS BENEDICT *3 or 6 servings*

Sauté six slices cooked ham briefly in butter. Place each on a toasted English muffin half and top each with a poached egg. Cover with Hollandaise sauce (page 449). If desired, garnish with a truffle slice.

PLAIN OMELET

To make an omelet select a nine- or ten-inch pan with round, sloping sides. Earmark it exclusively for omelets. To season the pan, rub the bottom with steel-wool soap pads until smooth and shiny. Cover the bottom with a few spoonfuls of salad oil and place the skillet over very low heat until the oil is nearly smoking. Cool pan overnight, pour out the oil and wipe with a dry clean cloth or paper towels. If, at a later date, omelets stick to the pan, season again, beginning with the soap-pad treatment.

To make an omelet for one, break three eggs into a small bowl and add one tablespoon cold water, a little salt and, if desired, a touch of Tabasco sauce. Beat eggs thoroughly with a fork until light and foamy. Place omelet pan over moderate heat. To determine when the pan is properly heated, flick drops of water into it. If they skitter about and disappear almost instantly, pan is ready. Quickly add one tablespoon butter and swirl around in pan. Pour the eggs into the pan. With left hand manipulating pan—flat on the burner—with a fore-and-aft motion, hold fork in the right hand and stir eggs with a circular motion, letting flat of fork touch flat of pan without scraping.

The fore-and-aft motion of the left hand prevents omelet sticking. The circular motion of the right hand causes layers to form, giving lightness to the omelet. When the omelet is cooked and ready to be folded, change position of left hand quickly. Hold handle with the fingers, the palm turned upward. If a fill-

(*cont'd*)

1. *To make an omelet*, heat pan, swirl butter around in it with a fork and add beaten eggs immediately.

2. With left hand shake pan, using fore-and-aft motion. Simultaneously stir eggs clockwise with fork.

3. When eggs are moist on top and set on bottom, quickly place filling on upper half near handle.

4. Change position of left hand as shown. Raise pan so it is on an angle. Roll omelet with fork.

5. Complete rolling, and, holding a warm plate in right hand, turn omelet out onto it. Garnish.

ing is used, place a little on the upper half of the omelet. Raise skillet to a forty-five-degree angle and, using a fork, start to roll omelet from the top down. Hold a warm plate in right hand and turn omelet out onto it.

OMELET CHASSEUR *6 servings*

6 tablespoons butter
2 teaspoons chopped shallot or scallion
3 chicken livers, cut into 3 or 4 pieces
3 mushrooms, sliced
Salt and freshly ground black pepper
1½ teaspoons flour
3 tablespoons dry white wine or chicken stock
18 small mushroom caps
Chopped parsley

1. In a skillet melt three tablespoons of the butter and add the shallot. Cook, stirring, one minute. Add the chicken livers and mushroom slices and sprinkle with salt and pepper. Cook gently, stirring, one minute, or until the livers are browned.

2. Sprinkle the mixture with flour and stir in the wine. Use as a filling for six three-egg omelets.

3. Melt the remaining butter in a skillet and in it sauté the mushroom caps. Garnish each omelet with three caps and sprinkle with parsley.

POTATO-ONION OMELET *4 servings*

1 teaspoon butter
½ cup cubed salt pork, lightly packed
1 large onion, chopped
1½ cups cubed, cooked, cold potatoes
2 teaspoons water
4 eggs, beaten
Salt and freshly ground black pepper

1. Melt the butter in an omelet pan, add the salt pork and cook over medium heat, stirring occasionally, until the butter and pork begin to brown. Add the onion and continue cooking until the onion is almost tender.

2. Add the potatoes, increase the heat slightly and sauté until the pork, onion and potatoes have browned. Drain off the fat.

3. Add the water to the eggs, season to taste with salt and pepper and pour over the mixture. Continue as for a plain omelet. Work rapidly, as the cooking time is one minute.

EGG AND SPINACH PIE, PAGE 28.

SPINACH AND SOUR-CREAM OMELET *6 servings*

2 pounds raw spinach
Salt
1½ tablespoons butter
¼ teaspoon nutmeg
Freshly ground black pepper to taste
1 cup sour cream
Paprika

(*cont'd*)

1. Trim off the tough stems from the spinach and discard. Wash the spinach leaves thoroughly in several changes of cold water until free from sand. Drain. Place the moist spinach in a saucepan, sprinkle with salt and cover tightly. Cook over moderate heat, stirring once or twice, six minutes or until tender. Drain and chop coarsely.

2. Add the butter, nutmeg, additional salt and pepper to taste and half the sour cream. Reheat gently over low heat without boiling.

3. Reserve six tablespoons of the mixture. Use the remainder as a filling for six three-egg omelets. Spoon the reserved mixture along the top of the folded omelets and top with the remaining sour cream. Sprinkle with paprika.

SPANISH OMELET *6 servings*

- 6 fresh tomatoes
- 3 tablespoons cooking oil
- 1 onion, chopped
- 1 green pepper, chopped
- 1 stalk celery, chopped
- 1 leek, chopped
- ½ bulb fennel, chopped, or ½ teaspoon crushed fennel seeds
- 1 clove garlic, minced
- 3 sprigs parsley, chopped
- 1 clove
- ½ teaspoon thyme
- ½ teaspoon orégano
- ½ bay leaf
- Pinch of saffron
- Salt and freshly ground black pepper

1. Peel the tomatoes, cut in half and gently press out the seeds and liquid. Chop the tomatoes.

2. Heat the oil in a pan and add the onion, green pepper, celery, leek, fennel, garlic and parsley. Sauté five minutes. Add the tomatoes and season with the clove, thyme, orégano, bay leaf, saffron and salt and pepper to taste.

3. Simmer the mixture gently until the vegetables are tender, about ten minutes. Discard the clove and bay leaf. Use to fill and garnish six three-egg omelets.

Note: Spanish sauce (page 453) may be substituted for the above filling.

FRITTATA ITALIANA *4 servings*

Frittata Italiana is an Italian omelet with ham and cheese.

- ½ cup sliced mushrooms
- 3 tablespoons butter
- 6 eggs, beaten
- 3 tablespoons heavy cream
- Salt and freshly ground black pepper to taste
- Pinch of basil
- 2 sprigs parsley, chopped
- 2 tablespoons grated Parmesan cheese
- 1 tablespoon olive oil
- ½ cup diced cooked ham
- Few drops of lemon juice
- 4 ounces mozzarella cheese, cubed

1. Preheat oven to hot (450° F.).

2. Sauté the mushrooms lightly in one tablespoon of the butter and set aside.

(*cont'd*)

3. Mix the eggs, cream, salt, pepper, basil, parsley and one tablespoon of the Parmesan cheese.

4. Heat the olive oil and one tablespoon butter in a heavy skillet until the butter turns white. Pour in the egg mixture and cook over very low heat until mixture is still soft on top. Remove from the heat.

5. Sprinkle the top with the mushrooms, ham, remaining Parmesan cheese, lemon juice, mozzarella and remaining butter, melted.

6. Place skillet in oven and bake until the cheese has melted, or about four minutes. Remove to a hot platter and serve immediately.

HOW TO SCRAMBLE EGGS *2 to 3 servings*

6 eggs, at room temperature
2 tablespoons butter
2 tablespoons heavy cream
Salt

1. Break the eggs into a small bowl and beat with a fork, whisk or egg beater until well mixed but not frothy.

2. Melt the butter in the top of a double boiler or skillet and add the eggs. Place the skillet over low heat, or the double boiler over boiling water. Cook, stirring constantly, until the eggs begin to set. Add the cream and continue stirring until the desired degree of firmness is reached. Season with salt and serve immediately.

Note: Tarragon, chives, parsley or chervil cooked with scrambled eggs complements their flavor. Garnishes include sautéed mushroom caps, anchovy fillets and chicken livers.

SALMON SOUFFLE *3 servings*

3 tablespoons butter
3 tablespoons flour
1 cup milk
4 eggs, separated
Salt, dry mustard and Worcestershire sauce to taste
1 cup fresh cooked salmon, or 1 small can salmon, drained
Hollandaise sauce (page 449)

1. Preheat oven to moderate (375° F.).

2. Melt the butter in a saucepan, stir in flour and blend with a wire whisk. Meanwhile, bring the milk to a boil and add all at once to the butter-flour mixture, stirring with the whisk until thickened and smooth. Cool the mixture.

3. Beat in, one at a time, the four egg yolks. Season with salt, mustard and Worcestershire.

4. Flake the salmon and blend well into the white sauce and egg mixture.

(*cont'd*)

1. *To make a soufflé*, first prepare a basic white sauce.

2. Let white sauce cool. Beat in egg yolks one at a time. Add seasonings.

3. Add whatever solid ingredients are to be used—in this case salmon—and blend well into the white sauce-and-egg-yolk mixture.

4. Using a rotary beater or an electric mixer, beat egg whites until they stand in peaks; do not overbeat.

5. Gently fold the beaten egg whites into the sauce, using a rubber spatula or wooden spoon. Do not overblend.

6. Pour into a soufflé dish and bake until firm in a moderate oven.

A well-puffed soufflé, for dessert or main course, is an easy triumph with modern equipment. A cheese soufflé is shown in the foreground. Ingredients for making assorted soufflés surround it. (Recipes for chocolate, strawberry and other dessert soufflés are to be found in Chapter 12.)

5. Using a rotary beater or an electric mixer, beat the egg whites until they stand in peaks. Do not overbeat. Fold the whites gently into the salmon mixture with a rubber spatula or wooden spoon, being careful not to overblend.

6. Pour into a two-quart soufflé dish, which may be greased or ungreased. Place in oven and bake thirty to forty minutes. Serve with Hollandaise sauce, if desired.

SOUR-CREAM SOUFFLES *4 servings*

- 1½ cups sour cream
- 1 cup sifted flour
- 1¼ teaspoons salt
- ¼ teaspoon freshly ground black pepper
- 2 tablespoons chopped chives
- ½ cup grated nonprocessed Gruyère or Parmesan cheese
- 5 eggs, separated

1. Preheat oven to moderate (350° F.).

2. Mix until smooth the sour cream, flour, salt and pepper. Stir in the chives and cheese.

3. Beat the egg whites until stiff but not dry. With the same beater, in a separate bowl, beat the yolks until thick and lemon-colored. Gradually add the yolks to the cream mixture, stirring constantly. Carefully fold in the egg whites.

4. Pour the mixture into four one-and-one-half-cup heatproof dishes, ungreased. Place in a shallow pan of hot water and bake until set, thirty to forty minutes. Serve immediately.

CHEESE SOUFFLE *4 to 6 servings*

- ¼ cup butter
- ¼ cup flour
- 1½ cups milk
- Salt
- Worcestershire sauce
- Cayenne pepper
- ½ pound Cheddar cheese, finely grated
- 4 eggs, separated

(*cont'd*)

1. Preheat oven to moderate (375° F.).

2. In a saucepan melt the butter over low heat and add the flour; stir with a wire whisk until blended. Meanwhile, bring the milk to a boil and add all at once to the butter-flour mixture, stirring vigorously with the whisk. Season to taste with salt, Worcestershire and cayenne pepper.

3. Turn off the heat and let the mixture cool two to three minutes. Add the cheese and stir until melted. Beat in the egg yolks one at a time and cool.

4. Beat the egg whites until they stand in peaks, but do not overbeat. Cut and fold the egg whites into the mixture. Turn into a two-quart casserole (greased or ungreased, as desired) and bake thirty to forty-five minutes.

CHEESE-HAM SOUFFLE *3 servings*

3 tablespoons butter
3 tablespoons flour
1 cup milk
¾ cup shredded Cheddar cheese
½ cup ground cooked ham
3 eggs, separated
Salt, paprika and cayenne pepper to taste

1. Preheat oven to moderate (375° F.).

2. In a saucepan melt the butter, add the flour and stir with a wire whisk until blended. Meanwhile, bring the milk to a boil and add all at once to the butter-flour mixture, stirring vigorously with the whisk. Stir in the cheese and ham.

3. When the cheese has melted, add a little of the hot mixture to the beaten egg yolks, mix and return slowly to the saucepan, stirring constantly. Let cool a little. Season with salt, paprika and cayenne.

4. Beat the egg whites until stiff. Fold them lightly but thoroughly into the cheese mixture.

5. Pour the mixture into a seven-inch soufflé dish that may be buttered or not, as desired. (Some say soufflés rise better if they have an ungreased surface to cling to on their way up.)

6. Bake until fairly firm, or about thirty to forty-five minutes.

EGGS A LA TRIPE *3 to 4 servings*

The name of this dish has nothing to do with tripe except in appearance. The sliced eggs in a Gruyère cheese sauce are said to resemble creamed tripe.

3 medium onions, sliced
3 tablespoons butter
2½ tablespoons flour
1 teaspoon salt
Freshly ground black pepper to taste
2 cups milk (may be part cream)
½ cup shredded Gruyère cheese
6 hard-cooked eggs, sliced

(*cont'd*)

1. In a heavy saucepan sauté the onions in the butter until tender but not brown. Add the flour, salt and pepper and blend well. Gradually add the milk and cook, stirring, until thickened.

2. Add the cheese, stir until melted and add the eggs. Reheat without boiling and serve on rice or toast. Or turn the mixture into a shallow six-cup casserole, dot with additional butter and broil until lightly browned.

EGGS FLORENTINE *6 servings*

This is a foremost luncheon dish. It may be prepared in advance and reheated quickly in a hot oven. The dish is poached eggs on a bed of spinach covered with a cream sauce.

¼ cup butter
¼ cup flour
1 cup milk
1 cup cream
Salt and freshly ground black pepper to taste
1½ pounds spinach, cooked and puréed
¼ teaspoon nutmeg
12 poached eggs
Grated Parmesan cheese

1. In a saucepan melt the butter, add the flour and stir with a wire whisk until blended. Meanwhile, bring the milk and cream to a boil and add all at once to the butter-flour mixture, stirring vigorously with the whisk until thickened. Season to taste with salt and pepper.

2. Combine the hot drained spinach with one-half cup of the sauce and season with nutmeg. Pour the spinach mixture into a shallow heatproof casserole and arrange the eggs on top. Spoon the remaining sauce over the eggs, sprinkle with Parmesan cheese and brown lightly under a broiler; or bake in a preheated hot oven (400° F.) until brown.

HERBED EGG TIMBALES *4 servings*

1½ cups light cream or milk, scalded
5 eggs, slightly beaten
¾ teaspoon salt
Freshly ground black pepper to taste
1 teaspoon grated onion
1 tablespoon minced fresh parsley or half as much dried
1 tablespoon minced fresh tarragon or half as much dried

1. Preheat oven to moderate (325° F.).

2. Add the scalded cream to the eggs, stirring. Mix in the remaining ingredients.

3. Pour the mixture into greased custard cups, filling the cups slightly more than three-quarters full.

4. Place the filled cups on a rack in a deep pan and pour simmering water

(*cont'd*)

around them. Bake until a knife inserted in the center comes out clean, twenty minutes or longer.

5. To serve, turn the timbales out on a serving dish and pour tomato sauce over them. Garnish with parsley or chopped chives.

MADRAS EGG CURRY *4 servings*

- 1 small onion, chopped
- 1 clove garlic, minced
- ¼ cup butter
- 1½ tablespoons curry powder
- 2 teaspoons tomato paste
- Water
- Salt
- Lemon juice
- 6 hard-cooked eggs, cut in half lengthwise

1. Sauté the onion and garlic in the butter two to three minutes. Add the curry powder, tomato paste and about one cup water, or enough to make a thin sauce. Simmer about ten minutes and add salt and lemon juice to taste.

2. Add the eggs, reheat and serve with rice and accompaniments such as chopped peanuts, raisins, grated orange rind, chopped parsley, chopped onion, chutney and coconut.

PICKLED EGGS *6 pickled eggs*

- 1 cup white vinegar
- ½ cup water
- 1 tablespoon mixed pickling spices
- 2 pieces ginger root
- ½ teaspoon salt
- 1 clove garlic
- 6 hard-cooked eggs

1. Boil together ten minutes all the ingredients except the eggs.

2. Place the peeled eggs in a jar and cover with the spiced vinegar. Refrigerate twenty-four hours before using. If desired, the eggs may be colored with pure vegetable dye added to the liquid; or beets may be pickled along with the eggs.

CURRIED STUFFED EGGS *6 servings*

- 6 hard-cooked eggs
- 2 tablespoons finely chopped gherkins
- ½ teaspoon freshly ground black pepper
- 1 teaspoon salt
- ¼ teaspoon curry powder, approximately
- 2 tablespoons mayonnaise

Split hard-cooked eggs lengthwise and remove the yolks. Mash the egg yolks and blend with the gherkins and spices. Add enough mayonnaise to make a firm paste. Add more curry powder if a stronger flavor is desired. Stuff the egg whites with the mixture.

CHEESE DISHES

ON CHEESE

Clifton Fadiman probably has written the ultimate essay on cheese. It appears in his volume *Any Number Can Play* (World Publishing Company, 1957). He quotes P. Morton Shand, who considered a love of cheese inherent in humanity, and Ben Gunn, who, isolated on Treasure Island, moaned wistfully that "Many's the long night I've dreamed of cheese—toasted mostly."

"Provided it be well and truly made there is really . . . no such thing as a *bad* cheese," Mr. Fadiman observed. "It may be dull, it may be naïve, it may be over-sophisticated. Yet it remains cheese, milk's leap toward immortality."

Mr. Fadiman also coined a word for cheese lovers. He calls them "turophiles," derived from the Greek word *turos,* meaning cheese.

New Yorkers have an opportunity to sample an extraordinary assortment of cheeses from here and abroad. There are mild cheeses, sharp cheeses, eloquent and dull cheeses. There is a cheese for every purse and palate.

In any discussion on cheese there is always a question of personal taste and judgment. Even when professionals break over cheese they are likely to argue over the categories in which cheeses should be placed. Is pont l'évêque a soft-ripening or semi-soft? And what of the excellent reblochon? Some say yes and some say no.

It is one man's opinion that crackers or crisp breads of any sort destroy the palatal pleasures of cheese. The bread-and-cheese cheeses deserve a crusty loaf and nothing else will do. Buttered toast is pardonable, but the crunchiness even of English water wafers distracts from a cheese's harmony.

One well-known restaurateur in this city has coined the phrase that "by the bread with which people eat cheese ye shall know them," discerning the discriminating palate by noting those who scorn his water biscuits and melba toast.

Generally speaking, the most worthy of these cheeses deserve a red wine, either lusty or light, depending on the nature of the cheese. However, slightly chilled beer will do.

In discussing cheese, the question is frequently asked as to what are the dessert cheeses. Here, too, there are gulfs as wide as a tall provolone.

"Dessert cheese?" one professional asked. "It's any cheese that captures your fancy after a meal."

Another equally experienced cheese enthusiast described a dessert cheese as any of the mild, creamlike cheeses such as the one known as gourmandise. The argument seems no more relevant than the difference between tweedle-dee and tweedle-dum.

Red wines and chilled beer are certainly not the only beverages that complement cheeses. The milder creamlike cheeses go well with champagnes and genuine Sauternes.

Fruit goes well with blue cheeses, soft-ripening, semi-soft and firm cheeses. Berries have an affinity for cheeses of the cream variety.

The statistics pertaining to the imports of cheese are fairly astonishing. According to Martin Fromer, general counsel of the Cheese Importers Association, the cheese imported in the greatest quantity each year is pecorino Romano, a hard, grating cheese from Italy. The next largest is Swiss cheese from Switzerland and third Edam and Gouda from Holland.

Both France and Denmark, of course, provide an impressive assortment of cheeses to this country. And France contributes the two cheeses that seem to be most admired by the largest audience of dedicated turophiles. These are Brie and Camembert, which appear on nine-tenths of the town's most elegant menus. They are almost invariably served as the penultimate dish at gala dinners sponsored by wine and food societies. France also sends us the noble Roquefort and two fairly recent notable blue-veined cheeses, bleu de Bresse and pipo crèm'.

Denmark offers among other cheeses the excellent Danish blue and tilsit.

Let it be noted that America is no sluggard when it comes to cheese production and quality. Among others, there is an excellent Brie-type cheese produced in Illinois. Vermont is famed for its Cheddar and California for its Monterey Jack. Domestically produced Liederkranz can hold its own with some of the soft-ripening cheeses such as Brie or Camembert.

There are many people who mistakenly believe that all of the cheeses imported into this country are pasteurized. It simply is not true. The same standards apply to the cheeses produced in this country and abroad. To wit, any cheese that is cured sixty days or longer need not be made from pasteurized milk. Younger cheeses must be made from pasteurized milk. It seems logical enough that the flavor of cheese is impaired by pasteurization.

The following is a listing by category of the most important cheeses available in New York. Some of the sources where they may be obtained are listed in Chapter 16.

BLUE-VEINED CHEESES

(Serve crumbled in salads; after the main course and before desserts with a crusty French or Italian loaf and red wine; with fruits such as pears.)

Bleu de Bresse (France)
Danish blue (Denmark)
Gorgonzola (Italy)
Nazareth blue (Israel)
Pipo Crèm' (France)
Roquefort (France)
Stilton (England)

SOFT-RIPENING CHEESES

(Serve after the main course and before desserts with a crusty French or Italian loaf and dry red wines.)

Brie (France)
Camembert (France)
Certosino (Italy)
Liederkranz (United States)

SEMI-SOFT CHEESES

(Serve after the main course and before desserts with a crusty loaf of French or Italian bread and dry red wines. Fontina and mozzarella are excellent "melting" cheeses. Feta, served cold, goes well with watermelon when in season.)

Beaumont (France)
Bel Paese (Italy)
Cantal (France)
Feta (Greece)
Fontina (Italy)
Gourmandise (France)
La Grappe (France)
Limburger (Germany)
Monterey Jack (United States)
Mozzarella (Italy)
Muenster (Germany)
Oka (Canada)
Pont l'Evêque (France)
Port du Salut (France)
Reblochon (France)
St. Paulin (France)
Tête de Moine (France)
Tomme de Savoie (France)
Tilsit (Denmark, Germany)
Wensleydale (England)

FIRM CHEESES

(Serve after the main course and before desserts with a crusty loaf of French or Italian bread and dry red wines. Gruyère is the best of all cheeses for fondues. Gruyère, Swiss, Cheddar and Cheddar-type cheeses in this category are excellent for soufflés and in cheese sauces.)

Black Diamond (Canada)
Cacciacavallo (Italy)
Caerphilly (Wales)
Cheddar (England, United States)
Cheshire (England)
Chèvre or goat cheese (France)
Christian IX (Denmark)
Coon (United States)
Double Gloucester (England)
Edam (Holland)
Gouda (Holland)
Gruyère (Switzerland)
Irish Blarney (Ireland)
Kasseri (Greece)
Lancashire (England)
Leicester (England)
Noekkelost (Norway)
Pineapple (United States)
Provolone (Italy)
Sage (America)
Swiss or Emmentaler (Switzerland)
Vacherin (Switzerland)

CREAM-TYPE CHEESES

(Serve after the main course with berries and champagne or sweet, well-chilled, white wines.)

Costello (Denmark)
Cottage cheese (United States)
Cream cheese (United States)
Crèma Danica (Denmark)
Crème Chantilly (France)
Double crème Gervais (France)
Petit Suisse (France)
Ricotta (Italy, United States)
Saint Florentin (France)
Triple crème (France)

(cont'd)

HARD OR GRATING CHEESES
(These cheeses are principally used grated over pasta such as spaghetti or lasagne. They may also be used sparingly in cheese sauces to produce a sharper flavor.)

Parmesan (Italy)
Pecorino (Italy)
Pepato (Sicily)
Romano (Italy)
Sbrinz (Switzerland)
Sap Sago (Switzerland)

Note: Many of the above cheese types are manufactured in the United States. The countries of origin are in parentheses. There is controversy among cheese experts as to whether Tallegio, Reblochon and Pont l'Evêque are soft-ripening or semi-soft cheeses but they are generally considered to be semi-soft.

SWISS CHEESE IN CRUST *6 squares or 12 triangles*

2¼ cups sifted flour
1 teaspoon salt
¾ cup shortening
6 tablespoons cold water
½ pound Swiss cheese, sliced
1 egg, beaten

1. Preheat oven to hot (425° F.).
2. Mix the flour and salt and chop in the shortening until the mixture looks like coarse cornmeal. Sprinkle the water over the mixture and mix lightly until all the flour is moistened. Divide the dough in half.
3. Roll one-half of the dough to one-eighth-inch thickness and cut into six three-and-one-half-inch squares. Place one two-and-one-half-inch square of cheese about three-eighths inch thick on half the squares. Moisten the edges of the dough, cover with the remaining squares, seal the edges and flute the rim. Prick the tops and brush with beaten egg.
4. Repeat with the remaining dough, or make turnovers by enclosing a triangle of cheese in each square and folding the dough over the top.
5. Place on an ungreased baking sheet and bake about fifteen minutes. Serve with a salad for a luncheon course.

QUICHE LORRAINE, PAGE 27.

CHEESE SOUFFLE, PAGE 309.

FONDUTA *6 servings*

¾ pound fontina cheese, diced
3 cups milk, approximately
2 tablespoons butter
6 egg yolks
¼ teaspoon white pepper
1 white truffle, sliced paper thin

1. Place the cheese in a dish and cover with the milk. Let stand at least six hours in refrigerator.
2. Place one tablespoon of the butter and the egg yolks in the upper part of a double boiler, add the cheese and milk and place over boiling water. Beat with a rotary beater while the cheese melts and until it begins to harden. When

(cont'd)

the cheese begins to thicken, remove from the boiling water, add the pepper, truffle and remaining butter and mix well. Serve on toast or with rice or polenta.

FONDUE, PAGES 47, 291.

MOZZARELLA IN CAROZZA *4 servings*

8 slices white bread
Flour
4 slices mozzarella cheese, ¼ inch thick
Olive oil
2 eggs, lightly beaten
Anchovy sauce (page 340)
4 lemon slices

1. Remove the crusts from the bread and cut off the tips of the corners.
2. Flour the cheese lightly and place each slice of cheese between two slices of bread.
3. Pour enough olive oil in a skillet to make a depth of one inch. Heat until hot but not smoking.
4. Dip the sandwiches in the lightly beaten eggs and fry in the hot oil, turning once, until the bread turns pale gold and the cheese starts to ooze out. Pour hot anchovy sauce over the sandwiches and garnish each with a lemon slice.

Webster's definition should settle the rabbit versus rarebit argument:
"Welsh rabbit. *A dish, variously made, of melted or toasted cheese, often mixed with ale or beer, poured over toasted bread or crackers;—a jocose term, like 'Cape Cod turkey' (codfish), that through failure to recognize the joke is commonly modified in cookbooks to* Welsh rarebit."

WELSH RABBIT I *4 servings*

½ pound sharp processed Cheddar cheese
¾ cup cream
1 teaspoon Worcestershire sauce
½ teaspoon prepared mustard

Melt the cheese in the top of a double boiler over simmering water. Add the cream gradually, stirring constantly. Add the seasonings and, when very hot, pour on toast.

WELSH RABBIT II *4 to 6 servings*

2 teaspoons Worcestershire sauce
½ teaspoon dry mustard
Dash of cayenne
Dash of paprika
½ cup ale or beer
1 pound sharp natural Cheddar cheese, shredded

Mix the seasonings in a skillet. Add the ale and let stand over very low heat until the ale is hot. Add the cheese and stir until it has melted. Serve on hot toast.

WHITE-WINE CHEESE TOAST *5 to 6 servings*

- 2 tablespoons butter
- 1½ tablespoons flour
- ½ cup milk
- ½ cup Gruyère cheese, grated
- 3 tablespoons dry white wine
- 1 clove garlic, minced
- 1 egg, beaten
- Salt and freshly ground black pepper to taste
- Grated nutmeg to taste
- French bread

1. Melt the butter in a saucepan, add the flour and stir with a wire whisk until blended. Meanwhile, bring milk to a boil and add all at once to the butter-flour mixture, stirring vigorously with the whisk. When the mixture has thickened, set it aside to cool to room temperature.

2. Add the cheese, wine, garlic, egg, salt, pepper and nutmeg to the sauce. Mix well.

3. Cut ten to twelve slices French bread diagonally and toast each slightly on one side. Spread each untoasted side with about three tablespoons of the cheese mixture about one-half inch thick. Broil under medium heat until the mixture is lightly browned and heated through.

RICE AND CHEESE CROQUETTES, PAGE 325.

RICE DISHES

Rice is one of the easiest of dishes to prepare and one of the most versatile. Here are two basic methods of cooking it.

BOILED RICE *4 servings*

- 2½ cups raw rice
- 2 quarts boiling water
- 2 tablespoons salt
- ½ cup butter

1. Rinse the rice and add it a little at a time to two quarts of violently boiling salted water. Cook over high heat, stirring occasionally, until the rice is tender, ten to fifteen minutes. Drain.

2. Melt the butter in a heatproof casserole and spoon the rice over it. Cover and place over the lowest heat possible, or place in the oven. Cook ten to fifteen minutes, or until the rice is fluffy and dry. The rice may be kept hot in a slow oven for nearly an hour.

STEAMED RICE *3 or 4 servings*

- 1 cup raw rice
- 2 cups cold water
- 1 teaspoon salt
- 1 tablespoon butter

(cont'd)

1. Combine the rice, water, salt and butter in a three-quart saucepan.

2. Place the saucepan over high heat and, when the water begins to boil, reduce the heat to low and stir the rice once with a fork.

3. Cover the saucepan tightly and simmer twelve to sixteen minutes, or until all the liquid is absorbed.

BROWNED RICE IN BOUILLON *6 servings*

¼ cup fat
1 large onion, minced
1 clove garlic, minced
1 cup raw rice
2 cups bouillon or chicken stock
Salt and freshly ground black pepper to taste

1. Heat the fat in a skillet, add the onion and garlic and sauté until the onion is transparent. Add the rice and sauté until the rice turns golden, adding more fat if necessary.

2. Put the rice mixture in a two-quart saucepan, add the bouillon and cover with a tight lid. Bring to a boil, reduce heat to as low as possible and simmer until the rice is tender, sixteen to twenty minutes. Remove the lid and allow the rice to dry.

RICE AND BEANS, ITALIAN STYLE *4 servings*

½ cup dried navy beans
Water
1 onion, chopped
1 stalk celery with leaves, chopped
2 tablespoons olive oil
1 cup canned tomatoes, undrained
1 teaspoon salt
Pinch of hot red pepper
½ cup raw rice
2 tablespoons grated Parmesan or Romano cheese

1. Soak the beans overnight in water to cover; or boil two minutes and let soak one hour. Simmer until tender, adding more water as needed.

2. Brown the onion and celery in the oil and add to the beans. Add the tomatoes, salt and pepper and water to cover.

3. Add the rice, cover tightly and cook, stirring often, until the rice is tender, or about twenty minutes. Add water as needed. When cooked, the mixture should have the consistency of a thick stew.

FRIED RICE WITH SHRIMP *4 servings*

½ cup salad or peanut oil
½ cup Chinese cabbage or finely diced celery
½ cup sliced water chestnuts (canned)
½ cup scallions, cut into thin diagonal strips
2 tablespoons finely chopped parsley
3 cups cooked rice
½ cup smoked ham (preferably Smithfield) cut into small cubes (optional)
Salt and freshly ground black pepper
3 tablespoons soy sauce or to taste
2 cups cooked, shelled shrimp
2 tablespoons butter
2 tablespoons water
4 eggs

(*cont'd*)

1. Heat the oil in a large skillet and add the vegetables. Cook quickly, stirring occasionally, three or four minutes.

2. Add the rice and ham and mix well, adding more oil if necessary. Season to taste with salt, pepper and soy sauce.

3. Add the shrimp and cook, stirring, until heated through.

4. Melt the butter in a separate skillet, add the water to the eggs and beat, then let them cook without stirring to make a pancake. Do not turn. Cut the pancake into thin strips and sprinkle over the fried rice.

JAMBALAYA *8 servings*

- 2 tablespoons fat
- 1 cup finely chopped onion
- 1 cup finely chopped green pepper
- 2 cloves garlic, minced fine
- 1 cup diced cooked chicken
- 1 cup diced cooked ham
- 12 tiny pork sausages, cut in pieces
- 2½ cups canned tomatoes, undrained
- 1 cup raw white rice
- 1½ cups chicken broth
- ½ teaspoon thyme
- 1 tablespoon chopped parsley
- ¼ teaspoon chili powder
- 1½ teaspoons salt
- ¼ teaspoon freshly ground black pepper

1. Preheat oven to moderate (350° F.).

2. Melt the fat in a large skillet and add the onion, green pepper and garlic. Cook slowly, stirring often, until the onion and pepper are tender. Add the chicken, ham and sausages and cook five minutes.

3. Add the tomatoes with their liquid, the rice, broth, thyme, parsley, chili, salt and pepper. Turn the mixture into a large casserole. Cover and bake until the rice is tender, about one and one-quarter hours.

Note: This dish may be baked for one hour, refrigerated and, at serving time, baked long enough to finish cooking the rice. Jambalaya may be made with seafood.

RICE A LA GRECQUE *About 4 cups*

- 3 tablespoons sweet butter
- 1 chopped onion
- 1 small clove garlic, crushed
- 3 or 4 leaves of green lettuce, shredded
- 2 fresh pork sausages, sliced
- 3 mushrooms, sliced
- 3 tomatoes, peeled, seeded and diced
- 1 cup raw rice
- 2 cups boiling water or chicken broth
- 1 teaspoon salt
- Dash of freshly ground black pepper
- ½ cup cooked peas
- 1 diced pimento
- 2 tablespoons raisins, sautéed in butter

1. Melt two tablespoons of the butter in a large saucepan and brown the onion in it. Add the garlic, lettuce, sausages, mushrooms and tomatoes. Add the rice and mix well together.

(*cont'd*)

2. Add the boiling water, salt and pepper. Cover tightly and cook over low heat twenty minutes. Mix well with a fork and add the remaining ingredients. Serve with lamb or poultry, or use for stuffing poultry or veal.

PILAFF GREEK STYLE *6 servings*

- ½ cup butter
- 2 cups raw long-grain rice
- 1 quart hot beef or chicken broth
- Salt and freshly ground white pepper

1. Melt the butter in a heavy skillet and sauté the rice, stirring, for five minutes, or until browned.

2. Add the broth, salt and pepper. Cover the pan with a cloth, then with a lid and simmer, without stirring, until the rice has absorbed all the liquid.

RISOTTO ALLA MILANESE *3 servings*

- Butter
- 2 tablespoons chopped beef marrow (optional)
- 3 tablespoons finely chopped onion
- 1 cup raw rice
- ¼ cup Marsala wine
- 1 quart boiling chicken stock, approximately
- Pinch of saffron
- Parmesan cheese, grated
- Mushrooms, sautéed in a little butter

1. Melt two tablespoons of the butter and the marrow (or an equal quantity of butter) in a heavy saucepan, add the onion and sauté until the onion is golden.

2. Add the rice and stir over medium heat until the rice becomes opaque, about three minutes. Add the Marsala and simmer until the wine has evaporated.

3. Add half the chicken stock and cook the rice, uncovered, over medium heat, stirring often. As the kernels absorb it, continue to add stock. Stir often. Toward the end of the cooking time (which must not exceed twenty minutes from the time the stock is first added) stir constantly.

4. Add the saffron, dissolved in a little additional stock.

5. When the rice is done (it should be creamy and not dry) stir in one tablespoon butter. Serve with Parmesan cheese and garnish with the mushrooms.

RISOTTO A LA SUISSE *5 servings*

- ½ medium onion, chopped fine
- ½ cup butter
- ½ cup dry white wine
- 1½ cups strong chicken or beef stock
- Salt and freshly ground black pepper
- 1 cup raw rice
- 4 ounces (about ½ cup) grated non-processed Gruyère cheese

1. In a heavy saucepan sauté the onion in the butter until the onion is golden. Add the wine, stock and salt and pepper to taste. Bring to a boil, add

(cont'd)

the rice and continue boiling five minutes, stirring constantly. Cover the pan, reduce the heat as low as possible and cook until the rice is tender, about fifteen minutes.

2. Remove the pan from the heat, fold in the cheese, cover and let stand about four minutes, or until the cheese has melted. Stir once again thoroughly and serve at once.

RISOTTO ALLA MARINARA

6 to 8 servings

- 2 tablespoons olive oil
- 2 medium onions, chopped
- 8 anchovy fillets, minced
- 2 tablespoons tomato paste
- 2 cups water
- 2 teaspoons chopped parsley
- 2 cups raw rice
- 1 sage leaf or 1 teaspoon powdered sage
- ¼ teaspoon salt
- ⅛ teaspoon freshly ground black pepper
- ½ cup dry white wine
- Grated Parmesan cheese

1. Heat the oil, add the onions and sauté until golden. When the onions are soft, add the anchovies and cook five minutes. Add the tomato paste and half the water and simmer, covered, twenty minutes.

2. Add the parsley, rice, sage, salt and pepper. Add the wine and cook until the wine is somewhat evaporated. Add the remaining water and cook until the rice is tender, about ten minutes. If the rice becomes too dry while cooking, add a little more water. Serve sprinkled with grated cheese.

RISOTTO A LA NORTON

6 servings

- ½ cup butter
- 2 small white onions, finely chopped
- 1 cup raw rice (preferably the Persian type available in foreign markets)
- 3 cups chicken bouillon, approximately
- ¼ teaspoon saffron
- Salt and freshly ground black pepper
- Truffles, if available—preferably white, otherwise black

1. Melt the butter in a large skillet, add the onions and cook until the onions are transparent.

2. Add the rice and a small amount of the bouillon. Cook, stirring constantly, until the rice is tender but not mushy, adding bouillon as it is absorbed.

3. Add the saffron and salt and pepper to taste and serve immediately, garnished with truffle slices.

RISOTTO WITH CHICKEN LIVERS AND MUSHROOMS

RISOTTO:

6 to 8 servings

- 3 tablespoons butter
- 1 onion, minced
- 2½ cups raw rice
- ¼ cup Marsala wine
- 2 quarts hot chicken stock

(cont'd)

1. Melt the butter in a heavy pot, add the onion and sauté until brown.

2. Stir in the rice and cook, stirring, until each grain is golden in color. Add the Marsala and cook slowly until it is absorbed into the rice. Add the hot chicken stock, two cups at a time, each time covering the pot. Allow the risotto to cook very slowly, without stirring, until the rice has absorbed all the liquid. When done, the rice should be fairly dry but not too soft.

SAUCE:

- 3 tablespoons butter
- 1 onion, finely sliced
- 1 thin slice raw ham (prosciutto, if possible) cut into matchlike strips
- 2 sage leaves or 2 teaspoons powdered sage
- 1 bay leaf
- 4 raw chicken livers, chopped
- ½ pound sliced mushrooms
- 1 sweetbread, parboiled, skinned and cut into dice
- Salt and freshly ground black pepper to taste
- 1 tablespoon Marsala
- 1 cup chicken stock

1. Melt the butter in a saucepan and sauté the onion, ham, sage and bay leaf until the mixture takes on a little color. Add the chicken livers, mushrooms and sweetbread. Cook until all the ingredients are well blended.

2. Add salt and pepper, the Marsala and stock. Simmer ten minutes.

3. Stir half the sauce into the risotto. To serve, place the risotto in a hot bowl, leaving a hollow in the center. Pour the remaining sauce into the well.

CHICKEN LIVER RISOTTO *6 servings*

- ¼ cup butter
- 5 chicken livers, cut into eighths
- ½ cup chopped onion
- ½ cup finely chopped mushrooms
- 1 cup raw long-grain rice
- 2½ cups boiling chicken stock
- 2 tablespoons chopped parsley
- Grated Parmesan cheese

1. In a heavy two-quart saucepan, melt the butter and brown the chicken livers. Remove the livers and keep hot. Add the onion to the saucepan and cook until transparent. Add the chopped mushrooms and cook three minutes longer.

2. Add the rice and cook, stirring constantly, two minutes. Add the stock, cover and simmer gently over low heat until the stock is absorbed and the rice is tender but firm, about twenty minutes. If the stock is absorbed and the rice is not done, add a little more liquid and cook longer.

3. Stir the livers and parsley into the rice and serve immediately with grated Parmesan cheese.

FLUFFY WILD RICE *3 to 4 servings*

Wash one-half cup wild rice in cold water. Cover with two cups boiling water. Cover and let stand twenty minutes.

Drain and repeat three times or more until rice is tender. Use fresh boiling

(*cont'd*)

water each time and add one and one-half teaspoons salt the last time. Season with salt, pepper and generous amounts of butter.

The rice may be kept warm in the oven or in a double boiler (cover if held longer than five minutes).

WILD RICE MINNESOTA STYLE *6 servings*

- 4 to 5 cups chicken broth
- 1½ cups wild rice, washed
- 1½ cups shredded celery
- ¾ cup chopped onion
- 1 three-ounce can mushrooms, drained
- 1 pimento, chopped
- Salt and freshly ground black pepper to taste

1. Preheat oven to moderate (375° F.).
2. Place all the ingredients except one cup of the broth in a six-cup greased casserole. Cover tightly and bake about one and one-half hours, adding more broth as necessary.

WILD RICE WITH SNOW PEAS *4 servings*

- 1 cup wild rice
- 2 scallions
- 1 tablespoon butter
- 1 teaspoon salt
- 2 cups or more chicken broth (canned, if desired)
- ¼ pound (1 cup) snow peas
- 4 large mushrooms
- 1 four-ounce can water chestnuts, drained
- 2 tablespoons peanut or salad oil
- ½ teaspoon salt
- ¼ teaspoon freshly ground black pepper
- ¼ cup toasted almonds

1. Wash the rice thoroughly, changing the water several times. Cut the green scallion stems diagonally into two-inch lengths. Chop the white part of the scallions fine.
2. Melt the butter in a large saucepan. Add the minced white scallion and sauté until tender. Add the rice, salt and two cups chicken broth. Bring to a boil, stir once and reduce the heat. Cover tightly and cook over low heat until the rice is tender and the liquid is absorbed, about thirty-five minutes. If necessary add more broth as the rice cooks.
3. Meanwhile, remove the ends and strings from the peas. Cut the mushrooms and water chestnuts into thin slices.
4. Heat the oil in a large skillet. Add the scallion stems, peas, mushrooms, water chestnuts and almonds and sauté only until the mushrooms are tender.
5. Transfer the cooked rice and vegetable mixture to a casserole. Add salt and pepper to taste and sprinkle with toasted almonds. Mix lightly and keep hot for serving in a very slow oven.

RICE AND CHEESE CROQUETTES *6 servings*

3 tablespoons butter
3 tablespoons flour
1 cup milk
1 cup shredded sharp Cheddar cheese
2 teaspoons grated onion
½ teaspoon salt, approximately
½ teaspoon dry mustard
⅛ teaspoon freshly ground pepper
Dash of cayenne pepper or Tabasco sauce
2 cups cooked rice
2 cups sifted bread crumbs
1 egg beaten with 2 tablespoons water
Fat for deep frying
Cheese pimento sauce (page 447)

1. Melt the butter in a saucepan, add the flour and stir with a wire whisk until blended. Meanwhile, bring the milk to a boil and add all at once to the butter-flour mixture, stirring vigorously with the whisk. Add the cheese, onion and seasonings and mix well. Add the rice and fold into the sauce. Chill.

2. Shape the mixture into twelve croquettes, roll in crumbs, then in beaten egg and again in crumbs. Let the croquettes dry.

3. Heat enough fat to cover the croquettes to 385° F. and fry until golden brown. Drain on absorbent paper. Serve with cheese pimento sauce.

MUSHROOM-RICE RING *6 servings*

1 cup raw rice
2 cups water
1 teaspoon salt
½ pound mushrooms
2 tablespoons butter
¼ cup hot bouillon or water
Freshly ground black pepper

1. Combine the rice with the water and salt and bring to a strong boil. Reduce the heat to very low, cover and cook fifteen minutes, or until the water is absorbed and the rice is dry and flaky.

2. Preheat oven to moderate (350° F.).

3. Chop the mushrooms and sauté them in butter three minutes. Add the bouillon.

4. Combine the rice and mushroom mixture and season to taste with salt and pepper.

5. Spoon the mixture into a greased seven-inch ring mold and set in a pan containing one inch hot water. Bake about thirty minutes.

6. Invert the rice on a platter and fill with two to three cups creamed fish or meat.

RICE WITH ASPARAGUS *5 to 6 servings*

1 bunch asparagus (2½ pounds)
½ cup dry white wine
1 cup raw rice
Salt and freshly ground black pepper
½ cup each grated Parmesan and non-processed Gruyère cheeses, mixed
6 tablespoons butter

(cont'd)

1. Cook the asparagus until tender in boiling salted water. Drain but reserve one cup of liquid in which vegetable was cooked.

2. Cook the rice (as for steamed rice, page 318) in the wine and reserved water seasoned with salt and pepper to taste.

3. Layer the cooked rice with the asparagus in a shallow buttered dish, saving the best-looking spears to arrange on top. Sprinkle with cheeses, dot with butter and broil until the cheese has melted and the top has browned.

RICE WITH CHILI PEPPERS AND CHEESE *6 servings*

1 cup rice
2 cups sour cream
Salt to taste
½ pound Cheddar cheese, cut into small cubes
1 six-ounce can peeled green chili peppers, drained and cut into thin strips
Butter
½ cup grated Parmesan cheese (optional)

1. Cook the rice until just tender as page 318, being careful not to overcook.

2. Preheat oven to moderate (350° F.).

3. Combine the rice with the sour cream and season with salt. Spread half the mixture in the bottom of a buttered casserole.

4. Sprinkle the rice mixture with the Cheddar cheese and strips of chili pepper. Top with the remaining rice mixture and dot with butter. Sprinkle with Parmesan cheese.

5. Bake, uncovered, thirty minutes and serve immediately.

RICE TOMATO CASSEROLE *3 or 4 servings*

¼ cup butter
1 medium onion, chopped
1 clove garlic, minced
½ green pepper, chopped
1 cup raw rice
2 eight-ounce cans tomato sauce, or 2 cups tomato juice
1½ cups boiling water
1 teaspoon salt
Freshly ground black pepper
⅓ cup chopped ripe olives (optional)
1½ cups grated American cheese

1. Heat the butter in a heavy saucepan, add the onion, garlic, green pepper and rice and cook, stirring, until lightly browned.

2. Reserve one-half cup tomato sauce or juice and add the remainder to the rice mixture. Add the boiling water and salt and pepper to taste. Simmer, covered, until the liquid has been absorbed.

3. Line a greased one-quart casserole with half the rice, and sprinkle with the olives and one cup of the cheese. Top with remaining rice.

4. Pour the reserved tomato sauce or juice over the top, sprinkle with the remaining cheese and broil quickly until the surface has browned, or bake in a hot oven (400° F.) until hot and browned.

BAKED BARLEY *6 servings*

2 cups pearl barley
3 cups hot chicken consommé
2 tablespoons butter

1. Preheat oven to slow (300° F.).
2. Place the barley in a heavy casserole and add half the consommé. Cover tightly.
3. Bake forty-five minutes. Add the remaining consommé, cover and bake forty-five minutes longer, or until tender. Stir in the butter.

PASTA DISHES

If Italy had contributed nothing but pasta dishes to the world of cuisine, it would have been sufficient for immortality. Store-bought pasta such as macaroni and spaghetti can be delicious. Homemade, it can be superb.

EGG NOODLE DOUGH *About 1 pound of dough*

3 cups sifted flour
4 eggs

1. Place the flour in a bowl, add the unbeaten eggs and mix with the hands until the dough can be gathered into a rough ball.
2. Turn out on a smooth surface and knead until all the crumbly particles have been incorporated. The dough should be very stiff. If necessary, work a little additional flour into the mixture. It should be stressed that the addition of more flour may be essential.
3. Divide the dough into thirds and, using one portion at a time, roll with a floured rolling pin into a very thin sheet. Let stand, covered with a towel, one-half hour or more. Roll the sheet of dough as for jelly roll and cut into strips of desired width. Lay out to dry well, and store until needed.
4. The noodles may be made in a pasta machine. To do this, divide the dough into thirds and press each into a flat rectangle. Use one piece at a time, keeping the remainder covered to prevent drying. Set the dial on the machine for the widest opening (No. 10) and run the dough through several times, gradually decreasing the size of the opening. As the strip of dough lengthens, fold it in half for each successive rolling. Use the No. 2 setting for the final rolling for cannelloni and ravioli. For noodles, use a No. 3 or 4 setting.
5. Shape and fill the dough immediately for cannelloni or ravioli. Let it dry briefly before running through the noodle cutter.

FETTUCCINE ALFREDO *6 servings*

1 recipe homemade noodle dough (page 327) cut into medium or wide noodles
Boiling salted water
1 to 1½ cups soft or melted sweet butter
2 cups grated Parmesan cheese
¾ cup heavy cream
Freshly ground black pepper

1. Cook the noodles in a large quantity of boiling salted water until tender. Allow about four minutes for thin noodles, longer for thick ones. Drain well.
2. Place noodles in hot casserole over low heat. Add butter, cheese and cream, a little at a time, tossing gently after each addition. Season with freshly ground black pepper to taste.

ROMAN NOODLES *4 servings*

1 small clove garlic
2 tablespoons olive oil
¾ pound mushrooms, sliced
1 or 2 anchovy fillets, minced
2 tablespoons softened butter
Salt and freshly ground black pepper
8 ounces freshly cooked noodles, drained
¼ cup grated Parmesan cheese

1. Brown the garlic lightly in the oil. Remove the garlic and sauté the mushrooms in the oil about five minutes.
2. Cream the anchovies with the butter, add to the mushrooms and season to taste with salt and pepper. Reheat.
3. Mix the mushrooms with hot noodles and serve with Parmesan cheese.

DUTCH NOODLES *3 or 4 servings*

½ cup blanched almonds
3 tablespoons butter
3 tablespoons poppy seeds
1 tablespoon lemon juice
8 ounces cooked noodles, drained
Salt and cayenne pepper to taste

1. Sliver the almonds and sauté until browned; or brown in a moderate oven (350° F.).
2. Melt the butter, add the almonds, poppy seeds and lemon juice and pour over the noodles. Add salt and cayenne and toss together.

GERMAN NOODLES *4 servings*

1 pound mushrooms, sliced
2 tablespoons butter
Salt and freshly ground black pepper to taste
Parsley
8 ounces cooked noodles, drained
2 tablespoons buttered fine bread crumbs

1. Preheat oven to moderate (375° F.).
2. Sauté the mushrooms in the butter over high heat five minutes. Season to taste with salt, pepper and chopped parsley. (*cont'd*)

3. Arrange the noodles and mushrooms in layers in a greased six-cup casserole. Top with the buttered bread crumbs and brown in the oven about ten minutes.

VIENNESE NOODLE PUDDING *4 servings*

8 ounces noodles
5 cups milk
2 teaspoons butter plus 3 tablespoons
3 eggs, separated
Salt and freshly ground black pepper to taste

1. Break the noodles into small pieces and cook in milk until well done. Let them cool but do not drain.
2. Grease an eight- or nine-inch frying pan with the two teaspoons butter. Preheat oven to moderate (350° F.).
3. Cream the remaining butter. Add the egg yolks one by one, beating steadily. Add the noodles with the milk. Beat the egg whites until stiff but not dry and fold into the noodles. Correct the seasonings.
4. Spread the mixture evenly in the greased pan and bake forty to fifty minutes, or until light brown in color. Let cool slightly. Loosen the rim and turn out on a warm platter. Cut into wedges and serve as a main luncheon dish or with meat at dinner.

STUFFED TUFOLI OR MANICOTTI *12 servings*

1 pound tufoli or manicotti
Melted butter
2 onions, chopped
3 cloves garlic, chopped
2 tablespoons olive oil
½ pound mushrooms, chopped
1½ pounds chopped lean beef (may be part veal)
1½ cups chopped mozzarella or Swiss cheese
1 cup soft bread crumbs
1 egg, slightly beaten
1½ teaspoons salt
½ teaspoon orégano
¼ teaspoon freshly ground black pepper
3 to 4 cups basic tomato sauce (page 341) or canned tomato sauce
1 cup grated Parmesan cheese

1. Cook the pasta in a large quantity of rapidly boiling salted water until half done, about twelve minutes. Drain and rinse in cold water. Return it to the pot and toss with a small amount of melted butter to prevent it from sticking together.
2. Preheat oven to moderate (350° F.).
3. Brown the onions and garlic lightly in the oil. Add the mushrooms and cook until wilted. Using the hands, blend the onion mixture with the beef, cheese, crumbs, egg, salt, orégano and pepper. Using a teaspoon, stuff the tufoli or manicotti with the mixture.

(*cont'd*)

4. Cover the bottoms of two eight-cup, shallow rectangular casseroles with a thin layer of tomato sauce and arrange a layer of the stuffed pasta on top. Cover lightly with more sauce and sprinkle generously with Parmesan cheese. If necessary, repeat the layers.

5. Bake about thirty minutes.

LASAGNE *About 12 servings*

- ½ pound lean ground beef
- 2 tablespoons olive oil
- 3 cups basic tomato sauce (page 341) or canned tomato sauce
- 1 recipe egg noodle dough (page 327) or 1-pound package of lasagne
- 1 pound ricotta or cottage cheese
- 1 pound mozzarella cheese
- 1 cup or more grated Parmesan cheese

1. Shape the meat into marble-sized balls and brown in the olive oil. Add the tomato sauce and let simmer until ready to use, then strain out the meat balls.

2. If homemade noodles are used, roll one-third of the dough at a time to wafer thinness and cut into strips about six by one and one-half inches. Cook in a large quantity of boiling salted water about twelve minutes, or until tender. Drain. (Follow directions on package if commercial pasta is used.)

3. Preheat oven to moderate (325° F.).

4. Using a baking dish about two inches deep, cover the bottom sparingly with tomato sauce and line the dish with a layer of lasagne. Dot with spoonfuls of ricotta, slivers of mozzarella and a little Parmesan cheese. Spread with the sauce and add all the meat balls. Repeat with another layer of lasagna, sauce and cheeses.

5. Bake about forty-five minutes. Cool slightly before serving.

CANNELLONI ALLA NERONE

About three dozen cannelloni, or approximately 12 servings

- 3 chicken breasts, boned
- ¾ cup butter
- 7 chicken livers
- 10 slices prosciutto (Italian ham) or 8 thin slices cooked ham
- 2 cups grated Parmesan cheese
- ½ cup flour
- 1 quart milk, scalded
- 1 cup heavy cream
- ¼ teaspoon white pepper
- Salt to taste
- 1 recipe egg noodle dough (page 327)

1. In a skillet, sauté the chicken breasts in one-quarter cup of the butter until the breasts are lightly browned.

2. Sauté the chicken livers briefly in the same skillet.

3. Grind the chicken breasts, livers and prosciutto, using the finest knife of a food grinder. Add one cup of the grated Parmesan cheese and mix.

4. In the top of a double boiler melt the remaining butter, add the flour and stir with a wire whisk until blended. Add the scalded milk to the butter-flour mix-

(*cont'd*)

ture, stirring vigorously with the whisk. Cook over boiling water, stirring, until thickened. Add the cream to the sauce and season with white pepper and salt to taste.

5. Add about one cup of the sauce to the ground mixture and mix well.

6. Using scissors, trim the edges of the rolled egg noodle dough to make it four inches wide. Cut across the dough at four-inch intervals to form squares.

7. Cook the squares of dough immediately in a large quantity of boiling water until tender, eight to ten minutes. Drain and spread the squares on damp towels.

8. Spread about two tablespoons chicken filling on each square and roll tightly. Arrange the rolls of filled dough in two layers in three 12x7½-inch buttered baking dishes. Sprinkle each layer with some of the remaining Parmesan cheese and cover with some of the reserved sauce. (This preparation may be done ahead.)

9. Dot the top of each dish with bits of additional butter and bake in a preheated moderate oven (375° F.) until the tops are lightly browned, twenty minutes or longer.

Note: The fillings for the cannelloni and the ravioli are interchangeable.

SPINACH-CHICKEN FILLING FOR PASTA *About 3 cups*

2 eggs, beaten
1 cup minced cooked chicken
1 cup chopped cooked spinach, well drained
½ cup fresh bread crumbs
¼ cup heavy cream
⅓ cup grated Parmesan cheese
2 teaspoons finely chopped parsley
1 clove garlic, finely chopped
½ teaspoon nutmeg
Salt and freshly ground black pepper to taste

Combine the ingredients and mix well. Use as a filling for ravioli, cannelloni or lasagne.

PASTA WITH EGGPLANT *6 servings*

The combination of pasta with vegetables is routine in Sicily and in many parts of Italy. Here is an incredibly good Sicilian pasta and eggplant dish.

3 small eggplants
½ cup olive oil
1 pound elbow macaroni or other pasta
2 cups canned tomato sauce or basic tomato sauce (page 341)
½ pound mozzarella cheese, cut into slivers
2 tablespoons butter
½ cup grated Parmesan cheese

1. Peel the eggplants and cut them into one-half-inch slices. Brown the slices in the oil and drain on absorbent paper.

(cont'd)

2. Cook the macaroni in four quarts or more boiling salted water until just tender but still firm. Drain well. Preheat oven to moderate (350° F.).

3. Return the macaroni to the pot, add the sauce and stir well.

4. In a large greased casserole, arrange the macaroni, eggplant and mozzarella in layers. Dot with butter and sprinkle with grated Parmesan cheese.

5. Place in oven and bake, uncovered, until bubbly and lightly browned, about twenty minutes.

RAVIOLI ALLA BARDELLI *12 servings*

- 1 small calf brain
- 2 cups roast beef, finely ground
- 1 cup lean roast pork, finely ground
- ¼ pound prosciutto, finely ground
- ⅛ pound mortadella sausage, finely ground
- 5 ounces (½ cup) Parmesan cheese, finely grated
- 1 egg
- 1 teaspoon nutmeg
- ½ teaspoon basil
- ½ teaspoon freshly ground black pepper
- Salt to taste
- Egg noodle dough (page 327)
- Chicken broth

1. Simmer the brain in water to cover twenty minutes. Drain and remove the membranes.

2. Grind the brain, using the finest knife of a food chopper. Mix with the meats, Parmesan cheese, egg and seasonings. Shape into marble-sized balls.

3. Knead and roll the egg noodle dough for ravioli and complete the shaping in a ravioli form. Fit the pan with a sheet of dough and press small balls of the filling into the depressions of the pan; the pressure releases any air trapped under the dough. Cover with another sheet of rolled dough. With a rolling pin, roll over the top of the pan; this automatically trims the edges of the dough and cuts the ravioli into twelve neat squares ready for cooking.

4. Boil the squares in chicken broth to cover about twelve minutes.

Note: The filling for cannelloni alla Nerone may be substituted in the recipe above.

PASTA WITH HERB SAUCE *4 to 6 servings*

- 1 pound fettuccelle or spaghetti
- ½ cup parsley leaves, minced
- ½ cup fresh basil leaves, minced
- ½ clove garlic, minced
- ½ cup olive oil
- 1 cup ricotta cheese, or creamed cottage cheese
- Dash of cayenne pepper

1. Cook the pasta according to package directions.

2. Meanwhile, combine the parsley, basil and garlic in a mortar. With a pestle pound them into a paste. Gradually work in the olive oil and cheese and season to taste with cayenne. Or blend ingredients in an electric blender.

3. Add the sauce to the cooked, drained pasta and gently mix in. Serve immediately.

1. *Ravioli.* A home pasta machine kneads egg noodle dough and rolls it to any thickness desired. Attachment cuts dough for noodles or spaghetti.

2. For fast and easy shaping of ravioli, a special pan, the Ravioli Chef, is used. Here pan is fitted with a sheet of dough.

3. Small balls of filling are pressed into depressions of pan. The pressure releases any air trapped under dough. Then another sheet of rolled dough is used to cover all.

4. Rolling over top of pan trims edges of dough and cuts the ravioli into twelve neat squares ready for cooking.

Homemade pasta, essential for many fine Italian dishes, is used (left to right) for fettuccine Alfredo, ravioli Bardelli, cannelloni alla Nerone, linguine with clam sauce. Parmesan cheese and black pepper may be added to taste.

PASTA E FAGIOLI *About 7 servings*

Pasta with beans: pasta e fagioli.

1 pound dried cranberry beans
6 or more cups bouillon
1 piece ham bone or 1 pound ham hock
1 onion, chopped
1 cup sliced celery
½ carrot, chopped
1 tomato, peeled and chopped, or ⅓ cup canned tomatoes
Salt and freshly ground black pepper
1 cup raw spaghetti, broken into 1-inch pieces and cooked

1. Boil the beans in the bouillon two minutes. Cover and let stand at least two hours.

2. Add the bone, onion, celery, carrot and tomato and simmer, uncovered, one hour. Season with salt and pepper.

3. Continue cooking the mixture until the beans are tender, or about one hour longer. Remove the ham bone or ham hock. Rub about half the beans through a sieve or put through a food mill. Return to the pot. Adjust the seasonings and reheat.

4. To serve, place a mound of hot pasta on each plate and top with beans.

SAUCES FOR PASTA, PAGE 340.

PASTA WITH CHEESE AND PARSLEY *6 servings*

5 medium onions, chopped
4 cloves garlic, minced
½ green pepper, minced
¼ cup olive oil
1½ cups minced parsley, tightly packed
1 teaspoon salt
Freshly ground black pepper
½ teaspoon orégano or thyme
½ cup sweet or sour cream
2 cups ricotta cheese (or creamed cottage cheese)
1 pound pasta (shells, elbows or other small forms)

1. Sauté the onions, garlic and green pepper in the oil until lightly browned, stirring often. Add the parsley, salt, pepper and orégano and cook, stirring, until the parsley is wilted but not brown.

2. Add the cream and mix. Add the ricotta and heat to serving temperature. To prevent curdling, do not heat to simmering.

3. Meanwhile, cook pasta according to package directions. Drain well, return to the pot and add the sauce. Toss until well mixed. Adjust the seasonings and serve on a hot platter.

SPAGHETTI WITH CHICKEN AND MUSHROOMS *6 servings*

- 1 three-pound chicken, disjointed
- ½ cup butter
- 1 teaspoon salt
- ½ cup chopped celery leaves
- 1 small onion, chopped
- 1 cup boiling water
- 1 pound mushrooms, sliced thick
- 3 tablespoons flour
- Heavy cream
- ⅔ cup grated Romano cheese
- ¼ cup dry sherry
- 1 pound of spaghetti, cooked according to package directions

1. Brown the chicken in three tablespoons of the butter. Add the salt, celery, onion and water and cover. Simmer until the chicken is tender, about thirty minutes. Cool, bone the chicken and cube the meat. Strain and reserve the broth.
2. Sauté the mushrooms in two tablespoons butter until tender. Add the chicken.
3. Melt the remaining three tablespoons of butter in a saucepan, add the flour and stir with a wire whisk until blended. Meanwhile, add to the chicken broth enough cream to make three cups of liquid. Bring to a boil and add all at once to the butter-flour mixture, stirring vigorously with the whisk. Stir in the cheese and add the chicken and mushrooms. Stir in the sherry and heat but do not boil. Correct the seasonings.
4. Serve over hot spaghetti.

SPAGHETTI WITH LOBSTER *6 servings*

- 2 live lobsters, about 1½ pounds each
- ⅓ cup olive oil
- 1 clove garlic, minced
- 1 small onion, chopped
- 1 teaspoon salt
- ¼ to ½ teaspoon cayenne pepper
- Freshly ground black pepper to taste
- 1 cup canned tomatoes, or 1 pound fresh tomatoes, peeled and chopped
- 2 tablespoons tomato paste
- 2 tablespoons water
- ⅔ cup dry white wine
- 1½ tablespoons chopped parsley
- 1 teaspoon orégano
- 1 pound pasta, cooked and drained

1. Wash the lobsters. Cut the spinal cord of each by inserting a knife where the tail and body meet. Turn the lobsters on their backs and split lengthwise. Cut each tail crosswise into three pieces. Cut off the claws and crack them.
2. Heat the oil in a large skillet, add the lobsters and cook over high heat three or four minutes, or until they are red. Add the garlic, onion and seasonings and cook, stirring, two minutes.
3. Add the tomatoes and tomato paste blended with the water and cook, turning constantly, about one minute.
4. Add the wine, parsley and orégano and cook about ten minutes, turning frequently.
5. To serve, drain the sauce onto spaghetti and toss to coat the pasta. Place on a platter and garnish with lobster.

CHICKEN AND SPAGHETTI CASSEROLE *6 to 8 servings*

Boiling salted water
1 three-pound chicken, quartered
1 onion stuck with 2 cloves
1 carrot, cleaned and sliced
1 stalk celery
8 peppercorns
1 pound raw spaghetti
2 cups canned whole-kernel corn, drained
2 cups canned tomatoes
1 cup green peas, cooked
½ pound fresh mushrooms, sliced and sautéed in a little butter
¾ cup grated Cheddar cheese

1. In a heavy kettle combine boiling water, chicken, onion, carrot, celery and peppercorns. Simmer, covered, until the chicken is fork tender, thirty to forty minutes.
2. Preheat oven to moderate (350° F.).
3. Remove the chicken from the kettle and cut the meat from the bones. Strain the broth, then bring it to a vigorous boil and add the spaghetti, stirring often with a two-pronged fork to keep ingredients from sticking together. Cook spaghetti until barely tender, nine or ten minutes.
4. Drain the spaghetti and combine it in a casserole with the chicken, corn, tomatoes, green peas and mushrooms. Sprinkle with cheese and bake, uncovered, thirty-five minutes.

NOODLE RING *6 servings*

¼ pound broad noodles
Water
3 tablespoons butter
2 tablespoons flour
½ cup light cream or milk
½ teaspoon salt
Dash of freshly ground black pepper
4 eggs, separated
¼ cup finely chopped parsley

1. Boil the noodles in three quarts salted water until barely tender. Drain and rinse in cold water.
2. Meanwhile, butter an eight-and-one-half-inch ring mold. Preheat oven to moderate (350° F.).
3. Melt the butter in a saucepan, add the flour and stir with a wire whisk until blended. Meanwhile, bring the cream to a boil and add all at once to the butter-flour mixture, stirring vigorously with the whisk. Season with salt and pepper. Cool slightly.
4. Beat the egg whites until stiff and set aside. Beat the egg yolks until foamy, using the same beater.
5. Add the egg yolks to the cooled sauce. Add the drained noodles and carefully fold in the egg whites and then the parsley.
6. Turn into the buttered ring mold and set in a pan of hot water. Bake about thirty minutes. Unmold and fill the center with creamed mixtures or sweetbreads and ham in sherry.

SPINACH AND RICOTTA DUMPLINGS *4 servings*

1 pound spinach, chopped
¾ pound ricotta or cottage cheese
½ teaspoon salt
2 egg yolks
5 tablespoons grated Parmesan cheese
Flour
¼ cup butter, melted

1. Cook the spinach until just tender. Drain well and press through a sieve.
2. Mix the spinach, ricotta cheese, salt, egg yolks and three tablespoons of the Parmesan cheese.
3. Drop the mixture from a spoon into flour and shape into small balls. Cook in a deep kettle of simmering water about five minutes. Remove with a perforated spoon to a hot platter.
4. Sprinkle the dumplings with butter and the remaining Parmesan cheese.

There are many forms of gnocchi, a dish that cannot be described in a word. The closest approximation is dumpling. Gnocchi may be made with potatoes, farina or, as in gnocchi Parisienne, with cream-puff paste.

GNOCCHI PARISIENNE *4 to 5 servings*

6 tablespoons butter
6 tablespoons flour
2 cups milk
½ cup heavy cream
Water
Salt and freshly ground black pepper
Cream-puff paste (see below)
Grated Parmesan cheese
Melted butter

1. Preheat oven to moderate (350° F.).
2. Melt the butter in a saucepan, add the flour and stir with a wire whisk until blended. Meanwhile, bring the milk to a boil and add all at once to the butter-flour mixture, stirring vigorously with the wire whisk. Stir in the cream and season to taste with salt and pepper.
3. Bring six quarts lightly salted water to a boil and fill a pastry bag fitted with a round tube (size twelve) with the cream-puff paste. Hold the bag over the boiling water and, as the paste comes through, cut it off in one-inch lengths. Poach the paste three to four minutes and remove from the water to drain.
4. Butter a shallow casserole or au gratin dish and add a thin layer of the cream sauce. Add one or two layers of the gnocchi, covering each with the cream sauce. Sprinkle each layer with grated Parmesan cheese and the top with melted butter.
5. Bake fifteen to twenty minutes.

CREAM-PUFF PASTE FOR GNOCCHI:

¼ cup butter
½ cup water
¼ teaspoon salt
Pinch of nutmeg
½ cup flour
2 eggs

(*cont'd*)

1. Bring the butter, water, salt and nutmeg to a rapid boil. Add the flour all at once and, stirring rapidly with a wooden spoon, lift the pan a few inches from the heat. Continue stirring thirty seconds, or until the paste comes away from the sides of the saucepan and forms a rough ball in the center. Remove from the heat.

2. Add the eggs, one at a time, beating vigorously after each addition until the paste is smooth.

GNOCCHI WITH POTATOES *5 to 6 servings*

- 3 medium potatoes
- 2 egg yolks
- ½ teaspoon salt
- 1 cup flour, approximately
- 1½ cups Italian-style tomato sauce, canned or homemade (page 341)
- 1 cup or more grated Parmesan cheese

1. For gnocchi, use a dry, mealy type of potato. Boil the potatoes in their jackets, peel and mash. Add the egg yolks and salt; whip until fluffy. Add the flour and mix, then knead until smooth, adding more flour as necessary to prevent sticking.

2. Divide the dough into six parts and shape each into a long roll about one-half inch in diameter. Cut into pieces about one inch long and press with the thumb or a fork. Sprinkle lightly with flour.

3. Add about a third of the gnocchi at a time to six quarts boiling salted water and cook about five minutes. Remove to a heated bowl and keep warm. Repeat until all the gnocchi have been cooked.

4. Add one cup of the tomato sauce and one-half cup of the cheese and toss lightly. Turn onto a serving platter and pour the remaining sauce over the top. Sprinkle with the remaining cheese.

GNOCCHI PARMIGIANA *About 6 servings*

- 3 cups milk
- ½ cup butter
- 1 teaspoon salt
- ¾ cup farina
- 2 cups grated Parmesan cheese
- 1 egg, lightly beaten

1. Combine two cups of the milk, one-quarter cup of the butter and the salt in a saucepan and bring to a boil. Mix the farina with the remaining milk and add to the boiling mixture. Cook, stirring, until thickened. Remove from heat.

2. Add one cup cheese and the egg and mix well. Turn into a nine-inch-square pan, cool and then chill until firm.

3. Preheat oven to hot (425° F.).

4. Cut the mush into small rounds, squares or diamonds and arrange in a greased shallow baking dish, preferably having only one layer with each shape of cereal slightly overlapping. Melt the remaining butter, pour over the top and sprinkle with the remaining cheese.

5. Bake until the top is golden brown, about twenty-five minutes.

BASIC POLENTA *About 4 cups*

1 quart water
1 teaspoon salt
1 cup cornmeal, yellow or white

1. Bring about two and one-half cups of water to a boil in the top part of a double boiler over direct heat. Add the salt.
2. Mix the cornmeal with the remaining water and add to the boiling water. Reduce the heat and cook, stirring constantly, until the mixture boils.
3. Place the pan over boiling water and cook, covered, about forty-five minutes, stirring occasionally.

VARIATIONS:

Polenta with Gorgonzola: Turn hot polenta into a serving dish. Make a depression in the center and fill it with butter and Gorgonzola cheese (three tablespoons or more of butter and three to four ounces of cheese). Spoon butter and cheese over each serving of polenta.

Polenta with Bel Paese: Turn hot cooked polenta into a greased nine-by-nine-inch pan and spread to make a layer about one-half inch thick. Chill. Cut into cubes, place in a greased shallow baking dish and sprinkle with bits of Bel Paese cheese and butter. Bake in a preheated hot oven (400° F.) until the polenta is hot and lightly browned, or about twenty-five minutes.

Grilled Polenta: Turn hot cooked polenta into a greased 9 by 9-inch pan. Spread to make a layer about one-half inch thick. Chill. Turn the polenta out of the pan and cut into squares, rectangles or as desired. Place the pieces on a cookie sheet that has been lined with foil and broil until brown and well crisped on both sides. If desired, brush with melted butter during broiling.

POLENTA LAYERS *6 servings*

1 cup yellow cornmeal
1 quart water
Salt
1 medium onion, chopped
1 clove garlic, minced
½ green pepper, chopped
2 tablespoons fat
1 pound chopped beef
½ cup soft bread crumbs
1 egg
Freshly ground black pepper to taste

1. Mix the meal with one cup of the cold water. Bring the remaining water to a boil with one teaspoon salt. Stir in the meal and cook, stirring, over moderate heat until thick.
2. Preheat oven to moderate (350° F.).
3. Sauté the onion, garlic and green pepper in the fat until tender. Add the beef, crumbs, egg and additional salt and pepper to taste. Mix well.
4. Turn half the cornmeal mush into a greased 8 by 4 by 3-inch loaf pan and spread evenly. Arrange the meat mixture on top and cover with the remaining mush.

(cont'd)

5. Cover the pan with a piece of greased aluminum foil or brown paper and bake about one hour. Serve with tomato sauce.

Note: The true polenta, made of a coarser yellow cornmeal than that used here, is the spaghetti of North Italy. It is most commonly served with a sauce of meat, fish or vegetables.

SAUCES FOR PASTA

ANCHOVY SAUCE *About ¾ cup*

½ cup olive oil (may be half butter)
8 cloves garlic, chopped
2 two-ounce cans flat anchovies, undrained
3 tablespoons chopped parsley

1. Heat the oil in a skillet and add the garlic. Reserving five anchovies for garnish, add the remainder to the oil and cook, stirring, until the garlic is lightly browned and the anchovies have disintegrated.

2. Pour the sauce over hot drained spaghetti and toss well until mixed. Add the parsley and toss with the spaghetti; or use for garnish with the reserved anchovies.

VARIATIONS:

Bagna Cauda: Add to the oil in the anchovy sauce above one-half cup butter and one sliced truffle. Serve over boiled meats or vegetables.

Green Anchovy Sauce: Sauté contents of one can anchovies, drained, in one-half cup olive oil along with one minced onion and one small minced green pepper. When onion is golden, add one-fourth cup minced parsley. Spoon over hot cooked pasta and sprinkle with grated Parmesan cheese.

SEAFOOD SAUCE *4 servings*

2 tablespoons olive oil
1 large onion, sliced thin
2 cloves garlic, minced
1 quart canned Italian tomatoes
1½ pounds raw shrimp, shelled and cut small
Pinch of orégano
Salt and freshly ground black pepper to taste

1. Heat the oil and sauté the onion until it is transparent. Add the garlic and continue cooking over low heat about three minutes. Add the tomatoes and cook over fairly high heat twelve minutes, leaving the pot uncovered.

2. Add the shrimp and season with the orégano. Reduce the heat and simmer about five minutes. Add salt and pepper to taste. Serve over one pound of hot cooked tagliarini or spaghetti.

(*cont'd*)

Note: In place of the shrimp, two cups of any of the following may be used: shelled raw clams without juice; raw oysters, cut small; crabmeat; lobster meat, cut small; raw baby squid, sliced thin.

The most versatile of vegetables is the tomato. Who could do without it? Here is a whole repertory of tomato sauces, any of which would do credit to Italy, Spain or the region around Nice.

BASIC TOMATO SAUCE *About 3 pints*

- 2 cups chopped onion
- 3 cloves garlic, chopped
- 3 tablespoons olive oil
- 3½ cups canned Italian-style plum tomatoes, undrained
- 2 small cans tomato paste
- 2 cups water or meat broth, approximately
- 1 bay leaf
- ½ teaspoon salt
- ¼ teaspoon freshly ground black pepper
- ½ teaspoon orégano, or ¼ teaspoon each orégano and basil

1. Sauté the onion and garlic in the olive oil until brown, stirring often. Add the tomatoes, tomato paste, water, bay leaf, salt and pepper. Simmer uncovered, stirring occasionally, about two hours. Add more water as necessary.

2. Add the orégano and continue cooking about fifteen minutes. Remove the bay leaf. The sauce should be thick. Serve over cooked spaghetti or use as an ingredient in such dishes as eggplant parmigiana (page 379), meat loaf, soups and stews.

VARIATIONS:

Meat Tomato Sauce: Brown one-half pound chopped beef in the fat before adding the onions and garlic.

Tomato and Wine Sauce: Substitute one cup dry red wine for one of the cans of tomato paste.

TOMATO SAUCE WITH MUSHROOMS *About 2½ cups*

- 3 tablespoons butter or olive oil
- ½ cup chopped onion
- 1 small clove garlic, finely chopped
- ½ cup chopped celery
- ⅔ cup sliced fresh mushrooms
- 2 cups canned Italian plum tomatoes
- 3 tablespoons tomato paste
- Salt and freshly ground black pepper to taste

1. Heat the butter in a saucepan and in it sauté the onion, garlic and celery. When the onion is transparent, add the mushrooms and cook three minutes longer, stirring occasionally.

2. Add the tomatoes and simmer fifteen minutes. Stir in the tomato paste

(cont'd)

and cook ten minutes longer. Season to taste with salt and pepper and, if a richer sauce is desired, add a little more melted butter.

VARIATION:

Tomato Sauce with Fennel Seeds: Omit the garlic and sauté one-fourth teaspoon thyme, one-half bay leaf and crushed red pepper to taste along with the onions. Add one-half to one teaspoon fennel seeds with the tomatoes.

SPAGHETTI SAUCE BOLOGNESE *4 to 5 cups*

1 cup dried white mushrooms
1 pound ground chuck
2 large onions, chopped
¼ pound prosciutto, sliced very thin
2 tablespoons sweet butter
2 tablespoons olive oil
4 cups canned Italian plum tomatoes
1 small can tomato paste

1. Wash the mushrooms well and soak in tepid water. When soft, chop fine and add to the meat.

2. Sauté the onions and prosciutto in the butter and oil over low heat until the onions are golden. Add the mixture of raw beef and mushrooms. Cook, stirring, until the meat has browned. Add the tomatoes and tomato paste and allow to simmer slowly, uncovered, about two hours, or until the sauce is thick.

MILANAISE SAUCE *5 to 6 cups*

2 ounces salt pork, diced
1 cup chopped onion
2 cloves garlic, minced
½ cup finely chopped carrot
1 bay leaf
Pinch of thyme
½ cup chopped parsley
4 cups canned Italian plum tomatoes, crushed
1 can tomato paste
1 quart chicken broth
Salt and freshly ground black pepper to taste
3 tablespoons butter
1 cup mushrooms, sliced
1 cup cubed, cooked ham, preferably prosciutto

1. Cook the diced salt pork over moderate heat, stirring occasionally, until it is rendered of fat. Add the onion, garlic, carrot, bay leaf and thyme and sauté until the onion is transparent.

2. Add the parsley, tomatoes, tomato paste and chicken broth and simmer, uncovered, one hour, or until the mixture reaches the desired thickness. Remove the bay leaf and season to taste with salt and pepper.

3. Melt the butter in a skillet and cook the mushrooms and ham in it until the mushrooms are wilted. Combine with the tomato sauce.

WHITE CLAM SAUCE *About 4 cups*

- ¼ cup butter
- 1 large clove garlic, finely chopped
- 2 tablespoons flour
- 2 cups clam juice, fresh or canned
- ¼ cup chopped parsley
- Salt and freshly ground black pepper to taste
- 1½ teaspoons dried thyme leaves
- 2 cups minced clams, fresh or canned

1. In a saucepan heat the butter, add the garlic and cook one minute over moderate heat. With a wire whisk stir in the flour. Add the clam juice, while stirring.

2. Add the parsley, salt, pepper and thyme and simmer gently ten minutes. Add the minced clams and heat through. Serve over linguine or spaghetti.

RED CLAM SAUCE *About 6 cups*

- 2 tablespoons olive oil
- 2 cloves garlic, finely chopped
- 1 onion, chopped
- 3 stalks celery, chopped
- ¼ teaspoon thyme
- ¼ teaspoon dried basil
- ½ teaspoon orégano
- Salt and freshly ground black pepper to taste
- 2 cups canned tomatoes
- 1 can tomato paste
- 1½ cups water
- 2 cups fresh or bottled clam juice
- 2 cups minced clams, fresh or canned
- ¼ cup butter
- ½ cup chopped parsley

1. In a heavy kettle, heat the oil, add the garlic, onion and celery and cook until the onion is transparent. Add the thyme, basil, orégano, salt, pepper, tomatoes, tomato paste and water. Bring to a boil, reduce the heat and simmer gently, uncovered, one hour.

2. After thirty minutes, add the clam juice.

3. Five minutes before serving add the clams and cook gently. Stir in the butter and parsley. Reheat until the butter melts. Serve with freshly cooked linguine or green noodles.

CHAPTER SEVEN

. . . .

VEGETABLES

STEAMED ARTICHOKES *8 servings*

8 large artichokes
Boiling salted water
8 coriander seeds (optional)
Juice of 2 lemons

1. Trim the tough outer leaves and stalks from the artichokes and drop the vegetables into boiling salted water to cover. Add the coriander seeds and lemon juice.

2. Simmer, covered, until the outer leaves pull off easily, about forty minutes. Serve hot with melted butter, Hollandaise or mousseline sauce, or cold with French dressing or sauce vinaigrette (see index).

STUFFING ARTICHOKES

1. Wash the artichoke and, using a sharp knife or scissors, cut off the top third of the vegetable.

2. Pull off the tough outside leaves around the base and discard. Using the fingers, open the center leaves carefully. Turn the artichoke over on a chopping board or other flat surface and press down firmly at the base to cause the leaves to spread open further.

3. Turn the artichoke right side up and pull the yellow and yellow-white leaves from the center.

4. Sprinkle the center, fuzzy portion of the vegetable with lemon juice to keep it from darkening. Using a soup spoon or other substantial spoon, carefully scrape and pull the fuzzy and prickly portion from the heart of the artichoke. It is important that the last bit of this "choke" be removed, because if swallowed it creates an unpleasant sensation in the throat.

5. Sprinkle the smooth, scraped artichoke bottom with additional lemon juice.

6. Using a sharp, heavy knife, cut off the stem of the artichoke flush with the base. The stem may be peeled and cooked and, when it is tender, used in the filling.

(cont'd)

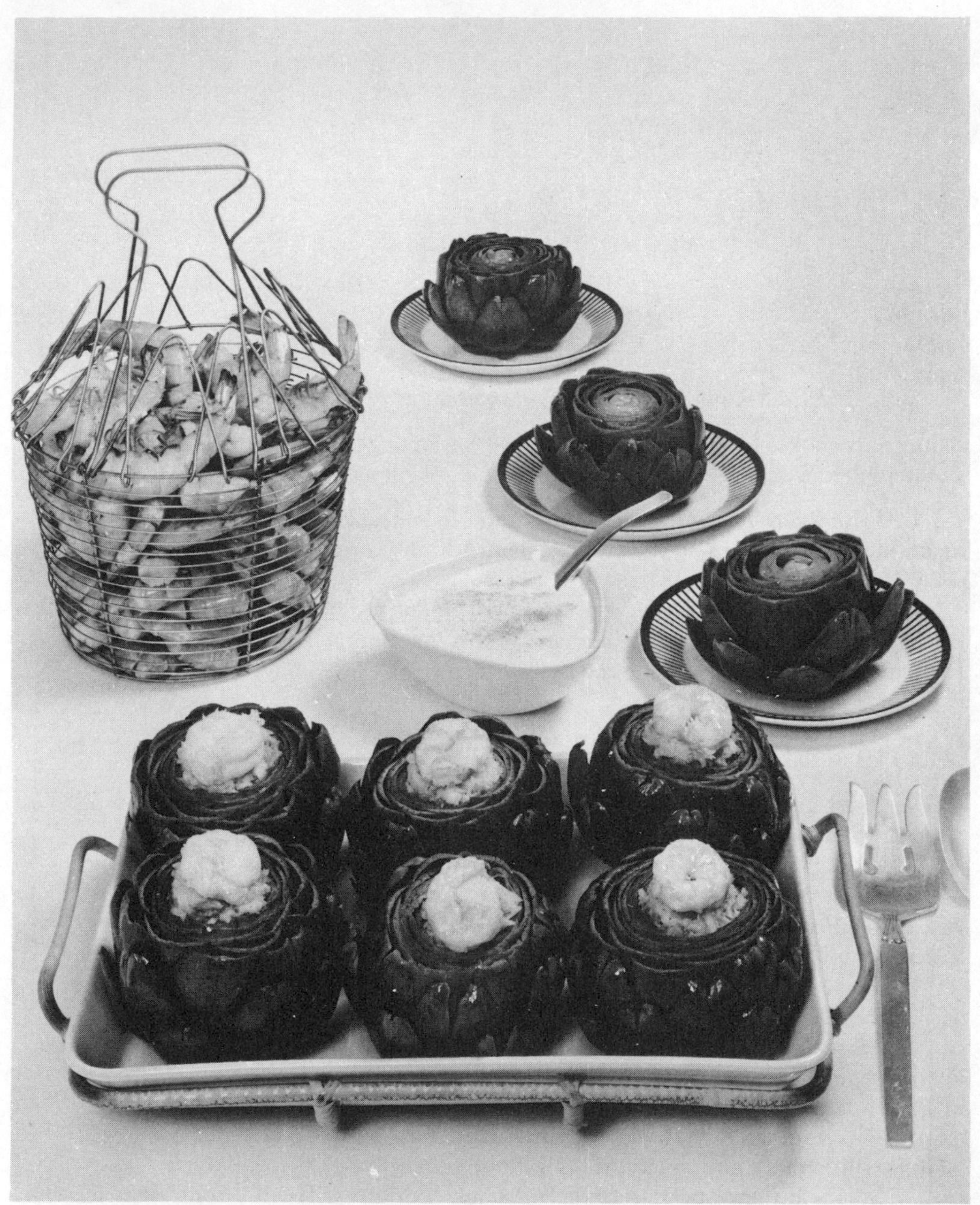

One of the most elegant and delicious of vegetables is the artichoke. It is a rare treat served hot or cold with a piquant sauce. In the foreground, artichokes are stuffed with a mixture of shrimp and fresh bread crumbs.

7. Stand the vegetable alongside the other artichokes in a deep kettle or saucepan so that they fit snugly together, or tie each with a string so that they will retain their shape.

8. Add salt, lemon juice and boiling water to cover. Cook, covered, twenty to thirty minutes, or until partly tender.

9. Using two spoons, remove the artichokes from the water and turn upside down to drain. When partly cool, fill the centers with stuffing and bake as directed.

BEEF-STUFFED ARTICHOKES *6 servings*

6 medium artichokes
1 tablespoon shortening
¾ pound ground beef
½ cup chopped onion
3 tablespoons chopped fresh parsley
1 cup soft bread crumbs
1 egg, beaten
2 teaspoons salt
⅛ teaspoon freshly ground black pepper
¼ teaspoon powdered ginger
¼ teaspoon whole orégano leaves, crumbled
6 slices fresh tomato
2 tablespoons olive oil
2 tablespoons buttered bread crumbs
2 tablespoons lemon juice

1. Prepare the artichokes for stuffing as page 347. Preheat oven to moderate (350° F.).

2. In a skillet heat the shortening, add the beef and onion and sauté until browned. Remove from the heat and stir in the parsley, bread crumbs, egg, one teaspoon of the salt, the pepper, ginger and orégano. Spoon the filling into the artichoke centers and top with a slice of tomato.

3. Combine the olive oil and remaining salt. Brush the artichokes and tomatoes with the mixture, place in a shallow baking pan and sprinkle with buttered crumbs. Fill the pan with boiling water to the depth of one inch and add the lemon juice. Cover closely with aluminum foil and bake one hour.

PARSLEY-STUFFED ARTICHOKES *6 servings*

6 medium artichokes
3 cups chopped parsley
1 clove garlic, finely chopped
1 teaspoon salt
⅛ teaspoon freshly ground black pepper
Juice of ½ lemon
Lemon wedges
1 tablespoon olive oil

1. Prepare the artichokes for stuffing as page 347. Preheat oven to moderate (350° F.).

2. Combine the parsley, garlic, salt and pepper and pack into the center of each artichoke. Arrange the artichokes in a baking dish just large enough to accommodate them snugly, or tie each with a string to retain the shape.

(*cont'd*)

3. To the dish add boiling water to the depth of one inch. Add the lemon juice and oil. Cover and bake thirty to forty-five minutes. Cool to room temperature before serving. Serve topped with thin lemon wedges.

SHRIMP-STUFFED ARTICHOKES *4 servings*

4 medium artichokes
1 cup cooked shrimp, shelled and deveined
1½ cups soft bread crumbs
¼ cup finely chopped onion
½ teaspoon salt
Fresh lemon juice
1 egg, beaten
Olive or salad oil

1. Prepare artichokes for stuffing (page 347). Preheat oven to moderate (350° F.).

2. Cut the shrimp into small pieces and combine with bread crumbs, onion, salt, two teaspoons of lemon juice and the egg. Spoon the mixture into the artichokes.

3. Place the artichokes in a small baking pan and pour boiling water around them to the depth of one inch. Add one tablespoon lemon juice and brush the artichokes generously with olive or salad oil. Cover with aluminum foil and bake thirty minutes.

Artichoke Hearts vs. Artichoke Bottoms: Artichoke hearts and artichoke bottoms are not the same. The heart (such as that purchased frozen) consists of a portion of the heart, the "choke" removed, and a few tender leaves. The bottom is precisely that. It is the bottom of the vegetable with all leaves and choke removed.

ARTICHOKE BOTTOMS WITH MUSHROOM SAUCE *8 servings*

16 large artichokes
Chicken stock or salted water to cover bottoms
2 tablespoons butter
2 tablespoons olive oil
¼ pound mushrooms, diced
Salt and freshly ground black pepper to taste
Dried tarragon to taste
½ cup cream
1 egg yolk, lightly beaten
1 tablespoon lemon juice

1. Cut off the top quarter of the artichokes and remove all stems and hard outer leaves. Cook in the stock until tender, twenty minutes or longer. Remove the remaining leaves and, with a spoon, remove the prickly choke, leaving only the bottoms.

2. In a skillet heat the butter and oil, add the mushrooms and cook until almost tender. Season with the salt, pepper and tarragon. Stir in the cream, egg yolk and lemon juice. Do not boil, but blend thoroughly over low heat.

3. Arrange the artichoke bottoms on a serving platter and spoon the mushroom sauce over them.

JERUSALEM ARTICHOKES *4 servings*

1 pound Jerusalem artichokes
Water
Salt to taste
¼ cup butter, melted
1 tablespoon finely chopped parsley or chives
Lemon juice to taste

1. Scrub the artichokes and pare them. Drop them in water to cover and add salt. Bring to a boil and simmer twenty-five to thirty-five minutes, or until tender.

2. Drain the artichokes and add the melted butter, chopped parsley or chives and lemon juice. Serve in place of boiled potatoes.

CHIPPED BEEF WITH ARTICHOKE HEARTS, PAGE 118.

ASPARAGUS

Remove the tough ends of the asparagus. Peel the stalks a few inches up from the end toward the tips. Stand the stalks in the lower part of a double boiler or deep kettle. Add boiling salted water to a depth of two inches, cover with the upper portion of the boiler or a lid and cook until just tender, twelve minutes or longer. (If it is more convenient, asparagus may be cooked in a heavy skillet with a tight-fitting cover.) Drain and serve with melted butter or with Hollandaise sauce (page 449), sauce Mornay (page 444), etc. Allow two pounds for four servings.

ASPARAGUS VINAIGRETTE

Pour vinaigrette sauce (page 455) over hot or cold cooked asparagus and let stand one hour, turning the asparagus once.

ASPARAGUS WITH FRESH TOMATO SAUCE

For the sauce, combine one-third cup mayonnaise, one and one-fourth teaspoons lemon juice, one-fourth teaspoon salt and a pinch of white pepper in the top part of a double boiler. Stir over hot, not boiling, water until heated through. Stir in one-third cup diced, peeled fresh tomato and serve over hot, freshly cooked asparagus. (Enough sauce for six servings.)

ASPARAGUS SOUR-CREAM CASSEROLE

Place cooked, drained asparagus in a greased casserole, sprinkle with salt and pepper and mix lightly with one cup sour cream. Top with one cup fresh bread crumbs which have been mixed with three tablespoons melted butter. Bake at 375° F. until crumbs are brown, about thirty minutes. (Enough for two and one-half pounds asparagus, or six servings.)

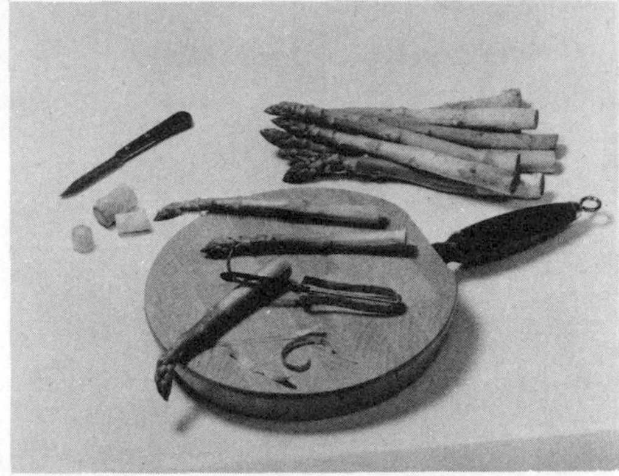

1. *Asparagus.* A potato parer with a swivel blade is a convenient device for peeling the lower part of asparagus spears.

2. To cook, place the vegetable upright in the bottom of a double boiler and cover with the inverted top.

3. Or, if it is more convenient, cook the asparagus in a heavy skillet equipped with a tight-fitting cover.

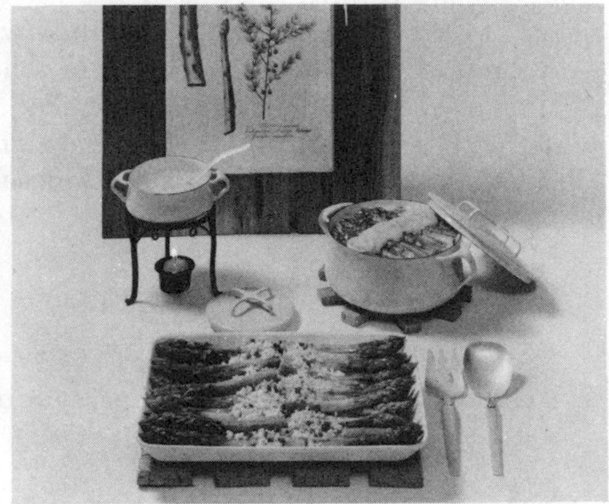

4. Asparagus, one of the most welcome signs of spring, is shown (foreground) with a classic polonaise garnish, and (rear) served with eggs and a cheese sauce.

BAKED ASPARAGUS WITH CHEESE *6 servings*

36 asparagus spears, cooked
Butter
Lemon juice
1 pound sliced Gruyère, Swiss or Fontina cheese
Grated Parmesan cheese

1. Preheat oven to hot (400° F.).

2. In a buttered baking dish, arrange a layer of asparagus, dot it with butter and sprinkle with lemon juice.

(cont'd)

3. Cover the asparagus with slices of cheese and sprinkle with a little of the grated Parmesan cheese. Alternate layers of asparagus and cheese, ending with a layer of sliced cheese sprinkled with Parmesan. Sprinkle with melted butter.

4. Bake until the cheese is melted and bubbling, eight to ten minutes.

RICE WITH ASPARAGUS, PAGE 325.

CREAMED ASPARAGUS WITH EGGS *6 servings*

¼ cup butter
¼ cup flour
1¾ cups chicken broth or milk
¼ cup light cream
Pinch of nutmeg
Salt and freshly ground black pepper to taste
3 hard-cooked eggs, sliced
1 cup cubed, cooked ham
24 asparagus spears, cooked and drained
Grated Parmesan cheese

1. Preheat oven to hot (400° F.).

2. In a saucepan melt the butter, add the flour and stir with a wire whisk until blended. Meanwhile, bring the chicken broth and cream to a boil and add all at once to the butter-flour mixture, stirring vigorously with the whisk until the sauce is thickened and smooth. Season with nutmeg, salt and pepper.

3. Place alternate layers of sauce, eggs, ham and asparagus in a buttered casserole, ending with a layer of sauce. Sprinkle with Parmesan cheese and bake five to ten minutes.

ASPARAGUS POLONAISE *4 servings*

Vegetables polonaise means that they are sprinkled with buttered bread crumbs and sieved egg.

6 tablespoons butter
¼ cup fine bread crumbs
2 pounds asparagus, cooked
1 hard-cooked egg, sieved
Chopped parsley

1. In a saucepan melt the butter, add the bread crumbs and sauté until lightly browned.

2. Sprinkle the crumbs and butter over hot, freshly cooked asparagus and then sprinkle with the sieved hard-cooked egg and chopped parsley.

ASPARAGUS AU GRATIN *6 servings*

¼ cup butter
¼ cup flour
1¾ cups chicken broth or milk
¼ cup light cream
¾ cup grated Cheddar cheese
¼ cup grated Parmesan cheese
Salt and freshly ground black pepper to taste
36 hot, freshly cooked asparagus spears

(*cont'd*)

1. In a saucepan melt the butter, add the flour and stir with a wire whisk until blended. Meanwhile, bring the chicken broth and cream to a boil and add all at once to the butter-flour mixture, stirring vigorously with the whisk until the sauce is thickened and smooth. Add the cheeses, salt and pepper and stir until the cheeses melt.

2. Place alternate layers of sauce and asparagus in a buttered casserole, ending with a layer of sauce. Sprinkle with additional Parmesan cheese and brown quickly under a preheated broiler or bake in a preheated hot oven (450° F.) five minutes.

SPANISH ASPARAGUS *4 servings*

- 2 pounds asparagus
- ¼ cup butter
- 1 small onion, minced
- 1 small bay leaf
- Salt and freshly ground black pepper to taste
- 3 tablespoons flour
- 2 cups chicken or veal stock
- Pinch of nutmeg
- 2 egg yolks
- 1 tablespoon lemon juice

1. Cook the asparagus until tender. Drain.

2. In a saucepan heat three tablespoons of the butter, add the onion, bay leaf, salt and pepper and sauté until the onion is tender but not brown, stirring often.

3. Stir in the flour, gradually add the stock and cook, stirring, until thickened. Add the nutmeg. Simmer five minutes and strain.

4. Beat the egg yolks until very light and add the lemon juice. Combine with a little of the hot sauce and add the egg mixture to the remaining sauce gradually, while stirring. Cook the mixture over boiling water in a double boiler, or over very low heat, stirring constantly, until thickened. Add the remaining butter.

5. To serve, place the asparagus on toast and pour the sauce over the top.

ASPARAGUS TIPS WITH PROSCIUTTO *4 servings*

- 24 asparagus tips
- 8 long thin slices of prosciutto or ham
- ½ cup butter, melted
- 3 tablespoons grated Parmesan cheese

1. Preheat oven to hot (400° F.).

2. Cook the asparagus in briskly boiling water until tender, about ten minutes. Drain well.

3. Wrap three asparagus tips in each slice of prosciutto and fasten with a toothpick. Place in a greased baking dish, sprinkle with half the butter and the cheese and bake five minutes. Remove from the oven and pour the remaining butter over the top.

GREEN BEANS

Remove ends and strings from beans. They may be left whole, snapped into one-inch lengths or French-cut into thin, lengthwise strips. Cook, covered, in a small amount of boiling salted water until barely tender. Drain and serve with melted butter. Allow one pound (about three cups) for four servings.

GREEN BEANS WITH WATER CHESTNUTS

Sauté one cup water chestnuts, drained and coarsely chopped, in three tablespoons butter about three minutes. Pour over three cups hot, drained beans and season with salt and a pinch of orégano.

GREEN BEANS WITH SOUR CREAM

Drain one small can whole mushrooms and brown lightly in two tablespoons butter. Add three cups hot, cooked green beans, cut French style, and one-half cup sour cream. Season with salt and freshly ground black pepper and heat through. Do not let boil. Serve immediately.

GREEN BEANS A LA NICOISE *6 servings*

½ cup olive oil
1 onion, sliced thin
1 cup canned Italian plum tomatoes
½ green pepper, chopped
½ cup chopped celery
¼ cup water
1 teaspoon salt
¼ teaspoon freshly ground black pepper
2 cloves
1 bay leaf
6 sprigs parsley
½ teaspoon dried chervil
1 pound green beans, cooked until tender and drained

1. In a skillet heat the oil, add the onion and cook until golden brown. Add the tomatoes, green pepper, celery, water, salt and pepper.
2. Tie the cloves, bay leaf, parsley and chervil in a small cheesecloth bag and add to the vegetables. Simmer, uncovered, about twenty-five minutes. Add the beans and continue simmering until the beans are hot. Remove the spice bag.

SAVORY GREEN BEANS *6 servings*

1½ pounds green beans
¼ cup oil
1 clove garlic, crushed
1 tablespoon chopped onion
¾ cup diced green pepper
¼ cup boiling water
1 teaspoon salt
1 teaspoon dried basil
½ cup grated Parmesan cheese

(*cont'd*)

1. Leave the beans whole, or cut into one-inch pieces.

2. Heat the oil and garlic in a heavy pan. Add the onion and green pepper and cook slowly three minutes. Add the beans, water, salt and basil, cover and simmer until the beans are tender, about fifteen minutes if whole.

3. Stir in half the cheese, turn the mixture into a serving dish and sprinkle with the remaining cheese.

FRESH LIMA BEANS

Cut off the rounded edges of the lima beans and shell like peas. Place the beans in a small amount of boiling salted water, cover and boil rapidly until tender, about twenty to thirty minutes. Allow two pounds (two and one-half cups shelled) or more for four servings.

LIMA BEANS WITH ROSEMARY

Season two and one-half cups hot, drained lima beans with two tablespoons butter and one-fourth teaspoon dried rosemary leaves. Blend well.

LIMA BEANS WITH CREAM *4 servings*

- 2 cups shelled fresh lima beans
- 2 tablespoons butter
- Salt and freshly ground black pepper to taste
- 2 teaspoons chopped fresh parsley
- ½ cup canned chicken consommé
- 1 tablespoon flour
- ½ cup light or heavy cream

1. Cook the beans as above. Drain.

2. In the same saucepan, melt the butter and add the beans, salt, pepper and parsley.

3. Gradually add the consommé to the flour and mix until smooth. Add the mixture to the beans and, when the sauce has thickened slightly, add the cream. Serve hot.

CREOLE LIMA BEANS *5 servings*

- 2 slices bacon
- 1 medium onion, chopped
- ¼ cup chopped green pepper
- 2 cups canned tomatoes
- 1 teaspoon sugar
- 2 cups canned or cooked baby lima beans, drained
- Salt and freshly ground black pepper to taste

1. Sauté the bacon until crisp and remove from the pan. Add the onion and pepper to the fat in the pan and cook until tender but not brown.

(*cont'd*)

2. Add the tomatoes and sugar, and cook about fifteen minutes, stirring occasionally. Add the beans and season with salt and pepper.

3. Simmer a few minutes longer. Serve hot, sprinkled with the crumbled bacon.

JAMAICAN BAKED BEANS *4 servings*

2 cups dried white pea beans
Water
¾ pound salt pork, cut into ½-inch cubes
1 teaspoon salt
1 small onion, studded with 4 cloves
½ cup brown sugar or molasses
¼ cup dark rum
2 teaspoons dry mustard
1 teaspoon freshly ground black pepper
Pinch of thyme

1. If unprocessed beans are used, soak them in one quart of water overnight. Soak the salt pork in cold water to cover two hours.

2. Drain the beans and put them in a large kettle. Add enough water to reach two inches above the beans. Add the salt and bring to a boil. Lower the heat and simmer the beans until they are barely tender. This will require about thirty to forty minutes for unprocessed beans, twenty minutes for the quick-cooking variety. Drain well.

3. Preheat oven to slow (250° F.).

4. Place the onion in the center of an earthenware casserole. Cover with a layer of half the drained beans and add a layer of half the salt pork. Add the remainder of the beans and top with the remaining salt pork.

5. Combine the sugar, rum, mustard, pepper and thyme and add to the beans. Add boiling water barely to cover and top the casserole with a tight-fitting lid. Bake four to five hours, or until tender, adding a little boiling water as necessary to keep the beans sufficiently moist. Uncover the casserole and let the beans cook thirty minutes longer without additional water.

BLACK BEANS IN RUM *6 servings*

1 pound dried black beans
Water
1 large onion, chopped
2 cloves garlic, minced
3 stalks celery, diced
1 minced carrot
Small herb bouquet (bay leaf, thyme and parsley, tied in cheesecloth)
Salt and freshly ground black pepper
3 tablespoons butter
2 jiggers (6 tablespoons) dark rum
Sour cream

1. Soak the beans overnight in water to cover; or boil two minutes and soak one hour or longer. Drain and add six cups of water.

2. Add vegetables and seasonings and simmer slowly until the beans are almost tender. Discard the herb bouquet.

3. Preheat oven to moderate (350° F.).

(cont'd)

4. Place the beans and their juice in a bean pot or casserole, add the butter and one jigger of the rum. Cover and bake until the beans are tender, about two hours. Add another jigger of rum and serve piping hot with cold sour cream.

RICE AND BEANS, ITALIAN STYLE, PAGE 319.

PASTA E FAGIOLI, PAGE 332.

FLAGEOLETS, BRETONNE STYLE *6 servings*

It is surprising that flageolets have such a small audience in the United States. The delightful green beans are the perfect accompaniment to roast leg of lamb.

FLAGEOLETS:

1 pound dried flageolets
5 cups water
1 onion studded with 5 or 6 cloves
2 teaspoons salt

1. Soak the beans overnight in the water; or boil two minutes and soak one hour or longer.

2. Add the onion and salt and bring to a boil. Reduce the heat, cover and simmer until the beans are tender, about two hours. Meanwhile prepare the sauce.

SAUCE:

2 tablespoons butter
1 onion, chopped
¼ cup tomato purée
4 tomatoes, peeled, seeded and chopped
3 cloves garlic, minced
Salt and freshly ground black pepper to taste
1 tablespoon chopped parsley

1. In a skillet heat the butter, add the onion and cook, stirring often, until brown.

2. Add the tomato purée, tomatoes, garlic, salt and pepper. Simmer the mixture about thirty minutes and add to the cooked beans. Reheat and top with the parsley. Serve with roast lamb and pan gravy.

RED BEANS AND RICE *6 servings*

1 pound dried kidney or other red beans
Water
½ pound salt pork, sliced
1 large onion, chopped
¼ cup minced celery, with a few leaves
¼ cup minced parsley (optional)
Salt and freshly ground black pepper to taste
4 cups hot cooked rice

1. Soak the beans in water to cover overnight; or boil two minutes and let soak one hour. Drain.

(cont'd)

2. Place the beans in a large pot with the salt pork and water to cover. Cover the pot and simmer. After one-half hour, add the vegetables and seasonings and cook until the beans are done, or one to one and one-half hours. Serve with hot rice.

INDIAN CHICK PEAS *6 to 8 servings*

- 2 cups dried chick peas
- 1½ quarts water
- 2 teaspoons salt
- ¼ cup butter
- 2 onions, chopped
- 1½ teaspoons turmeric
- ½ teaspoon powdered ginger
- ¼ teaspoon dried powdered mint, or 6 leaves fresh mint
- ½ teaspoon dried hot red peppers
- 2 tomatoes, peeled and chopped
- 1 can beef bouillon (about 1½ cups)

1. Soak the peas overnight in the water with the salt; or boil two minutes and soak one hour or longer.

2. Bring the peas to a boil, reduce the heat and simmer until almost tender, about thirty minutes. Drain, reserving the liquid.

3. In a skillet heat the butter, add the onions and cook until transparent. Add the seasonings and tomatoes and cook ten minutes. Add to the peas. Add the bouillon and enough of the liquid in which the peas were cooked to cover. Cover and simmer twenty minutes.

CHICK PEA SALAD, PAGE 427.

DRIED BEAN SALAD, PAGE 427.

CURRIED LENTILS *4 servings*

- 1 cup lentils
- 3 cups water or stock
- 2 large onions, chopped
- Salt
- 3 tablespoons butter or oil
- 1 clove garlic, minced
- 1 teaspoon curry powder

1. Combine the lentils and water. Add one of the onions and salt to taste and bring to a boil. Reduce the heat and simmer, covered, until the lentils are tender, thirty to forty minutes. Drain.

2. In a skillet heat the butter, add the remaining onion and the garlic and cook until they begin to brown. Add to the lentils. Add the curry powder and cook until the lentils are very tender, about ten minutes longer.

3. Serve plain or in a border of rice that has been garnished with fried onions, sliced lemon or sliced chicken.

LENTIL SALAD, PAGE 427.

CHEDDAR CHEESE AND LENTIL LOAF *5 servings*

½ pound Cheddar cheese
2 cups drained lentils, cooked or canned
½ small onion
½ teaspoon salt
¼ teaspoon freshly ground black pepper
¼ teaspoon thyme
1 cup soft bread crumbs, packed
1 egg, slightly beaten
1 tablespoon butter, softened

1. Preheat oven to moderate (350° F.).
2. Grind the cheese, lentils and onion together, and add the salt, pepper and thyme. Add the bread crumbs, egg and butter. Mix thoroughly.
3. Bake in a greased loaf pan forty-five minutes. Serve with tomato sauce.

CASSOULET *8 to 10 servings*

4 cups (2 pounds) small dried pea beans
2 quarts water
1 tablespoon salt
2 cloves garlic, minced
2 carrots, quartered
2 onions, each studded with 3 whole cloves
1 bouquet garni (parsley, celery, bay leaf and thyme tied in cheesecloth)
½ cup diced salt pork
3 tablespoons duck drippings or cooking oil
1½ pounds lean pork, cubed
1 pound boneless lamb, cubed
2 Bermuda onions, chopped
1 cup chopped shallots
1 cup thinly sliced celery
1 can (8 ounces) tomato sauce
1 cup dry white wine
1 garlic or Polish sausage
1 roasted duck removed from the bone and cut into bite-sized pieces (or canned preserved goose)

1. Combine the beans, water and salt in a large kettle, and let stand overnight; or boil two minutes and let soak one hour.
2. Add the garlic, carrots, onions studded with cloves, bouquet garni and salt pork. Bring to a boil. Reduce the heat and cook gently one hour. Skim the foam from the surface.
3. Heat the duck drippings or oil in a skillet. Add the meats and sauté until browned. Transfer to the bean mixture.
4. Sauté the onion, shallots and celery in the remaining drippings until tender. Add the tomato sauce and wine and simmer five minutes. Add to the beans. Add the garlic sausage, cover and simmer until the meats and beans are tender, about one hour, adding water if necessary to cover the beans. Skim off the excess fat. Discard the bouquet garni.
5. Transfer the mixture to a large earthenware casserole. Add the pieces of roasted duck or preserved goose. Bake, uncovered, in a preheated moderate oven (350° F.) thirty-five minutes.

The creation of music in honor of food and drink is not new. Bach wrote a cantata in praise of coffee and Schubert a trout quintet. One of the most unusual tributes to food was a musical essay written by one of South America's most illustrious composers, the late Heitor Villa-Lobos.

Once when Maestro Villa-Lobos was a guest in the home of Doña Dora Vasconcellos, the Brazilian consul general in New York, a special feijoada, Brazil's national dish, was served him. It was prepared by Noemia Faris, a shy, good-humored woman, the head of Doña Dora's kitchen staff.

The meal was an outstanding success and the composer was inspired to pen a brief composition in Miss Faris' autograph book titled "A Fugue Without End." The composer wrote beneath the piece that it was a "feijoada set to music for Noemia to remember Villa-Lobos." The composition was in four parts as any good feijoada should be. They were "Farina," "Meat," "Rice," and "Black Beans."

*A feijoada, pronounced "fay-*zhwah*-dah," is a most interesting meal, not too difficult to prepare and an excellent idea for autumn and winter entertaining.*

Noemia Faris' feijoada consists of black beans; several meats including sun-dried beef, sausage and salt pork; fluffy rice; sweet orange slices; chopped collards; and onions marinated in a powerfully hot French dressing. Roast pork usually accompanies the beans. Each of the foods is served from separate dishes to dinner plates and all is sprinkled liberally with an uncooked farina the Brazilians call farinha de mandioca.

The mandioca, linguiça defumada (sausage), carne seca (dried meat) and black beans may be obtained from many Spanish markets. In New York these are available at the Casa Moneo, 218 West Fourteenth Street.

FEIJOADA *6 servings*

3 cups dried black beans
Water
1 pound carne seca (sun-cured salted beef)
2 pounds raw smoked tongue
½ pound linguiça defumada (Portuguese sausage)
½ pound chuck beef
½ pound salt pork
Salt and freshly ground black pepper
2 large cloves garlic, chopped
2 teaspoons shortening

1. Wash the beans well and soak them overnight in water to cover. Soak the dried beef separately in water to cover. Drain the beans. Add six cups water and cook, covered, adding water as needed, until the beans are tender, or about two and one-half hours. As soon as the beans are cooking, begin adding the other ingredients.

2. Cut the carne seca into one-and-one-half-inch squares and add to the beans.

3. Peel the tongue and cut it into large cubes. Cover with water and bring to a boil. Simmer two minutes, drain and add to beans.

4. Prick the sausages with a fork, cover with water, boil a few minutes, drain and add to the beans.

(cont'd)

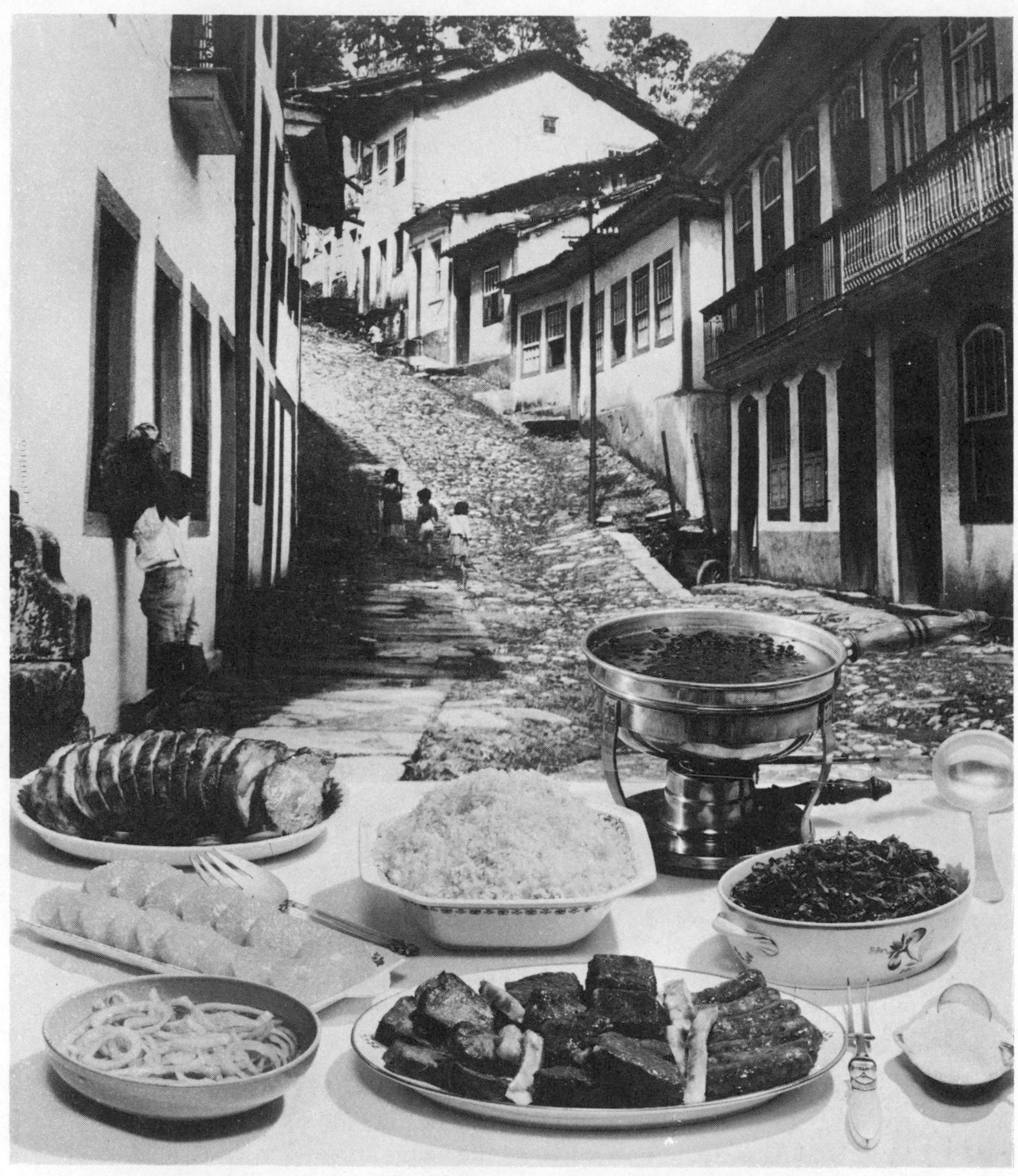

An authentic feijoada, the national dish of Brazil is pictured against the cobblestone streets of a Brazilian town, Ouro Prêto. The principal components of a feijoada are (clockwise): black beans in the chafing dish, collards, farina, meats, onion rings, oranges, roast pork and rice.

5. Cut the chuck in half and add to the beans.

6. Cut the salt pork into one-half-inch slices and add to the beans. Season the stew with salt and pepper.

7. When the beans are tender, brown the garlic lightly in the shortening. Add about one cup of the beans, mash and return to the large pot of beans. Adjust the seasonings.

8. Remove the pieces of meat to a hot platter and turn the beans into a chafing dish or bowl. Serve with braised pork loin, collards, onions in sauce (recipes follow), sweetened orange slices and hot rice. Cook the rice according to package directions, adding one and one-half tablespoons shortening and one-half teaspoon vinegar for each two cups uncooked, long-grain rice.

BRAISED PORK LOIN FOR A FEIJOADA *6 servings*

1 pork loin (10-inch cut), about 4 pounds
1 lemon
1 clove garlic
Tabasco sauce
Salt
¼ cup shortening
1 bay leaf

1. Have the butcher bone the loin and reserve the bone rack. Rub the meat with lemon juice, garlic, Tabasco sauce and salt.

2. Brown the loin in the shortening, turning to brown on all sides. Replace meat in bone rack and stand in a Dutch oven.

3. Add the bay leaf and a little water to the pot, cover and braise until tender, or about one and one-quarter hours.

COLLARDS FOR A FEIJOADA *6 servings*

1 tablespoon chopped onion
2 tablespoons shortening
1½ pounds collards, finely shredded
Salt

1. Sauté the onion in the shortening until it begins to brown.

2. Add the collards and salt and cook over low heat, stirring frequently, until the collards are tender, or about fifteen minutes.

ONIONS IN SAUCE FOR A FEIJOADA *6 servings*

1 large onion, sliced thin
¼ teaspoon salt
3 tablespoons Tabasco sauce
3 tablespoons olive oil
2 tablespoons vinegar

1. Cover the onion with boiling water, drain and rinse in cold water. Drain well.

2. Add the remaining ingredients and let stand at room temperature thirty minutes or longer.

PICADILLO WITH RICE AND BEANS *6 to 8 servings*

Picadillo is a Mexican meat hash. It is used in Mexico as a filling for pies, tamales, enchiladas and tacos.

BEANS:

1 cup dried black beans
3 cups water
½-pound ham hock
½ teaspoon salt
1 small onion, chopped
1 tablespoon chopped green pepper
1 large clove garlic, chopped
1 tablespoon oil

1. Boil the beans in three cups of water two minutes. Cover and let stand overnight.
2. Add the ham hock and salt and simmer, covered, until the beans are tender, or about two hours. Add more water if necessary.
3. Brown the onion, green pepper and garlic in the oil. Add to the beans and serve as a sauce for picadillo and rice.

PICADILLO:

1 onion, chopped
½ green pepper, chopped
1 tablespoon oil
1½ pounds chopped beef
2 cups canned tomatoes, undrained
1 tablespoon raisins
1 teaspoon capers
Salt and freshly ground black pepper
1 hard-cooked egg white, chopped
6 cups cooked rice
4 bananas sautéed in butter

1. Sauté the onion and green pepper in the oil until brown. Add the beef, tomatoes, raisins, capers, salt and pepper. Cook, stirring, until the mixture is almost dry.
2. Add the egg white and arrange the mixture on a warm platter with the rice. Garnish with the bananas.

BOILED BEETS

When cooking whole beets, leave on one inch of the stems and the root ends. Wash well and cook, covered, in boiling salted water to cover until tender when tested with a fork. Small young beets take one-half to one hour; older beets one to two hours. When tender, drain and slip off the skins. Allow two pounds of beets, with tops removed, for four servings.

BEETS IN SOUR CREAM *4 servings*

In the top part of a double boiler mix three cups cubed or sliced cooked beets with one-half cup sour cream, one-half to one tablespoon prepared horseradish, one teaspoon grated onion and one-fourth teaspoon salt. Heat, stirring occasionally, over hot water until mixture is at serving temperature. Garnish with chopped chives or parsley.

HARVARD BEETS *4 to 6 servings*

- 2½ cups sliced cooked or canned beets
- ⅓ cup sugar
- 2 teaspoons cornstarch
- ¼ cup vinegar
- 1 tablespoon butter

1. Drain the beets, reserving one-quarter cup of the liquid.
2. Combine the sugar and cornstarch and stir in the vinegar and beet liquid (or water). Cook, stirring, over low heat until the mixture is thickened and smooth.
3. Add the beets and the butter and cook until heated through.

GINGERED BEETS *About 4 servings*

- ⅓ cup sugar
- ¾ teaspoon ground ginger
- 2 teaspoons cornstarch
- ¼ cup cider vinegar
- 2½ cups cooked or canned baby beets, drained
- 2 tablespoons butter
- 1 tablespoon chopped parsley

1. Blend the sugar, ginger and cornstarch and gradually add the vinegar, stirring until smooth. Cook over medium heat, stirring, until thickened. Add the beets and butter and simmer ten minutes longer, stirring occasionally.
2. Serve piping hot, sprinkled with chopped parsley.

BEETS WITH ORANGE *6 servings*

- ½ cup sugar
- 1 tablespoon cornstarch
- ½ teaspoon salt
- ½ cup cider vinegar
- 2 tablespoons water
- Grated rind and juice of 1 orange
- 3½ cups cooked or canned small beets, drained
- 3 tablespoons butter

1. In a saucepan mix the sugar, cornstarch, salt, vinegar and water and bring to a boil. Stir until clear.
2. Stir in the orange rind and juice and the beets. Heat gently and, before serving, stir in the butter.

PICKLED BEETS, PAGE 498.

STUFFED BEETS, PAGE 420.

BROCCOLI

Wash broccoli well and drain. Remove and discard the large coarse leaves and cut off the tough lower parts of the stalk. If stalks are large, cut lengthwise into halves or quarters. Stand the stalks upright in a deep kettle, add one inch boiling salted water, cover and cook until stalks are just tender, about fifteen minutes. One bunch (about one and one-half pounds) yields four servings.

BROCCOLI WITH CAPERS

Sprinkle hot drained broccoli with bottled capers and melted butter mixed with a little of the juice from the bottle.

BROCCOLI AMANDINE

For four servings, cook one large bunch of broccoli as above; drain and arrange on a heated serving platter. To one-half cup melted butter add lemon juice to taste and one-fourth cup coarsely chopped toasted almonds. Sprinkle over the broccoli.

BROCCOLI WITH BLACK OLIVES *4 servings*

- 1 bunch (about 1½ pounds) fresh broccoli, trimmed
- 3 tablespoons olive oil
- 1 clove garlic, chopped fine
- Salt and freshly ground black pepper to taste
- ¼ cup small black olives, pitted and cut into small pieces
- 3 tablespoons grated Parmesan cheese

1. Parboil the broccoli about ten minutes in a small amount of salted water. Drain.
2. Heat the oil, add the garlic and sauté until lightly browned. Add the broccoli and season with salt and pepper. Cook slowly over low heat ten minutes, adding a little of the water in which the broccoli was cooked if the pan gets too dry.
3. Add the olives and heat two minutes longer. Serve immediately sprinkled with the grated cheese.

BRUSSELS SPROUTS

Remove any wilted leaves from the sprouts and cut a gash in each stem from tip toward sprout. Wash thoroughly. Simmer, uncovered, five minutes in salted water to cover. Cover and continue cooking six to twenty minutes longer, or until just tender. One quart of sprouts yields about six servings.

BRUSSELS SPROUTS WITH CARAWAY SEEDS *6 servings*

- 1½ pounds (1 quart) Brussels sprouts
- Chicken stock
- 3 tablespoons butter
- ¾ teaspoon salt or salt to taste
- ⅛ teaspoon ground black pepper
- 2 teaspoons whole caraway seeds

1. Wash the Brussels sprouts, trim off tough outer leaves and cut a small cross in the bottom of each.
2. Pour chicken stock to a depth of one inch in a saucepan. Bring the stock

(*cont'd*)

to a boil and add the sprouts. Return to the boil and simmer three minutes without a cover. Cover and cook seven to twenty minutes longer, or until just tender. Drain if necessary. Add remaining ingredients, toss lightly and serve at once.

BRUSSELS SPROUTS WITH BROWN BUTTER *6 servings*

Heat three tablespoons of butter over low heat until it begins to brown. Add one tablespoon of lemon juice and pour the mixture over one quart of hot, cooked Brussels sprouts. If desired, sprinkle with one-fourth cup shredded toasted almonds.

BUTTERED CABBAGE

Remove and discard discolored outer leaves from green cabbage. Wash, core, and cut into shreds or wedges. Cook, covered, in a small amount of boiling salted water or stock until just tender. Drain well. Season with salt and freshly ground black pepper and serve with melted butter.

CABBAGE A LA BRETONNE *4 servings*

1 medium-sized head cabbage
2 cups beef stock
2 eggs, well beaten
¾ cup light cream
½ teaspoon salt
Freshly ground black pepper and nutmeg to taste
3 tablespoons olive oil
3 tablespoons tarragon vinegar
2 teaspoons sugar
Paprika

1. Cut the cabbage into eight wedges and cook in the stock until tender. Drain and keep warm.
2. Mix the eggs, cream, salt, pepper and nutmeg.
3. Heat the oil, vinegar and sugar to boiling in the top of a double boiler over direct heat. Add, stirring, to the egg mixture. Return to the double boiler and cook over simmering water, stirring constantly, until thickened.
4. Remove the core from the cabbage and discard. Place the cabbage in a warm bowl and cover with the sauce. Sprinkle with paprika. Let stand a few minutes before serving.

CABBAGE IN SOUR CREAM *4 or more servings*

2 tablespoons butter
1 small head cabbage, shredded
1 egg, beaten
1 cup sour cream
2 tablespoons sugar
3 tablespoons vinegar or lemon juice
Salt and freshly ground black pepper to taste

(cont'd)

1. Melt the butter in a large skillet. Add the cabbage and cook, covered, until tender but not browned.

2. Mix the egg, sour cream, sugar, vinegar, salt and pepper. Pour over the cabbage and heat, stirring, until almost simmering; do not boil. Serve at once.

STUFFED CABBAGE

Cabbage is seldom thought of as company food, and perhaps its esteem in this regard is best illustrated by an incident in the life of a young Rumanian couple living in the United States.

Some time ago, when their funds were particularly low, they had invited to dinner a gentleman whose liking for steaks was well known. They were unable to provide his favorite dish and decided instead to serve one of their own—stuffed cabbage. But the husband struck on an idea.

"Maria," he said, "when we are seated at dinner, you come from the kitchen and say, 'Ion, what do you suppose happened? The steak fell on the floor.' I will say, 'No matter, Maria, we can have the stuffed cabbage.' "

When the night in question arrived and they were seated at the table the wife came from the kitchen and said, "Ion, what do you suppose happened? The stuffed cabbage fell on the floor."

"Maria," he said, "you mean the steak fell on the floor."

"No, Ion," she reiterated, "the stuffed cabbage fell on the floor."

Although it is not proposed that stuffed cabbage will ever replace steak as a national favorite, the dish can be a culinary delight. And it can be presented in a fashion to give it unusual eye appeal. Here is a European method of stuffing cabbage leaves to make them symmetrical with no strings attached.

1. Pull off the tough outer leaves from the cabbage and cut out the bottom core of the head with a paring knife. Cook the vegetable in boiling salted water to cover five minutes, or until the leaves separate easily. Invert and drain well.

2. Separate the individual leaves and dry them.

3. Place a square of cheesecloth on a flat surface. In the center of it place one of the large cabbage leaves, curly edge up. Insert a smaller cabbage leaf in the first and fill the smaller leaf with one or two tablespoons of the stuffing.

4. Bring the four corners of the cheesecloth together and twist the ends shut. This will shape the stuffed leaves into a compact round.

5. Remove the cheesecloth immediately and arrange the stuffed cabbage in a casserole with the sealed edge of the vegetable down.

6. Continue stuffing the leaves until all have been filled. The same square of cheesecloth may be used repeatedly.

ARMENIAN STUFFING FOR CABBAGE LEAVES *6 servings*

1 large cabbage
½ cup olive oil
2½ cups chopped onion
½ cup raw rice
½ cup finely chopped parsley
¼ cup raisins
¼ cup pistachio nuts
¼ cup tomato paste
½ cup water
¼ teaspoon allspice
¼ teaspoon cinnamon
1 teaspoon salt
¼ teaspoon freshly ground black pepper
2 cups chicken stock or canned chicken broth

1. Prepare the cabbage for stuffing as page 368.

2. In a skillet heat the oil, add the onion and cook gently until golden brown. Add the rice and cook, covered, over low heat one-half hour. Stir occasionally.

3. Add the remaining ingredients except the cabbage and stock and cook five minutes longer.

4. Strain the liquid into a heavy round casserole. Stuff the cabbage leaves with the rice mixture.

5. Arrange the stuffed leaves in the casserole and weight down with an inverted plate that fits loosely inside the casserole. Add enough chicken stock to reach the rim of the plate and simmer until done, about thirty minutes.

BEEF STUFFING FOR CABBAGE LEAVES *About 8 servings*

1 large head green cabbage
1½ tablespoons butter
1½ tablespoons olive oil
½ cup chopped onion
1 clove garlic, finely minced
1 pound ground chuck
2 cups cooked rice
3 tablespoons finely minced parsley
½ teaspoon thyme
1 teaspoon salt
¼ teaspoon freshly ground black pepper
1 cup bouillon
1 cup tomato sauce
1 bay leaf (optional)
Lemon slices

1. Prepare the cabbage for stuffing as page 368. Preheat oven to moderate (350° F.).

2. In a skillet heat the butter and oil, add the onion and garlic and cook until the onion is transparent. Remove to a platter. Add the meat to the skillet and cook until lightly browned. Return onion and garlic to skillet.

3. Add the rice, parsley, thyme, salt and pepper. Mix well and fill the cabbage leaves with the mixture.

4. Arrange the stuffed leaves in a casserole and add the combined bouillon and tomato sauce and, if desired, the bay leaf. Cover and bake one hour, adding more liquid if necessary.

5. Transfer the cabbage to a warm serving platter, garnish each serving with a lemon slice and sprinkle with additional parsley. Surround with the sauce remaining in the casserole, discarding the bay leaf if used.

HAM AND MUSHROOM STUFFING FOR CABBAGE LEAVES

About 8 servings

1 large head green cabbage
3 tablespoons butter
2 cups chopped mushrooms
2 cups cooked ham, cut into cubes
2 tablespoons chopped chives
¾ cup cooked rice
Freshly ground black pepper to taste
1 cup chicken or beef broth

1. Prepare the cabbage for stuffing as page 368. Preheat oven to moderate (350° F.).

2. In a saucepan heat the butter, add the mushrooms and sauté until wilted.

3. Combine with the remaining ingredients except the chicken broth and stuff the cabbage leaves.

4. Arrange the stuffed leaves in a casserole, add the broth, cover and bake one hour. If necessary, add more liquid. Serve with a stewed tomato glaze (see below).

STEWED TOMATO GLAZE FOR STUFFED CABBAGE:

3 tablespoons butter
½ cup onion, coarsely chopped
¼ cup celery, coarsely chopped
¼ cup green pepper, finely chopped
2½ cups canned tomatoes
Salt and freshly ground black pepper to taste
1½ tablespoons cornstarch
3 tablespoons cold water

1. In a saucepan heat the butter, add the onion, celery and green pepper and cook five minutes.

2. Add the tomatoes and bring to a boil. Reduce the heat and simmer gently fifteen minutes. Season with salt and pepper and thicken with the cornstarch blended with the water.

GEVULDE KOOL (Dutch stuffed cabbage)

4 to 5 servings

1 small head cabbage
¾ pound ground pork
¼ pound ground beef or veal
2 thin slices of bread that have been soaked in water
1 teaspoon salt
Freshly ground black pepper to taste
Nutmeg to taste
2 tablespoons butter

1. Remove eight to ten outer leaves from the cabbage and cook them in boiling salted water ten minutes. Reserve the remaining cabbage for salad or other uses.

2. Drain the cooked cabbage and put a leaf or two on a square of double-folded cheesecloth. Mix the meats with the bread and season with salt, pepper and nutmeg. Put a thin layer on the cabbage and arrange on the cloth.

3. Cover with a leaf or two, add another layer of meat and continue until

(*cont'd*)

the leaves and meat are used, ending with a layer of leaves. Gather the four corners of the cloth and tie. Lower into boiling salted water to cover and simmer, covered, one and one-half hours.

4. Preheat oven to hot (400° F.).

5. Remove the cabbage from the cloth and place in a greased baking dish. Dot with the butter and place in the oven until lightly browned.

GERMAN-STYLE RED CABBAGE *4 servings*

1 small head of red cabbage
2 tart red apples, cored but not peeled
2 tablespoons bacon fat or lard
Salt and freshly ground black pepper to taste
Water
3 tablespoons vinegar
1 teaspoon sugar
1 tablespoon flour

1. Remove the outer leaves of the cabbage and discard. Quarter, core and grate the cabbage into a skillet.

2. Slice the unpeeled apples and add to the cabbage. Add the fat, salt and pepper and bring to a boil with just enough water to cover. Cover, reduce the heat and simmer until tender but still crisp, about fifteen minutes. Drain, reserving the liquid.

3. Mix the vinegar, sugar and flour and stir in the reserved liquid. Cook, stirring, until thickened. Stir into the cabbage.

PIGS' KNUCKLES WITH SAUERKRAUT, PAGE 142.

SPARERIBS WITH KRAUT, PAGE 142.

CHOUCROUTE A L'ALSACIENNE, PAGE 141.

BUTTERED CARROTS

Scrape and peel the carrots; leave whole or cut up, as desired. Cook, covered, in a small amount of boiling salted water until tender. (Cooking time will depend on the size and age of the vegetables.) Drain well and season with salt, freshly ground black pepper and melted butter. Allow one pound of carrots for four servings.

GLAZED CARROTS *4 servings*

Cook four large or eight small carrots as above. Drain, then dry. Mix one-fourth cup sugar with one-half teaspoon ginger and roll the carrots in the mixture. Melt three tablespoons butter in a skillet and add the carrots, turning slowly and often over low heat until the carrots are glazed and a deep, appetizing brown.

CARROTS WITH HERBS *4 servings*

Cook five carrots, sliced, as above. Sauté a small minced onion in two tablespoons butter, add the drained carrots and season with a pinch of dried rosemary, a teaspoon of lemon juice and salt and freshly ground black pepper to taste. Serve sprinkled with chopped parsley.

CAULIFLOWER

Trim the cauliflower, removing outer leaves and part of the core and cutting off any blemishes. Score the core with a knife to facilitate cooking. Place in a kettle of boiling salted water to cover and add one teaspoon of lemon juice. Cover and simmer twenty-five to thirty minutes, or until just tender when tested with a fork. Do not overcook. (The cauliflower may be broken into flowerets and cooked for a shorter time.) Allow one large head for four servings.

CAULIFLOWER WITH ANCHOVY BUTTER

Combine one-half cup melted butter with one-half teaspoon anchovy paste. Blend well and pour over freshly cooked cauliflower.

CAULIFLOWER POLONAISE *4 servings*

Cook a large head of cauliflower until tender and drain. Place in a serving dish and cover lightly with one-half cup fresh bread crumbs that have been browned in two tablespoons butter. Sprinkle with one tablespoon chopped hard-cooked egg and one teaspoon chopped parsley.

MEXICAN-STYLE CAULIFLOWER *4 to 5 servings*

- 1 medium head of cauliflower, separated into flowerets
- 1½ cups tomato sauce
- 2 tablespoons chopped parsley
- ⅛ teaspoon cloves
- ¼ teaspoon cinnamon
- 1 tablespoon capers
- 2 tablespoons chopped olives
- 3 tablespoons grated cheese
- 2 tablespoons fine bread crumbs
- 1 tablespoon olive or salad oil

1. Preheat oven to hot (425° F.).
2. Cook the flowerets, covered, in a small amount of boiling salted water until barely tender. Drain.
3. Mix the tomato sauce, parsley, spices, capers and olives. Pour a little of the sauce into a heatproof baking dish, add cauliflower and cover with remaining sauce.
4. Sprinkle with the cheese, crumbs and oil and bake until brown.

BRAISED CELERY WITH MARROW SAUCE *6 servings*

1 onion, sliced
1 carrot, sliced
6 small hearts celery, or 3 large ones cut in half
Stock or water
Salt and freshly ground black pepper to taste
Marrow sauce

1. Place the onion and carrot slices in a saucepan or Dutch oven and arrange the celery over the top. Add enough stock just to cover and season with salt and pepper. Simmer, tightly covered, until the celery is tender, fifteen minutes or longer.

2. Remove the celery to a hot platter and cover with marrow sauce (see below).

MARROW SAUCE: *About 1½ cups*

1¼ cups Madeira wine
3 tablespoons chopped shallots
½ teaspoon thyme
½ teaspoon peppercorns
1 small bay leaf
1 can beef gravy, about 1¼ cups
2 three-inch marrow bones
1 teaspoon lemon juice
Salt and freshly ground black pepper to taste

1. Boil together until reduced to about one-half cup the wine, shallots, thyme, peppercorns and bay leaf. Add the beef gravy and simmer five minutes. Strain.

2. While the wine mixture is cooking, cover the marrow bones with water and simmer until the marrow at the ends of the bones looks translucent, about ten minutes. Push the marrow out of the bones and chop or cut into rings.

3. Add the marrow, lemon juice, salt and pepper to the wine mixture. Heat to simmering.

CELERY WITH TARRAGON *6 servings*

2 cups celery, cut into thin, matchlike strips about 2 inches long
1 cup strong chicken stock (canned, if desired)
1 teaspoon dried tarragon (or 2 teaspoons fresh tarragon) tied in a cheesecloth bag
Dry white wine
1 tablespoon butter
1 tablespoon flour
Salt and freshly ground black pepper to taste
Chopped fresh tarragon, if available

1. In a saucepan combine the celery, chicken stock and tarragon and cook until the celery is barely tender. Drain, reserving the cooking liquid. Discard the bag of tarragon.

2. Add enough white wine to the cooking liquid to make one cup and bring to a boil. Thoroughly blend together the butter and flour and gradually stir into the liquid. When the sauce is thickened and smooth, season with salt and pepper, add the celery and reheat. Serve sprinkled with fresh tarragon.

CELERY BRAISED IN CONSOMME *4 servings*

4 celery hearts
1 cup consommé
2 tablespoons butter
1 small onion, minced
2 tablespoons flour
4 slices buttered toast
Paprika or toasted almonds

1. Cut off part of the celery leaves. Cook the stalks, covered, in the consommé until tender. Remove the celery and keep warm. Reserve the broth.

2. Heat the butter in a saucepan, add the onion and sauté, stirring, until transparent. Blend in the flour. Gradually add the broth and cook, stirring, until thickened.

3. Place the celery on the toast and cover with sauce. Sprinkle with paprika or toasted almonds.

CREAMED CELERY *4 servings*

2 cups celery stalks, sliced crosswise
Salt and freshly ground black pepper to taste
2 tablespoons butter
1 tablespoon chopped onion (or ½ tablespoon chives, if available)
2 teaspoons flour
½ cup cream
¼ cup chicken broth

1. Place the celery, salt, pepper and butter in a saucepan with a tight-fitting cover. Cover and cook slowly, shaking the pan often, until the celery is almost tender, about fifteen minutes. Add the onion and continue cooking until tender. If the cover does not fit tightly it will be necessary to add a little water, but the celery should be almost dry at the end of the cooking time.

2. Blend in the flour and gradually add the cream and chicken broth. Bring to a boil and cook, stirring, until thickened.

VARIATIONS:

Creamed Celery Amandine: Add one-quarter cup shredded, toasted almonds to the creamed celery.

Scalloped Celery in Cheese Sauce: Prepare the creamed celery and add three-quarters cup grated American cheese to the mixture. Stir until the cheese has melted. Turn into a casserole, sprinkle the top with additional grated cheese or with buttered coarse crumbs and brown under a preheated broiler or in a preheated moderate oven (375° F.).

PUREE OF KNOB CELERY (CELERY ROOT) *4 to 6 servings*

Celery root, a knobby tuber that has a celery-like flavor, is sometimes called celeriac and sometimes celery knob.

4 large knob celery
2 medium potatoes
Chicken broth
Salt and freshly ground black pepper to taste
Whipped cream

(*cont'd*)

1. Peel the knob celery and potatoes. Cut into quarters. Boil the celery and potatoes separately in salted water until tender, about twenty minutes. Do not overcook.

2. Place the celery root in the container of an electric blender. Blend at low speed until smooth, adding enough chicken broth to aid the blending. Or the celery root may be put through a potato ricer.

3. Mash the potatoes and mix with the puréed celery. Season to taste with salt and pepper and fold in enough whipped cream to insure a smooth consistency.

CELERI REMOULADE, PAGE 40.

CELERY ROOT SALAD, PAGE 421.

BOILED PUREED CHESTNUTS *4 servings*

Chestnuts always bring to mind James Thurber's story of his grand-uncle who died of the chestnut blight. He was the only human being ever to do so and the only one who, to the family's embarrassment, needed the attention of a tree surgeon!

That blight has been the cause of more than embarrassment. Because of it we must now rely almost entirely on Italy and, to a lesser extent, Spain and Portugal for chestnuts. Shipments from those countries are at their peak during the winter holidays. Here is one excellent chestnut recipe which is an especially good accompaniment to venison or other game dishes.

1 pound chestnuts
1 teaspoon oil
Water
1 tablespoon vinegar
3 stalks celery
1 small onion, peeled
2 tablespoons butter
Salt to taste
¼ teaspoon or more freshly ground black pepper
2 or more tablespoons hot cream

1. Make a gash in the flat side of each chestnut. Place the nuts in a pan with the oil and shake until coated with the fat. Transfer to a moderate oven (350° F.) and heat until the shells and inner skins can be removed easily.

2. Cook the shelled nuts in boiling water to cover with the vinegar, celery and onion until tender. Drain, discard the celery and onion and purée or mash the chestnuts.

3. Beat in the butter, seasonings and cream.

CORN ON THE COB *6 servings*

One of the commonest faults in cooking corn on the cob is in overcooking it.

Boiling salted water
6 ears corn

1. Bring enough water to the boil to more than cover the corn when it is added to the kettle. Add one tablespoon of salt for each quart of water.

(cont'd)

2. Remove the husks from the corn and neatly break off or trim each end. Drop the corn into the boiling water and return to the boil. Turn off the heat immediately and let the corn stand in the water exactly five minutes. Serve with plenty of butter and a pepper mill.

TOMATOES STUFFED WITH FRESH CORN, PAGE 424.

OKRA WITH CORN, PAGE 385.

BAKED FRESH CORN *6 servings*

3 tablespoons butter
3 tablespoons flour
1½ teaspoons salt
Dash of freshly ground black pepper
1½ cups thin cream
2¼ cups cooked corn cut from the cob (8 to 9 medium ears)
3 beaten eggs
¾ cup buttered crumbs
Paprika

1. Preheat oven to moderate (350° F.).

2. Heat the butter in a saucepan, add the flour and blend with a wire whisk. Season with salt and pepper. Meanwhile, bring the cream to a boil and add all at once to the butter-flour mixture, stirring vigorously with the whisk until the sauce is thickened and smooth. Remove the sauce from the heat and add the corn. Slowly add the beaten eggs, stirring constantly.

3. Pour the mixture into a greased five- to six-cup casserole and top with the crumbs. Sprinkle with paprika and place in a shallow pan of hot water. Bake forty-five to fifty minutes.

ATJAR KETIMUN (cucumbers in turmeric) *8 to 10 servings*

This is a most refreshing accompaniment for curries or other highly condimented dishes. It is a chilled mixture of cucumbers and turmeric, of Indonesian origin.

5 cucumbers
3 tablespoons salt
2 shallots, minced
3 cloves garlic, minced
1 tablespoon fresh ginger, chopped, or 1 teaspoon ground ginger
2 tablespoons peanut oil
2 tablespoons ground Indonesian almonds (optional)
1½ teaspoons turmeric
1 tablespoon sugar
½ cup vinegar
¼ cup water

1. Peel the cucumbers and cut them lengthwise into quarters. Remove and discard the pulpy centers with the seeds. Cut the remaining quarters into bite-sized pieces and salt them heavily with two tablespoons of the salt. Place in the refrigerator for one hour or more.

2. Wash the cucumbers in a bowl of cold water and drain well. Press them in a clean towel to remove excess moisture.

(*cont'd*)

3. Sauté shallots, garlic and ginger in peanut oil until soft. Add the almonds, turmeric, remaining tablespoon of salt and sugar. Stir together, then add vinegar and water. Simmer ten minutes and pour the hot mixture over the cucumbers. Mix well and let stand in refrigerator at least one hour before serving as a side dish for curries.

Note: For sources for foreign ingredients see Chapter 16.

MASTE KHIAR (CUCUMBERS WITH YOGHURT), PAGE 422.

STUFFED EGGPLANT *6 servings*

3 medium eggplants
Boiling water
2 tablespoons olive oil
1 medium onion, chopped
2 cloves garlic, minced
1 green pepper, chopped
1 pound chopped beef
1¼ teaspoons salt
¼ teaspoon freshly ground black pepper
½ teaspoon orégano
½ cup grated Romano cheese
¼ cup dry bread crumbs
2 tablespoons tomato paste (optional)

1. Boil the eggplants in a large kettle of water, covered, for fifteen minutes. Drain and cut in half lengthwise. Carefully remove the pulp, leaving a shell one-half inch thick.

2. Preheat oven to moderate (350° F.).

3. In a skillet heat the oil, add the onion, garlic and green pepper and sauté until just tender.

4. Chop the eggplant pulp and combine with the sautéed mixture. Add remaining ingredients and mix well. Fill the shells with the mixture and place in a greased baking pan. Brush the tops with additional oil and bake about forty-five minutes. Serve with tomato sauce (page 454).

AUBERGINES A LA BOSTON *8 servings*

Aubergines à la Boston is eggplant in one of its most elegant forms. It is in a Gruyère cheese sauce. It is somewhat tedious to prepare but the game is worth the candle.

2 medium eggplants
2½ teaspoons salt
¼ teaspoon freshly ground black pepper
5 tablespoons flour
¼ cup salad or olive oil
3 tablespoons butter
1 cup finely chopped onions
Pinch of cayenne pepper
¾ cup milk
2 tablespoons grated Gruyère cheese (Swiss may be used)
2 tablespoons grated Parmesan cheese
¼ cup heavy cream
1 teaspoon dry mustard
1 cup sliced mushrooms

(cont'd)

1. Cut the unpeeled eggplants in half lengthwise. Cut gashes in the pulp and sprinkle each half with one-half teaspoon salt. Let stand thirty minutes.

2. Squeeze out the water and wipe dry. Mix the pepper and flour and dredge each half in the mixture. Reserve the remaining flour.

3. In a large skillet, heat half the oil, add two eggplant halves, cut side down, and cook slowly, covered, ten minutes. Turn and cook ten minutes longer. Remove from the pan and repeat the process with the remaining oil and eggplant.

4. In a saucepan heat two tablespoons of the butter, add the onion and cook until transparent. With a wire whisk stir in the reserved flour, the remaining salt and the cayenne. Add the milk and cook, stirring, until thickened.

5. Mix the cheeses and add half to the sauce. Blend in three tablespoons of the cream and the mustard. Sauté the mushrooms in the remaining butter and add.

6. Scoop out the eggplant pulp, leaving a shell one-half inch thick. Chop the pulp coarsely and add to the sauce. Mix well and spoon into the shells. Sprinkle the tops with the remaining cheese and broil until brown. Before serving, pour the remaining cream over the top. Serve hot.

EGGPLANT-LAMB CASSEROLE, PAGE 131.

MOUSSAKA A LA GRECQUE, PAGE 130.

MOUSSAKA A LA TURQUE, PAGE 128.

BROILED EGGPLANT *4 servings*

2 cloves garlic, minced
1 teaspoon grated onion
½ teaspoon salt
¼ cup olive oil or melted butter
1 medium eggplant

1. Mix the garlic, onion, salt and oil.

2. Peel the eggplant and cut into one-half-inch slices. Place on a greased baking sheet and brush with the seasoned oil. Broil in a preheated broiler about five inches from the source of heat five minutes, basting once with the seasoned oil.

3. Turn the slices, using a pancake turner, and brush with remaining oil mixture. Broil until tender, about two minutes longer.

4. Serve plain or with tomato sauce (page 454). Garnish with broiled bacon, if desired.

VARIATION:

Easy Eggplant Parmigiana: Broil the eggplant slices as directed. When tender transfer to a baking dish. Spread with tomato sauce and sprinkle generously with grated Parmesan cheese. Top each piece with a thin slice of mozzarella or mild American cheese and broil until lightly browned and bubbly. Serve as a luncheon or supper entrée.

EGGPLANT CASSEROLE *6 to 8 servings*

1 large eggplant
Boiling salted water
¼ cup butter
4 large onions, peeled and sliced
1 or 2 cloves garlic, finely chopped
¾ pound fresh mushrooms
4 large tomatoes, peeled and chopped
2 green peppers, seeded and cut in strips
2 teaspoons salt
1 teaspoon freshly ground black pepper
1 bay leaf
¼ teaspoon basil
¼ teaspoon orégano
⅛ teaspoon powdered cloves
¼ cup buttered bread crumbs

1. Preheat oven to slow (275° F.).

2. Peel the eggplant and cut into one-inch-thick slices. Cover with boiling salted water and simmer ten minutes. Drain well.

3. Melt the butter, add the onions and garlic and sauté until lightly browned. Remove stems from the mushrooms and reserve for another use. Add mushroom caps to the onions and garlic and cook, stirring, an additional five minutes. Add the tomatoes, green peppers, salt, pepper, herbs and spices and simmer ten minutes.

4. Place alternating layers of eggplant and sauce in a buttered two-quart casserole. Cover with buttered crumbs and bake one and one-half hours.

EGGPLANT PARMIGIANA *6 servings*

2 cups olive oil
1 clove garlic, finely minced
1 cup chopped onions
5 cups drained and chopped Italian tomatoes, fresh or canned
½ teaspoon dried basil
Salt and freshly ground black pepper to taste
2 tablespoons flour
1 whole egg, beaten
2 eggplants, peeled and cut into ⅓-inch slices
1 cup grated Parmesan cheese
½ cup diced mozzarella cheese
Butter

1. Heat one-quarter cup of the olive oil in a heavy skillet, add the garlic and onions and sauté until the onion is transparent. Add the tomatoes, basil, salt and pepper and cook, stirring occasionally, thirty minutes.

2. Preheat oven to moderate (350° F.).

3. Combine the flour, egg and one-quarter teaspoon salt. Dip the eggplant slices in the batter and fry in the remaining oil until lightly browned on both sides.

4. Place alternate layers of eggplant, sauce and cheeses in a large casserole. Dot the top with butter and bake thirty minutes.

PASTA WITH EGGPLANT, PAGE 331.

EGGPLANT FRITTERS *4 servings*

1 small eggplant
Water
1 egg, beaten
1 small onion, grated (optional)
½ teaspoon salt
⅛ teaspoon freshly ground black pepper
⅓ cup flour
1 teaspoon baking powder
2 tablespoons milk or tomato sauce, approximately
Fat for deep or shallow frying

1. Peel and cube the eggplant. Place in a saucepan with one-quarter cup water and cook, covered, until tender. Drain well and mash.
2. Stir in the egg, onion, salt and pepper.
3. Mix the flour and baking powder and stir into the eggplant mixture. Add enough milk to make a drop batter.
4. Drop the batter by tablespoonfuls into deep fat heated to 360° F. or into very shallow hot fat and cook until brown on all sides. Drain on absorbent paper.

BRAISED BELGIAN ENDIVE WITH WALNUTS *2 servings*

What a pity that most of us in this country know Belgian endive only as a salad ingredient! Once a taste for cooked endive is acquired the skillet takes precedence over the salad bowl.

4 large heads Belgian endive, halved lengthwise
¼ cup butter
¼ teaspoon dried basil
White pepper to taste
1 cup beef consommé
2 tablespoons chopped walnuts
1 tablespoon butter

1. Place the endive in ice water fifteen minutes to crisp. Dry gently with paper towels.
2. Heat a heavy skillet over medium heat. Add the butter and, when it has melted, sprinkle in the dried basil. Arrange the endive halves in the skillet and season lightly with pepper. Brown lightly, about two minutes on each side. Add one-quarter cup of the consommé and simmer, uncovered, until the endive is tender, twenty to twenty-five minutes. Add more of the consommé as necessary.
3. Brown the walnuts in the tablespoon of butter. Arrange the endive on preheated serving plates, garnish with the walnuts and serve piping hot.

ENDIVE AU GRATIN *6 servings*

18 heads of endive
Boiling water
Salt to taste
6 tablespoons butter
¼ cup flour
2 cups milk
¼ cup grated Gruyère or Swiss cheese
¼ cup grated Parmesan cheese
Dash of cayenne pepper

(*cont'd*)

1. Pour boiling water to a depth of one inch over the endive, add the salt, cover and cook until tender, about twenty minutes. Drain thoroughly and arrange in a shallow greased baking dish. Preheat broiler.

2. Meanwhile, melt the butter in a saucepan, add the flour and stir with a wire whisk until blended. Bring the milk to a boil and add all at once to the butter-flour mixture, stirring vigorously with the whisk until the sauce is thickened and smooth. Remove from the heat and thin out with a little heavy cream, if desired. Add the Gruyère cheese and half the Parmesan and stir until the cheese has melted. Pour over the endive.

3. Sprinkle with the remaining Parmesan cheese and add cayenne to taste. Broil until the sauce is bubbly and lightly browned.

As far as our palates are concerned we have much to learn from the residents of the Middle East. Stuffed grape leaves, hot or cold, are a treasure among foods. The leaves are available in most Greek grocery stores and in many fine food specialty shops. It is also possible to brine fresh grape leaves in the home.

HOW TO BRINE FRESH GRAPE LEAVES

Wash large green grape leaves and arrange them in stacks of thirty. Fold them over and tie with strings. Bring two quarts of water to a boil and add one-half cup salt. When the salt dissolves, dip bundles into the water and remove almost immediately. Pack the bundles tightly in sterilized jars; add a little of the brine and seal. They will be ready a week later and may be kept for months.

STUFFED GRAPE LEAVES *6 servings*

1 quart jar of grape leaves (purchased)
2 pounds ground lean lamb or beef
1 cup raw rice, washed and drained
Freshly ground black pepper to taste
2 teaspoons thyme
1 teaspoon orégano
1 small onion, grated
2 tablespoons butter
3 large onions, sliced
2 quarts canned tomatoes

1. Wash the grape leaves thoroughly in cold water to remove the salt.

2. Mix the meat with the rice, pepper, thyme, orégano and grated onion.

3. In a large kettle heat the butter, add the sliced onions and cook until transparent. Add half the tomatoes and heat.

4. Stuff the grape leaves (not too tightly) with the meat mixture, using about one tablespoon of the mixture for each leaf. Shape each into a neat package and place gently in the hot tomato sauce.

5. Heat the remaining tomatoes and pour over the top. Cover and simmer forty-five minutes to one hour.

COOKED GREENS

All greens should be washed well before cooking.

Most greens, if they are fresh and young, can be cooked in the liquid that clings to the leaves after they are drained. Place the greens in a kettle with a close-fitting lid and simmer until tender, three to ten minutes. Drain well and season with salt to taste. Serve with melted butter and, if desired, a little lemon juice. Edible greens include spinach, beet tops, dandelions, mustard greens, turnip greens and most members of the lettuce family.

If the greens are not particularly young, it is best to cook them until tender in a kettle with an inch or so of lightly salted water. In the South, greens are frequently cooked with salt pork for an hour or more.

BRAISED LEEKS *4 servings*

12 leeks
2 tablespoons butter
1 small white onion, minced
2 cups canned consommé
Salt and freshly ground black pepper to taste

1. Cut the tops off the leeks, leaving one or two inches of leaves. Trim the roots. Use the leek tops in soup. Cut the stalks in half lengthwise and wash thoroughly under running water, holding the leaves apart. Tie the leeks with string.
2. In a skillet, heat the butter, add the onion and sauté until golden brown. Add the leeks, consommé, salt and pepper. Cover and simmer until the leeks are tender, about fifteen minutes. Serve hot on toast, or chill and serve with French dressing.

LEEKS VINAIGRETTE, PAGE 422.

OVEN-BRAISED LETTUCE *6 servings*

6 heads Boston lettuce
Boiling salted water
3 slices bacon
2 tablespoons finely chopped onion
2 tablespoons finely chopped carrot
1 cup beef stock or canned consommé
Salt and freshly ground black pepper to taste
Chopped parsley
Melted butter

1. Preheat oven to moderate (325° F.).
2. Wash the lettuce and cook, covered, in a small amount of boiling salted water two minutes. Drain and press lightly with a dry cloth. Cut each head in half.
3. Line the bottom of a buttered casserole with the bacon and sprinkle with the chopped onion and carrot. Tuck the tops of the lettuce under and place flat on top of the vegetables. Add the stock and sprinkle with salt and pepper.
4. Cover with buttered waxed paper or aluminum foil and bake forty-five minutes.

(cont'd)

5. Transfer the lettuce to a warm serving dish and keep hot. Reduce the liquid in the casserole and pour over the lettuce. Before serving, sprinkle with parsley and melted butter.

STUFFED LETTUCE *4 or 5 servings*

- 1 pound ground meat, or a mixture of meats, such as pork, pork sausage, beef, liver, lamb, or fish
- 1 cup soft bread crumbs
- 1 egg
- 2 tablespoons milk or tomato juice
- ½ teaspoon salt
- ¼ teaspoon thyme
- Onion, garlic, green pepper and parsley to taste
- 1 large head Boston lettuce
- 2 cups beef or chicken broth

1. Mix thoroughly all ingredients except lettuce and broth. Shape into a ball.
2. Remove the stalk from the lettuce, loosen the leaves under running water and drain. Place a few large leaves on a square of white cloth and set the ball of meat mixture on them. Wrap the inner leaves around the ball of meat, and then cover with larger leaves.
3. Wrap the lettuce-covered meat in the cloth and tie securely with string. Place in boiling broth in a deep saucepan, lower heat and simmer, covered, one hour, turning once.
4. Remove the cloth carefully and serve in thick slices with a sauce made by thickening the broth in the pot.

MUSHROOM PIE *4 or 5 servings*

- ⅓ cup butter
- 1 or 2 medium onions, chopped
- 1 pound whole button mushrooms or large mushrooms sliced
- 1 tablespoon flour
- ½ cup light cream
- 1 tablespoon cognac or sherry
- Salt and freshly ground black pepper to taste
- Pastry for a 2-crust 8-inch pie

1. In a skillet heat the butter, add the onion and sauté until transparent.
2. Wipe the mushrooms with a damp cloth. Trim off the ends of the stems. Add to the onions and cook, stirring occasionally, four or five minutes. Stir in the flour, add the cream and bring to a boil, stirring.
3. Stir in the cognac, salt and pepper. Cool while making the pastry.
4. Preheat oven to hot (450° F.).
5. Line a glass pie plate with pastry. Using scissors, trim the edge of the pastry, allowing it to extend over the pan one-quarter inch. Place the trimmings on the remaining dough, pat and then roll to one-eighth-inch thickness. Using a pastry wheel or knife, cut into strips about one-half inch wide.
6. Turn the cooled mushroom mixture into the pastry-lined pan. Moisten the edge and arrange the strips of pastry over the top in lattice fashion, pressing

(*cont'd*)

the ends to the rim of the pie. Stand the pastry rim up inside edge of pan and flute with the fingers. For a glazed top, brush the pastry with milk or egg diluted with a little water.

7. Bake on the lower shelf of the oven until the crust is brown, about twenty minutes.

BROILED MUSHROOM CAPS *3 servings*

- 2 tablespoons fine bread crumbs
- 1 tablespoon chopped parsley
- ¼ clove garlic, minced
- 12 large mushroom caps
- 2 tablespoons cooking oil
- Salt and freshly ground black pepper to taste

1. Mix together the crumbs, parsley and garlic.
2. Brush the mushroom caps with oil and roll in the crumbs. Sprinkle with the salt and pepper.
3. Broil the mushrooms under moderate heat, about five minutes on each side. Sprinkle with more oil, if necessary. Serve as garnish for meats.

PAPRIKA MUSHROOMS *6 servings*

- 3 tablespoons butter
- 1 medium onion, chopped
- ¾ pound mushrooms, sliced
- ½ teaspoon salt
- ⅛ teaspoon freshly ground black pepper
- 1 teaspoon rose paprika
- 1½ tablespoons flour
- ¾ cup sour cream

1. In a skillet heat the butter, add the onion and sauté until golden. Add the mushrooms and cook, stirring, three to four minutes.
2. Stir in the seasonings and flour. Cook five minutes, then remove from the heat. Stir in the sour cream and heat gently. Do not let boil.
3. Serve on toast or in patty shells.

SAUTE OF WELL-SEASONED MUSHROOMS *3 servings*

- 3 tablespoons butter
- ½ pound mushrooms, chopped or sliced
- Salt and freshly ground black pepper to taste
- 1 onion, finely chopped
- 1 clove garlic, crushed
- 1 teaspoon finely chopped parsley

1. In a skillet heat two tablespoons of the butter, add the mushrooms and cook until golden brown. Season with salt and pepper. Remove the mushrooms from the pan.

(cont'd)

2. Add the remaining butter and heat. Add the onion, garlic and parsley and cook, stirring, about two minutes over high heat. Do not let brown.

3. Return the mushrooms to the pan and reheat.

STUFFED MUSHROOMS, PAGES 37, 38.

BOILED OKRA

Choose young, tender pods not more than two and one-half inches long. Wash the okra and cut off the stems without cutting into the pods. Cook, covered, in a small amount of boiling salted water until the okra is tender but not excessively soft, about eight minutes. Drain.

Some Southern cooks insist that a little acid (vinegar or lemon juice) added to the water in which the okra is boiled cuts its mucilaginous quality.

Boiled okra may be dressed with lemon juice and melted butter. Or it may be cooled, marinated in French dressing and served with mayonnaise.

OKRA WITH CORN *6 servings*

- ¼ cup butter
- 2 medium green peppers, seeded and diced
- ½ cup minced scallions, tops included
- 1½ cups corn cut from the cob (about 6 medium ears)
- 1½ cups sliced okra
- ⅔ cup boiling water
- ½ teaspoon salt
- ⅛ teaspoon freshly ground black pepper

1. Heat the butter in a skillet, add the peppers and scallions and sauté two to three minutes.

2. Add the remaining ingredients, cover and simmer until the vegetables are tender, about five minutes. Stir occasionally to prevent burning.

CREOLE OKRA *4 servings*

- 2 tablespoons butter or bacon drippings
- ¼ cup minced onion
- 3 tablespoons minced green pepper
- 1½ cups sliced okra
- 2 cups canned or fresh tomatoes, peeled and chopped
- Pinch of basil
- Salt and freshly ground black pepper to taste

1. Heat the butter, add the onion and green pepper and cook until soft but not brown.

2. Add the okra and sauté over moderate heat about five minutes, stirring constantly.

3. Reduce the heat, add the remaining ingredients and simmer, covered, about twenty minutes. Add a small amount of water if necessary to prevent scorching and give a moist consistency.

FRIED OKRA *6 servings*

3 dozen okra pods
2 eggs, lightly beaten
2 tablespoons milk
¾ teaspoon salt
½ cup fine dry crumbs
6 tablespoons shortening

1. Boil the okra pods until almost tender, about five minutes. Drain.
2. Mix the eggs with the milk and salt. Dip the pods in the crumbs, then in the egg mixture, then again in the crumbs.
3. Heat the shortening in a skillet, add the okra and sauté until brown, turning once.

CHICKEN-OKRA GUMBO, PAGE 210.

ONIONS BAKED IN THEIR SKINS

Wash medium onions, dry and bake in a preheated moderate oven (375° F.) until tender, or about one and one-half hours.

Cut a slice from the root end of each onion and squeeze out the center. Discard the skins. Season with butter, salt and freshly ground black pepper to taste.

ONIONS WITH CREAM AND SHERRY *6 servings*

12 medium onions, sliced
⅔ cup cream
3 tablespoons sherry
½ teaspoon or more salt
Freshly ground black pepper to taste
3 tablespoons butter

1. Boil the onions until tender yet firm, about ten minutes. Drain and turn into a greased baking dish. Preheat oven to moderate (350° F.).
2. Mix the cream, sherry, salt and pepper and pour over the onions. Dot with butter.
3. Cover and bake thirty minutes.

CREAMED ONIONS *6 servings*

Creamed onions are a most appetizing dish and almost as traditional as turkey on many Thanksgiving tables. An interesting variation includes a sprinkling of thyme as noted below.

18 small white onions
3 tablespoons butter
3 tablespoons flour
1½ cups milk
⅓ cup chopped parsley
¼ teaspoon paprika

1. To prevent weeping, cook the onions in their skins until tender, twenty minutes or longer. Drain and peel.
2. In a saucepan melt the butter, add the flour and stir with a wire whisk

(*cont'd*)

until blended. Meanwhile, bring the milk to a boil and add all at once to the butter-flour mixture, stirring vigorously with the whisk until the sauce is smooth and thickened. Add the sauce to the onions and reheat. Sprinkle with the parsley and paprika.

VARIATIONS:

Cheese: Add one-half cup grated sharp Cheddar cheese to the sauce before adding the onions.

Mushrooms: Sauté one-half pound sliced mushrooms in butter and add to the sauce with the onions.

Thyme: Stir one teaspoon or less of thyme into the sauce and omit the paprika.

FRENCH-FRIED ONIONS

Allow one large onion per serving. Cut the onions into one-quarter-inch slices, cover with a mixture of half water and half milk and let stand thirty minutes.

Drain the onions and dry on absorbent paper. Dredge the onions with flour and brown in deep fat heated to 360° F.

Drain on absorbent paper and sprinkle with salt to taste. Serve immediately.

ONIONS AU GRATIN *4 servings*

- 1 pound small whole white onions, or large onions sliced
- 2 tablespoons butter
- 2 tablespoons flour
- ½ cup cream or milk
- Salt and freshly ground black pepper to taste
- ¼ cup chopped parsley or pimento (optional)
- 1 cup coarse bread crumbs, buttered, or ¼ cup grated American or Parmesan cheese

1. Peel the onions and boil them in lightly salted water until just tender. Drain well, reserving one-half cup cooking liquid.
2. Melt the butter in a saucepan, add the flour and blend with a wire whisk. Meanwhile, bring the cream to a boil and add all at once to the butter-flour mixture, while stirring vigorously with the whisk. Add the reserved cooking water, salt, pepper and parsley.
3. Add the onions to the sauce and turn the mixture into a casserole. Sprinkle with buttered crumbs or grated cheese, or a mixture of both.
4. Brown under a preheated broiler or, if the dish has been prepared ahead, bake uncovered in a preheated moderate oven (375° F.) until heated through and brown on top.

VARIATION:

Vegetables au Gratin: Substitute any cooked vegetables such as peas, spinach or celery or a mixture of vegetables for part of the onions.

GLAZED ONIONS *4 servings*

20 small white onions
3 tablespoons butter
1 to 2 teaspoons sugar
¼ teaspoon salt

1. Place the unskinned onions in a saucepan, add one inch boiling water, cover and cook until tender, about twenty minutes. Drain, cool and slip off the skins.

2. Heat the butter in a saucepan or skillet, add the onions, sprinkle with the sugar and salt and cook slowly, shaking the pan or turning the onions until they become a light golden brown.

QUICK ONION KUCHEN *About 4 servings*

2 tablespoons butter
4 large onions, sliced
2 eggs, beaten
1 cup sour cream
¼ teaspoon salt
Freshly ground black pepper to taste
½ teaspoon caraway seeds (optional)
4 slices rye bread
2 to 4 slices bacon, halved

1. Preheat oven to moderate (375° F.).
2. Heat the butter, add the onions and sauté until tender.
3. Mix the eggs, sour cream, salt, pepper and caraway seeds.
4. Place the bread in a shallow greased baking dish and cover with the onions. Pour the sour cream mixture over the onions and place the bacon on top.
5. Bake until the bacon is crisp, about twenty-five minutes. Serve piping hot.

ONIONS STUFFED WITH NUTS *6 servings*

6 large Spanish or Bermuda onions
2 tablespoons butter
1 cup (packed) coarse dry bread crumbs or cooked rice
1¼ cups coarsely chopped Brazil nuts (or filberts, pecans or peanuts)
1 egg, lightly beaten
¼ teaspoon thyme
Salt and freshly ground black pepper to taste
Buttered crumbs

1. Peel the onions without cutting off root ends, so onions will remain whole. Cut a thick slice from the top of each. Boil the onions and the top slices in a large quantity of salted water until just tender, about thirty minutes. Drain and cool. Scoop out the centers to form cups, leaving one-third- to one-half-inch walls. Save the centers and invert the cups to drain.

2. Preheat oven to moderate (375° F.).

3. Chop the top slices and onion centers. In a skillet heat the butter, add the chopped onion and cook until most of the liquid that forms in the skillet evaporates. Add the remaining ingredients except the buttered crumbs and mix well.

(cont'd)

4. Stuff the onions with the mixture and top with the buttered crumbs. Place in a pan and add water barely to cover the bottom. Bake until the crumbs have browned, about twenty to thirty minutes. Serve with tomato, mushroom or cheese sauce.

ONIONS STUFFED WITH MEAT, POULTRY OR FISH

6 servings

- 6 large onions
- ¼ cup butter
- ½ green pepper, chopped
- ½ pound mushrooms, or 1 cup cooked meat, poultry, fish or shellfish
- 1 cup cooked rice, soft bread crumbs or mashed potatoes
- Salt and freshly ground black pepper to taste
- Soy sauce, curry powder or other desired seasoning
- ¼ cup sifted bread crumbs or grated Parmesan cheese

1. Prepare the onions for stuffing, as page 388. Preheat oven to moderate (375° F.).

2. Heat half the butter in a skillet, add the pepper and mushrooms and cook briefly. Add rice, seasonings and chopped onion. Stuff the onion shells with the mixture.

3. Sprinkle the tops with sifted crumbs and dot with bits of the remaining butter.

4. Place in a pan and add water barely to cover the bottom. Bake until the crumbs have browned, about twenty to thirty minutes.

ONIONS STUFFED WITH LIVER

4 servings

- 4 large onions
- 2 strips bacon
- ½ pound liver
- ¼ teaspoon salt
- ⅛ teaspoon freshly ground black pepper
- ½ cup soft bread crumbs, cooked rice or mashed potatoes
- 2 tablespoons grated cheese

1. Prepare the onions for stuffing as page 388. Preheat oven to moderate (375° F.).

2. Fry the bacon in a skillet until crisp. Remove the bacon and crush. Reserve.

3. Skin the liver and remove any veins. Fry in the bacon fat until almost no juice flows when the liver is pierced with a fork. Grind the liver with the reserved centers of the onions. Add the salt, pepper, bacon and bread crumbs and mix.

4. Stuff the onion shells with the mixture and sprinkle with the cheese. Place in a pan and add water barely to cover the bottom. Bake until the tops have browned, about twenty-five minutes. Serve with tomato, Spanish or brown sauce.

(cont'd)

VARIATION:

Liver-Stuffed Peppers: Substitute peppers for onions. Cut two large ones in half lengthwise, or cut a slice from the tops of four small peppers. Remove the seeds and pithy seed parts. Boil in water about six minutes and drain. Stuff each half pepper or small whole pepper with liver stuffing, adding one-quarter cup more soft crumbs and one teaspoon or more grated onion in place of the center portions of the onions. Bake as directed for stuffed onions.

BUTTERED PARSNIPS

Wash and peel parsnips. Leave whole, or slice if desired. Cook in a small amount of boiling salted water, covered, until tender, about twenty-five to thirty minutes for whole parsnips. Drain and serve with salt, freshly ground black pepper and melted butter. One and one-half pounds serves about four.

CANDIED PARSNIPS *6 servings*

6 parsnips, peeled
½ cup brown sugar, firmly packed
1 teaspoon salt
½ cup orange juice
1 teaspoon grated orange rind
⅓ cup butter

1. Boil the parsnips until almost tender, about twenty minutes. Drain and slice.
2. Preheat oven to moderate (375° F.).
3. Arrange the parsnips in layers in a greased casserole, sprinkling the layers with some of the sugar, salt, juice and rind and bits of butter. Bake twenty-five to thirty minutes.

BUTTERED FRESH PEAS

Shell peas just before cooking, wash and place in a small amount of boiling salted water. Add a pinch of sugar if desired. Cover and simmer until just tender (cooking time will depend on the size and age of the peas). Drain and season with salt and melted butter. One pound of peas will yield about one cup shelled.

FRESH PEAS FRENCH STYLE *4 servings*

2 cups shelled peas (about 2 pounds in the shell)
6 tiny white onions, peeled
5 to 6 lettuce leaves, shredded
3 sprigs parsley, tied together
½ teaspoon salt
Pinch of sugar
3 tablespoons butter
¼ cup water
1 teaspoon flour

1. In a saucepan combine the peas, onions, lettuce, parsley, salt, sugar and two tablespoons of the butter. Mix together and add the water.

(*cont'd*)

2. Cover closely and cook over medium heat until all but a little of the moisture evaporates, about thirty minutes.

3. Cream together the remaining butter and the flour. Add to the liquid in the pan and shake the pan in a circular movement to mix it in (stirring with a utensil breaks the peas). When the liquid has thickened and returned to a boil, remove the pan from the heat. Remove the parsley and serve.

HERBED NEW POTATOES WITH FRESH PEAS, PAGE 395.

PUREED GREEN PEAS *6 to 8 servings*

2 packages frozen peas, cooked
¼ teaspoon sugar
3 tablespoons butter
¼ cup flour
½ cup sweet cream
Salt and freshly ground black pepper to taste
¼ cup sour cream

1. Rub well-drained peas through a sieve or purée in a food mill. Add the sugar.

2. In a saucepan melt the butter, blend in the flour and cook, stirring, until lightly browned. Add the pea purée and sweet cream and bring to a boil, stirring constantly.

3. Season with salt and pepper, mix well and stir in the sour cream. Serve with braised sweetbreads (page 171).

PEAS AND CUCUMBERS WITH SOUR CREAM *4 servings*

1½ pounds fresh peas, shelled, or 1 package frozen peas
1 cucumber, peeled, seeded and diced
½ cup sour cream
2 tablespoons minced fresh dill, or 1 tablespoon dried dill

1. Cook the peas in boiling salted water until barely tender. Drain.

2. Cook the cucumber quickly in boiling water about two minutes, taking care not to overcook. The vegetable should remain crisp.

3. Just before serving, combine the cooked peas and cucumber with sour cream and dill in the top of a double boiler. Heat slowly over hot water only until the vegetables are warm.

MEAT-STUFFED GREEN PEPPERS *6 servings*

6 large green peppers
¼ cup olive oil
½ cup chopped onion
1 clove garlic, finely chopped
¾ pound ground veal, beef or pork, or a combination of the three
¾ cup grated Parmesan cheese
2 cups cooked rice
3 tablespoons chopped parsley
Salt and freshly ground black pepper to taste
3 tablespoons red wine (optional)
¾ cup tomato juice or stock

(*cont'd*)

1. Preheat oven to moderate (350° F.).

2. Trim the stem ends from the peppers and carefully remove the seeds and pith.

3. In a large skillet heat the oil, add the onion and garlic and sauté until the onion is transparent. Add the meat and stir until it is no longer red.

4. Stir in the remaining ingredients except the tomato juice and let cool slightly. Stuff the peppers with the mixture.

5. Place the peppers in a greased baking dish and pour the tomato juice around them. Bake until the peppers are tender, thirty to forty minutes. Baste occasionally with the pan liquid, adding more liquid to the pan as necessary.

PEPPERS STUFFED WITH FISH *4 servings*

- 2 large or 4 small green peppers
- 2 tablespoons butter or oil
- 1 small onion, chopped
- ¼ cup finely chopped celery leaves
- 1½ tablespoons flour
- ¾ cup milk or tomato juice
- 1 cup cooked fish
- 1 cup cooked rice
- ½ teaspoon salt
- Dash of Tabasco sauce
- ½ cup fine dry crumbs, buttered

1. Cut large peppers in half lengthwise, or cut a slice from stem ends of small ones. Remove seeds. Boil in salted water until almost tender; drain.

2. Preheat oven to moderate (375° F.).

3. Heat the butter in a saucepan, add the onion and celery leaves and sauté until tender. Blend in the flour, add the milk and cook, stirring, until thickened.

4. Add the fish and rice and season to taste with salt and Tabasco. Pile the mixture into peppers and sprinkle with buttered crumbs.

5. Arrange the peppers in a shallow baking dish, adding water barely to cover the bottom of the dish. Bake until the crumbs are brown, about twenty minutes.

CORN-STUFFED PEPPERS *4 servings*

- 4 small sweet green peppers, or 2 large ones
- 3 tablespoons butter
- 1 medium onion, chopped
- 2 cups corn cut from the cob
- ⅓ cup light cream
- ½ teaspoon salt
- ¾ teaspoon paprika
- Dash of cayenne pepper
- Grated cheese or buttered bread crumbs (optional)

1. Preheat oven to moderate (350° F.).

2. Prepare peppers as for peppers stuffed with fish (above) and parboil three minutes. Drain.

3. In a skillet heat the butter, add the onion and sauté until tender. Add the

(cont'd)

corn and cream and simmer, stirring occasionally, about three minutes. Season with salt, paprika and cayenne.

4. Stuff the peppers with the mixture and sprinkle with cheese. Place in a pan and add water barely to cover the bottom. Bake fifteen minutes.

LIVER-STUFFED PEPPERS, PAGE 390.

VEAL WITH PEPPERS, PAGE 160.

PIMENTOS STUFFED WITH CORN *4 servings*

1¼ cups cooked or canned corn
¾ cup soft bread crumbs
1 tablespoon chili sauce
1 to 2 tablespoons grated onion
3 tablespoons butter, melted
Salt and freshly ground black pepper
4 whole canned pimentos, well drained

1. Preheat oven to hot (450° F.).

2. Mix the corn, crumbs, chili sauce, onion, two tablespoons of the butter, and salt and pepper to taste.

3. Stuff the pimentos with the mixture and place in a shallow buttered baking dish. Top each with one-quarter tablespoon of the remaining butter and bake fifteen minutes.

Note: Any ground meat, poultry or fish may be substituted for the corn.

FRIED PLANTAINS *10 to 12 servings*

3 green plantains
4 cups water
2 tablespoons salt
2 cups melted lard or peanut oil

1. Peel the plantains and cut them into diagonal slices about two inches thick.

2. Combine the plantains with the water and salt and soak them for one hour. Drain and fry for five to seven minutes in fat heated to 350° F.

3. Remove the plantains with a slotted spoon and place on absorbent paper. Reserve the cooking fat.

4. Fold the paper over and mash the plantains with the palm of the hand. Return the plantains to the hot fat and cook five to seven minutes longer, turning once. Drain on absorbent paper and sprinkle with salt.

BAKED POTATOES

Thoroughly wash and dry potatoes. Grease lightly. Place on a rack in a preheated hot oven (425° F.) and bake until tender when tested with a fork, about forty to sixty minutes. When potatoes are done, remove from oven, split open and top with a lump of butter. Season to taste with salt and freshly ground pepper.

HASHED BROWN POTATOES *6 servings*

3 cups chopped cooked potatoes
1½ tablespoons flour
¾ teaspoon salt
½ cup light cream
¼ cup butter
Chopped parsley

1. Mix the potatoes with the flour and salt. Add the cream and blend well.

2. Heat half the butter in a heavy skillet and pour in the potato mixture, spreading evenly. Cook slowly until browned underneath. Invert on a plate, add the remaining butter to the pan and gently slide the potatoes back into the skillet, cooked side up. Brown the underside. Serve garnished with parsley.

DUCHESSE POTATOES *6 servings*

2 pounds (about 6 medium) potatoes
Boiling salted water
3 tablespoons butter
Salt and freshly ground black pepper to taste
¼ teaspoon nutmeg
2 whole eggs
2 egg yolks

1. Peel the potatoes and cut in half. Cook in boiling salted water to cover until soft but still firm.

2. Drain well and put through a food mill or a potato ricer. Beat the potatoes with a wooden spoon until smooth.

3. Add the butter, salt, pepper, nutmeg and eggs which have been lightly beaten with the egg yolks. Whip until fluffy.

Note: The potatoes may be made in advance and kept ready if they are brushed with melted butter to keep a crust from forming. The potatoes may be put through a pastry tube to use as a garnish for a meat or fish dish. They may be shaped decoratively with a pastry tube and browned under a broiler flame. They are also used in making potato croquettes.

MASHED POTATOES—WITH VARIATIONS *4 servings*

4 medium potatoes
Boiling salted water
½ onion
2 tablespoons butter
½ to 1 cup hot milk (may be partly thin cream)
Salt and pepper to taste

1. Peel the potatoes and cut into pieces. Cover with boiling salted water, add the onion, cover and cook until the potatoes are tender but not mushy. Drain the potatoes thoroughly and discard the onion. Return the potatoes to the pan and shake over low heat to dry.

2. Mash the potatoes thoroughly, until no lumps remain, using a potato masher, food mill or electric mixer. Return to the pan and place over low heat.

(*cont'd*)

Beat in the butter and add the milk, little by little, beating constantly with a wood spoon or an electric beater. Season with salt and pepper.

Note: Mashed potatoes may be held a short time over hot water in the top of a double boiler. Excessive heat develops an off-taste.

VARIATIONS:

With Cheese: Spread the mashed potatoes about two inches thick on a buttered heatproof platter. Sprinkle the top generously with grated cheese (Parmesan or a good Swiss) and brush with melted butter. Or spread with whipped cream to which grated cheese has been added. Slide under the broiler to brown.

With Scallions: Omit the onion in cooking the potatoes. Add to the mashed potatoes one-third cup finely minced scallions.

With Mushrooms: Sauté one-half pound sliced mushrooms in two tablespoons butter and add to the mashed potatoes.

Luncheon Dish Potatoes: Grease individual muffin cups, fill with hot mashed potatoes and make a depression in the top of each portion. Drop an egg in each depression. Bake in a preheated moderate oven (375° F.) until the eggs are set.

NEW POTATOES WITH DILL SEED–SOUR CREAM DRESSING

6 servings

2 pounds new potatoes
Boiling salted water
¾ cup sour cream
⅛ teaspoon ground white pepper
½ teaspoon dill seed

1. Scrape the potatoes and place in a saucepan with one-half inch boiling salted water. Cover, return to a boil and cook over medium heat until done, about twenty-five minutes. Shake the pan occasionally. Drain, remove the cover and cook a few minutes to evaporate any excess water.

2. Combine the sour cream, pepper and dill seed and toss lightly with the potatoes.

HERBED NEW POTATOES WITH FRESH PEAS

6 servings

2 pounds new potatoes
Boiling water
1¼ teaspoons salt
1 pound (1 cup shelled) fresh green peas, precooked
½ teaspoon ground basil
⅛ teaspoon freshly ground black pepper
2 tablespoons butter
¼ cup light cream
Fresh parsley for garnish

1. Scrape the potatoes and place in a saucepan with one-half inch boiling water and the salt. Cover and boil until done, about twenty-five minutes. Shake the pan occasionally.

(*cont'd*)

2. Five minutes before the potatoes are completely cooked, add the peas and basil. When the peas are heated through, remove from heat and drain if necessary.

3. Add the pepper, butter and cream and heat a few seconds. Turn into a serving dish and garnish with fresh parsley. Serve immediately.

POTATO PANCAKES *4 servings*

4 medium potatoes
1 medium onion
1 egg, lightly beaten
1 teaspoon salt
¼ teaspoon nutmeg (optional)
¼ teaspoon pepper, preferably white
½ teaspoon baking soda
Butter or bacon fat

1. Wash the potatoes and peel them, then drop them into cold water. Let stand one or two hours or overnight, if desired.

2. Grate the potatoes with a fine grater and press the potatoes to squeeze out excess liquid. Peel and grate the onion into the potatoes and add the egg, seasonings and soda. Mix well.

3. Heat butter in a large skillet and add one spoonful of the mixture for each pancake. They should not be too thick. Cook gently until golden brown on the bottom, turn and brown the other side. Add more butter to the skillet and continue cooking the pancakes in this fashion until all the mixture is used.

POTATOES RISSOLEES *8 servings*

8 large potatoes, peeled
½ cup butter or peanut oil
Salt to taste
Chopped parsley

1. Using a melon ball cutter, scoop rounds from large, firm potatoes. Cook the potato balls in boiling salted water eight to ten minutes. Drain well on a clean towel.

2. In a saucepan heat the butter, add the potatoes and sauté until golden brown. Shake the pan frequently so that the potatoes brown evenly.

3. Sprinkle with salt and chopped parsley and serve.

STUFFED ROASTED POTATOES *6 servings*

6 large baking potatoes
½ pound sausage meat
1 egg
Freshly ground black pepper to taste
1 teaspoon marjoram
2 to 3 tablespoons bread crumbs, approximately
Flour
Paprika

1. Preheat oven to moderate (325° F.).

2. Peel the potatoes, square the ends and trim so that they are of the same

(cont'd)

size and shape. With an apple corer, hollow out the inside, leaving a shell about one-half inch thick.

3. Mix the sausage meat with the egg, pepper and marjoram. Add enough crumbs for the mixture to hold its shape. Stuff the potatoes with the mixture and roll in flour. Dust with paprika.

4. Place in a pan around unstuffed duck or goose and bake until the potatoes are tender, about one hour. Baste with the drippings. Turn the potatoes once after thirty minutes.

ROQUEFORT-CHEESE-STUFFED BAKED POTATOES

6 servings

6 large baking potatoes
½ to ¾ cup sour cream
¼ cup crumbled Roquefort cheese
Salt and freshly ground black pepper to taste
4 green onions with tops, minced
Paprika

1. Preheat oven to hot (425° F.).

2. Thoroughly wash and dry the potatoes. Bake until soft, forty-five to sixty minutes.

3. Cut a slice from the top of each potato and scoop out the potato, being careful not to break the skin. Mash the potato well and beat in the sour cream, Roquefort cheese, salt and pepper. Add more sour cream, if necessary, to make the potatoes light and fluffy. Stir in the green onions.

4. Spoon the potato mixture into the shells, mounding it slightly. Place potatoes on a baking sheet. Dust the tops with paprika and return to the oven until lightly browned.

CHEESE POTATO STICKS

4 servings

4 large potatoes
¼ cup butter
Monosodium glutamate
Onion salt
Paprika
¼ cup grated Parmesan cheese

1. Scrub the potatoes without peeling. Cut into strips slightly larger than for French frying. Soak in ice water thirty minutes, drain and dry.

2. Preheat oven to hot (450° F.).

3. Arrange a single layer of potatoes in a shallow, greased baking pan. Brush with melted butter and sprinkle with monosodium glutamate, onion salt and paprika.

4. Bake twenty to thirty minutes, turning occasionally, until the potatoes are crisp and browned on the outside but still tender on the inside. Sprinkle with Parmesan cheese, shaking the pan so that the potatoes are evenly coated. Serve hot.

BRANDIED SWEET POTATOES *4 servings*

4 medium sweet potatoes
⅔ cup brown sugar, firmly packed
¼ cup water
2 tablespoons butter
¼ cup seedless raisins, or ½ cup chopped apple (optional)
¼ cup cognac

1. Wash the sweet potatoes but do not peel. Boil in water to cover until barely soft, about fifteen minutes. Drain, cool and peel. Slice into a greased casserole.
2. Preheat oven to moderate (350° F.).
3. Bring to a boil the brown sugar, water, butter and raisins. Add the cognac and pour the mixture over the potatoes.
4. Bake, uncovered, thirty minutes, basting several times with the syrup in the casserole.

TANGERINE SWEET POTATO CASSEROLE *6 servings*

2 pounds (about 6 medium) sweet potatoes, cooked and peeled
¼ cup butter, melted
6 tablespoons brown sugar, firmly packed
3 tablespoons dark rum
½ teaspoon salt
4 tangerines
2 tablespoons chopped pecans

1. Preheat oven to moderate (375° F.).
2. Whip together the sweet potatoes, two tablespoons of the butter, four tablespoons of the sugar, the rum and salt.
3. Peel the tangerines, removing the white membrane. Cut the sections from two of the tangerines into halves, removing the seeds. Fold into the sweet potato mixture. Turn into a greased two-quart casserole.
4. Snip the centers of the remaining tangerine sections with scissors and remove the seeds. Arrange the sections on top of the sweet potatoes.
5. Combine the remaining butter, sugar and the pecans. Sprinkle over the top and bake thirty minutes.

PUMPKIN RING *8 servings*

1 three-pound pumpkin
¼ cup butter, melted
¼ cup milk
3 eggs, well beaten
¼ cup fresh bread crumbs
1 tablespoon grated onion
½ teaspoon salt
⅛ teaspoon freshly ground black pepper

1. Cut the pumpkin into halves. Remove the seeds, stringy portion and outside shell. Cut into small pieces. Cover with boiling water and cook until tender,

(*cont'd*)

about twenty minutes. Drain and mash thoroughly, or put through a coarse sieve or food mill.

2. Preheat oven to moderate (350° F.).

3. Add the remaining ingredients to the pumpkin and mix well. Pack the mixture into a buttered one-quart ring mold. Set the mold in a pan of hot water and bake until firm, about forty-five minutes.

4. Turn out on a serving dish and fill the center with buttered peas, tiny whole onions or creamed mushrooms.

BAKED PUMPKIN WITH GINGER *8 servings*

1 three-pound pumpkin
¼ cup butter
¼ cup light brown sugar, firmly packed
3 tablespoons finely chopped preserved ginger
¼ teaspoon salt
⅛ teaspoon freshly ground black pepper

1. Preheat oven to moderate (350° F.).

2. Halve the pumpkin. Remove the seeds and stringy portion. Cut into two-inch diamonds. Pare each piece, then score deeply.

3. Melt the butter in a saucepan. Add the remaining ingredients and cook over low heat, stirring, until the sugar dissolves.

4. Arrange the pumpkin in a single layer in a shallow baking dish. Brush with the sugar mixture and bake, uncovered, until tender, about forty-five minutes, basting frequently.

SCALLIONS WITH CHEESE SAUCE *4 servings*

4 bunches scallions (green onions), trimmed
¾ cup water
1 bouillon cube
2 tablespoons butter
2 tablespoons flour
¼ cup heavy cream
¼ teaspoon salt
Dash of cayenne pepper or Tabasco sauce
¼ cup grated Parmesan cheese, or ½ cup grated American cheese
4 slices toast

1. Cook the scallions, covered, in water with the bouillon cube until just tender. Drain and keep warm. Reserve the liquid.

2. Melt the butter, add the flour and stir with a wire whisk until blended. Meanwhile, bring the reserved liquid and the cream to a boil and add all at once to the butter-flour mixture, stirring vigorously with the whisk. Season with salt and cayenne. Add the cheese and stir until melted.

3. Arrange the scallions on toast and cover with the cheese sauce.

ITALIAN SPINACH *6 servings*

2 pounds spinach, well washed and trimmed
3 tablespoons butter
3 tablespoons olive oil
1 clove garlic, finely chopped
Salt to taste
¼ teaspoon cayenne pepper
Coarsely grated Parmesan cheese

1. Cut the spinach into coarse shreds. Plunge into boiling salted water to cover and parboil thirty seconds. Drain well and place in a baking dish.

2. In a skillet heat the butter and olive oil. Add the garlic, salt and cayenne and cook over low heat five minutes. Combine the oil mixture with the spinach and sprinkle with cheese and additional butter, melted. Brown quickly under a broiler.

SPINACH SALAD, PAGE 417.

SPINACH WITH MUSHROOMS *6 servings*

2 pounds spinach, well washed and trimmed
Salt and freshly ground black pepper to taste
Butter
1 tablespoon chopped onion
1 pound mushrooms, sliced
3½ tablespoons flour
1¼ cups milk

1. Cook the spinach, covered, in a small quantity of boiling salted water until tender. (See cooked greens, page 382.)

2. Drain well, reserving the liquid. Chop the spinach coarsely. Boil down the reserved liquid to one-half cup.

3. Preheat oven to moderate (350° F.).

4. Season the spinach with salt, pepper and melted butter. Pack in buttered custard cups and place in a pan of hot water. Cover with a baking sheet and bake until thoroughly heated, about fifteen minutes.

5. Meanwhile, add one-half teaspoon salt to the onion and mushrooms and cook in two tablespoons butter until lightly browned, stirring constantly. Add the flour and mix well. Add the milk gradually and cook, stirring constantly, until thickened.

6. Add the spinach liquid, correct the seasonings and reheat. Turn the spinach out of the molds and serve with the sauce.

SPINACH RING *4 servings*

1 cup cooked spinach (approximately 1 ten-ounce package frozen spinach or 1½ pounds fresh spinach)
3 tablespoons butter
1 tablespoon chopped onion
3 tablespoons flour
1 cup half-and-half (very light cream)
3 eggs, separated
Salt, freshly ground black pepper and nutmeg

(cont'd)

1. Preheat oven to moderate (325° F.).

2. Drain the cooked spinach very thoroughly. Chop it very fine or put through a purée strainer. Reserve.

3. Melt the butter in a large skillet and sauté the onion until golden. Blend in the flour and slowly add the half-and-half, stirring. Cook, stirring, until smooth and thickened.

4. Reduce the heat to low. Beat the egg yolks and stir a little of the half-and-half mixture into them. Return to the hot mixture and cook one minute, stirring constantly. Add the spinach and season to taste with salt, pepper and nutmeg.

5. Remove the mixture from the heat. Beat the egg whites until stiff and fold into the mixture. Turn into a greased seven-inch ring mold and set the mold in a pan of hot water. Bake until set, or about thirty minutes.

6. Invert on a heated platter, fill with creamed mushrooms and eggs and serve immediately.

DANISH SPINACH RING *4 or 5 servings*

2 pounds spinach, trimmed
¼ cup cream or milk
4 eggs, beaten
½ teaspoon sugar
½ teaspoon salt

1. Wash the spinach well and place in a deep saucepan. Cover and cook, without additional water, until tender, about two minutes. Remove to a wooden bowl and chop. Return to the pot.

2. Add the cream and heat to simmering. Do not boil. Stir a little of the spinach into the eggs, then return this mixture to the pot. Add the sugar and salt.

3. Turn into a greased ring mold. Place on a rack in a pot and surround with a little boiling water. Cover the pot and steam about thirty minutes. Or set in a pan of boiling water and bake in a moderate oven (350° F.) until set, about thirty minutes. The ring is done when a knife inserted in the center comes out clean.

SPINACH AND SOUR CREAM OMELET, PAGE 305.

VIENNESE SPINACH *4 servings*

2 pounds fresh spinach, well washed and trimmed
1 tablespoon butter
1 tablespoon flour
½ cup sour cream
½ teaspoon minced onion
Salt and freshly ground black pepper to taste

1. Cook the spinach, covered, in a small amount of boiling salted water until just tender. Drain thoroughly and chop or put through a food mill.

(cont'd)

2. Melt the butter and blend in the flour. Add the sour cream and onion and cook, stirring constantly, until the mixture thickens.

3. Add the spinach to the mixture and heat gently. Season with salt and pepper to taste.

BAKED ACORN SQUASH WITH BACON *6 servings*

3 acorn squash
6 tablespoons butter
Salt and freshly ground black pepper
3 slices bacon, cut into halves
2 tablespoons brown sugar

1. Preheat oven to moderate (350° F.).
2. Cut the squash in half and spoon out the seeds. Arrange the squash halves, cut side up, on a baking sheet.
3. Drop one tablespoon of butter into the cavity of each half and season to taste with salt and pepper. Add half a slice of bacon to each half and one teaspoon of brown sugar. Bake forty-five minutes, or until the vegetable is tender when tested with a fork.

BAKED BUTTERNUT OR ACORN SQUASH

Preheat oven to hot (400° F.).

Cut butternut squash in half lengthwise, and then across into quarters; or cut acorn squash in half. Remove the seeds and fibers and brush cut surfaces with melted butter.

Place on a baking sheet, cover with foil and bake until almost tender when tested with a knife, about twenty-five minutes. Uncover, brush again with butter, and continue baking until tender and lightly browned.

STUFFED BUTTERNUT SQUASH *4 servings*

2 medium butternut squash
Water
1 cup broken medium-wide noodles
1 pound sausage meat
1½ tablespoons flour
½ cup water or broth
3 tablespoons brown sugar
¼ teaspoon dry mustard
Salt and pepper

1. Preheat oven to moderate (375° F.).
2. Cut each squash in half lengthwise and remove the seeds and fibers. Place, cut side down, in a baking dish, add about one-quarter cup water and bake until just tender, thirty minutes or longer.
3. While squash is baking, cook the noodles according to package directions and drain. Brown sausage meat and pour off excess fat. Mix the flour with the sausage, add the water or broth and heat to boiling. Add the noodles.

(cont'd)

4. Mix the sugar, mustard and salt and pepper to taste. Brush the cut surfaces of the squash halves with sausage fat and sprinkle with half the sugar mixture. Pile the sausage mixture into the squash and sprinkle with the remaining sugar mixture.

5. Return to the oven and bake fifteen minutes.

GLAZED BUTTERNUT SQUASH *4 servings*

1 two-pound butternut squash
½ cup brown sugar, firmly packed
½ teaspoon cinnamon
¼ teaspoon nutmeg or ginger
¼ teaspoon salt
3 tablespoons butter, melted

1. Peel, seed and slice the squash. Place on a rack in a pot with a tight-fitting cover, add water to cover bottom of pot, cover and steam until squash is nearly tender, twelve to fifteen minutes. Drain the squash well.

2. Preheat oven to hot (400° F.).

3. Arrange the squash in one or two layers in a greascd shallow baking dish. Mix sugar, spices and salt and sprinkle over the squash. Drizzle with the melted butter.

4. Bake until the squash is tender and somewhat glazed, fifteen to twenty minutes. For a deeper glaze, broil a few minutes.

MASHED BUTTERNUT SQUASH *4 servings*

1 two-pound butternut squash
2 tablespoons butter
1 to 2 teaspoons brown sugar
¼ teaspoon salt
Milk

1. Peel the squash and cut into slices of even thickness. Remove the seeds.

2. Place the squash slices on a rack in a pot with a tight-fitting cover, add water to cover the bottom of the pot and steam, covered, until tender, fifteen to twenty minutes.

3. Lift the squash to a bowl or drain off the water. Mash or put through a food mill. Add butter, brown sugar, salt and enough milk, if needed, to make mixture soft and fluffy. Reheat before serving.

SCALLOPED SUMMER SQUASH WITH CHEESE *4 to 5 servings*

3 tablespoons butter
1 onion, minced
1 clove garlic, minced
1 green pepper, chopped
4 medium tomatoes, peeled and chopped
½ teaspoon salt
Freshly ground black pepper to taste
1½ pounds summer squash
1 cup grated Parmesan cheese

(cont'd)

1. Heat the butter, add the onion, garlic and green pepper and sauté until tender and lightly browned. Add the tomatoes, salt and pepper and cook, stirring occasionally, while preparing the squash.

2. Peel the squash if the skin is not tender, and cut into slices or cubes. Add one-half cup boiling water, cover tightly and cook until the squash is just tender. Drain well.

3. Preheat oven to moderate (350° F.).

4. Turn half the squash into a deep pie pan or casserole. Cover with half the tomato sauce and half the cheese. Repeat the layers.

5. Bake until the cheese topping is bubbly and beginning to brown. Serve with crisp bacon, if desired.

BROILED TOMATOES WITH OLIVES *6 servings*

6 medium tomatoes
½ cup chopped cooked ham
½ cup chopped green olives
Fresh or dried basil to taste
3 tablespoons olive oil

1. Halve the tomatoes and leave inverted a few minutes to drain. Arrange, cut side up, in a shallow heatproof dish.

2. Mix the ham and olives and place a rounded tablespoon of the mixture on each tomato half. Sprinkle with basil and spoon the oil over the top.

3. Broil about three inches from high broiler heat until the tops are brown, about ten minutes.

STEWED TOMATOES WITH SWEET BASIL *4 servings*

5 large ripe tomatoes
6 tablespoons butter
Salt and freshly ground black pepper to taste
10 fresh leaves of sweet basil, cut in thin strips
2 Holland rusks, crumbled

1. Skin the tomatoes and remove the seeds. Dice the flesh and place in a saucepan. Add the butter, salt and pepper. Cover and stew slowly about five minutes, stirring occasionally.

2. Add the sweet basil and cook ten minutes longer. Add the crumbs and mix well. Cook until the tomatoes are soft. The crumbs will take up the excess liquid.

SAUTEED TOMATOES

Dip firm tomato slices into slightly beaten egg, then into fine cracker crumbs. Sprinkle with salt and pepper.

Brown on both sides in hot melted butter in a heavy skillet, about ten minutes.

DEVILED TOMATOES *4 servings*

4 tomatoes, halved
Salt and freshly ground black pepper to taste
Cayenne pepper to taste
2 tablespoons buttered bread crumbs
2 tablespoons butter
½ teaspoon prepared mustard
Dash of Tabasco sauce
2 teaspoons Worcestershire sauce
1 teaspoon sugar
1½ tablespoons vinegar
1 egg yolk

1. Place the tomato halves on a baking sheet, cut side up. Sprinkle lightly with salt, pepper and cayenne, and then with the buttered crumbs. Set aside.
2. Melt the butter in a very small saucepan. Add the mustard, Tabasco, Worcestershire, sugar, vinegar and a sprinkling of salt. Bring to a boil.
3. Beat the egg yolk and add a little of the vinegar mixture while stirring. Return to the saucepan and cook over low heat until thickened, stirring constantly.
4. Broil the tomatoes until the crumbs are brown and serve with a spoonful of sauce on each half.

GRILLED TOMATOES *6 servings*

3 medium tomatoes
Salt and freshly ground black pepper to taste
Cayenne pepper to taste
Butter
Bread crumbs

1. Cut the tomatoes in half, leaving the skin on. Sprinkle with salt, pepper and cayenne.
2. Dot the tomatoes with a few bits of butter and sprinkle with bread crumbs. Arrange, cut side up, on the rack of a broiling pan and broil under medium heat until the crumbs are brown and the tomatoes are tender.

ANCHOVY-STUFFED BAKED TOMATOES *6 servings*

6 large tomatoes
2 slices crumbled bread, crusts removed
1 seven-ounce can tuna, flaked
6 anchovies, chopped
1 small clove garlic, finely minced
½ teaspoon dry basil
Salt to taste
3 tablespoons dry bread crumbs or grated Parmesan cheese
3 tablespoons butter, melted

1. Preheat oven to moderate (375° F.).
2. Cut the tops from the tomatoes and discard. Scoop out the pulp and mince it, or rub it through a coarse sieve.
3. To the tomato pulp add the bread, tuna, anchovies, garlic and basil. Mix well.
4. Salt the tomato cups lightly and fill them with the mixture.

(cont'd)

5. Toss the crumbs or cheese in the butter until well mixed and sprinkle over the top.

6. Place the tomatoes in an oiled baking dish and bake about twenty minutes.

TOMATOES WITH BRAZIL NUT STUFFING *6 servings*

6 firm tomatoes
3 tablespoons butter
2 tablespoons finely chopped onion
1 cup fresh bread crumbs
1 cup ground Brazil nuts
½ teaspoon salt
⅛ teaspoon freshly ground black pepper
1 tablespoon lemon juice

1. Preheat oven to moderate (350° F.).

2. Remove the upper third of the tomatoes and reserve for another use. Press out the juice and seeds from the tomatoes, leaving the shells intact.

3. In a skillet heat the butter, add the onion and cook over low heat five minutes. Add the remaining ingredients and mix well. Stuff the tomatoes with the mixture.

4. Dot with additional butter and bake until browned, ten to fifteen minutes.

TOMATOES STUFFED WITH SHRIMP *4 servings*

4 large tomatoes
Salt
1 tablespoon butter
1 small onion, minced
1 cup cooked or canned shrimp
¼ cup soft bread crumbs
1 tablespoon chopped parsley or ⅛ teaspoon powdered basil
Freshly ground black pepper
2 tablespoons grated cheese, or buttered, dry, sifted crumbs

1. Preheat oven to moderate (350° F.).

2. Cut the stem ends off the tomatoes, remove the centers, sprinkle with salt and invert to drain.

3. In a skillet heat the butter, add the onion and sauté until tender. Add the shrimp, crumbs, parsley and salt and pepper to taste.

4. Stuff the tomatoes with the mixture and top with cheese. Bake fifteen to twenty minutes.

SICILIAN STUFFED TOMATOES *4 servings*

4 large tomatoes
¼ cup olive oil
1 small onion, chopped
4 anchovies, chopped
1 tablespoon capers
1 tablespoon chopped parsley
⅓ cup dry bread crumbs
1 tablespoon dry white wine
¼ teaspoon salt
Freshly ground black pepper to taste

(cont'd)

1. Preheat oven to moderate (350° F.).

2. Cut the tops from the tomatoes and scoop out the centers. Chop the centers and drain.

3. In a large skillet heat two tablespoons of the olive oil, add the onion and brown lightly. Add the tomato pulp, anchovies, capers, parsley, two tablespoons of the bread crumbs, the wine, salt and pepper and mix.

4. Fill the tomatoes with the stuffing. Mix the remaining crumbs with the remaining oil and spread over the top.

5. Bake in a greased baking dish about twenty minutes.

TOMATOES STUFFED WITH FRESH CORN, PAGE 424.

COLD RICE-STUFFED TOMATOES, PAGE 425.

PAULA'S COLD TOMATOES *6 servings*

- 2 pounds spinach, cooked briefly, thoroughly drained and finely chopped
- ¾ cup olive oil
- ½ cup pine nuts (pignoli)
- 2 medium onions, finely chopped
- 2 cloves garlic, finely chopped
- Salt and freshly ground black pepper to taste
- Monosodium glutamate to taste
- 6 medium tomatoes
- Sugar
- Dried or fresh basil to taste

1. Preheat oven to moderate (350° F.).

2. Drain the spinach thoroughly, then squeeze out the remaining moisture.

3. In a skillet heat one-quarter cup of the oil with the pine nuts and sauté until lightly browned. Add the onions and garlic and cook briefly until the onions are pale golden in color. Remove from the heat.

4. Add the spinach, one-quarter cup of the remaining oil, the salt, pepper and monosodium glutamate.

5. Cut the stem ends from the tomatoes, hollow them out and sprinkle the insides with salt, pepper, a little sugar and a pinch of basil. Stuff the tomatoes with the spinach mixture.

6. Arrange the tomatoes in a baking pan and pour the remaining oil over them. Bake until the tomatoes wrinkle, about fifteen minutes. Chill. At serving time, bring up to room temperature.

STEAMED WHITE TURNIPS

Peel young white turnips and dice in large cubes. Cook in boiling salted water to cover until soft, about thirty minutes.

Drain and toss in a little butter, shaking the pan frequently.

Serve sprinkled with chopped parsley.

TURNIPS IN SOUR CREAM *6 servings*

6 white turnips
Boiling salted water
1 tablespoon caraway seeds
¼ cup sour cream
½ teaspoon dried basil
Paprika
Lemon juice

1. Preheat oven to moderate (350° F.).
2. Cook the turnips in boiling salted water with the caraway seeds ten minutes. Drain and cool.
3. Peel and slice the turnips and place in a buttered casserole. Add the sour cream and basil, cover and bake until tender, about twenty-five minutes.
4. Sprinkle with paprika and a little lemon juice and serve hot.

TURNIP CASSEROLE *4 to 6 servings*

3 cups mashed cooked white or yellow turnips
3 tablespoons butter
4 teaspoons sugar
1½ teaspoons salt
⅛ teaspoon freshly ground black pepper
1¼ cups soft bread crumbs
2 eggs, beaten
1 tablespoon butter, melted

1. Preheat oven to moderate (350° F.).
2. Combine the turnips, butter, sugar, salt, pepper, three-quarters cup of the crumbs and the eggs. Mix well. Turn into a buttered one-quart casserole and top with the remaining crumbs mixed with the melted butter.
3. Bake until the top is browned, about thirty-five minutes.

PUREED RUTABAGAS (YELLOW TURNIPS)

Peel rutabagas and cut into cubes. Cook in boiling salted water to cover until soft, about thirty minutes. Drain well.

Purée by rubbing through a sieve or food mill, or in an electric blender.

Return to the pan and reheat to dry out the surplus water. Add butter and cream and stir until the purée has the consistency of mashed potatoes. Add salt and pepper to taste.

ZUCCHINI, ARMENIAN STYLE *6 servings*

2 pounds zucchini, washed and trimmed
1 cup ground lamb, preferably shoulder, or 1 pound lamb patties
½ cup raw rice
1 small onion, chopped fine
1 tablespoon chopped parsley
½ cup stewed tomatoes
Salt and freshly ground black pepper to taste

1. Peel the zucchini and cut into three-inch lengths. Scoop out the centers. Soak the vegetable in cold salted water about one-half hour. *(cont'd)*

2. Mix the lamb with the rice, onion, parsley, tomatoes, salt and pepper.

3. Drain the zucchini and fill the hollows with the lamb mixture. Arrange in a saucepan and add water to the depth of one inch. The water should not reach more than halfway up the sides of the zucchini.

4. Cover the pan tightly and simmer over low heat until the rice is tender, about one hour. Check from time to time to see that the water has not evaporated.

ZUCCHINI AU BON GOUT *6 servings*

6 small whole zucchini, scrubbed and trimmed
1½ cups peeled, chopped tomatoes
¾ cup bread cubes, cooked in butter until crisp
Salt and freshly ground black pepper to taste
Grated Parmesan cheese

1. Preheat oven to hot (450° F.).

2. Simmer the zucchini in a little water until barely tender, eight to ten minutes. Drain and, when cool, cut in half lengthwise. Scoop out the seeds from each half and invert the halves on paper towels to drain.

3. Arrange the zucchini, cut side up, in a baking dish and fill the cavities with equal parts chopped tomatoes and croutons. Sprinkle with salt, pepper and cheese.

4. Bake until heated through. Just before serving, brown under the broiler.

LES COURGETTES FLORENTINE *6 servings*

3 medium zucchini, washed and trimmed
2 pounds fresh spinach, well washed and trimmed
2 tablespoons butter
2 tablespoons flour
½ cup milk
½ cup cream
Salt and freshly ground black pepper to taste
¼ teaspoon nutmeg
¼ cup grated Gruyère or Parmesan cheese

1. Peel the squash and halve lengthwise. Scoop out the centers. Cook the vegetable in a little salted water until barely tender.

2. Meanwhile, cook the spinach until barely tender. Drain and chop coarsely.

3. Preheat oven to moderate (350° F.).

4. In a saucepan melt the butter, add the flour and stir with a wire whisk until blended. Meanwhile, bring the milk and cream to a boil and add all at once to the butter-flour mixture, stirring vigorously with the whisk until the sauce is thickened and smooth.

5. Remove the sauce from the heat and stir in the remaining ingredients.

(cont'd)

Stir in the chopped spinach and spoon the mixture into the squash halves.

6. Arrange the squash in a baking dish and sprinkle with additional grated Parmesan cheese and melted butter. Bake until heated through. Just before serving, brown quickly under the broiler.

ZUCCHINI AND MUSHROOM CASSEROLE *6 servings*

1 pound zucchini, trimmed and scrubbed
Pinch of fresh chopped or dried dill
1 clove garlic
Boiling salted water
½ pound mushrooms, sliced
3 tablespoons butter
2 tablespoons flour
1 cup sour cream
Buttered bread crumbs

1. Cut the zucchini crosswise into one-inch slices, add the dill and garlic and boiling salted water to cover, and return to a boil. Reduce the heat, cover and simmer gently until the vegetable is tender; do not overcook. Drain, reserving two tablespoons of the cooking liquid. Discard the garlic.

2. Sauté the mushrooms in butter five minutes, stirring occasionally. Stir in the flour and cook two minutes longer. Add the sour cream, zucchini and reserved cooking liquid, stirring constantly. Correct the seasonings and heat thoroughly but do not boil.

3. Transfer the mixture to a casserole and top with buttered bread crumbs. Brown quickly under high broiler heat.

STUFFED ZUCCHINI *6 servings*

1 cup ground ham
½ cup soft bread crumbs
½ teaspoon dry mustard
½ teaspoon salt
⅛ teaspoon freshly ground black pepper
2 tablespoons minced onion
½ cup grated cheese
2 pounds zucchini
¼ cup oil
1 clove garlic, crushed
1½ teaspoons cornstarch
½ cup canned tomato sauce

1. Preheat oven to moderate (350° F.).

2. Combine the ham, crumbs, mustard, salt, pepper, onion and cheese.

3. Wash the zucchini thoroughly and cut it into three-inch lengths. Scoop out the centers with an apple corer, leaving a shell one-quarter inch thick. Stuff with the ham mixture.

4. Place the zucchini in a baking pan and add the oil and garlic. Cover and bake until the squash are tender, forty-five to fifty-five minutes. Remove from the pan.

5. Mix the cornstarch with the tomato sauce and stir into the pan. Cook over low heat until thickened. Skim off the excess fat and spoon the sauce over the zucchini.

ZUCCHINI A LA GRECQUE, PAGE 425.

ZUCCHINI IN A SKILLET *4 servings*

- 2 tablespoons drippings or other fat
- 1 medium onion, sliced
- 1 cup chopped tomatoes, canned or fresh
- ¾ teaspoon salt
- Freshly ground black pepper to taste
- ½ bay leaf
- 3 medium zucchini, cut into 1-inch pieces

1. Heat the fat, add the onion and sauté until transparent. Add the tomatoes, salt, pepper and bay leaf. Simmer five minutes.

2. Add the zucchini to the sauce, cover and simmer until tender, about eight to ten minutes.

RUMANIAN GHIVETCH *6 to 8 servings*

This is a sort of Rumanian vegetable stew that resembles the famed ratatouille of Nice (below). Both of them contain almost everything except the garden fence.

- ½ head of cauliflower, separated into flowerets
- 2 potatoes, peeled and diced
- 2 carrots, sliced thin
- ½ unpeeled eggplant, cubed
- 1 seventeen-ounce can Italian plum tomatoes, drained
- ½ unpeeled yellow squash, sliced thin
- 2 medium onions, quartered
- ½ cup green peas
- ½ cup green beans, cut up
- 1 green or red pepper, seeded and sliced thin
- 2 stalks celery, cut fine
- Salt and freshly ground black pepper to taste
- 1½ cups bouillon
- ⅓ cup olive oil
- 2 cloves garlic, crushed
- ½ tablespoon chopped fresh dill or parsley

1. Preheat oven to moderate (350° F.).

2. Arrange the vegetables in layers in a three- to four-quart ungreased casserole and sprinkle each layer with salt and pepper.

3. Heat together the bouillon, olive oil and garlic. Add to the casserole. Sprinkle the dill over the top.

4. Cover the casserole and bake until all the vegetables are tender, one hour or longer. Serve lukewarm rather than piping hot.

RATATOUILLE NICOISE *5 to 6 servings*

This dish from the Riviera may be eaten hot or cold. Cold, it may serve as an appetizer. Add garlic according to conscience and social engagements.

- ⅓ cup olive oil
- 2 or more cloves garlic, peeled and chopped
- 1 large onion, sliced
- 2 zucchini, well scrubbed
- 1 small eggplant
- 3 tablespoons flour
- 2 green peppers, seeded and cut in strips
- 5 ripe tomatoes, peeled and sliced
- Salt and freshly ground black pepper to taste
- 1 tablespoon capers

(*cont'd*)

1. Heat the oil in a large skillet, add the garlic and onion and sauté until the onion is transparent.

2. Meanwhile, slice the squash and peel and cube the eggplant. Flour the pieces lightly.

3. Add the squash, eggplant and green peppers to the skillet, cover and cook slowly about one hour.

4. Add the tomatoes and simmer, uncovered, until the mixture is thick. Season with salt and pepper. Add capers during last fifteen minutes of cooking. Serve hot or cold.

CHAPTER EIGHT

SALADS, MOUSSES AND SALAD DRESSINGS

SALADS

An old culinary chestnut states that it takes four persons to make a sauce for salads: a spendthrift for oil, a miser for vinegar, a counselor for salt and a madman to stir the ingredients.

Whatever the qualifications for delivering a creditable salad dressing, the salad itself is no better than the greens that go into it. The rules for their preparation are relatively simple. The greens should be garden fresh and totally free from blemish. When brought into the kitchen they should be washed carefully in cold running water, then shaken firmly but gently to remove excess moisture. A little moisture goes a long way in helping to crisp the leaves; a lot of moisture shortens storage life.

The lettuce then should be placed in a clear plastic bag or in sheets of clear plastic. Foil also makes a good wrapping, and a vegetable hydrator aids crispness. The lettuce should be refrigerated until ready for use.

Since warmth can wilt the fragile leaves, salads should be tossed in chilled bowls and served on chilled plates. Salad dressings may be made in advance, although many responsible chefs and home cooks prefer to toss the greens with each dressing ingredient separately at the last moment. There seems to be an advantage in this. When the oil is added first and the greens are tossed, the leaves are individually coated with a film. The lemon juice or vinegar then is added, then the salt and freshly ground black pepper. The coating of oil is said to discourage wilting.

Here is one recommended method for preparing a salad in advance, ready to be tossed at the last minute. Combine the ingredients for salad dressing in the bottom of the salad bowl. Cover the dressing with an inverted saucer or small plate. Add the greens and cover the bowl with clear plastic wrap. Chill. When ready to serve, remove the saucer, toss the greens and serve immediately. Contrary to popular opinion, salad bowls should be washed after each use. The oil becomes rancid otherwise.

ITALIAN TOSSED SALAD *6 servings*

Salt
1 clove garlic, peeled
¼ cup olive oil
1 tablespoon lemon juice or wine vinegar
1 tablespoon mayonnaise
1 teaspoon dry mustard
Freshly ground black pepper
1 head romaine or other lettuce, cut into bite-sized pieces
1 fennel bulb, cut in julienne strips (optional)
⅓ cup walnut meats, coarsely chopped, or 3 anchovy fillets, chopped fine
1 tablespoon capers
2 hard-cooked eggs, sliced
Grated Parmesan cheese (optional)

1. Sprinkle the bottom of a salad bowl with salt and rub with the garlic. Add the oil, lemon juice, mayonnaise, mustard and pepper and stir with a wooden spoon until well blended.

2. Add the romaine, fennel, walnuts, capers and sliced egg and toss lightly with a fork and spoon. If desired, sprinkle with grated Parmesan cheese.

CAESAR SALAD *About 6 servings*

Salt
1 clove garlic, peeled
1 teaspoon dry mustard
1 tablespoon lemon juice
Tabasco sauce to taste
3 tablespoons olive oil
3 bunches romaine
1 tablespoon grated Parmesan cheese
1 can anchovies, drained
1 egg, boiled for sixty seconds
½ cup croutons

1. Sprinkle the bottom of a wooden salad bowl with salt and rub it with the garlic. Add the mustard, lemon juice and Tabasco and stir with a wooden spoon until the salt dissolves.

2. Add the olive oil and stir rapidly until the liquid blends.

3. Wash the romaine well and dry the leaves with a towel. Tear the leaves into bite-sized pieces and add them to the salad bowl. Sprinkle with Parmesan cheese, add the anchovies and break the egg over the salad.

4. Sprinkle with the croutons (bread cubes toasted lightly in olive oil) and mix gently but thoroughly with a wooden fork and spoon.

CHICORY AND FENNEL SALAD *6 servings*

Salt
1 clove garlic, peeled
½ cup olive oil
1 tablespoon wine vinegar
1 tablespoon mayonnaise
Freshly ground black pepper
1 head chicory, cut into bite-sized pieces
1 fennel bulb, cut in small thin strips
2 anchovy fillets, chopped
1 teaspoon capers
1 hard-cooked egg, sliced

(*cont'd*)

1. Sprinkle the bottom of a salad bowl with salt and rub it with the garlic. Add the oil, vinegar, mayonnaise and pepper. Stir with a wooden spoon until well blended.

2. Add the remaining ingredients and toss lightly with a fork and spoon.

WILTED DANDELION GREENS *3 to 4 servings*

1 quart coarsely shredded dandelion greens
4 strips bacon, diced
2 teaspoons sugar
½ teaspoon salt
Dash of freshly ground black pepper
¼ teaspoon dry mustard
3 tablespoons mild vinegar

1. Tough roots or stems should be removed from the greens before shredding them. Place the greens in a large bowl.

2. Cook the bacon until crisp. Add the remaining ingredients to the bacon and fat and heat, stirring, until the sugar has dissolved.

3. Pour the mixture over the dandelion greens and toss well.

VARIATION:

Wilted Lettuce: Prepare as above, substituting for dandelion greens an equal quantity of lettuce cut into bite-sized pieces.

SPINACH SALAD *6 servings*

1 pound raw spinach
Salt
1 clove garlic, peeled
2 tablespoons lemon juice
6 tablespoons olive oil
Freshly ground black pepper
2 hard-cooked eggs, cut into wedges
1 large ripe tomato, cut into wedges
½ red onion, sliced thin

1. Wash the spinach well in several changes of clear water. Using a pair of scissors, cut away the tough stems and discard. Drain the spinach leaves and chill in a damp, clean cloth. Tear into bite-sized pieces.

2. Sprinkle the bottom of a salad bowl with salt and rub with the garlic. Add the lemon juice and olive oil and chill the bowl. When ready to serve, add the spinach and sprinkle with pepper. Garnish with egg and tomato wedges and onion rings and toss lightly with a fork and spoon.

VARIATION:

Spinach and Avocado Salad: Prepare spinach salad as above and toss lightly with the onion rings, the eggs (coarsely chopped), and a large avocado, seeded and diced. Omit the tomato wedges. Serve immediately.

WATERCRESS–ENDIVE SALAD *6 to 8 servings*

1 bunch watercress
6 heads Belgian endive
½ cup olive oil
3 tablespoons wine vinegar
¼ teaspoon salt
Freshly ground black pepper
⅛ teaspoon paprika
1 teaspoon minced onion

1. Before untying the bunch of watercress, cut off part of the stems to make short sprays. Discard the remaining stems. Untie the bunch.
2. Crisp the watercress sprays and endive in ice water about fifteen minutes before using. Dry gently in paper towels.
3. Cut the endive heads in half lengthwise, beginning at the root ends. Cut into bite-sized pieces.
4. Combine the olive oil, vinegar and seasonings. Mix well.
5. Place the endive and watercress in a salad bowl and sprinkle with the salad dressing. Toss lightly.

CABBAGE A LA RUSSE *6 servings*

3 cups finely shredded white cabbage
2¾ teaspoons sugar
Salt and freshly ground black pepper to taste
Cayenne pepper to taste
12 prunes
½ green pepper, cut in strips
1 cup horseradish cream dressing (page 438)

1. Soak the cabbage in ice water for thirty minutes. Drain.
2. Add the sugar and toss. Season with salt, pepper and cayenne and toss again.
3. Plump the prunes in very hot water; remove the pits. Cut in narrow strips and mix thoroughly with the cabbage, adding the green pepper at the same time.
4. Mix with horseradish cream dressing. Chill. Serve in crisp lettuce cups.

COLE SLAW WITH CARAWAY *8 servings*

It is startling how caraway enlivens the flavor of cole slaw.

1 large firm head cabbage
1 small onion, peeled and finely chopped
Salt and freshly ground black pepper
Lemon juice to taste
¾ cup mayonnaise
1 tablespoon caraway seeds

1. Remove the hard core from the cabbage head and discard. Grate or chop the cabbage into fine shreds or cubes and sprinkle with the chopped onion, salt, pepper and lemon juice.
2. Add the mayonnaise and caraway seeds and blend the mixture well with the hands. Adjust the seasonings to taste and chill.

SALADE RUSSE

Salade Russe is a combination of equal parts cooked vegetables—carrots, turnips, celery root, beets and potatoes—cut into small cubes, plus cooked green peas.

The vegetables are marinated lightly in French dressing, drained and then mixed with enough mayonnaise to bind them together.

HONG KONG GARDEN SALAD *6 servings*

2 avocados, peeled and sliced
2½ cups canned bean sprouts, drained
1 pimento, cut in strips
½ cup slivered black olives
Finely chopped chives
½ cup French dressing (page 437)
Lime juice to taste

1. Combine three-quarters of the avocado slices with the remaining ingredients. Mix well and chill.

2. Serve on individual salad plates and garnish with the remaining avocado slices.

ARTICHOKES A LA GRECQUE *3 servings*

3 medium artichokes
3 cups water
Juice of half a lemon, or 2 tablespoons vinegar
½ cup olive oil
½ teaspoon salt
1 branch fennel, minced (optional)
1 stalk celery, minced
Few coriander seeds
4 peppercorns

1. Cut the artichokes into quarters. Remove the prickly choke and trim the pointed ends of the leaves until the leaves are about one inch long.

2. Mix the remaining ingredients in a pan and bring to a boil. Add the artichokes and cook, covered, until tender, fifteen to twenty minutes.

3. Cool the artichokes in the cooking liquid and serve in it.

ASPARAGUS VINAIGRETTE, PAGE 351.

AVOCADO PEAR GRAND DUC *2 servings*

¾ cup crabmeat (one 6-ounce can), picked over well
2 tablespoons mayonnaise
1 tablespoon tomato paste
1 teaspoon caviar
Juice of ½ lemon
Salt and freshly ground black pepper to taste
1 avocado, halved and pitted
1 hard-cooked egg, chopped
1 teaspoon chopped parsley
1 teaspoon chopped tarragon
1 teaspoon chopped chervil

(*cont'd*)

1. Combine all the ingredients except the avocado, egg and herbs. Mix well and stuff the avocado halves with the mixture.

2. Mix together the chopped egg, parsley, tarragon and chervil. Sprinkle the mixture over the stuffed avocado halves. Top each with additional caviar.

GUACAMOLE *About 1 cup*

Salt
1 clove garlic, cut
1 large ripe avocado, pitted
¼ teaspoon chili powder
1 teaspoon lemon juice
2 teaspoons minced onion
Mayonnaise

1. Sprinkle a bowl with a little salt and rub with the garlic. Mash the avocado in the bowl and season with one-quarter teaspoon salt, the chili powder and lemon juice.

2. Stir in the onion. If desired, the fleshy part of ripe tomatoes, diced, may be added; or sliced ripe olives; or crisp, crumbled bacon. Mix well.

3. Cover with a thin layer of mayonnaise to keep the mixture from darkening. Just before serving, stir well. Serve on crisp lettuce as a salad; or serve as an appetizer with tostadas, which may be purchased in cans.

GREEN BEAN SALAD

Dress cooked green beans while still warm with oil, vinegar, salt and freshly ground black pepper. Season with chopped dill or parsley and chopped scallions. Chill.

STUFFED BEETS *6 servings*

6 medium beets, cooked, peeled and chilled
½ cup cider vinegar
¼ cup water
½ cup water in which the beets were cooked
1 teaspoon salt
1 teaspoon sugar
4 hard-cooked eggs, coarsely chopped
2 teaspoons finely chopped chives
3 teaspoons chopped parsley
¾ cup mayonnaise
Freshly ground black pepper to taste

1. Hollow the beets with a melon cutter or sharp spoon, leaving a fairly thin rim. Cover the beet shells with the vinegar, water and beet juice. Add one teaspoon salt and the sugar and chill in the refrigerator one hour or more.

2. Combine the remaining ingredients, adding salt to taste. Stuff the beets with the mixture just before serving and serve on a bed of endive or chicory.

CELERY-BEET SALAD *6 servings*

2 hard-cooked egg yolks
1 raw egg yolk
5 tablespoons olive oil
1½ tablespoons wine vinegar
2 cups diced celery, chilled
Salt and freshly ground black pepper
1 cup sliced, cooked beets, chilled

1. Sieve the hard-cooked yolks into a bowl. Beat in the raw yolk, oil and vinegar.
2. Add the celery, toss and season to taste. Mound the mixture in the center of a round platter and circle with the beets. Additional oil and vinegar may be dribbled over the beets, if desired.

CELERY ROOT SALAD *6 servings*

2 celery roots (knob celery)
1 tablespoon finely chopped onion
½ cup olive oil
3 tablespoons lemon juice
1 tablespoon chopped parsley
Salt and freshly ground black pepper
Mayonnaise

1. Cook the celery roots, covered, in boiling salted water until tender. Cool, peel and slice into thin strips.
2. Combine the onion, oil, lemon juice, parsley, salt and pepper and blend well. Marinate the celery roots in the mixture overnight in the refrigerator. Serve garnished with mayonnaise.

CHINESE CUCUMBERS *3 servings*

2 medium cucumbers
Soy sauce
Vinegar
Salad oil

Slice the unpeeled cucumbers thin. Dress with equal parts of the remaining ingredients and chill thoroughly. Serve with grilled fish, hamburgers or ham steak.

STUFFED CUCUMBERS WITH GREEN MAYONNAISE *8 servings*

4 cucumbers
Water to cover
1 cup cooked green beans, chilled and diced
½ cup cooked green peas
Green mayonnaise (page 439)
Chives, finely minced

1. Cut unpeeled cucumbers in half lengthwise. Simmer in water to cover two minutes, remove from heat and place in ice water five minutes. Drain and

(*cont'd*)

dry thoroughly. When cold, hollow out the centers, leaving a shell one-quarter inch thick.

2. Pile the beans and peas into the cucumber shells, top with green mayonnaise and sprinkle with chopped chives. Serve cold.

MASTE KHIAR (cucumbers with yoghurt) *6 to 8 servings*

Cucumbers and yoghurt are as refreshing as brook water. This is an Indian and Pakistani dish.

4 cucumbers
¼ cup chopped fresh mint
3 eight-ounce containers plain yoghurt
Salt and freshly ground black pepper

1. Peel the cucumbers and cut into small cubes. Add the mint, two containers of the yoghurt and salt and pepper to taste. Mix and chill exactly two hours (the salad reaches its peak of flavor at the end of this time).

2. Drain off the excess water and add the remaining yoghurt. Stir the mixture and chill briefly.

CUCUMBER SALAD *6 servings*

¾ cup sour cream
1 teaspoon chopped onion or chives
½ teaspoon salt
Freshly ground black pepper to taste
2 tablespoons vinegar
2 medium cucumbers, pared and sliced thinly
Lettuce or other greens
Paprika

1. Mix the sour cream, onion, salt, pepper and vinegar. Add the cucumbers and toss lightly.

2. Serve on lettuce or other greens with a garnish of paprika.

Note: This salad, without greens, may also be served as an accompaniment to fish.

LEEKS VINAIGRETTE *4 servings*

1 bunch leeks
1 teaspoon prepared mustard
Salt and freshly ground black pepper
1 teaspoon lemon juice or 1 tablespoon vinegar
¼ cup olive or salad oil

1. Trim the leeks and cut them lengthwise almost but not to the root end. Wash thoroughly, making sure all the sand is removed. Tie leeks together neatly. Drop into boiling salted water and simmer until tender, fifteen to twenty minutes. Drain and cool.

2. Mix together the mustard, salt, pepper and lemon juice. Add the oil gradually, stirring until the ingredients are well blended. Marinate the leeks in the dressing an hour or longer and serve well chilled.

ITALIAN PEPPER SALAD *4 servings*

2 large green peppers
4 tablespoons salad oil
1 tablespoon wine vinegar
Salt and freshly ground black pepper to taste

1. Char the peppers on the outside by holding them on the tines of a fork in a moderately high flame of a gas burner. Turn them until they are black all over. Cool under running water and rub off the outer charred membrane.

2. Halve the peppers, remove and discard the seeds. Slice into thin lengths. Add the oil, vinegar, salt and pepper. Let stand thirty minutes at room temperature before serving.

Note: Italians like this salad best when made with White Caps, a slender, long yellowish-green pepper that becomes available locally in August. It is more tender than familiar types. Serve with broiled steaks.

RADISH SALAD *4 servings*

2 cups radishes
½ cup vinegar
2 teaspoons salt
Olive oil
Freshly ground black pepper
2 tablespoons capers
1 canned chili pepper, cut into strips

1. Slice the radishes and marinate in the vinegar and salt three hours. Drain.

2. Mix the radishes with olive oil to taste, sprinkle with pepper and garnish with the capers and chili pepper.

CHINESE RADISHES *3 servings*

20 radishes, sliced
1 green pepper, slivered
1½ tablespoons soy sauce
2 tablespoons vinegar
1 tablespoon sugar

Combine the ingredients and chill thoroughly. Serve with barbecued dishes.

TOMATO-CUCUMBER SALAD PLATTER *6 servings*

6 tomatoes
2 tablespoons finely chopped fresh basil
3 tablespoons finely chopped parsley
6 tablespoons finely chopped onion
6 cucumbers
⅓ cup wine or tarragon vinegar
⅔ cup olive oil
1 teaspoon salt
1 teaspoon sugar
3 tablespoons capers
Fresh snipped dill

1. Peel tomatoes; cut in halves. Combine basil, parsley and onion. Sprinkle over tomato halves. Chill.

(cont'd)

2. Peel cucumbers; slice. Combine vinegar, olive oil, salt and sugar. Pour over cucumber slices. Chill.

3. To serve, drain cucumber slices. Arrange in center of platter, sprinkle with capers and fresh dill. Arrange tomato halves around edge.

SLICED TOMATO SALAD

Dip large garden-ripe tomatoes in boiling water to loosen skins. Peel. Slice them thick and dress with oil, vinegar, salt, and, if possible, chopped fresh basil. Chill.

TOMATOES STUFFED WITH BASIL *6 servings*

6 ripe tomatoes
Salt
1 cup fresh basil leaves, closely packed
1 clove garlic
⅓ cup olive oil
¾ cup pine nuts (which may be purchased in almost any Italian grocery store)
½ cup freshly grated Parmesan cheese

1. Peel the tomatoes, core them and cut a slight depression in the center for stuffing. Squeeze the tomatoes gently to remove most of the seeds. Turn them upside down on a small layer of salt to drain.

2. Meanwhile, combine the remaining ingredients in the container of an electric blender and blend on low or high speed until well-puréed. Or purée in a mortar and pestle.

3. Salt the tomatoes both inside and out and spoon equal portions of the basil mixture into the center of each. Chill and serve cold.

TOMATOES STUFFED WITH FRESH CORN *4 servings*

4 ripe tomatoes
2 ears corn, cooked
1 tablespoon chopped onion
¼ to ½ green pepper, chopped
1 pimento, chopped (optional)
½ teaspoon salt
⅓ cup garlic French dressing
Dash of Tabasco
Lettuce
Mayonnaise

1. Core and peel the tomatoes. Remove the pulp, leaving a wall about one-third inch thick. Turn the tomato cups upside down to drain. Chop the pulp and drain in a sieve.

2. Cut the corn from the cobs and add the tomato pulp, onion, green pepper, pimento and salt.

3. Season the French dressing with Tabasco to taste and add to the vegetables. Toss all ingredients together and use to fill the tomato cups. Chill well.

4. Serve on lettuce with mayonnaise.

CREAM-CHEESE-STUFFED TOMATOES *6 servings*

6 firm ripe tomatoes
3 three-ounce packages cream cheese, at room temperature
2 ounces Roquefort or Danish blue cheese, at room temperature
1 tablespoon lemon juice
Tabasco sauce to taste

1. Peel the tomatoes and remove the cores. Chill. Cut in half for stuffing.

2. Combine the remaining ingredients and beat with a fork until the cheeses are well blended. Spoon the mixture onto the tomato halves and top with a sprig of parsley. Serve on a bed of lettuce.

Note: If desired, one-half cup chopped cucumber or one tablespoon chopped chives may be substituted for the Roquefort or blue cheese.

COLD RICE-STUFFED TOMATOES *6 servings*

½ cup raw rice
¼ cup oil
1 tablespoon vinegar
Salt and freshly ground black pepper to taste
1 teaspoon minced onion
1 tablespoon minced parsley
6 medium tomatoes
Boston lettuce or romaine

1. Cook the rice according to package directions. When tender and while still hot, add the oil and toss lightly. Add the vinegar, salt, pepper, onion and parsley. Toss lightly and let stand, covered, at room temperature three hours.

2. At serving time, cut the stem ends off the tomatoes. Hollow them out and mix the flesh with the rice. Pile the mixture lightly in the tomatoes and set on a bed of lettuce. If desired, serve with mayonnaise.

ZUCCHINI A LA GRECQUE *6 servings*

4 zucchini, trimmed and scrubbed
1 tablespoon finely chopped parsley
1 tablespoon finely chopped fresh tarragon, or 1 teaspoon dried tarragon
Pinch of thyme
½ teaspoon salt
Freshly ground black pepper
Dash of Tabasco sauce
1 bay leaf
1 tablespoon lemon juice
¼ cup olive oil
1 clove garlic
1 cup water

1. Cut the zucchini into slices one-quarter inch thick. Place with the remaining ingredients in a saucepan. Cover and bring to a boil. Reduce the heat and simmer until the zucchini is tender but firm, eight to ten minutes.

2. Let the mixture cool and refrigerate. Serve as an hors d'oeuvre or as a salad on lettuce leaves.

FRENCH POTATO SALAD *4 to 6 servings*

8 medium potatoes
1 teaspoon salt
½ teaspoon freshly ground black pepper
¼ cup wine vinegar
2 tablespoons consommé
2 tablespoons dry white wine
½ tablespoon dried tarragon leaves
1 tablespoon chopped parsley
½ cup oil

1. Cook the potatoes in boiling salted water until tender but still firm, about thirty minutes.

2. Peel the potatoes while still warm and cut into slices one-quarter inch thick. Place in a salad bowl.

3. In another bowl, combine the salt, pepper, vinegar, consommé and wine. Mix until the salt dissolves. Add the remaining ingredients and mix well. Pour over the potatoes and toss gently but thoroughly, until all the liquid is absorbed. May be served warm or cold.

GERMAN POTATO SALAD WITH SOUR CREAM *4 servings*

1 pound potatoes, boiled (about 4 medium potatoes)
1 teaspoon sugar
½ teaspoon salt
¼ teaspoon dry mustard
⅛ teaspoon freshly ground black pepper
2 tablespoons vinegar
1 cup sour cream
½ cup thinly sliced cucumber (optional)
Paprika

1. Slice potatoes while still warm. If new potatoes are used, slice in their jackets. Old potatoes should be peeled.

2. Mix the sugar, salt, mustard, pepper and vinegar. Add the sour cream and cucumber and mix. Pour over the potatoes and toss lightly until all the potatoes have been coated with dressing. Turn into a serving dish and sprinkle with paprika. Serve warm or cool.

SOUR CREAM POTATO SALAD *4 servings*

¼ cup sour cream
¼ cup mayonnaise
3 cups cooked potatoes, peeled and diced
1 teaspoon chopped onion or chives
Salt and freshly ground black pepper
Celery seed
Lettuce or other greens

1. Mix the sour cream and mayonnaise. Add to the potatoes.

2. Mix in the other ingredients except the greens. When thoroughly and lightly mixed, heap on a bed of the greens.

LENTIL SALAD *6 servings*

- 1 cup lentils
- 1 onion stuck with 2 cloves
- ½ bay leaf
- 3 cups water
- 1 teaspoon salt
- 2½ tablespoons oil
- 1½ tablespoons wine vinegar
- 1 raw onion, minced
- 2 tablespoons minced parsley
- Freshly ground black pepper to taste
- Quartered tomatoes

1. Place the lentils, the onion stuck with cloves and the bay leaf in a saucepan. Add water and salt and simmer until tender, thirty to forty minutes. Drain and discard bay leaf and onion.

2. Add the oil, vinegar and minced raw onion. Let cool to room temperature.

3. At serving time add the parsley and pepper and mix lightly. Garnish with tomatoes.

CHICK PEA SALAD *6 to 8 servings*

- 2 cups cooked or canned chick peas, drained
- ¼ cup chopped pimento
- ½ cup chopped green pepper
- 1 cup chopped celery
- Salt and freshly ground black pepper to taste
- ½ to ¾ cup mayonnaise or salad dressing
- 2 to 3 tablespoons prepared horseradish
- Lettuce

1. Combine the chick peas, pimento, green pepper, celery, salt and pepper and toss lightly. Combine the mayonnaise and horseradish and stir gently into the mixture.

2. Just before serving arrange on crisp lettuce.

DRIED BEAN SALAD *6 servings*

- 2 cups dried white Navy beans (either cooked or canned)
- ¼ cup olive oil
- Juice of 1 lemon
- Salt and freshly ground black pepper to taste
- Chopped parsley, dill and mint
- 4 scallions, chopped
- 1 tomato (optional)
- 1 hard-cooked egg (optional)

1. Drain the beans.

2. Place the oil, lemon juice, salt and pepper in a salad bowl and blend thoroughly.

3. Add the beans and mix well. Scatter chopped parsley, dill and mint and scallions over the beans. If desired, garnish with tomatoes and egg, cut in quarters.

KIDNEY BEAN AND EGG SALAD *6 servings*

2 cups canned kidney beans, drained
½ cup diced celery
¼ cup sweet pickle relish
2 hard-cooked eggs, sliced
1 tablespoon finely chopped onion
French dressing (page 437) to taste
Lettuce

1. Combine the kidney beans, celery, pickle relish, eggs and onion.
2. Pour dressing over the bean mixture and toss lightly. Chill thoroughly and serve on crisp lettuce.

COLD STUFFED GREEN PEPPERS *6 servings*

6 large green peppers
2½ cups cooked rice
2½ cups canned tomatoes, drained
6 green olives, pitted and chopped
2 tablespoons chopped pimento
1 tablespoon capers
¼ cup olive oil
Salt and freshly ground black pepper to taste
¼ cup chicken stock

1. Preheat oven to moderate (375° F.).
2. Remove a slice from the stem end of each pepper. Remove the seeds and membranes inside, being careful not to break the shells.
3. Plunge the peppers and their caps into boiling water to cover. Cover the pan and simmer until the peppers are almost tender, five to eight minutes. Drain.
4. Combine the rice, tomatoes, olives, pimento, capers, half the olive oil, the salt and pepper. Stuff the peppers with the mixture, filling them about three-quarters full. Replace the caps.
5. Arrange the peppers in a shallow baking dish and pour the stock and remaining oil around them. Bake about twenty minutes. Let cool to room temperature.
6. Remove the peppers from the pan and arrange on a bed of crisp salad greens. Surround with stuffed eggs and one and one-half cups each cooked green beans and carrots marinated two hours in French dressing.

COLD RICE WITH SHRIMP *5 servings*

1 cup raw rice
3 scallions
1 bunch chives
½ onion
1½ cups cooked, cleaned shrimp of small size
1 cup mayonnaise
Pinch of ginger
Salt and lemon juice to taste
Lettuce
Sesame seeds, toasted

1. Cook the rice according to package directions and cool.
2. Chop the scallions, chives and onion fine. Add to the cold cooked rice.

(*cont'd*)

Add the shrimp and mayonnaise. Season to taste with the ginger, salt and lemon juice and refrigerate until serving time.

3. Heap on lettuce and garnish with sesame seeds.

COLD RICE RAVIGOTE *5 to 6 servings*

1 cup raw rice
2 small green peppers
3 pimentos, chopped
1 pound cooked crabmeat, picked over and flaked
1 cup mayonnaise
½ teaspoon curry powder
Salt to taste
1 teaspoon lemon juice
Lettuce
Sliced pimentos
Minced chives

1. Cook the rice according to package directions. Cool.
2. Seed and chop the green peppers. Add to the rice. Add the pimentos and crabmeat.
3. Mix the mayonnaise with the curry powder, salt and lemon juice. Mix into the rice and crabmeat mixture and chill. Serve on lettuce garnished with sliced pimentos and chives.

RICE AND MEAT SALAD *2 servings*

⅔ cup cooked rice
⅓ cup leftover meat or poultry, sliced in thin strips
1 tablespoon minced green pepper
1 small white onion, chopped
French dressing (page 437) to taste

1. Combine the rice and meat in a bowl.
2. Add the remaining ingredients and toss lightly and carefully with a fork. Be careful not to crush the rice. Serve in lettuce cups if desired.

COLD RICE SALAD *6 servings*

1 cup raw rice
¼ cup salad oil
1 tablespoon wine vinegar
Salt and freshly ground black pepper to taste
6 water chestnuts, sliced
¼ cup minced parsley
¼ cup minced onion
Lettuce
Black olives
Mayonnaise

1. Cook the rice until tender.
2. Add the oil, vinegar, salt and pepper and cool. Add the water chestnuts, parsley and onion and mix gently. Add more oil and vinegar to taste.
3. Arrange on lettuce and garnish with black olives. Serve with mayonnaise.

CRAB LOUIS *4 servings*

1 cup mayonnaise
⅓ cup French dressing (page 437)
¼ cup chili sauce
2 tablespoons minced chives
2 tablespoons minced green olives
1 teaspoon horseradish
1 teaspoon Worcestershire sauce
Salt and freshly ground black pepper
Chilled lettuce, torn into bite-sized pieces
3 cups cooked crabmeat, flaked
4 hard-cooked eggs, quartered
Quartered tomatoes
Capers

1. Combine the mayonnaise, French dressing, chili sauce, chives, olives and seasonings. Chill.

2. Arrange the lettuce in a shallow, chilled salad bowl and mound the crabmeat on top. Spoon the dressing on top and garnish with hard-cooked egg, tomato quarters, and capers.

CHICKEN SALAD A LA CHINOISE *6 servings*

3 cups diced cooked chicken
1 cup canned bean sprouts, drained
2 stalks celery, diced
½ teaspoon salt
Freshly ground black pepper
French dressing (page 437)
¾ cup mayonnaise
Dash of soy sauce
Lettuce
Olives

1. Combine the chicken with the bean sprouts, celery, salt and pepper. Moisten with French dressing. Chill in the refrigerator.

2. Flavor the mayonnaise with the soy sauce. Mix with the chicken mixture.

3. Pile into crisp lettuce cups. Garnish with olives.

FRUIT SECTIONS WITH ROSEMARY *6 servings*

3 grapefruit
3 oranges
Ground rosemary

1. Using a sharp paring knife, peel the skin and outer pulp from the grapefruit and oranges. Slice from the outside toward the center, along each side of the membranes, to remove whole fruit sections. Discard the seeds.

2. Arrange alternate sections of grapefruit and orange in a windmill effect and sprinkle with rosemary. Chill.

CANTALOUPE FARMER'S STYLE *4 to 6 servings*

2 cantaloupes
French dressing (page 437)
1 large or 2 small cucumbers
Salt
½ cup sour cream
Lettuce leaves
Hard-cooked egg slices (optional)

(*cont'd*)

1. Cut the cantaloupes in half, peel and remove the seeds. Dice the meat and marinate in French dressing for half an hour in a cool place.

2. Peel and finely slice the cucumber and sprinkle with salt. Let stand one hour.

3. Drain the cantaloupe and cucumber thoroughly and mix with the sour cream. Arrange on crisp lettuce leaves and garnish with hard-cooked eggs.

MOUSSES AND ASPICS

QUICK ASPIC *About 1 quart*

3 cups chicken broth
1 cup tomato juice
4 envelopes unflavored gelatin
Salt and freshly ground black pepper
1 teaspoon sugar
2 egg shells, crushed
2 egg whites, lightly beaten
2 tablespoons cognac

1. In a saucepan combine the chicken broth with the tomato juice, gelatin, salt, pepper, sugar, egg shells and egg whites and heat slowly, stirring constantly, until the mixture boils up in the pan.

2. Remove the pan from the heat and stir in the cognac.

3. Strain the mixture through a sieve lined with a flannel cloth that has been rinsed in cold water and wrung out. If the aspic starts to set or becomes too firm it may be reheated, then brought to any desired temperature.

VARIATION:

Quick Fish Aspic: Substitute fish stock for chicken broth and proceed as above.

AVOCADO ASPIC RING *6 to 8 servings*

2 envelopes unflavored gelatin
½ cup cold water
3 cups seasoned chicken broth or consommé
2 avocados, halved
Lemon juice
1 to 2 teaspoons grated onion
1 cup diced celery, cucumber, cooked chicken or shrimp

1. Soften the gelatin in cold water. Heat, stirring, until dissolved. Add the broth and cool to room temperature.

2. Remove the seeds from the avocados, peel and cut into thin rings. Cut these in half to form crescents. Sprinkle with lemon juice.

3. Cover the bottom of a ring mold with gelatin and chill until set. Arrange

(*cont'd*)

the crescents on top and cover with a layer of soft gelatin. Chill. Arrange more crescents around the sides and add a thin layer of gelatin to hold them in place.

4. Mix the remaining gelatin with the onion, celery and remaining avocado, chopped. Turn into the garnished mold and chill until firm. Unmold.

AVOCADO-WATERCRESS RING *6 servings*

An avocado-watercress ring filled with shrimp and mushrooms is an ideal luncheon dish for summer.

6 ounces cream cheese
3 cups mashed avocado (about 3 avocados)
⅓ cup lime juice
¾ teaspoon salt
1 cup milk
1 tablespoon unflavored gelatin
¼ cup cold water
1 bunch watercress
1 pound shrimp, cooked, peeled and deveined
1 cup sliced raw mushrooms
French dressing (page 437) to taste
½ teaspoon crushed tarragon

1. Let the cream cheese soften at room temperature in a mixing bowl.
2. Combine the mashed avocado, lime juice and salt.
3. Mash the cheese with the back of a wooden spoon. Gradually blend in the avocado mixture and milk.
4. Soften the gelatin in water five minutes, then dissolve it over boiling water.
5. Meanwhile, chop the watercress stems into one-eighth-inch lengths. Add to the avocado mixture. Save the leaves for garnish.
6. Add the dissolved gelatin to the avocado mixture. Mix well. Turn into an oiled six-cup ring mold. Chill.
7. Combine the shrimp and mushrooms with the French dressing and tarragon. Mix well and chill.
8. To serve, unmold the avocado ring on a serving plate. Fill the center with marinated shrimp and mushrooms and garnish with watercress.

CHICKEN MOUSSE *8 to 10 servings*

6 tablespoons butter
¾ cup soft bread crumbs
½ teaspoon salt
¼ teaspoon nutmeg
2 cups light cream
3 cups cooked chicken, chopped
6 eggs, well beaten
½ cup dry sherry
3 large avocados, peeled and cubed
1½ cups mayonnaise

1. Preheat oven to moderate (350° F.).
2. Melt the butter in a large double boiler and add the crumbs, salt and nutmeg. Add the cream and cook over hot water ten minutes, stirring often. Mix the chicken, eggs and sherry and add to the sauce.

(cont'd)

3. Pour the mixture into a buttered two-quart mold, cover and bake until firm, or about fifty minutes. Cool and chill.

4. Toss the avocados with the mayonnaise. Unmold the mousse and surround with the avocado mixture.

COLD CRABMEAT MOUSSE *8 servings*

- ¼ cup butter
- ¼ cup flour
- 1 cup hot canned chicken broth
- 1 cup hot milk
- 2 envelopes gelatin
- ¼ cup water
- 2 six-and-one-half-ounce cans crabmeat, flaked and picked over well
- 1 tablespoon lemon juice
- 1 tablespoon chopped parsley
- ½ teaspoon paprika
- ½ teaspoon dry mustard
- Salt and freshly ground black pepper to taste
- 2 cups heavy cream, whipped

1. In a saucepan melt the butter, add the flour and stir with a wire whisk until blended. Meanwhile, bring the broth and milk to a boil and add all at once to the butter-flour mixture, stirring vigorously with the whisk.

2. Soften the gelatin in the cold water and add to the sauce. Cook, stirring, until the gelatin has dissolved.

3. Add all the remaining ingredients except the cream and refrigerate until the mixture starts to set.

4. Meanwhile, tie a band of waxed paper or aluminum foil around the top of a straight-sided bowl of six-cup capacity. Let the band rise two inches above the bowl.

5. Fold the cream into the partly set mixture. Turn into the prepared dish (the mixture may come to the level of the paper) and refrigerate until set.

6. To serve, remove the paper to expose the top of the soufflé. Garnish the top as desired with lobster claws, green pepper rings, etc.

COLD LOBSTER MOUSSE *6 to 8 servings*

- 1 tablespoon unflavored gelatin
- ¼ cup cold water
- ¾ cup mayonnaise
- 3 tablespoons lemon juice
- 1 cup minced celery
- ¼ small onion, grated
- 1½ cups minced, cooked lobster meat
- ⅓ cup heavy cream, whipped
- Salt and freshly ground black pepper to taste

1. Soften the gelatin in cold water, place over simmering water and stir until dissolved.

2. Add the gelatin to the mayonnaise, while stirring. Add the lemon juice.

3. Grind the celery, onion and lobster meat in a food chopper, using a fine

(*cont'd*)

1. *Fish mold of copper* has many uses other than ornamenting a wall. It is elegant for aspics.

2. To make a salmon mousse in aspic, chill mold on cracked ice; spoon in liquid aspic and swirl around to coat sides. Chill to set.

3. Use pimento strips dipped in aspic to outline fins; crescents of hard-cooked egg white dipped in aspic to simulate scales.

4. Fill center of mold with salmon mousse after the cutouts jell. Push the mousse through a pastry tube. Do not cover the "fins."

5. Add aspic after chilling till mousse jells thoroughly. Additional aspic will coat top and fill edges. Chill; unmold.

knife. Fold the vegetables and fish into the mayonnaise mixture. Fold in the whipped cream and season with salt and pepper.

4. Turn the mixture into a one-quart loaf pan or mold and chill until firm. Turn out and garnish with sliced cucumbers, tomatoes and lettuce or watercress.

SALMON MOUSSE WITH SOUR-CREAM DILL SAUCE

8 servings

- 1 envelope unflavored gelatin
- ¼ cup cold water
- ½ cup boiling water
- ½ cup mayonnaise
- 1 tablespoon lemon juice
- 1 tablespoon grated onion
- ½ teaspoon Tabasco sauce
- ¼ teaspoon paprika
- 1 teaspoon salt
- 2 cups canned salmon, drained and finely chopped
- 1 tablespoon chopped capers
- ½ cup heavy cream
- 3 cups cottage cheese
- Sour-cream dill sauce (page 453)

1. Soften the gelatin in the cold water, add the boiling water and stir until the gelatin has dissolved. Cool.

2. Add the mayonnaise, lemon juice, onion, Tabasco, paprika and salt and mix well. Chill to the consistency of unbeaten egg white.

3. Add the salmon and capers and beat well. Whip the cream, fold into the salmon mixture and turn into a two-quart oiled fish mold. Add the cheese to fill the mold. Chill until set.

4. Unmold on a serving platter and garnish with watercress, lemon slices and salmon roe. Serve with sour-cream dill sauce.

SALMON MOUSSE IN ASPIC

6 to 8 servings

- Quick aspic (page 431)
- Thin strips of pimento
- Thin crescents of hard-cooked egg whites
- 1 slice of truffle or black olive
- 2 cups canned salmon, drained and flaked (fresh cooked salmon may be used)
- Lemon juice to taste
- Salt and cayenne pepper to taste
- 1 envelope unflavored gelatin
- ½ cup cold water
- 3 tablespoons mayonnaise
- 3 tablespoons whipped cream

1. Place a one-quart fish mold on a bed of cracked ice and add a thin layer of chilled but still-liquid aspic. Swirl it around to coat the bottom and sides of the mold. Chill until set.

2. Outline the fins, tail and mouth with thin strips of pimento dipped in

(cont'd)

aspic and line the scales down the back with tiny, thin crescents of egg white dipped in aspic. Use a round slice of truffle or black olive for the eye.

3. Sprinkle chilled but still-liquid aspic over each piece of garnish to set into place and chill until firm.

4. Add a little additional chilled but still-liquid aspic to the mold and swirl it around to further coat the bottom and sides. Chill until firm.

5. Mash the salmon flakes and force the fish through a fine sieve.

6. Season the salmon with lemon juice, salt and cayenne pepper.

7. Soften the gelatin in the cold water, then dissolve it over hot water. Add the dissolved gelatin to the salmon mixture and mix thoroughly.

8. Fold in the mayonnaise and whipped cream. Chill slightly.

9. Using a pastry bag fitted with a large round tube, add the mousse to the mold, keeping it away from the sides. Chill in the refrigerator until the mousse is set.

10. Pour chilled but still-liquid aspic to cover over the mousse and chill until firm.

11. Quickly dip the mold in hot water three times. Wipe the base dry and invert the mold on a large glass or silver platter. Preferably, the platter should be coated with a thin layer of aspic and chilled before the fish is unmolded.

12. Garnish the platter with stuffed hard-cooked eggs.

TURKEY MOUSSE *6 to 8 servings*

2 envelopes unflavored gelatin
2 cups milk
¼ cup butter
3 tablespoons flour
½ teaspoon salt
Freshly ground black pepper to taste
1 cup thin mayonnaise (thinned with a little cream)
3 cups diced cooked turkey
1 cup diced celery
½ cup heavy cream, whipped
Cranberry sauce
Orange sections
Lettuce

1. Soften the gelatin in one-half cup of cold milk.

2. In a saucepan melt the butter, add the flour and stir with a wire whisk until blended. Meanwhile bring the remaining milk to a boil and add all at once to the butter-flour mixture, stirring vigorously with the whisk until the sauce is thickened and smooth. Season with salt and pepper.

3. Add the gelatin to the sauce and stir until dissolved. Add the mayonnaise and cool.

4. Add the turkey, celery and cream. Pour the mixture into a mold that has been rinsed in cold water. Chill until firm.

5. Unmold on a plate and garnish with slices of cranberry sauce and orange sections. Serve on beds of lettuce and top with additional mayonnaise.

SALAD DRESSINGS

FRENCH DRESSING *½ cup*

- 2 tablespoons cider vinegar, wine vinegar or lemon juice
- 6 tablespoons olive oil or other salad oil
- ¾ teaspoon salt
- Freshly ground black pepper
- 1 clove garlic, finely minced (optional)

Combine all the ingredients, blend thoroughly and chill.

ANCHOVY FRENCH DRESSING *About ¾ cup*

- 1 small can flat anchovy fillets, drained
- ½ cup olive oil
- 1 tablespoon lemon juice or to taste

Mash the anchovy fillets with a fork. Combine with the olive oil and lemon juice and mix until thoroughly blended.

FINES HERBES DRESSING *About 3 cups*

- ½ teaspoon dry mustard
- 2 teaspoons salt
- 1 teaspoon paprika
- ½ teaspoon freshly ground black pepper
- ½ teaspoon dried basil, finely chopped
- 2 cups salad oil
- ½ cup tarragon vinegar
- ¼ cup dry red wine
- ½ cup fresh parsley, chopped
- 2 cloves garlic, peeled and split

Combine all ingredients and shake well. Discard garlic before using. Use over salad greens, sliced tomatoes, cucumbers, etc.

HERB SAUCE *About ⅔ cup*

- ½ cup salad oil
- 3 tablespoons wine vinegar
- ⅛ teaspoon powdered thyme
- ⅛ teaspoon powdered marjoram
- ¼ teaspoon dried basil leaves, or 4 fresh basil leaves, chopped
- 1 tablespoon finely chopped onion
- 1 tablespoon water
- ½ teaspoon salt
- 1 tablespoon finely chopped parsley

Combine all the ingredients in a jar with a tight-fitting lid. Shake vigorously. Let stand ten minutes.

Serve over crisp salad greens.

HORSERADISH CREAM DRESSING *About 1¾ cups*

¾ cup heavy cream
¼ cup wine vinegar
Salt and white pepper to taste
3 tablespoons grated horseradish
1½ teaspoons finely chopped shallot or onion

1. Beat the cream until very stiff, then gradually beat in the wine vinegar.
2. When the mixture is the consistency of mayonnaise, add the salt and pepper. Fold in the horseradish and shallot.

NORTH AFRICAN LEMON DRESSING *About 1 cup*

Grated peel of 2 lemons
¼ cup lemon juice
1½ teaspoons salt
⅛ teaspoon red pepper or Tabasco sauce
2 cloves garlic, minced
⅔ to ¾ cup olive oil
½ teaspoon ground coriander
½ teaspoon ground cumin
½ teaspoon dry mustard
1 teaspoon sugar
½ teaspoon paprika

Combine all the ingredients in a jar with a tight-fitting lid. Refrigerate and shake well before using. Serve with fruit salads and cottage cheese, or with a salad made by alternating slices of tomatoes, sweet onions, cucumbers and sweet pepper rings.

LIME-MINT DRESSING *About 1 cup*

¾ cup olive oil or good-quality vegetable salad oil
¼ cup lime juice
1 teaspoon salt
¼ teaspoon white pepper
1 teaspoon finely chopped parsley
1 teaspoon finely chopped mint
1 teaspoon finely chopped chives
1 teaspoon prepared mustard

Mix all the ingredients, place a cube of ice in the dressing and beat until the mixture thickens to the consistency of medium cream sauce.

Use for tossed greens or coleslaw.

MAYONNAISE *About 2 cups*

2 egg yolks
1 teaspoon dry mustard
½ teaspoon salt
Pinch of cayenne pepper
¼ cup wine vinegar or lemon juice
1 cup olive oil
1 cup salad oil

1. Beat the yolks until thick and lemon-colored. Add the seasonings and half the vinegar. Beat well.

(*cont'd*)

2. Mix the oils and add, while beating, drop by drop at first and then in a gradually increasing amount as the mixture thickens. Do not overbeat.

3. Slowly add the remaining vinegar and beat well. Chill.

GREEN MAYONNAISE *About 1¼ cups*

10 sprigs fresh watercress
10 leaves spinach
10 stalks fresh tarragon or chervil
1 teaspoon lemon juice (optional)
1 cup mayonnaise

Simmer the washed greens in unsalted water two minutes. Drain and rinse in cold water. Press out the water and pound in a mortar until the greens are reduced to a pulp. Add the lemon juice and combine the mixture with the mayonnaise. Use with vegetable or fish salads.

ROQUEFORT CREAM MAYONNAISE *About 2 cups*

½ cup heavy cream
2 tablespoons Roquefort cheese
1 cup mayonnaise

Whip the cream until stiff. Crumble the cheese. Fold the whipped cream and cheese into the mayonnaise. Serve over greens or lettuce hearts.

MONA LISA DRESSING *About ½ cup*

½ teaspoon paprika
½ teaspoon horseradish
½ teaspoon English mustard
½ cup mayonnaise
1 tablespoon heavy cream

Add the paprika, horseradish and mustard to the mayonnaise and fold in the cream. If a lighter dressing is desired, the cream may be whipped.

Use for hearts of lettuce or romaine.

NICOISE SAUCE *About 2¾ cups*

½ cup tomato purée
1 green pepper, seeded and finely chopped
1 teaspoon chopped fresh tarragon and chives, mixed
2 cups mayonnaise

1. The purée should be about as thick as the mayonnaise. Cook, if necessary, to desired thickness and chill.

2. Combine the tomato purée with the green pepper, tarragon and chives. Fold into the mayonnaise and mix well.

RUSSIAN DRESSING A L'AUDELAN *About 2 cups*

1½ cups mayonnaise
½ cup finely chopped, cooked beets
1 tablespoon prepared horseradish or black caviar
Salt to taste

1. Mix the mayonnaise and the beets until the dressing is an even pink hue. If horseradish is used, mix it in thoroughly. Caviar should be folded in carefully but thoroughly. Add the salt.

2. Refrigerate the dressing at least two hours before serving.

SAUCE VERDE *About 1 cup*

Many nations have a green sauce specialty. This is the French.

1 cup parsley leaves, washed and drained
¼ cup capers in vinegar, drained
½ small can anchovy fillets
1 to 2 cloves garlic
1 tablespoon chopped onion
2 small sour gherkins
1 small boiled potato or a slice of white bread softened in water and drained
½ cup olive oil
Salt and freshly ground black pepper to taste
1 tablespoon wine vinegar

1. Chop together very fine the parsley, capers, anchovies, garlic, onion and pickles. Add the potato and grind with a pestle until a coarse, dry green paste is formed.

2. Place the mixture in a bowl and work in just enough of the olive oil (about one teaspoon) to form a slightly thinner but smooth paste. Add salt and pepper.

3. Continue to add the remaining oil slowly, mixing constantly, until the paste is of a smooth consistency. Add the vinegar and mix thoroughly.

SALSA VERDE *About ¾ cup*

And the Italian.

3 tablespoons vinegar
½ cup olive oil
¾ teaspoon prepared mustard
2 tablespoons mixed chopped parsley, chives, spinach and watercress
1 medium onion, chopped fine

Combine all the ingredients and mix well. Serve cold with chilled seafood, boiled beef, bollito misto (page 95) or salad.

SOUR CREAM AND CUCUMBER SAUCE *About 1½ cups*

1 cup sour cream
½ cup peeled, seeded and finely chopped cucumber
½ teaspoon salt
1 teaspoon finely chopped fresh dill, or ½ teaspoon dried dill
1 teaspoon finely grated onion

Thoroughly mix all the ingredients. Refrigerate one to two hours before serving.

CHAPTER NINE

SAUCES AND COMPOSED BUTTERS

SAUCES

BECHAMEL (WHITE SAUCE) *1 cup*

If the home cook could learn to make but one sauce this would be the most valuable. It is the basis for countless dishes.

2 tablespoons butter
2 tablespoons flour
1 cup milk
Salt and freshly ground pepper
Nutmeg (optional)

1. Melt the butter in a saucepan over moderate heat without letting it brown. Add the flour, accurately measured, and stir, preferably with a wire whisk, until it is well blended.

2. Meanwhile, bring the milk almost but not quite to the boiling point. While stirring the flour and butter mixture vigorously, add the hot milk all at once. When the mixture comes to a boil it will thicken automatically. Simmer, if time allows, for five minutes. Season to taste with salt and pepper and, if desired, a pinch of nutmeg.

Note: Some quarters recommend that the butter-flour roux be stirred on and off the heat for five minutes before the milk is added, taking care that the mixture does not brown. Although this does away with the raw taste of the flour, it is not absolutely essential.

VARIATIONS:

Thin White Sauce: Follow directions above, using one tablespoon butter and one tablespoon flour for each cup of milk.

Thick White Sauce: Use three tablespoons each of flour and butter for each cup of milk.

(cont'd)

Sauce Mornay: Add one-half to one cup grated Cheddar or American cheese to the hot sauce and stir over low heat until melted. Season with mustard and Worcestershire sauce to taste.

Sauce Velouté: Substitute chicken, beef or fish broth for the milk and proceed as for white sauce.

Mustard Sauce: Combine one teaspoon dry mustard with the flour when making white or velouté sauce.

Fresh Herb Sauce: Add one teaspoon freshly chopped herbs, such as parsley or fresh dill.

Dried Herb Sauce: Add one-half teaspoon dried herbs, such as thyme or orégano.

SAUCE CHAUD-FROID (JELLIED WHITE SAUCE) *About 5 cups*

3 tablespoons butter
¼ cup flour
1 quart clear chicken or turkey broth
2 envelopes unflavored gelatin
½ cup cold water
2 egg yolks
½ cup cream

1. Melt the butter in a saucepan and stir in the flour, using a wire whisk.
2. Bring the broth to a boil and add all at once to the butter-flour mixture, stirring vigorously with the whisk. When the mixture is thickened and smooth, continue cooking five minutes over very low heat.
3. Soften the gelatin in the cold water and add it to the sauce. Stir until gelatin is dissolved. Remove from heat.
4. Beat egg yolks with cream and stir into the hot sauce. Heat but do not boil. Cool but do not chill.

CREAM SAUCE *About 1¼ cups*

1 cup milk
1 thin slice of onion
1 sprig of parsley
2 tablespoons butter
2 tablespoons flour
Salt to taste
White pepper
Dash of nutmeg
2 tablespoons heavy cream

1. Combine the milk with the onion and parsley and bring it to the boil.
2. Meanwhile, melt the butter and, using a wire whisk, stir in the flour. Strain the hot milk into the butter-flour mixture, stirring vigorously with the wire whisk. When the mixture is thickened and smooth simmer it gently for five minutes, stirring occasionally with the whisk. If the sauce seems too thick add a little more milk. Add the seasonings and cream.

BROWN SAUCE *About 2 quarts*

One of the most versatile of all the bases of fine cuisine is a brown sauce. It is the foundation for many of the most glorious products of a French kitchen. This sauce is relatively easy to prepare and may be frozen.

- 5 pounds veal bones
- 1 large onion, quartered
- 5 small carrots, peeled and quartered
- 2 stalks celery with leaves, coarsely chopped
- ½ teaspoon thyme
- 1 teaspoon crushed peppercorns
- 3 bay leaves
- 3 cloves garlic, unpeeled
- 1 tablespoon salt
- ½ cup flour
- 3 quarts water
- 1¼ cups tomato purée
- ½ cup chopped green part of leeks, well washed
- 3 sprigs of parsley

1. Preheat the oven to hot (475° F.).

2. Combine bones, onion, carrots, celery, thyme, peppercorns, bay leaves, garlic and salt in a large roasting pan. Place in the oven and bake forty-five minutes. Reduce heat if necessary to prevent bones from burning. Sprinkle with flour and bake fifteen minutes longer.

3. Transfer the ingredients to a large kettle and add two cups of water to the roasting pan. Cook over moderate heat, stirring, to dissolve brown particles that cling to the bottom and sides of the pan. Pour liquid from roasting pan into the kettle and add remaining water, tomato purée, leeks and parsley. Bring to a rapid boil, reduce heat and simmer for two hours. Add more liquid if necessary and skim often to remove fat and foam as it rises to the surface. Cool and strain. This sauce may be frozen and defrosted as necessary. Or it may be stored tightly sealed for several weeks in the refrigerator.

FISH VELOUTE *About 5 cups*

- ¾ cup butter
- 1½ cups flour
- 5 cups fish stock (page 229)

1. Melt the butter in a large saucepan and stir in the flour.

2. When blended and smooth add five cups of hot fish stock and stir vigorously with a wire whisk. When sauce is thickened and smooth, cook about one hour, stirring occasionally.

Note: This sauce base may be frozen and defrosted as needed. Or it will keep a week or longer in the refrigerator.

BARBECUE BASTING SAUCE *1¾ cups*

- 1 cup peanut or sesame seed oil
- ¼ cup soy sauce
- ½ cup sherry

Combine the ingredients and use as a sauce for barbecuing chicken, shrimp or fish.

BEARNAISE SAUCE *1½ cups*

1 teaspoon chopped shallots
1 small sprig tarragon, chopped
1 small sprig chervil, coarsely chopped
2 peppercorns
Pinch of salt
¼ cup tarragon vinegar
5 egg yolks
¾ cup butter, melted
Pinch of cayenne pepper
1 teaspoon mixed tarragon and chervil, minced

1. Simmer the shallots, tarragon, chervil, peppercorns and salt in the vinegar over low heat until the vinegar has been reduced by two-thirds. Cool to lukewarm.

2. Add the egg yolks and beat briskly with a wire whisk. Place over low heat and gradually add the butter. Whisk until the sauce thickens. Strain. Season with cayenne and stir in the minced tarragon and chervil.

QUICK BEARNAISE *¾ to 1 cup*

The blender Béarnaise.

2 tablespoons white wine
1 tablespoon tarragon vinegar
2 teaspoons chopped tarragon
2 teaspoons chopped shallots or onion
¼ teaspoon freshly ground black pepper
½ cup butter
3 egg yolks
2 tablespoons lemon juice
¼ teaspoon salt
Pinch of cayenne pepper

1. Combine the wine, vinegar, tarragon, shallots and pepper in a skillet. Bring to a boil and cook rapidly until almost all the liquid disappears.

2. In a small saucepan heat the butter to bubbling, but do not brown.

3. Place the egg yolks, lemon juice, salt and cayenne in the container of an electric blender. Cover the container and flick the motor on and off at high speed. Remove the cover, turn the motor on high and gradually add the hot butter.

4. Add the herb mixture, cover and blend on high speed four seconds.

BORDELAISE SAUCE *About 2 cups*

2 tablespoons butter
2 tablespoons finely minced shallots
¾ cup dry red wine
1½ cups brown sauce (page 444) or canned beef gravy
2 tablespoons lemon juice
2 tablespoons minced parsley
Salt and cayenne pepper to taste
¾ cup sliced mushrooms, cooked in a little butter (optional)

1. Melt the butter in a saucepan and cook the shallots until they are transparent.

2. Add the wine and simmer until reduced one-half. Add the remaining ingredients and heat thoroughly.

BUTTER SAUCE *8 servings*

2 cups butter
3 to 4 tablespoons lemon juice
½ teaspoon Tabasco sauce
1 tablespoon Worcestershire sauce

Melt the butter over low heat. Add the remaining ingredients and beat well with a fork. Distribute among eight individual serving cups and serve with steamed hard-shell crabs, boiled lobster, etc.

DRAWN BUTTER *1¾ cups*

⅓ cup butter
3 tablespoons flour
½ teaspoon salt
⅛ teaspoon freshly ground black pepper
1½ cups hot water or fish stock
1 teaspoon lemon juice

1. Melt one-half the butter, add the flour, salt and pepper and stir until smooth.
2. Add the water, stirring constantly, and boil five minutes.
3. Add the lemon juice and remaining butter, bit by bit. Use for poached fish or shellfish.

VARIATION:

Egg Sauce: Add two coarsely chopped hard-cooked eggs to drawn butter (above). Serve over hot poached fish.

CAPER SAUCE *About 2½ cups*

3 tablespoons bacon fat or butter
3 tablespoons flour
1½ cups tongue or beef broth
½ cup heavy cream
2 tablespoons or more capers
Salt and freshly ground black pepper

1. Melt the bacon fat in a saucepan, add the flour and stir with a wire whisk until blended. Meanwhile, bring the broth to a boil and add all at once to the butter-flour mixture, stirring vigorously with the whisk. Cook, stirring, until thickened.
2. Add the cream, capers and salt and pepper to taste. Reheat before serving; do not boil. Serve with boiled tongue or beef.

CHEESE PIMENTO SAUCE *About 3 cups*

3 tablespoons butter
3 tablespoons flour
1½ cups milk
1½ cups grated sharp Cheddar cheese
⅓ cup chopped pimentos
Salt and cayenne pepper to taste

(cont'd)

1. Melt the butter in the top part of a double boiler, over direct heat, add the flour and stir with a wire whisk until blended. Meanwhile, bring the milk to a boil and add all at once to the butter-flour mixture, stirring vigorously with the whisk.

2. Add the cheese to the sauce, place over boiling water and cook, stirring often, until the cheese melts.

3. Add the pimento, salt and cayenne.

CHUTNEY SAUCE FOR HAM *About 1 cup*

½ cup bottled chutney, chopped
½ cup sugar
2 tablespoons lemon juice
¼ cup water

Mix all the ingredients and simmer until syrupy. Serve hot with hot baked ham.

CUCUMBER SAUCE *About 2 cups*

3 tablespoons butter
3 tablespoons flour
¼ cup clam juice (bottled)
1 cup milk
¼ cup cream
¼ cup chopped cucumber

1. Melt the butter and add the flour. Cook, stirring with a wire whisk, two or three minutes without letting the flour brown. Meanwhile, bring the clam juice and milk to a boil and add all at once to the butter-flour mixture, stirring vigorously with the whisk until the mixture is thickened and smooth. Cook over low heat ten minutes.

2. Just before serving, stir in the cream and cucumber. Serve hot with poached fish.

CURRY SAUCE *About 3 cups*

1 medium onion, chopped
1 clove garlic, chopped
1 stalk celery, diced
½ bay leaf
Sprig of parsley
¼ teaspoon powdered mustard
1 tart apple, diced
½ cup butter
¼ pound raw ham, chopped
2 tablespoons flour
½ teaspoon mace
1¼ teaspoons curry powder
2½ cups chicken broth

1. Cook together for eight minutes, stirring occasionally, the onion, garlic, celery, bay leaf, parsley, mustard, apple, butter and ham.

2. Add the flour, mace and curry powder and cook four minutes longer.

3. Add the broth and simmer one hour. Strain into another saucepan, rubbing the solids through a sieve.

FLEMISH SAUCE FOR POACHED SALMON OR TROUT

¾ to 1 cup

¼ cup butter
2 teaspoons imported mustard, preferably Dijon
Juice of 1 lemon
Salt and freshly ground black pepper
¼ teaspoon nutmeg
2 teaspoons chopped parsley
1 teaspoon chopped chives
4 egg yolks

1. In a saucepan, combine the butter, mustard, lemon juice, seasonings and herbs. Place the saucepan in a skillet containing simmering water (or use a double boiler) and stir with a wire whisk until the butter has melted.

2. Beat the egg yolks until thick and lemon-colored and stir them into the butter-mustard mixture. Continue beating vigorously over barely simmering water until the sauce thickens. Serve immediately over poached salmon or trout.

FRENCH QUARTER SAUCE *About ¾ cup*

2 tablespoons cider vinegar
6 tablespoons olive oil
3 tablespoons strong prepared mustard (preferably Dijon or Dusseldorf mustard)
1 clove garlic, minced
6 anchovy fillets, mashed to a pulp
½ teaspoon salt
1 tablespoon finely chopped parsley
1 tablespoon finely chopped chives

Combine all the ingredients and chill thoroughly. If desired, combine with one finely sieved hard-cooked egg. Serve over chilled shrimp.

GREEN GODDESS SAUCE *2 cups*

1 cup mayonnaise
1 clove garlic, minced
3 anchovies, chopped
¼ cup finely cut chives or green onions with tops
¼ cup chopped parsley
1 tablespoon fresh lemon juice
1 tablespoon tarragon vinegar
½ teaspoon salt
Freshly ground black pepper
½ cup sour cream

Blend all the ingredients except the sour cream. Fold in the sour cream. Serve with chilled cooked fish.

HOLLANDAISE SAUCE *About 1 cup*

Holland is a land of butter; small wonder this sauce is called Hollandaise.

3 egg yolks
1 tablespoon cold water
½ cup soft butter
¼ teaspoon salt
½ teaspoon lemon juice, or to taste

(cont'd)

1. Combine the egg yolks and water in the top of a double boiler and beat with a wire whisk over hot (not boiling) water until fluffy.

2. Add a few spoonfuls of butter to the mixture and beat continually until the butter has melted and the sauce starts to thicken. Care should be taken that the water in the bottom of the boiler never boils. Continue adding the butter, bit by bit, stirring constantly.

3. Add the salt and lemon juice. For a lighter texture, beat in a tablespoon of hot water if desired.

QUICK HOLLANDAISE SAUCE *About ¾ cup*

This recipe for Hollandaise sauce was first conceived by Ann Seranne, one of the nation's foremost food consultants.

Heat one-half cup butter to bubbling, but do not brown. Into an electric blender put three egg yolks, two tablespoons lemon juice, one-quarter teaspoon salt and a pinch of cayenne. Turn motor on low speed and add hot butter gradually. Blend about fifteen seconds, or until sauce is thickened and smooth.

HORSERADISH SAUCE *About 1½ cups*

3 tablespoons butter
3 tablespoons flour
1½ cups beef bouillon
Horseradish to taste

1. Melt the butter in a saucepan, add the flour and stir with a wire whisk until blended.

2. Add the boiling liquid all at once, stirring vigorously with the whisk until the mixture is smooth and thickened. Season with horseradish. Serve with boiled beef or tongue.

COLD HORSERADISH DRESSING *1¼ cups*

¼ cup horseradish, finely grated
1 cup sour cream
1 teaspoon sugar
Pinch of salt
Pinch of freshly ground black pepper
1 teaspoon dill, finely chopped

Mix together all the ingredients except the dill. Chill and, before serving, garnish with freshly chopped dill. Serve with smoked trout or whitefish or cold meats.

COLD HORSERADISH SAUCE A LA DRESDEN *About 2½ cups*

½ cup horseradish, freshly shredded
1 cup heavy cream, whipped
2 teaspoons sugar
Salt
Freshly ground black pepper

Mix all the ingredients and chill well before serving. Serve with smoked trout or whitefish.

MADEIRA SAUCE *About 1¼ cups*

2 tablespoons butter
2 tablespoons finely minced shallots or scallions
1½ cups brown sauce (page 445) or canned beef gravy
2 tablespoons lemon juice
¼ cup Madeira wine

1. Melt the butter in a saucepan and sauté the shallots for five minutes, taking care that the butter does not brown.

2. Add the brown sauce and lemon juice. When the liquid boils, add the wine and simmer gently five minutes.

MARCHANDS DE VIN SAUCE *About 2 cups*

6 tablespoons butter
6 scallions, minced
¾ cup dry red wine
1½ cups brown sauce (page 445) or canned beef gravy
2 tablespoons lemon juice

1. Heat four tablespoons of the butter until hot but not smoking. Slowly cook the scallions in it until wilted.

2. Add the wine and simmer, uncovered, until the liquid is reduced to one-quarter cup.

3. Add the brown sauce and lemon juice and heat. Add the remaining butter, bit by bit, swirling it in by rotating the pan gently.

MAYONNAISE, PAGE 438.

MAYONNAISE AND COGNAC SAUCE FOR SHRIMP *¾ cup*

¾ cup mayonnaise
1 teaspoon tomato purée
1 teaspoon cognac

Combine the ingredients and serve with chilled fresh shrimp.

SAUCE MOUSSELINE *2 cups*

This is Hollandaise with whipped cream.

1 cup butter, at room temperature
3 egg yolks
½ teaspoon salt
Juice of 1 lemon
½ cup heavy cream, whipped

1. Cut the butter into three parts. In the top of a double boiler combine one part of the butter with the beaten egg yolks. Place over hot, nearly boiling, water and beat constantly with a wire whisk until the butter has melted.

2. Add the second part of the butter and repeat the process; then add the

(cont'd)

third, beating constantly. When the sauce thickens, season with salt and lemon juice.

3. If the sauce begins to curdle while it is being made, add a little boiling water and continue beating until the sauce is smooth again. Fold the whipped cream into the sauce and serve at once.

MUSHROOM SAUCE *About 2 cups*

1 tablespoon chopped shallots or onion
¼ pound mushrooms, sliced thin
3 tablespoons butter
1 teaspoon lemon juice
1½ cups brown sauce (page 445) or canned beef gravy

Cook the shallots and mushrooms in the butter five minutes, stirring occasionally. Add the lemon juice and brown sauce and blend well. Bring to a boil and serve hot.

MUSHROOM-WINE SAUCE *6 servings*

2 tablespoons butter
1 tablespoon chopped parsley
½ clove garlic, chopped fine
1 small onion, chopped
1 tablespoon flour
1 cup chicken broth
⅛ teaspoon nutmeg
¾ pound mushrooms, thinly sliced
¼ cup dry sherry

1. In a saucepan heat one tablespoon of the butter, add the parsley, garlic and onion and cook over medium heat three minutes. Stir in the flour. Gradually add the broth, stirring constantly. Add nutmeg.

2. In a skillet heat the remaining butter, add the mushrooms and sauté five minutes. Combine with the sauce and simmer fifteen minutes. Add the wine and bring to a boil. Serve with roast meats or poultry.

SAUCE POIVRADE *About 1½ cups*

8 peppercorns, crushed
½ cup vinegar
1 cup brown sauce (page 445), or leftover thickened gravy
2 tablespoons red currant jelly

1. Mix together peppercorns and vinegar and simmer, uncovered, until reduced to one-quarter cup.

2. Add brown sauce and simmer one-half hour. Add jelly. Strain. Serve with venison or grilled chops.

REMOULADE SAUCE I (mayonnaise base) *About 2½ cups*

2 cups tart mayonnaise
1 clove garlic, finely minced
1 tablespoon finely chopped fresh tarragon or 1 teaspoon dried tarragon
2 hard-cooked eggs, finely chopped
1 teaspoon strong prepared mustard (preferably Dijon or Dusseldorf mustard)
1 tablespoon finely chopped parsley
1 teaspoon anchovy paste

Blend all the ingredients well and let stand one to two hours before serving.

REMOULADE SAUCE II (French dressing base) *About 1 cup*

3 tablespoons wine vinegar
1 to 2 tablespoons prepared mustard (preferably Dijon or Dusseldorf mustard)
2 tablespoons minced scallions
2 tablespoons minced celery
1 teaspoon fresh horseradish
1 tablespoon minced parsley
½ cup plus 1 tablespoon olive oil
Dash of red pepper
Salt and freshly ground black pepper

Combine the vinegar with the mustard, scallions, celery, horseradish and parsley. Beat in the olive oil, a little at a time, and season to taste with red pepper, salt and black pepper. Serve as a cocktail sauce for cold boiled shrimp.

SOUR-CREAM DILL SAUCE *About 2 cups*

1 egg
1 teaspoon salt
Pinch of freshly ground black pepper
Pinch of sugar
4 teaspoons lemon juice
1 teaspoon grated onion
2 tablespoons finely cut dill
1½ cups sour cream

Beat the egg until fluffy and lemon-colored. Add the remaining ingredients, blending in the sour cream last. Stir until blended and chill.

SPANISH SAUCE *2 cups*

1 large onion, minced
2 tablespoons chopped green pepper
1 small clove garlic, minced
2 tablespoons butter
2 cups canned Italian plum tomatoes
½ bay leaf
1 teaspoon salt
¼ teaspoon freshly ground pepper
Small pinch of cloves
¼ cup stuffed olives, chopped

1. Sauté the onion, green pepper and garlic in the butter until lightly browned, stirring often.

2. Chop the tomatoes in the can, using a knife. Add the tomatoes and re-

(cont'd)

maining ingredients to the sautéed mixture and simmer, partly covered, until thick, or about thirty minutes. Stir occasionally. Adjust the seasonings and remove the bay leaf.

3. Place two tablespoons of the sauce on an omelet before rolling it. Garnish with more sauce.

TARTAR SAUCE *About 1¼ cups*

1 cup mayonnaise
1 tablespoon finely chopped parsley
1 tablespoon finely chopped chives
1 teaspoon finely chopped tarragon
1 tablespoon finely chopped chervil (optional)
1 tablespoon capers
1 small sour pickle, finely chopped

Combine all the ingredients and blend well. If desired, add a little finely chopped garlic.

TOMATO SAUCE *About 9 cups*

3 cups chopped onion
3 large cloves garlic
⅓ cup olive oil
2 cups canned Italian tomatoes
2 six-ounce cans tomato paste
6 cups water
2 bay leaves
1 teaspoon orégano
2 stalks fresh basil (10 leaves) or ½ teaspoon dried basil
1½ teaspoons salt
Freshly ground black pepper to taste

1. Sauté the onion and garlic in the oil until the onion is well browned. Add the tomatoes, tomato paste, water and bay leaves. Simmer, partially covered, one hour, stirring frequently.

2. Add the orégano, basil, salt and pepper. Continue cooking, stirring often, until the sauce thickens, about one hour. Remove the basil and bay leaves.

Note: To store the sauce two to three weeks, fill sterilized jars with the hot sauce, seal, cool and refrigerate. For longer storage, fill the jars seven-eighths full, seal, cool and freeze.

SAUCES FOR PASTA, PAGE 340.

FRESH TOMATO SAUCE *2 cups*

1 clove garlic, minced
½ cup finely chopped onion
2 tablespoons olive oil
¼ cup finely chopped celery tops
½ cup finely chopped green pepper
2 cups finely diced ripe tomatoes
½ teaspoon sugar
1½ teaspoons salt
½ cup water
1 small bay leaf
4 whole black peppercorns
2 whole cloves
2 tablespoons tomato paste

(cont'd)

1. Sauté the garlic and onion in the olive oil in a heavy saucepan. Add the celery tops, green pepper, tomatoes, sugar, salt and water. Tie the bay leaf, peppercorns and cloves in a cheesecloth bag and add.

2. Cook slowly, uncovered, twenty minutes. Remove the spice bag.

3. Press the mixture through a coarse sieve. Stir in the tomato paste and heat.

TRUFFLE SAUCE FOR BEEF *About 1¾ cups*

1 small can truffles, with the liquid in which they are packed
¼ cup Madeira or dry red wine
1 tablespoon finely chopped shallots or onion
2 tablespoons butter
1½ cups brown sauce (page 445) or canned beef gravy
Maggi seasoning

1. Chop the truffles coarsely and reserve the liquid in the can. Combine the chopped truffles with the Madeira and cook over moderately high heat until the wine is reduced to about one tablespoon.

2. Cook the shallots in one tablespoon of the butter and add to the brown sauce. Cook three minutes and strain, if desired. Add the truffles and reduced wine. Add the truffle liquid in the can, the remaining butter and a few drops of Maggi seasoning. Spoon the sauce over cooked beef.

TUNA FISH SAUCE FOR COLD VEAL *1 cup*

1 medium clove garlic, peeled and sliced
3 to 4 ounces tuna and the oil in which it was packed (about half a 7-ounce can)
2 well-drained anchovies
¼ cup olive oil
2 tablespoons vinegar
2 tablespoons brine in which capers are packed
1 tablespoon light cream

Combine the ingredients in a blender and blend one minute at high speed. Serve with cold sliced veal.

VINAIGRETTE SAUCE *About 1 cup*

¾ cup olive oil
¼ cup lemon juice
Salt to taste
½ teaspoon dry mustard
Freshly ground black pepper
1 tablespoon chopped capers
1 teaspoon finely chopped pickles
½ teaspoon chopped parsley
½ teaspoon chopped chervil
½ teaspoon chopped chives

Combine all the ingredients well and chill.

Serve chilled with chilled seafood on the half shell or heat to lukewarm and serve with hot boiled beef.

COMPOSED BUTTERS

QUICK BLENDER BUTTER *About ¾ cup of sweet butter*

Those who yearn for country-fresh butter need only make their own in an electric blender. This is the sweetest butter imaginable and is made in seconds.

Into the container of an electric blender pour one cup heavy cream. Blend on high speed about fifteen seconds, or until the cream is whipped.

As soon as the cream begins to thicken around the blades, it is whipped. Add one-half cup cold water and one ice cube and blend on high speed two minutes. The ice serves to solidify the butter as it rises to the top of the liquid.

Spoon the fresh sweet butter from the top of the liquid into a cup to drain. Then knead smooth with a wooden spoon to extract any liquid that might be trapped in the butter.

HOW TO CLARIFY BUTTER

Place butter in the top of a double boiler over hot water. Place over heat and let stand just until the butter melts. When the whey (milky sediment) has separated from the melted fat, pour off the clear fat, which is the clarified butter, and discard the whey.

CURRY BUTTER *About ½ cup*

½ cup butter
½ teaspoon curry powder
Dash of freshly ground black pepper
Dash of paprika

Cream the butter, add remaining ingredients and beat until fluffy. Store in the refrigerator in a covered glass jar until ready to use. Re-cream before using.

Use as a substitute for regular butter in making sandwiches of egg salad, tomato and lettuce, cottage cheese and pickle, tuna fish, salmon or sliced cold meat.

Serve on broiled meat patties, broiled lamb, broiled fish, broccoli, cauliflower, onions and carrots, peas, broiled tomatoes or baked potatoes.

Or spread crackers with curry butter, heat ten minutes in a moderate oven and use as a base for canapés or as an accompaniment for fish, meat or vegetable salads, jellied soups, seafood or tomato juice cocktails.

FISH BUTTERS

Mustard Butter: Melt six tablespoons butter and add two tablespoons prepared mustard. Serve on broiled salmon.

Anchovy-Tomato Butter: To one-quarter cup creamed butter add four anchovies, chopped fine; one teaspoon tomato paste; one-half clove garlic, mashed; a pinch of black pepper. Use on smelts, mackerel, salmon, etc.

Piquant Butter: Cream six tablespoons butter and add one teaspoon Worcestershire sauce, two teaspoons finely chopped chutney and two teaspoons chili sauce. Serve on broiled fish steaks.

Anchovy Butter: Melt one-half cup butter and carefully pour it into another pan, leaving the residue behind. To the clarified butter add ten anchovy fillets, drained of oil and minced, one teaspoon minced parsley and the juice of one lemon.

Colbert Butter: Combine one-half teaspoon each softened beef extract and chopped fresh tarragon (or a pinch of dried tarragon) with one-half cup maître d'hôtel butter (page 458). Use for deep-fried fish.

GARLIC BUTTER *About ½ cup*

3 cloves garlic, minced
Salt and freshly ground black pepper to taste
½ cup softened butter

1. Combine all the ingredients and beat well with a fork.
2. Pile the butter in a serving dish and chill slightly. Use for making garlic bread or on grilled meats.

HERB BUTTER FOR MEATS *About ½ cup*

2 tablespoons finely chopped parsley
2 teaspoons chopped tarragon
2 tablespoons finely chopped chives
½ cup softened butter
Salt to taste
1 teaspoon dry mustard
Sherry or cognac to taste

1. Combine the ingredients and beat with a fork until the seasonings are blended into the butter.
2. Pile the butter in a serving dish and chill slightly. Serve on grilled meats.

HERB BUTTER FOR VEGETABLES *About ¼ cup*

¼ cup butter, at room temperature
1 teaspoon lemon juice
1 tablespoon chopped chives, chervil, tarragon or dill, or a mixture
Salt
Freshly ground black pepper to taste

(cont'd)

Cream the butter with the lemon juice. Add the herbs and blend well. Season to taste with salt and pepper.

Serve on cooked asparagus, cabbage, carrots, cauliflower, beans or other vegetables.

MAITRE D'HOTEL BUTTER *¾ cup*

½ cup softened butter
2 tablespoons minced parsley
2 tablespoons minced chives
2 tablespoons lemon juice

1. Cream the butter and mix with the remaining ingredients, adding the lemon juice a little at a time and stirring until well blended.
2. Turn the mixture onto waxed paper, form into a roll, wrap closely in paper and refrigerate. Serve on steak and other grilled meats.

MUSHROOM BUTTER *About 2 cups*

½ pound fresh mushrooms, sliced
¾ cup butter
¼ teaspoon freshly ground black pepper
¼ teaspoon salt
3 tablespoons sherry or cognac

1. Sauté the mushrooms in one-quarter cup butter five minutes. Turn them occasionally to brown on all sides.
2. Put the mushrooms and pan juices into the container of an electric blender, add the remaining ingredients, cover and blend until smooth. Serve on grilled meats.

RED WINE BUTTER FOR STEAK *About ¾ cup*

2 teaspoons minced shallots
9 ounces (1⅛ cups) dry red wine
¼ cup butter, at room temperature
1 teaspoon chopped parsley
Salt and freshly ground black pepper to taste

1. Cook the shallots and wine together in a shallow open pan until the liquid has reduced to one-quarter the original amount. Remove from the heat and cool.
2. Cream together the butter and parsley. Combine it with the wine-shallot mixture and season with salt and pepper.
3. Keep the creamed butter covered and under refrigeration. Add as desired to hot broiled meat.

CHAPTER TEN

BREADS

YEAST BREADS AND ROLLS

KNEADING BREAD

The cook who bakes good bread—firm, flavorful, fragrant—knows how to knead. The motion is simple but tricky to describe. When the dough, forming a sort of ball in shape, has been turned out of the bowl onto a lightly floured board, it should be folded over toward the cook, then pressed down and away from the cook with the heel of the hand. The ball is turned a quarter circle, the motion repeated, and so on until the texture is smooth and elastic. The board may be sprinkled lightly with additional flour from time to time; but no more flour should be kneaded in than is necessary. The kneading process takes eight to ten minutes.

ALLOWING DOUGH TO RISE

When making bread, the temperature of the dough should be kept as close as possible to 85° F. One good way to maintain this gentle warmth is to stand the bowl of dough in a large pan or a sink filled with lukewarm water. As the water cools, reheat it by adding hot water, but do not keep the dough warm over a hot burner. Dough may be shaped when doubled in bulk and an impression remains when pressed with a finger.

SHAPING LOAVES

After the dough has risen, punch down and divide into portions for the desired number of loaves. Form into balls and allow to rest about ten minutes on a lightly floured board. Shape into loaves by pressing the ball of dough into

(cont'd)

an oblong about 9 x 7 x 1 inches. Fold each end of the oblong to the center, overlapping the ends slightly. Press each side down firmly and pinch along the center to keep the ends sealed and the dough in shape. Place the loaves, sealed edges down, in greased bread pans. Brush the tops with melted shortening, cover with a towel and let rise until doubled in bulk.

ANADAMA BREAD *2 loaves*

- ½ cup cornmeal
- 1 cup cold water
- 1 package yeast
- 1½ cups boiling water
- 3 tablespoons butter
- ½ cup molasses
- 2 teaspoons salt
- 3 cups whole wheat flour
- 2½ to 3 cups sifted white flour

1. Mix the cornmeal with three-quarters cup cold water. Soften the yeast in the remaining cold water.
2. Add the cornmeal to the boiling water and stir over low heat until the mixture boils. Add the butter, molasses and salt and cool to lukewarm.
3. Combine the yeast with the cornmeal and mix. Add the whole wheat flour and enough white flour to give a fairly firm, non-sticky dough. Turn out on a floured board and knead until smooth and elastic.
4. Turn the dough into a greased bowl, grease the surface, cover with a towel and let rise in a warm place (80° to 85° F.) until doubled in bulk.
5. Knead lightly again and shape into two loaves. Place in greased loaf pans or on greased cookie sheets. Brush with oil. Cover and let rise until doubled in bulk.
6. Bake in a preheated hot oven (400° F.) fifteen minutes. Reduce the oven temperature to moderate (375° F.) and bake about thirty-five minutes longer.

CUBAN BREAD *2 loaves*

This is an adaptation of one of the most popular breads made at the James Beard Cooking School in New York.

- 1 package yeast
- 2 cups lukewarm water
- 1¼ tablespoons salt
- 1 tablespoon sugar
- 6 to 7 cups sifted flour

1. Dissolve the yeast in the water and add the salt and sugar, stirring thoroughly.
2. Add the flour, one cup at a time, beating it in with a wooden spoon. Or use the dough hook on an electric mixer at low speed. Add enough flour to make a fairly stiff dough.
3. When the dough is thoroughly mixed, shape it into a ball, place in a

(*cont'd*)

greased bowl and grease the top. Cover with a towel and let stand in a warm place (80° to 85° F.) until doubled in bulk.

4. Turn the dough out onto a lightly floured board and shape into two long, French-style loaves or round, Italian-style loaves. Arrange on a baking sheet heavily sprinkled with cornmeal and allow to rise five minutes.

5. Slash the tops of the loaves in two or three places with a knife or scissors. Brush the loaves with water and place them in a cold oven. Set the oven control at hot (400° F.) and place a pan of boiling water on the bottom of the oven. Bake the loaves until they are crusty and done, about forty to forty-five minutes.

FRENCH BREAD *1 loaf*

- 1 cup lukewarm water
- 1½ teaspoons salt
- 1 package yeast
- 1 tablespoon soft shortening
- 3½ to 3¾ cups sifted flour
- Sesame or poppy seeds

1. Combine the water and salt; add the yeast and stir until yeast is well dissolved. Add the shortening.

2. Stir in the flour, one-half cup at a time. Continue adding enough flour to make a stiff dough.

3. When the dough begins to leave the sides of the bowl, turn it out onto a lightly floured board. Knead until the dough is smooth and elastic and does not stick to the board.

4. Place the dough in a greased bowl, turning once to bring the greased side up. Cover with a damp cloth and let rise in a warm place (80° to 85° F.) until double in bulk, or about one and one-half to two hours. (Dough has doubled when two fingers, pressed into it, leave an indentation.)

5. Punch the dough down, fold over edges of dough and turn it upside down. Cover and let rise again until almost double in bulk, or thirty to forty-five minutes.

6. Roll the dough into an oblong, fifteen by ten inches. Starting from a wide side, roll the dough up tightly as for a jelly roll. Pinch the edges together to seal. With a hand on each end of the roll, roll gently back and forth to lengthen the loaf and taper the ends.

7. Place the loaf diagonally on a baking sheet that has been lightly greased and sprinkled with cornmeal. With a sharp knife, make one-quarter-inch slashes in the dough at two-inch intervals, or one lengthwise slash. Brush the top with cold water and let stand, uncovered, about one and one-half hours. Brush again with cold water.

8. Bake in a preheated hot oven (425° F.) ten minutes. Brush again with water, reduce oven temperature to moderate (375° F.) and bake ten minutes longer. Brush with water again, sprinkle with sesame or poppy seeds and continue baking until golden brown, or fifteen to twenty minutes longer.

Note: For more glaze and less crustiness, in place of the plain water brush with one egg white slightly beaten with one tablespoon water.

HIGH-PROTEIN BREAD *1 loaf*

- 1 package yeast
- 1 cup lukewarm water
- 2½ cups sifted flour
- 1½ teaspoons salt
- 2 teaspoons sugar
- 3 tablespoons full-fat soy flour
- 3½ tablespoons nonfat dry milk
- 2 teaspoons shortening

1. Dissolve yeast in water.

2. Combine all dry ingredients in a mixing bowl. Add the liquid and mix well. Add shortening and continue mixing until the dough is smooth.

3. Place the dough in a well-greased bowl, grease the top, cover and let rise in a warm place (80° to 85° F.) for one and one-half hours.

4. Punch dough down, fold over edges of dough and turn it upside down. Cover and let rise fifteen to twenty minutes.

5. Shape dough into a loaf and place in a greased bread pan 9 x 4 x 3 inches. Cover and let stand about fifty-five to sixty minutes in a warm place until dough fills the pan.

6. Bake in a preheated hot oven (400° F.) about fifty minutes.

SWEDISH JULBROD *2 loaves or about 20 servings*

A Christmas bread from Sweden.

- 2 packages yeast
- ¼ cup lukewarm water
- ¾ cup milk, scalded and cooled to lukewarm
- ½ teaspoon salt
- ⅓ cup sugar
- ½ cup butter, softened
- 3 eggs, lightly beaten
- 4¼ cups sifted flour
- 1 cup raisins
- 1 cup sliced citron
- 1 cup blanched almonds
- 1 to 3 teaspoons cardamom seeds
- ¼ cup confectioner's sugar

1. Soften the yeast in the water. Add the milk, salt, sugar, butter and eggs, reserving one egg white.

2. Mix a little flour with the raisins and citron. Add one-half cup of the almonds, shredded.

3. Remove the papery covering from the cardamom seeds and crush the seeds. Add with one-half of the flour to the yeast mixture and stir until smooth. Cover and let rise in a warm place (85° F.) until double in bulk, or about forty minutes.

4. Stir in the remaining flour and knead until smooth and elastic. Knead in the fruits and nuts. Turn the dough into a greased bowl, grease the top, cover and let rise about thirty minutes.

5. Cut the dough into sixths and roll each piece with the palms of the hands into a long strip. Braid three strips and shape into a ring on a greased baking sheet. Repeat for a second loaf.

6. Brush the loaves with the reserved egg white beaten with one tablespoon water. Cover with the confectioner's sugar and remaining almonds and let rise until doubled in bulk, or about thirty minutes.

(cont'd)

7. Bake in a preheated hot oven (450° F.) ten minutes. Reduce the oven temperature to moderate (350° F.) and bake about twenty minutes longer.

OLD-FASHIONED OATMEAL BREAD *3 loaves*

- 2 cups milk
- 2 tablespoons shortening
- ¼ cup brown sugar, packed
- 1¼ teaspoons salt
- 1 package yeast
- ¼ cup lukewarm water
- 2 cups regular rolled oats (not quick cooking)
- 5 to 6 cups sifted flour

1. Scald the milk and stir in the shortening, brown sugar and salt. Stir until dissolved and cool to lukewarm.
2. In a large mixing bowl, soften the yeast in the water. Stir in the lukewarm milk mixture, add the oats and sufficient flour to make a soft dough.
3. Turn the dough out on a lightly floured board. Knead until smooth and elastic, or about ten minutes; the dough will spring back when pressed with a finger.
4. Place the dough in a warm greased bowl, grease the surface, cover and let rise in a warm place (80° F.) until doubled in bulk, or about two hours; the dough will retain a finger imprint when pressed.
5. Turn the dough out on a lightly floured board, divide into thirds and shape into loaves. Place the loaves, sealed edges down, in greased 9 x 5½-inch bread pans. Brush the tops with melted shortening, cover and let rise until almost doubled in bulk, about one hour.
6. Bake in a preheated hot oven (400° F.) about forty-five minutes.
7. Remove from pans and cool the baked loaves on racks.

ONION RYE BREAD *3 loaves*

- 2 cups milk
- ¼ cup sugar
- 4 teaspoons salt
- ¼ cup salad oil
- 1 package yeast
- 1 cup lukewarm water
- 6 cups sifted white flour
- 3 tablespoons caraway seeds
- 1 cup chopped onion
- 2½ cups rye flour, approximately
- Cornmeal
- Cream

1. Scald the milk and add the sugar, salt and oil. Stir until the sugar has dissolved and cool the mixture to lukewarm.
2. Soften the yeast in the water and add to the milk mixture. Add the white flour and mix well. Stir in the caraway seeds, onion and two cups rye flour and mix.
3. Turn the dough out on a surface sprinkled with rye flour and knead until smooth and elastic, adding enough additional rye flour to give a fairly stiff dough. Place in a greased bowl, grease the top, cover with a towel and let stand in a warm place (80° to 85° F.) until doubled in bulk, about one hour.

(cont'd)

4. Punch the dough down by folding the edges into the center. Cover and let rise again until doubled in bulk.

5. Grease three loaf pans and sprinkle with cornmeal. Divide the dough into thirds, shape into loaves and place in the prepared pans. Brush the tops of the loaves with cream and then sprinkle with salt. Cover with a towel and let rise in a warm place until doubled in bulk, about one hour.

6. Bake in a preheated moderate oven (350° F.) one hour, or until the loaves have a hollow sound when tapped. Turn out on a rack to cool.

PANETTONE *1 large loaf*

The traditional Italian Christmas bread.

2 packages yeast
1 cup lukewarm water
½ cup butter, melted
2 teaspoons salt
½ cup sugar
2 eggs, beaten
3 egg yolks, beaten
5½ cups sifted flour, approximately
1 cup thinly sliced citron
1 cup seedless raisins

1. Soften the yeast in the water.

2. Mix the butter, salt, sugar, eggs and egg yolks. Add the yeast and butter mixture to five cups flour and stir until blended. Knead on a floured board until smooth and free from stickiness, adding more flour as needed. The dough should be soft. Knead in the citron and raisins.

3. Place the dough in a greased bowl, grease the surface, cover with a towel and let rise in a warm place (80° to 85° F.) until doubled in bulk, or about two hours.

4. Knead the dough again until smooth. Place in a greased three-quart pudding pan or other round pan, brush the top with melted butter, cover and let rise again until doubled in bulk, or about forty minutes. Using a sharp knife, cut a deep cross in the top of the loaf.

5. Bake in a preheated hot oven (425° F.) until the surface begins to brown, or about eight minutes. Reduce the oven temperature to slow (325° F.) and bake about one hour longer.

PUMPERNICKEL BREAD *3 or 4 loaves*

1½ cups cold water
¾ cup cornmeal
1½ cups boiling water
1½ tablespoons salt
1 tablespoon sugar
2 tablespoons shortening
1 tablespoon caraway seeds (optional)
1 package yeast
¼ cup lukewarm water
2 cups mashed potato, cooled
6 cups rye meal or flour
2 cups whole wheat flour, approximately

(*cont'd*)

1. Stir the cold water into the cornmeal. Add to the boiling water and cook, stirring constantly, until thick.

2. Add the salt, sugar, shortening and caraway. Let stand until lukewarm. Meanwhile, soften the yeast in the lukewarm water.

3. Add the potatoes and yeast to the cornmeal mixture. Add the rye flour and enough whole wheat flour to make a stiff dough, stirring first with a spoon, then with the hands.

4. Turn the dough out on a lightly floured board and knead until the dough is smooth and elastic and does not stick to the board.

5. Place the dough in a greased bowl, grease the surface, cover with a towel and let stand in a warm place (80° to 85° F.) until doubled in bulk.

6. Divide the dough into three or four portions and form into loaves. Place, seam side down, in greased loaf pans. Grease the tops of the loaves, cover and let rise until double in bulk.

7. Bake in a preheated moderate oven (375° F.) about one hour.

Note: On a cold day, stand the bowl of dough to rise in a pan of warm water about 120° F. in temperature. Add more hot water as needed to keep the water warm.

VARIATION:

Sour Dough Pumpernickel: After the dough has been kneaded the first time, put about one cup in a bowl. Cover and set aside at room temperature to ferment and sour for a week or so. When making a fresh batch of dough, add the sour dough to the liquids in place of one package of yeast.

SPIRAL BREAD *2 loaves*

1 cup scalded milk
2 tablespoons sugar
2½ teaspoons salt
¼ cup shortening
1 cup lukewarm water
2 packages yeast
7 cups sifted flour
Melted butter or salad oil
Filling (see page 469)

1. To the scalded milk add the sugar, salt and shortening. Stir and cool to lukewarm.

2. Pour water into a large bowl, add yeast and stir until dissolved. Add milk mixture.

3. Add four cups of flour, stir; then beat well. Add remaining flour and stir until dampened. Let stand ten minutes.

4. Turn dough out onto a floured surface and knead until smooth, about ten minutes. Place in a greased bowl, grease surface, cover and let rise in a warm place (80° to 85° F.) until double in bulk, about forty-five minutes.

5. Punch dough down, turn out on a smooth surface and let rest ten minutes.

6. Grease two 9 x 5 x 3-inch bread pans.

(*cont'd*)

1. To make a tasty spiral loaf of bread the dough is allowed to rise. It is punched down and turned out on a smooth surface.

2. The dough is allowed to rest ten minutes. It is then cut in half with a knife. Each half is shaped into a ball.

3. Each ball of dough is rolled into a rectangle about one-quarter inch thick. It is then brushed with lightly beaten egg.

4. A selected filling such as chopped parsley and scallions is spread over the dough to about one inch from the edges.

5. The dough is rolled somewhat tightly in a jelly-roll fashion. It is placed in greased pans, with sealed edges underneath.

6. After the loaves are left to rise about fifty to sixty minutes, they are baked one hour until brown in a 400° oven.

7. Cut dough in half and shape each half into a ball. Roll each into a rectangle about one-quarter inch thick and almost nine inches wide.

8. Brush with lightly beaten egg reserved from the selected filling recipe and then spread the filling over it to about one inch from the edges. Roll jelly-roll fashion and pinch edges to seal. Place in greased pans with seam side down.

9. Brush tops with melted butter or salad oil, cover with wax paper and let rise in a warm place until slightly higher in the middle than the edge, fifty to sixty minutes.

10. Meanwhile, preheat oven to 400° F.

11. Cut gashes in top of loaves if desired. Place in oven and bake one hour. Turn out and cool on rack.

HERB FILLING:

2 cups finely chopped parsley
2 cups finely chopped scallions
1 large clove garlic, minced
2 tablespoons butter
2 eggs, lightly beaten
¾ teaspoon salt
Freshly ground black pepper to taste
Tabasco sauce to taste

1. Cook parsley, scallions and garlic in butter over moderate heat, stirring often, until thoroughly wilted but not browned. Mixture should be reduced to about half the original volume. Cool.

2. Reserve about two tablespoons of the beaten eggs for later use in brushing over the dough. Add balance to vegetables and season with salt, pepper and Tabasco.

ANCHOVY FILLING:

4 two-ounce cans anchovy fillets, drained
2 small cloves garlic, minced
2 tablespoons tomato paste
1 whole egg
1 egg yolk
Cayenne pepper to taste
1 teaspoon paprika (for color)

1. Mash anchovies to paste with the garlic. Add the tomato paste and mix.

2. Beat the egg with the egg yolk until well mixed. Reserve two tablespoons for later use. Add balance to anchovy mixture. Add cayenne, paprika.

100% WHOLE WHEAT BREAD *2 loaves*

1 cup milk
¼ cup molasses
2 tablespoons shortening
2 teaspoons salt
1 package yeast
1 cup lukewarm water
6 cups whole wheat flour, approximately

1. Scald the milk and place in a deep bowl with the molasses, shortening and salt. Cool to lukewarm.

2. Meanwhile, soften the yeast in one-half cup of the water. Add the remaining water to the milk mixture and, when it is lukewarm, stir in the yeast.

(cont'd)

3. Sift the flour and return to the flour any bran remaining in the sieve. Set aside one cup. Add the remainder to the yeast mixture and stir until the flour is dampened. Add enough additional flour from the reserved cup to form a soft dough, stiff enough to leave the sides of the bowl and cling to the spoon in one ball.

4. Turn the dough out on a lightly floured board and knead until smooth and not sticky, about five minutes. Place in a greased bowl about three times the size of the dough. Turn the dough in the bowl and invert it so that the greased side is up. Cover with a towel and let rise in a warm place (80° to 85° F.) until doubled in bulk, or about two hours.

5. Punch the dough down, fold in the edges, cover and let rise again in a warm place about thirty minutes.

6. Turn the dough out on a board and cut in half. Shape into balls and let stand, covered, fifteen minutes. (This makes the dough easy to shape and gives the loaves a smooth crust.) Shape into loaves.

7. Place the loaves, smooth side up, in greased 9 x 4 x 3-inch loaf pans. Grease the tops, cover with a towel and let rise in a warm place until the dough comes slightly above the tops of the pans, or about one and one-half hours.

8. Bake the loaves in a preheated hot oven (425° F.) twelve minutes. Reduce the heat to moderate (350° F.) and bake about fifty minutes longer. The bread is done when it shrinks slightly from the sides of the pan. For a heavier crust, bake about fifteen minutes longer. Turn out of the pans immediately and cool on a rack before storing.

Note: To shorten the time of rising by about an hour, two packages of yeast may be used instead of one.

AMERICAN BRIOCHE *16 brioche*

½ cup milk
½ cup butter
⅓ cup sugar
1 teaspoon salt
1 package yeast
¼ cup lukewarm water
1 egg, separated
3 whole eggs, beaten
3¼ cups sifted flour

1. Scald milk and cool it to lukewarm.

2. Cream butter, adding sugar gradually. Add salt.

3. Soften the yeast in the water.

4. Blend milk, creamed mixture and yeast. Add the egg yolk, whole eggs and flour and beat with a wooden spoon for two minutes.

5. Cover and let rise in a warm place (80° to 85° F.) until more than double in bulk, about two hours or less.

6. Stir down and beat thoroughly. Cover tightly with foil and refrigerate overnight.

(cont'd)

7. Preheat oven to hot (425° F.); place rack near bottom.

8. Stir the dough down and turn out onto a floured board. Cut off slightly less than one-quarter of the dough and reserve. Cut remaining dough into sixteen pieces and form into balls of equal size. Place in well-greased brioche or muffin pans (2¾ x 1¼ inches deep). Cut the smaller piece of dough into sixteen pieces and shape into smooth balls. Moisten finger slightly and make a depression in each large ball. Place a small ball in each depression. Cover and let rise in a warm place until more than double in bulk, about one hour.

9. Beat the remaining egg white with a teaspoon of sugar. Brush over brioche. Bake until brown, or fifteen to twenty minutes.

FRENCH BRIOCHE *18 to 24 brioche*

1 package yeast
Lukewarm water
2 to 3 tablespoons sugar
4 cups sifted flour, approximately
1 cup soft butter
1 teaspoon salt
7 eggs
½ cup milk, scalded and cooled

1. Soften yeast in one-third cup lukewarm water. Add one teaspoon sugar and one cup flour. Mix and then knead until smooth. Place ball of dough in a bowl and cover with lukewarm water. Let rise until ball floats in water, about one hour or less.

2. Put remaining flour in a large bowl. Add the ball of dough, half the butter, remaining sugar, salt and two of the eggs, slightly beaten. Mix well with the fingers, adding enough milk to give a soft, nonsticky dough. Turn out on a lightly floured board and knead until smooth.

3. Work in the remaining butter and two more eggs. Repeat the kneading. Lift the dough and slap or bang it on the table until it is very smooth.

4. Add two more eggs, work them into the dough and repeat the kneading and banging on the table.

5. Shape the dough into a ball and place it in a greased bowl. Cover and let rise in a warm place (80° to 85° F.) until double in bulk.

6. Punch and stir the dough down. Shape into a ball, place in a clean greased bowl, cover tightly with foil and chill overnight or slightly longer.

7. To shape the brioche, turn the dough out onto a floured board. Cut off about one-sixth and reserve for topknots of buns. Divide remainder of the dough into eighteen to twenty-four portions and shape each into a ball. Place in greased brioche pans or muffin tins (2¾ x 1¼ inches deep). Cut reserved dough into the same number of small balls. Dampen a finger slightly and make a depression in the center of each large ball. Place a small ball in each of the depressions. Cover and let rise in a warm place until double in bulk, or about one hour.

8. Preheat oven to 450° F. and place rack near bottom.

9. Lightly beat remaining egg and brush over the tops of the brioche. Place in oven and bake until well browned, about fifteen minutes.

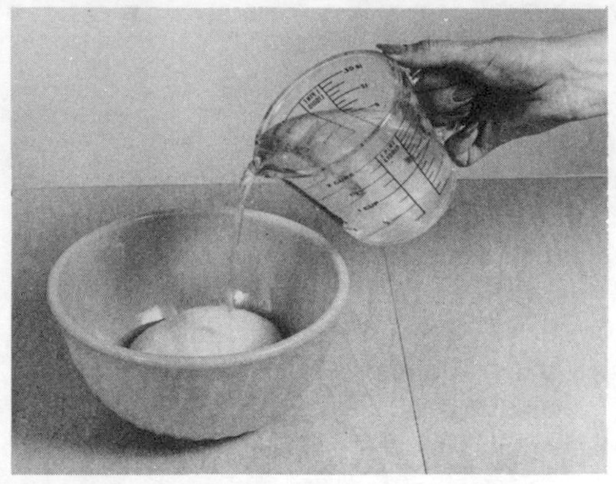

1. *Brioche.* To make sponge, dough is covered with water.

2. Later, sponge is mixed with the other ingredients.

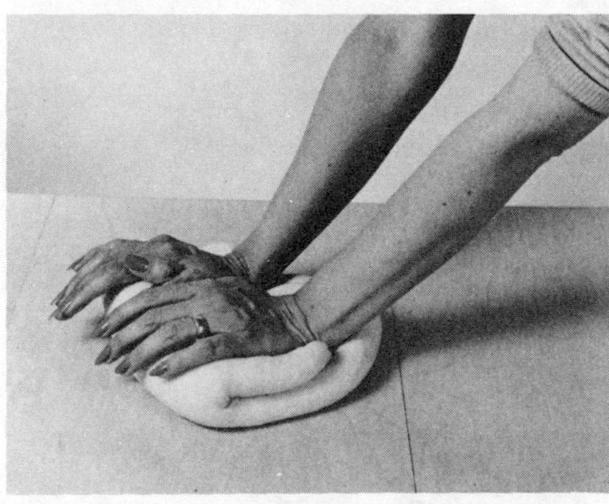

3. Brioche paste is then kneaded on a board until smooth.

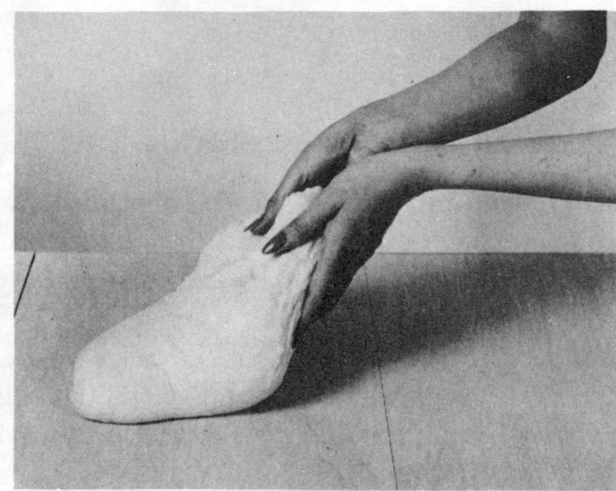

4. Eggs are added to the dough, which must then be smacked on the table.

5. When the dough rises, it is punched and stirred down.

6. Balls of dough are rolled and put in brioche tins.

7. A depression is made in each of the dough balls.

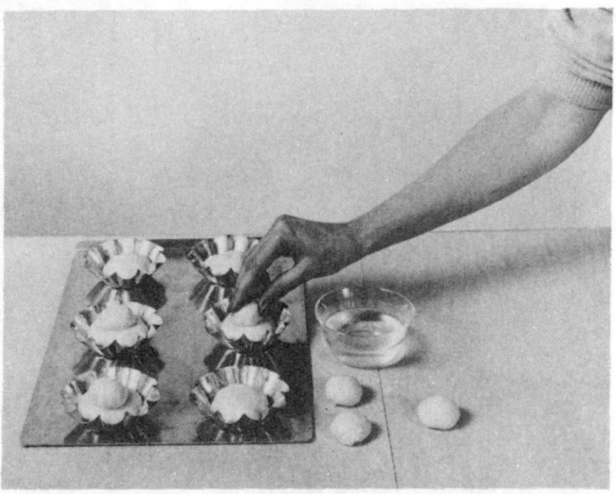

8. Topknots are added. The dough is brushed with butter, allowed to rise, and baked.

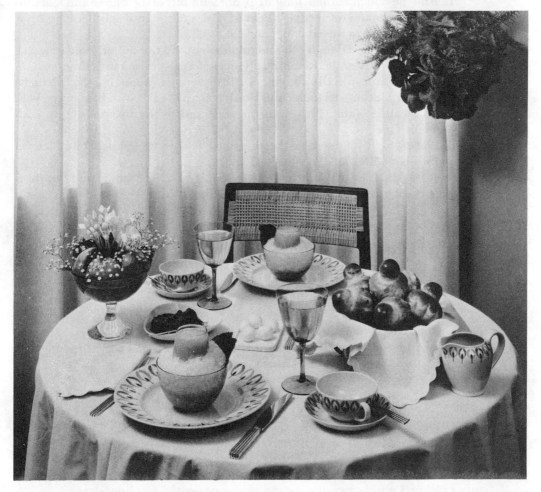

Golden brioche can be a festive addition to a leisurely weekend breakfast. Here brioche is shown with marmalade and butter, and glasses of orange juice encased in ice.

CROISSANTS *About 18 rolls*

Croissants, the traditional French breakfast bread, can be made from several doughs, including puff pastry (page 536). Here is one made with a yeast dough.

1 package yeast	½ teaspoon salt
¾ cup lukewarm milk	½ cup sweet butter
2 cups sifted flour	1 egg yolk

1. Dissolve the yeast in the milk.
2. Sift together the flour and salt and stir in the yeast mixture. Knead until smooth and elastic.
3. Place the dough in a greased bowl, grease the top of the dough and let rise in a warm place (85° F.) until doubled in bulk.
4. Roll the dough out in a long strip, dot with bits of the butter and fold into thirds. Turn so that an open edge is nearest. Pat and roll into another long strip, fold into thirds, wrap in waxed paper and chill well.
5. Roll the chilled dough out and fold the ends to the center. Fold again as above, wrap and refrigerate. Remove and repeat the process a fourth time.
6. The last time, roll the dough out a little thinner (about one-eighth inch) but do not fold. Cut into triangles and brush one tip of each with beaten egg yolk mixed with a little water. Roll from the wide end to the tip, pressing to seal. Shape into half moons.
7. Place on well-buttered cookie sheets, cover with waxed paper and let rise until doubled in bulk.
8. Brush the tops with beaten egg yolk and bake in a preheated hot oven (425° F.) twenty to twenty-five minutes. Serve hot or cold.

CRUMPETS *About 16 crumpets*

2 cups lukewarm water	¾ teaspoon salt
1 package yeast	1¾ cups sifted flour, approximately
¼ cup mashed potatoes (optional)	

1. Pour the water into a two-quart bowl. Add yeast and let stand until softened. Add potatoes, salt and flour. Mix well, using a wooden spoon, and then beat three minutes. The batter should be thin. Cover and let stand in a warm place thirty minutes.
2. Beat again three minutes and let stand thirty minutes longer. Repeat process once more.
3. Place a griddle over medium heat, grease it lightly and arrange six greased crumpet rings on it. When the griddle is hot, beat the batter briefly and spoon it into the rings, filling each about one-third full.
4. Bake until the surface is dry and the bottom is brown. Remove rings, turn crumpets and brown the second side very lightly. Cool on a rack.
5. Toast to heat. Serve with plenty of butter and, if desired, jam.

NUT TWISTS *2 dozen twists*

- ½ cup milk
- ½ cup shortening
- 3 tablespoons sugar
- 1½ teaspoons salt
- 1 teaspoon vanilla
- 2 packages yeast
- ¼ cup lukewarm water
- 3 cups sifted flour
- 3 eggs
- ¾ cup finely chopped nuts
- ½ cup sugar
- 1 teaspoon cinnamon

1. Scald the milk and combine with the shortening, sugar and salt. Cool to lukewarm. Add the vanilla and the yeast dissolved in the lukewarm water and mix well.
2. Blend in one and one-half cups of the flour and beat until smooth. Cover and let rest for fifteen minutes.
3. Add the eggs, one at a time, beating well after each addition. Blend in the remaining flour and mix thoroughly. The dough should be quite soft. Cover dough and let rise in a warm place (80° to 85° F.) about one-half hour.
4. Combine the nuts, sugar and cinnamon.
5. Divide the dough into small pieces with a tablespoon. Roll each piece in the sugar-nut mixture and stretch it to about eight inches in length. Twist into desired shapes.
6. Place on a greased baking sheet and let rise until almost double in bulk.
7. Bake in a preheated moderate oven (375° F.) twelve to fifteen minutes.

BASIC ROLLS *About 36 rolls*

- 2 cups milk
- ¼ cup shortening or butter
- ¼ cup sugar
- 2 teaspoons salt
- 2 packages yeast
- ¼ cup lukewarm water
- 5 to 6 cups sifted flour
- Melted shortening or butter

1. Bring the milk to a boil. Add shortening or butter, sugar and salt and cool to lukewarm.
2. Soften yeast in the lukewarm water and add to milk mixture.
3. Add about half the flour, mix and beat well. Add enough remaining flour to make a soft dough.
4. Turn out on a floured board, let rest ten minutes and then knead until smooth, about ten minutes.
5. Place dough in a greased bowl, grease surface, cover and let rise in a warm place (80° to 85° F.) until double in bulk.
6. Turn dough out on a floured board and knead lightly until surface is smooth. Shape as desired (see following directions) and place one inch apart on a greased baking sheet. Brush with melted butter, cover with a towel and let rise until double in bulk, thirty to forty minutes.
7. About ten minutes before rolls have risen preheat oven to 375° F.

(cont'd)

8. Brush rolls with additional melted butter, milk or egg diluted with a tablespoon of water and bake fifteen to twenty minutes or until brown.

VARIATIONS:

Parker House Rolls: Roll dough to one-quarter- to one-half-inch thickness and cut into two-inch rounds. Using the dull edge of a knife, make a crease slightly off center across each roll. Invert rolls, brush with melted butter and fold larger "half" over smaller half.

Biscuit Rolls: Roll dough one-half inch thick and cut into two-inch rounds.

Hamburger Rolls: Roll dough one-half inch thick and cut with a three-inch cutter.

Crescent Rolls: Using one-quarter of the dough at a time, roll dough into a round one-quarter inch thick. Use a nine-inch pan as a guide and cut the dough into a perfect circle. Cut into ten or twelve pie-shaped wedges, brush very lightly with melted butter and fold like jelly roll beginning with the outer edge. Curve each roll into a crescent on the baking sheet.

Finger Rolls: Shape dough into balls one to one and one-half inches in diameter. Roll and stretch under the hands until three to four inches long.

Cloverleaf Rolls: Cut risen dough in half and shape each half into a roll about twelve inches long. Cut into one-inch pieces and divide each piece into thirds. Shape into balls. Grease two-inch muffin cups, place three balls in each, brush the tops with melted butter and let rise until doubled in bulk.

Cinnamon Buns: Follow directions for whole wheat cinnamon buns (page 477).

CARAWAY BREAD STICKS, PAGE 49.

QUICK WHOLE WHEAT ROLLS *About 2 dozen rolls*

1¼ cups milk
¼ cup sugar
2½ teaspoons salt
3 tablespoons honey or molasses
¼ cup butter or other shortening
2 packages yeast
¼ cup lukewarm water
3½ cups whole wheat flour

1. Scald the milk and combine with the sugar, salt, honey and butter. Cool to lukewarm.

2. In a large bowl soften the yeast in the water. Add the lukewarm milk mixture and stir in enough flour to make a stiff dough.

3. Turn the dough out on a lightly floured surface and knead until smooth. Place in a greased bowl, grease the surface of the dough, cover with a towel and let rise in a warm place (80° to 85° F.) until doubled in bulk, about forty-five minutes.

4. Turn the dough out on an unfloured surface and shape into rolls (see basic roll variations, above). Brush the tops with melted butter, cover and let rise in a warm place until doubled in bulk, about one hour. Bake in a preheated hot oven (400° F.) about twenty minutes.

WHOLE WHEAT CINNAMON BUNS *18 buns*

Whole wheat roll dough (page 476)
Melted butter
1½ cups brown sugar, packed
1 tablespoon cinnamon
¼ teaspoon nutmeg
⅔ cup raisins

1. Follow the directions for the roll dough through the first rising. Turn out the dough onto a floured board, divide in half and roll each half into a thin rectangle about one-quarter inch thick and ten inches long. Brush with butter.
2. Mix the sugar, cinnamon and nutmeg. Sprinkle half the mixture and half the raisins on each sheet of dough. Roll tightly as for a jelly roll and cut each roll into nine equal portions. Place the buns, cut sides up, in two eight- or nine-inch greased round or square pans and brush with melted butter. Cover with waxed paper and let rise until doubled in bulk, about one hour.
3. Bake in a preheated moderate oven (350° F.) about thirty minutes. Serve warm, plain or sprinkled with confectioners' sugar, or cool and glaze with confectioners' icing (page 576).

SAFFRON BUNS *18 buns*

Saffron is undoubtedly the most expensive herb on earth, and for a very good reason. It is made with the dried stigmas of a crocus plant and literally thousands of the stigmas, harvested by hand, are necessary to yield a pound. A little saffron goes far, however.

¾ cup milk
¼ teaspoon powdered saffron
½ cup shortening
¼ cup granulated sugar
1 teaspoon salt
1 package yeast
¼ cup lukewarm water
1 egg, beaten
⅓ cup dried currants
¼ cup mixed candied fruit peel, chopped
1 teaspoon grated nutmeg
3½ to 4 cups sifted all-purpose flour
1 egg white, slightly beaten
1 cup confectioners' sugar
2 tablespoons hot water

1. Scald the milk with the saffron. In a large bowl, combine the milk mixture, shortening, sugar and salt. Cool to lukewarm.
2. Sprinkle the yeast on the water and stir until dissolved. Add the egg, currants, peel, nutmeg and enough flour to make a stiff dough. Knead until smooth and elastic.
3. Place in a greased bowl and brush the top with oil. Cover with a clean towel and let rise in a warm place (80° to 85° F.) until doubled in bulk.
4. Turn onto a lightly floured surface and knead one minute. Shape into eighteen two-inch balls and place in two greased eight-inch-square pans. Brush with egg white and cover with a towel. Let rise in a warm place until doubled in bulk.
5. Bake in a preheated hot oven (425° F.) twenty-five minutes, or until done. Cool on a wire rack. Frost with confectioners' icing (page 576).

QUICK BREADS

BAKING POWDER BISCUITS *16 2-inch biscuits*

2 cups sifted flour
2½ teaspoons baking powder
1 teaspoon salt
⅓ cup shortening
⅔ cup milk, approximately

1. Preheat oven to hot (425° F.).
2. Sift the flour, baking powder and salt into a mixing bowl.
3. With a pastry blender or two knives cut in shortening until mixture has the texture of coarse cornmeal.
4. Stir mixture gently with a fork while adding the milk. Use enough milk to form a dough that is soft but not sticky.
5. Knead on a lightly floured board until smooth, or about twenty strokes. Roll dough on the board until it is one-half inch thick. Cut with a floured biscuit cutter and place on a baking sheet at one-inch intervals.
6. Bake twelve to fifteen minutes, or until golden brown.

VARIATIONS:

Cheese Biscuits: Cut one-half cup grated sharp American cheese into the flour mixture with the fat.

Ham or Bacon Biscuits: Add two-thirds cup ground cooked ham or six slices cooked bacon, crumbled, to the flour-fat mixture before adding the milk.

Herbed Biscuits: Add two tablespoons each chopped chives and pimento and one tablespoon chopped parsley to the flour-fat mixture before adding the milk.

Orange Biscuits: Cut two tablespoons grated orange rind into the flour mixture with the fat. Top each biscuit with a cube of sugar that has been dipped in orange juice.

Drop Biscuits: Increase milk to one cup. Stir the dough lightly until just blended and drop by spoonfuls on greased baking sheet.

Watercress Biscuits: Add coarsely chopped leaves (washed and thoroughly dried) from one bunch of watercress to the dry ingredients.

BUTTERMILK BISCUITS *About 15 biscuits*

2 cups sifted flour
1 teaspoon salt
1 teaspoon baking powder
½ teaspoon soda
¼ cup shortening
¾ cup buttermilk, approximately

1. Preheat oven to hot (425° F.).
2. Sift together the dry ingredients. Cut in the shortening until the mixture resembles coarse cornmeal.

(cont'd)

3. Add enough buttermilk, while stirring lightly with a fork, to make a soft dough that separates from the sides of the bowl and forms a mound when stirred.

4. Turn onto a lightly floured board and knead lightly about thirty seconds. Roll to one-half-inch thickness and cut into rounds, using a floured biscuit cutter. Transfer to baking sheets and bake twelve to fifteen minutes.

ONION SQUARES *9 squares*

2 cups sliced onions
3 tablespoons butter
2 cups sifted flour
2 teaspoons baking powder
1 teaspoon salt
¼ cup shortening
2 tablespoons chopped parsley or ½ teaspoon caraway seeds
1 cup milk
⅓ cup sour cream or ½ cup grated cheese

1. Preheat oven to hot (425° F.).
2. Sauté the onions, covered, in butter until tender. Cool.
3. Sift together the flour, baking powder and salt. Chop in the shortening until the mixture resembles coarse cornmeal.
4. Add the parsley and milk and stir until all the flour is moistened.
5. Turn into a well-greased eight-inch-square pan. Spread onions over the top and cover with sour cream.
6. Bake about twenty minutes. Cut into squares and serve hot.

QUICK ONION KUCHEN, PAGE 388.

GARLIC BREAD, PAGE 50.

TEA SCONES *16 scones*

2 cups sifted flour
2 tablespoons sugar
3 teaspoons baking powder
½ teaspoon salt
⅓ cup butter
1 egg, beaten
¾ cup milk, approximately

1. Preheat oven to hot (425° F.).
2. Sift together the flour, sugar, baking powder and salt.
3. Chop in the butter with a pastry blender until the flour-coated particles of butter are the size of coarse cornmeal.
4. Add the egg and about three-quarters of the milk. Stir quickly and lightly, only until no flour shows. Add more milk if needed to make a soft dough.
5. Turn the dough out on a floured surface and knead gently about fifteen times. Cut the dough in half. Shape each half into a ball, press each down into a round about one-half inch thick and cut it into eight wedges like a pie.
6. Place the wedges on a greased cookie sheet without allowing the sides to touch. Glaze, if desired, with lightly beaten egg. Bake until deep golden brown, about twelve minutes.

Note: Scones may be cut also into two-inch rounds or into squares.

1. *Properly mixed muffins.* When liquid and dry ingredients are blended for muffins, the mixture should be stirred only until no flour shows. The batter looks lumpy and drops at once from the spoon. Such batter after baking gives perfect muffins. The grain is uniform and medium-fine with no elongated holes or tunnels. The crumb is moist and tender. The slightly rounded top is golden brown and glossy, with a pebbled surface.

2. *Overmixed muffins.* When liquid and dry materials are stirred and beaten until a muffin batter is smooth and elastic it forms ribbonlike strands that stretch when the spoon is lifted. Using too big a bowl encourages overbeating. Muffins made from such batter have uneven grain with tunnels running up toward the pointed top. They are tough and dry. The top is peaked and misshapen; the crust smooth, pale and lacking in gloss.

BASIC MUFFINS *12 3-inch muffins*

2 cups sifted flour
2 tablespoons sugar
2½ teaspoons baking powder
½ teaspoon salt
1 egg, well beaten
1 cup milk
¼ cup butter, melted and cooled slightly

1. Preheat oven to hot (400° F.).
2. Sift together the flour, sugar, baking powder and salt.
3. Mix the egg, milk and butter. Add the liquid mixture to the dry ingredients and stir only until the flour is moistened. Do not beat the batter until smooth.
4. Spoon into well-greased muffin tins, filling the cups about two-thirds full. Bake about twenty-five minutes and serve immediately.

(*cont'd*)

VARIATIONS:

Bacon Muffins: Add one-half cup crisp chopped cooked bacon to sifted dry ingredients. If desired, substitute part bacon fat for the butter.

Cheese Muffins: Eliminate sugar and add two-thirds cup grated sharp American cheese to the sifted dry ingredients. Sprinkle with paprika before baking.

Cranberry Muffins: Mix three-quarters cup chopped cranberries and one-quarter cup sugar. Add to the dry ingredients.

Nut Muffins: Add three-quarters cup finely chopped nuts to sifted dry ingredients.

Date Muffins: Add one-half cup sliced, pitted dates to sifted dry ingredients.

Upside-down Muffins: In the bottom of each muffin cup place one-half teaspoon butter and one teaspoon brown sugar. Add a few nuts or raisins or one stewed dried fig or apricot. Cover with batter and bake as directed.

BUCKWHEAT MUFFINS *12 muffins*

- ¼ cup shortening
- 3 tablespoons sugar
- 2 tablespoons molasses
- 1 egg, unbeaten
- 1½ cups sifted all-purpose flour
- 2 teaspoons baking powder
- ½ teaspoon soda
- ½ teaspoon salt
- ¾ cup fine buckwheat groats
- 1 cup buttermilk
- ¼ cup cut, seeded raisins

1. Preheat oven to hot (425° F.).
2. Cream the shortening until fluffy. Add the sugar and molasses and beat until light. Beat in the egg.
3. Sift together the flour, baking powder, soda and salt. Add to the creamed mixture. Add the groats and buttermilk and stir only until the dry ingredients are moistened. Add the raisins.
4. Fill greased 2½-inch-deep muffin pans one-half to two-thirds full and bake until the muffins are brown and done, or about twenty minutes. Serve hot.

POPOVERS *6 to 8 popovers*

An old recipe for popovers, typical of those in many early cookbooks, reads: "Get an iron popever pan blazing hot, grease it well and pour in the batter."

These cast-iron pans are found in few homes today, with the result that many home cooks are fearful of using substitutes. Fortunately, successful popovers can be baked in modern heavy aluminum tins, or oven glass and earthenware cups such as custard cups. The chief requirement is that the cups be deeper than they are wide. If the cups are of aluminum or metal that heats quickly, they do not have to be preheated; if glass or earthenware cups are used, it is well to preheat them while mixing the batter. Heated cups are greased just before filling.

No skill is required in mixing popovers. Success depends upon proper baking. The batter is thin—about as thick as heavy cream. In the hot oven the large amount of liquid forms steam,

(cont'd)

quickly causing the flour-and-egg mixture to expand and form a nearly hollow shell. This shell must be baked until it is rigid, to prevent collapse as the steam condenses on cooling. It is always a temptation to peek, but to prevent collapse the oven door should not be opened for at least thirty minutes of baking.

1 cup sifted flour
½ teaspoon salt
2 eggs
1 cup milk
1 tablespoon salad oil

1. Heat oven to hot (425° F.). Grease aluminum popover pans and set aside. If glass or earthenware cups are used, place these on a baking sheet in the oven to heat; remove and grease just before filling.

2. Measure all ingredients into a bowl and beat with a rotary beater until mixture is very smooth.

3. Fill cups a little less than half full and bake in the preheated oven, without peeking, about thirty-five minutes, or until the sides are rigid to the touch. If drier popovers are desired, pierce each one with a knife and bake five minutes longer.

SPOON BREAD *Serves 6 generously*

3 cups milk
¾ cup cornmeal (yellow or white)
2 tablespoons butter
1 teaspoon salt
2 eggs, separated
1 teaspoon baking powder

1. Scald two cups of the milk in a double boiler. Mix the remaining milk with the cornmeal, add to the scalded milk and cook, stirring frequently, thirty minutes. Cool slightly.

2. Preheat oven to moderate (375° F.).

3. Add the butter, salt and beaten egg yolks to the cornmeal mixture and mix well. Add the baking powder and mix. Fold in the egg whites, stiffly beaten.

4. Turn the mixture into a greased casserole and bake about thirty minutes.

CRACKLING CORN CAKES *About 12 corn cakes*

2 ounces salt pork, chopped
2 cups white cornmeal, preferably stone ground
1½ teaspoons baking powder
½ teaspoon soda
1 teaspoon salt
2 eggs, beaten
1 cup buttermilk, approximately

1. Cook the salt pork slowly, stirring frequently, until lightly browned.

2. Sift together the cornmeal, baking powder, soda and salt.

3. Mix the eggs, buttermilk and two tablespoons fat from the pork. Drain off remaining fat and reserve.

4. Add the liquid ingredients to the cornmeal. Add the salt pork cracklings

(cont'd)

and stir until the cornmeal is dampened. The batter should be stiff enough almost to hold its shape when dropped from a spoon.

5. In a skillet heat the reserved fat, discarding the sediment. Or, if desired, use another shortening. Drop the cornmeal mixture from a spoon into the fat to form cakes and brown slowly on both sides.

APPLE BREAD *1 loaf*

2 cups sifted flour
1 teaspoon baking powder
½ teaspoon soda
1 teaspoon salt
½ cup shortening
⅔ cup sugar
2 eggs
1 cup unpeeled, ground apples and juice
½ cup grated sharp cheese
¼ cup chopped nut meats

1. Preheat oven to moderate (350° F.).

2. Sift together the flour, baking powder, soda and salt.

3. Cream the shortening, add the sugar gradually and continue working until light and fluffy. Add the eggs, one at a time, beating about one minute after each addition. Add the apples, cheese and nuts and mix well.

4. Add the dry ingredients in two portions, mixing only until all the flour is dampened.

5. Turn into a greased 9 x 5 x 3-inch loaf pan. Push the batter well up into the corners of the pan, leaving the center slightly hollow. Bake one hour.

BANANA TEA BREAD *1 loaf*

1¾ cups sifted flour
2 teaspoons baking powder
¼ teaspoon soda
½ teaspoon salt
⅓ cup shortening
⅔ cup sugar
2 eggs, well beaten
1 cup mashed ripe bananas (2 to 3 bananas)

1. Preheat oven to moderate (350° F.).

2. Sift together the flour, baking powder, soda and salt.

3. Cream the shortening, add the sugar gradually and continue working until light and fluffy. Add the eggs and beat well. Add the flour mixture alternately with the bananas, a small amount at a time, beating after each addition until smooth.

4. Turn into a well-greased bread pan (8½ x 4½ x 3 inches) and bake about one hour and ten minutes.

VARIATIONS:

For raisin, nut or date banana bread, add one cup seedless raisins, one-half cup coarsely broken nut meats or one cup finely chopped dates to the batter.

BANANA BRAN BREAD *2 loaves and 2 custard cups*

- 1 cup ready-to-eat bran cereal
- 1 cup mashed ripe bananas (2 to 3 bananas)
- 3 tablespoons shortening
- ½ cup sugar
- ¼ cup boiling water
- 1 egg
- 1½ cups sifted flour
- 2 teaspoons baking powder
- ½ teaspoon baking soda
- ½ teaspoon salt

1. Preheat oven to moderate (350° F.).

2. Measure the bran, mashed bananas, shortening and sugar into a bowl. Add the water and stir until well mixed. Add the egg and beat well.

3. Sift together the flour, baking powder, soda and salt. Add to the banana mixture, stirring only until combined.

4. Fill two greased cans (baked bean cans) not more than two-thirds full. Bake any extra batter in greased custard cups.

5. Bake until a food pick inserted on the center comes out clean, or twenty-five minutes for custard cups, forty-five minutes to one hour for cans. Let cool five minutes, then remove from cans.

GINGERBREAD, PAGE 562.

ORANGE HONEY BREAD *1 loaf*

- 2 tablespoons shortening
- 1 cup honey
- 1 egg, well beaten
- 1½ tablespoons grated orange rind
- 2½ cups sifted flour
- 2½ teaspoons baking powder
- ½ teaspoon soda
- ½ teaspoon salt
- ¾ cup orange juice
- ¾ cup chopped nuts

1. Preheat oven to slow (325° F.).

2. Cream the shortening, add the honey and mix together thoroughly. Add the egg and grated orange rind.

3. Sift the flour with the baking powder, soda and salt and add to the creamed mixture alternately with the orange juice, stirring only until flour is dampened. Add the nuts.

4. Turn into a greased nine-inch loaf pan and bake one hour and ten minutes.

IRISH SWEET BREAD *2 loaves*

- 3 cups sifted flour
- 1½ teaspoons salt
- ¾ teaspoon soda
- ½ cup shortening
- ¼ cup sugar
- ¼ cup molasses
- 1 egg, unbeaten
- 1½ cups sour milk or buttermilk
- 1½ cups raisins, chopped
- 1½ cups currants
- ¼ cup chopped citron or chopped, candied lemon rind

(cont'd)

1. Preheat oven to slow (325° F.).
2. Sift together the flour, salt and soda.
3. Cream together the shortening and sugar and the molasses. Beat in the egg. Alternately add the dry ingredients and sour milk; stir in the fruit.
4. Pour the batter into two greased 8 x 4 x 2½-inch loaf pans and bake one and one-quarter hours.

SESAME TEA BREAD *1 loaf*

Until a decade ago the word "sesame" implied something out of the Arabian Nights to most Americans. Today sesame seeds enjoy a striking popularity throughout the land.

- 3 cups sifted all-purpose flour
- 1 teaspoon salt
- 2½ teaspoons baking powder
- ½ cup toasted sesame seeds
- ⅔ cup sugar
- ¼ cup shortening
- 2 eggs
- 1 teaspoon grated lemon rind
- 1½ cups milk
- 1 tablespoon untoasted sesame seeds

1. Preheat oven to moderate (350° F.).
2. Sift the flour, salt and baking powder together and mix in the toasted sesame seeds.
3. Cream the sugar and shortening together until fluffy and beat in the eggs. Blend in the lemon rind and milk. Add all at once to the flour mixture and mix only until the ingredients are blended, about thirty strokes. Use the cut-and-fold method of mixing and stop at the end of the fifteenth stroke to scrape down the bowl and spoon with a rubber spatula.
4. Turn the mixture into a well-greased, lightly floured 9 x 5 x 3-inch loaf pan. Sprinkle the untoasted sesame seeds over the top.
5. Bake one hour and ten minutes. Cool. Serve with sweet butter or cream cheese.

NEW ENGLAND BUTTERMILK DOUGHNUTS

About 3 dozen 3-inch doughnuts

For tender doughnuts the dough must be soft, not nearly so stiff as for bread. Plenty of flour on the pastry cloth or bread eliminates the handling that is undesirable. A fat thermometer registers the right heat—375° F. Higher than that means the doughnuts cook on the outside and not within, and lower than that means they become fat-soaked. Frying, too, causes the temperature of the fat to drop sharply.

- 4½ cups sifted flour
- ¼ teaspoon nutmeg
- ¼ teaspoon allspice
- 1½ teaspoons soda
- 1½ teaspoons cream of tartar
- 1½ teaspoons salt
- 3 eggs
- 1 cup sugar
- 3 tablespoons shortening, melted
- 1 cup buttermilk
- Fat for deep frying

(*cont'd*)

1. Sift together the flour, nutmeg, allspice, soda, cream of tartar and salt.

2. Beat the eggs until thick and lemon-colored and gradually beat in the sugar. Add the melted shortening and buttermilk, then add the flour mixture. Mix well, chill and turn out on a well-floured board or pastry cloth.

3. Roll to one-quarter inch thick; cut with a floured cutter.

4. Fry a few at a time in deep hot fat (375° F.) for three minutes or until brown, first on one side and then on the other.

BASIC PANCAKES

About 1 dozen 5-inch pancakes

1½ cups sifted flour
2½ teaspoons baking powder
¾ teaspoon salt
1 egg, well beaten
1¼ cups milk, approximately
3 tablespoons shortening, melted and slightly cooled, or salad oil

1. Sift together flour, baking powder and salt.

2. Mix egg, milk and shortening or oil. Three-quarters cup of milk will make thick pancakes; one and one-quarter cups of milk will make them thin enough for rolling.

3. Pour milk mixture into dry ingredients and stir only enough to moisten the dry ingredients. Do not beat or the pancakes will be tough. (For thinner pancakes, add more milk and mix lightly.)

4. Bake on a hot griddle, lightly greased if necessary. Turn pancakes only once.

VARIATION:

Dessert Pancakes: Sift three tablespoons sugar with dry ingredients and proceed as directed for basic pancakes.

BEER PANCAKES

About 2 dozen pancakes

3 cups sifted flour
3 teaspoons baking powder
1 teaspoon salt
1 tablespoon sugar
2 eggs, separated
1 cup beer
1½ cups milk
⅓ cup melted butter

1. Sift together the flour, baking powder, salt and sugar.

2. Beat the egg yolks with a fork. Stir in the beer, milk and butter and add to the dry ingredients. Beat until smooth.

3. Beat the egg whites until stiff. Fold into the batter.

4. Heat a griddle, grease lightly if necessary and drop the batter from the tip of a large spoon onto the griddle. Bake until the batter rises and the entire surface is dotted with holes. Turn and bake the second side. Serve hot with maple syrup, cottage cheese or jam.

SOUR CREAM PANCAKES *About 14 5-inch pancakes*

1 cup sifted flour
½ teaspoon salt
½ teaspoon baking soda
1¼ cups sour cream, approximately
1 egg, slightly beaten

1. Sift together the flour, salt and soda.
2. Combine the sour cream and egg. Pour into the flour mixture and stir just enough to moisten the dry ingredients. Do not beat.
3. Heat a griddle or skillet, grease if necessary and drop the batter by spoonfuls onto it. When bubbles break on top of the cakes, turn and bake on the other side.

VARIATIONS:

Buttermilk Pancakes: Substitute one cup buttermilk for the sour cream and add two tablespoons melted butter when combining the milk and egg.

Fruit or Nut Pancakes: Add to either sour cream or buttermilk batter one-half cup finely chopped apples or well-drained canned pineapple; or one-half cup chopped pecans or other nut meats.

BUCKWHEAT BLINI *36 blini*

1 cup milk
½ package yeast (½ tablespoon)
4 eggs, separated
½ teaspoon salt
1 teaspoon sugar
3 tablespoons butter, melted
1½ cups sifted buckwheat flour

1. Scald milk and allow it to cool to lukewarm. Add yeast and stir until softened.
2. Beat the egg yolks until thick. Add the yeast mixture and remaining ingredients except egg whites. Mix thoroughly.
3. Set in a pan of warm water, cover and let rise until double in bulk, about one and one-quarter hours.
4. Beat egg whites stiff and fold gently but thoroughly into batter.
5. Preheat a lightly buttered griddle until it is hot. Using one tablespoon of batter for each pancake, bake on top of stove until golden brown, turning once. If the blini begin to stick to the griddle, butter it lightly again. Serve with caviar and sour cream.

WHITE-FLOUR BLINI *42 blini*

2 cups milk
½ package yeast (½ tablespoon)
2 teaspoons sugar
3 cups sifted flour
3 eggs, separated
5 tablespoons butter, melted
½ teaspoon salt

(cont'd)

1. Scald the milk and allow it to cool to lukewarm. Add the yeast and stir until the yeast has softened.

2. Add the sugar and one and one-half cups of the flour and mix well. Cover and set in a pan of warm water until double in bulk, about one and one-quarter hours.

3. Beat the egg yolks with the butter and salt. Add to the batter. Add the remaining flour and beat until smooth. Cover and let rise as before until double in bulk, approximately thirty minutes.

4. Beat the egg whites until stiff and fold into the batter. Let the mixture stand for ten minutes.

5. Preheat a lightly buttered griddle until it is hot. Using one tablespoon of batter for each pancake, bake until golden brown on both sides, turning once. Serve with caviar and sour cream.

BASIC WAFFLE RECIPE *5 or 6 waffles*

2 cups sifted flour
3 teaspoons baking powder
1 teaspoon salt
2 tablespoons sugar
2 eggs, separated
1½ cups milk
6 tablespoons melted shortening or salad oil

1. Sift together the flour, baking powder, salt and sugar.

2. Beat egg yolks; add milk and melted shortening. Pour into flour mixture and stir just enough to moisten dry ingredients. Fold in egg whites which have been beaten until stiff but not dry.

3. Grease a hot waffle iron if necessary and pour batter to one inch from edge. Bake four to five minutes. Serve hot with melted butter and syrup or honey.

WHOLE WHEAT NUT WAFFLES *About 6 waffles*

2 cups whole wheat flour
2 teaspoons baking powder
½ teaspoon salt
3 eggs, separated
1½ cups milk
¼ cup melted shortening
½ cup chopped walnuts or filberts

1. Mix the flour with the baking powder and salt.

2. Beat the egg yolks and add the milk and shortening. Add to the flour mixture and mix until all the flour is moistened. Add the nut meats.

3. Fold in the egg whites, which have been stiffly beaten.

4. Bake in a hot waffle iron and serve with melted butter and heated syrup.

RYE FRITTERS *2 servings*

1 cup sifted all-purpose flour
1 cup rye meal (not regular rye flour)
1 teaspoon salt
1 teaspoon cinnamon
1 teaspoon baking powder
1 egg
2 teaspoons molasses
1 cup milk, approximately
Fat for deep frying

1. Sift together into a mixing bowl the flour, rye meal, salt, cinnamon and baking powder.

2. Beat the egg, add the molasses and pour into the flour mixture. Add two-thirds cup milk and mix thoroughly, adding more milk if necessary to make a medium stiff batter.

3. Drop the batter from a spoon slightly larger than a tablespoon into hot fat (360° F.). Fry about two and one-half minutes on each side. Serve hot with maple syrup and sausages.

CHAPTER ELEVEN

RELISHES AND PRESERVES

RELISHES

"Relish" is one of the most apt food words in the language. Relishes offer a fine contrast in flavors when served with savory dishes.

BEET-CABBAGE RELISH *5 pints*

1 cup chopped onion
1 quart cooked beets, shredded
1 quart cabbage, shredded
1 cup grated horseradish
4 teaspoons salt
1¾ cups vinegar
¾ cup sugar

1. Combine in a saucepan the onion, beets, cabbage, horseradish and salt.
2. Heat the vinegar, dissolve the sugar in it and add to the vegetables. Boil ten minutes. Pack in hot sterile jars and seal.

To Sterilize Jars: Place washed jars in a large kettle and cover with warm water. Cover the kettle and boil fifteen to twenty minutes. When ready to use, remove with tongs and drain. The jars should be hot when hot mixture is poured in to prevent breakage.

CABBAGE–GREEN TOMATO RELISH *About 4 pints*

2 quarts chopped green tomatoes
2 quarts chopped cabbage
2 cups chopped onion
½ cup chopped sweet red pepper
2 tablespoons salt
½ teaspoon ground allspice
1 teaspoon celery seed
1 tablespoon mustard seed
⅓ cup firmly packed brown sugar
1 pint cider vinegar

(*cont'd*)

1. Arrange the chopped tomatoes, cabbage, onion and red pepper in layers in a large saucepan, sprinkling each layer with salt. Let stand overnight. Drain.

2. Add the allspice, celery seed, mustard seed, sugar and vinegar. Boil uncovered, stirring occasionally, until there is just enough liquid left to moisten the ingredients well, or twenty-five minutes. Pack into hot sterile jars, filling the jars to the top. Seal.

SPICED CABBAGE *About 4 pints*

4 quarts shredded cabbage
½ cup coarse salt
Cider vinegar
½ to 2 cups sugar, depending upon sweetness desired
1 tablespoon white mustard seed
1 tablespoon prepared horseradish
1 teaspoon whole cloves
4 sticks cinnamon, broken

1. Place the cabbage in a stone crock or enamel pan in layers with the salt. Let stand overnight.

2. Press out all the juice and, if desired, rinse the cabbage in cold water to reduce the salt. Drain and measure.

3. In a saucepan, heat to simmering half as much vinegar as there is cabbage. Add the sugar, mustard seed and horseradish. Tie the cloves and cinnamon in cheesecloth and add. Cook, stirring, until the sugar is dissolved. Continue simmering fifteen minutes.

4. Pack the cabbage loosely in hot clean jars and fill to within one-half inch of the top of the jar with the hot spiced vinegar. Seal and process in boiling water (see below) twenty minutes.

Note: If desired, one-quarter cup mixed pickling spice may be substituted for the spices in the recipe.

Boiling-Water Bath: Adjust covers as manufacturer directs and place filled jars on a rack in a kettle containing boiling water. Add boiling water if needed to bring water an inch or two over tops of containers; do not pour boiling water directly on top of glass jars. Cover the kettle. When water returns to a rolling boil, begin to count processing time. Boil gently and steadily for the processing time recommended for the food you are canning. Add boiling water if necessary to keep containers covered during processing. Remove jars from the kettle immediately when processing time is up and seal at once as manufacturer directs.

CELERY RELISH *5 pints*

2 green peppers
2 sweet red peppers
1 pound (6 medium) onions
3 tablespoons salt
1¼ cups sugar
3 tablespoons mustard seed
½ teaspoon turmeric
⅔ cup light corn syrup
1⅔ cups distilled white vinegar
⅔ cup water
2 quarts (5 medium stalks) sliced celery

(*cont'd*)

1. Chop peppers and onions.

2. Combine salt, sugar, mustard seed and turmeric. Blend in the corn syrup, vinegar and water, cover and heat to boiling. Add vegetables, including celery. Simmer, covered, three minutes.

3. Pack into hot sterile jars, filling to within one-eighth inch of the top of the jar and making sure that the liquid covers the vegetables. Seal at once.

OLD-FASHIONED FRESH CORN RELISH *About 3 pints*

- 16 large ears fresh corn
- 1 quart (1 small head) finely chopped cabbage
- 1 cup diced celery
- 2 cups diced green pepper
- 1½ cups chopped onion
- 1 clove garlic, minced
- ¾ cup sugar
- ¼ cup fresh lemon juice
- ¾ cup water
- 1¼ cups cider vinegar
- 5 teaspoons salt
- 1 teaspoon celery seed
- 1½ tablespoons dry mustard
- 1 teaspoon turmeric
- ¼ teaspoon cayenne pepper
- ¾ cup chopped pimento

1. Cook the corn on the cob in boiling salted water to cover two to three minutes, using one teaspoon salt to one quart water. Cool the corn, cut from the cob.

2. Mix the corn with the cabbage, celery, green pepper, onion and garlic. Set aside while preparing the vinegar and spice mixture.

3. Combine the sugar, lemon juice, water, vinegar, salt and spices in a five-quart kettle. Bring to a boil. Add the vegetables and cook twenty-five minutes, stirring frequently. Stir in the pimento and heat.

4. Pack into hot sterile jars and seal at once. Keep four or five weeks before using.

OHIO CORN RELISH *About 1½ pints*

- 1 large cucumber, peeled and quartered
- 3 medium onions, peeled and quartered
- 1 green pepper, seeded and quartered
- 3 cups (about 12 ears) sweet corn, cut from the cob
- 2 medium tomatoes, peeled and seeded
- 1 cup sugar
- 2 tablespoons salt
- ½ teaspoon freshly ground black pepper
- 1 cup cider vinegar
- ½ cup water
- ½ teaspoon turmeric
- 1½ teaspoons mustard seed

1. Put the cucumber, onions and green pepper through a food grinder, using a medium blade. Combine with the corn and tomatoes in a large kettle.

2. Add the remaining ingredients, mix and bring to a boil. Stir almost con-

(cont'd)

stantly with a wooden spoon until the sugar dissolves. Cover and cook slowly over medium heat forty-five minutes.

3. Pour into hot sterile jars and seal at once. Keep four to five weeks before using.

CORN AND TOMATO RELISH *About 4 pints*

12 large ears fresh corn, cut from the cob
1 quart chopped, peeled onions
1 quart chopped, peeled ripe tomatoes
1 quart chopped, peeled cucumbers
3 green peppers, seeded and chopped
3 sweet red peppers, seeded and chopped
6 small hot red peppers, seeded and chopped
1 bunch celery, trimmed of leaves and tough outer stalks and minced
2 tablespoons turmeric
1 quart vinegar
2 tablespoons mustard seed
1 cup sugar
⅓ cup salt

1. Combine all the vegetables in a large, heavy saucepan.

2. Blend the turmeric with a little of the vinegar and add the mustard seed.

3. Dissolve the sugar and salt in the remaining vinegar. Add the vinegar and seasonings to the vegetables, bring to a boil and simmer, uncovered, one hour.

4. Pour into hot sterile jars and seal at once. Keep four or five weeks before using.

HENRY CREEL'S PEPPER HASH *4 pints*

1 dozen medium (7 cups ground) sweet green peppers
1 dozen medium (7 cups ground) sweet red peppers
2 medium (1 cup ground) onions
1 quart boiling water
2 cups cider vinegar
2 cups sugar
½ teaspoon salt

1. Wash the peppers, cut out the stems and remove the seeds. Put through a food chopper, using the coarse blade.

2. Peel the onions and put them through a food chopper, using the coarse blade.

3. Add the onion to the peppers. Add boiling water to cover and let stand ten minutes. Drain in a bag overnight or eight hours. Discard the liquid.

4. Add the vinegar, sugar and salt. Bring to the boiling point and boil twenty minutes. Pour into hot sterile jars and seal at once.

COOKED CRANBERRY ORANGE RELISH *About 12 servings*

1 pound cranberries, picked over and washed
2 cups sugar
½ cup water
2 teaspoons grated orange rind
½ cup orange juice
½ cup blanched almonds, slivered

(*cont'd*)

1. Combine all the ingredients except the almonds in a saucepan and cook until the cranberries pop open, about ten minutes.

2. Skim the foam from the surface, add the almonds and cool.

ONION RELISH *About 6 servings*

- 24 small white onions
- ⅓ cup olive oil
- ⅓ cup wine vinegar
- 1⅓ cups water
- 1 clove garlic, chopped
- ½ teaspoon salt
- ½ teaspoon dry mustard
- ½ teaspoon mustard seed
- ½ teaspoon freshly ground black pepper
- 1 clove
- 1 teaspoon sugar
- ⅓ cup light raisins
- Minced parsley or dill

1. Boil the unpeeled onions five minutes, drain and rub off the skins. Add the oil, vinegar, water, seasonings and sugar and simmer until the onions are just tender. Add the raisins and simmer three minutes longer. Chill.

2. Sprinkle generously with parsley or dill.

UNCOOKED TOMATO RELISH *4 pints*

- 2 quarts chopped, peeled tomatoes
- 1 cup chopped celery
- ¾ cup chopped onion
- ½ cup chopped green pepper
- 2 teaspoons salt
- 3 tablespoons sugar
- 1 tablespoon mustard seed
- ¼ teaspoon nutmeg
- ¼ teaspoon cinnamon
- ¼ teaspoon ground cloves
- 1 cup mild cider vinegar

Mix all the ingredients together thoroughly. Pour into sterile jars, cover and refrigerate. Use within two or three weeks.

SWEET MIXED RELISH *About 6 pints*

- 1 medium head of cabbage
- 7 green tomatoes
- 3 stalks celery
- 2 sweet red peppers
- 3 green peppers
- 1 tablespoon mustard seed
- 1 tablespoon celery seed
- 1 tablespoon salt
- 2 cups sugar, or more
- 1 quart mild cider vinegar

1. Put the cabbage, tomatoes, celery and green and red peppers through a food grinder, using the medium knife. Combine the vegetables in a large saucepan with the mustard seed, celery seed and salt. Add the two cups sugar, or more if a sweeter relish is desired, and the vinegar.

2. Cook slowly for about two hours, stirring occasionally. Pack into hot sterile jars and seal.

SPICY TOMATO KETCHUP *About 8 pints*

12 pounds ripe tomatoes
1 cup chopped onions
1 tablespoon salt
1 cup sugar
1 teaspoon black pepper
½ teaspoon celery seed
1 teaspoon mustard seed
1 tablespoon whole cloves
1 stick cinnamon, broken
1½ cups vinegar
¼ teaspoon cayenne pepper

1. Core and chop the tomatoes. Cook together tomatoes and onions until soft and press mixture through a fine sieve.

2. Return purée to heat and cook until reduced one-half, stirring occasionally. Add remaining ingredients including spices tied in a bag. Continue cooking, uncovered, to desired consistency, about four hours. Discard spice bag. Seal in hot sterilized jars.

PICKLES

PICKLED BEETS *About 3 pints*

2 pounds beets
1½ cups cider vinegar
1½ tablespoons dry mustard
½ teaspoon salt
1¼ cups sugar
2 medium onions, sliced (optional)
2 teaspoons celery seed

1. Cook the beets in water to cover until tender. Drain, reserving one cup of the cooking water. Slip off the skins and slice.

2. Heat the vinegar and reserved cooking water to a boil. Mix the mustard, salt and sugar. Add to the vinegar and let boil again.

3. Arrange the beets and onions in layers in clean canning jars. Add the celery seed and cover with the hot vinegar mixture. Seal, cool and store in the refrigerator. Let stand a few days before using. They will keep for weeks in refrigerator.

SPICED PICKLED CANTALOUPE *2½ pints*

2 quarts cantaloupe meat, cut in 1-inch squares
Water
¼ cup salt
4 cups sugar
1 cup vinegar
2 or 3 sticks whole cinnamon
1½ tablespoons whole allspice
1½ tablespoons whole cloves

(cont'd)

1. Select firm, slightly underripe cantaloupe. Cut in half, remove the seeds and rind and cut into one-inch squares.

2. Combine one quart cold water and the salt and stir to dissolve. Pour over the cantaloupe, cover and let stand three hours. Drain.

3. Add the sugar, vinegar and spices to three cups boiling water in a large enamel or stainless-steel pot. Bring to a boil, stirring until the sugar has dissolved. Add the drained cantaloupe meat and bring to a boil. Boil ten minutes, cool, cover and let stand overnight.

4. Drain the syrup from the cantaloupe. Bring the syrup to a boil and boil ten minutes. Add the cantaloupe and bring to a boil again. Reduce the heat and simmer gently about forty-five minutes, or until the cantaloupe is clear and transparent. Pour immediately into hot sterile jars and seal at once.

PICKLED CARROTS *About 2 pints*

1 quart small carrots of uniform size
Water
3 cups white vinegar
1 cup sugar
3 tablespoons mixed pickling spice, tied in a cheesecloth

1. Cook the carrots in water to cover until the skins slip easily and the carrots are half done. Peel.

2. Boil together ten minutes the vinegar, one-half cup water, the sugar and spice. Remove the spice bag.

3. Add the carrots and boil two to four minutes, or until almost tender. Pack in hot sterile jars and pour the syrup over them. Seal.

VARIATION:

Pickled Shoestring Carrots for Cocktails: Cut carrots after parboiling into uniform strips. Follow the above directions but do not boil the sticks in syrup; merely bring them to boiling point, pack and seal.

CAULIFLOWER PICKLE *Approximately 7 pints*

2 large heads cauliflower (approximately 4 pounds trimmed)
1 pound medium onions (about 12)
¼ cup salt
¾ cup sugar
1 teaspoon ground turmeric
2 teaspoons whole mustard seed
1 teaspoon whole celery seed
1 small dried hot red pepper
½ teaspoon whole cloves
1½ cups white vinegar
1½ cups water

1. Wash the cauliflower and break into flowerettes. Scald the onions, peel and slice. Mix with the cauliflower and salt and let stand overnight. Drain and rinse in cold water. If too salty, soak one hour in cold water and drain.

2. Combine the sugar, turmeric, mustard seed, celery seed and red pepper

(*cont'd*)

in an eight-quart kettle. Tie the whole cloves in a cheesecloth and add. Stir in the vinegar and water and boil five minutes.

3. Add the cauliflower and onions and boil until tender but still crisp, or five to ten minutes. Remove and discard cheesecloth bag and red pepper. Pack at once into hot sterile jars and fill the jars with the boiling liquid. Seal at once.

SWEET CUCUMBER AND GREEN-TOMATO PICKLE

7 half-pint jars

- 1 quart thinly sliced unpeeled cucumbers
- 1 quart thinly sliced green tomatoes
- 2 cups thinly sliced white onions
- ¼ cup salt
- 1 cup sugar
- 2 cups cider vinegar
- 1 tablespoon whole mustard seed
- ½ teaspoon whole celery seed
- 5 or 6 whole black peppercorns
- ½ teaspoon ground turmeric

1. Arrange alternate layers of cucumbers, green tomatoes, onions and salt in a bowl. Let stand six to eight hours, or overnight. Drain.

2. Combine the remaining ingredients in a four-quart kettle and bring to a boil. Add the cucumbers, tomatoes and onions and boil until the vegetables are clear, five to ten minutes.

3. Pack in hot sterile jars and seal at once.

KOSHER-STYLE DILL PICKLES *About 4 quarts*

- 3 dozen medium cucumbers
- 12 or more sprigs dill
- 5 cloves garlic
- 6 peppercorns
- 2 whole chili peppers (optional)
- 4 whole cloves
- 2 bay leaves
- 1½ cups salt
- 2 cups vinegar
- 2 gallons hot water

1. Wash and dry the cucumbers. Place half the dill, garlic, peppercorns, chili peppers, cloves and bay leaves in the bottom of a large stone crock. Add the cucumbers and top with the remaining seasonings.

2. Add the salt and vinegar to the water and stir until the salt has dissolved. Pour over the cucumbers, cover with a dinner plate and place a quart canning jar filled with water on the plate to keep the cucumbers under the brine.

3. Keep at an even temperature (68° to 72° F.) two to four weeks, removing the scum from the surface each day. Curing is finished when the pickles are well flavored and even-colored throughout. There should be no white spots. The pickles are ready to eat, but they must be canned for storage.

4. To can the pickles, pack them in hot clean glass canning jars. Strain the brine in which they were cured and boil it five minutes. Pour the boiling brine over the pickles and adjust lids. Process the jars ten minutes in a boiling-water bath (page 494).

QUICK DILL PICKLES I *2 quarts*

14 to 16 cucumbers, about 3½ inches long
2 tablespoons vinegar
4 cloves garlic, peeled
1 teaspoon whole mixed pickling spice
½ teaspoon whole mustard or celery seeds
4 bay leaves
2 small bunches fresh dill
2 grape leaves (optional)
1 quart water
½ cup coarse salt

1. Wash the cucumbers and drain. Pack in upright position in two sterile quart jars. Add half the vinegar, garlic, pickling spice, mustard, bay leaves, dill and grape leaves to each jar.

2. Bring the water and salt to a boil and pour over the cucumbers, filling the jars to within one-half inch of the top. Seal at once. Let stand in refrigerator at least one week before using and use within two to three weeks.

QUICK DILL PICKLES II *2 quarts*

2¾ to 3 pounds cucumbers (about 3½ inches long)
12 grape leaves
4 medium stalks fresh green dill
1 tablespoon mixed pickling spice
3¼ cups water
¼ cup cider vinegar
¼ cup salt

1. Choose firm, fresh cucumbers, clean grape leaves and fresh green dill. Wash the dill and cucumbers. Wipe the grape leaves but do not wash unless soiled.

2. Place a layer of grape leaves and dill in the bottom of two hot sterile quart jars or one half-gallon jar. Add one-third of the pickling spices and one-third of the cucumbers, fitting in as compactly as possible. Repeat the layers until the jars are filled.

3. Heat the water, vinegar and salt just to a boil. Skim and pour over the pickles, making sure they are covered well. Top with a layer of dill and grape leaves.

4. Seal with hot glass or enamel-lined lids, screwing down firmly and then turning back one-quarter inch. Let stand two weeks, wipe jars clean and screw lids down tightly.

PICKLED ONIONS *About 4 pints*

3 pounds small white onions
Water
½ cup salt
1 or more red chili peppers, seeded and quartered
½ teaspoon peppercorns
4 pieces ginger root
¼ to 1½ cups sugar (amount depends on whether cocktail onions or sweet onions are desired)
3 pints white vinegar

(*cont'd*)

1. Place the unpeeled onions in boiling water to cover and let stand two minutes. Drain, cover with cold water and peel.

2. Dissolve the salt in one quart water in an enamel, steel or earthenware container. Add the onions and enough additional water to cover. Let stand overnight. Rinse in cold water and drain.

3. Heat to boiling enough water to cover the onions. Add the onions and cook one minute. Drain and arrange in hot clean jars in layers with pepper, peppercorns and ginger root.

4. Bring the sugar and vinegar to a boil and pour over the onions to within one-half inch of the top of the jar. Seal.

PICKLED STUFFED PEPPERS *12 stuffed peppers*

- 12 green peppers
- 1 gallon water
- 1 cup plus 1 tablespoon salt
- 1½ quarts shredded or chopped cabbage
- 1 cup chopped onions
- 1 cup chopped celery
- 3 cloves garlic, minced
- 2 tablespoons white mustard seed
- 3 tablespoons celery seed
- ½ cup sugar
- 1 pint tarragon or other vinegar

1. Remove the stems and seeds from the peppers, leaving the shells whole. Mix the water with one cup of the salt, weight down the peppers and soak in the salted water overnight.

2. Mix the cabbage with the remaining salt and let stand while preparing the other ingredients. Press out all the liquid that has accumulated and add the onions, celery, garlic, mustard seed, celery seed and sugar. Mix well.

3. Drain the brined peppers and stuff with the cabbage mixture. Pack in sterile jars. Heat the vinegar to boiling and cover the peppers. Seal and store for three or four weeks before serving.

PICKLED SWEET RED PEPPERS *3 pints*

- 12 sweet red peppers
- 1 quart distilled white vinegar
- 2 cups sugar

1. Wash and seed the peppers and cut them into one-half-inch strips.

2. Boil the vinegar and sugar together five minutes.

3. While the vinegar-sugar mixture is boiling, pack the peppers into hot clean jars. Cover with the vinegar solution, filling to within one-half inch of the top of the jar. Adjust lids and process in boiling-water bath (page 494) ten minutes.

WATERMELON PICKLES *About 6 pints*

- Watermelon rind
- Limewater, made with 2 quarts cold water and 1 tablespoon lime (calcium oxide purchased in a drugstore)
- 2 tablespoons allspice
- 2 tablespoons whole cloves
- 10 two-inch pieces stick cinnamon
- 1 quart vinegar
- 4 pounds (9 cups) sugar

1. Select thick rind from a firm, not overripe, melon. Trim off the green skin and pink flesh. Cut into one-inch cubes enough trimmed rind to measure three quarts.
2. Soak for one hour in the limewater. Drain, cover with fresh water and boil until fork tender, ten minutes or longer. Drain.
3. Tie the spices in a cheesecloth, add the vinegar, one quart fresh water and sugar and bring to a boil. Add the watermelon rind and boil gently, uncovered, until clear. Add more water if the syrup becomes too thick. Remove the spice bag.
4. Pack the rind in hot sterile jars and fill the jars to the top with syrup. Seal tightly.

PRESERVES AND CONSERVES

BEET PRESERVES *About 3 pints*

- 2 pounds beets
- 4 cups sugar
- 1 tablespoon powdered ginger
- 1 cup coarsely chopped or slivered almonds
- 3 lemons, quartered and sliced

1. Cook the beets until tender in just enough water to cover. Drain, peel and dice.
2. Combine the beets with the sugar, ginger and almonds in a deep kettle. Cook over very low heat about thirty minutes.
3. Add lemons and continue cooking thirty minutes longer. Turn into a sterile crock or jelly glasses.

KUMQUAT PRESERVES *3 pints*

- 2 quarts (2 pounds) kumquats
- 2 tablespoons baking soda
- Water
- 2 cups corn syrup
- 2 cups sugar

(*cont'd*)

1. Remove the stems and leaves from the kumquats. Wash well and drain. Place in a deep kettle, sprinkle with baking soda, cover with boiling water and let stand until cool.

2. Wash three times in fresh water, using a vegetable brush to remove the oil. Drain. Cut crosses one-quarter inch deep in the stem and blossom ends. Drop one at a time into rapidly boiling water to cover. Cook until tender, about ten minutes.

3. Prepare a syrup by boiling together the corn syrup, sugar and three and one-third cups water for ten minutes. Add the drained kumquats. Boil slowly, stirring occasionally, until the fruit is partly transparent and the syrup thickens (226° F. on a candy thermometer), about twenty to thirty minutes. Remove from the heat and cover. Let stand overnight.

4. Reheat to boiling and pack the kumquats into hot sterile jars. Bring the syrup again to a boil and pour it over the fruit to within one-half inch of the top. Seal immediately.

LEMON PRESERVES *About 5 half-pints*

4 lemons
1 orange
Water
Sugar

1. Remove the peel from the lemons and orange. Cut the peel into paper-thin julienne strips and combine with the sliced or chopped fruit. Discard seeds.

2. Add one cup water for each cup pulp and peel. Let stand overnight.

3. Boil the mixture until the peel is tender. Cool.

4. Add one cup sugar for each cup fruit and juice. Cook until the syrup gives a jelly test—two drops form on the edge of a metal spoon and drop off simultaneously. Stir occasionally. Pour into hot sterile half-pint jars. Seal at once.

SPICED ORANGE WEDGES *8 servings*

4 oranges, unpeeled
Water
½ teaspoon soda
2 cups sugar
½ cup vinegar
12 whole cloves
3 pieces stick cinnamon

1. Cover the oranges with water. Add the soda and bring to a boil. Boil twenty minutes, or until easily pierced with a fork. Drain and cut each into eight wedges.

2. Combine the sugar with one and one-quarter cups water, the vinegar, cloves and cinnamon. Stir over low heat until the sugar has dissolved. Boil five minutes.

3. Add the orange wedges and simmer about twenty minutes. Cool, cover and refrigerate. Serve with fresh or smoked pork or duck.

PRESERVED ORANGE SLICES *About 2 pints*

6 large thin-skinned oranges
Water
2 cups sugar
⅓ cup lemon juice
¼ cup cognac (optional)

1. Wash the oranges and cut into one-half-inch slices. Cover with boiling water and cook until tender, or about one hour. Drain, discarding the water.

2. Boil together the sugar and two cups water five minutes, stirring until the sugar is dissolved. Add the lemon juice and orange slices and simmer until the orange rind is tender and translucent, or about one hour. Add water as necessary.

3. Place the orange slices in hot sterile jars. Cover with the boiling syrup, add the cognac and seal.

PICKLED SECKEL PEARS *About 4 quarts*

8 pounds Seckel pears
Water
10 two-inch pieces stick cinnamon
2 tablespoons whole cloves
2 tablespoons whole allspice
4 pounds (9 cups) sugar
1 quart cider vinegar

1. Wash the pears, remove the blossom ends only and prick the skins; or peel if desired.

2. Boil the pears ten minutes in water to cover; drain.

3. Tie the spices in a cheesecloth. Combine the sugar and vinegar with two cups water, add the spices and boil five minutes. Add the pears, cover and cook ten minutes longer, or until the pears are tender. Let stand overnight.

4. Remove the spice bag and reheat to boiling. Pack the pears in hot sterile jars. Return syrup to a boil and pour it over the pears, filling the jars to the top. Seal.

SPICED QUINCES *About 2 pints*

2 pounds quinces
2 cups white or cider vinegar
1 cup water
3 cups sugar
2 sticks cinnamon
1 tablespoon whole cloves
Few pieces of ginger root

1. Peel and core the quinces. Cut them into slices, cover with boiling water and cook until almost tender when pierced with a knife. Drain.

2. Boil for five minutes the vinegar, water, sugar, cinnamon, cloves and ginger root, stirring until the sugar is dissolved.

3. Add the quinces and cook until clear and tender.

4. Fill hot sterile jars with the quinces and cover to the top of the jars with boiling syrup. Seal immediately.

(cont'd)

VARIATION:

Spiced Pears: Substitute hard pears for quinces in this recipe. If a softer variety of pear—such as underripe Bartletts—is used, omit cooking in water and add the fruit directly to the syrup.

CRANBERRY FRUIT CONSERVE *About 4 8-ounce glasses*

1 pound (4 cups) fresh cranberries, picked over and washed
1½ cups water
2½ cups sugar
1 cup seeded raisins, chopped
1 apple, peeled, cored and chopped
Grated rind and juice of 1 orange
Grated rind and juice of 1 lemon
1 cup chopped walnuts

1. Cook the cranberries in the water until all the skins pop open. Add the sugar, raisins, apple, orange and lemon rind and juice. Boil together fifteen minutes.
2. Remove from the heat and add the walnuts. Pack in hot sterile jars and seal with melted paraffin.

GRAPE CONSERVE *About 4 pints*

4 pounds Concord grapes, washed and stemmed
1 orange
4 cups sugar
1 cup seedless raisins
½ teaspoon salt
1 cup chopped walnuts

1. Skin the grapes, reserving the skins. Boil the pulp ten minutes, stirring often. Sieve to remove the seeds.
2. Seed the orange and grind it coarsely. Add with the juice to the grape pulp. Add the sugar, raisins and salt.
3. Boil the mixture rapidly, stirring constantly, until thickened, or ten minutes. Add the grape skins.
4. Boil ten minutes longer. Add the nuts and reheat to boiling. Pack in sterile hot jars and seal.

Brandied tutti-frutti is an orchard in a crock. The time to start it is when the first perfect, firm-ripe fruit of summer comes on the market. As other fruits appear they are added to the crock and the end result is a fantastic dessert as is or a sauce for ice cream, puddings or cake.

BRANDIED TUTTI-FRUTTI I *About 6 quarts*

1 pound peaches
1 pound plums
1 pound pears
1 pound nectarines
3 pounds grapes (1 pound each green, red and blue)
7 pounds sugar

(*cont'd*)

1. Wash perfect, firm-ripe fruit. Rub the fuzz off the peaches with a clean cloth. With a fork, prick all over the peaches, plums, pears and nectarines. Do not prick or seed the grapes.

2. In a stone crock of at least eight quarts capacity, pack the fruits in layers with the sugar. Cover with the lid of the crock or waxed paper and let stand in a cool place until syrup forms. Stir up the sugar in the bottom of the container every three days.

3. After a week, when the fruit floats in the syrup, press down with a plate and a non-metal weight and cover with waxed paper. Stir occasionally from the bottom until the sugar is dissolved.

4. Let the fruit stand until fermentation is complete, a month or so. Pack in sterile jars, seal and store in a cool place.

Uses for Brandied Fruits: Use as a dessert or as a sauce for ice cream, cake or pudding. Or serve with crackers and cream cheese. In the South, brandied peaches are popular as an accompaniment to poultry and fresh and smoked hams. Any additional syrup may be used to flavor puddings and sauces.

BRANDIED TUTTI-FRUTTI II *Approximately 9 quarts*

- 1 pint cognac
- 1 pint peeled, sliced pineapple
- 1 pint strawberries
- 1 pint cherries
- 1 pint raspberries
- 1 pound apricots
- 1 pound nectarines
- 1 pound peaches
- 1 pint grapes
- Sugar

1. Into a stone crock of at least two and one-half gallons capacity, pour the cognac. Add the pineapple and an equal amount of sugar. Cover the crock tightly.

2. As each fruit comes into season, add it with an equal weight of sugar. Stir up the sugar from the bottom every three or four days to dissolve the sugar. If at any time fruits float in the syrup, weigh them down with a plate and non-metal weight.

3. When the juice ceases to bubble after the last addition of fruit and sugar, transfer the fruit and syrup to sterile jars and seal.

Note: The cognac is used at the beginning as a starter to help the fermentation. The crock must be kept in a cool dry place. All fruits should be added whole and unpeeled, unless otherwise stated. Apricots, nectarines and peaches should be pricked all over with a fork.

SPICED APPLES *6 pints*

- 5 pounds (15 medium) firm apples
- 6 cups sugar
- 2 cups white vinegar
- 4 sticks cinnamon, broken into 1-inch pieces
- 2 teaspoons whole cloves

(*cont'd*)

1. Peel, quarter and core the apples.

2. Combine the sugar, vinegar, cinnamon and cloves and heat to boiling. Add the apples and boil gently, uncovered, until tender but not broken.

3. Pack into hot sterile jars, filling to within one-quarter inch of the top and making sure the syrup covers the fruit. Seal immediately.

SWEET PICKLED CRAB APPLES *6 pints*

7 pounds crab apples
1 quart distilled white vinegar
8 cups sugar
¼ cup whole cloves
1 stick cinnamon
1½ teaspoons ginger

1. Wash crab apples and remove blossom ends. Prick each apple several times with a fork.

2. Heat the vinegar and sugar to boiling, add spices tied in cheesecloth and crab apples. Boil gently until the crab apples are tender but not broken. Remove the spice bag.

3. Pack the boiling mixture into hot sterile jars, filling to within one-quarter inch of the top of the jar and making sure that the syrup covers the fruit. Seal immediately, cool and store.

BRANDIED PEACHES I *About 1 quart*

1 quart cling peaches
1 cup sugar
1 cup cognac

1. Rub fuzz from peaches, or peel if desired. Pack into a clean quart jar in layers with the sugar until the jar is about three-quarters full.

2. Add the cognac and seal. Turn the jar upside down every day for four or five days to distribute and dissolve the sugar. Let stand about three months before using.

BRANDIED PEACHES II

Wash perfect peaches, ripe but not soft. Rub with a clean cloth to remove fuzz. Do not peel. Weigh. Weigh an equal amount of sugar. Prick the peaches all over with a fork.

In a stone crock or a glass, china or earthenware bowl, pack the peaches and sugar in alternating layers. Cover with the lid of the crock or waxed paper and let stand in a cool place until syrup forms. Stir up the sugar in the bottom of the container every three days.

After about a week, when the peaches float in syrup, press down with a plate and non-metal weight. Cover with waxed paper. Stir once a week from the bottom until the sugar is dissolved.

(cont'd)

Let the peaches stand until fermentation is complete, a month or so. Pack in clean jars, cover with syrup and seal. Store in a cool place.

BRANDIED PEACHES III

Wash perfect peaches, ripe but not soft. Rub off the fuzz with a clean cloth. Do not peel. Prick each peach twice with a fork and place in a saucepan.

For each pound of peaches use one cup each water and sugar. Combine the water and sugar and heat slowly until the sugar is dissolved. Bring to a boil and boil one minute.

Add the peaches to the syrup and boil until the peaches are tender, or five to seven minutes.

Pack the peaches in hot sterile jars and fill three-quarters full with the syrup. Finish filling with brandy. Seal and store in a cool place one month before using.

One pound of medium peaches fills a pint jar.

PEAR CHIPS *8 pints*

3 oranges
2 lemons
8 pounds cooking pears
7 pounds (15¾ cups) sugar
2 cups water
10 pieces dried ginger

1. Seed the oranges and lemons and grind the rind and pulp, reserving the juice. Peel the pears, core and slice in rings or lengthwise wedges.
2. Dissolve the sugar in the water and add the fruits, juices and ginger.
3. Bring the mixture to a boil, reduce the heat and simmer, covered, until the pears are transparent and the syrup is thick. Pack and seal.

APPLE BUTTER *4 pints*

3 quarts fresh sweet cider
8 pounds juicy ripe apples
2½ cups brown sugar, packed
2 teaspoons cinnamon
½ teaspoon allspice
½ teaspoon ground cloves
½ teaspoon salt

1. Boil the cider in a big stainless steel or enamel kettle until the amount is reduced one-half, or about thirty minutes.
2. Meanwhile, quarter and core the apples but do not peel them. Add to the reduced cider and cook over low heat until the apples are tender. Stir almost constantly. When the apples are cooked, force the mixture through a sieve and return to the kettle.
3. Add the sugar, spices and salt and cook over low heat until the mixture thickens, or about one-half hour. If necessary use an asbestos pad to insure low heat. Stir almost constantly.

(*cont'd*)

4. Pour at once into hot sterile jars and seal.

Note: To test apple butter for doneness, pour a little on a cold plate. When no rim of liquid separates around the edge of the butter, it is sufficiently thick.

CONCORD GRAPE BUTTER

6 or 7 6-ounce glasses

2 pounds Concord grapes
1½ tablespoons grated orange rind
1 cup water
2¼ cups sugar
½ teaspoon powdered cinnamon
¼ teaspoon powdered cloves
⅛ teaspoon grated nutmeg

1. Wash the grapes, drain and pull from the stems. Squeeze the pulp from the skins into a kettle, reserving the skins.
2. Cook the pulp slowly until soft, or about ten minutes. Put through a sieve to remove the seeds.
3. Return the pulp to the kettle, add the orange rind and water and cook ten minutes, stirring frequently with a wooden spoon. Add the skins and heat to boiling. Add the sugar and spices and cook over low heat, stirring frequently, until thick (see test for apple butter, above).
4. Pour into hot sterile jars and seal at once.

Note: If desired, the mixture may be puréed and reheated to boiling before canning.

HOME-CANNED APPLES

Peel and core tart apples and cut into pieces. To keep the fruit from darkening, drop it into water containing two tablespoons each of salt and vinegar for each gallon of water. Drain and rinse, then boil five minutes in heavy sugar syrup prepared by boiling together for five minutes equal parts of sugar and water. Each quart of fruit requires one cup of syrup.

Pack the hot fruit into hot sterile jars to within one-half inch of the top. Cover with the hot syrup, leaving one-half-inch space at the top of the jar. Adjust lids and process in boiling-water bath (page 494) fifteen minutes.

Two and one-half to three pounds of the apples yield one quart.

MINCEMEAT

Enough for about 10 8-inch pies

2 pounds lean beef, ground
1 pound beef suet, ground
3 quarts chopped tart apples
3 cups brown sugar, packed
1 cup molasses
1 quart cider
1½ pounds currants, washed
2 pounds raisins
½ pound citron, thinly sliced
Juice and peel of 1 orange, ground
Juice and peel of 1 lemon, ground
1½ teaspoons each cinnamon, mace, cloves, nutmeg, allspice and salt
1 pound broken nut meats (optional)
1 pint cognac

(*cont'd*)

1. Mix the beef, suet, apples, sugar, molasses, cider, fruits and peels in a large, heavy kettle. Bring to a boil, lower the heat and simmer, stirring frequently, about one and one-half hours.

2. Add the spices and continue cooking until thick, stirring almost constantly. Add the nuts and cognac and pack into sterile jars. Adjust lids and process either pints or quarts one and one-half hours in boiling water bath (page 494) or twenty minutes at ten pounds pressure in pressure canner. Seal.

. . . .

MARMALADES AND JELLIES

. . . .

ENGLISH MARMALADE *7 to 8 cups*

2 pounds Seville or bitter oranges
1 large lemon
9 cups cold water
8 cups sugar

1. Slice and seed the unpeeled oranges and lemon as thinly as possible. Cover with the cold water and let stand twenty-four hours.

2. Bring to a boil, add the sugar and remove from the heat. Stir until the sugar has dissolved. Let stand twenty-four hours.

3. Bring the mixture to a boil again and simmer gently two hours. When the peel is transparent and soft, bring to a rapid boil and cook about thirty minutes, or until two drops form on the edge of a metal spoon and drop off simultaneously. For a stiffer marmalade, continue cooking until the drops run together as they fall off.

4. Skim the foam from the surface and pour the marmalade into hot sterile jars. Seal tightly with jar tops or cover with a thin layer of melted paraffin. If paraffin is used, add a second layer after the first layer has cooled. Store in a cool dry place.

LIME MARMALADE *11 or 12 cups*

3 cups thinly sliced limes
1 cup thinly sliced lemons
2 quarts water
5 pounds (11¼ cups) sugar

1. Place the prepared fruits and water in an eight- to ten-quart kettle. Cover and cook until tender, fifteen minutes or longer.

2. Add the sugar, stir until dissolved and boil rapidly until the mixture gives a jelly test—two drops form on the edge of a metal spoon and drop off simultaneously—about forty-five minutes. For a stiffer marmalade, continue cooking until the drops run together as they fall off.

3. Skim the foam from the surface of the marmalade and fill hot sterile jars. Seal tightly with jar tops or cover with a thin layer of melted paraffin and, when cool, add another layer. Store in a cool dry place.

APPLE TOMATO MARMALADE *About 5 cups*

1 quart peeled and quartered tomatoes
1 quart peeled and chopped apples
2 lemons, seeded and ground
3 pounds (6 cups) sugar
1 ounce ginger root
4 whole cloves

1. Chop the tomatoes and drain in a sieve.

2. Add the apples and lemons to the drained tomatoes and cook fifteen minutes.

3. Add the sugar; add the ginger and cloves tied in a cheesecloth. Cook, stirring, until the sugar is dissolved; continue to cook until the mixture has the consistency of thin marmalade, stirring frequently. Remove the spice bag.

4. Pour into hot sterile jars and seal.

RIPE TOMATO MARMALADE *About 5 pints*

3 quarts peeled and sliced tomatoes
6 cups sugar
1 teaspoon salt
2 oranges
2 lemons
2 cups water
4 sticks cinnamon
2 teaspoons whole cloves

1. Mix the tomatoes, sugar and salt in a large kettle and set aside.

2. Peel the oranges and lemons and slice the peel very thin. Boil the peel in the water for five minutes and drain. Add peel to the tomatoes.

3. Slice the orange and lemon pulp, remove the seeds and add to the tomatoes.

4. Tie the cinnamon and cloves in a cheesecloth and add to the tomatoes.

5. Heat the tomato mixture to a boil. Cook rapidly, stirring almost constantly, until thickened, forty-five minutes or longer.

6. Remove the spice bag. Pour the marmalade into hot sterile jars and seal. Store in a cool, dry, dark place.

VARIATION:

Green Tomato Marmalade: Follow the cooking and canning directions for ripe tomato marmalade, omitting the oranges and spices and adding four additional lemons.

PINEAPPLE MARMALADE *6 or 7 cups*

3½ cups shredded or ground fresh pineapple (about 2 medium pineapples)
3 thinly sliced lemons
1 quart water
4½ cups sugar

1. Place the prepared fruits and water in a six-quart kettle and let stand overnight. Boil until the lemon is tender, about twenty minutes. *(cont'd)*

2. Add the sugar, stir until dissolved and boil rapidly until the mixture gives a jelly test—two drops form on the edge of a metal spoon and drop off simultaneously—about twenty-five minutes. For a stiffer marmalade, continue cooking until the drops run together as they fall off.

3. Skim the foam from the surface and pour the marmalade into hot sterile jars. Seal tightly with jar tops or cover with a thin layer of melted paraffin and, when cool, add another layer. Store in a cool dry place.

APPLE JELLY

Use sour red-skinned apples. Cut out stem and blossom ends but do not peel or core. Cut crosswise in one-quarter-inch slices and measure or weigh. (One pound measures about three cups.) Place apples in pot and add enough water barely to cover apples, not over two cups per pound of fruit. Cook gently until apples are very tender.

Turn apples into a cotton flannel jelly bag or several thicknesses of cheesecloth in a sieve and let juice drip several hours or overnight into a bowl. For additional juice, a second extraction may be made in this manner: Return the apple pulp to the pot and add an equal amount of water. Boil twenty minutes and drop in bag as for first extraction of juice. For the clearest jelly possible, use first extraction alone; for jelly that has good flavor but is less clear, combine extraction and jelly.

To make a batch of jelly, measure six cups of apple juice and four cups of sugar. In a three- or four-quart kettle bring the juice to a boil. Add sugar and cook, stirring, until sugar is dissolved. Boil rapidly until the jellying point has been reached, 220° to 222° F., or until two drops form on the edge of a metal spoon and then run together to form a sheet. Skim off foam. Pour immediately into hot sterile glasses, filling them to within one-quarter inch of the top. Pour a thin layer of melted paraffin over the top and cool. Add a second thin layer of paraffin, cool, cover with lid or foil and store in a cool place. (Yields six cups of jelly.)

VARIATIONS:

Apple-Rose Geranium Jelly: Place two rose geranium leaves in each glass before filling with boiling jelly.

Apple-Mint Jelly: Before pouring jelly into glasses add green food coloring and about one-half teaspoon mint extract.

Apple-Peeling Jelly: Substitute apple peelings and cores for sliced apples and proceed as directed for sliced apples. Six cups of peelings and cores yield about one and one-half cups jelly.

QUICK APPLE-ROSE GERANIUM JELLY *9 glasses*

5 cups sugar
1 box powdered pectin
1 quart bottled apple juice
Red food coloring
9 rose geranium leaves

(*cont'd*)

1. Measure the sugar into a bowl and set aside.

2. In a five- to six-quart pan, mix the pectin with the apple juice and stir until the pectin dissolves. Tint a light red. Place over high heat and stir until the mixture comes to a full rolling boil.

3. Add the sugar at once and return to a hard boil. Boil one minute, stirring constantly.

4. Remove the jelly from the heat and skim off the foam. Place a leaf in each of nine hot sterile glasses and pour jelly at once over the leaves in the glasses. The leaves will wilt but they give flavor to the jelly.

CRANBERRY JELLY *4 4-ounce glasses*

4 cups cranberries
3 cups boiling water
Sugar

1. Cook the cranberries in the water until soft. Strain the juice through a jelly bag.

2. Measure the juice and measure three-quarters cup sugar for each cup of juice.

3. Bring the juice to a boil, add the sugar and stir until dissolved. Cook rapidly five minutes, or until two drops form on the edge of a metal spoon and drop off simultaneously.

4. Pour the jelly into sterile glasses, cool and cover with paraffin.

Note: For best results, make the jelly in small amounts.

GRAPE JELLY *About 8 6-ounce glasses*

4 cups bottled Concord grape juice
7 cups sugar
½ bottle liquid fruit pectin

1. In a large saucepan mix the juice with the sugar and bring to a boil over high heat, stirring constantly. Immediately stir in the pectin.

2. Bring to a full rolling boil and boil hard one minute, stirring constantly. Remove from the heat, skim and pour at once into hot sterile glasses. Seal with melted paraffin.

HERB JELLY *6 6-ounce glasses*

2 cups herb infusion (see paragraph 1)
¼ cup vinegar
4½ cups sugar
Green food coloring
½ bottle liquid fruit pectin

1. To prepare the infusion, pour two and one-half cups boiling water on four tablespoons dried herbs or one cup fresh herb leaves and stems. Use basil, rosemary, sage, thyme, tarragon, marjoram or a combination of these herbs. Cover and let stand fifteen minutes. Strain and measure two cups into a big pan.

2. Add the vinegar and sugar and cook over high heat, stirring until the sugar dissolves. Stir in enough coloring to give the desired shade.

3. As soon as the mixture boils, stir in the pectin. Bring to a full rolling boil, stirring constantly, and boil hard one minute. Remove from the heat and skim off the foam. Pour into hot sterile glasses. Seal with melted paraffin.

PORT AND GRAPE JELLY *6 to 7 6-ounce glasses*

3 cups sugar
1 box powdered pectin
½ cup bottled grape juice
1½ cups port wine
1 cup water

1. Measure the sugar into a bowl.

2. Mix the pectin with the juice, port and water in a five- to six-cup saucepan. Stir until the pectin has dissolved. Place over high heat and stir until the mixture comes to a full rolling boil.

3. Add the sugar at once and return to a hard boil. Boil one minute, stirring constantly.

4. Remove the jelly from the heat, skim off the foam and pour at once into hot sterile glasses. Seal with paraffin.

ROSE PETAL JELLY *Approximately 8 6-ounce jars*

3 dozen fresh roses (2 quarts fresh petals, loosely packed)
1 quart boiling water
4 cups sugar
3 tablespoons lemon juice

1. Remove the petals from the roses and place in a large bowl. Add boiling water, cover and steep for twenty minutes or until all color is out of the petals.

2. Strain the liquid into a shallow wide pan. Add the sugar and lemon juice.

3. Cook over medium heat, stirring constantly, until the sugar is dissolved and the mixture comes to a full rolling boil. Maintain the full rolling boil until mixture gives a jelly test (two drops form on the side of a metal spoon, then flow together). Skim.

4. Pour into hot sterile jars and cover with melted paraffin.

CHAPTER TWELVE

DESSERTS

PIES AND PASTRIES

MAKING SUCCESSFUL PIE PASTRY

An experienced cook tosses together a batch of pastry quickly and easily and invariably turns out well-shaped pies with tender, crisp and somewhat flaky crusts. Some of the tricks which may help the novice in successful pastry making are:

Choice of Ingredients: Use all-purpose flour, not cake flour. Lard and hydrogenated vegetable shortenings are better than butter or margarine because they yield a tenderer product. Cold or ice water aids in producing flakiness.

Choice of Utensils: A pastry blender is an efficient tool for chopping in fat, but two knives will produce the same results. If the fingers are used, the heat from the hand softens the fat excessively and it is apt to be rubbed into the flour so thoroughly that the pastry is lacking in flakiness. Perhaps a fork is the best utensil for mixing as the water is added. Glass pie pans give a darker-colored crust than aluminum.

Amount of Water to Use: Fat particles coated with flour must be bound together with water, and for lightness there must be enough water present to form steam. The amount of water needed varies with the dryness of the flour. Use only enough water to dampen all the dough. Excess water toughens the crust and too little water makes it crumbly.

Rolling the Dough: Pat the dough all over with a rolling pin so the particles will stick together and roll without cracking. To prevent kneading and toughening the pastry, roll it from the center out toward the edge. A cloth-covered and well-floured board and rolling pin prevent sticking.

Fitting the Dough in the Pan: For a well-shaped pie, fit the dough into the pan without stretching. When pressing it to the pan do so by working from the rim to-

(*cont'd*)

ward the center, lifting the pastry at the edge if necessary to give extra fullness inside the pan. To prevent bulging of pastry, press out all air spaces between dough and the pan.

To Prevent Soaking of the Bottom Crust: Brush the dough with slightly beaten egg white or with shortening before adding the filling. Bake on the lower shelf of a hot oven at least ten minutes; for the whole time if the filling permits.

BASIC PIE PASTRY *Pastry for 9-inch pie or 6 tarts*

2 cups sifted all-purpose flour
1 teaspoon salt
⅔ cup shortening
⅓ cup cold water, approximately

1. Sift together the flour and salt.
2. Using a pastry blender or two knives, chop in the shortening until the mixture resembles coarse cornmeal.
3. Sprinkle water slowly over the top of the flour, while tossing the mixture up from the bottom of the bowl with a fork. After about three-quarters of the water has been added, press the dampened part of the dough into a ball and set aside. Add only enough water to dampen the remaining flour mixture. Press all the dough together and divide into two portions, one slightly larger than the other. If the kitchen is hot, chill the dough for one-half hour before rolling.
4. Place the larger ball of dough on a lightly floured pastry cloth or board, pat in all directions with a floured rolling pin and then roll from the center out in all directions, loosening the pastry and reflouring the cloth and rolling pin as necessary. Roll into a round one-eighth inch thick and two inches larger in diameter than the top of the pie pan.
5. Fold gently into quarters, place in the pan and unfold. Fit the dough into the pan loosely and press against the pan without stretching it. Trim the edge slightly larger than the outside rim of the pan. Add desired filling.
6. Stack the pastry trimmings on the remaining dough and roll until about one inch larger than the top of the pan. Fold gently into quarters and cut several small gashes to allow steam to escape.
7. Moisten the rim of the lower crust, place top crust on the filled pan and unfold. Do not stretch the pastry. Tuck the rim of the top beneath the edge of the undercrust and flute with the fingers, making a tight seal.
8. Bake as directed for the filling used.

VARIATIONS:

Baked Pie Shell: Line pie pan with pastry for bottom crust and prick well with fork around bottom and sides. Bake in preheated hot oven (450° F.) twelve to fifteen minutes, or until golden. Cool before adding desired filling.

Lattice-Top Pie Crust: Roll dough for top crust into a circle and cut into half-inch strips. Moisten the rim of the bottom crust with water and place half the strips parallel on the filled pie shell, spacing evenly. Repeat with remaining strips in opposite direction. Attach strips firmly to rim.

(cont'd)

Tart Shells: Cut pastry into five-inch rounds and fit over inverted muffin tins or custard cups; or line tart shells, fitting pastry loosely into pans and pressing it firmly around the sides. Prick well with fork and bake in a preheated hot oven (450° F.) ten to fifteen minutes, or until golden brown.

SWEET PIE PASTRY *6 tart shells or 2 9-inch pie shells*

2 cups sifted all-purpose flour
2 egg yolks
2 tablespoons sugar
1 cup butter, at room temperature
Grated rind of 1 lemon
Pinch of salt

1. Sift the flour into a mixing bowl. Make a well in the center and add the remaining ingredients.
2. Mix the center ingredients with the fingers of one hand or a pastry blender until blended. Quickly work in the flour. Add a small amount of ice water if necessary to moisten the dough so it can be gathered into a ball.
3. Wrap the dough in waxed paper and chill one hour. Roll out the pastry, fit it into the pans and bake on the bottom shelf of a preheated hot oven (450° F.) until brown, about fifteen minutes.

ALMOND CRUST *1 9-inch pie crust*

1½ cups blanched almonds
1 egg white
¼ cup granulated sugar

1. Preheat oven to moderate (375° F.).
2. Using a knife, chop the almonds fine. Do not put them through a food grinder.
3. Beat the egg white until stiff and gradually fold in the sugar. Fold in the chopped almonds and press the mixture firmly over the bottom and sides of an oiled nine-inch pie pan. Bake the crust until lightly browned. Remove to a rack and cool.

NUT-CRUMB CRUST, PAGE 548.

BRAZIL NUT CRUST *1 9-inch pie crust*

Brazil nuts
2 tablespoons sugar

1. Using an electric blender or food chopper, chop enough Brazil nuts to make one cup.
2. Blend the ground nuts with the sugar. Using the back of a tablespoon or the fingers, press the mixture against the bottom and sides of a nine-inch pie plate.
3. Bake the crust in a preheated hot oven (400° F.) until lightly browned, about eight minutes. Cool.

CRUMB CRUST *1 9-inch pie crust*

1⅓ cups vanilla wafer crumbs
¼ cup sugar
⅓ cup butter, melted

1. Preheat oven to hot (400° F.).
2. Combine the crumbs with the sugar and melted butter and mix thoroughly.
3. Press the mixture firmly against the sides and bottom of a nine-inch pie pan, using back of spoon.
4. Bake five minutes and cool.

CRUMB CRUST (BLENDER METHOD), PAGE 548.

MERINGUE CRUST *1 8-inch pie crust*

2 egg whites, at room temperature
⅛ teaspoon salt
⅛ teaspoon cream of tartar
½ cup granulated sugar
½ cup finely chopped walnuts or pecans
½ teaspoon vanilla extract

1. Preheat oven to slow (300° F.).
2. Combine the egg whites, salt and cream of tartar in a mixing bowl. Beat with electric mixer or egg beater until foamy throughout.
3. Add the sugar, two tablespoons at a time, beating after each addition until the sugar is blended. Continue beating until mixture will stand in very stiff peaks.
4. Fold in the nuts and vanilla and blend.
5. Spoon the mixture into a lightly greased eight-inch pie pan and make a meringue shell, spreading the meringue over the bottom and building up the sides one-half inch above the edge of the pan but not over the rim. If desired, the meringue can be squeezed through a pastry tube to make a fancy edge.
6. Bake fifty to fifty-five minutes. Cool.

MERINGUE PIE TOPPING *Topping for 8- or 9-inch pie*

3 egg whites
¼ teaspoon cream of tartar
6 tablespoons sugar

1. Beat the egg whites until light and frothy. Add the cream of tartar and continue beating until the whites are stiff enough to hold a peak.
2. Gradually beat in the sugar and beat until the meringue is stiff and glossy.
3. Pile the meringue lightly on cooled pie filling, spreading it until it touches the edges of the pastry to prevent the meringue shrinking.
4. Bake in a preheated hot oven (425° F.) until the top is brown, five to six minutes.

MERINGUE TART SHELLS *12 or more meringue shells*

6 egg whites, at room temperature
¼ teaspoon salt
2 teaspoons lemon juice
1⅔ cups granulated sugar

1. Beat the egg whites with the salt and lemon juice until they hold soft peaks.
2. Add the sugar gradually, beating until it has all been added. Continue beating until the meringue is glossy and stands in firm peaks.
3. Using a pastry bag, shape the meringue into three- to four-inch rounds on unglazed paper on a baking sheet. Build up the sides by laying coils of meringue one on top of the other to a depth of about one and one-half inches.
4. Bake in a preheated slow oven (275° F.) about one hour. Remove from the paper with a spatula.

APRICOT CREAM PIE *About 6 servings*

2 eggs, separated
1½ cups apricot whole fruit nectar
¼ teaspoon salt
½ cup sugar
1 envelope unflavored gelatin
1 tablespoon fresh lemon juice
½ cup heavy cream, whipped
Baked 8-inch pastry shell

1. Beat the egg yolks lightly and blend with the nectar, salt and half the sugar. Cook over hot water until slightly thickened, stirring constantly. Remove from the heat.
2. Soften the gelatin in the lemon juice and stir into the hot mixture. Cool until slightly thickened.
3. Beat the egg whites until stiff and gradually beat in the remaining sugar. Fold into the gelatin mixture. Fold in the whipped cream and pour the mixture into the pastry shell. Chill until firm.

BUTTERSCOTCH PIE *6 to 8 servings*

6 tablespoons butter
1 cup dark brown sugar, packed
1¼ cups water
1 egg yolk
1 envelope unflavored gelatin
¼ cup cold water
1 pint vanilla ice cream
Almond crust (page 521)
½ cup heavy cream, whipped
Slivered almonds, toasted

1. Melt the butter in a saucepan. Add the sugar and water and heat to a boil. Combine a little of the mixture with the lightly beaten egg yolk, then add to the mixture in the saucepan.
2. Soften the gelatin in cold water. Stir it into the sugar mixture until the gelatin dissolves. Add the ice cream, cut into pieces, and stir until melted.
3. Chill the mixture in the refrigerator until slightly thickened but not set. Turn into the prepared pie crust and chill until firmly set. When ready to serve, garnish with whipped cream and sprinkle with nuts.

CHOCOLATE CHIFFON PIE *6 servings*

1 envelope unflavored gelatin
½ cup sugar
¼ teaspoon salt
1 cup milk
2 eggs, separated
1 cup (6-ounce package) semisweet chocolate pieces
1 teaspoon vanilla extract
½ cup heavy cream, whipped
Brazil nut crust (page 521)

1. Combine the gelatin, half the sugar and the salt in the top of a double boiler. Stir in the milk, egg yolks and chocolate pieces. Place over boiling water and cook, stirring constantly, until the gelatin has dissolved and the chocolate has melted, about six minutes.

2. Remove from the heat and beat with a rotary beater until the chocolate is blended. Stir in the vanilla and chill until the mixture mounds slightly when dropped from a spoon.

3. Beat the egg whites until stiff but not dry. Gradually add the remaining sugar and beat until stiff. Fold into the gelatin mixture. Fold in the whipped cream.

4. Turn the mixture into the prepared crust and chill until firm. Garnish with additional whipped cream and sprinkle with chopped Brazil nuts.

GERMAN SWEET CHOCOLATE PIE *About 6 servings*

1 package (4 ounces) sweet cooking chocolate
3 tablespoons water
1 teaspoon vanilla extract
1 cup heavy cream
Baked meringue crust (page 522)

1. Place the chocolate and water in a saucepan over low heat. Stir until the chocolate has melted. Cool.

2. Add the vanilla to the chocolate. Whip the cream to a soft consistency. Fold the chocolate mixture into the whipped cream and pile into the cooled meringue shell. Chill about two hours before serving.

VARIATIONS:

German Sweet Chocolate Dessert au Café: Make German sweet chocolate pie but add one teaspoon instant coffee to the melted chocolate. If desired, omit the meringue shell and serve as a pudding in sherbet glasses. Chill as directed.

Brandied German Sweet Chocolate Dessert: Make German sweet chocolate pie as directed but add one tablespoon cognac with the vanilla. If desired, omit the meringue shell and serve as a pudding in sherbet glasses. Chill as directed.

COCONUT CREAM PIE *6 to 8 servings*

½ cup sugar
3 tablespoons cornstarch
¼ teaspoon salt
2 cups scalded milk
1 tablespoon butter
2 eggs, separated
1 teaspoon vanilla extract
1 cup grated fresh coconut
Baked 9-inch or deep 8-inch pie shell

(cont'd)

1. Preheat oven to moderate (325° F.).

2. Mix one-quarter cup of the sugar with the cornstarch and salt. Gradually stir in the scalded milk. Add the butter.

3. Cook the mixture in a double boiler, stirring constantly, until thickened.

4. Beat the egg yolks, add a little of the thickened mixture, blend and stir into the remaining hot mixture. Cook, stirring, until thickened. Cool slightly.

5. Add the vanilla and three-quarters cup of the coconut. Turn into the baked pie shell.

6. Beat the egg whites until foamy. Gradually add the remaining sugar and beat until stiff but not dry. Spread over the filling, making sure that the meringue touches the crust at all points. Sprinkle with the remaining coconut and bake until lightly browned, or about fifteen minutes.

Cool before serving.

Note: Packages of vanilla, coconut or other pudding mix may be used according to the directions on the package and this recipe followed from step 5 to the end.

EGGNOG CHIFFON PIE *6 servings*

⅔ cup milk or light cream
3 eggs, separated
½ cup sugar
Dash of salt
⅛ teaspoon nutmeg
1 envelope unflavored gelatin
2 tablespoons cold water
1 to 2 tablespoons rum
1 teaspoon vanilla extract
½ cup heavy cream, whipped
Baked 8-inch pie shell or crumb crust (page 522)

1. Scald the milk in the top of a double boiler.

2. Mix the egg yolks, half of the sugar, the salt and nutmeg and stir into the scalded milk. Cook, stirring constantly, over simmering water until the mixture coats a metal spoon.

3. Soften the gelatin in water, add to the custard and stir until dissolved. Strain the mixture.

4. Add the rum and vanilla, cool and chill in the refrigerator until the mixture begins to set.

5. Beat the egg whites until foamy, add the remaining sugar and beat again until stiff. Fold into the gelatin mixture.

6. Fold in the whipped cream.

7. Pour into the pastry shell and chill until firm. Sprinkle with nutmeg or garnish with whipped cream and then sprinkle with nutmeg.

LEMON MERINGUE PIE *6 servings*

1 cup granulated sugar
¼ teaspoon salt
¼ cup flour
3 tablespoons cornstarch
2 cups water
3 eggs, separated
1 tablespoon butter
¼ cup lemon juice
Grated rind of one lemon
Baked nine-inch pastry shell
Meringue pie topping (page 522)

(cont'd)

1. Combine the sugar, salt, flour and cornstarch and gradually stir in the water. Cook, stirring constantly, until thickened and smooth.

2. Gradually stir hot mixture into beaten egg yolks, return to low heat and cook, stirring, two minutes. (Reserve egg whites for meringue topping.) Stir in butter, lemon juice and rind and cool slightly. Pour into baked pastry shell and cool. Top with meringue and brown in oven, as directed.

KEY LIME PIE *6 to 8 servings*

1 cup sugar
¼ cup flour
3 tablespoons cornstarch
¼ teaspoon salt
2 cups water
3 eggs, separated
1 tablespoon butter
¼ cup fresh or bottled lime juice
Grated rind of 1 lime or 1 lemon
Baked 9-inch pie shell
Meringue pie topping (page 522)

1. Combine the sugar, flour, cornstarch and salt in a saucepan and gradually stir in the water. Cook, stirring constantly, until thickened. Gradually stir the mixture into the beaten egg yolks, return to low heat and cook, stirring, two minutes.

2. Stir in the butter, lime juice and rind and cool slightly. Pour into the baked pastry shell and cool.

3. Top with meringue and brown in the oven as directed.

NESSELRODE PIE *6 to 8 servings*

2 teaspoons rum
¼ cup diced candied fruit
2 envelopes gelatin
Sugar
½ teaspoon salt
2 cups cold milk
3 eggs, separated
⅓ cup sugar
1 cup heavy cream, whipped
Baked 9-inch pie shell
Candied fruits (optional)

1. Sprinkle rum over the candied fruit and set aside.

2. Combine the gelatin with one-quarter cup sugar and the salt in the top of a double boiler. Gradually stir in the milk and cook over hot water, stirring, until the gelatin has dissolved.

3. Gradually stir the gelatin mixture into the beaten egg yolks and return the mixture to the double boiler. Cook, stirring constantly, until the mixture coats a spoon and is slightly thickened. Cool. Add the candied fruits.

4. Beat the egg whites until stiff and gradually beat in one-third cup sugar. Carefully fold into the gelatin mixture. Fold in the cream.

5. Pour the mixture into the baked pie shell and chill until firm. If desired, garnish with candied fruits.

PUMPKIN PIE *6 servings*

Unbaked 9-inch pie shell
2 large or 3 small eggs
½ cup sugar
2 tablespoons molasses
½ teaspoon salt
1 teaspoon ginger
1 to 2 teaspoons cinnamon
¼ teaspoon cloves or allspice
2 cups cooked or canned pumpkin, strained
1½ cups milk, light cream or evaporated milk

1. Prepare the pie shell with a fluted standing rim. Brush lightly with egg white or shortening.
2. Preheat oven to hot (450° F.).
3. Beat the eggs with the sugar, molasses, salt and spices until well blended. Add the pumpkin and milk and mix well. Adjust the seasonings.
4. Turn the mixture into the prepared crust and bake on the lower shelf of the oven ten minutes. Lower the oven temperature to 400° F. and bake until a knife inserted in the center comes out clean, or about thirty minutes longer.

SOUR CREAM RAISIN PIE *4 to 6 servings*

1 cup seedless raisins
½ cup water
⅔ cup sugar
1 tablespoon flour
¼ teaspoon cloves
¼ teaspoon cinnamon
Grated rind of 1 lemon
1 egg, beaten
1 cup sour cream
Pastry for a 2-crust or lattice-top deep 8-inch pie

1. Preheat oven to hot (450° F.).
2. Cook the raisins, covered, in water until plump.
3. Mix the sugar, flour, cloves, cinnamon and lemon rind. Stir into the raisin mixture and cook, stirring, until thickened. Cool.
4. Mix the egg and sour cream. Add to the raisin mixture and blend.
5. Turn the mixture into a pastry-lined eight-inch pan, cover with pastry and cut slits for the escape of steam; or use pastry strips for a lattice top.
6. Bake ten minutes. Reduce temperature to moderate (350° F.) and bake until the custard is set, or about twenty minutes.

SOUR CREAM PUMPKIN PIE *6 servings*

1 nine-inch pie shell, three-quarters baked
1 cup sugar
¼ teaspoon salt
1 teaspoon cinnamon
½ teaspoon ginger
¼ teaspoon nutmeg
⅛ teaspoon ground cloves
1½ cups canned pumpkin purée
3 eggs, separated
1 cup sour cream
Whipped cream for garnish

(*cont'd*)

1. Preheat oven to hot (450° F.). Prepare pie shell, prick the crust as for baked pie shell (page 520) and bake until three-fourths done. Reduce heat to moderate (350° F.).

2. Combine one-half cup of the sugar with the salt and spices in the top of a double boiler. Blend in the pumpkin purée. Beat the egg yolks and stir into the mixture. Add the sour cream and mix well. Cook over hot, not boiling, water until thick, stirring constantly.

3. Beat the egg whites until they form soft peaks. Gradually beat in the remaining sugar. Fold into the pumpkin mixture.

4. Turn into the pie shell and bake forty-five minutes, or until the top has browned. Serve with whipped cream, if desired.

FRENCH RASPBERRY PIE *8 servings*

2 cups milk
1 vanilla bean
⅓ cup flour
½ cup sugar
¼ teaspoon salt
4 egg yolks
1 whole egg
¼ cup cream, whipped
Baked deep 9-inch pie shell
1 pint raspberries
1 six-ounce glass red currant jelly

1. In a double boiler, scald the milk with the vanilla bean. Remove the bean.

2. Mix the flour, sugar and salt. Add a little of the scalded milk, stirring until smooth. Add to the remaining milk in the double boiler and cook, stirring, until thickened.

3. Beat together the egg yolks and the whole egg. Add a little of the hot mixture and stir until smooth. Add to the remaining sauce and cook over simmering water, stirring constantly, until the mixture has thickened.

4. Strain the mixture, cool and fold in the whipped cream. Turn into the baked pie shell and cover with raspberries.

5. Melt the jelly over very low heat, stirring, and pour evenly over the raspberries. Chill.

RHUBARB PIE *6 servings*

Baked 9-inch pie shell
2½ cups sugar, approximately
1⅓ cups water
1¾ pounds rhubarb (5 cups cut)
6 tablespoons cornstarch
1 cup heavy cream, whipped

1. Cool the pie shell while preparing the filling.

2. Mix the sugar and one cup water and bring to a boil, stirring. Add the rhubarb and cook, stirring gently once or twice before the rhubarb starts to soften. Continue cooking without stirring until just tender. Remove the rhubarb with a slotted spoon and reserve.

(cont'd)

3. Reheat the syrup to boiling. Blend the cornstarch with the remaining water and add to the boiling syrup. Cook, stirring, until thickened and clear. If desired, add more sugar. Add the reserved rhubarb, cool five minutes and turn into the pie shell. Chill.

4. Before serving, garnish with whipped cream, sweetened if desired.

RUM CHIFFON PIE *6 servings*

2 eggs, separated
6 tablespoons sugar
2 envelopes gelatin
½ cup rum
½ cup hot milk
1 heaping cup crushed ice
1 cup heavy cream
Crumb crust (page 522)

1. Beat the egg whites until stiff and beat in two tablespoons of the sugar. Set aside.

2. In the container of an electric blender place the gelatin, rum and hot milk, cover and blend on high speed forty seconds. Add the remaining sugar and the egg yolks, cover and blend five seconds. Add the ice and cream, cover and blend twenty seconds.

3. Immediately pour the mixture into the beaten egg whites and fold gently until mixed. Pour into a nine-inch pie plate lined with the crumb crust and chill until set.

RUM CREAM PIE *Filling for 2 nine-inch pie crusts*

6 egg yolks
1 scant cup sugar
1 tablespoon gelatin
½ cup cold water
2 cups heavy cream
½ cup dark rum
Crumb crust (page 522)
Whipped cream and shaved chocolate for garnish

1. Beat the egg yolks with the scant cup of sugar until thick and lemon-colored.

2. Soak the gelatin in the cold water. Stir over hot water until thoroughly dissolved. Gradually add to the egg mixture, stirring.

3. Whip the cream until stiff and fold into the egg mixture. Flavor with the rum. Stir the mixture over cracked ice until it begins to set. Turn into the pie shell and chill until firm.

4. Garnish with whipped cream and, if desired, with shaved chocolate.

STRAWBERRY ICE CREAM AND MERINGUE PIE *6 servings*

Baked deep 8-inch pastry shell, chilled
1 quart strawberry ice cream
Meringue pie topping (page 522) flavored with 1 teaspoon vanilla extract

(*cont'd*)

1. Preheat oven to hot (450° F.).

2. Pack the ice cream firmly into the baked pie shell.

3. Spread the meringue lightly over the ice cream, making sure it touches the pastry at all points.

4. Bake until the meringue is a delicate brown, or three minutes. Serve immediately.

VARIATION:

Chocolate Pastry Shell: Use chocolate pastry and peppermint, vanilla or other suitably flavored ice cream. To make chocolate pastry, sift four teaspoons each cocoa and sugar with the flour in a standard recipe. Add three-fourths teaspoon vanilla with the water.

VELVET CUSTARD PIE *6 to 8 servings*

Unbaked 9-inch pie shell
4 eggs
⅔ cup sugar
½ teaspoon salt
½ teaspoon nutmeg
2⅔ cups milk
1 teaspoon vanilla extract

1. Preheat oven to hot (425° F.). Line a pie plate with pastry.

2. Beat the eggs with a rotary beater until they are thoroughly blended. Add the sugar, salt, nutmeg, milk and vanilla and stir until smooth. Pour the mixture into the pastry-lined pie plate.

3. Bake fifteen minutes. Reduce the oven temperature to moderate (350° F.) and bake until a knife inserted in the filling about one inch from the pastry edge comes out clean, about thirty minutes longer.

VINEGAR PIE *6 to 8 servings*

4 egg yolks
2 egg whites
1 cup sugar
¼ cup flour
½ teaspoon each nutmeg, cinnamon, allspice and cloves
Pinch of salt
1 cup sour cream
3 tablespoons melted butter
3 tablespoons cider vinegar
1 cup nutmeats (walnuts or pecans)
1 cup seedless raisins
Unbaked 9-inch pie shell

1. Preheat oven to hot (450° F.).

2. Beat the egg yolks.

3. Beat the egg whites until stiff. Fold in the sugar and mix with the yolks.

4. Sift the flour with the spices and salt and add, alternately with the cream, to the egg mixture.

5. Combine the butter and vinegar and mix with the nuts and raisins. Add to the flour mixture.

(cont'd)

6. Pour the mixture into a pastry-lined nine-inch pie pan and bake ten minutes. Reduce heat to 400° F. and bake five minutes. Reduce heat to moderate (350° F.) and bake until the filling begins to set, or about fifteen minutes.

7. Cool the pie and top with whipped cream.

TANGERINE CREAM TARTS *6 servings*

- 1 eight-ounce package cream cheese, softened
- 6 tablespoons orange Curaçao
- ¼ cup sugar
- 4 teaspoons cornstarch
- 1⅓ cups tangerine juice
- 3 tangerines
- 6 baked tart shells

1. Cream together the cheese and Curaçao.
2. In a saucepan, mix together the sugar and cornstarch. Gradually stir in the tangerine juice. Bring to a boil over medium heat and boil one minute.
3. Peel the tangerines, removing the white membrane. Snip the center of each section with scissors and remove the seeds. Add the tangerine sections to the sauce.
4. Spoon the cheese filling into tart shells made with sweet pastry (page 521) or plain pastry (page 520). Spoon the sauce over the filling. Chill until serving time.

CREAM PUFF SHELLS *10 large puffs*

When cream puff paste is baked it is one of the apparent miracles of cuisine. The paste expands to many times its original size and a mass of air occurs in the center. Nonetheless, it is one of the easiest of foods to prepare. The only "secret" is to add the flour all at once and fearlessly to the water-butter mixture. Cream puff paste is not only baked; it may be deep fried to produce air-filled beignets soufflés.

- 1 cup water
- ½ cup butter
- ¼ teaspoon salt
- 1 cup sifted all-purpose flour
- 4 eggs

1. Preheat oven to hot (450° F.).
2. Combine the water, butter and salt and bring to a boil. Remove from the heat and add the flour all at once. Stir vigorously until the mixture leaves the sides of the pan and forms a ball around the spoon. If a ball does not form almost immediately, hold the saucepan over low heat and beat briskly a few seconds. Cool slightly.
3. Add the eggs, one at a time, and beat until the mixture is smooth and glossy after each addition.
4. Drop the mixture by rounded tablespoonfuls onto a greased baking sheet, leaving two inches between the puffs to permit spreading.
5. Bake fifteen minutes. Reduce the oven temperature to moderate (350° F.)

(*cont'd*)

1. *To make cream puffs or éclairs,* flour is added all at once to boiling water and butter. Mixture is stirred rapidly until paste ball forms.

2. Eggs are added one at a time. Mixture is beaten well after each addition until the paste is waxy, firm, and exceptionally smooth.

3. To make éclairs, the paste is forced out of a pastry tube onto a baking sheet. To make cream puffs it is dropped from a spoon.

4. Cream puffs or éclairs are baked in a hot oven. When they are done, no bubbles of fat remain on surface; sides feel rigid.

5. Many fillings complement cream puff shells. Here shells are filled with smooth pastry cream, then frosted and chilled.

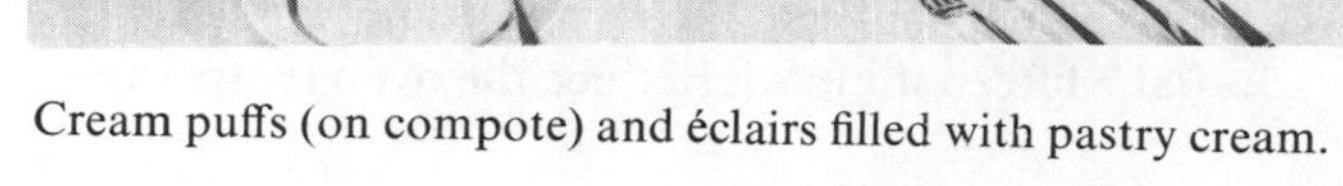

Cream puffs (on compote) and éclairs filled with pastry cream.

and bake until no bubbles of fat remain on the surface and the sides of the puffs feel rigid, about thirty minutes longer. Cool. Cut a cap off each puff and fill with pastry cream (see below). Replace the cap.

VARIATIONS:

Eclairs: Using a spoon or large round pastry tube, shape the cream puff mixture on a baking sheet into finger lengths. Bake, cool and slit each puff at the side. Fill with pastry cream (see below) and frost with melted chocolate or any chocolate icing.

Beignets Soufflés: Flavor cream puff mixture with one-quarter teaspoon orange extract or one tablespoon rum and drop by tablespoons into deep hot fat (370° F.). Fry until brown on all sides. Serve hot, sprinkled with confectioners' sugar.

PASTRY CREAM: *About 3 cups*

- 1/3 cup sugar
- 3 1/2 tablespoons cornstarch or 6 tablespoons flour
- 6 lightly beaten egg yolks
- 2 cups milk
- 1 teaspoon vanilla extract

1. Mix sugar, cornstarch and egg yolks in a saucepan. Scald the milk and pour it gradually over the egg yolk mixture, stirring rapidly with a wire whisk.
2. Cook over low heat or in the top of a double boiler, stirring rapidly with the whisk, until the mixture is thickened and smooth. Do not allow the pastry cream to boil. Cool and stir in the vanilla.

DANISH PASTRY *About 24 pastries*

- 4 3/4 cups sifted all-purpose flour, approximately
- 1 1/2 cups butter
- 1 1/2 packages dry yeast
- 1 1/4 cups lukewarm milk
- 1/4 cup sugar
- 1 egg, beaten

1. Measure one-third cup flour onto a board or into a bowl. Add the butter and chop the flour and butter together with a pastry blender or two knives. Roll the mixture between two sheets of waxed paper into a twelve-by-six-inch rectangle. Chill.
2. Sprinkle the yeast on the warm milk and let stand until softened and the mixture has cooled. Add the sugar and egg. Add the remaining flour gradually and mix with a wooden spoon until a soft dough is formed. Turn the dough onto a floured surface and knead until smooth.
3. Roll the dough on a generously floured board into a fourteen-inch square. Place the butter-flour mixture on one half of the dough and fold the other half of the dough over it. Press around the edges to seal.
4. Pat the dough with a rolling pin and then roll it out into a paper-thin sheet. Fold the sheet of dough into thirds. Repeat the patting, rolling and folding process three times. If the butter mixture softens and begins to ooze out upon rolling, chill the dough before continuing. *(cont'd)*

1. *Danish pastries.* To fashion envelopes, place filling in center of a pastry square. Fold corners toward center; press down edges.

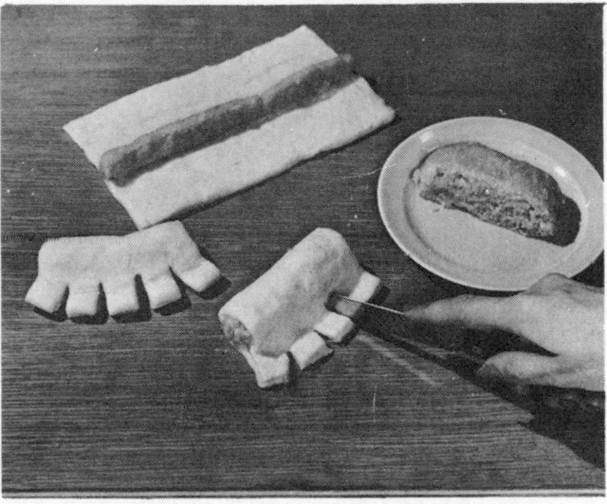

2. To make cockscombs, place filling across pastry rectangle. Fold side over. Cut in lengths; gash as shown.

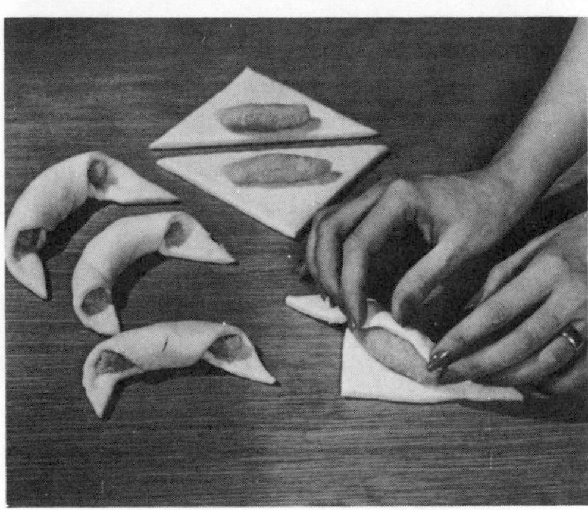

3. To shape pastry crescents, cut the dough into triangles, fill them and roll from triangle base to apex.

4. A breakfast fit for a royal Dane. Pictured is an assortment of filled Danish pastries, served with cups of steaming coffee.

5. Cut the finished dough into three equal portions. Roll and shape into envelopes, combs and crescents (page 535) and fill. Save any trimmings and stack them neatly to preserve the pastry layers. Chill and use to make additional pastries.

6. Place the pastry shapes on lightly greased baking sheets. Cover and set aside to rise until half doubled in size. While the pastries are rising, preheat oven to hot (400° F.).

7. Brush the envelopes and crescents with slightly beaten egg diluted with a

(*cont'd*)

little water and bake on the lower shelf of the oven until brown, about twenty minutes. Cool on racks.

8. If desired, frost the crescents and envelopes with one-half cup confectioners' sugar blended with one tablespoon milk and one-half teaspoon vanilla.

VANILLA CREAM FILLING FOR DANISH PASTRIES: *Enough for 8 pastries*

½ cup milk
1 tablespoon flour
1 egg yolk
1 tablespoon sugar
½ teaspoon vanilla extract

1. Mix all the ingredients except the vanilla in the top of a double boiler.
2. Cook the mixture over boiling water, stirring constantly, until thick. Cool the mixture, stirring occasionally. Add the vanilla.

ALMOND PASTE FILLING FOR DANISH PASTRIES: *Enough for 8 pastries*

¼ pound almonds, blanched
½ cup sugar
1 egg

1. Grind the blanched almonds and mix with the sugar.
2. Add the egg and work until smooth.

PRUNE FILLING FOR DANISH PASTRIES: *Enough for 8 pastries*

½ cup puréed prunes
¼ cup ground almonds
1 teaspoon grated orange rind

Mix all the ingredients together.

CHEESE FILLING FOR DANISH PASTRIES: *Enough for 8 pastries*

1 cup creamed cottage cheese
1 egg, well beaten
1 tablespoon sugar
1 tablespoon butter, melted
Pinch of salt
Pinch of nutmeg
Pinch of cinnamon

Blend the first four ingredients thoroughly and season to taste with salt and spices.

SHAPING DANISH PASTRIES:

Envelopes: Using one portion of the dough, roll it into a strip about five inches wide and one-quarter inch thick. Trim the edges to make it four inches wide and cut it into four-inch squares. Spread the center of each square with one tablespoon filling, fold the corners into the center, press down.

Cockscombs: Using one portion of dough, roll it into a strip five inches wide and one-quarter inch thick. Place a strip of filling about one-half inch in diameter down the center and fold the dough over it. Press around the edges and trim evenly. Sprinkle with sugar and chopped almonds and cut into four-inch lengths. Gash the side of each piece four times, cutting in about three-quarters of an inch toward the filling. *(cont'd)*

Crescents: Roll the remaining dough into a strip about five inches wide and one-quarter inch thick. Trim the edges to make it about four inches wide. Cut into squares and then cut into triangles. Place a tablespoon of filling on the wide side and roll up, twisting the ends if necessary to cover the filling.

PUFF PASTRY

If all the pastries used in cuisine were ranked in order of excellence, puff pastry would undoubtedly lead the list. In a phrase it is the pastry of kings and the king of pastry. It is also the most difficult to prepare and, for dedicated cooks, the most interesting.

What is puff pastry? It is a flaky, air-filled, butter-rich product of the oven with infinite uses. It is the basis for patty shells, fruit turnovers, cream horns, croissants, palm leaves and pie crusts.

One of the pitfalls in making puff pastry is not getting enough "elasticity" into the dough before the butter is enclosed in it. To achieve this, the dough must be kneaded for at least twenty minutes. Puff pastry, incidentally, is best made during winter months, since the butter has a better consistency in cold weather.

Someone has noted, with some exaggeration, that a description of making puff pastry can be as intricate as describing how to play golf to someone who has never heard of the game. To facilitate the exposition, method photographs as well as recipes are given. The method is that of Mrs. Paula Peck, an exceptionally accomplished instructress at the James Beard Cooking School in New York.

- 2 cups sweet butter
- 4 cups (1 pound) unsifted all-purpose flour
- 1 teaspoon salt
- 1 tablespoon lemon juice
- 1⅓ cups water

1. Work the butter into a brick shape measuring 3 by 5 by 1½ inches.
2. Spoon three tablespoons of flour onto waxed paper and coat butter with it. Wrap butter in waxed paper and refrigerate.
3. Place remaining flour in a large mixing bowl. With the fingers make a well in center of flour. Add salt, lemon juice and one cup of water.
4. Using the fingertips in a circular motion, work flour and water mixture to make a rather firm, slightly sticky dough. Gradually add remaining one-third cup water if the dough seems to require it.
5. Knead dough twenty minutes or more. It is almost impossible to overwork it. Pound dough on the table occasionally and, while working, dip the fingers into water and dab a few drops into dough to prevent it from becoming hard and dry. The dough has been worked sufficiently when it becomes smooth, satiny and elastic. Shape dough into a ball and leave for fifteen minutes.
6. Place ball on a well-floured cloth. Cut a cross in the center, then roll out four "ears" from the cross, leaving the center a thick cushion.
7. Place the chilled butter on the cushion center. Butter must not be too firm. Stretch the four rolled-out portions over the butter, overlapping them and sealing edges and corners. There will be a cushion on bottom and one on top

(*cont'd*)

formed by the overlapping ears of dough. Wrap the whole in foil and chill twenty minutes.

8. On a well-floured cloth, gently roll dough as evenly as possible into a rectangle measuring approximately 8 by 18 inches, slightly less than one-third inch thick. Use a firm, even motion. Do not roll over the ends of the dough with the roller until the dough is eighteen inches long. Then the rolling pin may be rolled over the ends but at a right angle to the former motion.

9. Brush off excess flour from dough and bring each end of the rectangle to center. Press dough firmly.

10. Fold the dough in half, pocketbook fashion, to make four layers of dough. Wrap in waxed paper; chill one-half hour.

11. Place the dough again on a floured cloth with one of the two open ends facing you.

12. Roll the dough into a rectangle once more, brush off excess flour and fold as before. Repeat the rolling and folding three more times, chilling the dough for at least one-half hour between each rolling and folding.

13. When the dough has been rolled, folded and chilled five times it is ready for use. The final chilling, however, should be for three hours.

PATTY SHELLS OR VOL-AU-VENTS: *Approximately 1 dozen*

1. Preheat oven to hot (450° F.).

2. Roll puff pastry to a thickness of one-eighth inch. For each patty shell, cut three three-inch circles of dough with a biscuit cutter. Place the first circle on a baking sheet and brush it with egg yolk. Do not let egg drip on sides.

3. Using a slightly smaller cutter, cut out center of second pastry circle to make a ring. Turn this ring over and place it on perimeter of the first pastry circle. Brush with egg yolk.

4. Press the smaller biscuit cutter into the third pastry circle but do not cut through it. Place this on top of the ring and brush with egg yolk. Bake ten minutes. Reduce heat to 350° and bake twenty minutes longer, or until golden and dry.

5. Remove the indented center of the topmost layer of the pastry with a sharp knife. Return the shell to a 350° oven to dry. Fill the vol-au-vents with creamed mixtures such as chicken or seafood, covering with the removed centers.

CREAM HORNS: *Approximately 2 dozen*

1. On a floured cloth roll puff pastry in strips to a thickness of one-eighth inch. Each strip should be thirty inches long if cream horn tubes are five and one-half inches long. If tubes are smaller, shorter strips can be used.

2. Starting at the narrowest end of each tube, wind a strip of dough around it, slightly overlapping the edges. Do not stretch pastry around tube. Chill.

3. Preheat oven to hot (450° F.).

4. Brush top and sides, but not the bottom, with beaten egg. Coat brushed part with granulated sugar. Place tubes one inch apart on a paper-lined cookie sheet.

(cont'd)

1. *Puff pastry.* Work butter into brick shape. Coat with flour; wrap in waxed paper; place in refrigerator.

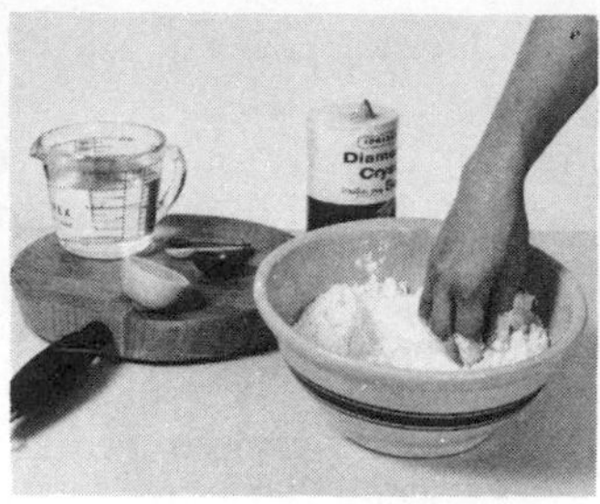

2. Place flour in bowl; make a well in center and add the salt, lemon juice and water.

3. Using fingertips in circular motion, work ingredients to make firm, slightly sticky dough.

4. Knead and pound dough twenty minutes or more. Wet fingers often to keep dough moist.

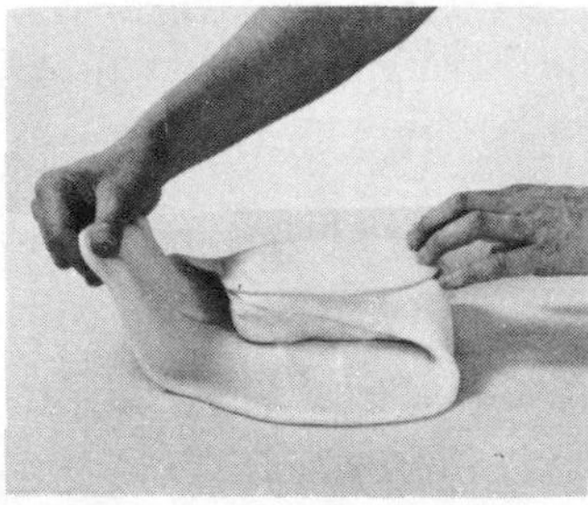

5. When dough is ready, roll out into four "ears," wrap butter in the middle. Seal, then chill.

6. Roll dough on floured cloth into an 8 x 18 inch rectangle one-third of an inch thick.

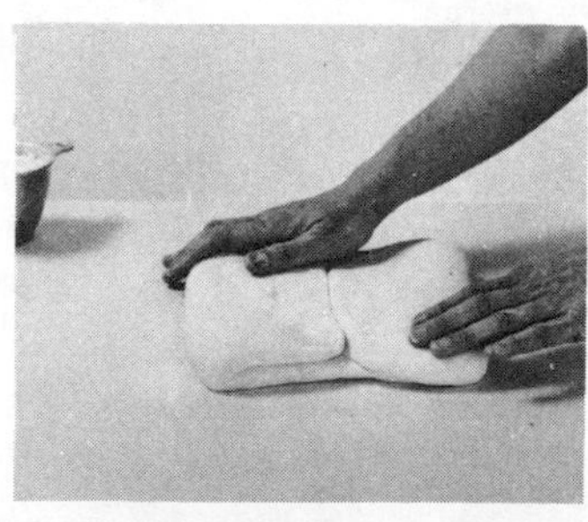

7. Brush off excess flour and bring each end of rectangle to center. Press down firmly.

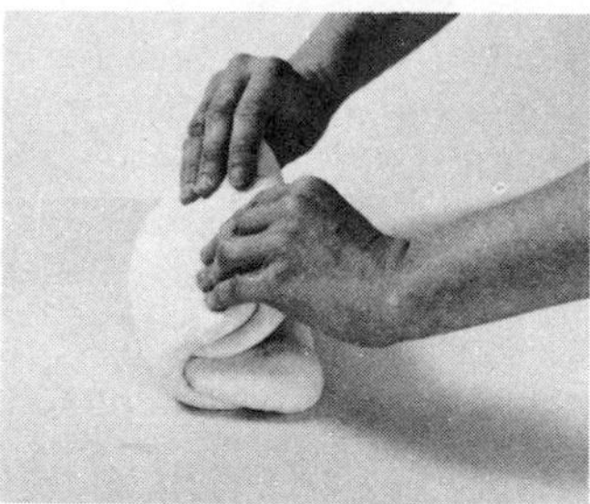

8. Bring one-half of the dough over the other half. This produces four layers of dough.

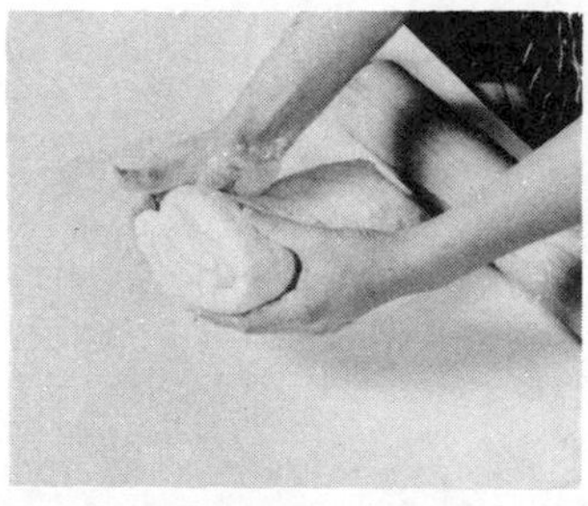

9. Turn one end of dough toward you. Roll again into 8 x 18 inch rectangle and fold as before.

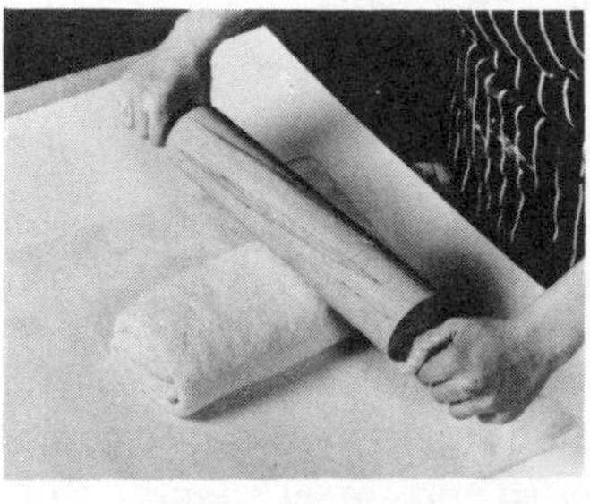

10. Dough should be rolled and folded for a total of five times. Chill dough after each rolling.

11. For a patty shell, use biscuit cutter to make three circles. Brush first one with egg.

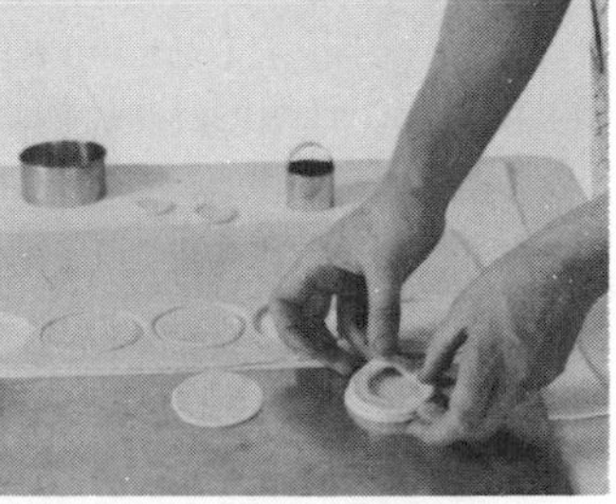

12. Use a smaller cutter on second circle to make a ring. Place upside down on first circle.

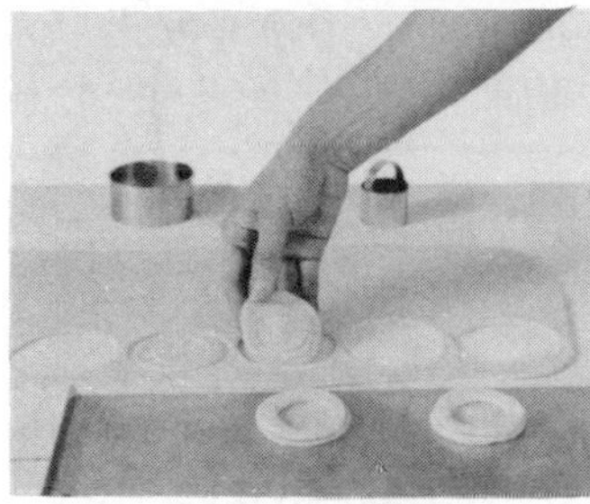

13. Third circle is pressed with small cutter, but not cut through. Use to top egg-brushed ring.

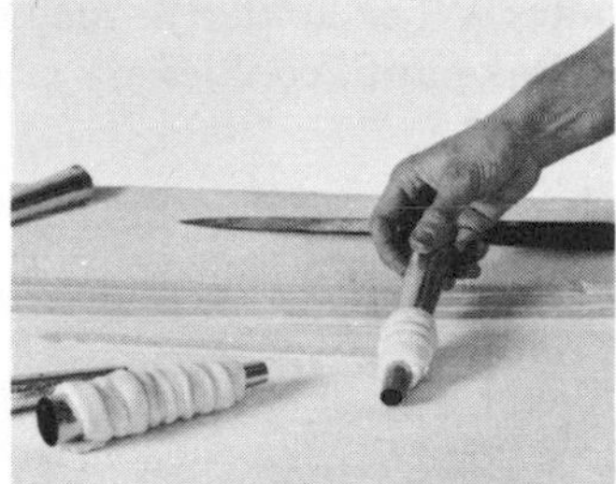

14. To make cream horns, the strips of puff pastry are wrapped around metal baking tubes.

15. To make palm leaves, dough is folded to produce six layers. Dough is sliced with knife.

Elegance from the oven: Puff pastry may be used to make patty shells (on the stand), sugar-coated palm leaves (center) and cream horns filled with whipped cream.

5. Bake ten minutes, then reduce heat to 350° and bake until pastry is golden. Remove tubes from pastry immediately by twisting them free. Serve cold, filled with whipped cream or pastry cream (page 533).

PALMIERS OR PALM LEAVES: *Approximately 2 dozen*

1. On a cloth liberally sprinkled with granulated sugar, roll the puff pastry (or puff paste trimmings) into a square one-eighth inch thick. Determine center of square and fold each side into thirds toward center so ends meet exactly. Fold in half to make a compact roll. Wrap in waxed paper and chill two hours.

2. Preheat oven to hot (450° F.).

3. Cut roll into half-inch-wide slices. Dip each slice into sugar and place slices one and one-half inches apart on a cookie sheet.

4. Bake eight minutes. When golden at the bottom, turn with a spatula and reduce heat to 375° F. Bake until cookies are crisp and no white spot shows in centers.

MOCK PUFF PASTRY (FOR TARTS) *6 tart shells*

3 cups sifted all-purpose flour
¾ teaspoon salt
3 tablespoons shortening
2 eggs, slightly beaten
⅔ cup milk, approximately
¾ cup butter

1. Sift together the flour and salt. Add the shortening and rub or chop it thoroughly into the flour.

2. Mix the eggs and milk. Add to the dry mixture and mix well, adding a little more milk if necessary to make a fairly stiff dough.

3. On a floured pastry cloth, roll the dough into a thin sheet. Cut the butter into small pieces and arrange over the center third of the pastry. Fold unbuttered portions of the pastry over the butter. Press around the edges to seal and pat the edges with a rolling pin. Fold the pastry once more, as before, into thirds. Pat the edges and then pat the entire surface and roll into a thin sheet. Fold into thirds once again and chill.

4. Divide the dough in half and roll each half into a strip about one-sixth inch thick. Cut into three squares and line three four-inch tart shells. To do this, fit the pastry loosely into the pans, pressing it firmly around the sides. Trim the edge, flute with the fingers and prick the sides and bottom of the pastry well with a fork. Place the tarts on a baking sheet and bake on the bottom shelf of a preheated hot oven (450° F.) until brown, about fifteen minutes. Cool on a rack before filling.

Note: Stack the scraps of pastry as they are trimmed from the tarts (this incorporates air between the layers and helps keep it flaky), pat it and roll it as before for extra tarts.

STRUDELS

3 cups sifted all-purpose flour
⅔ cup lukewarm water
1½ tablespoons salad oil
1 egg plus 1 yolk, well beaten
¼ teaspoon salt

Melted butter or salad oil
2 or more tablespoons fine dry bread crumbs
Strudel filling (see below and page 543)

1. Sift the flour into a bowl. Reserving two tablespoons of water, combine the remainder with the oil, egg, egg yolk and salt. Add to the flour and stir into a smooth dough, adding the remainder of the water if necessary. The dough should be stiff.

2. Place the dough on a floured board and knead three minutes. Cover with a warm bowl and let stand thirty minutes.

3. Cover a table at least thirty inches square with a tablecloth and rub flour into the cloth evenly. A double face, pressure-sensitive tape is excellent for holding the cloth firm by securing the edges to the underneath rim of the table.

4. Using a lightly floured rolling pin, roll the dough in every direction to make it into as perfect a circle as possible. Place the backs of the hands under the dough, and, using a gentle hand-over-hand motion, stretch in all directions.

5. Pull the extremities of the dough with the fingers and anchor them over the table's edge to facilitate the stretching.

6. With an ordinary pair of kitchen scissors, trim off the overhanging edges as neatly as possible. With a pastry brush, brush the entire surface of the dough generously with melted butter or salad oil. Sprinkle lightly and as evenly as possible with fine dry bread crumbs.

7. Place the filling in an even roll the full width of the dough and approximately two inches from one of the ends. Carefully fold the two inches of dough over the filling. Pat the dough, if necessary, to make it adhere. Fold the two parallel sides of the dough toward the center, taking care to totally enclose the filling.

8. Lift the edge of the tablecloth closest to the filling and continue lifting to make the dough roll over and over itself. The dough may be rolled directly onto a baking sheet. Slice in half, if necessary, or curve into a horseshoe shape. Brush with melted butter.

9. Bake in a preheated moderate oven (350° F.) until golden brown, about twenty-five to thirty minutes.

10. Slide the strudel onto a bread board and cut into two-inch pieces.

APPLE STRUDEL FILLING:

6 tart apples, peeled and cored
1 cup raisins
1 cup chopped walnuts or almonds

1 cup sugar
1 teaspoon cinnamon

(*cont'd*)

1. *Apple strudel.* Follow the instructions for making strudel dough. Place the ball of dough on the floured cloth.

2. Using a lightly floured rolling pin, roll the dough in every direction to make it into as perfect a circle as possible.

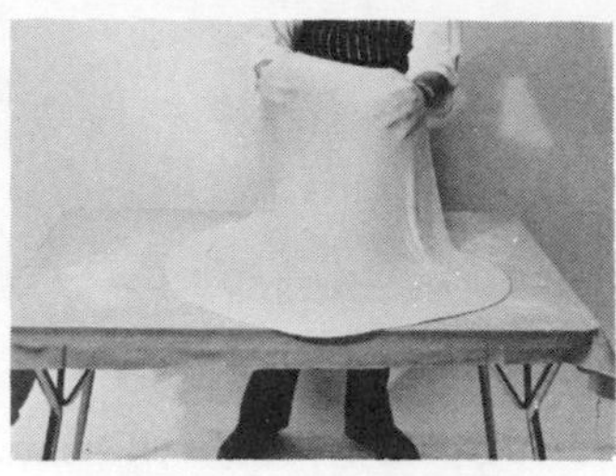

3. Place the backs of the hands under the dough and, using a gentle hand-over-hand motion, stretch in all directions.

4. The extremities of the dough may be pulled by the fingers and anchored over the table's edge to facilitate the stretching.

5. With an ordinary pair of kitchen scissors, the overhanging edges should be trimmed off as neatly as possible.

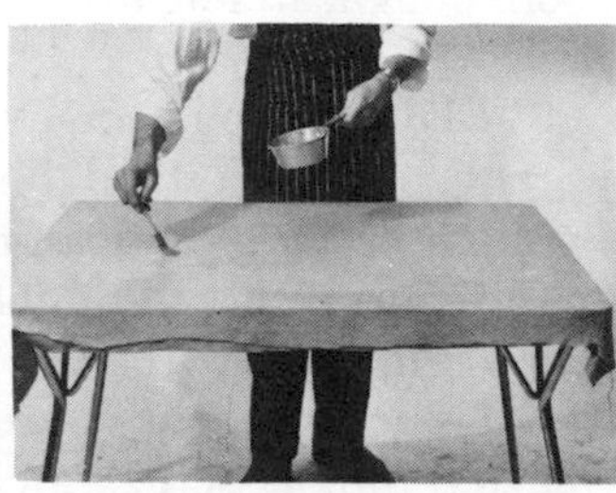

6. With a pastry brush, the entire surface of the dough should be brushed generously with melted butter or oil.

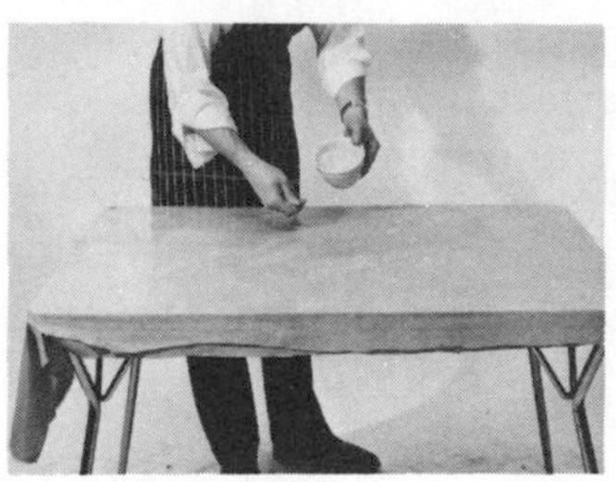

7. The dough is then sprinkled lightly and as evenly as possible with two or more tablespoons of fine dry bread crumbs.

8. The filling is placed in an even roll the full width of the dough and approximately two inches from one of the ends.

9. The two inches of dough are carefully folded over the filling. Pat the dough, if necessary, to make it adhere.

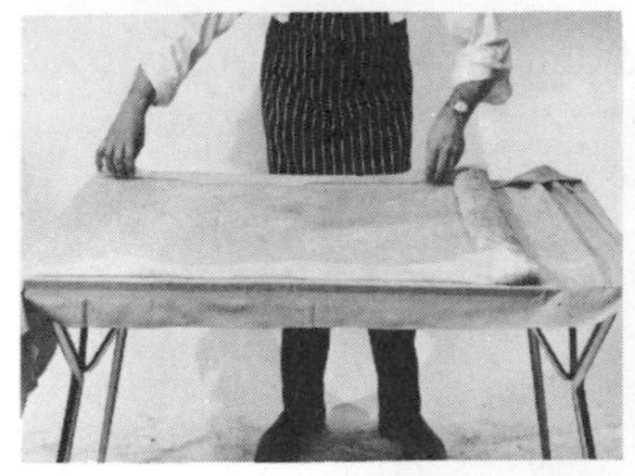

10. Fold the two parallel sides of the dough toward the center. Care should be taken to see that filling is totally enclosed.

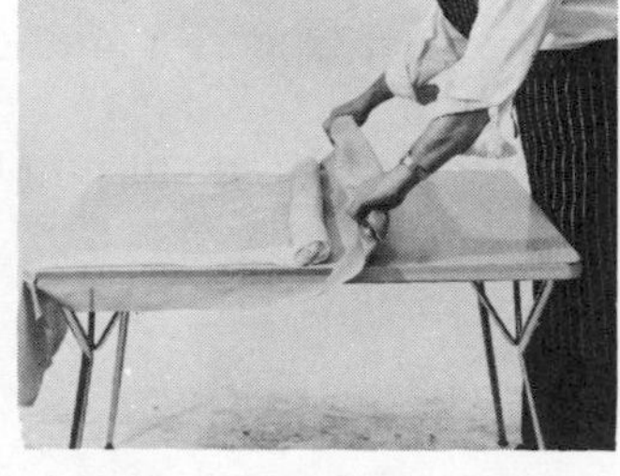

11. Lift the edge of the tablecloth close to the filling, and continue lifting to make dough roll over and over itself.

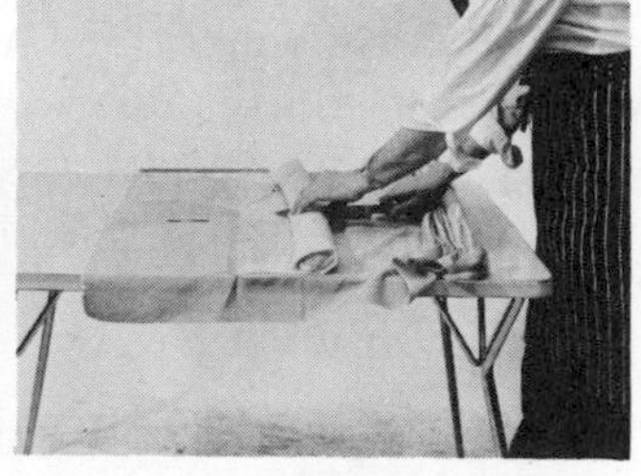

12. Dough may be rolled directly onto baking sheet. Slice in half, if necessary, or curve it into a horseshoe shape.

Apple strudel made with nuts, raisins and cinnamon is an excellent dessert to serve with coffee or afternoon tea.

Cut the apples into thin slices and mix with remaining ingredients. Use as filling for one strudel.

CHERRY STRUDEL FILLING:

2 pounds sweet black cherries, pitted

1 cup chopped walnuts or almonds

½ cup sugar

Combine all ingredients. Use as filling for one strudel.

CAKES

AMBROSIA CAKE *12 or more generous servings*

2 eight-inch cake layers (see below)
½ recipe pastry cream (page 533)
Kirsch to taste (optional)
2 bananas, sliced
Peeled wedges of two oranges
Vanilla boiled frosting (page 573)
¾ cup shredded coconut

1. Cut a thin slice from the top of one of the cake layers to flatten it. Spread it with pastry cream. If desired, the cream may be seasoned to taste with kirsch.
2. Cover the pastry cream with half the banana slices and orange wedges. Top with the second cake layer and use a spatula to remove any pastry cream that may drip over the side of the cake.
3. Frost the top and sides of the cake with vanilla frosting and coat sides with the coconut.
4. Just before serving garnish the top symmetrically with the remaining banana slices and orange wedges.

AMBROSIA CAKE LAYERS *2 8-inch layers*

2 cups sifted cake flour
3 teaspoons baking powder
½ teaspoon salt
½ cup butter
1 cup granulated sugar
2 eggs
1 teaspoon vanilla extract
¾ cup milk

1. Preheat the oven to moderate (375° F.).
2. Sift together the flour, baking powder and salt.
3. Cream the butter, add sugar gradually and beat until light and fluffy. Add the eggs, one at a time, beating well after each addition. Add the vanilla.
4. Add dry ingredients alternately with milk, stirring only enough to blend thoroughly. Do not beat. Pour into two greased eight-inch layer cake pans.
5. Bake twenty-five minutes, or until a cake tester inserted in the center of each cake comes out clean. Cool.

ANGEL CAKE *12 to 16 servings*

1 cup sifted cake flour
1½ cups superfine granulated sugar
1¼ cups egg whites (10 to 12), at room temperature
1¼ teaspoons cream of tartar
¼ teaspoon salt
1 teaspoon vanilla extract
¼ teaspoon almond extract

(*cont'd*)

1. Preheat the oven to moderate (325° F.).
2. Sift the flour four times with one-half cup of the sugar.
3. Beat the egg whites until foamy. Add the cream of tartar and salt and beat until soft moist peaks form when the beater is withdrawn.
4. Add the remaining sugar, about two tablespoons at a time, beating it in after each addition. Add vanilla and almond extract.
5. Sift about one-quarter cup of the flour-sugar mixture at a time over the meringue and cut and fold it in just until no flour shows.
6. Turn into an ungreased ten-inch tube pan and bake about one hour. Invert pan and let cake cool in pan.

BABAS AU RHUM *6 servings*

¼ cup milk
¼ cup butter
1 package yeast
¼ cup lukewarm water
2 egg yolks
¼ cup granulated sugar
1 egg
½ teaspoon grated lemon rind
2 tablespoons dried currants
1¾ cups sifted all-purpose flour
Hot rum syrup (page 616)
2 ounces (¼ cup) dark rum

1. Scald the milk, add the butter and blend. Cool to lukewarm.
2. Sprinkle the yeast on the water and stir until dissolved.
3. Beat the egg yolks and gradually add the sugar. Vigorously beat in the whole egg. Add the milk mixture, dissolved yeast, lemon rind and currants.
4. Stir in the flour and beat until smooth. Cover the batter and let rise in a warm place (80° to 85° F.) until doubled in bulk, about one hour. Stir down.
5. Spoon into six individual well-greased baba molds or small custard cups, filling them two-thirds full. Let rise, uncovered, until the batter reaches the tops of the molds, about thirty minutes. Fifteen minutes before babas are ready, preheat the oven to moderate (350° F.).
6. Bake until a cake tester comes out clean, about twenty minutes. Remove from the molds and cool on a cake rack. If desired, wrap in foil and freeze.
7. Marinate the babas in hot rum sauce several hours before serving. To serve, ignite two ounces heated dark rum in a ladle and pour over the babas.

Note: Baba molds may be purchased in many fine specialty shops with imported cooking utensils.

BUCHE DE NOEL *10 to 12 servings*

One of the most charming of the traditional French holiday cakes is the bûche de Noël, or Christmas log. When finished the cake looks deceptively like a log.

1 cup sifted cake flour
¼ teaspoon salt
1⅓ cups granulated sugar
4 eggs, separated
1 teaspoon vanilla extract
Rum syrup (page 546)
Mocha cream frosting (page 575)
Decorative frosting II (page 577)

(cont'd)

1. Line a 10½ by 15½-inch jelly roll pan with waxed paper.
2. Preheat oven to hot (400° F.).
3. Mix the flour, salt and half the sugar. Sift together three times.
4. Beat the egg whites until stiff. Gradually beat in the remaining sugar. Fold in the vanilla and egg yolks, which have been stiffly beaten. Fold in the flour-sugar mixture, about three tablespoons at a time.
5. Pour the batter into the prepared pan in parallel strips running lengthwise of the pan. Spread evenly and bake until firm in the center, or about fifteen minutes.
6. Turn the cake out onto waxed paper, or a towel that has been sprinkled with confectioners' sugar. Remove the pan lining and cut off all the edges of the cake. Roll the cake as for jelly roll, without removing the paper or towel. Cool and chill briefly. (The paper or towel will be on the inside of the roll.)
7. Unroll, brush with half the rum syrup and spread with mocha cream frosting. Roll as a jelly roll, this time removing the paper or towel. Wrap in waxed paper and chill thoroughly, or until the frosting becomes firm.
8. Remove the waxed paper and cut off the ends of the cake diagonally for use as "branches."
9. Brush the outside of the cake and the "branches" with the remainder of the rum syrup. Set "branches" aside. Frost cake with mocha cream, using a pastry bag and notched tube and running the strips lengthwise of the cake to give the appearance of bark.
10. Attach the "branches" to the "log" and press into the frosting. Frost with mocha cream.
11. Frost the ends of the "log" and "branches" with alternating rings of mocha cream and yellow decorative frosting, forcing both through pastry tubes. Chill the "log" until the mocha cream is firm.
12. Decorate the log as desired with flowers, "Noël," etc., using decorative frosting and forcing it through different tubes. Serve the cake promptly, storing it in a cool place until serving time so that the butter in the mocha frosting does not soften.

RUM SYRUP FOR A BUCHE DE NOEL:

¼ cup sugar
¼ cup water
1½ tablespoons rum

Boil the sugar and water together until syrupy, or about three minutes. Cool and add the rum.

COTTAGE CHEESECAKE WITH STRAWBERRY GLAZE

10 to 12 servings

1 six-ounce package zwieback
1 cup granulated sugar
¼ cup butter, melted
1½ pounds cottage cheese
¼ cup sifted all-purpose flour
¼ teaspoon salt
6 eggs, separated
1 cup sour cream
Rind and juice of 1 lemon
Strawberry glaze (page 547)

(cont'd)

1. Preheat oven to moderate (325° F.).

2. Roll the zwieback into fine crumbs. Grease a nine-inch spring-form pan and dust the sides with zwieback crumbs. Mix the remaining crumbs with one-quarter cup of the sugar and the butter and press onto the bottom of the pan. Bake five minutes. Cool.

3. Press the cottage cheese through a fine sieve. Add half the remaining sugar, the flour, salt, egg yolks, sour cream, lemon rind and juice. Whip until thoroughly blended.

4. Beat the egg whites until stiff, adding the remaining sugar gradually. Fold into the cheese mixture.

5. Turn the mixture into the prepared pan and bake at 325° F. about one and one-half hours. Cool in the pan and glaze as directed.

STRAWBERRY GLAZE:

1 quart strawberries
⅓ cup sugar
¼ cup water
1 tablespoon cornstarch
1 teaspoon butter

1. Wash and hull the strawberries. Crush enough berries to make one-half cup.

2. Boil the crushed berries, sugar, water and cornstarch two minutes, stirring. Add the butter. Strain and cool.

3. Arrange the whole berries over the top of the cheesecake and pour the glaze over the berries. Chill.

REFRIGERATOR RUM CHEESECAKE *10 to 12 servings*

2 envelopes unflavored gelatin
1 cup granulated sugar
¼ teaspoon salt
2 eggs, separated
1 cup milk
1 teaspoon grated lemon rind
1 tablespoon lemon juice
2 tablespoons light rum, or 2 teaspoons rum flavoring
3 cups (1½ pounds) creamed cottage cheese
Nut-crumb crust (page 548)
1 cup heavy cream, whipped

1. Mix the gelatin, three-quarters cup of the sugar and the salt in the top of a double boiler.

2. Beat the egg yolks, add the milk and add to the gelatin mixture. Cook over boiling water, stirring, until the gelatin dissolves and the mixture thickens slightly, or about ten minutes.

3. Remove the mixture from the heat and add the lemon rind, lemon juice and rum. Cool.

4. Whip the cottage cheese with an electric beater until smooth, or rub through a sieve into a large bowl. Stir in the cooled gelatin mixture. Chill, stirring occasionally, until the mixture mounds slightly when dropped from a spoon.

5. While the gelatin mixture is chilling, prepare the nut-crumb mixture and set aside.

(cont'd)

6. Beat the egg whites until stiff but not dry. Gradually add the remaining sugar and beat until very stiff. Fold into the gelatin-cheese mixture. Fold in the whipped cream and turn into pan lined with nut-crumb crust. Chill before serving.

NUT-CRUMB CRUST:

2 tablespoons melted butter
1 tablespoon sugar
¼ cup finely chopped nuts
⅔ cup graham cracker crumbs
¼ teaspoon cinnamon
¼ teaspoon nutmeg

1. Mix together all the ingredients.
2. Sprinkle half the crumb mixture on the bottom of an eight-inch spring-form pan. Turn the cheesecake mixture into the pan and sprinkle with the remaining crumbs. Chill until firm.

BLENDER CHEESECAKE *6 servings*

This is perhaps the quickest-made cheesecake ever developed.

1 envelope unflavored gelatin
1 tablespoon lemon juice
Yellow peel of 1 lemon
½ cup hot water or milk
⅓ cup granulated sugar
2 egg yolks
8 ounces cream cheese
1 heaping cup crushed ice
1 cup sour cream
Crumb crust (see below)

1. In an electric blender place the gelatin, lemon juice, peel and hot liquid. Cover and blend on high speed forty seconds.
2. Add the sugar, egg yolks and cheese, cover and blend ten seconds. Add the ice and cream, cover and blend fifteen seconds.
3. Pour the mixture into a four-cup spring-form pan lined with half a recipe for crumb crust and sprinkle with the remainder. Chill until set.

CRUMB CRUST (BLENDER METHOD):

15 graham crackers
1 tablespoon sugar
½ teaspoon cinnamon
¼ cup butter, melted

1. Break five crackers into quarters and place in the container of an electric blender. Blend to crumbs by flicking the motor on and off high speed four times. Empty the crumbs into a bowl and continue until all the crackers are crumbed.
2. Stir in the sugar and cinnamon. Add the melted butter and mix until all the crumbs are moistened.
3. Press the crumbs against the sides and bottom of a buttered spring-form pan or nine-inch pie plate. Chill before adding the filling.

ONE-BOWL CHOCOLATE CAKE *12 servings*

2 cups sifted cake flour
2 teaspoons baking powder
½ teaspoon soda
¼ teaspoon salt
½ cup plus 2 tablespoons cocoa
1½ cups granulated sugar
½ cup plus 2 tablespoons shortening
½ cup warm water
⅔ cup milk
2 eggs
1 teaspoon vanilla extract

1. Preheat oven to moderate (350° F.).

2. Sift together in the bowl of an electric mixer the flour, baking powder, soda, salt, cocoa and sugar. Add the shortening, water, milk, eggs and vanilla and blend on very low speed until the ingredients are moistened. Mix three minutes on medium (No. 3) speed, scraping the bowl frequently to insure complete blending. Do not include the scraping time in the three minutes.

3. Pour the mixture into two nine-inch layer cake pans that have been greased and lined with waxed paper circles cut one-eighth inch smaller than the bottoms of the pans.

4. Bake until the cake rebounds when pressed gently in the center, twenty-five to thirty minutes. Cool in the pans on a cake rack ten minutes before removing from the pans. Cool and frost as desired.

SWEET CHOCOLATE CAKE *10 to 12 servings*

1 four-ounce package sweet cooking chocolate
½ cup boiling water
1 cup butter, at room temperature
2 cups granulated sugar
4 eggs, separated
1 teaspoon vanilla extract
2½ cups sifted cake flour
1 teaspoon baking soda
½ teaspoon salt
1 cup buttermilk

1. Preheat oven to moderate (350° F.).

2. Melt the chocolate in the boiling water. Cool.

3. Cream the butter, add the sugar and cream until light and fluffy. Add the egg yolks, one at a time, beating after each addition. Add the vanilla and melted chocolate and mix until well blended.

4. Sift the flour with the soda and salt. Add the sifted dry ingredients alternately with the buttermilk to the butter mixture, beating after each addition until the batter is smooth.

5. Fold in the stiffly beaten egg whites and pour the batter into three eight- or nine-inch greased layer pans, lined on the bottom with waxed paper. Bake thirty-five to forty minutes. Cool.

6. Frost the top and between the layers with coconut-pecan frosting (page 576) or other desired frosting. Do not frost the sides of the cake.

RED DEVIL'S FOOD CAKE

2 nine-inch layers

1¾ cups sifted cake flour
1½ cups granulated sugar
⅓ cup cocoa
1¼ teaspoons soda
1 teaspoon salt
½ cup shortening
1 cup milk
2 eggs
1 teaspoon vanilla extract

1. Preheat oven to moderate (350° F.). Grease the bottoms of two nine-inch layer cake pans, line with waxed paper and grease the paper.
2. Sift together in a large bowl or the bowl of an electric mixer the flour, sugar, cocoa, soda and salt. Add the shortening and two-thirds cup of the milk and mix. Beat two minutes by hand or at medium speed in the mixer. Add the remaining ingredients and beat two minutes longer.
3. Turn the batter into the prepared pans and bake on the lower shelf of the oven until the cake rebounds to the touch when pressed lightly in the center, thirty to thirty-five minutes.
4. Cool the cake in the pan five minutes. Turn out on a rack, remove the paper, cool and frost as desired.

SOUR CREAM FUDGE CAKE

12 servings

2 cups sifted cake flour
1½ cups granulated sugar
1 teaspoon soda
1 teaspoon salt
⅓ cup shortening
1 cup sour cream
3 squares (ounces) unsweetened chocolate, melted
2 eggs
1 teaspoon vanilla extract
¼ cup hot water

1. Preheat oven to moderate (350° F.). Grease the bottom of a 13 by 9 by 1½-inch pan, line with waxed paper and grease the paper.
2. Sift together the flour, sugar, soda and salt. Add the shortening and sour cream and beat two minutes. Add the chocolate, eggs, vanilla and hot water and beat two minutes longer.
3. Turn the batter into the prepared pan and bake until the cake rebounds to the touch when pressed gently in the center, about thirty-five minutes.
4. Cool the cake in the pan five minutes. Turn out on a rack, remove the paper and cool. Frost as desired. To serve, cut into squares.

MINNESOTA FUDGE CAKE

10 to 12 servings

5 eggs
2½ cups granulated sugar
4½ squares (ounces) unsweetened chocolate
1¾ cups milk
¼ cup butter
½ cup vegetable shortening
1½ teaspoons vanilla extract
½ teaspoon red food coloring
1½ teaspoons soda
½ teaspoon salt
3 cups sifted cake flour

(cont'd)

1. Preheat oven to moderate (350° F.).

2. Beat one of the eggs and combine it with one cup of the sugar, the chocolate and three-quarters cup of the milk in a saucepan. Cook, stirring, over low heat, until the chocolate melts and the mixture thickens. Cool to room temperature.

3. Mix the butter and shortening and add the remaining sugar gradually. Cream until fluffy. Add the vanilla and coloring. Add the remaining eggs, one at a time, beating well after each.

4. Sift the dry ingredients together and add to the butter mixture alternately with the remaining milk, beating well. Beat until smooth. Blend in the chocolate mixture.

5. Pour into three nine-inch greased layer pans, lined in the bottom with waxed paper, and bake twenty-five to thirty minutes. Cool and frost as desired.

FRESH COCONUT CAKE

1 9-inch cake

- 2¼ cups sifted cake flour
- 1½ cups granulated sugar
- 4 teaspoons baking powder
- 1 teaspoon salt
- ½ cup vegetable shortening
- 1 cup coconut milk (page 139)
- 1 teaspoon vanilla extract
- 4 medium egg whites, unbeaten

1. Preheat oven to moderate (350° F.). Grease two nine-inch layer cake pans, line with waxed paper and grease the paper.

2. Into the bowl of an electric mixer sift the flour, sugar, baking powder and salt. Add the shortening, three-quarters cup of the coconut milk and the vanilla. Beat two minutes at low to medium speed, scraping the bowl and beaters as necessary.

3. Add the egg whites and the remaining coconut milk and beat two minutes longer.

4. Turn the batter into the prepared pans and bake until a cake tester inserted in the center of the cake comes out clean, about twenty to thirty minutes.

5. Cool the cake on a rack ten minutes before removing from the pans.

6. When the cake is completely cool, spread a lemon filling (prepared from a packaged mix) between the layers. Frost with vanilla boiled frosting (page 573) or with sweetened whipped cream. Sprinkle with freshly grated coconut.

HUNGARIAN CREAM CAKE

3 8-inch or 2 9-inch layers

- 3 cups sifted cake flour
- 3 teaspoons baking powder
- 1 teaspoon salt
- 3 eggs
- 1½ teaspoons almond extract
- 2 teaspoons vanilla extract
- 1½ cups granulated sugar
- 2 cups heavy cream
- Strawberry cream filling (page 552)

(cont'd)

1. Grease three eight-inch or two nine-inch layer cake pans. Line with waxed paper and grease the paper. Preheat oven to moderate (350° F.).

2. Sift together three times the flour, baking powder and salt.

3. Beat the eggs with a rotary beater until light and foamy. Add the almond and vanilla extracts. Add the sugar gradually, beating well after each addition. Add the dry ingredients alternately with the cream, beating until just smooth after each addition.

4. Pour the batter into the prepared pans and bake until the cake starts to shrink from the sides of the pan, about forty-five minutes. Turn out on cake racks, remove the paper, turn right side up and cool. Fill and frost with strawberry cream or other desired filling.

STRAWBERRY CREAM FILLING:

Whip stiff one cup heavy cream. Stir in two tablespoons cognac or rum. Into half the cream fold one-quarter cup sliced, lightly sweetened strawberries. Spread between the layers. Pile the remaining cream on top and garnish with whole berries.

SICILIAN CREAM CAKE *12 servings*

- 1 large sponge cake
- 1¼ pounds ricotta cheese
- 1 cup granulated sugar
- 1 teaspoon vanilla extract
- 2 tablespoons cognac, rum or crème de cacao
- 3 tablespoons chopped semisweet chocolate bits
- 1 tablespoon chopped candied fruit
- Pinch of salt
- Powdered sugar

1. Split the cake into three layers of equal size.

2. Combine the cheese, sugar, vanilla and cognac and beat well with a wooden spoon until smooth and fluffy, or blend well in an electric blender.

3. Add the remaining ingredients except the powdered sugar and mix thoroughly.

4. Spread one of the layers with the cheese mixture and place another layer on top. Repeat with the remaining cheese mixture and sponge cake layer. Refrigerate the cake several hours. Dust the top with powdered sugar before serving.

CRUMB AND NUT CAKE *3 8-inch layers*

- 1 cup shortening
- 1 cup sugar
- 4 eggs
- 2 teaspoons vanilla extract
- 3 cups fine graham cracker crumbs
- 1 cup finely chopped nuts
- 3 teaspoons baking powder
- 1 cup milk

1. Preheat oven to moderate (350° F.).

2. Blend the shortening, sugar, eggs and vanilla. Combine the crumbs, nuts

(cont'd)

and baking powder and add to the shortening mixture alternately with the milk. Pour into three greased eight-inch layer cake pans one and one-fourth inches deep.

3. Bake thirty to thirty-five minutes. Turn out on a rack to cool. Put the layers together with chocolate cream frosting (page 574).

REVANIE (GREEK NUT CAKE) *48 pieces*

12 eggs, separated
1½ cups granulated sugar
1 teaspoon vanilla extract
¾ pound (3 cups) ground walnuts
¾ pound (3 cups) ground almonds
16 pieces of zwieback, ground or crushed very fine
Grated rind of one orange
Rum syrup (page 616)

1. Preheat oven to moderate (350° F.). Grease a 16 x 13 x 3-inch pan (a roasting pan will do).

2. Beat the egg whites until stiff and set aside. Beat the yolks with the sugar until light and lemon colored. Add vanilla to the yolks while beating.

3. Mix the nuts, zwieback and rind together.

4. Gradually fold the beaten egg whites into the yolks. Fold in the nut mixture.

5. Pour batter into prepared pan and bake exactly one hour. While baking, prepare the syrup. Pour the hot syrup over the cake the moment it is removed from the oven. Cool and, before serving, cut into diamond shapes.

DUNDEE CAKE *1 round loaf*

1 cup sultanas or other raisins
½ cup currants
2¼ cups sifted all-purpose flour
1 teaspoon baking powder
½ teaspoon salt
¾ cup butter
¾ cup sugar
3 eggs
½ cup milk
¼ cup candied orange peel or citron, shredded or chopped, or grated rind of 1 small orange
¼ cup chopped or shredded blanched almonds
10 or 12 blanched almonds, split

1. Grease a round 9 by 3½-inch pan or casserole. Line the bottom with waxed paper and grease the paper. Preheat oven to moderate (325° F.).

2. Chop the raisins. Wash the currants and dry them. Set aside until ready to use.

3. Sift together flour, baking powder and salt.

4. Whip the butter well. Add sugar gradually and whip until fluffy. Add the eggs, one at a time, beating until very fluffy after each.

(*cont'd*)

5. Add flour mixture and milk alternately to the butter mixture, stirring after each addition only until well mixed. Do not beat.

6. Fold in the raisins, currants, orange peel or citron and the shredded almonds. Turn into prepared pan and arrange the split almonds over the top.

7. Bake about one hour and fifteen minutes, or until the cake has begun to shrink from the sides of the pan. Cool fifteen minutes before removing from the pan.

JAMAICA SPICED BLACK FRUITCAKE *2 loaf cakes*

- 3¼ cups dried currants
- 2¼ cups seedless raisins
- 2 cups seeded raisins, chopped
- 1¼ cups sliced citron
- 1½ cups dried figs, chopped
- 1 cup cooked and drained dried prunes, pitted and chopped
- 1½ cups blanched whole almonds, toasted and sliced
- 1 cup chopped, pitted dried dates
- 1 cup glazed whole cherries, sliced
- ½ cup glazed orange peel, chopped
- 3 cups dark Jamaica rum
- 1 cup butter
- 2 cups dark brown sugar, firmly packed
- 1½ teaspoons each cinnamon, allspice and nutmeg
- 5 eggs
- 2 cups sifted all-purpose flour
- 2 teaspoons baking powder
- ½ teaspoon salt

1. Prepare the fruits and almonds and mix well. Stir in the rum and allow to soak one week.

2. Preheat oven to slow (275° F.).

3. Soften the butter in a large mixing bowl and gradually blend in the sugar and spices. Beat in two of the eggs.

4. Sift the flour with the baking powder and salt and add one cup to the butter-sugar mixture. Beat in the remaining eggs, stir in the rum-soaked fruit, undrained, and add the remaining flour. Mix well.

5. Line two greased 9 by 5 by 3-inch bread pans with brown or waxed paper and grease the paper lightly. Divide the batter equally between the two pans. Place a large shallow pan of hot water beneath the cake pans in the oven to prevent the cake from drying. Bake the cake until a toothpick or cake tester inserted in the center comes out clean, or two and one-half hours.

6. Cool in the bread pans one hour. Remove to a wire cooling rack, remove the paper and let rest until cold. Wrap in aluminum foil and store in a tightly closed tin box. Moisten occasionally with Jamaican rum. Age at least one month before serving and serve, if desired, with brandied foamy sauce (page 615).

Note: If desired, half the batter may be baked in a 9 by 5 by 3-inch pan and the rest steamed in a six-cup pudding mold for three hours. Place the inverted mold in hot water so that the water reaches halfway up the side of the mold.

HELEN McCULLY'S WHITE FRUITCAKE

1 10-inch tube cake or 2 loaves

- 1½ pounds almonds, blanched and coarsely shredded
- ½ pound candied citron, chopped
- ¼ pound candied pineapple, chopped
- ¼ pound candied cherries, halved
- ½ pound golden raisins
- 4 cups sifted all-purpose flour
- 1½ cups butter
- 2 cups sugar
- 6 eggs, separated
- ¾ cup milk
- ¼ cup cognac
- 1 teaspoon almond extract
- 1 teaspoon cream of tartar

1. Preheat the oven to slow (275° F.). Grease one 10-inch tube pan or two 9 by 5 by 3-inch loaf pans. Line with brown paper and grease the paper.

2. Mix together the almonds, fruits and one-half cup of the flour. Set aside.

3. Cream the butter until smooth, adding the sugar gradually. Beat the egg yolks lightly, add them to the creamed mixture and beat well.

4. Combine the milk, cognac and almond extract. Add to the creamed mixture alternately with remaining flour.

5. Beat the egg whites until foamy, then add cream of tartar. Continue beating until stiff. Pour the batter over the fruits and nuts. Mix well. Fold in egg whites.

6. Lift the batter into the prepared pans and press down firmly with the palm. Bake in tube pan three hours and fifteen minutes or in loaf pans two hours and fifteen minutes.

7. Let stand thirty minutes. Turn the cakes upside down onto a wire rack. Peel off paper and store in an airtight container several days.

Note: This cake may be frosted with layers of almond paste (page 558), milk frosting (page 558), and confectioners' icing (page 576).

JAMAICA LIGHT FRUITCAKE

10 pounds of cake

- 1 pound currants
- 1 pound prunes
- 1 pound dates
- 1 pound seedless raisins
- 2 cups dry white wine
- 2 cups rum
- 6 cups all-purpose flour
- 4 teaspoons baking powder
- 1 teaspoon cinnamon
- 1 teaspoon nutmeg
- 2 cups butter, at room temperature
- 2 cups granulated sugar
- 8 eggs, well beaten
- 1 teaspoon vanilla extract

1. Wash the currants and prunes and dry. Pit the prunes and dates and cut them into small pieces. Mix all the fruits with the wine and rum and let stand three days, stirring every day.

2. Preheat oven to slow (300° F.).

3. Sift together the flour, baking powder, cinnamon and nutmeg.

(cont'd)

4. Cream the butter, add the sugar and cream well. Add the eggs and vanilla and mix well. Add the flour mixture gradually, stirring until blended. Fold in the prepared fruit and liquor.

5. Grease four 8½ by 4¼ by 2¼-inch pans, line with waxed paper and grease the paper. Fill not more than three-quarters full with the batter.

6. Place a shallow pan of hot water on the bottom of the oven; place the cakes on a rack in the middle of the oven and bake about three hours. Remove the pan of water thirty minutes before the cakes are done.

7. Remove the cakes with the paper and place on a rack to cool. Wrap in fresh waxed paper or aluminum foil and store in an airtight container in a cool place. Allow at least two weeks, preferably longer, for aging.

WATERMELON PICKLE FRUITCAKE *2 loaves*

3 cups sifted all-purpose flour
1½ teaspoons baking powder
½ teaspoon salt
7 ounces candied cherries, halved
6 ounces candied pineapple, shredded
2 cups drained watermelon pickle, shredded
12 ounces white raisins
6½ ounces pecans, chopped
4½ ounces almonds, blanched and coarsely shredded
1 cup butter
2 cups sugar
5 eggs
½ cup sherry

1. Preheat the oven to slow (300° F.). Grease two 9 by 5 by 3-inch loaf pans, line with waxed paper and grease the paper.

2. Sift together the flour, baking powder and salt. Mix several tablespoons of this mixture into fruits and nuts.

3. Cream the butter until smooth, adding sugar gradually. Add the eggs, one at a time, beating well after each.

4. Stir in the flour mixture alternately with sherry. Mix in fruit-nut mixture. Transfer batter to pans, pressing down.

5. Bake two hours. Cool, remove from pans and peel off paper.

6. Wrap the cakes in foil and store them in an airtight container about one month before serving. Sprinkle several times a week with a light shower of sherry.

ORANGE FRUITCAKE *1 10-inch cake*

2½ cups sifted cake flour
1 teaspoon baking powder
½ teaspoon salt
6½ ounces pitted dates, chopped
4½ ounces walnuts, chopped
1 cup butter
2 cups granulated sugar
2 eggs
1 teaspoon soda
1 cup buttermilk
1 teaspoon vanilla extract
Grated rind and juice of 2 oranges

(*cont'd*)

1. Preheat the oven to slow (300° F.). Grease a ten-inch tube pan.

2. Sift together the flour, baking powder and salt. Stir several tablespoons of this mixture into the chopped dates and nuts.

3. Cream the butter until smooth, gradually adding one cup sugar. Add the eggs, one at a time, beating well after each addition.

4. Stir the baking soda into the buttermilk and add to the creamed mixture alternately with the flour mixture.

5. Add vanilla, dates, nuts and orange rind and mix well. Pour into pan and bake one hour and twenty minutes.

6. Meanwhile, boil together the orange juice and remaining one cup sugar. When cake is done, pour over the top.

Note: This cake will keep two to three weeks if wrapped in foil or Saran and stored in the refrigerator.

NOVA SCOTIA BLACK FRUITCAKE *2 loaf cakes*

- 4 ounces candied citron, coarsely chopped
- 2 ounces candied lemon peel, coarsely chopped
- 2 ounces candied orange peel, coarsely chopped
- ½ pound candied cherries, halved
- 1 pound candied pineapple, shredded
- 1 pound golden raisins
- ½ pound seeded raisins
- 4 ounces currants
- ½ cup dark rum, cognac or sherry
- 4 ounces almonds, blanched and shredded
- 4 ounces walnuts or pecans, coarsely chopped
- 2 cups sifted all-purpose flour
- ½ teaspoon mace
- ½ teaspoon cinnamon
- ½ teaspoon baking powder
- 1 tablespoon milk
- 1 teaspoon almond extract
- ½ cup butter
- 1 cup granulated sugar
- 1 cup brown sugar, packed
- 5 eggs

1. Mix the fruits. Add rum, cover and let stand overnight.

2. Preheat the oven to slow (275° F.). Grease one 10-inch tube pan or two 9 by 5 by 3-inch loaf pans. Line with waxed paper and grease the paper.

3. Combine the fruits, the nuts and one-half cup flour.

4. Sift together the remaining flour, mace, cinnamon and baking powder. Mix the milk with the almond extract.

5. Cream the butter until smooth, adding sugars gradually. Add the eggs, mix well and add the milk mixture. Add flour mixture; mix well.

6. Pour the batter over the fruits and nuts and mix thoroughly. Fill the pans and press batter down firmly.

7. Bake tube cake about four hours, loaves about three hours. Let cakes stand thirty minutes. Turn out onto a rack and peel off the paper.

8. Wrap cooled cakes in cheesecloth soaked in rum, cognac or sherry. Place

(*cont'd*)

in a crock or deep kettle and cover tightly. As the cloth dries, dribble a little of the same liquor over it. Let ripen one month before frosting with a layer of each of the following two frostings. When dry, spread the milk frosting evenly with confectioners' icing (page 576).

ALMOND PASTE:

1 pound almonds, blanched
1 pound sifted confectioners' sugar
3 egg whites, lightly beaten
1 teaspoon almond extract

1. Grind the almonds finely.
2. Add remaining ingredients; mix thoroughly. Spread over the cake. Let dry.

MILK FROSTING:

1 teaspoon butter
1½ cups sugar
1 tablespoon light corn syrup
½ cup milk
½ teaspoon almond extract

1. Cook the butter, sugar, corn syrup and milk to 234° F., stirring. Cool.
2. Add the almond extract and beat until of a soft fudge consistency. Spread over almond paste. Let dry.

GENOISE *2 9-inch or 3 8-inch layers*

The genoise is a superb French pastry. It does not contain a leavening agent other than the air that is beaten into the eggs. Originally it was necessary to beat the eggs by hand over low heat in order to give the eggs volume. With today's electric mixers the method is greatly simplified. It is important, however, that the eggs be at room temperature or warmer and that the mixing bowl of the electric mixer be warmed before the beating begins.

The power of electric mixers varies. Care should be taken that the mixer does not become overheated.

Finally, the utmost care must be taken when folding the flour and butter into the genoise batter.

6 eggs, at room temperature or warmer
1 cup extra-fine granulated sugar
1 teaspoon vanilla extract
1 cup sifted cake flour
¼ cup butter
Quick butter frosting (page 573) or rich butter cream (page 573)
Praline powder (page 559)

1. Warm the bowl of an electric mixer. Beat the eggs with the sugar and vanilla at the highest speed until the mixture stands in stiff peaks when the beater is withdrawn. Depending on the power of the mixer, this should take from five to thirty minutes. It is important not to underbeat the mixture. Scrape the sides of the bowl with a rubber spatula from time to time so the ingredients will be well blended.

(cont'd)

The genoise, one of the most sumptuous of cakes, is made quickly in a modern electric mixer. A three-layered version of the cake, frosted with butter cream and spread with crushed praline, is shown.

The versatile nature of the genoise is depicted in the easily made petits fours shown. The cake is frosted with a butter icing, cut into small shapes and decorated with nuts and candied fruits.

2. Meanwhile, grease two nine-inch or three eight-inch cake pans that are one and one-half inches deep. Line the pans with waxed paper and grease the paper. Melt the butter and cool to lukewarm. Set heat control at moderate (350° F.) and place rack in the lower third of the oven.

3. Divide the flour into six to eight portions and sift over the egg mixture a portion at a time. Use a rubber spatula to fold the flour in gently after each addition.

4. Add the butter, about a teaspoon at a time, and fold it in gently but completely.

5. Turn the batter into the prepared pans and bake thirty-five to forty minutes. When done, the cake will rebound to the touch when pressed gently in the center.

6. Turn the cakes out onto a cooling rack, remove the paper and let cool. Frost with desired frosting and genoise praline powder (see below).

GENOISE PRALINE POWDER:

1 cup granulated sugar	⅓ cup water
⅛ teaspoon cream of tartar	1 cup blanched almonds

1. Boil the sugar, cream of tartar and water, stirring until the sugar dissolves. Add the almonds and cook without stirring until the almonds have browned and the syrup is a golden brown color. Turn into a buttered pan and cool until brittle.

2. Turn the brittle out of the pan, break into pieces and, using about a quarter at a time, cover with a towel and crush to a powder with a mallet or rolling

(cont'd)

pin. (Yields enough for use with either butter cream or butter frosting over a three-layer, eight-inch genóise.)

TO FROST THE GENOISE:

Reserve half the praline powder and add the remainder to the selected frosting. Spread frosting between the layers and over the top and sides of the cake. Stand the cake on waxed paper and toss the remaining powder over the sides, pressing it in gently. Any powder on the paper may be used for a border around the top of the cake.

If the rich butter cream is used, chill the cake after frosting until ready to serve.

PETITS FOURS

Frost a sheet of genoise cake (page 558) smoothly with quick butter frosting (page 573) or rich butter cream (page 573). Cut the sheet with cookie cutters or a knife into desired shapes. Garnish with candied cherries cut in half or into sixths for petals of flowers, angelica cut into diamonds for leaves, whole or chopped nuts, candy sprinkles, melted chocolate, coconut, etc.

BASKET CAKE

Hollow out a loaf of genoise cake (page 558), leaving a three-quarter-inch base and rim. Use decorative frosting (page 576) with a stem tube to draw a lattice on the sides of the cake. Fill the cake with fruits, pastry cream (page 533), flavored whipped cream or ice cream.

For the handle of the basket, use a strip of angelica. If the angelica is too dry to bend, let it stand in boiling water for a minute or so to soften slightly.

HONEY BALLS (TEIGLACH) *About 3 dozen*

6 eggs
1 teaspoon ground ginger
2 tablespoons salad oil
1 tablespoon cognac
3 heaping cups all-purpose flour
2 pounds honey
2 cups granulated sugar
Water
2 teaspoons ground ginger
Grated coconut (optional)

1. Beat the eggs and stir in the ginger, oil and cognac. Add the flour and stir to make a smooth, soft dough, stiff enough to handle.

2. Divide the dough into four parts and roll each part into a long rope the thickness of a pencil. Cut the dough into two-inch lengths.

3. Tie each two-inch segment of dough into a knot and press the ends together. Roll each knot gently between the palms of the hands to make it round.

(cont'd)

4. In a large kettle, combine the honey, sugar, one cup of water and the ginger. Heat to a rolling boil and drop the rounded knots into it, a few at a time, to prevent lowering the temperature. Cook ten minutes, uncovered, without stirring. Cover and cook thirty to forty minutes in constantly boiling syrup until the balls are a deep, golden brown.

5. Twenty minutes before the balls are done, turn them over in the liquid with a long wooden spoon.

6. When the balls are done, remove the kettle from the heat and pour into it one cup of rapidly boiling water. Turn the teiglach once more with a wooden spoon.

7. Set the kettle aside to cool. Spoon the balls into a crock and pour the syrup over them. If desired, roll each ball in coconut before serving.

HONEY CAKE (LEKACH) *35 to 40 honey cakes*

- 4 eggs
- 1 cup granulated sugar
- 1 cup honey
- ½ cup strong black coffee
- 2 tablespoons salad oil
- 3½ cups sifted all-purpose flour
- 1½ teaspoons baking powder
- 1 teaspoon soda
- ¼ teaspoon ground cloves
- ½ teaspoon allspice
- ½ teaspoon cinnamon
- ½ cup chopped nuts
- ½ cup raisins
- ½ cup citron, finely cut
- 2 tablespoons cognac

1. Preheat oven to slow (300° F.). Line a 10 by 15 by 2¼-inch pan with waxed paper.

2. Beat the eggs lightly. Add the sugar gradually and continue beating until the mixture is light and fluffy.

3. Combine the honey and coffee and stir it into the oil. Blend the mixture into the eggs and sugar.

4. Sift the flour, baking powder, soda and spices together. Stir in the nuts, raisins and citron and blend the mixture into the egg mixture. Stir in the cognac and pour the batter into the prepared pan.

5. Bake one hour. Cool and cut into squares.

PAIN D'EPICE *2 loaves*

- 1½ cups water
- 1 teaspoon anise seed
- 1 cup honey
- 1¼ cups granulated sugar
- 3 teaspoons soda
- 4½ cups sifted all-purpose flour
- ¼ teaspoon salt
- 1 teaspoon cinnamon
- ½ teaspoon nutmeg
- 3 tablespoons chopped citron
- 3 tablespoons chopped candied orange peel

1. Bring the water with the anise seed to a boil and set aside.

2. Preheat oven to moderate (350° F.).

(cont'd)

3. Add the honey and sugar to the water and stir until the sugar has dissolved. Add the soda.

4. Sift together the flour, salt, cinnamon and nutmeg. Add the citron and orange peel and mix. Add the honey mixture to the dry ingredients and stir until smooth.

5. Turn the mixture into two 8½ by 4½ by 2¾-inch greased loaf pans and bake about one hour.

GINGERBREAD *Serves 8*

- 1 tablespoon vinegar
- ¾ cup milk
- 2 cups sifted flour
- 2 teaspoons baking powder
- ¼ teaspoon soda
- ½ teaspoon salt
- 1½ to 2 teaspoons ground ginger
- 1 teaspoon ground cinnamon
- ¼ teaspoon ground cloves
- ⅓ cup shortening
- ½ cup sugar
- 1 egg
- ¾ cup molasses

1. Preheat oven to moderate (350° F.). Grease an 8 x 8 x 2-inch pan.

2. Add the vinegar to the milk and set aside. Sift together twice the flour, baking powder, soda, salt and spices.

3. Cream the shortening, add the sugar gradually and cream well. Add the egg and whip until fluffy. Add the molasses and mix.

4. Add dry ingredients, about one-quarter at a time, alternately with the by this time curdled milk. Stir only until mixed after each addition. Turn into prepared pan and bake forty-five to fifty minutes, or until bread rebounds to the touch when pressed gently in the center.

PEANUT RING CAKE *8 servings*

- ½ cup shortening
- ½ cup molasses
- ½ cup fresh roasted or salted peanuts
- ½ cup granulated sugar
- 1 teaspoon cinnamon
- ½ teaspoon ground ginger
- ¼ teaspoon salt
- 1 egg
- 2 cups sifted cake flour
- 2 teaspoons baking powder
- ¾ cup buttermilk
- ½ teaspoon soda

1. Preheat oven to moderate (350° F.).

2. Beat half the shortening with half the molasses until well blended and spread the mixture in a five-cup ring mold. Sprinkle with chopped peanuts.

3. Blend the remaining shortening and molasses with the sugar and stir in the cinnamon, ginger and salt. Add the egg and beat well. Sift together the flour and baking powder and stir into the molasses mixture alternately with the milk mixed with soda. Turn the batter into the prepared ring mold and bake forty-five minutes.

4. Allow the cake to stand for one minute and turn out onto a cake rack to cool.

SPICED POUND CAKE *1 9-inch tube cake*

1 cup butter
1½ teaspoons ground nutmeg or mace
½ teaspoon salt
1⅔ cups granulated sugar
5 eggs
2 cups sifted cake flour

1. Have all the ingredients at room temperature. Soften the butter and add the nutmeg and salt. Beat four minutes by electric beater or eight minutes by hand.

2 Gradually blend in the sugar until fluffy, beating two minutes by electric beater or eight minutes by hand.

3. Beat in four of the eggs, one at a time. Total beating time should be one minute by electric beater or two minutes by hand.

4. Stir in all the flour at one time and beat two minutes by electric beater or five minutes by hand.

5. Blend in the remaining egg, fifteen seconds by electric beater or thirty-three strokes by hand. Turn the mixture into a well-greased, lightly floured 9 by 3½-inch tube cake pan.

6. Place in a cold oven and set the control at slow (300° F.). If the cake is mixed by electric beater, bake two hours; if mixed by hand, bake one and one-half hours. (Since the electric beater entraps a little more air into the batter, it produces a cake that is a little thicker and lighter.)

7. Cool the cake in the pan ten minutes. Turn out on a wire rack to finish cooling.

STRAWBERRY ROLL *6 servings*

4 eggs, at room temperature
¾ teaspoon baking powder
1 teaspoon salt
Granulated sugar
1 teaspoon vanilla extract
¾ cup sifted cake flour
Confectioners' sugar
9 ounces cream cheese, at room temperature
3 tablespoons Grand Marnier
1 quart strawberries, sliced

1. Preheat oven to hot (400° F.).

2. Beat the eggs, preferably in an electric mixer, with the baking powder and salt until thick and light-colored, gradually adding three-quarters cup granulated sugar. Add the vanilla and fold in the flour.

3. Turn into a 15½ by 10½-inch jelly roll pan that has been greased and lined with greased paper. Bake thirteen minutes.

4. Turn from the pan onto a towel that has been dusted with confectioners' sugar. Quickly remove the paper and cut off the crisp edges of the cake. Roll, jelly-roll fashion, with the towel inside and enwrapping the cake. Chill.

5. Cream the cheese until fluffy with the Grand Marnier and three tablespoons sugar. Unroll the cake, spread with cheese and distribute the sliced berries over the cheese. Roll, jelly-roll fashion, and chill until cold. Serve with additional berries crushed and sweetened to taste.

GINGER ROLL *8 to 10 servings*

1¼ cups sifted all-purpose flour
⅓ cup granulated sugar
1¼ teaspoons soda
1 teaspoon each ginger, cinnamon, nutmeg and allspice
⅓ cup butter, melted
⅓ cup molasses
1 egg, well beaten
½ cup warm water
Confectioners' sugar
1 cup heavy cream, whipped

1. Preheat oven to moderate (350° F.). Grease a 10½ by 15½-inch jelly roll pan and line with paper; grease the paper.

2. Sift together twice the flour, sugar, soda and spices. Add the melted butter, molasses, egg and water and stir until smooth. Spread the mixture in the prepared pan. Bake until the cake rebounds when pressed with a finger, or fifteen minutes.

3. Let the cake cool briefly in the pan. Cover with a thin cloth wrung out in cold water and finish cooling in the refrigerator.

4. Remove the cloth, sprinkle the cake with sugar, turn out on waxed paper and remove the paper adhering to the under side of the cake.

5. Spread with cream and roll. Wrap in waxed paper and chill until ready to serve.

NUT ROLL *12 servings*

6 eggs, separated
¾ cup granulated sugar
1 teaspoon baking powder
1½ cups grated pecans
1½ cups heavy cream
Sugar and vanilla to taste

1. Preheat oven to moderate (350° F.). Grease a jelly roll pan, line with paper and grease the paper.

2. Beat the egg yolks with the sugar until thick.

3. Mix the baking powder with the pecans and fold into the egg yolks.

4. Whip the egg whites until stiff and fold into the batter. Spread in the prepared pan and bake twenty minutes.

5. Cover the cake with a damp towel and chill in the refrigerator. Turn the cake out on the towel and remove the paper.

6. Whip the cream until stiff and flavor with sugar and vanilla. Spread on the cake and roll like a jelly roll. Chill until serving time.

SAVARIN *8 to 10 servings*

1 package yeast
¼ cup lukewarm water
1½ cups sifted all-purpose flour
1 tablespoon sugar
½ teaspoon salt
2 large or 3 small eggs
¼ cup milk
⅔ cup butter, at room temperature
1 teaspoon grated lemon rind
Hot rum syrup (page 616)

(cont'd)

1. Soften the yeast in the water five minutes, then stir until blended.

2. Combine the flour, sugar and salt in a mixing bowl. Stir in the yeast and eggs, beaten slightly with the milk. Beat until the batter is smooth, about one hundred strokes. Add the butter and lemon rind and beat until the butter is blended into the batter, about fifty strokes.

3. Spoon the batter into a nine-inch ring mold, filling it half full, cover with a towel and let rise until the batter just fills the mold, about one hour.

4. Bake in a preheated hot oven (400° F.) thirty to thirty-five minutes, or until browned.

5. Carefully turn the savarin out of the mold and spoon over it hot rum syrup until the cake is saturated. Keep warm and serve filled with whipped cream. If desired, the savarin may be served blazing. To do this, pour one-quarter cup warm rum over the warm savarin and set ablaze. Accompany with warm zabaglione sauce (page 603).

BANANA SHORTCAKE *9 servings*

3 cups sifted all-purpose flour
½ teaspoon salt
4 teaspoons baking powder
2 tablespoons sugar
½ cup butter
1 cup milk, approximately
2 tablespoons butter, melted
1½ cups any marmalade
3 bananas, sliced
1 cup cream, whipped

1. Preheat oven to hot (425° F.).

2. Sift together the flour, salt, baking powder and sugar. Using a pastry blender, chop in the butter until well mixed. Add the milk all at once and then more if necessary to give a soft dough. Turn the dough out on a floured surface and knead about thirty times.

3. Press half the dough into a greased 8 by 8-inch pan. Brush with the two tablespoons melted butter. Press the second half of the dough into an eight-inch square and place on top. Bake until brown, about twenty minutes.

4. Slide a cookie sheet between the layers to separate them. Place the bottom layer on a serving plate, spread generously with half the marmalade and cover with half the banana slices. Cover with the remaining shortcake and spread with marmalade and banana. Top with whipped cream.

FRESH STRAWBERRY SOUR CREAM SHORTCAKE *6 servings*

2 cups sifted all-purpose flour
3 teaspoons baking powder
¾ teaspoon salt
Granulated sugar
1 three-ounce package cream cheese
Butter
1 egg, beaten
½ cup milk, approximately
1 quart fresh strawberries
1 cup sour cream

(*cont'd*)

1. Preheat oven to hot (450° F.).

2. Sift together the flour, baking powder, salt and one-quarter cup sugar. Add the cream cheese and two tablespoons butter, cutting them in with a pastry blender or two knives until the mixture resembles coarse cornmeal.

3. Pour the beaten egg into a measuring cup. Add enough milk to make three-quarters cup and gradually stir into the flour mixture. Knead the dough about twenty seconds.

4. Pat half the dough into a greased round eight-inch layer cake pan. Brush the surface with melted butter. Pat the remaining half of the dough over the top.

5. Bake until done, about twenty minutes. Remove to a cooling rack.

6. When the cake is cold, split the layers apart and place one on a large serving plate.

7. Wash, hull and slice the strawberries. Add one-third cup sugar and let stand ten minutes. Spoon the strawberry mixture between and over the top of the shortcake layers.

8. Top with sour cream sweetened to taste.

SPONGE CAKE *1 10-inch cake*

6 eggs
1 tablespoon lemon juice
1 packed teaspoon grated lemon rind
1 cup sifted cake flour
¾ teaspoon salt
1 cup granulated sugar

1. Preheat oven to moderate (325° F.). Lightly grease and flour the bottom, not the sides, of a ten-inch tube pan.

2. Break the eggs into the large bowl of an electric mixer, add the lemon juice and grated rind and beat the mixture at highest speed until soft peaks can be formed, or twelve to sixteen minutes.

3. While the eggs are being beaten, sift together the flour and salt onto a piece of waxed paper.

4. Continue beating the eggs at highest speed (after soft peaks can be formed) and pour the sugar in a fine stream over them, taking two and one-half to three minutes to add all the sugar.

5. Change to lowest speed and sift the flour and salt over the surface of the mixture as the bowl turns, taking two and one-half to three minutes to add all the flour. Scrape the sides of the bowl and beat at lowest speed one-half minute.

6. Pour the batter into the prepared pan and bake fifty minutes, or until a toothpick inserted in the center comes out clean.

7. Invert the cake pan and set it on a rack to cool. Prop it up if necessary so that the air can circulate between the cake and the tabletop. Let the cake cool at room temperature before removing it from the pan.

SPONGE LAYERS *2 8-by-8-inch layers*

¾ cup sifted cake flour
1 teaspoon baking powder
¼ teaspoon salt
4 eggs, separated
¾ cup granulated sugar
½ teaspoon almond extract
2 tablespoons water

1. Preheat oven to moderate (375° F.).
2. Sift together the flour, baking powder and salt.
3. Beat the egg whites until stiff, adding half the sugar gradually.
4. Beat the egg yolks until thick and add the remaining sugar gradually. Beat until very thick and add the almond extract. Add the water gradually while beating and fold in the egg white mixture. Sift about one-third of the flour mixture at a time over the top and fold in.
5. Turn the mixturc into a jelly-roll pan that has been lined with waxed paper. Bake about eighteen minutes. Turn out on a cooling rack, remove the paper and cut in half. Fill with any desired filling.

MORAVIAN SUGAR CAKE *About 3 dozen squares*

2 packages yeast
⅔ cup lukewarm water
½ cup granulated sugar
1½ teaspoons salt
1 cup butter
1 cup milk, scalded
2 eggs, slightly beaten
5 cups sifted all-purpose flour, approximately
Cinnamon
Nutmeg
2 cups light brown sugar
Confectioners' sugar (optional)

1. Soften the yeast in the water.
2. Add the sugar, salt and three tablespoons of the butter to the milk. Cool to lukewarm, stirring until the sugar is dissolved. Add the yeast and eggs. Add the flour, a cup at a time, and stir until blended. Dough must be soft.
3. Turn out on a floured board and knead the dough until smooth. Place in a greased bowl, grease the surface, cover and let rise in a warm place (80° to 85° F.) until doubled in bulk, or about one and one-quarter hours.
4. Press portions of the dough into three greased pans 7 by 11 inches for thick cakes, or into two pans 11 by 15 inches for thinner cakes. Grease the surfaces, cover and let rise until doubled, or about thirty minutes.
5. Pinch the dough all over with the thumb and finger to make holes in it. Sprinkle lightly with cinnamon and nutmeg and very generously with the light brown sugar. Dot with bits of the remaining butter.
6. Bake in a preheated oven (400° F.) until brown with a bubbly topping, or about twenty minutes. Serve warm or reheat. Traditionally, the cake is sprinkled with confectioners' sugar before serving. Cut into squares.

Torten are a Viennese version of cake. Their texture is somewhat heavier than the typical American cake but they are delicious nonetheless.

APFELTORTE *6 to 8 servings*

1 cup butter
Granulated sugar
1 egg, beaten
6 almonds, ground
1¾ cups sifted all-purpose flour
½ teaspoon salt
4 or 5 apples
¾ cup water
Whipped cream

1. Preheat oven to hot (400° F.).
2. Cream the butter and one-third cup sugar well. Add the egg and almonds. Sift in the flour and salt and mix smoothly. Spread two-thirds of this dough in a deep nine-inch spring-form cake pan and bake twenty minutes. Let cool in pan.
3. Wash, pare, core and slice the apples into small sections.
4. Boil one-half cup sugar and the water together until the syrup spins a thread from the edge of the spoon. Place a few apple sections at a time in the syrup and cook until soft but not broken. Let apples cool.
5. Let the syrup cook a little longer to thicken it.
6. Arrange apple sections in neat rows on the torte and pour the syrup over them. Force the remaining dough through a pastry tube, decorating the top with a border and criss-crossing strips over the apples.
7. Return the torte to the hot oven and bake until the garnishing dough is done and beginning to turn golden brown.
8. Remove outer rim of pan and let the torte chill on the base. Serve with whipped cream.

CHESTNUT TORTE *12 servings*

1¾ pounds fresh chestnuts, or ⅔ pound dried chestnuts
8 eggs, separated
½ cup granulated sugar
¼ cup almonds, ground
1 tablespoon sifted dry bread crumbs
1 tablespoon cognac or maraschino, or 2 teaspoons vanilla, or ½ teaspoon almond extract
1 cup heavy cream

1. If fresh nuts are used, make gashes in the flat side of each. Boil about twenty minutes in water to cover and drain. Remove the shell and inner skin. Return to pot, cover and boil in water to cover until tender, about five minutes. Drain and press through a sieve or food mill.

If dried chestnuts are used, soak overnight in water to cover. Add enough additional water to cover and boil, covered, until tender, about an hour. In a pressure cooker cook fifteen minutes at fifteen pounds pressure. Drain and press through a sieve or food mill.

2. Preheat oven to moderate (350° F.). Grease the bottom of a nine-inch spring-form pan.

(cont'd)

3. Beat the egg yolks, add the sugar and beat well. Add the chestnut purée (reserving one-fourth cup for garnish), almonds, crumbs and flavoring.

4. Beat egg whites until stiff and fold into mixture. Pour into pan and bake until firm in the center, about one hour.

5. Just before serving the cake (after it has cooled) whip the cream, sweeten and flavor to taste (cognac is recommended flavoring) and spread over top. Arrange the remainder of the chestnut purée as a border around the outer rim.

SPICY FIG TORTE *12 servings*

- ¾ cup grated blanched almonds
- ¼ cup candied orange peel, finely minced
- ¾ cup dried figs, finely minced
- ½ cup sifted dry white bread or matzos crumbs
- ½ teaspoon cinnamon
- ¼ teaspoon each nutmeg, allspice and cloves
- ½ teaspoon baking powder
- 1 tablespoon cognac
- 5 eggs, separated
- 1 cup less 2 tablespoons granulated sugar
- Confectioners' sugar
- Whipped cream

1. Preheat oven to moderate (325° F.). Grease the bottom of a nine-inch spring-form pan.
2. Mix the almonds, peel, figs and crumbs. Mix the spices and baking powder and add to the almond mixture. Add the cognac and mix with the fingers.
3. Beat the egg yolks until foamy. Gradually add the sugar and beat until thick. Add the almond mixture and mix well.
4. Beat the egg whites until stiff but not dry. Fold into the batter until no white shows.
5. Turn the batter into the prepared pan and bake one hour. Invert the pan on a rack, cool and remove the sides of the pan. Sprinkle the top of the cake with confectioners' sugar and serve with whipped cream.

LINZERTORTE *12 servings*

- 1 cup butter
- 1 cup sifted all-purpose flour
- 1½ cups unpeeled almonds, grated
- ½ cup granulated sugar
- ⅛ teaspoon cloves
- ⅛ teaspoon cinnamon
- 2 egg yolks
- ⅓ cup raspberry jam
- ½ egg white, slightly beaten
- 1½ tablespoons confectioners' sugar

1. Preheat oven to moderate (325° F.).
2. Crumble or chop the butter into the flour. Add the almonds.
3. Mix the sugar with the cloves, cinnamon and egg yolks. Add to the flour mixture and knead the dough until smooth and well blended.

(*cont'd*)

4. Turn two-thirds of the dough into a nine-inch ungreased cake pan with a removable bottom. Press dough over the bottom and halfway up the sides. Spread with jam.

5. Roll egg-sized balls of the remaining dough between the palms to make long rolls about one-third to one-half inch in diameter and about eight inches long. Place the rolls on a baking sheet and chill until firm.

6. Using a spatula, lift the rolls and arrange lattice-style over the jam. Fasten to the dough around the rim of the pan by pressing lightly.

7. Brush with egg white and bake on the lower shelf of the oven about one hour and fifteen minutes.

8. Set the pan on a rack and partly cool the cake before removing the rim of the pan. Before serving, sprinkle the cake with confectioners' sugar and, if desired, slivered almonds.

MANDELTORTE *12 servings*

6 eggs, separated
1 cup sugar, sifted
3 tablespoons lemon juice
1 teaspoon grated lemon peel
½ teaspoon almond extract
1 teaspoon cinnamon
1 cup blanched, grated almonds (about ⅓ pound)
½ cup fine dry bread or matzos crumbs
½ teaspoon salt
Lemon filling (see below)

1. Preheat oven to moderate (350° F.).

2. Grease two eight-inch layer pans. Line the bottoms with waxed paper and grease the paper.

3. Beat the egg yolks until light. Gradually add the sugar and continue to beat until creamy. Beat in the lemon juice, peel, almond extract and cinnamon. Thoroughly fold in the almonds and crumbs.

4. Beat the egg whites and salt together until stiff but not dry. Fold into the batter until no egg white shows.

5. Pour the batter into the prepared pans and bake until the top is firm to the touch, or about forty minutes.

6. Invert the pans on a rack, cool and then remove the cakes. When thoroughly cool, remove the paper and layer the cakes together with lemon filling. Frost with any desired white icing and decorate with whole almonds.

LEMON FILLING:

2½ tablespoons lemon juice
6 tablespoons orange juice
⅓ cup water
½ cup sugar
2 tablespoons flour
⅛ teaspoon salt
3 egg yolks
½ teaspoon grated lemon rind

Combine the ingredients in the top of a double boiler. Cook, stirring, over simmering water until thick. Cool.

PRUNE TORTE *10 to 12 servings*

1½ cups cooked prunes, drained
1 cup brown sugar, packed
½ cup granulated sugar
¾ cup butter
3 eggs
⅓ cup milk
2½ cups sifted all-purpose flour
2 teaspoons baking powder
½ teaspoon salt
½ teaspoon soda
1 teaspoon cinnamon
1 cup coarsely chopped walnuts
Whipped cream

1. Preheat oven to moderate (375° F.).
2. Pit the prunes and cut into small pieces.
3. Cream the sugars and butter together thoroughly. Blend in the eggs and milk.
4. Sift together the flour, baking powder, salt, soda and cinnamon. Blend into the creamed mixture. Stir in the prunes and walnuts. Spread the mixture in the bottoms of two greased nine-inch layer cake pans.
5. Bake thirty minutes and cool.
6. Put the layers together with whipped cream and spread cream over the top. Cut into wedges to serve.

SACHER TORTE *6 to 8 servings*

This cake originated in the famed Sacher Hotel in Vienna.

⅓ cup butter, at room temperature
6 tablespoons granulated sugar
½ cup (3 ounces) semisweet chocolate pieces, melted
4 egg yolks
½ cup plus 1 tablespoon sifted flour
5 egg whites
2½ tablespoons apricot jam

1. Preheat oven to moderate (325° F.). Grease and lightly flour a deep eight-inch spring-form cake pan.
2. Cream the butter, add the sugar gradually and cream until fluffy. Add the chocolate and mix thoroughly, scraping the bottom of the bowl several times.
3. Add the egg yolks one at a time and mix well after each addition. Stir in the flour until no particles show.
4. Beat the egg whites until stiff but not dry and gently fold them into the batter until no white shows.
5. Turn the batter into the prepared pan and bake on the lower shelf of the oven until the cake shrinks from the sides of the pan and rebounds to the touch when pressed gently in the center, or about one hour and fifteen minutes.
6. Let the cake stand ten minutes on a cooling rack before turning out of the pan. (The cake will shrink slightly on cooling.) Turn the cake out on the rack, turn right side up and let it finish cooling.
7. Stand the rack and cake on waxed paper and spread the top of the cake with jam. Pour any desired chocolate icing over the cake and spread it quickly to coat the top and sides.

WALNUT CAKE *1 loaf*

- 2 cups sifted all-purpose flour
- 1 teaspoon baking powder
- ½ teaspoon salt
- ¾ cup chopped walnuts
- ¾ cup butter
- ¾ cup granulated sugar
- 3 eggs
- 1 teaspoon vanilla extract
- ¼ cup milk

1. Sift together the flour, baking powder and the salt. Add the chopped walnuts and mix. Grease a 9½ by 5¼ by 2¾-inch loaf pan, line with waxed paper and grease the paper.
2. Preheat oven to moderate (325° F.).
3. Whip the butter until soft. Add the sugar gradually and whip until fluffy. Add the eggs one at a time, beating until very light and fluffy after each. Add vanilla.
4. Add the dry ingredients and the milk alternately to the butter mixture, stirring only until all the flour is dampened.
5. Turn the batter into the prepared pan and bake about one and one-quarter hours, or until a toothpick inserted in the center comes out clean. Cool in pan ten minutes before turning out on rack.

ZUPPA INGLESE *8 servings*

Zuppa inglese, or English soup, is not a soup at all. It is a very fine Italian dessert cake with rum and candied fruits.

- ½ cup granulated sugar
- ¼ cup flour
- ¼ teaspoon salt
- 2 cups scalded milk
- 4 egg yolks
- ½ cup light rum
- ½ teaspoon vanilla extract
- 2 tablespoons crème de cacao
- 2 sponge layers, purchased or homemade (page 567)
- 1 cup heavy cream, whipped
- 2 tablespoons candied fruits, chopped fine

1. Mix the sugar, flour and salt in the top of a double boiler. Add the milk gradually, stirring. Cook, stirring, over boiling water until thickened.
2. Beat the egg yolks until blended. Gradually add part of the milk mixture to the yolks, while stirring. Return to the hot mixture and cook over simmering water, stirring constantly, until thickened. Cool and chill.
3. Divide the mixture into three parts. Add one tablespoon rum to one part, the vanilla to the second and the crème de cacao to the third.
4. Split the sponge cake layers to make four layers and place one on a serving plate. Sprinkle with one-fourth of the remaining rum and spread with one of the three custard mixtures. Repeat with the second and third layers. Cover with the fourth layer of cake and sprinkle it with the remaining rum. Chill overnight in the refrigerator.

(cont'd)

5. At serving time, spread whipped cream over the top and sides of the cake and sprinkle the top with candied fruits.

. . . .

FROSTINGS

. . . .

VANILLA BOILED FROSTING

Frosts tops and sides of 2 8- or 9-inch cake layers

2½ cups granulated sugar
⅓ cup light corn syrup
½ cup water
2 egg whites
1½ teaspoons vanilla extract

1. Bring to a boil the sugar, corn syrup and water, stirring until the sugar dissolves. Continue cooking to 242° F. (syrup forms a firm ball in cold water).
2. In an electric mixer or a large bowl, beat the egg whites until stiff but not dry. Add the syrup in a fine stream while beating constantly.
3. Add the vanilla and continue beating until the frosting will hold its shape when dropped from the beater back into the bowl.
4. Spread the frosting quickly on the cake.

ALMOND PASTE, page 558.

QUICK BUTTER FROSTING

Frosts tops and sides of 2 9-inch or 3 8-inch layers

¼ cup butter, at room temperature
1 pound (3½ cups) sifted confectioners' sugar
¼ teaspoon salt
4 to 5 tablespoons heavy cream
1 teaspoon vanilla extract

Cream the butter, add about one cup of the sugar and the salt and cream well. Add the remaining sugar alternately with the cream, using enough cream to give a slight gloss and a good spreading consistency. Add the vanilla.

RICH BUTTER CREAM

Frosts tops and sides of 2 9-inch or 3 8-inch layers

1 cup granulated sugar
⅛ teaspoon cream of tartar
⅓ cup water
6 egg yolks
1 cup butter, at room temperature
1 teaspoon vanilla extract

1. Mix the sugar and cream of tartar. Add the water and bring to a boil, stirring until the sugar dissolves. Continue boiling to 246° (a drop of the mixture forms a firm ball in cold water). Set aside to cool to lukewarm.

(*cont'd*)

2. Beat the egg yolks in an electric mixer or with a rotary hand beater until very thick and fluffy. Add the syrup slowly while beating. Beat until cool.

3. Add the butter, a tablespoon at a time, beating well after each addition. Beat until very smooth and creamy. Chill until firm enough to spread. After frosting, chill the cake until ready to serve.

CHOCOLATE BUTTER CREAM *Frosts tops of 2 8-inch layers*

1 cup (6-ounce package) semisweet chocolate pieces
¼ cup boiling water or coffee
2 tablespoons confectioners' sugar
4 egg yolks
½ cup butter
2 tablespoons rum

1. Place the chocolate in the container of an electric blender, cover and blend on high speed six seconds. Turn the motor off and scrape the ground chocolate away from the sides with a knife.

2. Add the liquid, cover and blend six seconds. Add the sugar, egg yolks, butter and rum and blend fifteen seconds, or until smooth.

3. In warm weather, chill to spreading consistency. Frost cake and refrigerate.

CHOCOLATE CREAM FROSTING *Frosts tops of 2 8-inch layers*

1 cup (6-ounce package) semisweet chocolate pieces
¼ cup water
1 teaspoon instant coffee
¼ cup granulated sugar
4 egg yolks
½ cup butter

1. In the top of a double boiler heat the chocolate, water, coffee and sugar. Stir occasionally until the mixture is smooth.

2. Beat in the egg yolks one at a time and cook over boiling water three minutes, stirring constantly. Cool to lukewarm and beat in the butter bit by bit.

FUDGE FROSTING *Frosts tops and sides of 2 9-inch layers*

3 cups granulated sugar
3 tablespoons light corn syrup
1 cup milk
4 ounces (squares) unsweetened chocolate
⅓ cup butter
1 teaspoon vanilla extract

1. Cook the sugar, syrup, milk and chocolate, stirring, until the sugar dissolves. Continue cooking to 232° F. (the syrup forms a very soft ball in cold water). Stir occasionally to prevent scorching.

2. Remove from the heat, add the butter and cool without stirring until the bottom of the saucepan feels lukewarm. (*cont'd*)

3. Add the vanilla and beat until the frosting is creamy and barely holds its shape. Spread quickly on the cake before the frosting hardens.

BLACK WALNUT FUDGE FROSTING

Frosts tops and sides of 2 9-inch layers

- 1½ cups brown sugar, packed
- ¾ cup granulated sugar
- ¼ teaspoon salt
- ½ cup milk
- 1½ tablespoons corn syrup
- 2 tablespoons butter
- 2 teaspoons vanilla extract
- ⅔ cup coarsely chopped black walnut meats
- 1 to 2 tablespoons light cream

1. Combine the sugars, salt, milk and syrup in a saucepan, bring to a boil, stirring constantly, and boil rapidly until the mixture reaches 234° to 238° F. (syrup forms a soft ball in cold water).

2. Remove the syrup from the heat, add the butter and cool without stirring.

3. Add the vanilla and beat with a spoon until the frosting is as thick and creamy as fudge.

4. Stir in the nuts. Add the cream, a teaspoonful at a time, beating until the frosting is the correct consistency to spread on a cake.

MILK FROSTING, PAGE 558.

MOCHA CREAM FROSTING

Frosts tops and sides of 2 8-inch layers

- ⅔ cup granulated sugar
- ⅓ cup water
- 2 egg yolks
- 1 cup soft butter
- 1½ squares (ounces) unsweetened chocolate, melted
- 1 tablespoon very strong coffee
- 1½ tablespoons rum

1. Boil together the sugar and water to 240° F. (syrup forms a soft ball in cold water).

2. Beat the egg yolks until fluffy. Add the syrup gradually, while beating, and continue beating until the mixture is cool.

3. Add the butter, bit by bit, until it has all been beaten in. Beat in the chocolate, coffee and rum.

EASY PENUCHE ICING

Enough icing for 2 8-inch layers

- ½ cup butter
- 1 cup brown sugar, packed
- ¼ cup milk
- 1¾ to 2 cups sifted confectioners' sugar

1. Melt the butter in a saucepan, add the brown sugar and boil, stirring, over low heat two minutes. Add the milk and return to a boil, stirring constantly. Cool to lukewarm.

2. Gradually add the confectioners' sugar. Place the pan in ice water and stir until the icing is thick enough to spread.

CARAMEL FROSTING

Frosts tops and sides of 2 9-inch layers

3 cups light brown sugar, packed
1 cup light cream
½ teaspoon salt
⅓ cup butter
1 teaspoon vanilla extract

1. Cook the sugar, cream and salt, stirring, until the sugar dissolves. Continue cooking to 234° F. (the syrup forms a very soft ball in cold water).
2. Remove from the heat, add the butter and cool without stirring until the bottom of the saucepan feels lukewarm.
3. Add the vanilla and beat until the frosting is creamy and barely holds its shape. Spread quickly on the cake before the frosting hardens.

COCONUT-PECAN FROSTING

Frosts top and between layers of 3 9-inch layers

1 cup evaporated milk, or half evaporated milk and half fresh milk
1 cup granulated sugar
3 egg yolks
½ cup butter
1 teaspoon vanilla extract
1 can (3½ ounces) flaked coconut
1 cup chopped pecans

1. Combine the milk, sugar, egg yolks, butter and vanilla in a saucepan. Cook over medium heat, stirring constantly, until the mixture thickens.
2. Add the flaked coconut and pecans. Beat until cool and of a spreading consistency.

CONFECTIONERS' ICING

1 cup sifted confectioners' sugar
2 tablespoons milk
¼ teaspoon almond extract

Mix all ingredients until smooth.

DECORATIVE FROSTING I

About 1 cup

1 egg white
1 cup confectioners' sugar
½ teaspoon vanilla extract
⅛ teaspoon cream of tartar
Food coloring (optional)

1. Beat the egg white with the sugar, vanilla and cream of tartar until the mixture is stiff and holds up in sharp peaks when the beater is withdrawn.
2. Tint with food coloring if desired.
3. Force it through decorating tubes to make the desired designs.

DECORATIVE FROSTING II *About 1 cup*

2 tablespoons softened butter
1 cup confectioners' sugar
Dash of salt
½ teaspoon vanilla extract
1 tablespoon or more milk or cream
Food coloring

1. Cream the butter, add about half the sugar and cream until fluffy.
2. Add the salt and vanilla. Add remaining sugar and milk alternately, using enough liquid to give a good spreading consistency. Beat until the frosting stands in sharp peaks.
3. Divide the frosting into three portions; color one green, another yellow and the third pink. Apply with decorating tubes.

COOKIES

ALMOND MACAROONS *About 3 dozen*

½ pound (1 cup) almond paste
1 cup confectioners' sugar
3 egg whites, approximately
Dash of salt
½ teaspoon vanilla
Granulated sugar

1. Preheat oven to slow (300° F.).
2. Chop the almond paste, add the sugar and work with the fingers until blended.
3. Add the egg whites, one at a time, blending well after each addition. Use only enough egg white to make a soft "dough" that will hold its shape when dropped from a spoon. Add the salt and vanilla.
4. Force the mixture through a plain round pastry tube, well apart, in rounds on unglazed paper that has been fitted onto a cookie sheet. Sprinkle with granulated sugar.
5. Bake about twenty minutes. Remove the sheet of macaroons to a damp cloth, paper side down, to loosen the cookies for easy removal from the paper. Cool on a rack.

ROLLED MARZIPAN COOKIES

Prepare almond macaroon mixture (above), using a minimum of egg white. The mixture must be stiff. Pat and roll to one-quarter inch thickness on a board dusted with a mixture of equal measures of flour and confectioners' sugar. Cut into shapes, using a small floured cookie cutter. Bake as for almond macaroons, cool and ice with confectioners' icing (page 576)). If desired, before the frosting hardens, decorate with candied fruits, small candies or colored sugar.

BRANDY SNAPS *80 cookies*

¼ cup light corn syrup
¼ cup molasses
½ cup butter
1 cup sifted flour
⅔ cup granulated sugar
1 teaspoon ground ginger
2 teaspoons brandy

1. Preheat the oven to slow (300° F.).
2. Heat the syrup and molasses to boiling. Remove from heat and add butter.
3. Sift together the flour, sugar and ginger. Add gradually, while stirring, to molasses mixture. Mix well. Add brandy.
4. Drop by half-teaspoonfuls three inches apart on a greased cookie sheet. Bake ten minutes.
5. Remove from oven, loosen one cookie at a time and roll over handle of a wooden spoon. Slip off carefully. Serve filled with whipped cream.

BROWNIES *12 to 18 brownies*

4 squares (ounces) unsweetened chocolate
⅓ cup butter
2 eggs
1 cup sugar
½ cup sifted all-purpose flour
½ cup chopped walnuts or pecans
1 teaspoon vanilla extract
¼ teaspoon salt

1. Preheat oven to moderate (350° F.). Grease a 9 by 9-inch pan, line with paper and grease the paper.
2. Melt the chocolate and butter together. Beat eggs with sugar until fluffy and add to chocolate mixture.
3. Add flour, blend and add nuts, vanilla and salt. Stir until well mixed.
4. Spread batter in prepared pan. If desired, garnish top with additional walnut or pecan halves. Bake for about twenty-five minutes. Cool in pan, turn out, remove paper and cut into squares or bars.

VARIATION:

Black and White Brownies: Halve the amount of chocolate in the recipe above and add it, melted, to half the batter. Spread the white batter in a layer in the prepared pan, then pour chocolate layer over the top and spread evenly. Bake as above.

BUTTER COOKIES *2 to 2½ dozen cookies*

½ cup butter, at room temperature
⅓ cup sugar
1 egg
¼ teaspoon salt
½ to 1 teaspoon vanilla extract
¼ teaspoon grated orange rind or ⅛ teaspoon nutmeg
1 cup sifted all-purpose flour
Nuts (optional)

(*cont'd*)

1. Preheat oven to moderate (375° F.).

2. Cream the butter and sugar thoroughly. Add the egg, salt, vanilla and fruit rind and mix. Add the flour and mix well.

3. Shape the dough into small balls and flatten with the hand; or chill the dough and put it through a cookie press. Garnish with nuts if desired.

4. Place on a lightly greased cookie sheet and bake until the edges are light brown, or about twelve minutes.

DATE AND NUT BARS *40 bars*

1 cup pecans or walnuts
½ cup dates
¾ cup sifted all-purpose flour
3 eggs
1½ cups brown sugar, firmly packed
¾ teaspoon baking powder
¼ teaspoon salt

1. Preheat oven to moderate (350° F.). Grease, line with paper and grease again a 10 by 10-inch pan.

2. Chop nuts coarsely. Pit dates and chop. Add one tablespoon flour and mix with fingers until dates are coated and mixed with nuts. Set aside.

3. Beat eggs, add sugar gradually and beat until fluffy.

4. Sift together remaining flour, baking powder and salt. Add to egg mixture and stir until well mixed. Stir nuts and dates into the batter.

5. Spread in prepared pan and bake for about twenty minutes, or until cake rebounds to the touch when pressed gently in the center. Cool slightly, turn out of pan and cut into bars one by two and one-half inches.

GINGERBREAD MEN *About 30 cookies*

⅔ cup shortening
½ cup packed brown sugar
2 teaspoons ginger
1 teaspoon cinnamon
¼ teaspoon cloves or allspice
1½ teaspoons salt
1 egg
¾ cup molasses
3 cups sifted all-purpose flour
1 teaspoon soda
½ teaspoon baking powder

1. Cream together the shortening, brown sugar, spices and salt. Add the egg and mix thoroughly. Add the molasses and blend.

2. Sift together twice the flour, soda and baking powder. Add to the molasses mixture and stir until blended. Chill.

3. Preheat oven to moderate (375° F.).

4. Using a third to a quarter of the dough at a time, roll it to one-eighth inch or slightly thicker on a lightly floured pastry cloth with a floured, covered rolling pin.

5. Cut with gingerbread man cutter or any other cutters desired. If no cutters are available, fold a sheet of heavy paper lengthwise and draw half the desired

(*cont'd*)

shape (half of head, neck, one arm, etc.) next to the fold. Cut out the figure and unfold to make a symmetrical pattern. Grease one side of pattern, place on rolled-out dough and cut around outline with a floured sharp knife. Transfer carefully to greased baking sheet and repeat with remaining dough. Before baking, press raisins into the dough for eyes, nose and buttons on suit. Use half a slice of candied cherry for mouth.

6. Place in oven and bake eight to ten minutes. Cool on a rack. If desired, decorate with decorative frosting (pages 576, 577).

VARIATION:

Gingerbread Cookies: Roll the dough to five-eighths inch thickness on a floured pastry cloth or board. Using floured springerle boards or rolling pin, press out the desired shapes and cut apart with a floured knife. Place on greased baking sheets and bake ten to twelve minutes.

KOURAMBIEDES (Greek butter cookies) *About 4 dozen*

These crumbly cookies, coated with confectioners' sugar, are traditionally served in Greek homes at all festive occasions. At weddings they are served as a good luck token.

2 cups sweet butter, at room temperature
Confectioners' sugar
1 egg yolk
1½ tablespoons cognac or brandy
4½ cups cake flour, sifted twice
Whole cloves (optional)

1. Cream the butter in an electric mixer until thick and lemon-colored. Sift three-quarters cup confectioners' sugar and add it gradually to the butter. Add egg yolk, creaming well. Add cognac.

2. Gradually work in the flour to make a soft dough that will roll easily in the palm of the hand without sticking. If sticky, refrigerate the dough for one hour.

3. Preheat oven to moderate (350° F.).

4. Pat and shape the dough into balls one and one-half inches in diameter. If desired, stud each cake with a whole clove.

5. Place on ungreased baking sheet and bake until sandy colored (not brown), about fifteen minutes. Cool and sift over generously with confectioners' sugar.

LADY FINGERS *About 18 whole lady fingers*

½ cup sifted cake flour
⅔ cup sifted confectioners' sugar
⅛ teaspoon salt
3 eggs, separated
½ teaspoon vanilla extract

1. Preheat oven to moderate (350° F.).
2. Sift together three times the flour, half the sugar and the salt.

(*cont'd*)

3. Beat the egg whites until stiff and gradually beat in the remaining sugar. Beat the egg yolks until thick and lemon-colored, and fold with the vanilla into the egg white mixture. Sift the flour mixture, a third at a time, over the eggs and fold in carefully.

4. Line ungreased baking sheets with unglazed paper. Press the batter through a pastry bag onto the paper, or shape with a spoon into strips about 4 by ¾ inches.

5. Bake twelve to fifteen minutes, or until golden brown. Remove from paper with a spatula and cool on a rack.

VARIATION:

Sponge Cookies: Make batter for lady fingers and drop by teaspoonfuls on unglazed paper. Bake as directed above.

GERMAN LEBKUCHEN *3 to 4 dozen*

- 4 eggs
- 2 cups sugar
- 2 cups honey
- 2½ cups blanched almonds, cut in small pieces
- 3 cups sifted all-purpose flour
- ½ teaspoon soda
- 1 tablespoon ground cloves
- 1 teaspoon cinnamon
- ½ cup candied orange peel
- ½ cup candied lemon peel
- ¼ cup citron

1. Beat the eggs well, add the sugar a little at a time and beat until light and fluffy. Add the honey and almonds and stir just enough to mix.

2. Sift the flour, soda and spices together, add the fruit cut in paper-thin strips and mix well so that the fruit is completely covered with flour. Combine the two mixtures and refrigerate to chill.

3. Preheat oven to moderate (350° F.).

4. Spread the mixture one-quarter inch thick on a buttered baking sheet and bake thirty minutes. Cool slightly and cut into desired shapes with cookie cutters.

MADELEINES *3½ to 4 dozen madeleines*

Marcel Proust immortalized these plain French sweets in Swann's Way *when he wrote of them evocatively in a poetic passage that begins:*

"... my mother, seeing that I was cold, offered me some tea.... She sent out for one of those short, plump little cakes called 'petites madeleines,' which look as though they had been molded in the fluted scallop of a pilgrim's shell. And soon ... I raised to my lips a spoonful of the tea in which I had soaked a morsel of the cake."

- 4 eggs, at room temperature
- ¼ teaspoon salt
- ⅔ cup granulated sugar
- 1 teaspoon vanilla
- 1 cup sifted all-purpose flour
- ½ cup butter, melted and cooled

1. Grease well and flour pans for four dozen madeleines. If only half this many are available, cut the recipe in half and make it again. This is because the

(*cont'd*)

butter, on standing, settles to the bottom and causes a heavy rough layer. Place racks near the bottom of the oven and preheat the oven to hot (400° F.).

2. Beat the eggs with the salt, adding sugar gradually, until the mixture stands in very stiff peaks. Add vanilla.

3. Sift about one-quarter of the flour at a time over the egg mixture and fold it in until no flour shows.

4. Add the butter about a tablespoon at a time and fold it in as quickly as possible. Fill the prepared pans about three-quarters full, place in oven immediately and bake until brown, about ten minutes.

LAYERED NUT BARS *18 bars or 36 tea-sized squares*

THE BASE:

1 cup sifted all-purpose flour
1 cup firmly packed brown sugar
½ cup shortening (may be half butter)

1. Preheat oven to moderate (350° F.).
2. Grease, line with paper and grease again a 9 by 9-inch square pan.
3. Mix flour and sugar. Cut in shortening and mix till crumbly. Press into prepared pan and bake for fifteen minutes. While this is baking, prepare topping.

THE TOPPING:

2 tablespoons flour
½ teaspoon baking powder
¼ teaspoon salt
2 eggs
1 cup packed brown sugar
1 teaspoon vanilla extract
¾ cup chopped pecans or walnuts
1 cup flaked coconut

1. Combine the flour, baking powder and salt.
2. Beat eggs until very light. Add sugar gradually and beat till fluffy. Add vanilla.
3. Add dry ingredients; mix and add nuts and coconut.
4. Pour over baked base. Return to oven and bake about thirty minutes. Cool in pan, turn out and cut into bars or squares. If desired, serve sprinkled with confectioners' sugar.

PRESSED COOKIES *6 dozen*

1 cup soft butter
1 cup brown sugar, packed
½ cup extra-fine granulated sugar
2 eggs, beaten
2 teaspoons vanilla
4 cups sifted all-purpose flour
½ teaspoon salt
1 teaspoon baking powder
½ teaspoon soda
2 tablespoons milk

1. Preheat oven to hot (400° F.).
2. Cream the butter with the sugars, add the eggs and vanilla and cream well.

(*cont'd*)

3. Sift together the dry ingredients and add alternately with the milk to the creamed mixture. Mix well.

4. Force the dough through a cookie press onto an ungreased cookie sheet. Use different stencils in the press to give different shapes. Or the dough may be shaped into small balls, flattened with a fork and baked. Garnish with nuts, raisins and coconut, if desired.

5. Bake about ten minutes.

CHINESE SESAME SEED COOKIES *6 dozen cookies*

4 cups sifted all-purpose flour
2 teaspoons baking powder
½ teaspoon salt
1 cup butter, at room temperature
1¾ cups granulated sugar
2 eggs
3 tablespoons toasted sesame seeds
¼ cup water

1. Sift together the flour, baking powder and salt.

2. Cream the butter and sugar together, beat in the eggs and stir in the sesame seeds. Add the flour mixture alternately with the water. Chill the dough three to four hours.

3. Preheat oven to moderate (375° F.).

4. Drop the chilled dough from a teaspoon onto ungreased cookie sheets. Flatten to one-sixteenth inch thickness with a glass covered with a damp cloth. Bake until the cookies are lightly browned around the edges, about ten minutes.

Note: These cookies are of a plain butter type. If desired, the dough may be flavored further by adding vanilla extract, nutmeg or a mixture of spices before baking. To provide a more pronounced sesame seed flavor, top each with additional seeds after flattening and before baking. Sesame seed cookies make an excellent accompaniment for the less exotic ice creams, such as vanilla or chocolate.

SCOTCH SHORTBREAD *16 to 20 wedges*

⅔ cup butter, at room temperature
½ cup confectioners' sugar
1½ cups plus 2 tablespoons sifted all-purpose flour
½ teaspoon salt

1. Preheat oven to moderate (325° F.).

2. Cream the butter, add the sugar gradually and beat until fluffy. If desired, use an electric mixer at medium speed.

3. Sift the flour and salt into the creamed mixture and blend thoroughly with the hand.

4. Press the mixture into a nine-inch pie pan and pinch the edge to form a fluted rim. Prick the surface with a fork. Mark into sixteen to twenty wedges, cutting about halfway through the dough.

5. Bake until firm when pressed gently in the center, or about fifty minutes;

(*cont'd*)

the shortbread should not be brown. In an aluminum pan bake on the lower shelf; in a glass pan bake on the center shelf.

6. Cool the shortbread in the pan. To serve, place right side up on a cutting board and cut in wedges where marked.

SPRINGERLE COOKIES

About 3 dozen

- 4 cups sifted all-purpose flour
- 1 teaspoon baking powder
- ½ teaspoon salt
- 4 eggs
- 2 cups granulated sugar
- 1 teaspoon grated lemon rind
- 2 to 3 tablespoons anise seeds

1. Sift together the flour, baking powder and salt.
2. Place the eggs, sugar and lemon rind in the bowl of an electric mixer and beat about thirty minutes at medium speed. Beat in the flour mixture, one-half cup at a time. Chill the dough, covered, overnight.
3. Roll the dough to five-eighths inch thickness on a pastry cloth generously spread with flour.
4. Flour chilled springerle boards or rolling pin. Press into or roll slowly over the dough, bearing down firmly and evenly to leave clear-cut designs. With a floured knife, cut the cookies apart.
5. Sprinkle greased cookie sheets with anise seeds and transfer the cookies to the sheets. Let stand overnight, uncovered, at room temperature.
6. Bake in a preheated moderate oven (325° F.) fifteen minutes, or until thoroughly dried.

CRISP SUGAR COOKIES

About 5 dozen

- 2 cups sifted all-purpose flour
- 1 teaspoon baking powder
- ½ teaspoon salt
- ½ cup shortening
- 1 cup sugar
- 1 egg
- ¼ cup milk
- ½ teaspoon lemon extract

1. Sift together the flour, baking powder and salt.
2. Cream together the shortening and sugar and mix in the egg. Add the dry ingredients alternately with the milk and lemon extract and blend. Chill the dough overnight.
3. Preheat oven to hot (400° F.).
4. Roll the dough to five-eighths inch thickness on a floured pastry cloth. With floured springerle boards or rolling pin, press out the desired shapes and cut apart with a floured knife.
5. Transfer to greased cookie sheets and bake seven to ten minutes.

Springerle cookies, crisp anise-flavored holiday sweets, may be made in a variety of patterns and in different shapes and sizes. Shown are antique and modern springerle molding boards carved of wood.

VIENNESE CRESCENTS *6 dozen crescents*

When this recipe was first published in The Times, *one food authority wrote that it was, in her opinion, the greatest cookie recipe ever devised.*

¼ vanilla bean
1 cup sifted confectioners' sugar
1 cup walnut meats
1 cup butter, at room temperature
¾ cup granulated sugar
2½ cups sifted all-purpose flour

1. Chop the vanilla bean. Pound it in a mortar or pulverize it in an electric blender with about one tablespoon of the sugar. Mix with the remaining confectioners' sugar. Cover and let stand, preferably overnight. Reserve while cookies are baked.
2. Preheat oven to moderate (350° F.).
3. Cut the walnuts with a sharp knife into very small pieces. Pound the pieces to a paste, using a mortar and pestle.
4. With a wooden spoon or the fingers, mix the walnuts, butter, granulated sugar and flour to a smooth dough. Shape the dough, about a teaspoon at a time, into small crescents, about one and one-half inches in diameter.
5. Bake on an ungreased cookie sheet until lightly browned, or fifteen to eighteen minutes. Cool one minute. While still warm, roll the cookies in the prepared vanilla sugar.

. . . .

PUDDINGS, CUSTARDS AND OTHER DESSERTS

. . . .

BREAD-AND-BUTTER PUDDING *About 8 servings*

3½ cups scalded milk
1-inch piece vanilla bean or 1 teaspoon vanilla extract
4½-inch length French bread (center portion, not the crusty end)
¼ cup softened butter
½ cup seedless raisins
3 eggs or 5 egg yolks
⅓ cup sugar
⅛ teaspoon salt
Nutmeg

1. In the top of a double boiler heat the milk and, if used, the vanilla bean. Place over simmering water and cook fifteen minutes. Cool. Discard the vanilla bean, if used, or add the vanilla extract.
2. Cut the French bread into slices one-quarter inch thick and spread butter on one side of each slice. Arrange the slices in a six-cup casserole with the buttered side down, sprinkling the raisins between the layers.
3. Beat the eggs with the sugar and salt and add the scalded milk, stirring. Pour over the bread. Let stand thirty minutes. Sprinkle with nutmeg.
4. Set the casserole in a pan of hot water and bake in a preheated moderate oven (350° F.) until a knife inserted in the center comes out clean, about one hour. Serve warm.

NEW ENGLAND BREAD PUDDING *6 servings*

3½ cups milk
¼ cup butter
2 cups dry bread cubes
½ cup sugar
2 eggs, slightly beaten
½ cup sherry
1 teaspoon cinnamon
1 teaspoon mace
1 teaspoon nutmeg
1 cup seedless raisins
½ cup thinly sliced citron (optional)

1. Preheat oven to moderate (375° F.).
2. Scald the milk, add the butter and pour the hot liquid over the bread cubes. Soak about five minutes, then add the sugar, eggs, sherry and spices. Add the raisins and citron.
3. Pour the mixture into a buttered baking dish. Set the dish in a pan of hot water and bake until a knife inserted in the center comes out clean, or one hour.

ORANGE BREAD PUDDING *4 servings*

1 cup bread cubes
¾ cup scalded milk
¾ cup orange juice
Grated rind of 1 orange
4 egg yolks, beaten
½ cup sugar
⅛ teaspoon salt
Butter
Whipped cream

1. Preheat oven to moderate (375° F.).
2. Soak the bread cubes in milk ten minutes. Add the orange juice and rind, egg yolks, sugar and salt. Stir until the sugar has dissolved.
3. Pour into well-buttered individual molds, dot with butter and place the molds in a pan of hot water. Bake thirty minutes, or until the tip of a knife inserted one inch from the outside edge comes away clean. Chill. Unmold and serve with whipped cream.

HASTY PUDDING *6 servings*

1 quart milk
½ cup yellow cornmeal
3 tablespoons butter
1 cooking apple, pared and diced
½ cup molasses
1 teaspoon salt
½ teaspoon nutmeg

1. Preheat oven to slow (250° F.). Butter a covered two-quart baking dish.
2. Bring one and one-third cups of the milk to a boil and gradually add the cornmeal, stirring constantly. Remove from the heat and add the butter, apple, molasses, salt and nutmeg. Mix well and add the remaining milk.
3. Pour the mixture into the baking dish and cover. Bake three to three and one-quarter hours.
4. Serve hot either plain or with heavy fluid cream, unsweetened whipped cream or vanilla ice cream.

Note: The classic pudding omits the apple.

INDIAN PUDDING *6 servings*

- 1 quart milk
- ½ cup yellow cornmeal
- 2 tablespoons melted butter
- ½ cup molasses
- 1 teaspoon each salt and cinnamon
- ¼ teaspoon ginger
- 2 eggs

1. Scald the milk and pour slowly on the cornmeal, stirring constantly. Cook the mixture over hot water twenty minutes.
2. Preheat oven to moderate (350° F.).
3. Combine the butter, molasses, salt, cinnamon and ginger. Beat the eggs well and add, with the molasses mixture, to the cornmeal.
4. Pour the mixture into a greased baking dish and place in a pan of hot water. Bake one hour. Serve hot with hard sauce (page 615), plain or whipped cream, or vanilla ice cream.

PLUM PUDDING *24 servings*

- 6 cups fine crumbs from day-old bread (see page 29)
- 1½ teaspoons salt
- 1½ teaspoons cinnamon
- 1 teaspoon nutmeg
- ½ teaspoon ground cloves
- 1¼ cups light brown sugar, packed
- 1½ cups scalded milk
- 12 eggs, well beaten
- ¾ pound beef suet, ground
- 3 cups seeded raisins
- 1 cup currants
- ½ cup candied orange peel, chopped or sliced
- ½ cup candied lemon peel, chopped or sliced
- ½ cup candied citron, chopped or sliced
- ½ cup dates, cut up
- 1 cup chopped apples
- ½ cup cognac, rum or cider

1. Mix the crumbs, salt, spices and brown sugar. Add the milk and let stand until cool.
2. Add the eggs and suet and mix. Add the fruits and cognac and mix with hands, to separate the fruit.
3. Turn the mixture into two greased two-quart molds, cover with lids or foil and stand on a rack in an inch of water in a pot with a tight cover. Steam five to six hours, adding more boiling water as necessary. Serve with hard sauce.

STEAMED FIG PUDDING *10 servings*

- 1 cup dried black figs
- ⅓ cup finely chopped citron
- ⅓ cup finely chopped candied lemon peel
- 1 cup chopped walnuts
- 1¼ cups sifted flour
- 1 teaspoon soda
- ½ teaspoon salt
- ¼ cup shortening
- 1 teaspoon cinnamon
- ½ teaspoon ground cloves
- 1 cup brown sugar, firmly packed
- 2 eggs
- 1 cup grated raw carrot
- 1 cup grated raw potato

(*cont'd*)

1. Cover the figs with boiling water and let stand ten to fifteen minutes. Drain. Clip the stems and chop the fruit fine. Mix with the citron, peel and nuts.

2. Sift the flour with the soda and salt. Add one-half cup to the fruits and nuts and mix.

3. Cream the shortening with the spices and sugar until fluffy. Beat in the eggs, one at a time. Add the grated vegetables. Gradually stir in the remaining flour, beating until smooth. Mix in the fruits and nuts.

4. Fill a greased one-and-one-half-quart mold about two-thirds full and cover with a lid or foil. Stand on a rack in an inch of boiling water in a pot with a tight cover. Steam two hours, adding more boiling water as necessary. Serve hot with hard sauce (page 615).

PUMPKIN PUDDING *6 servings*

1½ pounds fresh pumpkin
4 eggs, separated
¾ cup light cream
2 to 4 tablespoons rum
¾ cup light brown sugar, packed
½ teaspoon each ground ginger, cloves and nutmeg
¾ teaspoon cinnamon
½ teaspoon salt
Whipped cream

1. Remove the seeds and peel from the pumpkin and cut into small pieces. Cook in boiling water until tender. Drain and mash thoroughly. Cool slightly.

2. Preheat oven to moderate (350° F.).

3. Beat the egg whites until stiff.

4. Beat the egg yolks until thick and lemon colored. Combine the yolks with the pumpkin purée, cream, rum, brown sugar and seasonings. Mix thoroughly until blended. Fold in the beaten egg whites.

5. Place the mixture in a buttered one-quart soufflé dish and bake forty to forty-five minutes. Serve at once with sweetened, flavored whipped cream.

OLD-FASHIONED RICE PUDDING *6 servings*

1 quart milk
¼ cup raw long-grain rice
½ cup sugar
½ teaspoon salt
½ cup seeded raisins (optional)
1 teaspoon vanilla extract
¼ teaspoon grated nutmeg

1. Preheat oven to slow (300° F.).

2. Mix the milk, rice, sugar and salt in a six-cup buttered casserole and bake, uncovered, two hours, stirring the mixture every half hour.

3. If the raisins are not soft and fresh, let them stand in water to cover while the pudding bakes. Drain and add to the pudding. Add the vanilla and nutmeg and mix carefully.

4. Bake the pudding without stirring about one-half hour longer, or until the rice is very tender. Serve warm or cold.

ZARDA (an Indian rice pudding) *12 servings*

- 2⅓ cups raw long-grain rice
- Water
- 1 teaspoon salt
- ¼ teaspoon powdered saffron
- 2 cups sugar
- 1½ cups butter
- 2 whole cardamom seeds, shelled
- 5 whole cloves
- Juice of 1 lemon
- ¼ cup light or dark raisins
- ¼ cup unroasted pistachios
- ¼ cup blanched almonds, sliced and toasted
- ¼ cup unsalted cashews, Brazil nuts or filberts, sliced and toasted
- 1 cup heavy cream, whipped

1. Cook the rice in six cups of boiling water with the salt and saffron until half done, about ten minutes. Use enough saffron to give a rich yellow color. Drain.

2. Boil the sugar with three and three-quarters cups water for one minute, stirring until the sugar has dissolved.

3. In the bottom of a heavy four-quart Dutch oven or other large kettle, heat the butter. Add the cardamom and cloves and cook over low heat ten minutes. Add all but one-half cup of the syrup and boil one minute.

4. Add the rice to the mixture and cook, stirring gently, until the butter is absorbed, or about ten minutes.

5. Add the lemon juice, raisins and nuts. Cook over fairly high heat five minutes. Continue cooking over very low heat until the rice is tender, stirring when necessary. If the rice is not quite tender when the syrup has been absorbed, add the remaining syrup and cook over low heat until the rice is dry and soft.

6. Remove the mixture from the heat and let stand, covered, ten minutes. Serve warm with whipped cream.

JELLIED ALMOND CREAM *6 servings*

- 1 envelope unflavored gelatin
- ¼ cup cold water
- 1½ cups milk
- ¾ cup almond paste
- 3 eggs, separated
- 1 teaspoon vanilla extract
- 1 cup heavy cream, whipped
- ½ cup sugar

1. Soften the gelatin in cold water.

2. Scald the milk in a double boiler, add the almond paste and stir until blended.

3. Beat the egg yolks and gradually add the almond milk. Return to the double boiler and cook over hot water, stirring constantly, until the mixture is slightly thickened. Add the softened gelatin and vanilla. Chill until beginning to set.

4. Fold in the whipped cream. Beat the egg whites, adding the sugar gradually, and fold into the almond mixture.

5. Turn into a glass serving dish and chill until firm. If desired, garnish the top with candied fruit.

ALMOND BAVARIAN CREAM *12 servings*

- 1 cup almonds
- 1½ cups milk
- ½ cup sugar
- 6 egg yolks, slightly beaten
- 1 teaspoon vanilla extract
- 2 envelopes unflavored gelatin
- 1 pint heavy cream, whipped

1. Blanch and chop the almonds coarsely. Toast if desired.
2. Combine one cup of the milk with the sugar, egg yolks and the chopped almonds. Cook over low heat, stirring, until thickened. Add the vanilla.
3. Soak the gelatin in the remaining milk, add a little of the hot custard and stir until dissolved. Combine the two mixtures and set aside to cool. When it starts to thicken, fold in the whipped cream.
4. Oil a two-quart mold and pour the mixture into it. Chill about two hours in the refrigerator.
5. Unmold and serve with crushed fruit or berries and additional whipped cream.

To Blanch Almonds: Pour boiling water over almonds and let them stand two or three minutes, or until the skins slip off easily. Drain and remove the skins.

COCONUT BAVARIAN CREAM *6 servings*

- 1 envelope unflavored gelatin
- ¼ cup cold water
- 2 cups milk, scalded
- 2 eggs, separated
- ¼ cup extra-fine granulated sugar
- ⅛ teaspoon salt
- 1 teaspoon vanilla extract
- ½ cup heavy cream, whipped
- ½ cup shredded coconut, toasted

1. Soften the gelatin in the cold water and then dissolve in the scalded milk. Mix the slightly beaten egg yolks, sugar and salt. Add the hot gelatin mixture gradually and stir until the sugar has dissolved.
2. Chill the mixture in the refrigerator until it begins to set. Add the vanilla, beat until foamy and fold in the stiffly beaten egg whites. Mix well and fold in the whipped cream and coconut. Pour into sherbet glasses and chill well.
3. Garnish with toasted coconut, candied cherries or whipped cream.

COFFEE BAVARIAN CREAM *4 to 6 servings*

- 1 tablespoon (1 envelope) unflavored gelatin
- ¼ cup cold water
- 2 eggs, separated
- ½ cup sugar
- ¼ teaspoon salt
- ½ cup milk
- ½ teaspoon vanilla extract
- ½ cup strong black coffee
- 1 cup heavy cream

1. Soften the gelatin in the water.
2. Beat the egg yolks in the top part of a double boiler and add one-quarter

(*cont'd*)

cup of the sugar and the salt. Gradually add the milk. Cook over hot water, stirring constantly, until slightly thickened.

3. Add the softened gelatin and stir until dissolved. Add the vanilla and coffee and chill until slightly thickened.

4. Beat the egg whites until stiff. Gradually add the remaining sugar, beating constantly. Whip the cream until slightly stiff. Fold into the gelatin mixture with the egg whites.

5. Pour the mixture into a one-quart mold which has been rinsed out in cold water and chill until firm.

STRAWBERRY BAVARIAN CREAM *6 servings*

1 package (10 ounces) frozen strawberries
2 envelopes unflavored gelatin
¼ cup cold water or milk
¼ cup sugar
2 eggs
1 heaping cup crushed ice
1 cup heavy cream

1. Defrost the berries and heat one-half cup juice to simmering. In the container of an electric blender place the gelatin and liquids, cover and blend forty seconds.

2. Add the sugar and eggs, cover and blend five seconds. Add the berries, cover and blend five seconds. Add the ice and cream, cover and blend twenty seconds.

3. Pour the mixture into an oiled four-cup mold or spoon into serving dishes. Chill several hours.

VANILLA BAVARIAN CREAM *8 to 10 servings*

1 envelope plus 1½ teaspoons unflavored gelatin
⅓ cup cold water
6 egg yolks
¾ cup sugar
¼ teaspoon salt
1½ cups milk
1½ teaspoons vanilla extract
1½ cups heavy cream, whipped
Fruit for garnish

1. Soften the gelatin in cold water and set aside for later use.

2. Beat the egg yolks in the top of a double boiler until light and lemon colored. Gradually beat in the sugar. Add the salt.

3. Scald the milk and gradually stir it into the egg mixture. Cook over hot, not boiling, water until thickened, stirring constantly.

4. Blend in the softened gelatin and vanilla. Chill until the mixture begins to thicken, stirring occasionally to prevent a crust from forming on the surface.

5. Fold in the whipped cream and turn the mixture into a one-and-one-half-quart mold rinsed in cold water. Chill until firm.

6. When ready to serve, turn out on a serving plate. Garnish with fresh or frozen strawberries, or other fruit.

CHARLOTTE RUSSE WITH KIRSCH *8 to 10 servings*

8 egg yolks
1 cup sugar
2 cups milk
1 inch vanilla bean (optional)
2 envelopes unflavored gelatin
¼ cup cold water
¼ cup kirsch
2 cups heavy cream
12 lady fingers, split

1. Combine the egg yolks and sugar and work the mixture with a wooden spoon until smooth. Bring the milk to a boil with the vanilla bean. Add it gradually to the yolk mixture, stirring rapidly with a wire whisk. Cook over boiling water until the mixture thickens.

2. Soften the gelatin in the cold water and add it to the custard, stirring until the gelatin dissolves. Remove the vanilla bean. Cool the custard but do not let it set. Add the kirsch.

3. Whip the cream until it stands in moist peaks and fold it into the custard.

4. Line a two-quart mold with lady fingers. Outline the bottom first by placing a small round of lady finger in the center. Cover the bottom with a daisy-petal pattern with the small round as a center. Stand lady fingers side by side upright and close together around the sides. Pour the custard mixture into the mold and chill until set, about two hours. Unmold and serve. The charlotte may be served with fruit sweetened to taste and flavored with kirsch.

CHARLOTTE NESSELRODE *8 servings*

1 package lady fingers
1 tablespoon gelatin
¼ cup cool water
½ cup scalded milk
⅓ cup sugar
Pinch of salt
1½ teaspoons vanilla extract
2 tablespoons rum
1 cup cream, whipped
¾ cup bottled nesselrode mix

1. Split the lady fingers and arrange in a one-quart oiled mold.

2. Soften the gelatin in the water and add to the scalded milk. Add the sugar and salt and stir until the gelatin and sugar are dissolved. Set in a pan of ice water. Add the vanilla and rum and whip until the mixture begins to set.

3. Fold in the cream and nesselrode mix. Turn into the prepared mold and chill until firm. Unmold and serve garnished with whipped cream.

CHARLOTTE MALAKOFF *10 to 12 servings*

Lady fingers
½ cup sweet butter
½ cup granulated sugar
½ cup grated blanched almonds
¼ cup kirsch
2 cups heavy cream, whipped

1. Line the greased bottom of a six-cup charlotte or other pudding mold with waxed paper. Split lady fingers and place vertically around the inside walls, arranging them so that they touch. *(cont'd)*

2. Cream the butter until soft and gradually add the sugar. Cream until light and fluffy. Beat in the almonds and kirsch. Gently fold the mixture into the whipped cream.

3. Turn the mixture into the mold and chill in the refrigerator at least two hours.

4. To serve, unmold the charlotte onto a serving dish and remove the waxed paper. Decorate, if desired, with a little whipped cream pressed through a pastry bag fitted with an open star tube.

CARAMEL CUSTARD *5 servings*

¾ cup sugar
3 eggs
Pinch of salt
2 cups milk, scalded
½ teaspoon vanilla extract

1. Preheat oven to moderate (350° F.).

2. Heat one-half cup of the sugar slowly in a small heavy skillet, stirring constantly with a wooden spoon until the sugar melts, is free from lumps and turns a light caramel in color. Pour a spoonful of the syrup in each of five custard cups and let stand until slightly cooled.

3. Beat the eggs slightly with the remaining sugar and the salt. Add the milk slowly, while stirring. Add the vanilla. Strain and pour the strained mixture carefully into the prepared cups so as not to disturb the caramel.

4. Place the cups in a pan of hot water (the water should be almost level with the tops of the cups) and bake until a knife inserted in the center comes out clean, or about forty minutes. Remove immediately from the water and cool quickly. Chill if desired.

5. To serve, run a knife around the edge of the custards, turn out and serve with whipped cream if desired.

CREME BRULEE *6 to 8 servings*

3 cups heavy cream
6 tablespoons sugar
6 egg yolks
2 teaspoons vanilla extract
½ cup light brown sugar

1. Preheat oven to slow (300° F.).

2. Heat the cream over boiling water and stir in the sugar.

3. Beat the egg yolks until light and pour the hot cream over them gradually, stirring vigorously. Stir in the vanilla and strain the mixture into a baking dish.

4. Place the dish in a pan containing one inch of hot water and bake until a silver knife inserted in the center comes out clean, or thirty-five minutes. Do not overbake; the custard will continue to cook from retained heat when it is removed from the oven. Chill thoroughly.

(cont'd)

5. Before serving, cover the surface with the brown sugar. Set the dish on a bed of cracked ice and put the crème under the broiler until the sugar is brown and melted. Serve immediately or chill again and serve cold.

ENGLISH CUSTARD *3½ cups*

3 cups milk
⅓ cup sugar
1½ tablespoons flour
5 egg yolks
1 teaspoon vanilla extract

1. Heat the milk in the top of a double boiler.
2. Mix the sugar and flour. Add the egg yolks and blend well. Add the milk, stirring with a wire whisk. Return to the double boiler and cook over simmering water, stirring constantly, until thickened. Cool quickly by placing the pan in cold water. Strain and add the vanilla.
3. Chill thoroughly and serve if desired with fresh strawberries or other berries lightly sweetened.

BAKED ORANGE CUSTARD *5 to 6 servings*

1 cup heavy cream
3 eggs, slightly beaten
1 cup orange juice
1½ teaspoons finely grated orange rind
¼ cup sugar
⅛ teaspoon salt

1. Preheat oven to moderate (325° F.).
2. Combine all the ingredients and blend well. Pour the mixture into custard cups and place in a pan of hot water.
3. Bake until a silver knife inserted in the center comes out clean, forty to fifty minutes.

CHOCOLATE FONDUE *4 servings*

2 squares (ounces) unsweetened chocolate
1 cup milk
1 cup soft bread crumbs
1 tablespoon butter
½ cup sugar
¼ teaspoon salt
3 eggs, separated

1. Preheat oven to moderate (350° F.).
2. Add the chocolate, broken into pieces, to the milk. Heat until the chocolate melts and stir until blended. Add the crumbs, butter, sugar and salt.
3. Beat the egg yolks slightly, stir in a little of the hot milk and return to the milk mixture, stirring. Cool.
4. Beat the egg whites until stiff and fold into the cooled mixture. Turn into a five-cup greased baking dish and bake about forty minutes. Serve hot with whipped cream.

MANJAR BLANCO *About 2 cups*

Manjar blanco is a Chilean sweet made with milk, sugar and vanilla or cinnamon. It requires about an hour to prepare and Chilean children cry for it. It has a delicate caramel flavor.

- 6 cups milk
- 1½ cups sugar
- 2-inch piece vanilla bean or 1-inch cinnamon stick

Bring all the ingredients to a boil, lower the heat and simmer. Stir the mixture frequently until it begins to thicken, and then constantly until done, when it will have the consistency of custard and a caramel color.

Note: There are numerous ways in which manjar blanco is eaten. It may be spread on buttered bread or used as a filling for baked apples or French pancakes.

MONT BLANC AUX MARRONS *12 servings*

The name of this dessert comes about because of its shape. A mound of chestnut purée is topped with vanilla-flavored sweetened whipped cream.

- 1½ pounds chestnuts
- 3 cups milk
- 2-inch piece vanilla bean
- ¾ cup sugar
- ⅓ cup water
- 2 tablespoons butter
- ¼ teaspoon salt
- 1½ cups cream, whipped
- Vanilla and sugar to taste

1. Cut a cross in the flat side of each chestnut. Cover with water and boil fifteen minutes. Drain, cover with cold water, shell and peel off the brown skin. The skin is easier to remove while the chestnuts are wet and warm.
2. Scald the milk with the vanilla bean in a double boiler. As each chestnut is peeled, add it to the milk. Cook over boiling water until the chestnuts are very tender, about thirty minutes. (The milk may be used later for a pudding.)
3. While the chestnuts are cooking, boil the sugar and water to 230° F. (syrup forms a soft ball in cold water).
4. Purée the drained chestnuts in a food mill or sieve. Add the sugar syrup, butter and salt and blend well.
5. Force the chestnut mixture through a ricer, letting it fall into a nine-inch ring mold. Place any purée that falls outside into the mold. Turn out on a serving plate and chill.
6. Fill the center with whipped cream, flavored with vanilla and sweetened to taste.

MOUSSE AU CHOCOLAT I *8 servings*

- 1 cup (6-ounce package) semisweet chocolate pieces
- 5 tablespoons boiling water
- 4 eggs, separated
- 2 tablespoons dark rum

(cont'd)

1. Put the chocolate pieces into the container of an electric blender and blend on high speed six seconds.

2. With the motor off, scrape the chocolate from the sides of the container with a knife. Add the water and blend on high speed ten seconds. Add the egg yolks and rum and blend three seconds or until smooth.

3. Fold the chocolate mixture into the stiffly beaten egg whites. Spoon the dessert into individual serving dishes and chill one hour before serving.

MOUSSE AU CHOCOLAT II *8 servings*

4 squares (ounces) unsweetened chocolate
¾ cup sugar
¼ cup water
5 eggs, separated
1 teaspoon vanilla extract or 1 tablespoon cognac or 2 tablespoons sherry

1. Combine the chocolate, sugar and water in the top of a double boiler. Heat until the chocolate has melted, stirring occasionally.

2. Add the egg yolks, one at a time, while the double boiler is still over the heat, beating hard after each addition.

3. Remove the mixture from the water and let cool while beating the egg whites stiff. Fold the whites in gently but thoroughly and flavor with vanilla, cognac or sherry.

4. Turn the mixture into a dessert bowl or individual sherbet glasses and let stand in the refrigerator at least twelve hours.

OEUFS A LA NEIGE (floating island) *8 to 10 meringues*

This is one of the most delectable of desserts. Mounds of egg white are poached in milk, then the milk is made into an English cream. The two are served together.

2 cups milk
1 vanilla bean
5 egg whites
⅔ cup sugar
Caramel (page 598)
English cream (page 598)

1. Pour the milk into an eight- or nine-inch skillet and add the vanilla bean. Over low heat let the milk warm to a point where bubbles appear around the edge.

2. Meanwhile, beat the egg whites until foamy. At this point, gradually start to add the sugar, continuing to beat until the egg whites are stiff.

3. Remove the skillet from the heat and drop the beaten egg whites on the milk in very large, rounded spoonfuls.

4. Return the skillet to very low heat; the surface of the milk should barely quiver. Cook the mounds of egg white two minutes. Using a skimmer or two forks, turn and cook two minutes on the other side, or until the meringues are firm to the touch.

(cont'd)

5. Remove the meringues to a towel and drain. Reserve the milk and vanilla bean for the English cream.

6. Pile the meringues in a shallow bowl and chill. To serve the dessert, fill a crystal bowl with the chilled English cream, float the poached meringues on top and trickle the caramel over the meringues.

CARAMEL:

Melt one-half cup sugar in a small heavy skillet over very low heat, stirring constantly with a wooden spoon. Remove from the heat and add one-quarter cup water. Return the skillet to very low heat and simmer until the syrup is slightly thick and smooth. Trickle over the meringues.

If desired, the caramel may be prepared in advance, kept at room temperature and reheated just before use.

ENGLISH CREAM: *2½ cups*

Milk reserved from cooking the meringues
½ vanilla bean, reserved from cooking the meringues
5 egg yolks
½ cup sugar

1. Strain the milk from the meringues into a two-cup measure. Add enough fresh milk to fill it. Pour the milk into the top of a double boiler, add the half vanilla bean and, over boiling water, heat the milk to a point where bubbles appear around the edge.

2. Blend the egg yolks with the sugar, using a fork. Add the hot milk gradually, stirring constantly.

3. Return the mixture, with the bean in it, to the top of the double boiler and cook over simmering water, stirring constantly, until the mixture thickens and coats a metal spoon.

4. Chill the mixture quickly by holding the top of the boiler in ice water; stir occasionally while the mixture cools. Strain and chill.

BOULES SUR CHOCOLAT *12 servings*

This is a variation of floating island but the poached meringues are on a chocolate custard.

4½ cups milk
4-inch piece vanilla bean, or 2 teaspoons vanilla extract
2¼ cups superfine granulated sugar
8 egg whites, at room temperature
Chocolate custard (page 599)

1. Combine the milk with the vanilla bean and one-fourth cup sugar. Slowly heat to simmering.

2. Meanwhile, beat the egg whites until stiff. Continue beating, adding the remaining two cups of sugar gradually, until the meringue holds its shape.

3. Using two spoons, drop egg-shaped balls of meringue on the simmering

(*cont'd*)

milk and simmer until they are firm, turning once. Carefully remove and set on a clean towel. Remove the vanilla bean and reserve the milk. If a bean is not used, add the extract.

CHOCOLATE CUSTARD:

⅔ cup sugar
⅔ cup cocoa
8 egg yolks
4 cups hot milk, reserved from the meringue

1. Mix the sugar, cocoa and yolks in a six-cup saucepan. Slowly add the hot milk, while stirring, and cook over very low heat, stirring constantly, until the mixture coats a metal spoon.

2. Remove the mixture from the heat and cool. Pour into glass serving bowl and set the meringues on top. Chill.

PAVE AU CHOCOLAT *8 servings*

4 squares (4 ounces) unsweetened chocolate
½ cup butter, softened
¾ cup sifted confectioners' sugar
4 egg yolks
¼ cup cognac
¾ cup water
2 packages lady fingers

1. Melt the chocolate over hot, not boiling, water.

2. Meanwhile cream the butter in a mixing bowl, add the sugar gradually and cream until smooth. Add the egg yolks, one at a time, and stir them in thoroughly. Add the melted chocolate and mix.

3. Combine the cognac with the water in a shallow pan. Dip the lady fingers quickly into the liquid and make a row of one-third of the lady fingers down an oblong platter. Cover with a coating of the chocolate mixture (allow one-third of the mixture for frosting between the layers and use the remainder for the top and sides). Build up two more layers of lady fingers with the chocolate filling between them. Ice the top and sides of the loaf with the chocolate mixture and refrigerate three hours.

PEARS A LA JOINVILLE *6 servings*

Sugar
1½ cups milk
1 cup light cream
2–inch piece vanilla bean, or 1 teaspoon vanilla extract
4 eggs
2 egg yolks
¼ teaspoon salt
Fresh pear halves, poached

1. Preheat oven to slow (300° F.).

2. Melt three-quarters cup sugar in a heavy saucepan, stirring constantly, until smooth and caramel-colored. Pour into a nine-inch ring mold and let stand until set.

(cont'd)

3. In a saucepan scald the milk and cream with the vanilla bean.

4. Combine the eggs and egg yolks in a large bowl and beat until fluffy. Add one-quarter cup sugar and the salt and beat until thick and lemon-colored.

5. Remove the vanilla bean, if used, from the milk. If a bean is not used add the extract. Gradually pour the milk into the egg mixture, beating constantly until thoroughly mixed. Pour the custard mixture through a fine strainer into the ring mold and set the mold in a baking pan. Fill the pan with hot water to within three-quarters inch of the top of the mold.

6. Bake one and one-quarter hours, or until a silver knife inserted in the center comes out clean. Remove from the water and cool quickly on a wire rack or ice to prevent overcooking and separation. Refrigerate until cold.

7. When ready to serve, unmold on a serving plate and fill the center with fresh pear halves that have been poached until tender in sugar syrup flavored with vanilla.

8. If desired, garnish with whipped cream, candied cherries and pistachio nuts.

POTS DE CREME AU CHOCOLAT *4 servings*

2 cups heavy cream
2 teaspoons sugar (optional)
4 ounces sweet chocolate, melted
3 egg yolks

1. Preheat oven to moderate (325° F.).

2. Heat the cream and sugar in a double boiler over boiling water. Stir until the sugar has dissolved.

3. Add the chocolate and stir until the mixture is blended.

4. Beat the egg yolks and pour the hot cream over them, a little at a time, stirring vigorously.

5. Pour the mixture into crème pots or individual heatproof dishes. Place the pots in a pan of hot water about one inch deep. Bake until a knife inserted in the center comes out clean, or about fifteen minutes. Chill.

POTS DE CREME A LA VANILLE *6 servings*

6 egg yolks
½ cup granulated sugar
⅛ teaspoon salt
2 cups light cream
1¼ teaspoons vanilla extract

1. Preheat oven to moderate (325° F.).

2. Beat the egg yolks until light and lemon-colored. Gradually beat in the sugar and salt. Stir in one-quarter cup of the cream. Scald the remaining cream and gradually stir into the mixture. Add the vanilla. Strain through a fine sieve into six individual half-cup crème pots or custard cups. Cover with crème pot covers or aluminum foil.

(*cont'd*)

3. Place in a baking pan on the lower shelf of the oven. Pour enough boiling water into the pan to cover two-thirds of the pots or cups. Bake fifteen minutes, or until a silver knife inserted into the center comes out clean. Cool and chill before serving.

RICE GRETE *8 servings*

- 3½ cups milk
- ⅔ cup raw rice, washed and drained
- ½ teaspoon salt
- 2 tablespoons sugar
- 1 teaspoon vanilla extract
- ¼ cup blanched almonds, finely chopped
- 1 cup heavy cream, whipped
- 1 No. 2½ can pitted Bing cherries in heavy syrup
- 5 teaspoons cornstarch

1. Bring the milk to a boil in a large saucepan. Immediately stir in rice, lower heat, cover and cook forty to forty-five minutes, stirring occasionally.
2. Remove from heat and add salt, sugar, vanilla and almonds. Mix. Cool the mixture, then chill in the refrigerator.
3. Add the whipped cream in three portions, folding it in thoroughly after each addition.
4. Drain the cherries, reserving one and one-half cups of the juice. (Or add enough water to make one and one-half cups.)
5. Mix two tablespoons of the juice with the cornstarch to make a smooth paste. Place remaining juice in a saucepan, stir in the cornstarch mixture and heat until thickened, stirring constantly. Remove from heat, add cherries. Serve lukewarm over the rice.

RIZ A L'IMPERATRICE *12 servings*

This is perhaps the finest and most elegant of rice desserts. It is made with rice and cream and is garnished with crystallized fruits.

- Water
- 1 cup raw long-grain rice
- 3 cups milk
- ¼ teaspoon salt
- ½ vanilla bean
- 1 envelope unflavored gelatin
- ¼ cup cold water
- ½ cup sugar
- 4 egg yolks
- 1 cup finely shredded crystallized fruits
- ¼ cup kirsch
- 1 cup heavy cream, whipped
- Angelica and candied cherries
- 1 glass red currant jelly

1. In a heavy three- or four-quart saucepan, bring four cups water to a boil. Add the rice, boil two minutes and drain. Return the rice to the saucepan.
2. Add one and one-third cups of the milk, the salt and vanilla bean. Cook, covered, over very low heat until the rice is tender, about thirty minutes. If the rice becomes too dry before it is soft, add more milk. *(cont'd)*

3. While the rice is cooking, soften the gelatin in water and make a custard: Mix the sugar and egg yolks, add the remaining milk and cook over lowest heat or in a double boiler, stirring constantly, until the mixture coats a metal spoon. Add the gelatin to the custard and stir until dissolved. Strain into the rice, mix well and chill until beginning to set.

4. Marinate the shredded fruits briefly in two tablespoons of the kirsch.

5. Taste the dessert and, if greater sweetness and flavor are desired, add sugar and vanilla extract to the whipped cream. Fold the whipped cream and fruits into the rice, turn the mixture into a two-quart mold and chill until set.

6. Unmold and decorate with candied cherries and shapes cut from angelica. Serve with a sauce made by whipping the jelly and remaining kirsch together.

VARIATION:

Strawberry Impératrice: Substitute two cups sliced strawberries for the crystallized fruits and marinate in one-fourth cup kirsch while the custard is being prepared. Fold strawberries and cream into the rice. Omit the whipped currant jelly sauce and instead heat one-half cup currant jelly with a teaspoon of water until liquefied. Dip two cups whole strawberries into the jelly and use to garnish the mold. Serve with whipped cream, plain or flavored with kirsch and sweetened to taste.

MALTAISE RICE MOLD *6 to 8 servings*

In French menu parlance the name maltaise almost invariably signifies oranges.

1½ cups raw long-grain rice
Water
3½ cups milk
½ teaspoon salt
⅓ cup sugar
1½ teaspoons grated orange rind
½ cup orange juice
¾ cup heavy cream, whipped
2 cups orange sections
⅓ cup Grand Marnier

1. Soak the rice in water thirty minutes, then drain well. Turn into a heavy saucepan, add the milk and salt and bring to a boil. Partly cover and simmer thirty minutes. Cover tightly, remove from the heat and let stand ten minutes.

2. Stir in the sugar, rind, juice and cream. Turn the mixture into an oiled nine-inch ring mold and chill four hours or overnight.

3. Unmold the dessert and fill the center with orange sections that have been marinated thirty minutes in Grand Marnier.

RICE ROMANOFF *6 servings*

1 cup raw long-grain rice
1 quart water
Salt
3 cups heavy cream
3 tablespoons kirsch, Grand Marnier or cognac
3 tablespoons sugar
20 almonds, blanched and shaved
24 macaroons, soaked in kirsch, Grand Marnier or cognac
Strawberry sauce (page 617)

(cont'd)

1. Cook the rice in lightly salted water twenty to twenty-five minutes, or until it is very tender; do not stir. Drain the rice and set aside to cool.

2. Whip the cream until stiff and flavor with kirsch, Grand Marnier or cognac and sugar. Stir in the almonds. Mix the cream thoroughly with the rice.

3. Place one-third of the rice cream in a large glass serving bowl. Arrange half the macaroons on top. Add another third of rice cream, then the remaining macaroons. Finish with rice cream.

4. Chill the dessert several hours and decorate, if desired, with additional whipped cream. Serve with strawberry sauce.

CHOCOLATE SPONGE *6 servings*

8 ounces dark sweet cooking chocolate
2 tablespoons butter
½ cup evaporated milk
4 eggs, separated
1 teaspoon unflavored gelatin
¼ cup water
6 tablespoons whipped cream

1. In a saucepan melt the chocolate with the butter and milk over low heat. Remove from the heat. Cool briefly and stir in the beaten egg yolks. Cook very slowly, stirring, one minute.

2. Soften the gelatin in the cold water and add to the hot mixture. Fold in stiffly beaten egg whites and chill. Serve with whipped cream.

ZABAGLIONE *4 servings as a dessert; 6 as a sauce*

6 egg yolks
6 tablespoons sugar
⅔ cup Marsala

1. Beat the egg yolks and gradually add, while beating, the sugar and the wine.

2. Place the mixture over boiling water and whip vigorously with a wire whisk until the custard foams up in the pan and begins to thicken. Do not overcook. Serve warm in sherbet glasses or as a sauce.

There was a time when the making of soufflé was a somewhat tricky affair. That was in the days when stoves were wood-burning or coal-burning and it was difficult to maintain a constant oven temperature. With today's ranges it is easier to succeed than to fail in making a perfect soufflé.

CHOCOLATE SOUFFLE *6 servings*

2 tablespoons butter
2 tablespoons flour
¾ cup milk
Pinch of salt
2 squares (ounces) unsweetened chocolate
⅓ cup sugar
2 tablespoons cold coffee
½ teaspoon vanilla extract
3 egg yolks, lightly beaten
4 egg whites, stiffly beaten
Whipped cream

(cont'd)

1. Preheat oven to moderate (375° F.).

2. In a saucepan melt the butter, add the flour and stir with a wire whisk until blended. Meanwhile, bring the milk to a boil and add all at once to the butter-flour mixture, stirring vigorously with the whisk. Add the salt.

3. Melt the chocolate with the sugar and coffee over hot water. Stir the melted chocolate mixture into the sauce and add the vanilla. Beat in the egg yolks, one at a time, and cool.

4. Fold in the stiffly beaten egg whites and turn the mixture into a buttered two-quart casserole sprinkled with sugar. Bake thirty to forty-five minutes, or until puffed and brown. Serve immediately with whipped cream.

GINGER SOUFFLE *4 servings*

3 tablespoons butter
3 tablespoons flour
1 cup milk
⅓ cup sugar
⅛ teaspoon salt
1 tablespoon cognac
⅛ teaspoon powdered ginger
½ cup drained preserved or crystallized ginger, finely chopped or ground
4 eggs, separated

1. Preheat oven to moderate (375° F.).

2. In a saucepan, melt the butter, add the flour and stir with a wire whisk until blended. Meanwhile, bring the milk to a boil and add all at once to the butter-flour mixture, stirring vigorously with the whisk. Add the sugar, salt, cognac and ginger. Remove from heat.

3. Beat in the egg yolks one at a time. Cool. Beat the egg whites until they stand in peaks and fold into the mixture. Transfer to a two-quart casserole and bake thirty-five to forty-five minutes. Serve immediately.

SOUFFLE AU GRAND MARNIER *5 servings*

3 tablespoons butter
3 tablespoons flour
¾ cup milk
3 tablespoons orange marmalade
4 egg yolks, lightly beaten
¼ cup Grand Marnier
6 egg whites

1. Preheat the oven to moderate (375° F.).

2. Melt the butter in a saucepan and stir in the flour.

3. Add the milk gradually, stirring with a wire whisk, and cook over low heat until the mixture thickens. Stir in the marmalade and the egg yolks. Add the Grand Marnier.

4. Beat the egg whites until stiff and fold them into the soufflé mixture. Butter a one-and-one-half-quart soufflé dish and sprinkle the bottom and sides with sugar. Pour the soufflé mixture into it and bake until puffed and golden brown, about thirty to forty-five minutes.

BANANA SOUFFLES *6 servings*

6 bananas
1 tablespoon potato starch or cornstarch
Confectioners' sugar
Pinch of salt
½ cup milk
1 tablespoon anisette or pernod
2 egg yolks, slightly beaten
3 egg whites

1. Cut off a thin slice lengthwise from each banana. Carefully lift out the fruit from the bananas without breaking the skin. Reserve the skins. Put enough of the bananas through a potato ricer, sieve or food mill to yield two cups of purée. Reserve any remaining fruit for another use.

2. Combine the potato starch or cornstarch with one tablespoon confectioners' sugar, the salt and the milk and cook, stirring constantly with a wire whisk, until the mixture thickens. Add the banana purée, anisette or pernod and egg yolks. Bring to a boil, stirring constantly, and remove from the heat. Cool.

3. Preheat the oven to modcrate (350° F.).

4. Beat the egg whites until they are stiff but not dry and fold them into the banana mixture. Pile the mixture into the reserved banana skins until they are two-thirds full. Sprinkle with confectioners' sugar and bake ten to fifteen minutes, or until the soufflés are puffed and browned. Serve as a dessert.

Note: The soufflés must be served as soon as they are removed from the oven.

STRAWBERRY SOUFFLE *6 servings*

2 cups sliced fresh strawberries, or frozen strawberries defrosted
½ cup orange juice
½ cup Curaçao
Sugar to taste
3 tablespoons butter
3 tablespoons flour
1 cup milk
4 eggs, separated
Whipped cream

1. Preheat oven to moderate (375° F.).

2. Combine the strawberries, orange juice, Curaçao and sugar to taste.

3. In a saucepan melt the butter, add the flour and stir with a wire whisk until blended. Meanwhile, bring the milk to a boil and add all at once to the butter-flour mixture, stirring vigorously with the whisk. Stir in the slightly beaten egg yolks and cool.

4. Fold in stiffly beaten egg whites.

5. Drain the excess juice from the strawberries and reserve. Place the strawberry mixture in the bottom of a buttered soufflé dish sprinkled lightly with sugar. Pour the soufflé mixture on top and bake until puffed and golden brown, thirty to forty-five minutes.

6. Serve immediately with whipped cream flavored with the reserved strawberry juice.

SWISS MERINGUE *1 vacherin or 12 individual shells*

8 egg whites, at room temperature
¼ teaspoon salt
¼ teaspoon cream of tartar
2 cups granulated sugar
1½ teaspoons vanilla extract

1. Beat the egg whites until frothy. Add the salt and cream of tartar and beat well.

2. Add the sugar gradually, while continuing to beat. Add the vanilla and continue beating until the mixture is glossy and stiff, but not dry.

3. Cover baking sheets with waxed paper and, using a spoon or pastry bag, shape the meringue into any desired form.

4. Bake in a very slow oven (225° F.) until firm and dry but still white, forty-five to sixty minutes. If necessary, turn off the oven heat. Remove the meringues from the paper while warm.

VARIATIONS:

Meringue Shells: Use a spoon or pastry bag to shape Swiss meringue into large ovals or rounds. Bake in a very slow oven (225° F.) until the meringues are dry, about one hour.

Meringues Glacées: Place ice cream between the shells. Garnish with whipped cream and nuts.

COEUR A LA CREME *6 servings*

This is an enchanting dessert that must be made in a special heart mold. The molds are generally available wherever fine imported housewares are sold. They are also made in New York at the Lighthouse for the Blind. This is a fine dish for Valentine's Day.

1 pound cottage cheese
1 pound cream cheese, softened
Pinch of salt
2 cups heavy cream
Crushed strawberries, fresh or frozen and defrosted

1. Combine thoroughly the cottage cheese, cream cheese and salt. Gradually add the heavy cream, beating constantly until the mixture is smooth.

2. Turn the mixture into individual heart-shaped baskets or molds (which have been lined with one layer of cheesecloth) with perforated bottoms. Place on a deep plate and refrigerate to drain overnight. One large basket may be used.

3. When ready to serve, unmold the hearts onto chilled plates and serve with crushed sweetened strawberries. Garnish, if desired, with whole fresh strawberries.

BUDINO DI RICOTTA *4 servings*

This is an Italian ricotta cheese "pudding."

½ pound ricotta
¼ cup grated milk chocolate
¼ cup finely chopped walnuts
2 tablespoons cream, approximately

(*cont'd*)

1. Cream the ricotta, add the chocolate and nuts and blend thoroughly.

2. Add enough cream to make a smooth consistency. If desired, two tablespoons of either chopped candied fruits or maraschino cherries may be added.

3. Serve in sherbet glasses with cookies.

PASKHA *24 or more servings*

And this is a Russian pot cheese dessert.

5 pounds pot cheese
18 egg yolks
3 tablespoons vanilla extract
1½ cups sugar
1 cup heavy cream
1½ pounds (3 cups) butter
½ pound mixed candied fruits
½ to 1 cup blanched, shredded almonds

1. Line a colander with cheesecloth and set it in a pan. Turn the cheese into it, cover with cloth and place a plate and heavy weight on top. Let stand in the refrigerator to drain eight hours.

2. Force the cheese through a food mill, coarse sieve or potato masher.

3. Beat the egg yolks until very light and fluffy. Add the vanilla and sugar and beat until well blended. Add the heavy cream and blend.

4. Melt the butter over low heat and cool to lukewarm. Add gradually to the yolk mixture and mix well. Add the candied fruits, nuts and cheese. Mix with a wooden spoon or the hands.

5. Line a paskha mold or flowerpot with doubled cheesecloth, dampen the cloth and add the cheese mixture. Stand the mold in a pan and refrigerate several hours. Turn out on a platter and decorate with colored candies and fresh flowers. If desired, dyed Easter eggs may be arranged around the base.

Crêpes are nothing more than French pancakes. They should be made in special crêpe pans, available wherever fine imported cooking utensils are sold. A crêpe pan is a small "spider" large enough for making one crêpe at a time.

BASIC CREPE RECIPE *24 crêpes*

3 cups sifted flour
4 eggs
4 egg yolks
1 quart milk
2 teaspoons sugar
1 teaspoon salt
¼ cup clarified butter (page 456)

1. Mix the flour, eggs and egg yolks with a wire whisk. Add the milk, sugar and salt and beat until all the ingredients are thoroughly blended.

2. Melt the butter in a small container and skim off the foam. Pour off and reserve the fat, or clarified butter. Discard the sediment in the bottom of the container.

(*cont'd*)

Crêpes with a difference include: (foreground, left to right) crêpes Marcelle, crêpes with pineapple cubes, crêpes Gil Blas topped with hard sauce; and (rear, around the chafing dish) crêpes Alaska.

3. Heat a four-inch skillet and brush it with the clarified butter. Pour in one tablespoon of the batter and tilt the pan immediately so that the batter will spread over the entire bottom of the pan. Cook the crêpe quickly on both sides.

4. Repeat the process until all the crêpes are cooked, stacking them on a plate as they are finished. If the crêpes are to be sauced later, cover with waxed paper to prevent drying.

CREPES SUZETTE *4 to 6 servings*

This is the best known of the dessert crêpe recipes.

4 lumps sugar
1 orange
½ cup butter
1 jigger (3 tablespoons) maraschino
1 jigger (3 tablespoons) Curaçao
1 jigger (3 tablespoons) kirsch
12 crêpes (page 607)

1. Rub the lumps of sugar on the orange skin until they are covered with the aromatic oil. Squeeze the orange and reserve the juice.
2. Crush the sugar with half the butter and cream well.
3. Place the rest of the butter in a flat skillet or a chafing dish and, when it melts, add the orange butter. Add the orange juice, maraschino and Curaçao and stir with a wooden spoon until well blended. Add the kirsch and ignite. Keep the sauce barely simmering over a spirit lamp or other low flame.
4. Add the crêpes one at a time and, using a fork and large spoon, turn each crêpe over in the sauce, then fold into quarters. Serve hot.

CREPES GIL BLAS *6 servings*

These crêpes, named for Lesage's picaresque hero, are served with a cream sauce flavored with kirsch.

¼ cup butter
1 cup confectioners' sugar
⅛ teaspoon salt
1 teaspoon or more kirsch
½ teaspoon grated lemon rind
¼ cup light cream (optional)
6 crêpes, made from basic recipe (page 607) plus 1 teaspoon grated lemon rind stirred into the batter

1. Cream the butter, add the sugar and salt and cream well.
2. Add the kirsch, lemon rind and enough cream to make a fluffy mixture. Serve with hot crêpes.

CREPES ALASKA *6 servings*

Many desserts made with ice cream are called "Alaska." Here, ice cream is sandwiched between two crêpes, hot sauce is added and the effect is most unusual.

4 lumps sugar
1 orange
5 tablespoons butter
1 teaspoon lemon juice
¼ cup cointreau
¼ cup Grand Marnier
½ cup warmed cognac
12 warm crêpes (page 607)
6 scoops vanilla ice cream
½ cup slivered almonds, toasted

1. Rub the lumps of sugar on the orange skin until they are covered with the aromatic oil. Squeeze the orange and reserve the juice.

(*cont'd*)

2. Crush the sugar with three tablespoons of the butter and mix until creamy.

3. Place the remaining butter in a flat skillet or in a chafing dish and add the lemon juice and liqueurs. Add the warmed cognac and ignite.

4. Place one crêpe on each of six dessert plates and top each crêpe with a scoop of vanilla ice cream. Cover with another crêpe and spoon the hot sauce over them. Sprinkle with toasted almonds.

KAISER SCHMARREN *8 pancakes*

Kaiser Schmarren are crêpes made with almonds and raisins.

⅔ cup butter
3 eggs
1 cup sifted flour
1 cup milk
1 teaspoon sugar
¼ teaspoon salt
½ cup almonds, blanched and sliced
½ cup golden raisins
Confectioners' sugar
Cinnamon

1. Stand measuring cup of butter in boiling water and let the butter melt. Pour off the melted yellow fat, discarding the milky liquid that settles at the bottom.

2. In a six-cup bowl, using a rotary beater, beat until smooth the eggs, flour, milk, sugar and salt.

3. Heat about two tablespoons of the melted butter in a nine-inch heavy skillet. Sprinkle one tablespoon each almonds and raisins in the pan. Add about one-third cup of the batter and brown over medium heat, about three minutes. Turn to brown on the second side. Remove to a warm plate.

4. Repeat the process until all the nuts, raisins and batter are used, using one tablespoon of the melted butter for each pancake.

5. Cut each pancake into small squares and sprinkle with powdered sugar and cinnamon.

CREPES MARCELLE *6 servings*

Crêpes Marcelle are filled with a cognac-flavored pastry cream.

Pastry cream
1 teaspoon vanilla extract
2 tablespoons orange juice
1 tablespoon grated orange rind
1 tablespoon cognac
2 macaroons, crushed
6 crêpes (page 607)
Confectioners' sugar

1. Prepare pastry cream as for crêpes with pineapple (page 611), following steps 1 through 3.

2. Stir in the vanilla, orange juice, orange rind, cognac and crushed macaroons. Spoon the mixture down the center of the crêpes and roll. Place the crêpes on an ovenproof platter and sprinkle with confectioners' sugar.

3. Place the platter under a hot broiler and broil until the crêpes are lightly glazed.

CREPES WITH PINEAPPLE *6 servings*

This is an unusually delicious crêpe recipe. The crêpes are filled with a pastry cream and pineapple mixture.

⅔ cup sugar
3½ tablespoons cornstarch
½ teaspoon salt
2½ cups milk
3 egg yolks, lightly beaten
1 teaspoon vanilla extract
2 tablespoons pineapple juice
1 tablespoon kirsch
6 crêpes (page 607) at room temperature
Pineapple cubes

1. Mix the sugar, cornstarch and salt in a bowl. Scald the milk and pour over the dry ingredients, stirring constantly.
2. Place the mixture in a saucepan and cook over very low heat, stirring, until the mixture thickens. Cover and cook ten minutes longer.
3. Add, stirring, a little of the hot mixture to the egg yolks. Add the yolks to the remaining mixture and cook over hot water, stirring, until thickened, two minutes.
4. Cool the pastry cream and add the vanilla, pineapple juice and kirsch. Spoon the mixture down the center of the crêpes and roll. Garnish with pineapple cubes.

SWEDISH PANCAKES *About 3 dozen pancakes*

1 cup sifted flour
2 tablespoons sugar
¼ teaspoon salt
3 eggs, beaten
3 cups milk
Clarified butter (page 456)

1. Sift together the flour, sugar and salt. Add the eggs and milk gradually, stirring until well blended. Let stand two hours.
2. Heat a Swedish pancake pan or ordinary skillet and brush generously with clarified butter. Beat the batter again, pour into the pan a tablespoon at a time, and fry on both sides until nicely browned.
3. Place on a very hot platter and serve immediately with lingonberry sauce (page 616).

. . . .

DESSERT SAUCES

. . . .

APRICOT SAUCE *About 2 cups*

¾ cup sugar
1½ cups canned apricot nectar
2 teaspoons lemon juice

(*cont'd*)

In a saucepan combine the sugar and apricot nectar. Bring to a boil and cook five minutes. Remove from the heat and stir in the lemon juice. Serve hot with babas au rhum, savarin rings, etc.

BLUEBERRY SAUCE *About 2 cups*

- Water
- ¼ cup sugar
- 1 tablespoon lemon juice
- 1 teaspoon cornstarch
- 1 cup blueberries

1. Bring three-fourths cup water and the sugar to a boil and stir until the sugar has dissolved. Add the lemon juice.
2. Mix the cornstarch with one tablespoon water and add, stirring, to the syrup. Cook, stirring, one minute.
3. Add the blueberries and cook one-half minute. Serve warm.

BUTTERSCOTCH SAUCE *About 2 cups*

- 1 cup dark corn syrup
- 1 cup sugar, or ½ white and ½ light brown sugar
- ¼ teaspoon salt
- ½ cup light cream
- 2 tablespoons butter
- 1 teaspoon vanilla extract

1. Combine all the ingredients except the vanilla in a saucepan and cook over medium heat, stirring constantly, until the mixture comes to a full rolling boil. Boil briskly five minutes, stirring occasionally. Remove from the heat.
2. Add the vanilla and serve warm.

Note: The sauce may be stored in the refrigerator. To reheat, place in a pan of hot, not boiling, water, until the sauce has thinned to pouring consistency.

GINGER CARAMEL SAUCE *1½ cups*

- 1¼ cups brown sugar
- ⅔ cup light corn syrup
- 1 tablespoon syrup from preserved ginger
- ¼ cup butter
- ½ cup heavy cream
- 3 to 4 tablespoons chopped preserved ginger
- ½ teaspoon vanilla extract

1. Combine the sugar, corn syrup, ginger syrup and butter in a saucepan and stir over low heat until the sugar has dissolved. Continue cooking until the mixture forms a firm ball in cold water (242° F. on a candy thermometer).
2. Remove the syrup from the heat and add the cream, chopped ginger and vanilla. Cool. This sauce is recommended for vanilla and coffee ice cream.

CHERRY SAUCE *About 2½ cups*

1 pound sweet cherries, pitted
½ cup water
⅓ to ½ cup white corn syrup or sugar
1 tablespoon cornstarch
Lemon juice
Kirsch, cognac, sherry or cherry liqueur (optional)

1. Place the cherries, one-quarter cup of the water and the syrup in a saucepan and bring to a boil.
2. Blend the cornstarch with the remaining water and add, stirring, to the cherries. Cook, stirring, until clear or about one minute.
3. Add lemon juice and kirsch to taste. Serve warm or cold over puddings or ice cream.

Note: The sauce may be stored in the refrigerator.

CHOCOLATE SOUR CREAM SAUCE *About 1½ cups*

1 cup (6-ounce package) semisweet chocolate bits
½ cup sour cream
⅛ teaspoon salt
½ teaspoon cinnamon
¼ cup milk

1. Fill a skillet half full of water and bring almost to the simmering point. Pour the chocolate bits into a saucepan and place in the skillet.
2. Stir until the chocolate has melted and blend in the sour cream, salt, cinnamon and milk. To serve, spoon over individual portions of cake.

HOT FUDGE SAUCE *About 2½ cups*

½ cup cocoa
1 cup sugar
1 cup light corn syrup
½ cup light cream or evaporated milk
¼ teaspoon salt
3 tablespoons butter
1 teaspoon vanilla extract

1. Combine all the ingredients except the vanilla in a saucepan. Cook over medium heat, stirring constantly, until the mixture comes to a full rolling boil. Boil briskly three minutes, stirring occasionally.
2. Remove the mixture from the heat and add the vanilla. Serve warm.

Note: The sauce may be stored in the refrigerator. To reheat, place in a pan of hot, not boiling, water until the sauce has thinned to pouring consistency.

CHOCOLATE MINT SAUCE *4 to 6 servings*

10 large chocolate peppermint patties
3 to 4 tablespoons cream

1. Melt the patties over hot water, stirring occasionally.
2. Add the cream and blend well.

BITTER CHOCOLATE SAUCE *About 1½ cups*

4 squares (ounces) unsweetened chocolate
2 tablespoons butter
2 tablespoons white corn syrup
6 to 8 tablespoons sugar
¾ cup milk
Dash of salt

1. Melt the chocolate with the butter over hot water. Add thc corn syrup and sugar and blend.
2. Add the milk and salt and cook, stirring, ten minutes.

SHERRY CUSTARD *About 8 servings*

6 eggs, separated
⅔ cup sugar
¾ cup sweet sherry
¼ teaspoon salt
Cherries or strawberries

1. Mix the egg yolks and sugar in the top of a one-and-one-half-quart double boiler. Set over simmering water and beat with a rotary beater until fluffy. (Do not let the water boil.)
2. Add the sherry gradually and continue beating until the mixture resembles whipped cream. Cool quickly and chill.
3. Before serving, beat the egg whites with the salt until stiff. Fold into the chilled custard and turn into a glass serving dish. Serve plain or garnished with cherries or strawberries.

SOFT CUSTARD SAUCE *About 2½ cups*

4 egg yolks
3 tablespoons sugar
2 tablespoons flour
Dash of salt
2 cups scalded milk
1 teaspoon vanilla extract

1. Mix the egg yolks, sugar, flour and salt. Add the milk slowly, while stirring.
2. Cook the mixture in the top of a double boiler over hot water, stirring constantly, until the mixture thickens and coats a metal spoon.
3. Set the pot in cold water for five minutes, stirring occasionally. Strain and add the vanilla.

BROWN SUGAR CUSTARD SAUCE *About 1 cup*

1 cup brown sugar, packed
⅓ cup water
2 egg yolks
⅛ teaspoon salt
2 to 4 tablespoons sherry or cognac

(cont'd)

1. Boil the sugar and water, stirring, until the sugar is dissolved, or about one minute.

2. Beat the egg yolks with the salt and add the syrup gradually, while beating. Cook, stirring, over hot water until thickened. Add the sherry and serve hot over pudding.

BRANDIED FOAMY SAUCE *About 2 cups*

½ cup butter
1⅓ cups sifted confectioners' sugar
Dash of salt
1 egg, separated
2 tablespoons cognac
½ cup heavy cream, whipped
Dash of ground nutmeg

1. Soften the butter and gradually blend in the sugar. Add the salt and egg yolk and beat well.

2. Cook over hot, not boiling, water, stirring constantly, until the mixture is light and fluffy, or six to seven minutes. Remove from the heat and stir in the cognac. Chill.

3. Fold in the egg white, beaten until it stands in soft peaks. Fold in the whipped cream just before serving.

4. Serve over fruitcake and sprinkle with nutmeg.

GRAND MARNIER SAUCE *About 2½ cups*

½ cup milk
½ cup cream
1-inch piece vanilla bean
2 egg yolks
¼ cup sugar
½ teaspoon cornstarch
2 ounces Grand Marnier
½ cup heavy cream, whipped

1. Scald the milk and cream with the vanilla bean. Discard the bean.

2. Beat the egg yolks with the sugar. Add the cornstarch and liquid and cook, stirring, until thickened. Strain and chill.

3. Add the Grand Marnier and fold in the whipped cream. Serve with additional whipped cream.

HARD SAUCE *About 2 cups*

1 cup sweet butter, softened
1 cup confectioners' sugar
¼ cup brandy, rum or sherry
Nutmeg

Cream the butter and the sugar well. Add the brandy a few drops at a time and beat until fluffy. Add the nutmeg to taste and chill.

FRESH LINGONBERRY SAUCE *About 2 cups*

2 cups fresh lingonberries
1 cup water
½ cup sugar

1. Wash and pick over the lingonberries, removing the stems, leaves and spoiled fruit.

2. Place the water and sugar in a saucepan over high heat and bring quickly to a boil. Boil the sugar syrup about thirty seconds, then add the berries. Reduce the heat and simmer gently fifteen to twenty minutes. Cool and serve.

RUM MINT SAUCE *About 1½ cups*

2 cups sugar
1 cup water
½ cup fresh mint leaves, packed
1 teaspoon grated lemon rind
¼ cup lemon juice
⅓ to ½ cup rum

Boil together the sugar, water, mint and lemon rind two minutes. Strain and chill. Add lemon juice and rum.

FRESH RASPBERRY SAUCE *About 2 cups*

2 cups raspberries
½ cup sugar, approximately
1 tablespoon cornstarch
1 tablespoon lemon juice
1 tablespoon cognac

1. Mix the raspberries with the sugar and heat, stirring frequently, to a boil. Strain and add more sugar if desired.

2. Mix the cornstarch with two tablespoons of cooled raspberry juice. Heat the remaining juice to a boil, stir in the cornstarch and cook, stirring, until thickened.

3. Cool and add the lemon juice and cognac. Serve over vanilla ice cream.

RUM SYRUP *About 1½ cups*

1 cup water
1 cup sugar
2 slices lemon
1 slice orange
2-inch stick cinnamon
1-inch piece vanilla bean
1 clove
½ cup rum

(cont'd)

1. Bring all the ingredients except the rum to a boil, stirring until the sugar has dissolved. Simmer five minutes.

2. Strain and add the rum.

STRAWBERRY SAUCE *About 2 cups*

2 cups fresh or defrosted frozen strawberries
½ cup sugar
½ cup water
Kirsch, Grand Marnier or cognac

1. Rub the strawberries through a fine sieve or squeeze through cheesecloth wrung out in cold water. Discard the pulp.

2. Combine the sugar and water in a saucepan and bring to a boil. Reduce the heat and simmer gently five minutes.

3. Combine the sugar syrup with the sieved strawberries and flavor with kirsch, Grand Marnier or cognac. Chill well.

STRAWBERRIES JUBILEE, PAGE 624.

ZABAGLIONE, PAGE 603.

FRUIT DESSERTS

GLAZED APPLES *6 servings*

6 medium apples, peeled and cored
1 tablespoon sugar
⅔ cup apple cider
1 cup currant jelly, melted
½ cup heavy cream, whipped

1. Preheat oven to slow (300° F.).

2. Dust the apples with sugar and set in a baking dish. Add the cider and bake thirty-five minutes, basting several times with the juice. Test the apples with a fork: they are cooked when they are soft inside but still hold their shape.

3. Mix the jelly with the juices in the bottom of the baking dish and pour over the apples to glaze them. Refrigerate and serve cold with whipped cream.

CARAMEL APPLES *6 servings*

6 medium apples
3 tablespoons butter
⅛ teaspoon salt
3 tablespoons brown sugar
½ teaspoon cinnamon
Whipped cream

(cont'd)

1. Pare and core the apples and cut them into eighths.

2. Melt the butter in a heavy skillet with a tight-fitting cover and add the apples. Cover and cook over low heat ten minutes, or until the apples soften.

3. Sprinkle with salt, sugar and cinnamon and cook, uncovered, fifteen to twenty minutes longer. Serve while warm with whipped cream.

APPLE CRISP *6 servings*

6 tart apples
1 cup sugar
¼ teaspoon ground cloves
½ teaspoon cinnamon
2 teaspoons lemon juice
¾ cup sifted flour
⅛ teaspoon salt
6 tablespoons butter
¼ cup chopped nut meats
Whipped cream or ice cream

1. Preheat oven to moderate (350° F.).

2. Peel, core and slice the apples into a bowl. Add one-half cup of the sugar, the spices and lemon juice. Mix lightly and pour into a buttered one-and-one-half-quart casserole.

3. Blend the remaining sugar, flour, salt and butter to a crumbly consistency. Add the nuts and sprinkle over the apple mixture. Bake forty-five minutes, or until the apples are tender and the crust is nicely browned. Serve with whipped cream or ice cream.

APRICOTS A LA COGNAC *6 servings*

1 pound dried apricots
⅔ cup sugar
Cognac to cover

Combine all the ingredients and let stand at least twenty-four hours. The flavor is improved if the fruit is allowed to steep in cognac for upward of a week. Serve chilled.

BANANAS CARIBBEAN *8 servings*

4 medium bananas
¼ cup brown sugar, packed
½ cup fresh orange juice
¼ teaspoon nutmeg
¼ teaspoon cinnamon
½ cup sherry
1 tablespoon butter
2 tablespoons light rum

1. Preheat the oven to hot (450° F.).

2. Peel the bananas and split them in half lengthwise. Place in a buttered 10 x 6 x 2-inch baking dish.

3. Combine the brown sugar with the orange juice, spices and sherry. Heat and pour over the bananas. Dot with butter.

(*cont'd*)

4. Bake ten to fifteen minutes, or until the bananas are tender, basting once or twice.

5. Remove from the oven and sprinkle with rum.

FLAMING GLAZED BANANAS *4 servings*

Select four yellow or green-tipped bananas, remove the skins and cut in half lengthwise.

Melt one-half cup butter in the glazer pan of a chafing dish, arrange the bananas in it and sprinkle with one-quarter cup lemon juice and three-quarters cup sugar. Turn the bananas occasionally until lightly browned.

If desired, add one cup canned Bing cherries and heat thoroughly.

Add one-third cup warmed cognac and set ablaze.

CHERRIES JUBILEE *6 servings*

1 can pitted black cherries
1 tablespoon sugar
1 tablespoon cornstarch
¼ cup warmed kirsch or cognac
Vanilla ice cream (optional)

1. Drain the cherries, reserving the juice.

2. Mix the sugar with the cornstarch and add one cup of the reserved juice, a little at a time. Cook three minutes, stirring constantly. Add the cherries and pour the kirsch over the top. Ignite the kirsch and ladle the sauce over the cherries.

3. Serve over vanilla ice cream if desired.

FIGS IN CREME DE CACAO *6 servings*

1 dozen fresh figs
1 cup sour cream
2 tablespoons crème de cacao
½ teaspoon cocoa

1. Wash and drain the figs and, using a sharp knife, peel them.

2. Combine the sour cream and crème de cacao in a mixing bowl. Mix well. Dip the figs in this mixture, coating them entirely. Set the figs on end in a serving bowl. Dust with the cocoa and refrigerate to chill thoroughly.

FRESH FIGS CURACAO *6 servings*

12 fresh figs, peeled and quartered
1 tablespoon cognac
1 cup sour or sweet cream
⅓ cup Curaçao

1. Marinate the figs in the cognac thirty minutes or longer.

2. Mix the cream and Curaçao. Fold in the figs and any cognac which they have not absorbed.

GINGERED FIGS *6 to 8 servings*

1 pound dried figs
Water
2 lemons
1 large piece ginger root
Sugar
Cream

1. Wash the figs and clip off the stems. Add cold water to cover, two tablespoons lemon juice and one tablespoon very thinly sliced lemon rind.
2. Add the ginger root and bring mixture to a boil. Boil until the figs are puffed and soft, or twenty to thirty minutes. Drain, reserving the liquid. Place the figs in a serving dish.
3. Measure the liquid and return it to the saucepan. Add half as much sugar as liquid and simmer until syrupy. Add one tablespoon lemon juice and four slices of lemon.
4. Pour the syrup over the figs, chill and serve with cream.

CHILLED SLICED ORANGES IN RED WINE *6 servings*

¾ cup sugar
1 cup water
1 cup dry red wine
2 cloves
Stick cinnamon
2 slices tangerine
2 slices lemon
6 large navel oranges

1. Dissolve the sugar in the water and add the wine. Tie the cloves, cinnamon, tangerine and lemon in cheesecloth. Bring the wine mixture to a boil, add the cheesecloth bag and boil until the liquid becomes syrupy. Remove the bag and discard.
2. Meanwhile, skin the oranges and, with a sharp knife cut off all the white membrane. Remove the segments. Add the fruit to the syrup and refrigerate until extremely cold.
3. Serve the dessert cold with a garnish, if desired, of slivered orange peel.

PEACH MELBA *6 servings*

1 package frozen raspberries
½ cup currant jelly
1½ teaspoons cornstarch
1 tablespoon cold water
6 canned peach halves
Vanilla ice cream

1. Place the raspberries in a saucepan and allow to thaw. Mash the berries with a spoon, add the jelly and bring to a boil over low heat. Add the cornstarch mixed with the water and cook, stirring, until clear. Strain, if desired, and cool.
2. Place a canned peach half, cut side up, in each of six individual dessert dishes. Top each with a scoop of ice cream and pour the cooled sauce over the top.

PEARS A LA BORDELAISE *6 servings*

6 fresh pears
Lemon juice
½ cup red Bordeaux wine
1 cup sugar
1 3-inch piece stick cinnamon
1 small piece lemon peel
2 tablespoons rum or cognac (optional)

1. Peel and core the pears, cutting each into lengthwise halves. To prevent the pears from darkening, brush them with lemon juice or drop into water containing a little lemon juice.

2. In a saucepan combine the wine, sugar, cinnamon and lemon peel. Bring to a boil, stirring. Add two or three pear halves at a time and cook gently until tender. Repeat the process until all the pears have been cooked.

3. Cook the syrup until reduced to about one-half the original quantity. Pour over the pears and chill.

4. If desired, add rum before serving. Pour over the pears and ignite at the table.

PEARS FLAMBE *6 servings*

6 fresh pears
¾ cup sugar
Water
1-inch piece vanilla bean, or ½ teaspoon vanilla extract
1 cup apricot preserves
2 tablespoons cornstarch
½ cup rum

1. Peel and core the pears, cutting each into lengthwise halves.

2. In a saucepan combine the sugar, one and one-half cups water and vanilla. Bring to a boil, stirring. Add two or three pear halves at a time and cook gently until tender. Repeat the process until all the pears have been cooked.

3. Cook the syrup until it has been reduced to about one cup. Add the apricot preserves and bring to a boil, stirring. Add the cornstarch, blended with two tablespoons cold water, and cook until thickened and clear. If the sauce is not thick enough to coat the pears, thicken with additional cornstarch blended with a little water.

4. Pour the sauce over the pears and keep hot in a chafing dish or oven.

5. When ready to serve, heat the rum, pour over the pears and ignite at the table.

PEARS MARY GARDEN *4 servings*

4 table pears
1 cup sugar
Water
½ cup raspberry jam
1 teaspoon cornstarch
1 tablespoon kirsch
¼ cup candied cherries
1 cup whipped cream

(cont'd)

1. Peel the pears, cut them in half and remove the cores.

2. Boil the sugar and one cup water together three minutes, stirring until the sugar has dissolved. Add the pears, lower the heat and simmer until the pears are tender. Cool the pears in the syrup, then drain well.

3. Heat the jam, stirring, until softened. Strain. Mix the cornstarch with one tablespoon cold water and add to the strained jam. Bring to a boil, cool and add the kirsch.

4. Pour warm water over the cherries and let stand until soft. Drain and dry. Add to the jam mixture.

5. To serve, turn the raspberry-cherry sauce into a serving dish, arrange the cooled pears over the sauce and garnish with the whipped cream, using a pastry tube if desired.

PEARS WITH RASPBERRY PUREE *6 servings*

Water
Sugar
½ teaspoon vanilla extract
3 peeled ripe pears, halved
1 package frozen raspberries, defrosted
1 teaspoon cornstarch
Kirsch (optional)
Blanched, slivered almonds

1. Combine one and one-half cups each water and sugar and boil five minutes. Add the vanilla and pears and simmer until the fruit is tender. Drain and chill.

2. Combine the raspberries with one tablespoon sugar. Mix the cornstarch with two tablespoons cold water and combine with the raspberries. Simmer three minutes and mash through a sieve. Chill and add kirsch to taste.

3. Spoon over the pears and sprinkle with almonds.

PEARS HELENE *6 servings*

What a splendid idea! Poached pears with ice cream and hot fudge sauce. To cap the climax: crystallized violets, generally available where fine imported foods are sold.

3 table pears
2 cups water
⅔ cup sugar
1 teaspoon vanilla extract
1 quart vanilla ice cream
6 rounds of sponge cake (optional)
Crystallized violets
Hot fudge sauce (page 613)

1. Peel, halve and core the pears. Combine the water and sugar and bring to a boil. Add the pears and reduce the heat. Simmer, covered, until the pears can be pierced easily with a paring knife, five minutes or longer. Turn once.

2. Add the vanilla and let the pears cool in the syrup.

3. At serving time, divide the ice cream on six dessert plates. If desired, the ice cream may be set on rounds of sponge cake.

(*cont'd*)

4. Drain the syrup from the pears. Place a half, rounded side up, on each portion of ice cream and garnish with violets. Serve the hot sauce separately.

Note: Canned pear halves may be substituted. Omit the cooking and flavor the syrup from the can to taste with vanilla. Let the pears stand in the syrup three hours before serving.

PEARS WITH GINGER *6 servings*

6 firm cooking pears
Water
¾ cup sugar
⅛ teaspoon powdered ginger
1 slice lemon

1. Peel the pears, cut in half and remove the cores.
2. Drop the pears into two cups boiling water, cover and simmer ten minutes. Add the sugar, ginger and lemon, cover and cook until tender, or ten to fifteen minutes. Cool.

PRUNE WHIP WITH PORT WINE *6 servings*

½ pound dried prunes
Water
⅔ cup granulated sugar
Lemon rind
1 cup port wine
1 cup heavy cream
3 tablespoons confectioners' sugar
Slivered blanched almonds

1. Soak the prunes overnight in water to cover. Drain. Place them in a small kettle and add the sugar, lemon rind and water to cover. Bring to a boil and cook until the prunes are tender.
2. Drain, leaving the prunes in the kettle. Add the port and cook ten minutes longer. Remove the stones and put the prunes through a sieve, or purée in an electric blender. Add a little more port if necessary to make the prunes moist; add more sugar to taste.
3. Whip the cream and mix half of it with the prunes. Sweeten the remaining cream with confectioners' sugar and use as a garnish. Top with almonds.

CARDINAL STRAWBERRIES *4 servings*

1 quart fresh strawberries
¼ cup raspberry jam
2 tablespoons sugar
¼ cup water
1 tablespoon kirsch
¼ cup slivered, blanched almonds

1. Wash and hull the strawberries.
2. Combine the jam, sugar and water in a saucepan and simmer about two minutes. Add the kirsch and chill.
3. Arrange the strawberries in four individual serving dishes. Pour the chilled raspberry sauce over the fruit and sprinkle with the slivered almonds.

STRAWBERRIES CHANTILLY *12 servings*

2 quarts ripe strawberries, washed
¾ cup superfine granulated sugar
2 cups heavy cream
⅓ cup kirsch
Plain cake

1. Hull and halve the strawberries.
2. Ten minutes before serving time, add the sugar.
3. Just before serving, whip the cream, add the kirsch and fold in the berries. Pile in the center of a plain cake that has been baked in a ten-inch tube pan.

STRAWBERRIES JUBILEE *6 servings*

½ cup water
⅓ cup sugar
2 teaspoons arrowroot or cornstarch
1 pint strawberries, washed and hulled
2 ounces kirsch
1 quart vanilla ice cream

Mix the water, sugar and arrowroot. Heat, stirring, to a boil and add the strawberries. Return to a boil, stirring only enough to blend. Add the kirsch and ignite.

Serve the flaming sauce over ice cream.

STRAWBERRIES A LA NINO *4 servings*

28 fresh strawberries
3 ounces (6 tablespoons) tawny port
4 canned figs
3 ounces (6 tablespoons) kirsch
2 cups sweetened whipped cream
4 scoops French vanilla ice cream
4 macaroons
2 teaspoons Grand Marnier, Cointreau or orange-flavored cordial

1. Wash strawberries and rinse under cold water just enough to remove sand. Cut off stems. Place in a large bowl and add port. Puncture the fruit with a fork so that it will absorb the wine. Chill in the refrigerator at least one hour.
2. Remove strawberries from the refrigerator, add figs, mix together and partially crush. Add the kirsch and mix. Add the whipped cream and mix again. Add the ice cream and stir just enough to blend in with the other ingredients.
3. Transfer the mixture to four individual glasses or a deep dessert dish. Crush the macaroons and sprinkle over the dessert.
4. Sprinkle the cordial over the macaroons and serve immediately.

TANGERINES IN KIRSCH

Peel tangerines and separate the segments. Arrange in a glass serving dish and sprinkle with powdered sugar. Sprinkle with kirsch and refrigerate two hours before serving.

GINGERED FRUIT WITH CHEESE *6 to 8 servings*

This is an extraordinary combination: whipped cream cheese with gingered fruit. The fruit is available in Oriental grocery stores.

1 small can preserved gingered fruit
¾ pound whipped cream cheese
Saltine crackers

1. Chill the fruit well and have the cream cheese at room temperature.
2. Place the fruit in a bowl over a container of cracked ice. Serve with cream cheese and crisp saltine crackers.

Note: The fruit should be speared with a food pick and dipped in the cream cheese.

MACEDOINE OF FRUIT IN VERMOUTH *6 servings*

½ cup sweet or dry vermouth
¼ cup sugar
¼ teaspoon cinnamon
1 small to medium pineapple, cut in wedges
3 navel oranges, peeled and cut in sections
18 large grapes, halved and seeded

1. Combine the vermouth, sugar and cinnamon and let stand in the refrigerator one hour.
2. Pour off the liquid and discard the sugar sediment. Pour the liquid over prepared fresh fruit and marinate at least one hour in the refrigerator before serving.

ICE CREAMS, SHERBETS AND FROZEN DESSERTS

FRESH PEACH ICE CREAM *About 1½ quarts*

2 cups crushed ripe peaches
1⅓ cups sugar
1 teaspoon almond extract
⅛ teaspoon salt
2 tablespoons flour
2 eggs, slightly beaten
1½ cups milk
2 teaspoons vanilla extract
2 cups heavy cream

1. Mix the peaches with one-third cup of the sugar and the almond extract.

(*cont'd*)

2. Mix the remaining sugar, salt and flour in a pan. Blend in the eggs and one-quarter cup of the milk. Add the remaining milk and cook over low heat until the mixture coats a metal spoon, stirring constantly. Remove from the heat and cool. Add the vanilla and cream.

3. Pour into the two-quart can of an ice cream freezer and place the can in the freezer tub. Cover with the lid, put on the gear case and adjust until the handle turns easily. Pack with one part ice-cream salt to eight parts crushed ice. Turn the crank until the mixture is half frozen (when resistance is felt, after about fifteen minutes' turning).

4. Add the crushed peaches. Pack the tub with additional salt and ice in the above proportions and turn the crank fairly rapidly until too hard to turn, at which point the mixture will have frozen.

5. Remove the gear case, lid and dasher. Cover the can with aluminum foil, replace the lid and stop up the hole in the top of the lid. Drain the water from the tub and pack with one part salt to four parts ice. Let stand two hours.

VARIATION:

In Freezer Trays: Follow steps 1 and 2 above. Pour the mixture into freezer trays and freeze until the mixture is frozen one-half inch around the edge. Remove from the trays and beat vigorously until smooth and fluffy. Fold in the peaches, return to the trays and freeze until firm.

PISTACHIO ICE CREAM

About 1 quart

½ cup sugar
1 tablespoon cornstarch
1 cup light cream
½ cup milk
2 eggs, slightly beaten
½ teaspoon salt
1 teaspoon vanilla extract
½ teaspoon almond extract
1 cup heavy cream, whipped
½ cup finely chopped pistachio nuts

1. Set the refrigerator control for fast freezing.

2. Mix the sugar and cornstarch in the top of a double boiler. Add the light cream and milk and bring to a boil over direct heat, stirring constantly.

3. Mix the eggs with the salt and add a little of the hot mixture, stirring. Return to the top of the double boiler and cook, stirring, over simmering water until the mixture thickens. Cool.

4. Add the flavorings, pour the mixture into freezer trays and freeze until firm.

5. Transfer the mixture to a bowl, break up the lumps and beat in an electric mixer or by hand until soft but not mushy.

6. Fold in the whipped cream and nuts. Return to the freezer trays and freeze until firm.

VANILLA ICE CREAM *About 1½ quarts*

- 2 cups milk
- ¾ cup sugar
- 4 teaspoons flour
- ¼ teaspoon salt
- 3 egg yolks or 2 whole eggs
- 2 teaspoons vanilla extract
- 2 cups light cream

1. Scald the milk in the top of a double boiler.
2. Mix the sugar, flour and salt. Add the hot milk, stirring, and return to the double boiler. Stir over boiling water until thickened.
3. Beat the egg yolks or whole eggs and add a small portion of the hot mixture. Return to the remaining hot mixture and cook, stirring occasionally, until the mixture coats a metal spoon. Chill thoroughly.
4. Add the vanilla and cream and freeze in a hand-crank or electric freezer, following the instructions given with either (or directions for fresh peach ice cream, page 625).

VARIATION:

Chocolate Ice Cream: Add two ounces unsweetened chocolate, grated or shredded, to the milk and proceed as for vanilla ice cream.

FRENCH VANILLA ICE CREAM *1½ quarts*

- 1½ cups milk
- 2½ cups light cream
- 1 vanilla bean
- 8 egg yolks
- ¾ cup sugar
- ¼ teaspoon salt

1. Scald the milk, cream and vanilla bean in the top of a double boiler. Remove vanilla bean.
2. Blend the egg yolks with the sugar and salt. Stir in some of the scalded milk and return to the mixture in the double boiler. Cook, stirring, until thick (the mixture will coat a metal spoon).
3. Remove from the hot water and cool quickly in cold water, stirring occasionally. Chill thoroughly. Freeze in a hand-crank or electric freezer, following instructions given with either (or see directions for fresh peach ice cream, page 625).

LEMON MILK SHERBET *About 1 quart*

- 2 egg whites
- ¼ cup sugar
- 1 cup light corn syrup
- 2 cups milk
- ½ teaspoon grated lemon rind
- ⅔ cup lemon juice

1. Set the refrigerator control for fast freezing.
2. Beat the egg whites until stiff but not dry. Gradually beat in the sugar.

(*cont'd*)

Add, while beating, the corn syrup, milk, lemon rind and juice. Pour into freezer tray and freeze until almost firm.

3. Turn into a cold bowl, break up the lumps and beat with a rotary hand or electric beater until smooth. The mixture should be mushy but not melted. Turn again into the tray and freeze until firm.

Note: For storage, set the cold control midway between normal and fast freezing.

VARIATION:

Lime Mint Milk Sherbet: Follow the recipe for lemon milk sherbet, substituting lime rind and juice for the lemon. Remove the leaves from about twelve stalks of mint, crush and add to the corn syrup. Add one-quarter cup water and boil two minutes. Cool, strain and proceed as with plain corn syrup in the recipe.

ORANGE RUM SHERBET *About 1½ pints*

2 teaspoons unflavored gelatin
¾ cup cold water
¾ cup sugar
1 cup orange juice
1½ tablespoons lime juice
½ cup light rum
1 tablespoon grated orange rind
Few grains salt

1. Soften the gelatin in one-quarter cup of the water.

2. Combine the remaining water and the sugar and boil one minute. Add the gelatin and stir until dissolved. Add the orange and lime juice, rum, orange rind and salt. Strain and cool.

3. Pour into freezing tray; set refrigerator at point for freezing ice cream and freeze to a mush.

4. Place the mixture in a chilled bowl and beat with a rotary beater until smooth. Return to the tray and freeze, stirring several times, until almost firm. (Too hard a sherbet has an unpleasant texture.)

RASPBERRY SHERBET *About 1½ pints*

¾ cup sugar
1 cup warm water
½ cup light corn syrup
¼ cup lemon juice
1 container frozen raspberries, thawed and puréed
2 egg whites

1. Set refrigerator control for fast freezing.

2. Dissolve the sugar in the water, stirring. Add the corn syrup, lemon juice and raspberry purée. Freeze until firm around the edges.

3. Beat the egg whites until stiff.

4. Turn the partially frozen mixture into a chilled bowl and whip until smooth but not melted. Quickly fold in the egg whites and freeze until firm.

STRAWBERRY SHERBET *1½ quarts*

- 1 cup water
- 1¼ cups sugar
- ¾ cup light corn syrup
- 1 quart ripe strawberries, washed and hulled
- 1 cup evaporated milk, thoroughly chilled
- 1 tablespoon lemon juice
- 2 egg whites, stiffly beaten

1. Set the freezer control at the coldest point.
2. Heat the water with the sugar, stirring until the sugar has dissolved. Add the corn syrup, blend well and cool.
3. Reserving a few whole strawberries for garnish, purée the balance by rubbing through a sieve or beating in a blender. Add to the syrup. Add the milk and lemon juice.
4. Turn the mixture into a freezer tray with the capacity of about five cups. Freeze until firm.
5. Turn the mixture into a bowl, break up the lumps with a wooden spoon and then beat with an electric or hand beater until no lumps remain and the mixture is a thick mush.
6. Fold in the egg whites, return the mixture to the freezer tray and freeze until firm.

To Serve: Line the bottom and sides of a bowl with lady fingers and fill with the sherbet. Garnish with the reserved whole strawberries.

COUPES

Although the combination of ice creams with various flavors is common in America, the idea is of French origin. In France, coupes are almost invariably served in the open-shaped glasses commonly associated with champagne. They may be served in any stemmed glass, however.

Coupes may be garnished with whipped cream, candied fruits, chopped nuts, candied flowers, mint leaves and chopped fresh or canned fruit.

The most famous coupe is perhaps the coupe Melba, named in honor of Dame Nellie Melba, the Australian operatic soprano.

Coupe Melba: Top vanilla ice cream with half a peach and spoon over it puréed raspberries sweetened to taste. Garnish with whipped cream and toasted slivered almonds.

Coupe Romanoff: Top vanilla ice cream with fresh sweetened strawberries marinated in kirsch. Spoon over them sweetened puréed raspberries and garnish with whipped cream.

Coupe Jacques: Arrange vanilla ice cream by spoonfuls vertically in a serving glass. Cover each spoonful with mixed fruits cut in small cubes to fill the space between the ice cream mounds.

Coupe Eugénie: Mix vanilla ice cream with broken preserved chestnuts and

(*cont'd*)

1. *The versatile meringue velvet* may be frozen in various shapes and garnished, here with almonds.

2. A rare treat for summer menus would be this Palermo cassata. It is made with layers of vanilla ice cream, sponge cake, raspberry ice and frozen meringue velvet.

3. A molded creation with a pistachio ice cream shell is this Sicilian cassata. The shell is filled with softened orange ice and frozen meringue velvet before it is refrozen. It is garnished with whipped cream.

refreeze in the freezing unit of the refrigerator. Garnish with whipped cream and more chestnuts.

FROZEN MERINGUE VELVET

About 3 quarts

- 1 cup chopped or diced candied fruit
- ½ cup maraschino
- 1⅔ cup granulated sugar
- ½ cup water
- 6 egg whites, stiffly beaten
- 1¾ cups coarsely chopped toasted hazel nuts or almonds and pistachios
- 1 quart heavy cream, whipped

1. Marinate the candied fruit in the maraschino until ready to use.
2. In a saucepan combine the sugar and water. Bring to a boil and cook

(*cont'd*)

until the syrup reaches the soft-ball stage (236° F. on a candy thermometer).

3. Add syrup in fine stream to egg whites while beating. Continue beating until mixture forms stiff peaks. Chill.

4. Add nuts to marinated fruits; fold into chilled meringue.

5. Fold in whipped cream, blending the two mixtures well. Freeze.

CASSATA DESSERTS:

Sicilian Cassata: Freeze a round three-quart mold. Soften one quart of pistachio ice cream to stiff spreading consistency and spread over the inside of the mold. Refreeze immediately. Repeat the process with softened orange ice. Refreeze. Fill center with frozen meringue velvet (see recipe) and freeze until firm.

Palermo Cassata: Freeze a 9½ x 5¼ x 2¾-inch bread pan. Pack one pint vanilla ice cream in a smooth layer in the bottom of the pan. Add a layer of sponge cake and freeze until firm. Cover with one pint softened raspberry ice and refreeze until firm. When firm, fill the pan with frozen meringue velvet (see recipe), using about three cups. Freeze until firm. Unmold before serving.

ROYAL EGG YOLK VELVET

About 4 quarts

2 cups sugar
½ cup water
8 egg yolks
¼ teaspoon salt
¼ cup rum or cognac
6 cups heavy cream, whipped

1. In a saucepan, combine the sugar and water. Bring to a boil and cook until the syrup registers 236° F. on a candy thermometer. If a candy thermometer is not used, cook to the soft ball stage. To make this test, spoon a few drops of syrup into cold water. If a soft ball forms, it is ready to be used.

2. Beat the egg yolks with the salt until they are very thick. Add the syrup in a fine stream while beating and continue beating until the mixture forms peaks when the beater is withdrawn. Chill the mixture.

3. Add the rum or cognac and fold in the whipped cream.

4. Turn the mixture into several small molds or paper cups and freeze.

VARIATIONS:

Chocolate Velvet: Mix two-thirds cup cocoa with sugar and water before cooking.

Coffee Velvet: Mix three tablespoons powdered coffee with sugar and water before cooking.

Fruit or Nut Velvet: Stir three-quarters cup toasted nuts or candied fruit into mixture before freezing.

Tortoni: Stir five finely chopped almonds into mixture before freezing. Sprinkle with additional crushed almonds.

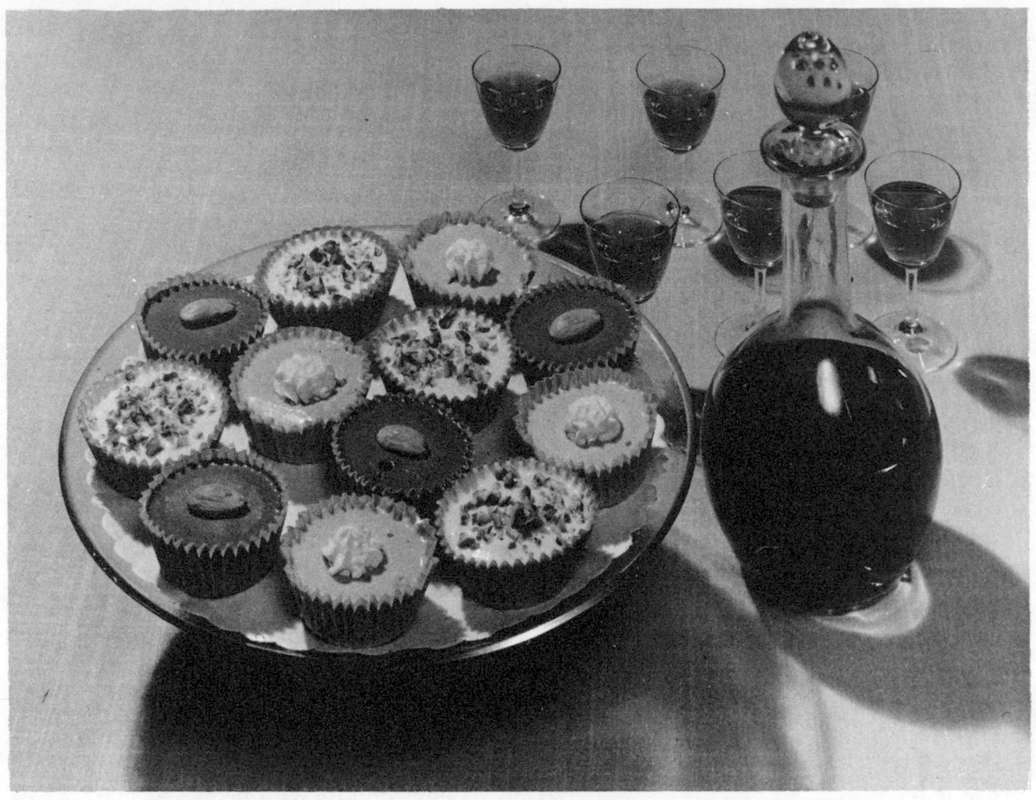

Summer desserts are made with a basic recipe for royal egg velvet, with various flavors.

MINT PARFAIT *6 servings*

1 cup sugar
1 cup water
3 egg whites, stiffly beaten
Salt
Green food coloring
¼ cup green crème de menthe
2 cups heavy cream, whipped

1. Dissolve the sugar in the water and bring to a boil. Cook rapidly five minutes.
2. Pour the syrup in a fine stream into the egg whites, beating constantly. Beat until the meringue is thick and cool.
3. Add the salt, food coloring and crème de menthe. Fold in the whipped cream and freeze in freezer tray.

FROZEN APRICOT MOUSSE *About 1½ pints*

1 cup cooked, sweetened dried apricots
2 eggs
⅓ cup sugar
½ teaspoon vanilla
Few grains of salt
1 cup heavy cream, beaten stiff

(*cont'd*)

1. Mash the apricots thoroughly, or press through a sieve.

2. Beat the eggs until light and fluffy. Beat in the sugar gradually. Combine with the apricot pulp, vanilla and salt and fold in the cream.

3. Turn into refrigerator tray and place in the freezing compartment. Set control at lowest temperature and freeze until firm.

4. Reset temperature control to normal.

SOUFFLE GLACE AUX FRAISES *8 servings*

1 cup milk
1 cup light cream
1-inch piece vanilla bean or 1 teaspoon vanilla extract
4 egg yolks
½ cup sugar
2 cups heavy cream, whipped
2 cups strawberries, sweetened
2 to 4 tablespoons kirsch

1. Fold waxed or glazed paper lengthwise and tie around the top of a one-and-one-half-quart soufflé dish to make a three-inch standing rim. Remove the ends of a tall slender can and stand in the center of the dish. Place the dish in the freezer and set control for fast freezing.

2. Scald the milk and cream with the vanilla bean in a double boiler. Discard vanilla bean.

3. Beat the egg yolks with the sugar until thick and light. Stir in a little of the hot milk mixture and add the yolks to the milk, stirring. Cook over simmering water, stirring, until the custard is thick. Strain through a fine sieve and cool quickly. Chill.

4. Fold in the whipped cream and turn into the prepared mold. Cover with paper and freeze until firm.

5. To serve, remove the paper collar and can and fill the center with kirsch-flavored strawberries.

FROZEN VANILLA SOUFFLE *8 to 10 servings*

4 egg yolks
1 cup sugar
⅛ teaspoon salt
1 cup milk
1 cup light cream
4-inch piece vanilla bean, or 1½ teaspoons vanilla extract
2 cups heavy cream, whipped
Shaved chocolate or powdered cocoa

1. Beat the egg yolks in the top of a double boiler until light and lemon-colored. Gradually beat in the sugar. Stir in the salt and one-quarter cup of the milk.

2. Split the vanilla bean and place in a saucepan with the light cream and remaining milk. Heat until scalded, cool and remove the vanilla bean. Gradually stir the milk mixture into the egg mixture and cook over hot, not boiling, water, stirring constantly, until the mixture coats a metal spoon. Cool.

(*cont'd*)

3. Fold in the whipped cream and turn the mixture into a one-quart soufflé dish with a three-inch band of heavy brown paper or foil tied around the outside at the top. This will give the mixture the illusion of a hot soufflé when frozen.

4. Place in a freezer for six to eight hours, or overnight. Remove the paper rim and serve from the dish. Garnish with shaved chocolate or powdered cocoa.

TANGERINES EN SURPRISE *6 servings*

This is a colorful and delicious dessert. Tangerine shells are hollowed out, filled with a tangerine sherbet mixture, then frozen. A sprig of mint serves as a "stem."

10 to 12 tangerines
2 cups water
Sugar
2 tablespoons corn syrup
2 tablespoons grated tangerine peel
2 tablespoons lemon juice
Red and yellow food coloring
2 egg whites
Fresh mint

1. Cut the tops off six of the tangerines. With a spoon, gently scoop out the fruit sections. Reserve the shells and tops.

2. Remove the seeds from the sections and extract the juice by pressing the sections in a potato ricer. Use enough additional tangerine sections to make two cups juice.

3. Combine the water, one cup sugar and the corn syrup and boil briskly five minutes. Add the grated tangerine peel and cool.

4. Add the tangerine and lemon juices and a few drops of red and yellow food coloring to the syrup mixture. Strain the mixture through a fine sieve and pour into a shallow pan. Freeze until mushy.

5. When the ice is partly set, beat the egg whites with two tablespoons sugar until stiff. Fold into the ice and continue to freeze until the ice is solid.

6. Using an ice cream scoop, fill each tangerine shell with two scoops of the ice. Cover each with a tangerine top. Assemble in a pan, wrap with foil and return to the freezer until ready to serve. Garnish each with a sprig of mint before serving.

CANDIES

NUT BRITTLE *2 pounds*

2 cups granulated sugar
1 cup brown sugar, packed
½ cup light corn syrup
½ cup water
⅛ teaspoon salt
¼ cup soft butter
⅛ teaspoon soda
1½ cups pecans, walnuts or peanuts, coarsely chopped

(*cont'd*)

1. Boil the sugars, syrup, water and salt together until a little of the mixture turns very brittle in cold water (300° F. on a candy thermometer). Stir the mixture only until the sugar is dissolved.

2. Add the butter and soda, stirring only until mixed. Add nuts and pour at once onto a greased heatproof surface. Smooth out and mark into squares or stretch the candy into a thin sheet. Loosen from sheet before it cools and hardens and break into squares or rough pieces.

CANDIED FLOWERS

Rose petals, whole pansies, violets, mint leaves or other flowers as desired
1 ounce gum arabic
1 cup water
1 tablespoon corn syrup
1 cup granulated sugar

1. Dip the flowers in water gently, then dry carefully so as not to bruise the petals.

2. In the top of a double boiler, over hot water, dissolve the gum arabic with one-half cup of the water. Let the mixture stand until cold.

3. Using a soft brush, coat the flowers, petals or leaves with the gum arabic. Allow each piece to dry thoroughly. It is best to stick each flower on a pin so that no part touches any surface.

4. Mix the corn syrup and sugar with the remaining water and bring to a boil. Cook to 238° F. (syrup forms a soft ball in cold water).

5. Allow the syrup to stand until it is cold. Then dip the flowers gently into the syrup. Remove the flowers and sprinkle them with finely granulated sugar. Place them on waxed paper to dry.

Note: Flowers done in this way can be kept for months. A simpler method, if they are to be used immediately, is to brush the petals with slightly beaten egg white, dip them in finely granulated sugar and place them on a plate well spread with sugar. Sprinkle more sugar over the petals and allow them to stand in a warm place until thoroughly dry.

VANILLA DIVINITY *36 squares or 1¼ pounds*

2⅓ cups granulated sugar
½ cup light corn syrup
½ cup water
¼ teaspoon salt
2 egg whites
Red, green or yellow food coloring (optional)
1 teaspoon vanilla extract
1 cup pecans or walnuts, coarsely chopped

1. Cook the sugar, corn syrup, water and salt to 264° F., or until it forms a hard, almost brittle ball if dropped in cold water, stirring only until the sugar is dissolved.

2. When the syrup is almost ready, beat the egg whites in an electric mixer or with a rotary hand beater until stiff. Add the syrup in a fine stream, beating con-

(*cont'd*)

stantly. Replace the beater with a wooden spoon when the mixture becomes heavy. If desired, color the mixture pink, green or yellow. Add the vanilla and continue beating until the mixture just holds its shape when dropped from a spoon.

3. Add the nuts, mixing quickly. Drop as speedily as possible, by rounded teaspoonfuls, on lightly greased surface; or turn the divinity into a greased 8 x 8-inch pan. Coat with melted semisweet chocolate and sprinkle with chopped nuts if desired. Cool, turn out of the pan, invert the candy and cut it into squares.

VARIATIONS:

Almond Divinity: Substitute toasted slivered almonds for the pecans or walnuts and one-half teaspoon almond extract for the vanilla.

Fruit Divinity: Substitute three-quarters cup any chopped, candied fruit or raisins for the pecans or walnuts.

Coconut Divinity: Substitute flaked coconut for the pecans or walnuts.

Ginger Divinity: Substitute one-third cup chopped candied ginger for one-third cup nuts.

CREAM TAFFY

About 120 1-inch pieces, or 1 pound 3 ounces of candy

2 cups granulated sugar
¾ cup water
¼ cup light corn syrup
¼ teaspoon salt
1 cup heavy cream
1 teaspoon vanilla extract

1. In a three- or four-quart saucepan, cook the sugar, water, corn syrup and salt to 250° F. (hard ball in cold water), stirring only until the sugar is dissolved.

2. Add the cream and cook slowly, stirring as needed to prevent sticking, to 260° (almost brittle). Pour into greased pan.

3. When cool enough to handle, pour the vanilla into center and gather the corners toward it so that none will be lost. Remove taffy from the pan and pull until rather firm and a light cream color, first dipping fingers in cornstarch if necessary to prevent sticking.

4. Stretch into a long rope about three-quarters inch in diameter. Lay the rope on a greased surface and cut it at once into one-inch pieces.

5. Wrap pieces separately in foil, Saran or waxed paper.

When Making Taffy: Taffy should be pulled with the fingers rather than the whole hand to produce the appropriate lightness. If the taffy is too sticky to handle, dust the fingers with cornstarch. If this does not help, try butter, but only as a last resort, for it tends to make the taffy stringy. However, when used to grease pans, butter improves taffy's flavor.

WHITE TAFFY

About 60 1-inch pieces, or 1 pound 2 ounces of candy

2 cups granulated sugar
½ cup light corn syrup
⅔ cup water
⅛ teaspoon salt
1 teaspoon vanilla extract

(*cont'd*)

1. Grease one 9 by 9-inch pan, or two 8 by 8-inch pans if two people are going to pull the taffy. Also grease a large surface for cutting the candy.

2. Cook all ingredients except the vanilla to 268° F. (the mixture makes a firm, nearly brittle ball in cold water), stirring only until the sugar is dissolved. Pour into the greased pans.

3. When cool enough to handle, pour the vanilla into the center of the candy and fold the corners over it so that it will not be lost. Pull, using the fingertips, until the candy is rather firm and white.

4. Stretch into a long rope about three-quarters inch in diameter. Lay the rope on the greased surface and cut it at once into pieces of desired size. Separate the pieces to prevent sticking together. Serve on a buttered plate or, if the candy is to be kept, wrap each piece in waxed paper, foil or transparent Saran and store in a sealed container.

Note: The taffy may be colored and flavored with a suitable flavoring oil before pulling. For example, color the taffy pink and flavor it with wintergreen; color it pale green and flavor it with spearmint; color it yellow and flavor it with lemon; or leave the taffy white and flavor it with peppermint.

MEXICAN ORANGE CANDY *About 1¾ pounds*

3 cups sugar
¼ cup boiling water
1 cup evaporated milk
Few grains salt
2 teaspoons grated orange rind
1 cup nuts

1. Place one cup of the sugar in a heavy saucepan over medium heat and cook, stirring occasionally, until the sugar begins to melt. Then stir constantly until all the sugar is melted and deep golden brown in color. Add the boiling water to the caramelized sugar and cook to a smooth syrup, stirring constantly.

2. Add the remaining sugar, milk and salt and cook over medium heat to 238° F. (mixture forms a soft ball in cold water), stirring constantly. Add the orange rind. Cool and stir in the nuts. Beat until crystalline. Drop from a teaspoon onto waxed paper.

PRALINES *About 30 pralines*

1½ cups sugar
⅓ cup light New Orleans molasses
1 cup light cream (or ½ cup heavy cream plus ½ cup milk)
1 tablespoon butter
Dash of nutmeg
1½ cups pecan meats, coarsely chopped

1. Combine the sugar, molasses, cream, butter and nutmeg in a two-quart saucepan. Bring to a boil and continue to boil over medium heat, stirring occasionally, to 240° F. (mixture forms a firm ball in cold water), thirty-five to forty minutes.

2. Remove from heat and let stand three minutes. Add the nuts and drop the mixture from a teaspoon onto waxed paper or foil.

NOUGAT *About 1¾ pounds*

- 2½ cups shelled almonds
- ½ cup pistachios
- 1 cup sugar
- ½ cup water
- 3 tablespoons light corn syrup
- ½ teaspoon salt
- 2 egg whites, at room temperature
- ½ cup honey
- 1 teaspoon vanilla extract

1. Blanch the almonds and, while soft, cut lengthwise into slivers. Brown lightly in a moderate oven (350° F.), stirring often.

2. Blanch the pistachios and let dry by spreading out on paper towels. (To blanch nuts, cover with boiling water, let stand five minutes, drain and slip off the skins.)

3. In a one-quart saucepan combine the sugar, water, half the corn syrup and the salt. Cook together, stirring, until the sugar dissolves. Cook to 290° F. (syrup forms a brittle ball in cold water). Remove from the heat.

4. In a large bowl, beat the egg whites until stiff but not dry. Add the cooked syrup gradually, while beating.

5. Boil together the honey and remaining corn syrup to 290° F. Add gradually, while beating, to the egg white mixture. Add the almonds and pistachios.

6. Stand the bowl of mixture on a rack in a pan of boiling water and steam, stirring occasionally, until a spoonful of the candy, cooled, is not sticky to the touch, or about one and one-half hours. Add the vanilla.

7. Line an 11 by 7-inch pan with wafer paper, turn the nougat into the pan and cover with wafer paper. Place a pan of the same size on top of the candy and press with a heavy weight. Let stand overnight or longer.

8. Turn the candy out of the pan and cut into 1½ by ½-inch bars. Wrap immediately in freezer wrap or waxed paper. Store in a covered tin box in a cool place.

CHAPTER THIRTEEN

ON WINE

There is nothing that complements food better than wine. It is a drink that is well within the reach and purse of most men and, if one is to believe Pasteur, it is the healthiest of liquids to drink. Wine stimulates conversation, sharpens the wit and brings forth all that is most generous in the inner man. And yet more precious and bewildering nonsense has been written about wine than any other adjunct of gastronomy.

For some obscure reason, some authorities seem bent on making the drinking of wine a ritual more complicated than chess. They have succeeded in inhibiting a large section of the public and depriving them of one of the greatest pleasures known to man.

One volume, venerated by some, lists twelve steps to the enjoyment of wine. It begins with the admonition that the wine must be studied when it is poured, inhaled, then swirled in the mouth. Finally, the author adds, the wine must be discussed.

Inhaling the bouquet at the same time as the wine is being drunk can be a risky business for the amateur. And while swirling wine in the mouth may add to the enjoyment of the dedicated connoisseur, it may appear boorish if inexpertly done. As to the discussion of wine, this is tantamount to saying that it is impossible to relish a game of golf or bridge without a post-mortem. It is not farfetched to say that wine can be enjoyed with meals in solitude.

"White wine with white meat and red wine with red meat" is only a broad generalization and should not be taken too seriously. Roast chicken is admirably suited to the red wines of Bordeaux, roast turkey to those of Burgundy. While it is hard to conceive anyone *wanting* to drink a red wine with fish or a white wine with rare roast beef, it is most surely a question of personal choice.

The notion that a rosé wine complements all foods is questionable, and a pity it is that many people deprive themselves of the joys of the whites and the reds through their indecision as to what wines to serve and their desire to be "correct."

The choice may well depend on a sauce. If the sauce is a lusty tomato concoction in the South Italian tradition, an Italian red wine is thoroughly appropriate whether the sauce is served on chicken, veal or simply boiled spaghetti.

In essence it would seem that dry white wines are best suited to all fish and seafood, to pork, to such a delicate dish as sweetbreads; sweet white wines to desserts. Red wine is most appropriate with pâtés, beef, lamb, mutton, game and pasta dishes. Chicken, turkey, other poultry and veal are suited to either red or white wines except when the poultry or veal is served in cream sauces, when it is best suited to dry white wines. Rosé wines may be served with almost any dish, though they come off best with cold meat platters, curries and aspics.

A dry champagne is universally considered the one drink that complements all foods and may be served before, during and after a meal. Sweet white wines should be served with desserts.

WINE GLASSES

There was an era when it was proper to have a particular glass for each wine type. There was a glass for Burgundy, one for Bordeaux, another for Rhine, Moselle and so on. There were and still are three glasses for champagne alone, the flute, the coupe and the tulip. Although the flute and the coupe have a certain elegance, the tulip is best suited to the drink since the upper part of the glass tapers inward and this is said to help retain the sparkle in the liquid.

The present trend is toward a single glass for all drinks.

An all-purpose wine glass should have a long stem and a large bowl; the rim should be tapered inward; it should be crystal clear and the glass as thin as possible. If it meets these conditions it is suitable for still wines, sparkling wines, fortified wines such as sherry and port and for brandies.

THE SERVICE OF WINES

As a general rule, during the course of a single meal white wines are served before red wines, young wines before old ones and dry wines before sweet wines. The order is sheer logic.

Consider a meal including fish and beef. The fish, best suited to a dry white wine, always precedes the beef, best suited to a red wine. It is common sense in menu planning to proceed from the light to the rich. And if a fine old wine were followed by a young wine, the latter would suffer by contrast.

The purpose of a wine basket is to act as a cradle for fine old wines. The wine, lying on its side, is taken from the rack and placed in the basket to prevent jostling. This keeps the deposits resting in peace where they fell. Opening a bottle of wine when it is in a wine basket requires great skill and should not be essayed by nonprofessionals.

Few people have cellars and most of the wine that is drunk today is young wine free from deposit. A wine basket is totally nonessential for these wines and thus becomes a decorative conceit. It is valid as a table ornament but serves no other purpose.

Wines which have a deposit should properly be decanted, since it takes an expert skill to pour such wines at table directly from the bottle. To decant, the wine should be poured while lying on its side into a decanter. A candle or flashlight held behind the bottle will indicate at what point the dregs begin to enter the decanter. If this seems a tiresome procedure, the bottle should be placed upright for a period of at least twenty-four hours, then very carefully poured at table, taking care that the bottle is not joggled and no dregs enter the glasses of the guests.

To open a bottle of wine properly, the foil wrapping covering the cork should be carefully trimmed, a quarter to half an inch down, with a knife. The top of the foil is then removed and discarded and the top of the cork wiped with a clean napkin. The point of a corkscrew, inserted into the dead center of the cork, is screwed into the cork and the cork carefully withdrawn. The rim of the mouth of the bottle is then wiped once more with a clean napkin.

The host pours a small amount of wine into his own glass and samples it. This gesture is made for two reasons. If bits of cork were left in the bottle they will probably enter the first glass receiving wine. It also gives the host an opportunity to note whether the wine is spoiled. If air has entered the bottle it may have become sour. If the wine is a white wine and has great age, "madeirization" may have set in, which is to say it has a dank, dark-brown taste which is unpleasant.

Fine red wines of whatever age should be uncorked from thirty minutes to an hour before they are served. This permits the wine to breathe and gives depth to the flavor.

Because the character of a wine from any given vineyard may vary from year to year it is impossible to offer a valid list of wines whose quality is guaranteed to give pleasure. Although 1959 was hailed as an outstanding year in Europe's vineyards, this does not mean that most bottles wearing that date will be "great." In any good year the best wines may be extraordinary, but in every harvest there are many that are commonplace.

The obvious method of getting to know wines is by trial and error. Select a wine or wines that please your palate and stick with it. Needless to say, fine wines do not come in gallon jugs and cost one dollar per.

A sounder method for an amateur is to discover a wine merchant who is truly reputable and who has a knowledge of wine to match his character. They are admittedly rare, but once discovered they can be invaluable. It is also an aid to be familiar with the name of the shipper on the label.

WINE TEMPERATURE

Temperature is important in the service of wine and there is no hocus-pocus involved in achieving these temperatures. In general, white wines and rosé wines should be chilled on the bottom or lower shelf of the refrigerator or in a wine bucket with ice and kept chilled throughout the meal.

Dry red wines are usually served at a temperature slightly cooler than room temperature. Except in hot climates, however, they may be served at room temperature.

Champagnes should be served well chilled. The best method of chilling champagne is in the refrigerator or in a bucket filled with ice. When champagne is to be served on sudden notice, it may be chilled in a bucket of ice but with coarse salt added to further lower the temperature. Care should be taken that the salt does not enter the bottle after it is opened. Swizzle sticks should never be served with champagne except to an invalid whose stomach cannot support the sparkle. Swizzle sticks destroy in a second what required a miracle of years to produce.

The ideal temperatures at which wines should be served are as follows:

Dry white wines:	47° to 54°
Sweet white wines:	44° to 47°
Young dry red wines:	54° to 60°
Old red wines:	59° to 65°
Champagnes:	42° to 45°

CHAPTER FOURTEEN

BEVERAGES

BREWED TEA, ENGLISH STYLE

Partially fill a teapot with boiling water and let stand. Meanwhile, into a kettle measure as much water as desired for making tea, allowing one cup per person. Place the kettle on high heat and bring to a full boil.

Drain and dry teapot and add one teaspoon of tea or one tea bag for each cup of water in the kettle. Pour the boiling water over the tea, cover the pot and let it steep for three to five minutes. Serve immediately.

If more tea is desired, discard old leaves and restart with fresh leaves.

The English frown on the use of tea bags. They consider them suitable only for picnics. Use tea leaves, if possible.

CAFE BRULOT *16 servings*

3 broken sticks cinnamon
Shredded peel of 2 oranges
Shredded peel of 1 lemon
1 teaspoon whole allspice
16 demitasse cubes sugar
1 cup cognac or bourbon
5 cups strong, dark-roasted, freshly made coffee

1. In a chafing dish, mix the cinnamon, fruit peels and allspice. Add the sugar.
2. Add all but one tablespoon of the cognac and let it warm. Ignite the remaining tablespoon and add flaming to the dish. When the cognac in the dish ignites, ladle the flaming liquid over the sugar to melt it.
3. Add the coffee and stir well. When piping hot, ladle into demitasse cups, using a strainer.

BORANI *About 8 servings*

This could be called a Pakistani cocktail. Made with yoghurt and highly seasoned with black pepper it is surprisingly refreshing.

2 cups yoghurt
Salt and freshly ground black pepper to taste
1 quart water
8 strips lemon peel
⅛ teaspoon chili powder
½ teaspoon fresh chopped mint or ¼ teaspoon dried mint *(cont'd)*

1. Combine the ingredients in a cocktail shaker or in a mixing bowl. Shake well or beat with a wire whisk until well blended.

2. Adjust the seasonings according to taste. Refrigerate until ready to use in well-chilled cocktail glasses.

BLOODY MARY

A bloody Mary is any drink made with tomato juice and vodka. It may be served over ice cubes or it may be shaken with crushed ice and strained into a chilled glass such as a sour glass. An excellent recipe for a bloody Mary is made with one part vodka, two parts tomato juice, the juice of half a lemon, one teaspoon Worcestershire sauce, salt and freshly ground black pepper to taste. Pour these ingredients over crushed ice in a cocktail shaker and shake vigorously. Strain into a sour glass.

MARTINI

The original martini was a sweet drink made with gin and Italian vermouth. Eventually a dry vermouth was substituted and today it is a recommended ingredient for the martini. Actually, martinis can be divided into three categories. These are the martini, the dry martini and the extra-dry martini. Generally speaking a simple martini is made with three parts gin and one part dry vermouth; a dry martini contains four to seven parts gin and one part dry vermouth; the extra-dry martini is made by using gin in any proportion and a dash of vermouth as a gesture. The liquids should be poured over cracked ice, stirred until thoroughly chilled, then strained into martini glasses. Garnishes for the martini and dry martini are green olives plain or stuffed; for the extra-dry martini a twist of lemon peel. The Gibson is a dry martini garnished with a pickled onion.

MANHATTAN

There are principally two categories of manhattan, the sweet and the dry. The sweet version is made with one part sweet vermouth, two parts Bourbon or rye whiskey and, if desired, a dash of Angostura bitters. The dry manhattan is made with one part dry vermouth and two parts Bourbon or rye whiskey. These ingredients are poured over ice cubes and are stirred until chilled. The drink is then poured into a manhattan glass. A sweet manhattan is garnished with a maraschino cherry; a dry manhattan with an olive or a twist of lemon.

WHISKEY SOUR

A whiskey sour is made with one part sugar syrup, two parts lemon juice and eight parts rye or Bourbon. The ingredients are poured over shaved ice or cracked

(*cont'd*)

ice and are shaken vigorously in a cocktail shaker. The liquid is then strained into sour glasses and garnished, if desired, with a maraschino cherry and half an orange slice.

OLD-FASHIONED

To make an old-fashioned place one small lump of sugar in an old-fashioned glass and add barely enough lukewarm water to dissolve it. Sprinkle with Angostura bitters and crush with a muddler until thoroughly blended. Add a little rye or Bourbon whiskey and stir until sugar is thoroughly dissolved. Add cracked ice to fill the glass and pour over it one or two jiggers of rye or Bourbon.

DAIQUIRI

The daiquiri is made by shaking one part sugar syrup, two parts lime juice and eight parts light rum with finely crushed ice. The cocktail should be strained into a cocktail glass.

TOM COLLINS

To make a Tom Collins combine one tablespoon of sugar syrup, the juice of one lemon and two jiggers of gin. Stir well and add ice cubes to fill the glass. Add carbonated water to taste, stir once and serve.

TALL DRINKS

Americano: Pour into an eight-ounce glass over cracked ice an ounce of Italian bitters such as Carpano, three ounces (two jiggers) sweet vermouth and enough soda water to fill the glass. Stir slightly. Garnish with a twist of lemon peel.

Black Velvet: Pour chilled champagne and chilled stout slowly and simultaneously into a fourteen-ounce glass.

Screwdriver: Pour over cracked ice in a tall glass one and one-half ounces vodka (one jigger) and four ounces orange juice. Or substitute grapefruit juice. Stir.

PINEAPPLE-ORANGE PUNCH *6 servings*

2 cups unsweetened pineapple juice
2 cups orange juice
¼ cup lemon juice
1 pint any flavor sherbet
Fresh mint sprigs

1. Mix the juices.
2. Divide the sherbet into six tall glasses, add the juices and stir slightly. Garnish with mint.

BORDELAISE CHAMPAGNE PUNCH

One of the finest apéritifs made in France is called Lillet. It is excellent when served over an ice cube with a twist of orange peel. It also makes an extraordinary punch when poured over ice with champagne. To make the punch pour any desired amount of champagne over ice and add Lillet to taste. Add twists of orange peel if desired.

SUMMER PUNCH *About 8 servings*

1 six-ounce can frozen lemon juice
⅔ cup light corn syrup
1 quart ginger ale
1 tray ice cubes

1. Empty the lemon juice into a large pitcher and stir in the syrup.
2. At serving time, add the ginger ale and ice cubes. Mix well and serve immediately.

SHERRIED GRAPEFRUIT JUICE *6 servings*

2 cups grapefruit juice, fresh or made with juice concentrate
¾ cup dry sherry

Combine the liquids and chill well.

MULLED WINE *About 12 servings*

1 quart burgundy or claret
Yellow peel of 1 orange and 1 lemon
2 to 3 inches stick cinnamon
1 whole nutmeg, crushed
6 whole cloves
1 tablespoon sugar

1. Mix all the ingredients in a saucepan and simmer gently five to ten minutes.
2. Strain to remove the spices and serve hot.

BASIC TEA FORMULA FOR PUNCH *1 quart*

1 quart water
¼ cup tea in bulk, or 12 tea bags

In a saucepan bring the water to a rolling boil. Remove from the heat. Add the tea immediately and let steep five minutes. Stir and, if bulk tea was used, strain. If tea bags were used, remove them. Cool the tea to room temperature.

LUCHOW'S MAY WINE BOWL *8 to 10 cups*

½ cup dried woodruff
¼ cup superfine granulated sugar
½ cup cognac
2 bottles Rhine or Moselle wine
1 bottle champagne or charged water
½ cup whole fresh strawberries (*cont'd*)

1. Tie the woodruff in a small piece of cheesecloth. Place it in a bowl and add the sugar, cognac and one-half bottle of the wine. Cover closely and let stand overnight.

2. Strain the woodruff-wine mixture into a punch bowl containing ice cubes or a large chunk of ice. Add the remaining still wine, champagne and strawberries. Serve in stemmed glasses.

JAMAICAN PUNCH *About 25 servings*

¼ pound lump sugar
Oranges
1 quart clear, strong tea
2 cups lemon juice
1 quart gin
2 cups (1 pint) Jamaica rum
1 teaspoon Angostura bitters
1 quart chilled ginger ale
Garnishes

1. Rub sugar lumps on the oranges so they may absorb the oil from the orange rind.

2. Place the sugar in a punch bowl. Add the cool tea and mix until the sugar has dissolved. Add the lemon juice, gin, rum and bitters.

3. When ready to serve, pour in the ginger ale. Add a large block of ice and garnish with mint, cherries, orange slices, etc.

TROPICAL TEA PUNCH *About 25 cups*

1 quart freshly brewed tea
1 cup sugar
2 cups (1 pint) cognac
½ cup (4 ounces) light rum
1 can frozen pineapple chunks, defrosted, with liquid
2 bottles dry champagne, chilled
Fresh peeled fruit, cut in cubes, and melon balls for garnish

1. When the tea has cooled to room temperature, stir in the sugar until it has dissolved.

2. Combine the tea, cognac, rum and pineapple chunks. Chill thoroughly. Meanwhile, fill a ring mold or a star mold with water and freeze.

3. When ready to serve, pour the tea mixture into a punch bowl. Unmold the ice and add to the bowl. Pour in the champagne and garnish with fresh fruit and melon balls.

SPARKLING BURGUNDY PUNCH *About 24 servings*

1 quart freshly brewed tea
¼ cup (2 ounces) rum
¼ cup (2 ounces) cognac
Juice of 2 lemons
1 quart sparkling water, chilled
1 bottle sparkling Burgundy
1 cup sugar syrup made by briefly boiling 2 cups sugar with 1 cup water

(cont'd)

1. When the tea has cooled to room temperature, add the rum, cognac and lemon juice. Chill.

2. When ready to serve, pour the mixture into a punch bowl. Add sufficient ice to chill and stir in the sparkling water and sparkling Burgundy. Sweeten to taste with sugar syrup and serve immediately.

AGE OF INNOCENCE CUP *About 60 punch cups*

1 quart freshly brewed tea
2 quarts cold water
2 cups fresh lemon juice
1 quart fresh orange juice
6 cups (1½ quarts) fresh cranberry juice
1 quart ginger ale, chilled
2 cups sugar syrup, made by briefly boiling 2 cups sugar with 1 cup water

1. When the tea has cooled to room temperature, pour into a punch bowl. Add the remaining ingredients except the ginger ale and sugar syrup.

2. Just before serving, add a block of ice to the bowl and pour in the ginger ale. Sweeten to taste with sugar syrup.

SWEDISH GLOGG *About 20 punch cup servings*

¾ cup water
3 cardamom seeds
8 whole cloves
2 tablespoons grated orange peel
¼ cup blanched almonds
½ cup seedless raisins
1 cup prunes
1 bottle (24 ounces) red Bordeaux wine
1 bottle (24 ounces) port
1¾ cups vodka
Sugar to taste (optional)

1. Bring the water to a boil, add the spices and orange peel tied in a cheesecloth bag, cover and simmer ten minutes.

2. Add the almonds, raisins, prunes and enough additional water to cover the fruit. Cover and simmer twenty minutes.

3. Add the Bordeaux wine, port and vodka. Bring to a boil and remove immediately from the heat. Cool and allow to stand in the refrigerator in a covered container overnight or longer. When ready to serve, remove the spice bag. Reheat the punch and add sugar to taste. Serve in heated mugs or small glasses with a few almonds and seedless raisins in each.

CHAMPAGNE PUNCH *20 servings*

6 lumps sugar
Dash of bitters
1 cup high-quality cognac
3 bottles chilled French champagne

(*cont'd*)

1. Place the sugar lumps in a punch bowl. Sprinkle with bitters and add the cognac.

2. At serving time, uncap the champagne and add to the bowl. Add ice. If desired, decorate with fruit.

CHAMPAGNE WEDDING PUNCH *About 70 servings*

- 10 fifth bottles brut champagne
- ¾ cup cognac
- ¾ cup yellow Chartreuse
- ¾ cup Cointreau
- 3 fifths sparkling water
- Sugar to taste
- Slices of fresh oranges, lemons and pineapples
- Fresh mint

1. Mix all the liquids, adding sugar to taste.

2. Set a block of ice in a punch bowl and pour in the mixture. Garnish with the fruit slices and mint sprigs.

JAMES BEARD'S PUNCH *50 to 60 servings*

- 5 quarts strawberries
- 5 cups finely granulated sugar
- 5 bottles Moselle
- 10 bottles champagne
- 3 bottles claret

Place hulled strawberries in a large glass bowl set in cracked ice. Sprinkle with sugar and pour the Moselle over them. Let stand two to six hours. When ready to serve, add chilled champagne and claret for the color. Serve with a berry in each glass.

MOSELLE PUNCH *20 to 30 servings*

- 6 oranges, sliced very thin
- 1 cup finely granulated sugar
- 2 bottles Moselle or other dry white wine
- 1 large block of ice
- 3 bottles champagne, chilled

1. Place the orange slices in a bowl and sprinkle with sugar. Pour one bottle of the Moselle over the fruit and let stand one hour or longer.

2. Pour the mixture over the block of ice in a punch bowl. Add the remaining Moselle and the champagne.

TOM AND JERRY *12 8-ounce servings*

- 12 eggs, separated
- 6 tablespoons sugar
- Grated nutmeg
- 1 cup (8 ounces) Jamaican rum
- 1½ cups (12 ounces) whisky or brandy
- Hot milk or boiling water

(*cont'd*)

1. In an electric mixer, beat the egg yolks until thick and lemon colored. Gradually add the sugar and one teaspoon grated nutmeg, beating until the mixture is very thick. Beat the egg whites until stiff and fold into the mixture. Stir in the rum and chill several hours.

2. To serve, transfer the mixture to a punch bowl or pitcher. Ladle or pour about a tablespoon of the mixture into each preheated mug. Add a jigger (one ounce) whisky or brandy to each serving and fill the mug with hot milk or boiling water. Stir and top with grated nutmeg.

EGGNOG *About 40 punch-cup servings*

12 eggs, separated
1 cup granulated sugar
1 cup bourbon whisky
1 cup cognac
½ teaspoon salt
3 pints heavy cream
Grated nutmeg

1. In an electric mixer, beat the egg yolks with the sugar until thick and lemon colored. Slowly add the bourbon and cognac, while beating at slow speed. Chill several hours.

2. Add the salt to the egg whites and beat until almost stiff, or until the beaten whites form a peak that bends slightly. Whip the cream until stiff. Fold the whipped cream into the yolk mixture, then fold in the beaten egg whites. Chill one hour.

3. When ready to serve, sprinkle the top with freshly grated nutmeg. Serve in punch cups with a spoon. If desired, add one or two cups milk to the yolk mixture for a thinner eggnog.

CHAPTER FIFTEEN

HERBS AND SPICES

One of the most surprising developments in the world of food has occurred on American spice shelves since the end of World War II. The public appetite has been sharpened for seasonings that were scarcely known to any but professional chefs two decades ago.

"Such popular herbs as orégano, rosemary, basil and tarragon were common to our forefathers," a spokesman for the American Spice Trade Association said recently. "By the twenties, however, they were almost unknown.

"There's a curious thing about whole spices, too. Until the early nineteenth century most homes had spice mills or mortars and pestles for grinding their spices. Commercially ground spices were unknown; yet by the time of World War II few Americans had ever seen a peppercorn or fresh ginger. Now, black and white peppercorns, whole nutmegs and such seeds as mustard, anise, fennel, caraway, poppy and cardamom are commonplace."

Spices, whether fresh or dried, should be added to dishes according to taste. Many sources state that the pungency of dried herbs is twice that of fresh herbs; but this is relative, since the flavor of dried herbs diminishes with age and the keeping condition of the herb on the shelf. Dried herbs should be kept in tightly closed containers and away from heat.

ALLSPICE, WHOLE

Fish and Shrimp: Add 4 or 5 whole allspice to the cooking water when poaching fish or cooking shrimp.

Fruit Compote (dried and fresh): Add 4 or 5 whole allspice to the syrup before cooking the fruit.

Meats:

Beef, lamb and veal: Add 4 or 5 whole allspice to stews and pot roasts.

Poultry: Add 4 or 5 whole allspice when fricasseeing chicken.

Soups: Add 4 or 5 whole allspice to the stock pot when making soup from beef, ham bone, lamb, poultry, seafood or veal. Especially delicious in green pea and ham soup.

ANISE SEED

Appetizers:

Cheese canapés, shellfish canapés: Sprinkle tops lightly with whole anise seed.

Mild-flavored cheese: Blend whole anise seed to taste with cream cheese, cottage cheese and other mild-flavored cheese.

Fruits:

Fruit compotes (dried or fresh): Add a few whole anise seed to syrup when cooking the fruit.

Raw fruits: Dip fruit lightly into whole anise seed to give unusual flavor variation.

Fruit pies: Instead of cinnamon or nutmeg, sprinkle ¼ teaspoon whole anise seed over fruit pies before baking.

Cookies: Sprinkle whole anise seed on tops of cookies before baking.

BASIL LEAVES

Eggs: Add a small amount of basil to scrambled eggs, egg soufflés, deviled eggs or egg sandwich mixtures.

Fish and Shellfish: Add basil to taste to chowders, stews, and baked, broiled and poached fish.

Stuffing: Add basil to fish (or other seafood) and eggplant stuffing.

Tomatoes: Add basil to taste to most cooked tomato dishes, salads, aspics and soups.

BAY LEAF, WHOLE

Appetizers:

Tomato juice, clam and tomato bouillon: Add 1 bay leaf to ingredients, heat and chill.

Fish: Add 1 to 2 bay leaves to chowders, court bouillon, kabobs, marinades, stews and pilaffs.

Meats: Place a bay leaf in the bottom of a roasting pan for beef, lamb or veal oven roast or pot roast. Add 1 bay leaf to the cooking water of corned beef and tongue. Add 1 to 2 bay leaves to beef, lamb, poultry or veal stews and fricassees.

Sauces: Add ½ bay leaf to ingredients for tomato, meat or seafood sauces.

Soups: Add 1 to 2 bay leaves to soup stocks made from any of the meats, poultry or seafood.

Stuffings: Crush a bay leaf and add to stuffings for fish, pork or poultry.

CARAWAY SEED, WHOLE

Appetizers: Add caraway seed to taste to cheese spreads, dips or wafers.

Breads:

Rye bread, onion bread: Add 1 tablespoon whole caraway seed to the dough and sprinkle over the top before baking.

Biscuits and rolls: Mix caraway seed with coarse salt and sprinkle on the tops before baking.

Cakes and Cookies: Mix caraway seed with the batter or sprinkle on the top before baking.

Fruit:

Baked apples: Mix caraway seed with sugar and spoon into the cavities before baking.

Apple pies: Mix 1 teaspoon caraway seed with the flour for pastry using 2 cups flour.

Meats: Add to beef, lamb or veal stew. Tie seeds in a bag before adding if desired.

CARDAMOM SEED, WHOLE

Beverages:

Coffee: Place a whole cardamom seed in the cup. Fill with hot coffee.

Hot spiced wines: Crush cardamom along with other spices, tie in a bag, add to wines and heat.

Fruits:

Baked apples, dried or fresh fruit salad: Mix fruit with whole cardamom seed. Remove seed before serving. Chill.

Fruit compote: Add 2 to 3 whole seed to the syrup.

Grape jelly: Crush 3 to 4 cardamom seed, tie in a bag and add to the jelly while it is cooking.

CELERY SEED

Appetizers: Add celery seed to taste to cheese, seafood or ham mixtures for canapés or sandwiches or sprinkle the seed lightly on the tops.

Tomato or vegetable juice cocktail: Add ¼ to ½ teaspoon celery seed to the juice and heat.

Meats:

Beef, lamb, pork and veal: Add 1/4 to 1/2 teaspoon celery seed to meat loaf, stew, pie and stuffing. Add 1/4 teaspoon celery seed to each cup flour used in pastry for meat pies.

Salads: Add celery seed to taste to fruit, seafood, chicken, potato, cabbage and other vegetable salads. Add 1/4 to 1/2 teaspoon celery seed to French dressing or mayonnaise.

Vegetables: Add celery seed to taste to stewed tomatoes, eggplant, potatoes, cabbage and cucumbers.

CHERVIL LEAVES

Cheese: Add chervil to taste to cottage or cream cheese for dips, canapé and sandwich spreads and salads.

Eggs: Add chervil to taste in scrambled eggs, omelets, egg casseroles and creamed eggs.

Meats:

Beef, lamb, pork and veal: Mix chervil with salt and black pepper and rub on all sides of oven roast before cooking. Add to pot roasts and stews shortly before cooking time is up.

Salads:

Beet, celery, cucumber, lettuce, potato, tomato, cooked vegetable and raw vegetable salads: Blend with salad dressing and add.

Sauces:

Béarnaise, butter, cream and tomato sauce: Add chervil to sauces shortly before cooking time is up.

Soups:

Spinach soup, tomato soup: Add chervil to taste shortly before cooking time is up.

Vegetables:

Beets, eggplant, spinach, braised lettuce: Add chervil to taste to melted butter or margarine. Pour over vegetables.

STICK CINNAMON

Beverages:

Coffee, hot chocolate: Use stick cinnamon as a muddler for stirring. Gives a delicious flavor.

Desserts:

Baked custard, bread or rice pudding: Place a cinnamon stick in casserole, add custard or pudding mixture and bake.

Dessert sauces: Add a cinnamon stick to the mixture when making apple, chocolate, lemon or orange sauce.

Fruits:

Fruit compotes (dried and fresh): Add a stick of cinnamon to the syrup when cooking fruit.

Spiced jam and jelly: Add 2 to 3 sticks of cinnamon to conserve, jam and jelly mixtures. Remove and discard before ladling the mixture into jars.

Spiced canned fruit for meat accompaniments: Tie stick cinnamon, whole allspice and cloves in a bag and add to the syrup drained from the can. Boil 3 minutes. Add fruit and cook 2 minutes.

CLOVES, WHOLE

Appetizers:

Cranberry juice cocktail, tomato juice cocktail: Add 3 to 4 whole cloves, heat and chill.

Beverages:

Hot cider, hot tea, mulled wine, hot chocolate: Add 1 to 2 whole cloves for each serving.

Fruit (all fruits):

Baked fruit, preserves, jam or jelly, stewed and poached fruit: Tie 6 to 8 whole cloves in a bag and add while cooking. Allspice and cinnamon may be added also.

Sauces:

Chocolate, fruit (all fruits), tomato, meat and fish sauces: Add 2 to 3 whole cloves while cooking. Remove from sauce and discard when serving.

Soup:

Soup stocks (beef, ham, lamb, poultry and veal), and bean, beet, onion, potato, tomato and pea soups: Add 3 to 4 whole cloves while cooking. Remove and discard before serving.

Vegetables:

Beets, carrots, squash, sweet potatoes: Add 2 to 3 whole cloves to the cooking water.

CORIANDER SEED

Beverages:

Coffee: Crush coriander seed and place one in each coffee cup. Fill with hot coffee.

Fruits:

Apples, pears, dried fruit: Add coriander seed while cooking.

Marinades:

Beef, lamb and pork roasts, kebabs, fish, poultry: Add coriander seed to marinades. Heat and pour over meat. Let stand several hours in refrigerator.

Soup Stocks: Add ¼ teaspoon coriander seed to soup stock while it is cooking.

CUMIN SEED

Appetizers:

Canapés and sandwich spreads: Blend cumin seed to taste with Cheddar, cream and cottage cheeses and chicken salad. Use as spread for canapé or sandwich filling.

Bread: In bread recipes, replace caraway seed with cumin seed, using half the amount.

Cheese: Sprinkle Cheddar, cottage, cream cheese with cumin seed before serving.

Cookies: Sprinkle over cookies before baking.

Eggs: Add cumin seed to taste to deviled eggs, sandwich spreads and salads.

Meats:

Meat balls, meat loaf, hamburgers, curry, chile con carne and Mexican dishes: Add cumin seed to taste.

Marinade: Add cumin seed to taste to marinade for kebabs.

Pies: Add ¼ teaspoon cumin seed to fruit pies along with other spices before putting on top crust.

Pilaff: Add cumin seed to taste to fish, poultry or meat pilaffs.

DILL SEED

Cheese Dishes:

Canapés, sandwiches, salads: Add dill seed to taste or sprinkle over the top.

Fish:

Halibut and herring, salmon and other fat fish: Add a few dill seed to the sauces or, if poached, add to the water.

Meats:

Lamb chops: Sprinkle chops with a few dill seed before broiling.
Lamb roast: Place a few dill seed in roasting pan before cooking.
Lamb stew: Add ¼ to ½ teaspoon dill seed to the stew while it is cooking.

Pie:

Apple pie: Sprinkle a few dill seed over apples before baking.

Salads:

Cabbage, cucumber, beet, tossed green, potato and seafood salads: Add dill seed to taste.

Salad Dressings:

Boiled dressing, French dressing, sour cream dressing: Add dill seed to taste.

Soups:

Cabbage, beet, dried bean, cucumber and tomato soups: Add dill seed to taste.

Vegetables:

Beets, broccoli, Brussels sprouts, cabbage, cucumbers, snap beans, sauerkraut, turnips: Add ½ teaspoon dill seed to cooking water or add to the melted butter and pour over vegetables.

DILL WEED

Fish:

Shrimp, lobster, salmon and other fish or seafood: Add to the water before poaching. Use sprigs of fresh dill as a garnish for poached fish platters.

Meats:

Meat loaves, meat balls: Blend with meats before cooking.

Salads: Almost all cold vegetable, fish or seafood salads benefit by the addition of fresh or dried chopped dill.

FENNEL SEED

Bread and Rolls: Sprinkle fennel seed over the tops before baking.

Cakes and Cookies: Sprinkle over tops before baking.

Cheese: Sprinkle on mild-flavored cheeses, such as mild Italian cheese.

Fish and Shellfish:

Baked: Sprinkle fennel seed over the top before baking.
Poached: Add a few fennel seed to the cooking water.

Fruits:

Baked apples: Mix fennel seed with sugar.
Apple pie: Sprinkle fennel seed lightly over the top before baking.

Meat and Poultry (beef, lamb, pork, chicken and duck):

Stews and braised: Add ¼ to ½ teaspoon fennel seed to water before cooking.
Roasts: Place a few fennel seed in the roasting pan before cooking.

Pilaff:

Seafood
Lamb
Poultry } Add ¼ to ½ teaspoon fennel seed to the rice mixture before cooking.

Salads: Blend ¼ to ½ teaspoon fennel seed with dressing for seafood and green vegetables.

Sauerkraut: Add fennel seed to taste while cooking.

GINGER

Beverages: Ginger syrup for carbonated beverages.

Fruit:

Apples and pears: Add ginger to the syrup when poaching or stewing apples and pears.

Spiced fruit: Tie a ginger root, along with whole allspice, cloves and stick cinnamon, in a bag and add to syrup when making spiced fruit, using either fresh or canned fruit.

Meats: Add ginger root or powdered ginger to any meat stews while cooking. Use with chicken, beef, veal and pork. Ginger is most frequently used with meats cooked in the Oriental manner.

Soup stocks: Add ginger to the pot when making beef, lamb, veal or chicken stock.

MACE

Appetizers:

Tomato juice: Add a blade of mace to the juice, heat and chill. Remove before serving.

Sauces: Add mace to sauces for chicken or seafood.

Soup Stock: Add 1 to 2 blades of mace to the pot when making chicken or fish stock for soup or consommé.

Vegetables: Add mace to the cooking water of snap beans, carrots, onions, celery, potatoes, cauliflower.

MARJORAM

Egg Dishes: Add a small amount of marjoram to creamed and scrambled eggs, omelets and soufflés.

Fish: Sprinkle lightly over fish before baking.

Meats: Sprinkle lightly over beef, lamb, or veal roast or add to stews 10 to 15 minutes before cooking time is up. Add to meat loaf or meat balls.

Poultry: Rub inside and outside of chicken, duck or turkey lightly with crushed or ground marjoram before cooking. (Omit if birds are stuffed with herbed stuffing.)

Salads: Add marjoram leaves to taste to vegetables, chicken, egg or seafood salads.

Shellfish: Add marjoram to taste to bisques, chowders, casseroles, salads, and sauces for seafood.

Stuffings: Add marjoram to taste to stuffings for poultry, fish, onions, squash and eggplant.

Vegetables: Add marjoram to cooking water for carrots, kale, onions, peas, spinach and zucchini.

MUSTARD SEED

Pickles: Add mustard seed to beet, cucumber, green tomato, snap bean, cabbage and onion pickles and relish. The amount varies with the size of the recipe.

Vegetables: Add ½ teaspoon mustard seed to the cooking water for broccoli, Brussels sprouts and cabbage. Add mustard seed to taste to sauerkraut before cooking. Add ¼ to ½ teaspoon mustard seed to coleslaw.

NUTMEG

Beverages: Sprinkle a few grains of grated nutmeg in hot or cold milk drinks, such as chocolate milk and eggnog.

Fruit: Add grated nutmeg to apple and pear desserts.

Puddings: Add grated nutmeg to bread, butterscotch, banana, chocolate, custard, rice and tapioca puddings.

Sauces: Add grated nutmeg to apple, custard, lemon, mushroom and orange sauces.

Vegetables: Sprinkle grated nutmeg over snap beans, lima beans, corn, cauliflower, kale, potatoes, spinach, squash and sweet potatoes.

OREGANO LEAVES

Appetizers:

Tomato juice, vegetable juice, tomato-clam juice: Add orégano to taste. Heat and chill.

Meat:

Beef, lamb, pork and veal roast and stews: Mix orégano with salad or olive oil and rub over roast. Add orégano to stews about 10 minutes before cooking time is up.

Marinades: Add orégano to marinades for kebabs, roasts and chicken.

Poultry: Mix orégano with salad or olive oil and rub over chicken before broiling or roasting. Or mix orégano with flour along with salt and ground black pepper for dredging chicken before frying.

Salads: Add orégano to taste to potato, kidney bean, seafood, tomato, green vegetable and meat salads. Add orégano to taste to salad dressings.

Sauces: Add orégano to taste to cream sauces, spaghetti, chili, tomato and meat and seafood sauces.

Seafood: Rub orégano over fish before broiling or baking. Rub inside of fish with orégano before stuffing. Mix orégano with butter and pour over baked or broiled fish before cooking, using about ¼ teaspoon orégano to 2 tablespoons melted butter. Mix orégano with batter or flour or bread crumbs for coating fish, shrimp, scallops or seafood croquettes for deep frying.

Soup:

Tomato soup, seafood broths, soup or chowder, bean soup, corn soup, green pea soup: Add orégano to taste 5 minutes before cooking time is up.

Vegetables: Add about ¼ teaspoon orégano to each 2 tablespoons melted butter or margarine and pour over onions, peas, spinach, green beans, potatoes, corn; mix lightly. Sprinkle orégano in stewed tomatoes 5 minutes before cooking time is up or sprinkle over sliced fresh tomatoes. Add orégano to water in which kale, mustard or turnip greens are cooked.

PARSLEY, CHOPPED OR FLAKED

Bouquet Garni: Tie parsley in a bag along with 2 to 3 other herbs and add to stews, soups, etc., 10 to 15 minutes before cooking time is up for a fresh herb flavor.

Garnish: Sprinkle over canapés, soups, vegetable juice cocktail, salads, fish and other seafood, casseroles and vegetable dishes.

Sauces: Add parsley to taste to egg, meat, poultry and seafood sauces.

Salads: Add parsley to taste to all seafood, poultry, potato and egg salads.

Stews: Add parsley to taste to beef, chicken, fish, lamb or veal stews 10 to 15 minutes before cooking time is up.

Vegetables: Add to melted butter and toss lightly with all vegetables.

BLACK PEPPER

Appetizers:

Tomato juice, vegetable juice, tomato-clam broth: Add whole black pepper and heat. Serve the juices chilled and the broth hot.

Cheese: Add freshly ground black pepper to cheese sauces, cheese spreads for canapés and sandwiches.

Eggs: Sprinkle black pepper over eggs.

Marinades: Add black pepper to marinades for fish, poultry, beef or lamb roasts and kebabs.

Soups: Add black pepper to the pot when making stock from beef, lamb, poultry or seafood. Add black pepper to Brunswick stew. Add freshly ground black pepper to seafood bisque, oyster stew and chicken soup.

Vegetables: Freshly ground black pepper is delicious over vegetables, especially over corn, cucumbers and tomatoes.

POPPY SEED

Bread, Cakes and Cookies: Toast poppy seed in moderate oven (350° F.) 18 minutes or heat in a pan over low heat. Sprinkle, while warm, over unbaked cakes, cookies, bread and rolls. Stir poppy seed into jam, fruit and honey fillings for coffeecakes and sweet rolls.

Noodles: Sprinkle toasted poppy seed over cooked noodles and toss lightly with butter or margarine.

Salads: Sprinkle fruit salads with poppy seed.

ROSEMARY LEAVES

Beverages:

Fruit punches: Steep ½ to 1 teaspoon rosemary leaves 5 minutes in hot fruit juice, cool and add to the cold punch mixture.

Egg Dishes: Add a pinch of rosemary to egg casseroles, omelets and scrambled eggs.

Fish Dishes: Add a pinch of rosemary to fish or shellfish casseroles and stews, or sprinkle rosemary over fish before broiling or baking.

Meat: Rub beef, lamb, pork or veal lightly with rosemary before roasting; add rosemary to stews 10 to 15 minutes before cooking time is up.

Poultry: Sprinkle inside of chicken or turkey or duck lightly before cooking. Add rosemary to creamed chicken to taste.

Soups: Add rosemary to taste to chicken, peas, spinach, potato and fish soups.

SAFFRON (a little goes a long way)

Bouillabaisse (fish and shellfish): Add about ¼ teaspoon.

Breads and Rolls: Sift ¼ to 1 teaspoon saffron with the flour; the amount depends upon the size of the recipe.

Chicken: Add ¼ to ½ teaspoon to chicken dishes; the amount varies with the size of recipe.

Pilaffs: Add ¼ to ½ teaspoon to pilaffs made with chicken, lamb or seafood.

Saffron Rice: Add ¼ to ½ teaspoon saffron to rice.

SAGE LEAVES

Bread:

Sage biscuit or sage corn bread: Add ground or rubbed sage to the dry ingredients, using about ¾ teaspoon to 2 cups flour or corn meal. Serve with chicken or seafood.

Cheese:

Cheddar, cottage and cream cheeses: Add ground or rubbed sage to taste and serve as a spread for canapés and sandwiches or with salads. This is especially delicious with salads made of poultry, seafood or raw green vegetables.

Meat:

Beef, lamb, pork or veal roasts or stews: Rub sage over outside of roast before cooking. Add sage to taste when making homemade pork sausage. Add sage to taste to stews 5 to 10 minutes before cooking time is up. Add sage to taste to stuffed lamb roast, veal or pork chops.

Marinades: Add sage to marinade for beef, lamb, pork or veal roasts, kebabs, chicken or fish.

Poultry:

Chicken, turkey or goose: Sage-fried chicken—Mix sage with flour into which roll chicken before frying, add about ¾ teaspoon sage to ¾ cup flour. Add sage to taste to stuffing for chicken, turkey and goose.

Salad Dressings: Add sage to taste to French dressing or mayonnaise for poultry, seafood or vegetable salads.

Soups:

Chicken and seafood soups and chowders: Add sage to taste.

Vegetables:

Lima beans, onions, zucchini squash, eggplant, peas, potatoes and tomatoes: Add a pinch of ground sage to each 2 tablespoons melted butter or margarine. Pour over cooked vegetables and toss lightly.

SAVORY LEAVES

The flavors of summer and winter savory are markedly similar. The major difference between the herbs is size and color.

Eggs: Add savory to taste in all egg dishes.

Chicken: Add savory to the melted butter used to broil or bake chicken. Add savory to chicken or meat pies.

Meats (beef, lamb, pork, ham and veal):

Hamburgers: Add savory to taste along with salt and black pepper to hamburger meat.

Roasts: Rub surface of meat with a mixture of savory to taste, salt and black pepper.

Stews: Add savory to taste 10 to 15 minutes before cooking time is up.

Salads: Add savory to taste to tomato and green vegetable salads.

Sauces: Add savory to taste to fish and meat sauces shortly before cooking time is up.

Seafood: Add savory to taste in seafood casseroles, pies, chowders and soups. Rub savory on fish before broiling or baking.

Soups: Add savory to taste to tomato, vegetable, seafood and bouillon 10 to 15 minutes before cooking time is up.

Stuffing: Add savory along with sage to stuffing for poultry, fish and pork.

SESAME SEED

Toast sesame seed in a moderate oven (350° F.) 20 minutes or heat in a pan over low heat.

Bread and Rolls: Brush bread and rolls with whole beaten egg and sprinkle generously with toasted sesame seed before baking.

Cakes and Cookies: Stir toasted sesame seed instead of chopped nuts into cake or cookie batter or sprinkle over the top before baking.

Mild-Flavored Cheeses: Mix toasted sesame seed with cheese canapé or sandwich spreads or sprinkle with toasted sesame seed.

Garnishes: Sprinkle toasted sesame seed instead of buttered bread crumbs over fish and casseroles before baking. Sprinkle over fruit, vegetable, seafood, chicken or egg salad.

Soups: Sprinkle cream soups lightly with toasted sesame seed just before serving.

Vegetables: Mix toasted sesame seed with melted butter or margarine, pour over asparagus, green beans, carrots, potatoes, squash and spinach.

TARRAGON LEAVES

Appetizers:

Tomato juice, vegetable juice: Add tarragon to taste, heat and chill.

Eggs: Add tarragon to taste to scrambled eggs, omelets, deviled eggs, egg sandwich spreads and soufflés.

Fish and Shellfish: Rub tarragon on both sides of fish before broiling or baking or add to melted butter used for basting.

Meats: Rub tarragon on both sides of steaks or lamb or pork chops before cooking.
Marinades: Add tarragon to marinades for beef, lamb, pork, fish or chicken.

Poultry:
Chicken and duck: Add tarragon to melted butter used for basting chicken or duck while cooking or sprinkle lightly with tarragon before cooking.

Salads: Mix tarragon to taste with salad dressing used on cabbage, chicken, seafood, tomato and green salads.

Sauces: Add tarragon to taste to Béarnaise, Hollandaise, mayonnaise, mustard, tartar, tomato and egg sauces.

Soups: Add tarragon to taste to chicken, consommé, mushroom, seafood or tomato soups shortly before cooking time is up.

THYME LEAVES

Appetizers:
Clam juice cocktail, tomato juice cocktail, vegetable juice cocktail: Add thyme to taste. Heat and chill.
Tomato-clam broth: Add thyme to taste, heat and serve hot.

Cheese Dishes: Add thyme to taste to cottage or cream cheese and use for sandwiches or canapés.

Egg Dishes: Add thyme to taste to scrambled eggs, egg sandwich spreads, deviled eggs and creamed eggs.

Meats: Mix thyme to taste with salt and ground black pepper, and rub over oven roast or pot roast beef, lamb, pork or veal. Add thyme to taste to any meat stews shortly before cooking time is up.

Poultry: Add thyme to taste to broiled, baked, creamed or fried chicken or croquettes.

Salads:
Cheese, chicken or seafood: Blend thyme to taste with salad dressing and add to mixture.

Seafood: Add thyme to butter for baking or broiling all seafoods, or sprinkle with thyme before cooking.

Soups:
Chicken bouillon and soup, onion, potato, seafood, tomato and vegetable soups: Add ½ teaspoon thyme or thyme to taste shortly before cooking time is up.

Stuffings: Use thyme to taste in stuffings for fish, pork or poultry.

Vegetables:
Snap beans, carrots, eggplant, mushrooms, onions, potatoes and squash: Add thyme to taste to melted butter or margarine and pour over vegetables.

CHAPTER SIXTEEN

SOURCES FOR INGREDIENTS

The following is a list of sources where many of the unusual ingredients listed in some of this book's recipes may be purchased.

All addresses Manhattan unless otherwise specified.

Sources for fine imported foods:

Abraham & Straus, 420 Fulton Street, Brooklyn.
Allerton Fruit Shop, 546 Madison Avenue.
B. Altman's Delicacies Shop, Fifth Avenue at 34th Street.
Bloomingdale's Delicacies Shop, Lexington Avenue at 59th Street.
Bon Voyage Shop (Charles & Company), 683 Madison Avenue.
Charles & Company, 340 Madison Avenue.
Dilbert's, 22 West 34th Street.
Fraser Morris & Co., 872 Madison Avenue.
Gimbels Department Store, Broadway and 33rd Street.
Ellen Grey, 712 Madison Avenue.
Hammacher Schlemmer & Co., Inc., 145 East 57th Street.
Macy's Department Store, Herald Square.
Madison Fruits and Grocery, 18 East 58th Street.
Maison Glass, 52 East 58th Street.
Martin's Fruit Shop, 1042 Madison Avenue.
William Poll's Gourmet Shop, 1051 Lexington Avenue.
Rahmeyer's International Delicatessen, 1022 Third Avenue.
Service Delicacies, 1032 Lexington Avenue.
Seven Day Shopping Center, Charlottesville, Va.
Suburban Delicatessen, 1188 First Avenue.
Sutton Terrace Delicatessen, 1165 York Avenue.
Vendôme Tables Delicacies, 15 East 48th Street.

Imported cooking utensils:

Bazar Français, 666 Sixth Avenue.
The Bridge Company, 498 Third Avenue.

Cathay Hardware Corporation, 49 Mott Street. (Chinese.)
La Cuisinière, 903 Madison Avenue.
Soupçon Gift and Food Shop, 147 East 70th Street.

Fine imported and domestic cheese:

Bloomingdale's Delicacies Shop, Lexington Avenue at 59th Street.
The Cheese Shop, 271 Greenwich Avenue, Greenwich, Conn.
Cheese Unlimited, 1263 Lexington Avenue.
Cheeses of All Nations, 235 Fulton Street.
John Delucia, 89 Mulberry Street. (Provolone.)
F. W. Hearn, 67 Fulton Street.
Macy's Grocery Department, Herald Square.
Manganaro Foods, 488 Ninth Avenue.
Fraser Morris & Co., 872 Madison Avenue.
Old Denmark, 135 East 57th Street.
William Poll's Gourmet Shop, 1051 Lexington Avenue.

Freshly roasted coffee:

Dick Coffee Company, 414 West 42nd Street.
Empire Coffee Mills, Inc., 323 West 42nd Street.
House of Yemen, 486 Ninth Avenue.
Porto Rico Importing Company, 194 Bleecker Street.
Rohrs Coffee Roasting Establishment, 1492 Second Avenue.
Schapira Coffee Company, 117 West 10th Street.
Schweitzer Coffee Company, 204 East 59th Street.
J. Stavridis, 483 Third Avenue.

Fresh fish:

Frank Campanile, 211 East 59th Street.
M. Citarella, 2135 Broadway.
Eugene Clark, 1129 Lexington Avenue.
G. Imperato & Sons, 896 Third Avenue.
King of the Sea Retail Shop, 885 Third Avenue.
Leonard's Fish Market, 1241 Third Avenue.
Park East Fish Market, Inc., 1007 Lexington Avenue.
L. Petrosino & Sons, 236 Fulton Street.
Pisacane Market, 1050 Second Avenue.
Rosedale Fish & Oyster Market, 1132 Lexington Avenue.
Wynne & Treanor, 712 Madison Avenue.

Game, fresh or frozen:

Gourmet Meat Co., Inc., 826 Washington Street.
Iron Gate Products Co., Inc., 424 West 54th Street.

E. Joseph, 183 Van Brunt Street, Brooklyn.
Maryland Market, 412 Amsterdam Avenue.
George H. Shaffer Market, 1097 Madison Avenue.

Stone-ground grains by mail:

Byrd Mill, Louisa, Va.
Clarks Falls Grist Mill, North Stonington, Conn.
Grist Mill of the Vermont Guild, Weston, Vt.
Mill O'Milford, Inc., Danbury, Conn.
Mystic Seaport Stores, Inc., Mystic, Conn.
Rose Mill, Milford, Conn.
Vermont Country Store, Weston, Vt.

Country hams by mail:

Homestead Stock Farm, Trenton, Tenn.
Nicholson and Weede, Franklin, Va.
Olde Salem Country Ham, 885 Northern Boulevard, Winston-Salem, N.C.

Virginia or Smithfield hams by mail:

Gwaltney, Inc., Smithfield, Va.
Jordan's Old Virginia Smokehouse, 1435-L, East Cary Street, Richmond, Va.
V. W. Joyner, Smithfield, Va.
Seven Day Shopping Center, Barracks Road and Route 29, Charlottesville, Va.
Smithfield Ham and Products Co., Smithfield, Va.
Smithfield Packing Co., Smithfield, Va.
Thalhimer Fine Food Shop, 7 Broad Street, Richmond, Va.
(*Smithfield hams are also available in many fine food sources in most metropolitan centers.*)

Fresh herbs in season:

B & M Market, 201 East 59th Street.
Balducci's, 1 Greenwich Avenue.
Mayo Food Market, 1592 York Avenue.
New Star Market, 1214 Third Avenue.
M. Nicola, 271 West Fourth Street.

Dried spices and herbs:

Atlas Importing Company, 1109 Second Avenue.
Ye Olde Herb Shop, 46 Dey Street.

Indonesian spices:

A Bit of Bali, Woodstock Hotel, 127 West 43rd Street.
Mrs. De Wildt, Box 25, Harvey Cedars, New Jersey.

Shallots by mail:

Les Eschalottes, 706 Lafayette Street, Paramus, N.J.

Vanilla beans by mail:

L. A. Champon & Co., 230 West 41st Street.

Caribbean vegetables and groceries:

C. Constant, 502 Ninth Avenue.
Marcus Matza, Stand 461, New York Public Market, 114th Street and Park Avenue.

Continental pastries:

William Greenberg Desserts, 1181 Madison Avenue.
Leonard Baking Company, 1412 Third Avenue.

French pastries:

Colette French Pastry, Inc., 1136 Third Avenue.
La Marjolaine, 50–17 Skillman Avenue, Woodside, L. I.
La Vie en Rose, 43–16 Greenpoint Avenue, Long Island City.

German specialties:

George Kern, Inc., 496 Ninth Avenue.
Schaller & Weber, Inc., 1654 Second Avenue.

Greek pastries:

Liberty Oriental Pastry Co., 281 Audubon Avenue.
Poseidon Confectionery Company, 629 Ninth Avenue.

Greek specialties:

M. G. Couphopoulos, 306 West 40th Street.
Kassos Brothers, 570 Ninth Avenue.
New International Importing Co., 517 Ninth Avenue.

Hungarian specialties:

Paprikas Weiss, 1504 Second Avenue. (Strudel leaves, rose paprika, etc.)
H. Roth & Son, 1577 First Avenue. (Strudel leaves, spices, etc.)

Italian breads and pastries:

Ferrara Pastry Shop, 195 Grand Street.
Napoli-Palermo Bakery, 173 First Avenue.
J. Pappalardo, 110 Mulberry Street.

Italian specialties:

Joseph Bovera, 625 Ninth Avenue.
Manganaro Foods, Inc., 488 Ninth Avenue.
Solimeo & Schiraldi, 165 First Avenue. (Sausages.)

Near and Middle Eastern foods:

Alwan Brothers, 183 Atlantic Avenue, Brooklyn.
Fouad Alwan Pastry Shop, 189 Atlantic Avenue, Brooklyn.
Kalustyan Orient Expert Trading Corp., 397 Third Avenue.
M. Kehayan, 380 Third Avenue.
Malko Brothers–Cassatly, 197 Atlantic Avenue, Brooklyn.
Malko Importing, 185 Atlantic Avenue, Brooklyn.
Sahadi Importing Company, 187 Atlantic Avenue, Brooklyn.
Trinacria Importing Company, 415 Third Avenue.

Oriental foods:

China Food Center, Inc., 20 East Broadway.
Katagiri & Co., 224 East 59th Street. (Japanese.)
Oriental Food Shop, 1302 Amsterdam Avenue.
Wing Fat Company, 35 Mott Street.
Wo Fat Company, 16 Bowery Street.

Scandinavian foods:

Fredricksen & Hagen, 5706 Eighth Avenue, Brooklyn 20, N. Y.
Nyborg & Nelson, 937 Second Avenue.
Old Denmark, 135 East 57th Street.
Scandinavian Delicacies, 1098 Third Avenue.

Scandinavian pastries:

Haakon Petterson Bakery, 5909 Eighth Avenue, Brooklyn 20, N. Y.
Swedish Kondis, 204 East 58th Street.

Scotch specialties:

Drewes Brothers, Inc., 6815 Fourth Avenue, Brooklyn.

Spanish foods:

Casa Moneo, 218 West 14th Street.

CHAPTER SEVENTEEN

TABLES, WEIGHTS AND MEASURES

WEIGHTS AND MEASURES

1 teaspoon = ⅓ tablespoon
1 tablespoon = 3 teaspoons
2 tablespoons = ⅛ cup (1 ounce)
4 tablespoons = ¼ cup
5⅓ tablespoons = ⅓ cup
8 tablespoons = ½ cup
16 tablespoons = 1 cup
⅜ cup = 5 tablespoons
⅝ cup = 10 tablespoons
1 cup = ½ pint
2 cups = 1 pint
2 pints = 1 quart
4 quarts = 1 gallon
8 quarts = 1 peck
4 pecks = 1 bushel
1 pound = 16 ounces
1 fluid ounce = 2 tablespoons
16 fluid ounces = 1 pint
1 jigger = 1½ fluid ounces (3 tablespoons)

ROASTING MEATS

Permit meat to stand at room temperature for an hour or two before roasting. Preheat oven to desired temperature and place the meat, fat side up, on a rack in an open roasting pan. Season with salt and pepper or other seasonings if desired. Do not cover the meat during the roasting. Basting is unnecessary.

For best results, use a meat thermometer with the bulb inserted in the center of the thickest part of the lean meat before it is placed in the oven. Make sure the bulb does not touch the bone. (See the table on page 685 for the proper interior temperature for various cuts of meat.) If the roast is not cut immediately

(cont'd)

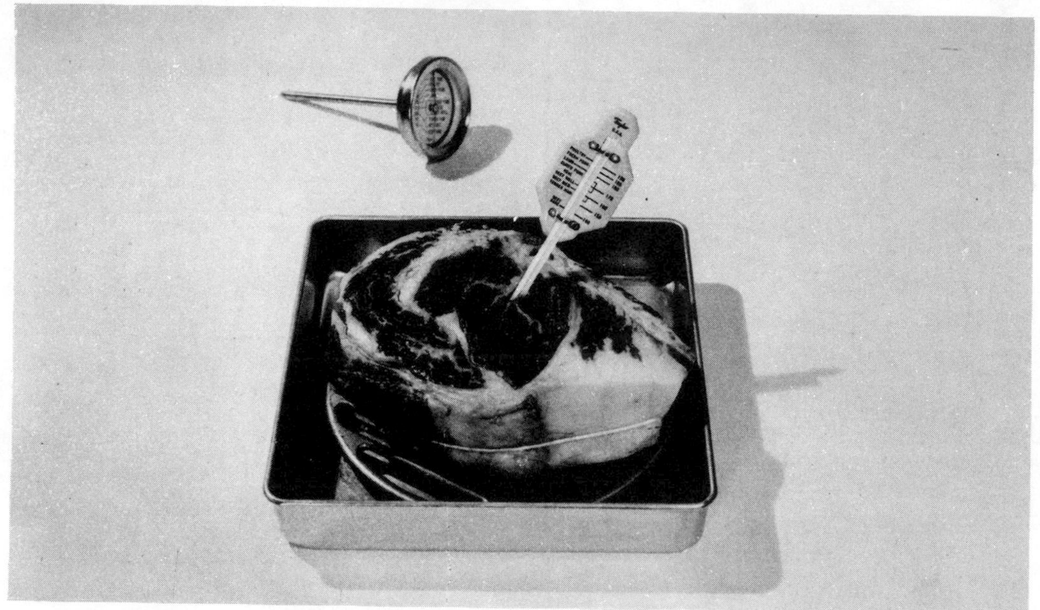

To determine the exact moment when meat is rare, medium or well done, use a thermometer.

upon removal from the oven it will continue to cook, possibly as long as thirty to forty-five minutes, with a corresponding temperature rise.

Although a meat thermometer is the only accurate method of judging the proper degree of doneness, the timetable on page 685 may serve as a general guide to approximate cooking time.

DEEP-FAT FRYING

For cooks without a deep-fat thermometer or a heat-regulated deep fryer, the temperature of hot fat may be judged by the time a one-inch cube of bread will turn golden brown in the fat.

345° to 355° will take about 65 seconds
350° to 365° will take about 60 seconds
375° to 385° will take about 40 seconds
385° to 395° will take about 20 seconds

APPROXIMATE CAN SIZES

Can Size	*Weight*	*Contents*
6 ounce	6 ounces	¾ cup
8 ounce	8 ounces	1 cup

(*cont'd*)

No. 1	11 ounces	1⅓ cups
12 ounce	12 ounces	1½ cups
No. 303	16 ounces	2 cups
No. 2	20 ounces	2½ cups
No. 2½	28 ounces	3½ cups

CONVERSION TABLE FOR FOREIGN EQUIVALENTS

The question frequently arises as to how European measurements for recipes may be translated into American terms. Here are scales for such conversions:

DRY INGREDIENTS

Ounces	*Grams*	*Grams*	*Ounces*
1	28.35	1	0.035
2	56.70	2	0.07
3	85.05	3	0.11
4	113.40	4	0.14
5	141.75	5	0.18
6	170.10	6	0.21
7	198.45	7	0.25
8	226.80	8	0.28
9	255.15	9	0.32
10	283.50	10	0.35
11	311.85	11	0.39
12	340.20	12	0.42
13	368.55	13	0.46
14	396.90	14	0.49
15	425.25	15	0.53
16	453.60	16	0.57

Pounds	*Kilograms*	*Kilograms*	*Pounds*
1	0.454	1	2.205
2	0.91	2	4.41
3	1.36	3	6.61
4	1.81	4	8.82
5	2.27	5	11.02
6	2.72	6	13.23
7	3.18	7	15.43
8	3.63	8	17.64
9	4.08	9	19.84
10	4.54	10	22.05
11	4.99	11	24.26
12	5.44	12	26.46
13	5.90	13	28.67
14	6.35	14	30.87
15	6.81	15	33.08

(cont'd)

CONVERSION TABLE FOR FOREIGN EQUIVALENTS (*cont'd*)

LIQUID INGREDIENTS

Liquid Ounces	*Milliliters*	*Milliliters*	*Liquid Ounces*
1	29.573	1	0.034
2	59.15	2	0.07
3	88.72	3	0.10
4	118.30	4	0.14
5	147.87	5	0.17
6	177.44	6	0.20
7	207.02	7	0.24
8	236.59	8	0.27
9	266.16	9	0.30
10	295.73	10	0.33

Quarts	*Liters*	*Liters*	*Quarts*
1	0.946	1	1.057
2	1.89	2	2.11
3	2.84	3	3.17
4	3.79	4	4.23
5	4.73	5	5.28
6	5.68	6	6.34
7	6.62	7	7.40
8	7.57	8	8.45
9	8.52	9	9.51
10	9.47	10	10.57

Gallons	*Liters*	*Liters*	*Gallons*
1	3.785	1	0.264
2	7.57	2	0.53
3	11.36	3	0.79
4	15.14	4	1.06
5	18.93	5	1.32
6	22.71	6	1.59
7	26.50	7	1.85
8	30.28	8	2.11
9	34.07	9	2.38
10	37.86	10	2.74

TIMETABLE FOR ROASTING MEATS
(Courtesy National Live Stock and Meat Board)

ROAST	WEIGHT	OVEN TEMPERATURE CONSTANT	INTERIOR TEMPERATURE WHEN REMOVED FROM OVEN	APPROXIMATE TIME PER POUND
	Pounds	*Degrees F.*	*Degrees F.*	*Minutes*
BEEF				
Standing ribs	6–8	300	140	18–20
			160	22–25
			170	27–30
Standing rib (1 rib)	2	350	140	33
			160	45
			170	50
Rolled rib	5–7	300	140	32
			160	38
			170	48
Standing rump (high quality)	5–7	300	150–170	25–30
Rolled rump (high quality)	4–6	300	150–170	25–30
PORK—FRESH				
Loin—*Center*	3–5	350	185	35–40
Half	5–7		185	40–45
Ends	2–3		185	45–50
Picnic shoulder	4–6	350	185	30–35
Boned and rolled	3–5	350	185	40–45
Cushion	3–5	350	185	35–40
Boston butt	4–6	350	185	45–50
Fresh ham, whole	10–12	350	185	30–35
PORK—SMOKED				
Ham*—*Whole*	10–14	300	160	18–20
Half	5–7	300	160	22–25
Butt	3–4	300	160	40–45
Smoked shoulder butt	2–4	300	170	35
Picnic	5–7	300	170	35
LAMB				
Leg	5–8	300	175–180	30–35
Shoulder	4–6	300	175–180	30–35
Boned and rolled	3–5	300	175–180	40–45
Cushion	3–5	300	175–180	30–35
VEAL				
Leg roast	5–8	300	170	25–35
Loin	4–6	300	170	30–35
Rib (rack)	3–5	300	170	30–35
Shoulder	5–8	300	170	25–35
Boned and rolled	4–6	300	170	40–45

* *Hams now on market which require shorter cooking period due to method of processing.*

INDEX

ABOUT THE AUTHOR

Food News Editor for *The New York Times* for many years, Craig Claiborne is well known for his books and articles on cuisines around the world and for his knowledge of the art and enjoyment of cooking. He has traveled widely and has prepared and tasted countless dishes of every variety from many lands and cultures. In 1953-1954 he was a student in cuisine and table service at the Ecole Hôtelière, the professional school of the Swiss Hotelkeepers' Association, Lausanne, Switzerland. Upon his return to the United States he was on the staff of *Gourmet* magazine, where he wrote a column and features.

Born in Mississippi in 1920, Claiborne attended high school there. He went to Mississippi State College for two years, and received his Bachelor in Journalism degree from the University of Missouri in 1942.

He served with the U.S. Navy from 1942 to 1945 in both the European and Far Eastern theaters. From 1945 to 1949 Claiborne was assistant director of publicity for the American Broadcasting Company, midwest division, in Chicago. The next year he attended the Alliance Française in Paris. With the outbreak of the Korean War, he again served in the U.S. Navy. From 1950 to 1953 he was a lieutenant aboard a destroyer escort.

Among his cook books are *Cooking with Herbs and Spices, Craig Claiborne's Kitchen Primer* and *The New York Times International Cook Book.*

Craig Claiborne lives in New York City and on eastern Long Island. He is the publisher, with Pierre Franey, of *The Craig Claiborne Journal,* a semimonthly newsletter about menus, recipes, wines, restaurants and cookery around the world.

ABOUT THE AUTHOR

[illegible]